JAMES K. CROSSFIELD

PANZERTRUPPEN
**The Complete Guide to the
Creation & Combat Employment of
Germany's Tank Force
1943-1945**

Also by Thomas L. Jentz
GERMANY'S PANTHER TANK: THE QUEST FOR COMBAT SUPREMACY
PANZERTRUPPEN: 1933-1942

Contents

INTRODUCTION

Having failed to win their strategic objectives, the **Heer** (German Army) was overextended deep in enemy territory facing numerically superior forces in the Fall of 1942. Now it was the Allies turn to launch the offensives that would keep the **Heer** off balance. With few exceptions the days of employing massed Panzer formations to gain strategically decisive objectives had come to an end. And, these few exceptions were almost invariably failures. Forced onto the defensive the **Panzertruppen** modified their tactics becoming expert at counterattacks that spoiled their opponents drives and inflicted heavy casualties. They became so proficient that the Allied armies took years to retake territory that the **Heer** had overran in a few weeks or months. This book presents how the **Panzertruppen** fought during their defensive struggle with details on the units, organizations, type of Panzers, and tactics.

Many other books have successfully covered the history of the Panzertruppen at division, corps, army, and army group level. These have dealt with the strategic decisions of the high command, the successes and the mistakes. A listing of other books that have very thoroughly related the history of the higher level strategy and tactics are listed as Appendix E. After reading many of these published accounts, I was still left with many unanswered questions. How many Panzers were actually available with each unit at the start of each campaign? When were new units formed and committed to action? What was their organization and equipment? What were the Panzers armament, armor protection, and capabilities? What tactics were used by the smaller units from platoons up to regiments? How did they survive in the face of overwhelming numerical superiority?

The answers to all of these questions were obtained by digging through original records for the past twenty-five years. The content of this book is derived solely from these original records consisting of war diaries, reports, and technical and tactical manuals written during the war. No attempt has been made to analyze the content or to interject personal opinion. The story is told as recorded by those responsible for decisions in developing the Panzertruppen and by those who fought in the Panzers. The only editing of reports was done to eliminate information that was not pertinent to understanding development or tactics of the Panzers and Panzer units.

In presenting how the Panzers fared in combat, only original combat and experience reports written directly after the actions were used to relate the thoughts of the troops that fought in the Panzers. This establishes a foundation for the reader to evaluate their performance free from the influence of assumptions, generalities, opinions, and other uninformed statements expressed by armchair armor experts. The reader should be aware that many of these original experience reports are biased in that they do not describe routine activity but were written to relate the unusual. Most of the German reports were written with the motive of initiating improvements to the Panzers or changing tactics.

Throughout this book, I have retained the names of the Panzers, Panzer units, rank, and title as they were used in the original reports. These names can not be translated without loss of identity and meaning. As each new name is introduced, the American equivalent is included in parenthesis when the equivalency is not obvious (i.e. **Division, Brigade, Regiment, Bataillon, Kompanie**). The **Panzer-Abteilung** frequently is mistranslated as being a detachment or a unit. It is not a German battalion which at the time consisted of five companies. With its two to four **Panzer-Kompanien** under command, it is roughly the equivalent of an American tank battalion. To somewhat ease the impact of German terms on the English speaking reader, I have inserted hyphens to break up some of the longer names and have blatantly hacked off suffixes that are normally appended to German nouns. A glossary of terms is included as Appendix F.

Many thanks are due to George Wagner (now retired) of the Captured Records Section at the National Archives for his advice and guidance in digging my way through the mountain of available records. I would also like to thank his replacement, Robin Cookson, who has been a great help in locating the odd box of records. Thanks are also due to Heer Meyer and Heer Loos at the Militaerarchiv and Heer Nielges and Frau Kuhl at the Bildarchiv for their friendly assistance in extracting data from the massive collection of documents and photographs. Special thanks go to Werner Regenberg (specializing in research on units outfitted with captured tanks) and Leo Niehorster (specializing in unit organizations) for reviewing and providing additional details for the list of Panzer units presented in Appendix A. Thanks are also due to Steve Zaloga for providing data on the T-70 and IS-2 Soviet tanks as presented in Appendix D. Any omissions or mistakes are my own and may be largely due to my stubborn refusal to use any data that could not be verified in original records.

The research was the fun part, providing constant rewards as long-sought-after facts and figures were finally discovered. The hard part was beating the data into some semblance of order and the tedious hours of translation so that the information would be made available to the many interested readers who don't have a command of the German language. Peter Frandsen is thanked for his efforts in reviewing the manuscript as a representative for the average armor enthusiast. Thanks are also due to professional proofreader Stanley Thawley for his role in degermanizing sentence structure in the translations.

Any difficulty you may find while attempting to read through this book as if it was a light work of fiction is entirely your own fault for even attempting to embark on such an endeavor. It took over five times the length of World War II to compile this information. There is much more information contained in these two volumes than any single person actively involved with the Panzertruppen knew at the time. It is impossible for the most casual observer to even start to comprehend the most obvious facts after a few hours of light reading. Don't be quick to jump to conclusions. Keep an open mind, absorb the information at face value, and then apply it to analyze and understand how armored battles were fought in World War II.

This book is intended for those interested in facts and figures. As such it should be studied in conjunction with many other fine books on the subject. Your reward will be new discoveries on practically every page that debunk the old myths, propaganda, and erroneous military intelligence which have been insidiously infiltrated into our common knowledge and many published histories on World War II.

Tom Jentz
Germantown, Maryland
6 June 1996

21

Defeat in North Africa

The German forces had overextended and lost the initiative in North Africa. From now on they were forced to react to their opponent's moves. With very few exceptions, the days of employing massed Panzer formations to gain strategically decisive objectives had come to an end. But even decimated Panzer units were still very dangerous opponents, expert at counterstriking and inflicting serious casualties.

Panzerarmee Afrika settled into a heavily mined defensive belt running parallel to the British positions at El Alamein and held the **Panzer-Regiments** in reserve. When the British launched their major offensive during the night of 23/24 October 1942, **Panzer-Regiment 5** and **8** were positioned where they could strike at any armored force that managed to break through the static defenses. Their operational strength reported for the evening of 23 October 1942 was:

	PzII	PzIII	PzIIISp	PzIV	PzIVSp	PzBef	Total
Pz.Rgt.5:							
Available	19	53	43	7	15	6	143
Operational	18	43	43	6	15	3	128
Pz.Rgt.8:							
Available	14	43	44	3	15	2	121
Operational	12	38	43	2	15	1	111

In preventing the British from achieving a complete break through, the **Panzer-Regiments** lost 1 **Pz.Kpfw.II**, 18 **Pz.Kpfw.III**, 20 **Pz.Kpfw.III Sp.**, 1 **Pz.Kpfw.IV**, and 10 **Pz.Kpfw.IV Sp.** as total write-offs during the period from 24 to 29 October. This battle of attrition had left the **Panzer-Regiments** with the following operational strengths to face the renewed British assault in Operation Supercharge on 2 November 1942:

	PzII	PzIII	PzIIISp	PzIV	PzIVSp	PzBef	Total
Pz.Rgt.5	9	28	20	4	11	3	75
Pz.Rgt.8	5	15	27	3	5	1	56

The following excerpts from the war diary of the **15.Panzer-Division** relate how **Panzer-Regiment 8** attacked and held up the British advance – for one more day:

2 November 1942

*0200 - Contact between **Panzer-Grenadier-Regiment 115** and **Panzer-Regiment 8** was disrupted.*

0220 - Intercepted enemy radio message: Our tanks have passed through the gap in the minefield and are now advancing on a wide front.

*0320 - The forward elements of the enemy have broken through to the headquarters of **Panzer-Regiment 8** and the main body is located on the Otto-Piste (track). Contact with **Panzer-Regiment 8** is not available.*

*0445 - Telephone contact with **Panzer-Regiment 8** was restored.*

0505 - As dawn broke enemy tanks could be seen on the telegraph track from the division command post. Artillery fire and shells fired by tanks are hitting close to the division command post.

0636 - Our Panzers are advancing from the southwest toward the northeast on the Otto-Piste. The enemy is pulling back. The burning tanks are the enemy's.

*The **21.Panzer-Division** has reached the Otto-Piste near A.P.412. From there they intend to strike south to hit the enemy in the flank at A.P.411.*

*0705 - Orders to **Panzer-Artillerie-Regiment 33**: The enemy is located at A.P.411 with 80 tanks. **21.Panzer-Division** has been given the assignment to immediately attack south. **Panzer-Regiment 8** is attacking toward the east to close the gap. **I.Abteilung/Panzer-Regiment 8** is still at the old location. **II.Abteilung/Panzer-Regiment 8** is in the area of A.P.507. Artillery to commence firing.*

This **Pz.Kpfw.IV Ausf.F2** and **Pz.Kpfw.III Ausf.L** of **Panzer-Regiment 5** were knocked out at El Alamein. (TTM)

ORGANIZATION AND STRENGTH OF PANZER UNITS
At El Alamein on 23 October 1942

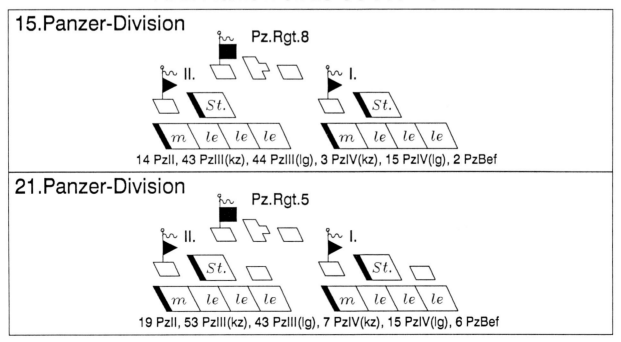

15.Panzer-Division

Pz.Rgt.8

14 PzII, 43 PzIII(kz), 44 PzIII(lg), 3 PzIV(kz), 15 PzIV(lg), 2 PzBef

21.Panzer-Division

Pz.Rgt.5

19 PzII, 53 PzIII(kz), 43 PzIII(lg), 7 PzIV(kz), 15 PzIV(lg), 6 PzBef

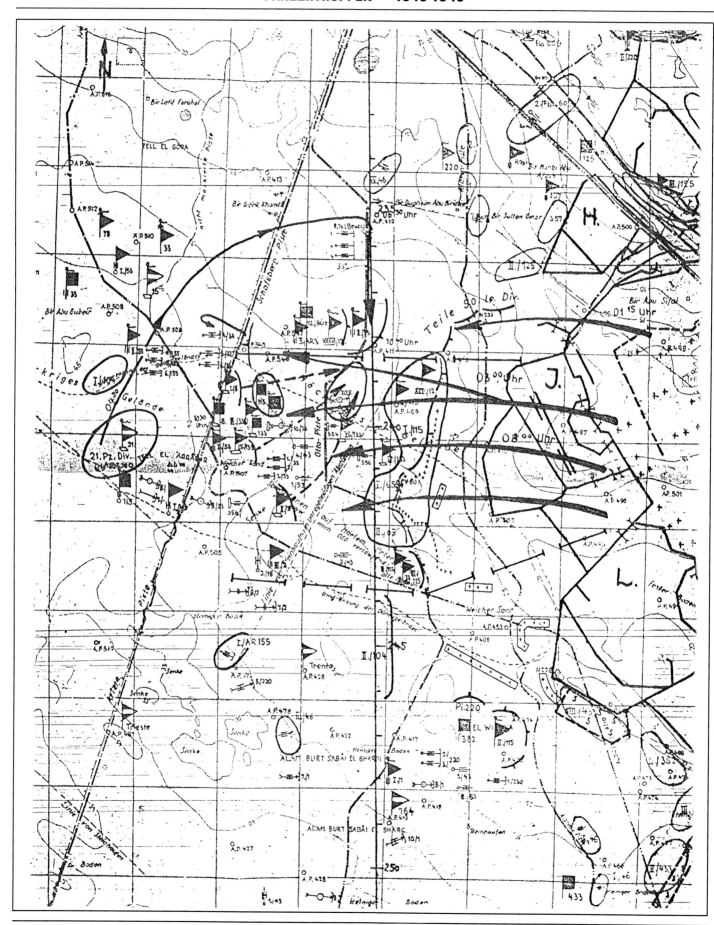

*0735 - The commander of the **I.Abteilung/ Panzer-Regiment 8**, Ritterkreuztraeger Hauptmann Stiefelmayer, was reported killed.*

*0740 - **Panzer-Regiment 8** accompanied by Italian tanks is attacking in a generally northeasterly direction. The **I.Abteilung** still has nine operational Panzers. The attack is slowly gaining ground to the north.*

*0803 - **II.Abteilung/Panzer-Regiment 8** reported: There are now 90 to 100 enemy tanks. We are still located at the old position.*

*0810 - Orders to Oberst Teege: **21.Panzer-Division** is attacking south and has crossed assault line 236. Commence attack.*

*0915 - Up to now, **II.Abteilung/Panzer-Regiment 8** knocked out 30 enemy tanks. The artillery had succeeded in knocking out 15 enemy tanks. **I.Abteilung/Panzer-Regiment 8** reported that 20 were knocked out.*

*0940 - Situation of **Panzer-Regiment 8** at about 0940: On the southeast wing only four Panzers are combat ready near the old position of the **I.Abteilung**.*

*Hauptmann Stiefelmayer was killed. Contact with the infantry in the forward line has still not been reestablished. To the left of the **I.Abteilung**, the Italian tanks, which had pulled back slightly, have been pulled forward again. Beside them to their left, the **II.Abteilung** with 12 Panzers (1.5 km north of A.P.507) extends up to the telegraph track. The regimental command post is behind the right wing of Hauptmann Siemens on the telegraph track. The enemy can be pushed back only very slowly. **Panzer-Regiment 8** is pushing further forward toward the north and northeast.*

*1040 - The advanced elements of the **21.Panzer-Division** are located on height A.P.411. A **Panzer-Kompanie**, swung out to the right, is seeking to gain contact with the right wing of **Panzer-Regiment 8**.*

1130 - Orders to Oberst Teege: Attack toward Point 32, then turn toward the north. The Panzers have been promised additional artillery support.

*1200 - The **21.Panzer-Division** is at A.P.411 facing east. **Panzer-Regiment 8** should gain contact by advancing, facing east along the Otto-Piste toward 411. The **Flak** batteries are to take over flank protec-*

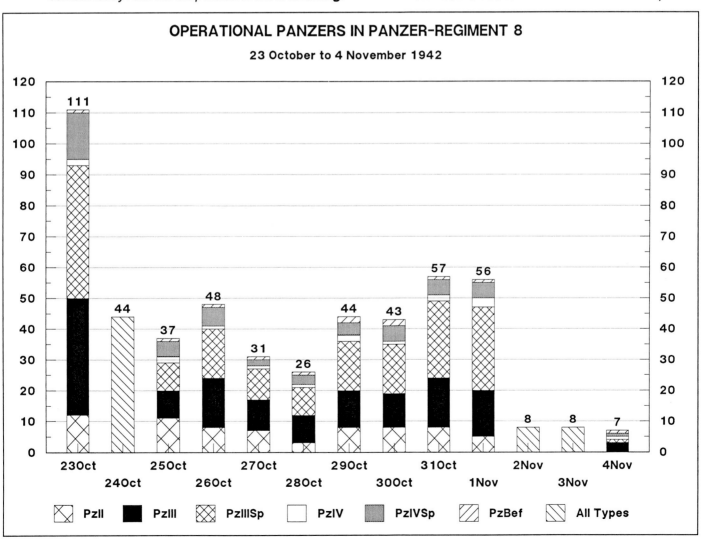

OPERATIONAL PANZERS IN PANZER-REGIMENT 8

23 October to 4 November 1942

tion. Objective: Push forward to the east until the old positions are regained.

*1215 - **II.Abteilung/Panzer-Regiment 8** is in contact with **Panzer-Regiment 5** on the telegraph track.*

*1240 - Orders to **Panzer-Regiment 8**: Quickly start to attack. New attack direction toward A.P.411 to establish contact with the **21.Panzer-Division**. Pull the Italians along.*

*1255 - **Panzer-Regiment 8** reported: Up to now, 60 enemy tanks have been knocked out.*

*1303 - **II.Abteilung/Panzer-Regiment 8** is attacking again. They have only five Panzers in action.*

*1335 - Report from **II.Abteilung/Panzer-Regiment 8**: The enemy is attacking from the east toward the southwest. The **21.Panzer-Division** (**Panzer-Regiment 5**) is hanging back.*

*1335 - Orientation from Major von Heuduck, Ia **21.Panzer-Division**: 200 enemy tanks are driving southwest from minefield J.*

*1410 - **II.Abteilung/Panzer-Regiment 8** reported: 70 enemy tanks are attacking from the southeast.*

*1425 - **Panzer-Regiment 8** repeated that **Panzer-Regiment 5** is not following the attack. Cooperation must occur. Closing up requested.*

*1605 - Oberst Teege was killed. Hauptmann Siemens took over command of the rest of **Panzer-Regiment 8**.*

*1645 - Report from **Panzer-Regiment 8**. Enemy covering itself with a heavy smokescreen.*

*1845 - **Chef des Stabes Deutsches Afrikakorps** oriented the division commander on the army commander's new decision: The army will prevent further destruction of the divisions by the far superior enemy tanks and artillery in the old stationary positions by pulling units back to the west in short stages in rearguard actions and build up a new defensive front.*

The time for divisions to break contact has not been determined.

This **Pz.Kpfw.IV Ausf.G** was abandoned during the retreat following the battles at El Alamein. (NA)

For tonight, the division expects further infantry attacks supported by heavy artillery and tank action. The defensive forces are exceedingly weak in both Panzers and artillery, compared to the opposing sectors. Italian troops are no longer available.

*The combat force of **Panzer-Regiment 8** has sunk to eight operational Panzers. Its commander was killed. The backbone of the division has been broken.*

Today's Results: About 60 enemy tanks destroyed.

The retreat out of Egypt continued back across Libya to the positions at Marsa el Brega, where Rommel had achieved his first success in North Africa on 31 March 1941. Here **Panzerarmee Afrika** rested and took stock, reporting that between 23 October and 2 December, 29 **Pz.Kpfw.II**, 94 **Pz.Kpfw.III**, 67 **Pz.Kpfw.III Sp**, 8 **Pz.Kpfw.IV**, 23 **Pz.Kpfw.IV Sp**, and 8 **Pz.Bef.Wg.** had been lost as total write-offs. On 2 December 1942, the Panzer strength was reported as 4 **Pz.Kpfw.II**, 8 **Pz.Kpfw.III**, 22 **Pz.Kpfw.III Sp**, 16 **Pz.Kpfw.III(75)**, 2 **Pz.Kpfw.IV**, 12 **Pz.Kpfw.IV Sp** for a total of 64, of which all but 11 were operational. An additional 22 **Pz.Kpfw.IV Sp** were on the way to North Afrika, 11 joining each of the **Panzer-Regiments** in late December 1942.

The first unit sent as reinforcements was **Panzer-Abteilung 190**, which was originally intended to join its parent formation the **90.leichte Division**. On 8 November 1942, six **Pz.Kpfw.III** arrived at Bengasi with part of the **2.Kompanie/ Panzer-Abteilung 190** and joined up with **Panzerarmee Afrika**. Allied forces also landed in French North Africa on 8 November 1942 and were advancing toward Tunisia. In response, the rest of the **2.Kompanie** and the balance of **Panzer-Abteilung 190** landed in Bizerte, Tunisia in the period between 12 and 22 November 1942.

Rommel had also been promised a **Tiger-Abteilung**. The first elements of this unit, **schwere Panzer-Abteilung 501**, landed at Bizerte, Tunisia on 23 November 1942. A total of 20 Tigers and 25 **Pz.Kpfw.III(75)** were shipped to Tunisia for the **schwere Panzer-Abteilung 501**.

The **10.Panzer-Division** was also ordered to Tunisia in response to the Allied landings in French North Africa. The bulk of **Panzer-Regiment 7** landed in Tunis in the period from 27 November to 5 December 1942. Ships carrying most of the **5.Kompanie** and **8.Kompanie** were sunk on 3 December 1942. In total, 2 **Pz.Kpfw.II**, 16 **Pz.Kpfw.III**, 12 **Pz.Kpfw.IV**, and 3 **Pz.Bef.Wg.** were lost in transit out of the original 21 **Pz.Kpfw.II**, 105 **Pz.Kpfw.III**, 20 **Pz.Kpfw.IV** and 9 **Pz.Bef.Wg.** shipped with **Panzer-Regiment 7**.

As elements of units landed in Bizerte and Tunis, they were rapidly organized into ad hoc **Kampfgruppen** and quickly sent out to stop the British and American units driving eastward to occupy Tunisia. The commander of the **schwere Panzer-Abteilung 501**, Major Lueder, given command of one of these **Kampfgruppen** wrote the following combat report dated 16 December 1942 on the initial actions of Tigers in Tunisia:

The first Tigers of the **1.Kompanie/schwere Panzer-Abteilung 501** were loaded onboard a ship in Reggio on 21 November. The **Abteilung** commander, Major Lueder, flew in advance to Tunis on 22 November and upon arrival was assigned command of a **Kampfgruppe** until his **Abteilung** arrived. On 4 December, he again took over command of the elements of his **Abteilung** that had arrived, which up to then had been led by Hauptmann Baron von Nolde until he was wounded and then by Leutnant Vermehren.

Up to 1 December, four Tigers and four **Pz.Kpfw.III** had arrived in Tunisia. On 1 December, three Tigers and four **Pz.Kpfw.III** were operational. One Tiger was out of action due to problems with the engine.

*After being assigned security tasks, the Tigers were moved to an assembly area 7 kilometers east of Djedeida. The order to attack came at 1300 hours, and the Panzers immediately started toward Djedeida to gain contact with the oncoming enemy tank force moving northwestward. At 1500, the Panzers encountered the first enemy activity, weak infantry forces 3 kilometers northwest of Djedeida. The **Kompanie** was hit by heavy artillery fire from the heights north of Tebourba and also repeatedly attacked by strafing aircraft. Hauptmann Baron von Nolde fell when an artillery shell exploded while he was walking toward a Tiger.*

The attack was carried forward against enemy tanks in the olive groves 5 kilometers west of Djedeida. The field of view and the field of fire were very limited in the thick olive groves. Enemy tanks could only be fought at close range. Hauptmann Deichmann, who left his Panzer to obtain a better view, fell when hit in the stomach by a rifle shot. The Tigers were hit by General Lee tanks firing at a range of 80 to 100 meters. This resulted in deep penetrations, but the last 10 mm of the side armor held. This proved that the armor was excellent.

*Two General Lee tanks were knocked out at a range of 150 meters. Others were eliminated by the **8.8 cm Flak** guns. The rest pulled back. At dusk, the Tigers pulled back to the old **Stuetzpunkt** and **Panzer-Grenadiere** took over the forward defense line. One Tiger had fallen out due to engine failure and remained in the olive groves. A **Pz.Kpfw.III** was dispatched to guard the Tiger.*

Lessons: Although it was undesirable to send only a few Tigers into action, this was necessary due to the enemy situation and the shortage of our own forces. The approach march was engaged by long-range enemy artillery fire that couldn't be suppressed.

It is especially difficult to direct Panzers in combat in olive groves because the thick tree crowns take away the commanders' and gunners' view. An attacking Panzer is easily knocked out by well-sited dug-in defenses.

In spite of unfavorable conditions, the crews' trust in their Tigers has greatly increased because of the quality of the armor.

*One Tiger and three **Pz.Kpfw.IIIs** were operational on 2 December 1942. With two additional **Pz.Kpfw.IIIs** from **Panzer-Abteilung 190** attached, and accompanied by an*

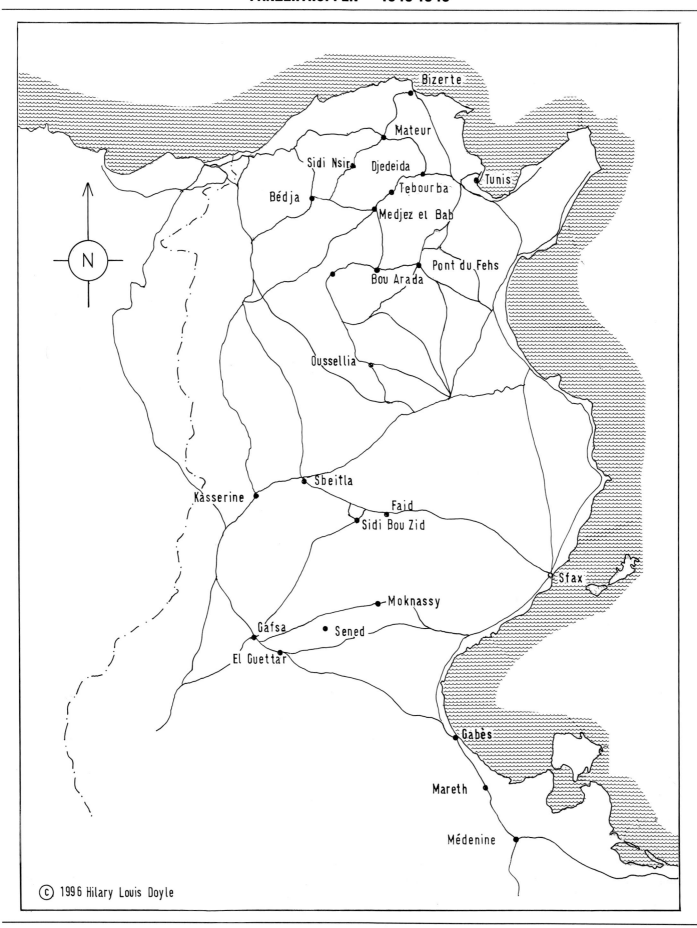

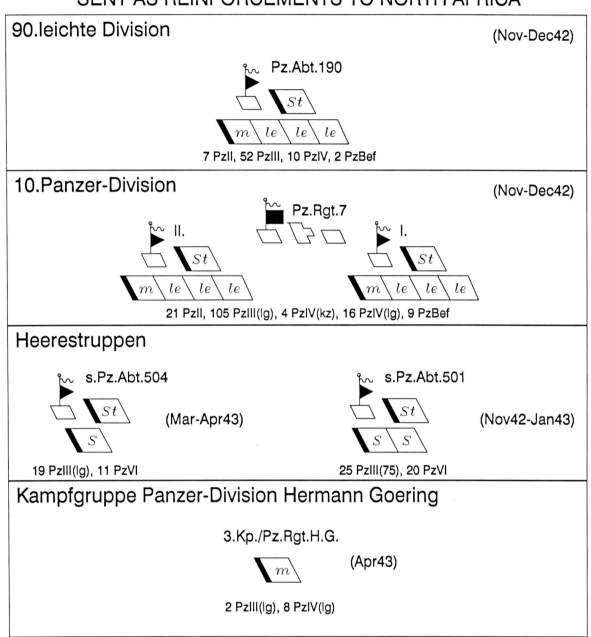

ORGANIZATION AND STRENGTH OF PANZER UNITS SENT AS REINFORCEMENTS TO NORTH AFRICA

90.leichte Division (Nov-Dec42)

Pz.Abt.190

7 PzII, 52 PzIII, 10 PzIV, 2 PzBef

10.Panzer-Division (Nov-Dec42)

Pz.Rgt.7

II.   I.

21 PzII, 105 PzIII(lg), 4 PzIV(kz), 16 PzIV(lg), 9 PzBef

Heerestruppen

s.Pz.Abt.504 (Mar-Apr43)

s.Pz.Abt.501 (Nov42-Jan43)

19 PzIII(lg), 11 PzVI

25 PzIII(75), 20 PzVI

Kampfgruppe Panzer-Division Hermann Goering

3.Kp./Pz.Rgt.H.G. (Apr43)

2 PzIII(lg), 8 PzIV(lg)

infantry Kampfgruppe, the unit advanced westward from Djedeida to attack Point 186.4 east of Tebourba. Strong defenses were emplaced in the olive groves east of Tebourba. Four anti-tank guns, six General Stuart light tanks, two American armored halftracks, and some trucks were shot up. Our own losses included three **Pz.Kpfw.III**, of which one was a total write-off. The infantry took over the defense line at dusk. The Panzers were pulled back to guard Djedeida.

Lessons: Combat in the olive groves was unavoidable because Tebourba is completely surrounded by olive groves except in the northwest.

Close cooperation between the Tigers and escorting Panzers is necessary. The shortage of command resources makes itself felt, especially the missing **Befehlspanzer** and the resulting lack of communication with the next higher command.

One Tiger and two **Pz.Kpfw.IIIs** were operational on 3 December 1942. The unit again attacked toward Point 186 along the combat route taken the previous day. The Panzers were engaged by enemy artillery and mortar fire from positions on the heights that couldn't be spotted. In addition, they were attacked by strafing aircraft. Three anti-tank guns, a

Two **Pz.Kpfw.III Ausf.N**s from the **Stabskompanie/schwere Panzer-Abteilung 501** in Tunisia. (BA)

mortar position, and three ammunition carriers were destroyed.

A Tiger was hit in the area of the final drive by an enemy 7.5 cm self-propelled anti-tank gun. It was sent back to the starting point because its ability to remain operational appeared questionable. Both **Pz.Kpfw.IIIs** carried the attack further forward up to the olive groves southwest of Point 196.

The unit took up a hedgehog formation, remaining in the olive groves overnight. Several infantry losses occurred due to the bitterly fighting, scattered enemy troops. At 0300 hours, the order was received to disengage from the opponent. The Panzers returned to Djedeida, taking along the wounded and dead. Another anti-tank gun and an ammunition carrier were destroyed on the return march.

Lessons: The lessons of the previous days were confirmed. When fighting in close terrain with limited visibility, close cooperation with infantry forces is necessary, especially when attacking through woods.

Maintenance on the vehicles was performed on 4 and 5 December. This was difficult and time consuming because of the lack of the **Werkstatt-Kompanie**.

Three Tigers and four **Pz.Kpfw.IIIs** were operational on 6 December 1942. Three additional Tigers were being repaired. Before dawn the Panzers moved within 4 kilometers east of El Bathan and into El Bathan by 1030. The commander of the **10.Panzer-Division**, Generalleutnant Fischer, person-

ally gave the orders to take the heights east of the pass west of Tebourba and to engage the enemy artillery supposedly located on the other side of the pass. The objective was reached without encountering any enemy activity. The enemy battery didn't fire and therefore couldn't be spotted. The units turned south and pushed forward the **Fallschirmjaeger** attack on Point 145 from El Bathan. Fleeing enemy columns and tanks were observed as soon as the Tigers appeared. The fleeing enemy could only be engaged with difficulty, because the hilly terrain constantly provided cover for the opponent. Point 145 was secured and attempts were made to gain contact with **Kampfgruppe Gehrhardt**, who was expected from the southeast. One Tiger was hit in the idler wheel and roadwheels by a self-propelled enemy 7.5 cm anti-tank gun. However, it remained drivable. From covered positions on the heights northwest of Medjerda, medium enemy batteries fired at the Tigers without success. The territory that had been gained was secured for the night in cooperation with the **Fallschirmjaeger** that had arrived.

Lessons: The morale effect of Tigers was especially noticeable on this day. Without problems the Tigers easily managed the march through the mountainous terrains.

On 7 December 1942 the Tigers were pulled back to an area 1 kilometer south of El Bathan. The **Kompanie** was assigned tactically to **Panzer-Regiment 7 (Kampfgruppe Gehrhardt)**.

On 8 December 1942 the Panzers had to move to slightly higher terrain because the ground was no longer crossable due to persistent rainfall.

*On 9 December, both Panzers (one Tiger and one **Pz.Kpfw.III**) arrived that had taken part in the march from Bizerte to capture and disarm the Ville navy base. It rained throughout the day. At 2000 hours, attack orders came in for the 10th.*

*On 10 December 1942, five Tigers and 4 **Pz.Kpfw.IIIs** were operational out of the seven Tigers and 5 **Pz.Kpfw.IIIs** available. Near Massicault, the unit joined the formation of **Panzer-Regiment 7**. Two Tigers were assigned to the lead company; the rest followed in reserve behind the main body of the **Kampfgruppe**. The objective was Medjez el Bab. Movement was restricted to the roads, the ground being too soft because of rain.*

*Enemy resistance was first encountered 8 kilometers southwest of Furma. From hull-down positions, enemy tanks fired at the lead Panzers. One Tiger shot up two enemy General Stuart tanks and four armored half-tracks. The advance continued. Six kilometers short of Medjez el Bab, the Panzers came under fire from several enemy batteries. The column took up defensive positions. The plan was to continue the attack after the **Panzer-Grenadiere** arrived and to advance on Medjez el Bab from the north on both sides of the river.*

*During the approach march, the enemy tanks that had been driven off assembled in the high ground north of Furma and attacked our artillery positions. The Tigers, which were immediately sent to the rear, encountered 20 to 25 General Stuart tanks and shot up 12 without suffering a single loss. Additional enemy tanks were knocked out by elements of **Panzer-Regiment 7**. The night was spent on the road from Furma to Medjez el Bab.*

*On 11 December 1942, the captured territory was mopped up by **Kampfgruppe Gehrhardt**. The Tiger took over defensive positions facing south against reported enemy tanks. Only several enemy armored cars were spotted; they immediately pulled back. At 2000 hours, orders were received to pull the Tigers out and send them to a **Stuetzpunkt** 7 kilometers east of Djedeida at the disposal of the Armee.*

*Lessons: If only a few Tigers are available, it is entirely suitable to incorporate the Tigers into a Panzer advance. Two Tigers, assigned to the lead, served as battering rams and drew fire from dug-in defensive weapons that were difficult to spot. The rest of the **Kompanie**, pulled along in reserve, was to engage any threats expected to the flanks from enemy tanks.*

Tigers may not open fire too early against enemy tanks, in order to keep retreating enemy tanks within the effective range of our weapons as long as possible.

Tigers can maintain the convoy speed of the lighter tanks without reaching or exceeding the ordered limit of 30 kilometers per hour.

The previous methods used in employing Tigers in Tunisia were the result of the prevailing conditions. We should

*strive for employment of pure Tiger formations including their escort tanks as the **Schwerpunkt**.*

Seven of the eight available Tigers were operational on 16 December 1942.

On 17 December 1942, Major Lueder also wrote the following report on the effectiveness of enemy heavy weapons and the usefulness of their own heavy weapons:

I. Enemy weapons:

A. Enemy Tanks: The 7.5 cm gun of the M3 (General Lee) couldn't penetrate through the Tiger's armor at a range of 150 meters. The last 10 mm of the side armor held up against a hit on the side armor that had been guided by the sheet metal fender over the track.

*The 3.7 cm gun of the M2 (General Stuart) is apparently very accurate. Fire was especially heavily directed at the driver's visor, commander's cupola, and the gap between the turret and hull. In one case, a shell fragment jammed the turret, temporarily taking the Tiger out of action. It is proposed that a deflector channel be added like those installed on the **Pz.Kpfw.II** and **III**.*

*B. Enemy anti-tank guns: At ranges of 600 to 800 meters, the 3.7 cm and 4 cm anti-tank guns penetrate through the front and side of the hull of the **Pz.Kpfw.III**. They succeed only in damaging the Tiger's roadwheels and track which in no case results in immobilizing the Tiger.*

In one case, at an estimated range of 600 to 800 meters, a self-propelled 7.5 cm anti-tank gun hit a Tiger on the right front by the final drive. The Tiger was out of service temporarily due to the resulting failure of the weld seam.

C. Enemy artillery: Up to now only minor roadwheel damage has been caused by shell fragments. Most hits on the Tiger lay in the suspension components, causing high wear on the roadwheels, rubber tires, track links, and track pins. Jamming the interleaved roadwheels has not occurred, and no Tigers were immobilized.

II. Our weapons:

*A. The **8.8 cm Kw.K.** gun is very accurate. Up to now, the Tiger has fired only at the M3 (General Lee) at ranges of 100 to 150 meters. The front and side armor were cleanly penetrated. The M2 (General Stuart) was shot through at all ranges.*

*We should strive to supply the Tigers solely with **Panzer-Kopfgranaten** with tracers for better observation of each shot.*

*An enemy battery was engaged at a range of 7600 meters by using a gunner's quadrant. The enemy battery was silenced after six shots were fired at it. It is proposed that the **Tiger-Kompanie** be outfitted with a **Feldfunksprecher f** (radio set "f") to enable forward observers to direct their fire. In addition, the inverted image rangefinders should be exchanged for converging image rangefinders. Large errors result from using the former type in terrain with no discernible landmarks.*

*B. The **7.5 cm Kw.K. (kurz)** has proven to be very successful in engaging mass targets with **Sprenggranaten** (high explosive shells). The effectiveness of the **Hohlgranate** (shaped charge shells) has not been established, because up to now only the Tigers have fought with enemy tanks.*

The initial attempt by the Allies to quickly occupy all of Tunisia was thwarted. Engagements to control the numerous passes continued with the Germans managing to regain and hold significant territory. In the interim, **Panzerarmee Afrika** had retreated back to and held off the British Eighth Army on the Mareth Line in southeastern Tunisia.

The Germans exploited the lull in the Allied attacks by launching limited counterstrikes including Operation "Fruehlingswind" on 14 February 1943. The **10.Panzer-Division** with **Panzer-Regiment 7** (minus the **II.Abteilung/Panzer-Regiment 7**) supported by a **Tiger-Kompanie** from the **schwere Panzer-Abteilung 501** and the **21.Panzer-Division** with **Panzer-Regiment 5**, hit the southern end of the Allied line at Sidi Bou Zid. The 3rd Battalion of the 1st U.S. Armored Regiment, starting the day with 53 Sherman tanks, was decimated after being hit from the front and then from the right rear. They were left with only six Shermans tanks at the end of the day. The 2nd Battalion of the 1st U.S. Armored Regiment was sent in the next day with 54 Sherman tanks. All but four Shermans that remained behind as rearlink tanks were knocked out by the **Pz.Kpfw.IIIs** and **Pz.Kpfw.IVs** of

the **I.Abteilung/Panzer-Regiment 7** and **Panzer-Regiment 5** without any assistance from the Tigers.

But this success was an isolated event. Any remaining offensive strength in the Panzer units was lost in an attack that failed to dislodge the British forces facing the Mareth Line and in Operation "**Ochsenkopf**" in attacks that failed to gain control of the passes near Beja, Tunisia.

The last Panzer units sent to Tunisia were the **Stab** and **1.Kompanie/schwere Panzer-Abteilung 504** and the **3.Kompanie/Panzer-Regiment Hermann Goering**. The following notes made by the company commander for their war diary reveal how the **3.Kompanie/Panzer-Regiment Hermann Goering** was employed in defensive positions awaiting Allied attacks in the final phases of the campaign in Tunisia:

8 April 1943: At 1300 hours, drove into positions in the Tina valley with 5 Panzers without incident. Intermittent light harassing artillery fire.

9 April 1943: Uneventful. Light harassing artillery fire. Three Pz.Kpfw.IVs arrived toward evening.

10 April 1943: At 0130 hours, took up new defensive positions in two groups, one on each side of the road. Toward 1000 hours, enemy tanks gathered. Leutnant Lahusen counted 33 tanks. Artillery fire landed on both groups.

11 April 1943: From 1000 to 1430 hours, strong artillery fire landed on the group on the right side of the road. Changed

This Tiger from the **1.Kompanie/schwere Panzer-Abteilung 504** was abandoned after the turret was jammed. The loader's hatch was also shattered by a hit. (TTM)

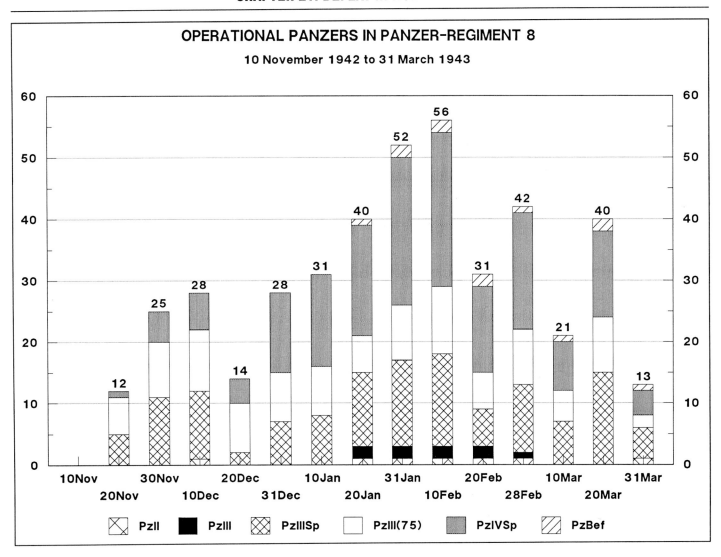

OPERATIONAL PANZERS IN PANZER-REGIMENT 8

10 November 1942 to 31 March 1943

Legend: PzII | PzIII | PzIIISp | PzIII(75) | PzIVSp | PzBef

positions to hull down. Two Panzers were out of action due to damage to an idler wheel and roadwheels.

12 April 1943: After 0100 hours, reoccupied the position of the right group. Entire day uneventful.

13 to 17 April 1943: Uneventful. Occasional light harassing artillery fire on both groups.

18 April 1943: Uneventful throughout the day. About 2300 hours, after a short heavy artillery preparation, a British patrol of about 30 men attacked the left group. After about two hours the enemy patrol was thrown back by *A 24* with support from the Panzers.

19 to 21 April 1943: No unusual activity. Harassing fire and surprise barrages during the day and night.

22 April 1943: Quiet all day. Some harassing fire, increasing toward evening. *3./A 24* reported that the British were assembling in a Wadi in front of the main battle line. In spite of this, no action occurred through the night.

23 April 1943: In the morning, 12 British tanks were spotted which joined in the attack against the neighbor on the right. They drove along the eastern side of the Djebel Egel and halted about 2500 meters away from the Kompanie po-

sition. Four *Pz.Kpfw.IVs* opened fire. Two British tanks were destroyed; the rest turned back. At the end, an artillery barrage hit our positions.

At 2200 hours, Leutnant Lahusen with four *Pz.Kpfw.IVs* drove over to the neighbor on the right. The remaining five Panzers supported the *3./A 24* in repulsing an enemy platoon that had broken into the main defense line.

24 April 1943: Three *Pz.Kpfw.IVs*, on guard since 0300 hours by the right-hand neighbor, covered the disengagement of *T 3*. After 0445 hours, all of the Panzers in the **Kompanie** were located in the *T 3* sector. With the support of the Panzers, **Bataillon Lersch (T 3)** was assigned to cover the disengagement of their right-hand battalion. For this purpose **Bataillon Lersch** took up a hedgehog formation. The Panzers of the **Kompanie** were dispersed in this hedgehog formation. One man was wounded by a shell fragment from light artillery fire.

About 1830 hours, Feldwebel Fragel was ordered to reconnoiter the zone in front of the position with an infantry group. During this action, he destroyed an artillery forward observation post and threw back an American infantry company.

*25 April 1943: **T 3** was pulled back after 0000 hours. The **Panzer-Kompanie** took up hull-down positions in a Wadi. The day passed quietly.*

*26 April 1943: At 0000 hours, the **Panzer-Kompanie** was pulled back further and took up alert positions in the mountains. No activity. The **Kompanie** rested.*

*27 April 1943: About 0100 hours, the **Kompanie** changed positions and took up positions behind the **5./734** north of the Medjerda valley. Uneventful.*

28 April 1943: No activity.

*29 April 1943: The British broke into the position of the **5.Kompanie** in the afternoon. During the night, two **Pz.Kpfw.IVs** (Leutnant Lahusen and Unteroffizier Sondermann) drove a British infantry unit off the ridge and remained guarding the ridge until morning.*

*30 April 1943: About 1300 hours, the **5.Kompanie** reported a British attack supported by 18 tanks. The **Panzer-Kompanie** was formed into two groups and drove into positions on line with the **5.Kompanie**. After a short exchange of fire, the right group under Leutnant Lahusen had to pull back after receiving hits on a gun, gearbox, and final drive.*

*The left group under Oberleutnant Muenzner spotted four enemy tanks on the slope on which the **5.Kompanie** was located. Oberfeldwebel Kirschbaum laid down a smokescreen on the position up to the opponent. Under cover of this smokescreen, Oberleutnant Muenzner drove to the next ridge and shot up two enemy tanks at a range of 25 meters. Oberfeldwebel Kirschbaum also drove to the same ridge and was knocked out by an enemy tank. The driver let the Panzer roll back down. Oberfeldwebel Kirschbaum had been killed, the gunner and loader wounded.*

*The commander's Panzer shot up an artillery forward observation post on the ridge. Following this action, nothing more was seen of any British on the ridge. During the night, the infantry counterattacked the ridge and found it unoccupied. At night, the damaged Panzers were towed back to the **Werkstatt**.*

In addition to the Panzers sent to Tunisia with the units, from 1 November 1942 to 1 May 1943 a total of 68 **Pz.Kpfw.III** and 142 **Pz.Kpfw.IV** had been shipped to North Africa as replacements, of which 16 **Pz.Kpfw.III** and 28 **Pz.Kpfw.IV** were reported as having been sunk in transit. But these reinforcements were insufficient to deal with the combined tank strength of the American and British forces. Worn down by attrition (only 44 **Pz.Kpfw.III**, 25 **Pz.Kpfw.IV** and 1 Tiger were reported as operational in the last strength report compiled on 4 May), the last of the Panzer units had surrendered in Tunisia by 13 May 1943.

Surrounded at Stalingrad to the Counteroffensive to Retake Kharkov

When the Russians launched their major offensive to envelop Stalingrad, the **Panzertruppen** on the Eastern Front were organized as shown in the Order of Battle dated 15 November 1942 and with the strength shown in the table on the Operational Panzers at the Start of the Russian Offensive. The **6.Armee** with three Panzer-Divisions and two **Infanterie-Division (mot)** were still tied up in their attempt to capture Stalingrad. The **4.Panzer-Armee** with the **16.** and **29.Infanterie-Division (mot)** were south of Stalingrad and the **22.Panzer-Division**, **27.Panzer-Division**, and **Panzer-Verband 700** were west of Stalingrad. These were the only **Panzertruppen** that stood in the way of the Russian offensive that succeeded in quickly enveloping and entrapping the **6.Armee** in Stalingrad.

But this wasn't the only Russian offensive designed to cut off the overextended German forces. On 25 November 1942, the Russians launched another offensive farther to the west against **Heeresgruppe Mitte**. Details on what it was like to be isolated and surrounded as a result of a major Russian offensive were recorded by Oberleutnant Graf Rothkirch, company commander in **Panzer-Regiment 31** as follows:

*24 November 1942 - The **Kompanie** was deployed on the left sector of the division with seven gun-armed Panzers: one Panzer in Wassilki, two Panzers in the Zungenwaeldchen and four Panzers along with a **Pz.Kpfw.II** in the woods south of Wassilki where the company command post was located. Deserters reported that a major Russian offensive was planned to start the next day.*

25 November 1942 - The battalion ordered an increased alert status after 0400 hours. About 0600 hours, firing from all calibers, the opponent's artillery preparation suddenly struck in unheard-of force. The 32 cm rockets were fired in salvoes for the first time. Similar to the Stalinorgan, within a few seconds 30 to 40 rockets rained down on the position. In the woods it was barely possible for the crews to get into their Panzers. There was no chance to bring along any provi-

sions such as food or blankets. This situation would cause great discomfort in the coming days.

*The four Panzers took up positions along the wood line. Communication was maintained by messengers with the infantry company to the right. About 0730 hours, a message came in that tanks were approaching. Utilizing mutual fire support tactics, the four Panzers drove into positions directly behind the infantry dugouts. Three T34 tanks could be observed beyond our firing range as they broke through between Cholm-Beresuiski and into our own position. Because the Russians were laying down heavy caliber artillery shells and rockets on the infantry positions and it was also apparent that the Panzers were receiving aimed artillery fire, orders were given to move back to the wood line to the rear. Two Panzers took over covering the area to the northeast while the other two Panzers set off to hunt down the T34 tanks that had broken through. It took one and one-half hours for the two Panzers to stalk and kill two of the T34 tanks. The third was destroyed by a Pak Sfl. (self-propelled anti-tank gun) positioned in the woods. At the same time, the **Pz.Kpfw.III 5 cm kurz** located in the Zungenwaeldchen had destroyed three Christie tanks. The Panzer located in Wassilki destroyed a T34 tank on the west bank of the Ossug.*

*The Russian artillery barrage continued in the same intensity until about 1430 hours. About 1530 hours, the **Kompanie** commander received an order from the **Kampfgruppe** to advance with four Panzers to Gradjakino and destroy enemy tanks found there. The order was immediately carried out. The Panzer in Wassilki and both Panzers in the Zungenwaeldchen remained behind. Even at long range, communication by radio worked excellently.*

*A **Gruppe** under Oberfeldwebel Doleski joined the **Kompanie** commanded by Oberleutnant Graf Rothkirch in Gradjakino. That same evening, the entire **Kompanie** was ordered to take over anti-tank defense behind the battalion. The **Kompanie** now consisted of two **Pz.Kpfw.III** or **IV** with 7.5 cm Kw.K. kurz, three **Pz.Kpfw.III 5 cm Kw.K. lang**, two*

ORDER OF BATTLE – 15 NOVEMBER 1942

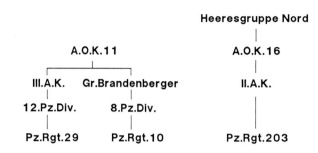

```
                                                      Heeresgruppe Nord
                                                             |
                              A.O.K.11                                    A.O.K.16
                          ┌──────┴──────────┐                                |
                      III.A.K.      Gr.Brandenberger                      II.A.K.
                          |                 |                                |
                     12.Pz.Div.        8.Pz.Div.                             |
                          |                 |                                |
                     Pz.Rgt.29        Pz.Rgt.10                         Pz.Rgt.203
```

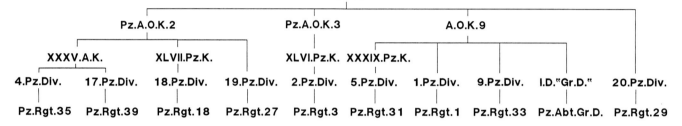

```
                                         Heeresgruppe Mitte
        ┌────────────────────────────────────┬──────────────────────────────────────────────────┐
     Pz.A.O.K.2                          Pz.A.O.K.3                          A.O.K.9
  ┌──────┴──────┐      ┌──────┴──────┐        |          ┌────────┬─────────┬──────────┬──────────┐
XXXV.A.K.           XLVII.Pz.K.            XLVI.Pz.K. XXXIX.Pz.K.
┌───┴───┐         ┌───┴───┐
4.Pz.Div. 17.Pz.Div. 18.Pz.Div. 19.Pz.Div. 2.Pz.Div. 5.Pz.Div. 1.Pz.Div. 9.Pz.Div. I.D."Gr.D." 20.Pz.Div.
   |        |          |          |          |         |         |         |          |          |
Pz.Rgt.35 Pz.Rgt.39 Pz.Rgt.18 Pz.Rgt.27 Pz.Rgt.3 Pz.Rgt.31 Pz.Rgt.1 Pz.Rgt.33 Pz.Abt.Gr.D. Pz.Rgt.29
```

```
                                            In Reserve
                                           11.Pz.Div.
                                               |
                                           Pz.Rgt.15
```

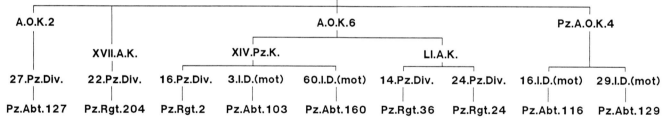

```
                                         Heeresgruppe B
   ┌────────────────────────────────────────────┬───────────────────────────────────────────┐
 A.O.K.2                                       A.O.K.6                                   Pz.A.O.K.4
   |              ┌──────┐      ┌───────────┴────────────┐        ┌──────┴──────┐     ┌──────┴──────┐
27.Pz.Div.     XVII.A.K.            XIV.Pz.K.                   LI.A.K.
   |              |        ┌───────┬────────────┐        ┌───────┴───────┐
   |          22.Pz.Div. 16.Pz.Div. 3.I.D.(mot) 60.I.D.(mot) 14.Pz.Div. 24.Pz.Div. 16.I.D.(mot) 29.I.D.(mot)
Pz.Abt.127   Pz.Rgt.204  Pz.Rgt.2  Pz.Abt.103  Pz.Abt.160  Pz.Rgt.36  Pz.Rgt.24  Pz.Abt.116  Pz.Abt.129
```

```
                                         Heeresgruppe A
                                           Pz.A.O.K.1
                         ┌───────────────────┬──────────────────┐
                     III.Pz.K.           XXXX.Pz.K.           LII.A.K.
                  ┌──────┴──────┐
             13.Pz.Div.  23.Pz.Div.   3.Pz.Div.        SS-Div.Wiking
                  |         |             |                  |
             Pz.Rgt.4  Pz.Rgt.201    Pz.Rgt.6          SS-Pz.Abt.5
```

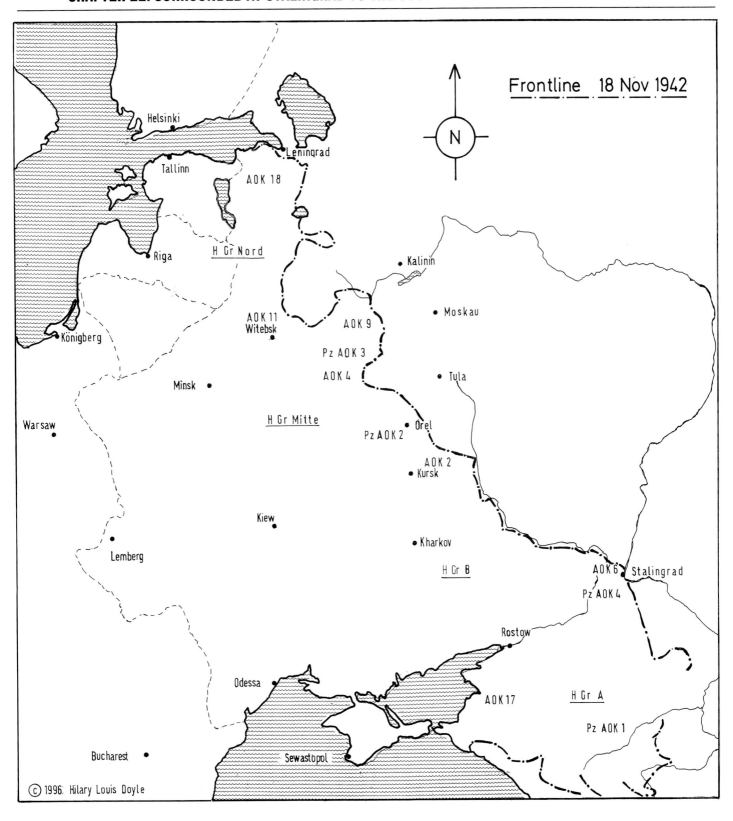

Frontline   18 Nov 1942

N

Helsinki

Leningrad

Tallinn

AOK 18

Riga

H Gr Nord

Königberg

Kalinin

AOK 11
Witebsk

AOK 9

Moskau

Pz AOK 3

Minsk

AOK 4

Tula

H Gr Mitte

Orel

Warsaw

Pz AOK 2

AOK 2

Kursk

Kiew

Lemberg

Kharkov

H Gr B

AOK 6   Stalingrad

Pz AOK 4

Rostow

Odessa

AOK 17

H Gr A

Pz AOK 1

Bucharest

Sewastopol

© 1996; Hilary Louis Doyle

Pz.Kpfw.III 5 cm Kw.K. kurz, one **7.5 cm Pak 40 Sfl.**, and one **7.62 cm Pak 36 Sfl**. The night passed quietly.

26 November 1942 - As on the previous day, the same artillery barrage started at 0600 hours. The positions occupied during the night had to be abandoned because they could be directly observed by the enemy. The Panzers divided, taking up positions in two depressions. Several minutes later, a tank attack was reported on the left sector of the battalion. The **Kompanie** set off to counterattack. The Russian attack passed by the battalion out of range of our weapons toward Cholm-Beresuiski. The **Kompanie** had to maneuver very skillfully in order not to be spotted by the exceptional enemy artillery observers and be decimated. In addition, anti-tank guns and dug-in enemy heavy weapons opened up an unheard-of barrage. Two of our Panzer were already hit by artillery and anti-tank shells but could still be repaired by the proficient crews during the action.

After an hour and a half, it was no longer possible to hold the positions. The **Kompanie** again divided, taking up positions in both depressions. This also lay under very strong artillery fire, which hit another Panzer but didn't cause any damage. Two Panzers were requisitioned to secure the **Panzer-Schlucht** (ravine) surrounding the battalion's sector on the right. Keen all-round observation was necessary. The necessity for being alert was proven by the fact that three T34 tanks suddenly broke into the position from the rear. These tanks were immediately surrounded without spotting the Panzers and within several minutes were shot to pieces. The **Kompanie** also destroyed a towing vehicle and successfully engaged five anti-tank guns.

At dusk, the **Kompanie** was pulled into the right battalion sector for overnight security. A KW I tank broke through from behind and was knocked out. This tank exploded scattering parts in a 300 meter radius over the field. These positions were held overnight and maintained the next day with only short movements.

27 November 1942 - No tank kills were made today. The **Kompanie** limited itself to wiping out Russian infantry and shooting up enemy convoys. The **Pak Sfl.** and two Panzers were hit by anti-tank rifles.

The spirit and morale of the crews must be especially mentioned. By this evening, the crews had already been sitting in their Panzers for two and one-half days. During this time they didn't have anything to eat and knew that supplies weren't expected because the ring had been closed around them since 26 November. They received fuel and ammunition in frighteningly small quantities. Sleep couldn't be considered, not even for the coming night. Happy and confident faces were always seen in spite of the fact that the situation had started to become very serious. This is proof that the men appropriately fought with the roten **Teufel** (the red devil unit symbol for **Panzer-Regiment 31**) on their steel giants.

After today, two Panzers were positioned to guard the left wing of the battalion during the night because the Russians constantly attacked there at night. Their main task was to support the effort to eliminate enemy infantry. Both of these Panzers were pulled back again at dawn.

28 November 1942 - The defensive tasks and positions remained the same as before. A mounted reconnaissance patrol was wiped out, a radio post destroyed, and an anti-tank rifle and several infantry shot up.

A *Pz.Kpfw.II* arrived today with ammunition, mainly armor piercing, some food, and also 60 liters of fuel. Since yesterday, there had been rumors that the Russians had broken through the main defense line southeast of us, and were pursuing with an unbelievably large number of tanks. Our attacks that should free us appear to have run into the sand, because the noise of combat moved farther away. A certain nervousness became noticeable after this occurred. Only the local successes, which should occur again today, bolstered the undiminished good mood.

About 1530 hours, an Oberfeldwebel arrived at the company command post totally spent, collapsed, and reported that six tanks had broken into our positions and were rolling toward our infantry positions and the battalion command post. Four Panzers attacked within a few minutes. Two T60, one T34, and a heavy American tank with two gun turrets were knocked out and went up in flames within 10 minutes. A fifth tank was knocked out by a Pak and a T34 tank fled. This attack was aided by the fact that the **Kompanie** could choose

OPERATIONAL PANZERS AT START OF RUSSIAN OFFENSIVE									
	PANZERKAMPFWAGEN								
Organization	II	38t	III kz	III lg	III 75	IV kz	IV lg	Bef	Date
Heeresgruppe A									
1.Pz.Armee									
3.Pz.Div.	13		19	25		5	3		18Nov
13.Pz.Div.	4		7	14		1	3		18Nov
23.Pz.Div.	5		12	15		4	4		18Nov
SS-Wiking			3	12		1	7		18Nov
Heeresgruppe B									
22.Pz.Div.	2	5		12	10	1	10		18Nov
2.Armee									
27.Pz.Div.	9	22	5	10	12	2	5		10Nov
4.Pz.Armee									
16.Inf.Div.	8			16	7		11	1	16Nov
29.Inf.Div.	7			23	9		18	2	16Nov
6.Armee									
14.Pz.Div.			1	21	7	1	6	5	18Nov
16.Pz.Div.				21		1	9		18Nov
24.Pz.Div.	5		9	17	5	5	12	2	18Nov
3.Inf.Div.	3			22	3		4		18Nov
60.Inf.Div.	4			12		2	3		18Nov
Heeresgruppe Mitte									
11.Pz.Div.	11		9	49			6	3	18Nov
2.Pz.Armee									
4.Pz.Div.	2		12			5			18Nov
17.Pz.Div.	9		30			18		3	18Nov
18.Pz.Div.	5		22		6	4	9	2	18Nov
19.Pz.Div.	7	37	8			3	10	3	18Nov
3.Pz.Armee									
2.Pz.Div.	11		10	8	12	4	8	1	18Nov
9.Armee									
1.Pz.Div.	3	7	16	8	6	5	6	4	18Nov
5.Pz.Div.	15		23	10	7	10	6	7	18Nov
9.Pz.Div.	26		30	32		7	5	2	18Nov
20.Pz.Div.	4	22	14			11	5	6	18Nov
Inf.GD	7		1			7	12	3	18Nov
I./Pz.Rgt.15	3		2	28			3	1	18Nov
Heeresgruppe Nord									
11.Armee									
8.Pz.Div.		14						1	18Nov
12.Pz.Div.	1		24	17		2	18	3	18Nov
16.Armee									
Pz.Rgt.203			7			2			18Nov
18.Armee									
1./s.Pz.Abt.502				9	7		PzVI 6	1	18Nov

the direction to attack, driving with the wind in the heavy snow-storm. The Russians had to fight facing into the blowing snow. Four prisoners were brought in.

The totally spent *Oberfeldwebel* let himself be lifted into his *Panzer* and very successfully took part in the attack. Again proof of the men's good spirits which must be highly regarded in these situations.

29 November 1942 - At dawn today, without infantry sup-port on the left wing of the battalion, two *Panzers* captured a Russian fieldwork and rolled up part of our own earthworks that the Russians had occupied for several days. During the evening, in the same sector a KW I tank was knocked out that had been destroying our positions by firing at a range of 80 meters. A prisoner was brought in who was exceptionally well oriented on the situation and dramatically portrayed for us the precariousness of our situation.

The so-called *Panzer-Schlucht* lay under heavy mortar fire all day. Toward evening, yelling Hurrah, the Russians charged the right sector and were already within 5 meters of our earthworks when the *Panzer* crews mounted up. Imme-diately, five *Panzers* drove off to surround the *Panzer-Schlucht* from all sides. This attack was beaten back in ex-actly the same way as four other attempts. A deserter stated

that 150 had been killed and wounded. These earthworks were occupied by only 10 *Pioniere*, so it is readily apparent that the prevention of a break-in was earned entirely by the *Panzer* crews.

30 November 1942 - Today began with the sad loss of a *Pz.Kpfw.IV* that couldn't pull back out of its position because of lack of fuel and was wiped out by a direct hit. All day long the Russians laid down heavy artillery fire on the position, especially on the *Panzer-Schlucht*. Having reinforced the ring around us, the opponent could see in from all sides. They precisely spotted the *Panzers* and concentrated fire on these, their most dangerous opponents. It was necessary to con-tinuously change positions, even if only for a few meters. We didn't know where we should move to at the end. The de-fense still completely held up in spite of this. Every *Panzer* was hit additional times. A *Pz.Kpfw.III 5 cm Kw.K. lang* (tac-tical number 32) was destroyed. A *Pak Sfl.* was shot to pieces. The Russians moved into position 80 meters away, ready to attack.

Orders came to break out of the ring about 1300 hours. At 1615 hours, the *Panzer-Grenadiere* disengaged from the enemy. The *Panzers* took over the wounded, covered the rear of the *Panzer-Grenadiere*, and followed them at about

A replacement **Pz.Kpfw.IV Ausf.G** in mint condition passes a **Pz.Kpfw.III Ausf.L** that is being repaired. (WR)

1645 hours. All of the wounded were brought along. The immobilized Panzers were blown up.

The battalion arrived in Cholm-Beresuiski one hour later.

1 December 1942 - About 0300 hours, the combined battalions commanded by Stieber and Ihle broke through the woods south of Wassilki. The Russians pursued by the hundreds. However, the breakout was achieved without significant losses.

The **Kompanie** was now attached to **Infanterie-Regiment 195**. Disregarding warnings of the consequences, all of the Panzers, even those that weren't operational, were employed for anti-tank defense of the **I.Bataillon/Infanterie-Regiment 195**. This resulted in the loss of a **Pz.Kpfw.III** that could have been recovered. After enormous difficulties, the **Kompanie** managed to free itself from being assigned subordinate to **Infanterie-Regiment 195** about 1400 hours.

At about 1600 hours, the commander of **Panzer-Regiment 31** was informed of the arrival of the remains of **Kampfgruppen** Rothkirch, Kettner, and Doleski in Kropotowo with a strength of one **Pz.Kpfw. 7.5 cm kurz**, two **Pz.Kpfw.III 5 cm lang**, five **Pz.Kpfw.III 5 cm Kw.K. kurz**, and one **7.62 cm Pak Sfl.**

The **6.Panzer-Division**, which had been resting and refitting in the West since the Spring of 1942, was rapidly loaded on rail cars and sent to the **4.Panzer-Armee** to attempt to break through to the encircled German forces at Stalingrad. As related by the following excerpts from their war diary, **Panzer-Regiment 11** went into action directly after being unloaded:

3 December 1942 - At Remontnaja

The **2.Kompanie** was unloaded from the rail transport and pulled into bivouac west of Remontnaja.

1015 hours - The Division Ia called: The enemy is attacking Pochlebin from the north. The **6.Panzer-Division** has pulled the **1.** and **5.Kompanie/Panzer-Regiment 11** into Kotelnikowo. **Panzer-Regiment 11** is to prepare for combat.

1030 hours - The division ordered: All **Kompanien** of **Panzer-Regiment 11** are to be sent forward. The regimental

commander is to move to division headquarters. The **1.**, **2.**, **5.**, and **8.Kompanien** are to be assigned to the commander of the **II.Abteilung** (Baeke). The **Stab II.Abteilung**, 2. and **8.Kompanien** are to move to Swenitschnyj. **Abteilung Baeke** will report directly to **6.Panzer-Division**.

1100 hours - The opponent had swept through Pochlebin from north to south with tanks and overrun the **3.Kompanie/Panzer-Grenadier-Regiment 114**, which had been guarding the village.

1300 hours - The **6.** and **7.Kompanien** were unloaded from rail transport in Gaschun, southwest of Remontnaja. The commander and elements of the **Stabs-Kompanie I.Abteilung** had also arrived in the interim. The **Kompanien** were ordered to bivouac east of the **Regiment**, if possible, so that they can be quickly moved to the front.

The opponent's tanks south of Pochlebin had turned west toward Kajorekij and were repulsed by our **Panzer-Jaegern** that were located there. The **1.** and **5.Kompanie/Panzer-Regiment 11** and the **II.Bataillon/Panzer-Grenadier-Regiment 114** were sent in by the division to attack this enemy.

1400 hours - Division Ia called that the opponent appears to have turned away. One speculates that on 4 December the enemy will move out of Pochlebin and attempt to envelop Kotelnikowo. The division ordered the **Stab I.Abteilung** with the **6.** and **7.Kompanien** to move to Korolew, west northwest of Ssemitschnaja.

It is foreseen that after presenting the results of reconnaissance to the division commander on 4 December, the commander of **Panzer-Regiment 11** will take over command of both its **Abteilungen**.

1900 hours - The **1.** and **5.Kompanie** had encountered enemy tanks south of Pochlebin as night fell. Positioned behind a ridge, the enemy had let both Kompanien come on. One enemy tank was knocked out. One of our Panzers burned out, with one killed and one wounded. Darkness ended the battle.

During the night the **6.** and **7.Kompanien** were diverted to Ssemitschnyj. The march was extraordinarily difficult because of the slick ground. It was thawing weather and the trails were muddy. The regimental commander and the

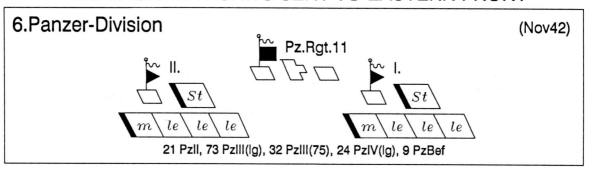

ORGANIZATION AND STRENGTH OF PANZER UNITS
REPLACEMENT UNITS SENT TO EASTERN FRONT

6.Panzer-Division
(Nov42)

Pz.Rgt.11

21 PzII, 73 PzIII(lg), 32 PzIII(75), 24 PzIV(lg), 9 PzBef

I.Abteilung commander were also ordered to move there in the early morning of 4 December.

The *3.Kompanie* was unloaded from rail transport in Remontnaja and remained there under orders from the division. The *4.Kompanie* was to be pulled forward to Ssemitschnaja and unloaded with orders to remain there.

4 December 1942 - At Ssemitschnaja

The commander with the *Regiments-Stab* remained with the division in Ssemitschnaja for the night of 3/4 December in order to be available to attack on 4 December with two *Abteilungen* (six *Kompanien*) in the event that aerial reconnaissance spotted strong enemy forces near Pochlebin.

0245 hours - The adjutant was ordered to the Division Ia. Reconnaissance had reported noise from tanks at Pochlebin during the night. The division assumed that the enemy was reinforcing, especially with tanks, and ordered: The entire *Panzer-Regiment* was to attack as early as possible. The following forces are available:

Abteilung Baeke with *Stab II.Abteilung*, 1., 2., 5., and 8.*Kompanien*

Abteilung Loewe with *Stab I.Abteilung*, 4., 6., and 7.*Kompanien*

II.(SPW) Bataillon/Panzer-Grenadier-Regiment 114

1.(Sfl.) Kompanie/Panzer-Jaeger-Abteilung 41

I.Abteilung/Artillerie-Regiment 76 with one *leichte* and one *schwere Batterie*

The *4.Kompanie*, ordered to move to Ssemischnyj directly after unloading from rail transport in Ssemitschnaja, had problems during unloading and didn't arrive in Ssemitschnyj until 0645 hours.

0530 hours - The regimental commander briefly oriented the *Abteilung* commanders in Ssemischnyj and then drove to the commander of *Panzer-Grenadier-Regiment 114* in order to use the reconnaissance reports available there to plan the attack. Unnecessary delays occurred because of poor reconnaissance sent in too late by the *Grenadier-Regiment*. The results of the reconnaissance contained nothing about the enemy tanks. The advanced observation posts had only spotted enemy infantry moving into the defile between Pochlebin and Majorskij.

The Regiment commander decided to immediately attack Pochlebin from the west and northwest and set the time for disseminating orders as 0830 hours at the command post of *Panzer-Grenadier-Regiment 114*. The *Abteilung* commanders were informed to move their *Kompanien* into the assembly areas.

0830 hours - The following orders were given out: Attack Pochlebin from the west and northwest to destroy the enemy and take Pochlebin. The attack will continue up to the Akssej River north of Pochlebin. Clean out the area around and north of Pochlebin.

1.Kompanie/Panzer-Regiment 11 and *1.Kompanie/Panzer-Jaeger-Abteilung 41* should hold the right wing and prevent the enemy from pulling out to the south. The main body of the *II.Abteilung/Panzer-Regiment 11* with its right

wing on Majorskij is to attack Pochlebin with the main effort to the left through Point 76.6. Starting at Point 94.4, *I./Abteilung/Panzer-Regiment 11* is to attack Pochlebin from the northwest, with the main effort to the left through the Komlowaja defile 2 kilometers north of Pochlebin. *II.Bataillon/Panzer-Grenadier-Regiment 114* is to follow between the Panzer-Abteilungen in the event that the enemy retreats to the north in order to be able to move forward to the road from Pochlebin to Wessely. The *I.Abteilung/Artillerie-Regiment 76* with two *Batterien* is to support the attack and at the beginning of the attack is to fire on Pochlebin and the hills close to Pochlebin in order to cause the enemy to start moving and thereby create targets for the Panzers. The *schwere Flak* in Kotelnikowo have orders to fire at Pochlebin when they receive the radio message that the *Panzer-Regiment* has started to attack.

0945 hours - *I.Abteilung/Panzer-Regiment 11* reported that they had arrived at the assembly area. The regimental commander ordered the attack to start.

0955 hours - The attack began but the *II.Abteilung* only gained ground slowly. In a frontal attack on the hills by Pochlebin, the *II.Abteilung* encountered heavy, well-aimed fire from excellently camouflaged enemy tanks and anti-aircraft guns. In a short time, three Panzers of the *8. mittlere Kompanie* had been hit. The Panzers exploded. In addition, several Panzers of the *2.Kompanie* were burning because the fuel cans fastened on the rear deck of the Panzers were hit. Because of ignited fuel cans, the commander of the *2.Kompanie* had to leave his burning Panzer and was severely wounded while outside his Panzer. Loss of the commander caused a significant reduction in the combat value of the *Kompanie*.

Because of the difficulty in orientation, *I.Abteilung/Panzer-Regiment 11*, which was supposed to attack Pochlebin from Point 94.4, started out too far north and was pulled even farther north because it wanted to cut off the enemy retreating to the north.

By radio, the regimental commander gave the *I.Abteilung* orders to turn toward Pochlebin, drove across the battlefield toward the *Abteilung*, and brought them back from the north to attack Pochlebin and to support the hard-pressed, halted *II.Abteilung*. The attack of the *I.Abteilung* relieved the pressure on the *II.Abteilung*, and their attack again gained ground. The hills and village of Pochlebin were taken from the west and north at 1200 hours. As a result of the wide swing of the *I.Abteilung*, a hole occurred between the *Panzer-Abteilungen* which the opponent cleverly exploited to break out. Elements of both *Panzer-Abteilungen* and the *SPW-Bataillon* immediately turned but couldn't prevent part of the enemy forces mounted on horses from breaking out. This didn't alter the success of the attack.

II.Bataillon/Panzer-Grenadier-Regiment 114, which up to now had followed the battle, was now ordered to mop up the battlefield. Depressions in the terrain, deeply cut by gullies, favored the enemy dug-in on the ground in front of

Pochlebin. The enemy let the Panzers roll past and then rejoined in the defense. Thus, an increasing number of Panzers were fired at from close range, especially by the long anti-tank rifles.

After Pochlebin was taken, the enemy infantry and dismounted cavalry units were pushed together in the ravine between Pochlebin and Majorskij. By nightfall, the **5.Kompanie** supported by two **SPW-Kompanien** had mopped up the enemy, only a few of which had still offered resistance.

Shortly before nightfall, the **Panzer-Regiment** assembled on the south side of Pochlebin. The battlefield was totally quiet. The results of the battle included 10 tanks knocked out, 14 guns captured, and 1200 counted prisoners. Another 800 prisoners were later reported by the **SPW-Bataillon** which remained in Pochlebin. Cleaning up the battlefield the next day brought in a large number of anti-tank rifles, machine guns and other captured equipment such as about 800 horses.

The battle was victoriously decided by the swift attack of the main body of the **Panzer-Regiment**, consisting of about 90 Panzers. The **3.Kompanie** and the **leichten Zuege** from the **Regiments-Stab** and **Stab II.Abteilung/Panzer-Regiment 11** weren't unloaded until the day of the battle. A number of Panzers had suffered mechanical breakdowns during the nighttime approach march to the assembly areas because of the difficult condition of the trails, marsh, and mud.

A significant part of the success was due to the **II.Abteilung/Panzer-Regiment 11** and by the incisive and self-sacrificing combat of the **1.** and **8.Kompanie**. Special recognition was earned by Oberleutnant Ranzinger, commander of the **8.Kompanie**, who mounted up again in another Panzer as each of three Panzers that he was in were knocked out.

Our losses were one **mittlere Kranken-Panzer-Wagen** and one **SPW** as well as a **7.62 cm Pak Sfl.**, eight killed, and 28 wounded. Five Panzers were lost as total write-offs (of which one had already been lost on 3 December) and 12 Panzers were temporarily out of action (of which five had broken down prior to the battle).

Another view of this same battle was recorded in the combat report from the **II.Abteilung/Panzer-Regiment 11**:

At 1000 hours on 4 December 1942, the **Abteilung** was located in the assembly area on the height northwest of Majorskij with orders to reoccupy Pochlebin, which had been captured by the Russians the day before, and to destroy any enemy forces found there.

The **Abteilung** formed up with the **5.Kompanie** to the right front, **8.Kompanie** left, **2.Kompanie** echeloned to the left rear, and the **Abteilung-Stab** behind the **8.Kompanie**. The **I.Abteilung** was on the left and the **II./Panzer-Grenadier-Regiment 114** behind the **I.Abteilung**.

About 1000 hours, the **Abteilung** received orders from the **Panzer-Regiment** to quickly start because the Russians were pulling out to the north. In a smooth advance toward the

northwest, receiving artillery fire, the **Abteilung** arrived on the heights southwest of Pochlebin about 1045 hours.

As they crossed over the ridge southwest of Pochlebin, the **Abteilung** was hit by heavy anti-tank gun fire from the western edge of the village. Especially heavy fire was returned by the **2.** and **8.Kompanien**, who had moved to positions closer to the village. The **2.** and **8.Kompanien** knocked out a number of anti-tank guns. In addition, the **8.Kompanie** shot up five T34 tanks that were pulling back to the north.

In spite of this, Russian anti-tank guns managed to knock out four of the **8.Kompanie** Panzers. Three Panzers of the **2.Kompanie** were also knocked out of action and many others damaged. During this firefight, the **5.Kompanie** went into position to engage the enemy anti-tank guns, infantry, and cavalry south of Pochlebin. The **5.Kompanie** managed to destroy several anti-tank guns.

About 1205 hours, the **Abteilung** received a radio message that the **Kompanie** commanded by Scheibert had arrived 800 meters north of the village of Pochlebin. After this the **Abteilung** advanced toward Pochlebin again. The **Abteilung** succeeded in storming past the south edge of Pochlebin and destroyed the strong infantry opponent defending themselves with anti-tank rifles and hand grenades against our attack. On orders from the commander, the **5.Kompanie** advanced further toward the southeast to destroy the infantry dug-in in field positions and foxholes and captured 352 prisoners.

At 1430 hours, the **Abteilung** assembled east of Pochlebin and on orders from the **Regiment** started the return march to Maiorskyj and Ssemitschnyj.

The **7.Kompanie** remained behind with **Bataillon Kueper** to defend Pochlebin.

Losses:	8.Kompanie	4 Pz.Kpfw.IV knocked out, of which three were total write-offs.
	2.Kompanie	3 Panzers knocked out
	5.Kompanie	1 gun barrel failure
	Stabs-Kompanie	Sanitaets-M.T.W. knocked out.

Personnel losses: 8 dead and 24 wounded.

Panzer tactics employed to combat the Russian armored spearheads during this period are also revealed in the following report sent by General von Machensen, commander of the **1.Panzer-Armee** to General Guderian on 21 March 1943:

While assigned to the **1.Panzer-Armee**, the **11.Panzer-Division** reported comparatively very high tank kills, which initiated the thought that this division had exploited a lesson that was not generally known. I therefore asked the division commander, Generalleutnant Balck, to write the report that I have enclosed. Even though it doesn't contain secret methods, it is still full of new insights. In addition, Generalleutnant Balck verbally explained:

1. Well-trained, older Panzer crews are the decisive fac-

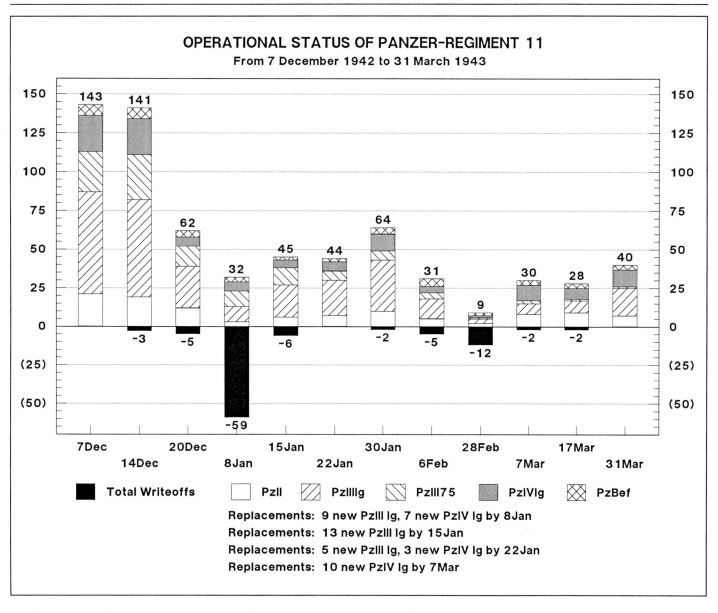

OPERATIONAL STATUS OF PANZER-REGIMENT 11
From 7 December 1942 to 31 March 1943

Total Writeoffs — PzII — PzIIIlg — PzIII75 — PzIVlg — PzBef

Replacements: 9 new PzIII lg, 7 new PzIV lg by 8Jan
Replacements: 13 new PzIII lg by 15Jan
Replacements: 5 new PzIII lg, 3 new PzIV lg by 22Jan
Replacements: 10 new PzIV lg by 7Mar

tor for success. Their experience, in addition to their calmness and self-assuredness gained through previous successes, is the basis for all of the great achievements. Young replacement crews sent to the unit must first be trained. It is preferable to start off with fewer Panzers than to set out with young crews who lack combat experience.

2. Whenever possible, let an identified opponent advance. The one that rashly charges forward is disadvantaged. An attempt should be made to fall on the enemy from the flank whenever possible from an ambush position. In addition, in order to surprise the enemy, it is often useful to prepare for combat while it is still dark!

3. Cunningly and skillfully stalking the opponent like a hunter works. This is especially successful against tanks in built-up areas. Dismounted crew members scout on foot to locate especially suitable tanks to attack and establish a plan of attack for each individual action before the attack. Tank-versus-tank actions in built-up areas are always conducted

methodically step-by-step, employing mutually covering fire support, and often last an hour or longer for each enemy tank.

Experience in Combat Against Tanks by Generalleutnant Balck, commander of the **11.Panzer-Division**, dated 12 March 1943:

During the period from 28 June 1942 to 11 March 1943, the division knocked out 1000 tanks, of which 664 were knocked out by **Panzer-Regiment 15** and 336 by other weapons. Of the latter, 65 were destroyed by tank-hunter teams in close combat. This compares to our own losses of 50 Panzers as total write-offs.

The division notes that, disregarding any small inaccuracy, they consider these numbers to be correct, because whenever possible they themselves examined the number of kills claimed. Confirmation of the claims by the troops was constantly confirmed by the numbers of knocked-out tanks that the **Pionier-Bataillon** reported that they had blown up with explosives. When Barenkowa was taken, the troops reported 27 kills. A follow-up count on the next day revealed 54 Russian tanks. Therefore, the troops had not included in their claims tanks that had been destroyed by the **Luftwaffe** or had been abandoned in previous battles.

This achievement was due mainly to the high morale of the troops, their determined will to fight, and the quality of their commanders.

The following three main points result from looking back to determine what contributed to these successes:

1. The division must understand the enemy tank unit in order to force him to fight under unfavorable conditions.

2. All weapons and all available means are to be concentrated to fight tanks.

3. The tactics employed by the Panzer-Regiment and individual Panzers.

Point 1: Whenever possible, the attack should be initiated in the rear of the enemy tank unit. Three times this Winter the division's Panzers started to attack the enemy in the rear at the same time that the enemy started to attack. On 8 December 1942, 39 tanks were knocked out near Sowchos Nr.79 without losing a single Panzer as a total write-off, and on 19 December, 35 tanks were knocked out in comparison with two total write-offs for us. An enemy unit was surrounded on 25 December 1942, but his destruction didn't occur until a few days later by troops from the **6.Panzer-Division** because the **11.Panzer-Division** had only eight Panzers left to oppose at least 30 enemy tanks.

When our Panzer attack unexpectedly encountered an enemy position, usually the enemy was forced and seduced to immediately conduct fragmented and unplanned counterstrikes. These cost the enemy high losses, if one skillfully let them close in. The first successful attack on 19 December 1942 was followed by strong, fragmented, and unconcentrated Russian tank counterstrikes in which 30 enemy tanks were knocked out in comparison to one Panzer loss as a total write-off. On 20 February 1943, the division struck the Russian Rollbahn near Nowa Alexandrowka. Here numerous tank counterattacks were defeated in the same way, resulting in 15 Russian tanks kills, and not a single Panzer was lost as a total write-off.

If an opponent in a defensive position isn't surprised by an unexpected approach, surprise can be achieved by tactical means. On 24 January 1943, the division attacked the 5-kilometer-long village of Meschnytschkaja. An open plain, 3 kilometers wide, lay in front of the village. An enemy tank force drove up and down the village street, constantly shifting superior forces into position at the right time and frustrating every attempt to break in. A fake attack by **Panzerspaehwagen** and **Pz.Kpfw.II** on the northern end of the village under cover of a heavy smokescreen was set up for the next day. The fake attack was staged to draw the Russian tanks to the northern end of the village, then to attack the southern end supported by strong artillery and Stuka

preparations, and attack from the rear those Russian tanks that were drawn toward the northern end.

The plan was completely successful. Almost all of the Russian tanks massed in front of the fake attack at the northern end of the village and were enveloped from the rear by our own Panzers. Twenty-one enemy tanks were knocked out in comparison to the loss of one Panzer as a total write-off. The entire Russian armored force was destroyed.

Finally, the Panzers must be held strictly together, regardless if there are many or a few enemy tanks. Never employ them scattered. Expressly create a **Schwerpunkt!**

Point 2: The basic requirements are to strictly follow tactical guidelines for digging in, emplacement, and employment of anti-tank guns, mines, and close-combat tank-hunter teams.

If the terrain is not covered with woods or clumps of brush and depressions aren't available, the defensive positions must be disguised artificially. Deep, slit trenches in short runs with numerous foxholes are cover against tanks and restrict those tanks that have broken into the position from working forward. The prerequisite is that enemy infantry be separated from the tanks by centrally directed concentrated artillery fire.

An interesting example of how all available elements cooperated in the destruction of the enemy is: On 27 February 1943, **Panzer-Pionier-Bataillon 209** set up a defense east of Barwenkowo. Enemy tanks were expected, their direction of attack known. The **Bataillon** had laid a mine barrier during the night, guarded by an **8.8 cm Flak** gun. At dawn, five Russian tanks charged at high speed. Two ran onto mines; one was destroyed by the **Flak** gun. The other two broke into the village at high speed and were destroyed by close-combat teams. The first tank was destroyed by the commander of **Panzer-Pionier-Bataillon 209**, the second tank by the next oldest officer.

Point 3: The **Panzer-Regiment** reported the following:

Attacks against Russian tanks are governed not only by the tactical specifications but mainly by the quality of the opposing enemy tank crews. This depends upon making the enemy insecure and to instigate movements that draw him out of favorable positions that can't be approached. If the enemy is attack happy, then immediately take up good positions with a good field of fire, move some of the Panzers into flanking positions, kill the engines so that the enemy can be heard, and then let the enemy close in on our front.

In combat in towns it is very advantageous to have **Panzer-Grenadiere** out front to seek out the enemy tanks and give timely warnings to our Panzers. However, in practice this is possible only when enemy infantry are not present. If an advanced guard is not out, four guns must be constantly ready to provide overwhelming fire to force the enemy to reveal his position and pull out of his cover. The **Pz.Kpfw.IV** can be held back from combat in towns and employed only in difficult situations.

Often the next position must first be scouted by the commander on foot. Attacks over open ground against enemy tanks under cover (edge of towns, wood lines, etc.) is prepared by a fake attack that draws the enemy tanks to a specific location. But the actual attack will charge rapidly to a different location.

In general, night attacks against enemy tanks result in losses without success and are difficult. Defend against night attacks by taking up good positions, let the enemy get close, and then suddenly open fire.

Everything depends on preventing a surprise encounter with an enemy defense line, constantly guarding against a sudden attack in the flank, and opening fire from the greatest possible number of guns. When hit by effective enemy fire, immediately withdraw and approach from a new direction. In terrain providing poor visibility, attack frontally with weak forces, and if possible, strike the enemy in the flank with strong forces.

In conclusion, it can be said that the division believes that it has achieved its success only by the coordination of all three of these points. Failure in one of the three areas cancels out success.

Connected to this, the value of a good repair service must be pointed out. In addition, all Russian tanks should be immediately blown up in order to prevent later recovery and repair by the enemy.

Even though they were successful in winning numerous local engagements, the weakened Panzer-Divisions did not succeed in breaking through to relieve Stalingrad and were continuously forced to retreat west. As shown in the <u>Panzer Strength</u> chart for July 1942 to March 1943, operational strength rapidly deteriorated as broken down and damaged Panzers were left behind in territory controlled by the Russians. Reinforcements sent in December 1942 and January 1943 consisted of the **7.Panzer-Division, Panzer-Abteilung 138, schwere Panzer-Abteilung 503, 2.Kompanie/schwere Panzer-Abteilung 502**, the **Panzer-Lehr-Kompanie 233**, and the **5.Kompanie/Fuehrer-Begleit-Bataillon**. In addition, 162 **Pz.Kpfw.III** and **40 Pz.Kpfw.IV** were sent as replacements to **Heeresgruppe B** and **Don**.

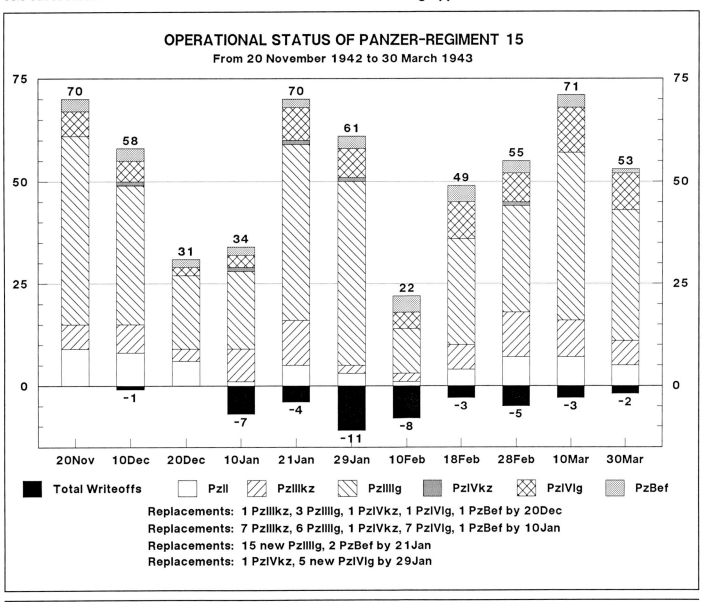

OPERATIONAL STATUS OF PANZER-REGIMENT 15
From 20 November 1942 to 30 March 1943

Replacements: 1 PzIIIkz, 3 PzIIIlg, 1 PzIVkz, 1 PzIVlg, 1 PzBef by 20Dec
Replacements: 7 PzIIIkz, 6 PzIIIlg, 1 PzIVkz, 7 PzIVlg, 1 PzBef by 10Jan
Replacements: 15 new PzIIIlg, 2 PzBef by 21Jan
Replacements: 1 PzIVkz, 5 new PzIVlg by 29Jan

Again the Russians launched offensive strikes which threatened to cut off the retreat of the **1.Panzer-Armee** and **4.Panzer-Armee** and capture the rail center at Rostov. The newly arrived **schwere Panzer-Abteilung 503** was sent in with their Tigers to counter this threat. Results of their first action were reported to **Heeresgruppe Don** at 0845 hours on 7 January 1943 as follows:

Panzer-Abteilung 503 went into combat at midday on 5 January with 16 *Pz.Kpfw.VI* and 23 *Pz.Kpfw.III (7.5 cm) kurz* operational out of the available 20 *Pz.Kpfw.VI* and 25 *Pz.Kpfw.III (7.5 cm) kurz.*

By the evening of 6 January, they probably knocked out 18 enemy tanks, of which 14 were definitely T34 tanks. Whether the total number of kills is accredited solely to **Panzer-Abteilung 503** *is being clarified by a liaison officer who was sent because radio contact with the* **Abteilung** *has been disrupted.*

Our own losses after one and a half days in combat were:

	Pz.Kpfw.VI	Pz.Kpfw.III (7.5) kurz
Totally destroyed	1 (towed back)	2
Damaged by hits	5 (light)	7 (4 light)
Mechanical breakdown	5 (3 already repaired)	2

The armor on two Pz.Kpfw.VIs was penetrated by enemy 7.62 cm anti-tank guns, once in the side armor and once in the vertical rear armor. The shells didn't enter the fighting compartment.

Ten **Pz.Kpfw.VI** *and 12* **Pz.Kpfw.III (7.5 cm) kurz** *were operational again on 7 January.*

The high losses from one and a half days in combat resulted from:

OPPOSITE: A column of Tigers from the **schwere Panzer-Abteilung 503** cresting a hill. The "13" stenciled on the commander's cupola designates the 13th step in the procedure for sealing the Tiger for submerged fording. (CHY)

ORGANIZATION AND STRENGTH OF PANZER UNITS
REPLACEMENT UNITS SENT TO EASTERN FRONT

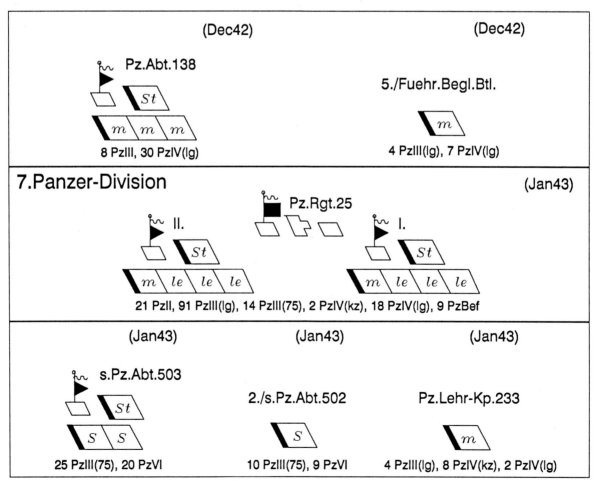

(Dec42)

Pz.Abt.138

St

m *m* *m*

8 PzIII, 30 PzIV(lg)

(Dec42)

5./Fuehr.Begl.Btl.

m

4 PzIII(lg), 7 PzIV(lg)

7.Panzer-Division   (Jan43)

Pz.Rgt.25

II.   *St*   *m* *le* *le* *le*   I.   *St*   *m* *le* *le* *le*

21 PzII, 91 PzIII(lg), 14 PzIII(75), 2 PzIV(kz), 18 PzIV(lg), 9 PzBef

(Jan43)   (Jan43)   (Jan43)

s.Pz.Abt.503

St

S *S*

25 PzIII(75), 20 PzVI

2./s.Pz.Abt.502

S

10 PzIII(75), 9 PzVI

Pz.Lehr-Kp.233

m

4 PzIII(lg), 8 PzIV(kz), 2 PzIV(lg)

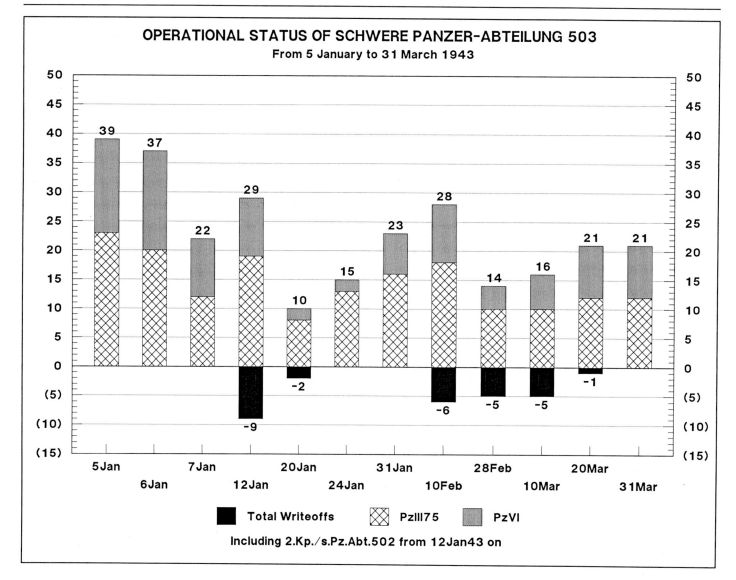

OPERATIONAL STATUS OF SCHWERE PANZER-ABTEILUNG 503
From 5 January to 31 March 1943

Legend: Total Writeoffs | PzIII75 | PzVI

Including 2.Kp./s.Pz.Abt.502 from 12Jan43 on

a. Commanders and drivers who still are not totally familiar with the equipment, which results in breakdowns, primarily transmission damage. The main cause of this was that the period of retraining from Porsche Pz.Kpfw.VI to Henschel Pz.Kpfw.VI was too short.

b. Commanders are still not correctly familiarized and mainly lack combat experience, especially in combat on the Eastern Front. Desire is present but experience is lacking in coordinated actions.

*In its first action, **Panzer-Abteilung 503** prevented a strong enemy tank force from penetrating to Proletarskaya.*

A graphic description of what it was like to fight in a Tiger was recorded by Leutnant Zabel in the following account of his impression of the enemy's ability to inflict battle damage to a Tiger:

*On 10 and 11 February 1943 in an attack on the collective farm west of Sserernikowo, **Kampfgruppe Sander** faced greatly superior forces. The Tigers in the lead platoon drew most of the enemy fire on themselves. The fire came mostly from the right flank and the front from tanks, anti-tank guns, and infantry with anti-tank rifles, all opening fire at the longest range possible.*

At the beginning of the attack, my Tiger was hit on the front of the superstructure by a 7.62 cm anti-tank gun. The track links, which had been fastened to the superstructure front plate by a steel bar, were shot away. We heard a dull clang and felt a slight jolt inside the Tiger. At the same time, we observed many near misses striking the ground to the front and the side of the Tiger.

Shortly thereafter, I received a hit on the commander's cupola from a 4.5 cm anti-tank gun. The brackets holding the glass vision block flew off. The block became welded tight but visibility was eliminated by the impact of the shell fragments. A second hit on the cupola knocked brackets loose from the turret ceiling. At the same time, a heat wave and a cloud of acrid smoke enveloped the crew. Two hits from 4.5 cm anti-tank shells and 15 hits from anti-tank rounds were counted on the cupola after the battle.

The loader's hatch, somewhat stuck and therefore about half open, received several hits from anti-tank rifles which knocked some brackets off. Other rounds striking the hatch jammed the hinges so that it could be opened only with the aid of a wrecking bar after the battle.

The enemy bathed the Tiger with machine gun fire on both days. The smoke dischargers mounted on the turret side were riddled, setting them off. This smoke filtering into the crew compartment became so thick and strong that for a short time the crew couldn't function.

The closer the Tiger approached the collective farm, the greater the intensity of the enemy defensive fire. Each hit on the Tiger was accompanied by a sharp clang, a slight jolt, acrid clouds of smoke, a shimmering yellow flash, and a detonation.

The nerves of the crew were stretched thin. We paid no attention to hunger, thirst, or time. Even though the attack lasted over 6 hours, the crew thought that only a short time had elapsed at the time.

After another 7.62 cm anti-tank shell struck the gun mantle, the brackets holding the gun snapped, the recoil cylinder began losing fluid, and the gun remained at full recoil. The shaking caused by additional hits damaged the radio, a gas tube, and the gear lever by the driver. The engine caught fire when the shield protecting the exhaust muffler was shot away, but the fire was rapidly extinguished.

An explosive charge thrown on top of the Tiger from the side was sensed as a dull explosion accompanied by heat and smoke enveloping the Tiger and the crew.

We counted 227 hits from anti-tank rifle rounds, 14 hits from 5.7 cm and 4.5 cm anti-tank guns, and 11 hits from 7.62 cm guns. The right track and suspension were heavily damaged. Several road wheels and their suspension arms were perforated. The idler wheel had worked out of its mount. In spite of all this damage, the Tiger still managed to cover an additional 60 kilometers under its own power.

The hits had caused the failure of several welded joints and caused the fuel tank to start leaking. The tracks had received several hits, but these didn't especially hinder the Tiger's mobility.

In conclusion it can be said that the armor on the Tiger can withstand the most intense punishment that the enemy can deliver. The crew can head into combat secure in the knowledge that they are surrounded by sufficient armor to keep out the most determined anti-tank round.

The **Pz.Bef.Wg. Ausf.J** belonging to the **I.Abteilung/SS-Panzer-Regiment 3** had a pistol port for the radio operator instead of a machine gun ball mount. (HLD)

A **Pz.Kpfw.III Ausf.M** being retrieved by another **Pz.Kpfw.III Ausf.M** after it had broken through the ice while attempting to cross a river during the offensive to retake Kharkov. (BA)

The area around Rostov was held until early February 1943, allowing the **1.Panzer-Armee** and **4.Panzer-Armee** to retreat to the West and set up a new defensive line anchored on the Mius River. The Russian Winter Offensive again threatened to cut off the forces under **Heeresgruppe Don** by spearheads thrusting well to their rear toward the rail center of Dnepropstrovsk. Strong reinforcements in the form of three **SS-Divisions**, each with a complete **Panzer-Regiment** and a **schwere Panzer-Kompanie**, and the **II./Panzer-Regiment "Grossdeutschland"** with the **13.schwere Panzer-Kompanie/Panzer-Regiment "Grossdeutschland"** arrived in early February 1943. This allowed General Manstein to launch a major counteroffensive which succeeded in cutting off major Russian forces, stabilizing the front, and recapturing Kharkov.

In response to the question on the basis of their success in combating tanks during the Winter battle around Kharkov, on 3 April 1943 **Infanterie-Division "Grossdeutschland"** reported:

1. In the period from 7 March to 20 March 1943, 250 T34, 16 T60 or T70 and 3 KW-I tanks were knocked out.

2. The number of kills scored by each type of weapon were:

> *188 by **Pz.Kpfw.IV 7.5 cm lang**,*
> *41 by **Sturmgeschuetz 7.5 cm lang**,*
> *30 by **Pz.Kpfw.VI (Tiger)**,*
> *4 by **7.5 cm Pak (mot Zug)**,*
> *4 by **7.5 cm Pak (Sfl)**,*
> *1 by a direct hit from a **s.I.G.**,*
> *1 using a **Hafthohlladung** (hand-held shaped charge).*

(**Panzer-Regiment Grossdeutschland** began with 5 **Pz.Kpfw.II**, 20 **Pz.Kpfw.III 5 cm L/60**, 10 **Pz.Kpfw.IV 7.5 cm L/24**, 75 **Pz.Kpfw.IV 7.5 cm L/43**, 9 **Pz.Kpfw.VI 8.8 cm L/56**, 2 **Pz.Bef.Wg. 5 cm L/42**, and 26 **Flammpz.III**. Their losses as total write-offs amounted to 1 **Pz.Kpfw.III 5 cm L/60**, 1 **Pz.Kpfw.IV 7.5 cm L/24**, 11 **Pz.Kpfw.IV 7.5 cm L/43**, and 1 **Pz.Kpfw.VI**.)

3. Degradation of the Russian armor steel was not noticeable. However, the armor steel is darker and finished rougher. The tanks reveal that they were produced in a short time, because there is no evidence of any close tolerance work. The turret of the T34 is not made from a single piece; instead it is assembled from numerous pieces. In many T34 tanks the armor walls were created from pieces of 1 cm thick steel with 6 cm filling of cast iron or other material and then a second piece of 1 cm thick steel.

4. Leadership of the enemy tanks is on the whole poor, even though there is an officer in almost every tank. Training and morale of the Russian tank crews have declined noticeably. Training usually occurs at the tank assembly plants. When halted the accuracy of the enemy tanks is good. The radio communications have apparently improved (American radio sets). It is noticeable that panic sets in when Tigers appear.

In general, the Russians cannot carry out concentrated armor attacks. Instead, they charge forward with four to nine

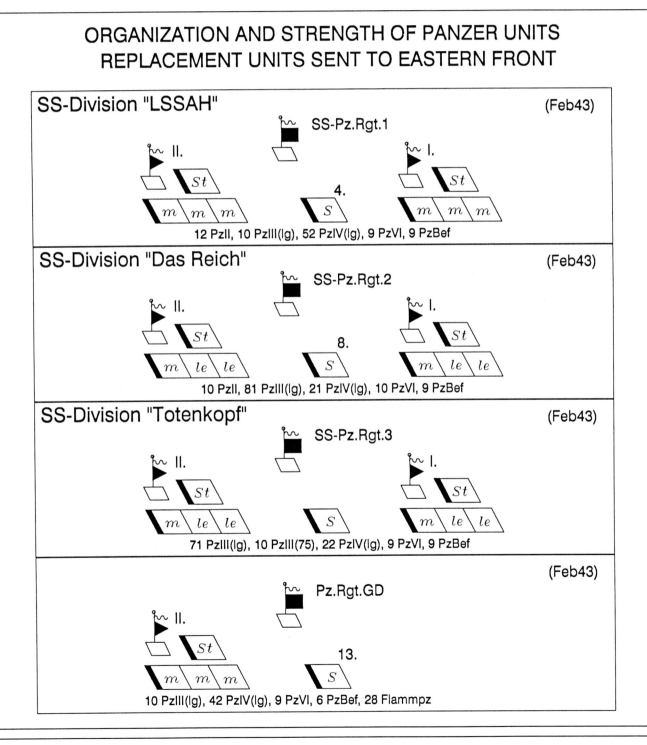

ORGANIZATION AND STRENGTH OF PANZER UNITS
REPLACEMENT UNITS SENT TO EASTERN FRONT

SS-Division "LSSAH" (Feb43)

SS-Pz.Rgt.1

II.   I.

St   4.   St

m \ m \ m   S   m \ m \ m

12 PzII, 10 PzIII(lg), 52 PzIV(lg), 9 PzVI, 9 PzBef

SS-Division "Das Reich" (Feb43)

SS-Pz.Rgt.2

II.   I.

St   8.   St

m \ le \ le   S   m \ le \ le

10 PzII, 81 PzIII(lg), 21 PzIV(lg), 10 PzVI, 9 PzBef

SS-Division "Totenkopf" (Feb43)

SS-Pz.Rgt.3

II.   I.

St   St

m \ le \ le   S   m \ le \ le

71 PzIII(lg), 10 PzIII(75), 22 PzIV(lg), 9 PzVI, 9 PzBef

(Feb43)

Pz.Rgt.GD

II.

St   13.

m \ m \ m   S

10 PzIII(lg), 42 PzIV(lg), 9 PzVI, 6 PzBef, 28 Flammpz

tanks and pull additional tanks into action with radio messages that often give a false situation report in order to lift their own morale.

5. Success hinges on starting the enemy tanks moving during our attack. The Tiger is especially suitable for this. When you get onto their flanks or into their rear, they dissolve into total confusion and are no longer capable of conducting orderly countermeasures. Then it is very easy to shoot up the enemy tanks.

In addition to the **Tiger-Kompanie** in the **Panzer-Regiment**, we should attempt to issue three or four Tigers (without the associated **Pz.Kpfw.III 5 cm lang**) to each **Panzer-Abteilung**. This is recommended because the Tiger is very suitable for breaking through well-dug-in anti-tank gun positions and in addition is used to start enemy tanks rolling that are firing at long range while halted.

In general the Russian tanks carry 100 rounds (75 high explosive and 25 armor piercing) of main gun ammunition. The quality of the ammunition has not diminished. The armor-piercing shells not only penetrate through the armor but also break up inside. Most of the time all five crew members are severely wounded when an armor-piercing shell penetrates.

Our own **Panzerkopfgranate** are exceptionally effective and amazingly accurate. However, to the contrary, due to its large dispersion the **HL/B-Granaten** (shaped charge shells) is usable at a maximum range of 500 meters. If a hit is obtained at long range by expenditure of a high number of rounds, the effect of the **HL/B-Granate** is good. However, the troops have no faith in the **HL/B-Granate**. It is desired that the supply of **Panzer-Kopfgranaten** be increased.

On 27 April 1943, the **Generalinspekteur der Panzertruppen** responded to this experience report from **Infanterie-Division "Grossdeutschland"**:

The following position is taken on the proposed use of Tigers stated in the second paragraph of Section 5. The proposal to issue three or four Tigers to every **Panzer-Abteilung** is decisively rejected. The Tiger is a **Schwerpunktwaffe** within the **Panzertruppe**. Dispersing them into the two **Panzer-Abteilung** is an idiotic squandering of this valuable equipment. The maintenance needs - especially for a Tiger - are not guaranteed in a normal **Panzer-Abteilung**. The repair service would need to be completely reorganized.

The **13.(Tiger) Kompanie/Panzer-Regiment Grossdeutschland** reported on their experience in employing **Pz.Kpfw.VI (Tiger)** from 7 to 19 March 1943 in the area of Poltawa-Belgorad:

The recent combat assignments have placed especially high demands on the **Pz.Kpfw.VI (Tiger)**. The **Tiger-Kompanie** is a self-sufficient unit within the **Panzer-Regiment** in addition to the two **Panzer-Abteilungen**. Due to the especially strong armor protection and armament of the nine **Pz.Kpfw.VI**, it is self-evident that this unit should be constantly employed as the lead element. It is also necessary to employ individual Panzers for scouting. The **Pz.Kpfw.VI** must endure these combat assignments without any type of care or necessary technical support, even including long periods without changing the oil. The Panzers are attacking during the day and then must stand guard at night which prevents any form of maintenance being performed. This resulted in the first automotive failures occurring after about five to six days in action; this could absolutely have been prevented through routine care and maintenance.

The primary failures occurred from damage to the running gear and to a lesser extent problems with the preselector system for shifting the transmission. The latter problem was partially traced back to the necessity for changing the transmission oil, because the lubrication ability of the oil was greatly reduced through excessive overtaxing and strong temperature swings. Engine failures occurred in the fewest cases of mechanical breakdowns.

In order for the highly complicated **Pz.Kpfw.VI** to receive the necessary care and maintenance, so that problems are recognized and corrected as soon as the first indications appear, it is urgently necessary to assign a second **Tiger-Kompanie** to the **Panzer-Regiment**. In this way it would be possible to employ both Tiger units alternatively. It would be necessary to combine the **Tiger-Kompanien** together within the **Panzer-Regiment**, more in the sense of a **schwere Abteilung** than assigning one **Tiger-Kompanie** to each **Panzer-Abteilung**. So, while one **Tiger-Kompanie** is employed as the lead in the lead **Panzer-Abteilung**, the second **Tiger-Kompanie** can be held in regimental reserve and accomplish maintenance tasks. The assignment of a **Tiger-Kompanie** as a **schwere Kompanie** to each **Panzer-Abteilung** will not change the current situation, because each **Panzer-Abteilung** will strive to maximize the use of the **schwere Panzers**. This will result in overwhelming tasks assigned from the start and therefore make it impossible to perform routine care and maintenance tasks.

The highly complicated Tiger must be as carefully maintained as combat aircraft in the **Luftwaffe**. Not until this is achieved will it be guaranteed that the Tiger has proven to be an extraordinary weapon.

The **Pz.Kpfw.III** as part of a **Tiger-Kompanie**: The previous combat actions have also shown that the **Pz.Kpfw.III**, originally intended to be a security vehicle for each Tiger, has not evolved to withstand hits from enemy weapons. The opponent's defensive weapons take it under fire in preference to firing at the Tiger. In addition, it would aid in improving the number of operational Panzers by having a pure company made up of only one type of Panzer. A very inefficient and complicated repair staff for the **Tiger-Kompanie** is necessary only because of transporting **Pz.Kpfw.III** repair parts in addition to the difficulties with Tiger repair parts. In this case, it is appropriate to reduce Tiger units to only one type of Panzer - the **Pz.Kpfw.VI**.

Pionier-Zug: In most cases during an attack it is not possible to scout for fords through streams and rivers or for the load capacity of bridges because of the lack of trained experts. It would be beneficial to incorporate a **Pionier-Zug** mounted on **M.T.W.** (armored half-tracks) as an organic part of a Tiger-Kompanie. Then this combat-powerful **Pionier-Zug** could accomplish these tasks and, if necessary, also reinforce bridges, prepare ramps on river banks, or clear mines. The suggested equipment for this platoon should be one **1 ton M.T.W. (Sd.Kfz.250)**, six **3 ton M.T.W. (Sd.Kfz.251)**, and three tracked trucks.

General and technical experience: During a scouting patrol two Tigers encountered about 20 Russian tanks to their front, while additional Russian tanks attacked from behind. A battle developed in which the armor and weapons of the Tiger were extraordinarily successful. Both Tigers were hit (mainly by 7.62 cm armor piercing shells) 10 and more times at ranges from 500 to 1000 meters. The armor held up all round. Not a single round penetrated through the armor. Also hits in the running gear, in which the suspension arms were torn away, did not immobilize the Tiger. While 7.62 cm anti-tank shells continuously struck outside on the armor, on the inside, undisturbed, the commander, gunner, and loader selected targets, aimed, and fired. The thin tendrils of smoke, coming from the fuming crinkling paint where the armor had been hit, were sucked in by the ventilator.

The end result was 10 enemy tanks knocked out by two Tigers within 15 minutes.

First-round hits were usually achieved with the **8.8 cm Kw.K.** gun at ranges between 600 to 1000 meters, At these ranges, the **Panzer-Granate** absolutely penetrated through the frontal armor of T34 tanks. After penetrating through the frontal armor, usually the **Panzer-Granate** still destroyed the engine at the rear of the tank. In very few cases could the T34 be set on fire when fired at from the front. Shots from the same range hitting the side of the hull toward the rear or the rear of the tank resulted in 80 percent of the cases in the fuel tanks exploding. Even at ranges of 1500 meters and longer, during favorable weather it is possible to succeed in penetrating the T34 with minimal expenditure of ammunition. Experiments in shooting at the T34 with **Sprenggranaten** could not be conducted because **Sprenggranaten** are available in very limited quantity at the present time.

Mobility: In one case two Tigers were sent to follow five T34 at a distance of about 2 kilometers. The Tigers couldn't manage to close the range even though the snow wasn't deep and the ground was hard. In no way was the Tiger less maneuverable than the T34. The Tiger is well suited as a lead tank because of its good mobility. The relatively quick acceleration is especially astounding for a tank which is especially important for deployment in a lead **Kompanie**. Loose snow drifts up to 1.5 meters deep were no obstacle.

Engines: Coolant temperatures under load held at an average temperature of 60 degrees C after the crew compartment heaters were removed from all of the **Pz.Kpfw.VI.** This temperature is almost too low for a Maybach engine.

After the heaters were removed, engine fires no longer occurred and sufficient air cooling of the exhaust pipes was achieved. All engines require routine intensive care if they are to run smoothly without problems. Sometimes after a long operation, flames 50 cm high shot out of both exhaust pipes and could be seen at long distances at night.

Armament: The **8.8 cm Kw.K.** gun proved to be a dependable and effective weapon. No problems or breakdowns occurred in the electrical firing circuit. **Sprenggranaten** were fired at an moving artillery column at a range of 5000 meters. A direct hit was achieved with the third round. Horses and men immediately lay in the snow. With **Panzer-Kopfgranaten**, penetrating hits were scored on T34 tanks with minimal ammunition expenditure at ranges of 1500 meters and longer.

Armor: In every case the armor is proof against hits from 7.62 cm armor-piercing and high explosive shells. In one case, the commander's cupola was hit on the weld at its base by a 7.62 cm armor piercing shell which tore and rotated the commander's cupola from its seat. The hit also ripped open the cupola in two locations. The vision block holders were torn out entirely. The commander was severely wounded.

As a result of further experience, all of the Nebel-**Abwurfvorrichtungen** (smoke candle dischargers) were taken off. In several cases the **Nebelkerzen** (smoke candles) themselves had ignited when hit. The crew had to immediately evacuate because engine's combustion air was drawn in from the fighting compartment. In one case the driver died of smoke poisoning.

Fordability: In almost all cases in which Tigers broke through the ice in water about 1 meter deep, water came in even though the drain valves on the bottom were closed. Water flowed out of every opening in the hull when the Tigers were recovered. Because Tigers have to detour around bridges and ford rivers, there is an urgent need to achieve 100 percent fordability at depths of at least 1.30 meters.

With the exception of known childhood diseases, the Pz.Kpfw.VI has proven itself to be good. Already, it can be said that its reliability is superior to the Pz.Kpfw.III and IV. When routine care and maintenance are accomplished (that means one day for maintenance for three days in action), even the way it is now, the Tiger can achieve exceptional success. But it is an urgent need that only old experienced drivers be employed, at best mechanics, and especially well-trained, technically competent personnel be assigned to the maintenance section. The main emphasis should be placed on knowledge of the integral workings of the component parts and knowledge of the care of the vehicle during driver's training. Practical driving should be secondary. Only after the driver has grasped the basics of the steering gear and transmission will he be able to drive correctly.

On 11 April 1943 the **Panzeroffizier** on staff by the **Chef General Stab des Heeres** commented on the report from the **Tiger-Kompanie** of **Infanterie-Division "Gross-Deutschland"**:

A Tiger from the **schwere Kompanie/SS-Panzer-Regiment 2** being towed by a train of three 18-ton **Zugkraftwagen**. (BA)

Employing Tigers as the lead units is not self-evidently correct. Situations will occur where this is necessary or useful. The controlling factors are the tasks and the number of operational Tigers. If there are only nine Tigers in the Division, their assignment to the point means that the Tigers will not be available when they are needed to attack enemy tanks. Losses will frequently occur due to mines and bridge failure, plus getting hung up in uncrossable terrain. In addition, immobilized Tigers will frequently block the way.

*In order to maintain the high operational and production value of the Tigers, it is necessary to concentrate the Tigers in units so that concentrated purposeful employment, maintenance, and care can be achieved. That is why the **General der Schnellen Truppen** has repeatedly proposed the creation of **Tiger-Abteilungen** consisting of three **Kompanien** (which has been ordered in the interim) and to assign these **Tiger-Abteilungen** as an organic part of **Panzer-Divisions**. This was first achieved with **schwere Panzer-Abteilung 501** assigned to the **10.Panzer-Division**.*

*A **Pionier-Zug** is found in the **Stabs-Kompanie** of the **Tiger-Abteilung**. Assigning a **Pionier-Zug** to each **Tiger-Kompanie** cannot be justified.*

*The results achieved with the **8.8 cm Kw.K.** gun are the same as those calculated and are known.*

The very good mobility of the Tiger is known. However, because the T34 has 19 metric horsepower per ton and the Tiger 11.5 per ton, the acceleration and speed of the T34 may be superior to the Tiger.

A usable crew compartment heater is planned for the Tiger for the Winter of 1943/44.

*The deficiencies of the **Nebelabwurfvorrichtung** are known. However, because smoke can't be dispensed with, the **General der Schnellen Truppen** has requested a mortar be installed on the turret that can shoot both **Nebel** and **Sprenggranaten**. Experiments are still ongoing.*

On 14 May 1943, General Guderian, **Generalinspekteur der Panzertruppen**, took the following position on the experience report from the **13.Kompanie (Tiger)/Panzer-Regiment "Grossdeutschland"**:

*1. The experience report states that it is self-evident that the **Tiger-Kompanie** is constantly employed as the point unit. Fundamentally, this statement cannot be endorsed.*

The Tiger unit is the most valuable and strongest weapon in a Panzer unit. If it is used as the point unit, it will quickly bring localized success because of its high combat power. However, they will have insufficient force at the start of a decisive battle that could mean destruction of the opponent in the depths of his position, because the Tigers will suffer heavy breakdowns due to mines, hits, and terrain obstacles. Therefore, they will enter the decisive phase of the battle already greatly depleted.

Fundamentally a point unit has increased fuel consumption. Because the Tiger already has a limited radius of action, when it is used as a lead vehicle the situation must occur that it will be short of fuel at the start of the decisive phase of the battle.

*2. The request for a second **Tiger-Kompanie** is incorrect. Fundamentally we should strive to employ the Tigers concentrated in a **Panzer-Abteilung** with three **Kompanien** for a total of 45 Tigers.*

*3. Outfitting Tiger units with the **Pz.Kpfw.III** or **Pz.Kpfw.IV** is not deemed necessary. However, since the **Tiger-Abteilung** must have its own reconnaissance capability, the **Generalinspekteur der Panzertruppen** has requested the creation of an **Aufklaerungszug (SPW)** (reconnaissance platoon mounted on armored half-tracks) as a trial unit for **schwere Panzer-Abteilung 503**. Based on the experience gained by **schwere (Tiger) Panzer-Abteilung 503**, the **Generalinspekteur der Panzertruppen** will propose the assignment of an **Aufklaerungszug** to each **schwere (Tiger) Panzer-Abteilung**.*

Farther to the north, the **Panzertruppen** under **Heeresgruppe Mitte** had also succeeded in stabilizing the situation in March 1943. The Panzers' ability to knock out enemy tanks during these battles is related in the following detailed report compiled by the **5.Panzer-Division** for the period from 22 February to 20 March 1943. This shows the relative effectiveness of each type of Panzer as well as the ranges at which the Panzers were firing:

Type and Number of Pz.Kpfw.	Number and Type of Enemy Tanks Knocked Out and Effect of Types of Ammunition Used
7.5 cm Kw.K. L/43 in 4 **Pz.Kpfw.IV**	17 KW-I, 26 T34, 1 T26, 1 Mark II, 3 Mark III, 1 General Lee. **Pzgr.39** was fired at ranges from 1200 to 1600 meters. Every hit caused a destructive effect with the tank going up in flames. Two to three **Pzgr.39** rounds were expended per tank killed. **Gr.38 HL/B** ammunition was seldom used. One to five rounds were required to set an enemy tank on fire.
7.5 cm Kw.K. L/24 in 9 **Pz.Kpfw.III** and 5 **Pz.Kpfw.IV**	1 KW-I, 6 T34, 1 T60, 4 T26, 1 Mark II, 4 Mark III, 2 General Lee. **Gr.38 HL/B** had a destructive effect when fired at ranges under 600 meters at the hull and rear of the KW-I. The T34 was also engaged by firing at the hull. Three to six rounds of **Gr.38 HL/B** were required to kill each enemy tank.
5 cm Kw.K. L/60 in 10 **Pz.Kpfw.III**	2 KW-I, 18 T34, 3 T70, 7 T60, 4 T26, 2 Mark II, 6 Mark III, 2 General Lee, 3 type not reported. Only the hull and rear of the KW I and T34 were engaged at ranges under 150 meters. Very seldom does the tank catch on fire. Two to five rounds of **Pzgr.39** or **Pzgr.40** were expended to kill each KW-I or T34. One to three rounds were expended to kill each lighter tank.
5 cm Kw.K. L/42 in 17 **Pz.Kpfw.III**	5 T34, 2 T60, 4 Mark II, 3 Mark III, 3 General Lee, 3 type not reported. Same ammunition use and effect as **5 cm Kw.K. L/60**.

The Panzers in **Panzer-Regiment 31** accounted for 145 of the 214 tanks destroyed by the **5.Panzer-Division**. 6937 rounds of all types of 5 cm and 7.5 cm tank gun ammunition were expended. **Panzer-Regiment 31** lost a total of 23 Panzers (2 **Pz.Kpfw.II**, 8 **Pz.Kpfw.III 5 cm L/42**, 3 **Pz.Kpfw.III 5 cm L/60**, 6 **Pz.Kpfw.III 7.5 cm L/24**, 3 **Pz.Kpfw.IV 7.5 cm L/24**, and 1 **Pz.Kpfw.III 7.5 cm L/43**) as total write-offs from all causes. They received only one **Pz.Kpfw.III 5 cm L/42** and one **Pz.Kpfw.IV 7.5 cm L/24** as replacements during this same period.

Their ability to knock out the "technically" superior T-34 and KW-I tanks with their **Pz.Kpfw.IIIs** and **Pz.Kpfw.IVs** is even more impressive when it is recognized that these Panzer units were frequently handicapped by orders from superiors who didn't understand the tactics these Panzers needed to use in order to succeed in combat. As shown by the following accounts, the **Panzertruppen** were encountering major problems when they were attached to infantry units, even within their own division. Oberleutnant von Prondzynski, commander of the **1.Kompanie/Panzer-Regiment 31** in support of **Infanterie-Regiment 337** reported:

*On 8 March, I arrived about midnight at the regimental command post in Dynnaja and reported to the regimental commander. He ordered me to move to the command post of **Infanterie-Regiment 337** and report to them with all of the* *available operational Panzers refueled and filled with ammunition. I was further ordered to attack with the infantry and take the heights at dawn.*

*At 0330 hours, I marched out of Dynnaja with one **Pz.Kpfw.IV lang**, two **Pz.Kpfw.IV kurz**, and two **Pz.Kpfw.III kurz**. I reached the Jasenok valley south of Bukan about 0530 hours. One **Pz.Kpfw.III kurz** dropped out due to engine trouble during the move. This Panzer remained in the valley while I was accompanied to the **Infanterie-Regiment 337** command post by an officer from **Panzer-Regiment 33**. There I received the following briefing and assignment from the commander, Oberst Kokott: The enemy captured Point 206 on 7 March, advanced further west to the road from Bukan to Osslinka, and occupied the clumps of bushes along the road north of the grain mill. These clumps of bushes are being used by the enemy as an assembly area and it must be calculated that they are occupied with strong forces especially with heavy weapons, above all anti-tank rifles and guns.*

*The **Panzer-Gruppe** with two Infanterie Kompanien is to attack Point 206 and occupy it.*

*Battle Plan: With infantry from the right-hand company mounted on the Panzers, the **Panzer-Gruppe** is to start from the Jasinok valley toward the clumps of bushes along the road, halt there until these are completely cleaned out, and then strike in one bound to the small depression southeast of these clumps of bushes. From there, the Panzers are to strike in another bound to Point 206, await for the infantry to arrive and take up defensive positions, and return to the starting point in order to get ready for the next assignment, an attack on Point 218.*

The commander also remarked that at the moment the Panzers move out of the clumps of bushes, they must calculate that they will be engaged frontally by anti-tank and tank gun fire. During the bound toward the height, heavy anti-aircraft gun fire from the left and other fire from all weapons from both flanks should be expected.

*I informed the commander that I could not promise any success from this attack because as a result of the experience of the previous days I must assume that 1. the infantry would not follow and 2. the enemy defense was sufficiently strong to knock out all of the Panzers in a short time. An officer from **Panzer-Regiment 33** present at the command post also stated that, based on his experience in several actions in this sector, the attack was hopeless from the start. Then Oberst Kokott warned that the attack must be conducted in accordance with the orders of the commanding general. Because I knew that both the **5.Panzer-Division** and my **Panzer-Regiment** had been briefed on the attack orders, I didn't see any possibility that this attack order would be rescinded by anyone informed by me.*

*I immediately got in contact with the commander of the **Infanterie-Kompanie** on the right and came to an agreement with him on the strength of the infantry that were to ride on the Panzers and the plan of attack. Thereafter, I wanted to start from the Jasenok valley with the Panzers in line and,*

*with all weapons, firing quickly charge to the clumps of bushes along the road. This should pin down the enemy infantry from the start and accelerate the advance of our own **Infanterie**.*

*The start of the attack set for 0615 hours, was delayed for 15 minutes because an additional two Panzers arrived at 0615 hours. As planned, the charge happened very quickly. Together with the **Infanterie**, the Panzers came within short range of the clumps of bushes when heavy tank gun, anti-tank gun, and anti-tank rifle fire suddenly commenced. Five Panzers immediately fell out. The crews had to dismount and because of heavy machine gun fire pulled back to the starting point. The Panzer advancing on the far left got into the clumps of bushes unnoticed by the enemy. Later, this Panzer had to be pulled back because our own infantry didn't follow and enemy tanks were located in the same clumps of bushes.*

*I reported the course of the attack to the commander of the **208.Infanterie-Division** and by telephone to the command post of the regiment.*

This wasn't an isolated incident, as reported by Leutnant Hagen of the **7.Kompanie/Panzer-Regiment 31** on the employment of two detached Panzers on 9 March 1943:

*On 9 March, with a **Pz.Kpfw.III 5 cm kurz** (Tactical Nr. 522) and a **Pz.Kpfw.IV 7.5 cm lang** (Tactical Nr.882) commanded by Oberfeldwebel Becker of the **8.Kompanie**, I was ordered to report to **Panzer-Grenadier-Regiment 14** commanded by Oberstleutnant von Baath.*

About 0700 hours, I received the following order: "From Dynnaja drive east on the paved road and report to Hauptmann Munser at the command post." When I reached the Autobahn I counted 18 enemy tank moving toward the paved road echeloned in depth at a range of 500 to 1800 meters. Hauptmann Munser gave me orders to destroy several enemy tanks from a position on the paved road and then drive down the paved road in order to destroy additional tanks.

*I drove about 150 meters back from the paved road into a hull-down position because at this location the Autobahn ran along a ridgeline and several enemy tanks were already firing at us. I explained to Hauptmann Munser that it was impossible to carry out this order because by driving along the Autobahn we would show the side of our Panzers to enemy fire and my weapons were inferior to the numerous enemy tanks, some of which were heavy tanks. In the presence of the troops, my tactical handling was laid out as cowardice, with a cursing reproach amplified by the words: "All you **Panzersoldaten** prefer to drive backward instead of forward!"*

During the afternoon of the same day I received a new order from Hauptmann Munser to advance past the main battle line with my two Panzers without infantry escort in order to frighten the enemy tanks on the east side of the paved road. To carry out this order, in order to destroy a few enemy tanks both Panzers would have had to be driven between the enemy tanks. I then explained to Hauptmann Munser that it was also impossible to carry out this order and also that there were two 44-ton tanks, several T34 tanks, and other light tanks that would immediately knock out my Panzers on the ridge, while my own Panzers guns were ineffective at these ranges. In addition, two 7.62 cm anti-tank/aircraft guns and two 4.7 cm anti-tank guns were in position east of the Autobahn. I explained to Hauptmann Munser that driving into the middle of the Russian position with my two Panzers would be ineffectual and impossible. I was forced to let the enemy tanks advance and then to destroy them at close range.

*Hauptmann Munser replied: "You have one **7.5 cm lang Pz.Kpfw.** and that is 50 percent of your vehicles. Therefore in order to destroy the Russian tanks, you are to immediately drive over the main battle line between the enemy tanks."*

*It was also impossible to follow this order and I made Hauptmann Munser aware of the divisional order that employment of Panzers advancing over the main battle line was only allowed by direct orders from the division. Again in the presence of the troops, my handling was laid out as cowardice, with the declaration that I was subordinate to the Hauptmann and must carry out every one of his orders. Hauptmann Munser stated: "All you **Panzersoldaten** are worthless and are not useful for anything in battle." My objection that it was useless to award the enemy a prize of our Panzers because of their high value and effectiveness when correctly employed tactically was characterized as absurd, with the additional statement: "These two Panzers don't play a large role even if they are knocked out by the enemy." I couldn't afford the consequences of this order and remained with my Panzers in a hull-down position on the paved road. I reported the situation to the regimental command post by radio.*

The tactics employed by the **Panzertruppen** were evolving, forced by the circumstances of fighting defensive actions instead of engaging in major offensive campaigns directed at strategic targets. In an attempt to establish new tactical doctrine, the commander of the **LVII.Panzer-Korps** posed the following questions to the commander of the **17.Panzer-Division**:

1. During an attack how should the increasingly strong anti-tank defenses be suitably disposed of?
2. Which conclusions are to be drawn for Panzer tactics?

The commander of the **17.Panzer-Division** replied on 24 April 1943:

1. The Panzer tactics that led to the great successes in the years 1939, 1940 and 1941 must be viewed as outdated. Even if today it is still possible to breach an anti-tank defensive front through concentrated Panzer forces employed in several waves behind each other, we still must consider past experience that this always leads to significant losses that can no longer be endured by our production situation. This action, often employed in succession, leads to a very rapid reduction in the Panzer strength. Already within the past sev-

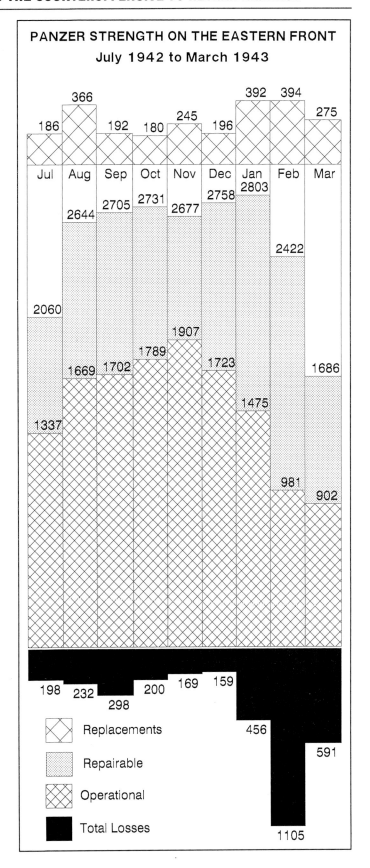

PANZER STRENGTH ON THE EASTERN FRONT
July 1942 to March 1943

eral days, the picture of a **Panzer-Division** is distorted, resulting in major difficulties for higher commanders.

The evolution of Panzer tactics is logical. The early success of a new weapon, caused by its shock effect and temporary invincibility of the attacker, always finds its end in the development of a corresponding defense. Production-wise, Panzer production is not capable of keeping up with the production of defensive weapons. Probably thousands of anti-tank rifles and dozens of anti-tank guns can be produced for one Panzer.

The following conclusions are to be drawn from these perceptions:

2. The new **Panzer-Taktik**, which out of necessity has already been successfully employed by the divisions during this campaign, is sketched out as follows:

The Panzers no longer build the core of the **Panzer-Division** around which the other weapons are grouped more or less as supporting weapons. The Panzer is a new weapon that is to be employed together with the older weapons and is equal to them. In coordination with other weapons, the Panzers still have their purpose, even if their numbers have sunk far below the authorized strength.

Their importance as new weapons is based on the fact that Panzers combine in themselves both of the elements important in an attack - mobility and firepower. They are not based on Panzers being indestructible or less destructible because of their armor.

Panzer-Division combat is characterized by possessing all mobile elements. Therefore, the commander has the capability to choose and build up a **Schwerpunkt** during an action. This principle excludes the creation of rigid inflexible plans for employment of the Panzer unit before an attack. Inflexible employment, specified in the scope of combat plans laid out before an action, is replaced by assembling and directing mobile units during an action to attack weak positions or suitable targets recognized by the division commander himself.

The battle will be initiated by an infantry attack. The infantry attack provides necessary information on the strength of the anti-tank defense front, its extent and depth. Once the anti-tank defense front is identified, following the old classical principles on the command of mobile units, the Panzers will be ordered to attack the flank or if possible the rear of the enemy defensive position. This attack will only be carried out by the Panzers alone, if it can achieve complete surprise. If surprise cannot be guaranteed, then prior to the flank attack, fire superiority of artillery and of the Panzers themselves is used to degrade the enemy anti-tank defense front so that it can be described as shaken or at least shattered. If surprise can be guaranteed, then in exceptional cases an attack can succeed against the flank of an anti-tank defense front without preparatory fire.

Even in the most favorable conditions against the flanks or rear, an attack against the enemy anti-tank defense fronts cannot be carried out only with the Panzers' weapons. It re-

quires artillery support. However, experience has shown that a Panzer attack, advancing against the flank and rear, outranges the artillery group that has been assigned to cooperate with them. Self-propelled artillery batteries are needed which use their mobility to move to firing positions in the same formation with the Panzers and thereby conform to the mobility of the Panzer unit.

3. Now that these principles for the new **Panzer-Taktik** have been laid out, their practical employment will be explained.

a. The employment of Panzers as the first attack wave against a strong, dug-in, prepared defensive position always results in too large a number of losses and therefore is incorrect.

b. The employment of Panzers against self-supporting anti-tank positions is possible under the prerequisite conditions that it be ordered by a "neutral" commander on the spot in close cooperation with the other weapons after building a **Schwerpunkt** and directed by the "neutral" commander himself as the battle progresses.

c. The employment of Panzers promises the greatest success if at the same time that it is employed and directed by the "neutral" commander on the spot, it hits the opponent in the flank shortly after the attack commences, as long as the enemy anti-tank weapons have not yet been pulled into prepared positions. Also, in this latter case, the direction and timing of the attack must be ordered by the "neutral" commander on the spot. (Using this last method, an enemy division was completely destroyed at both Kuteinikowskaja on 5 January and near Bol.Talowaja on 27 January 1943 by the vastly understrength 17.Panzer-Division).

4. The new tactics depend upon the cooperation of the three main branches of the army - infantry, Panzers, and artillery - during the entire duration of a battle. This cooperation can be guaranteed only by the commander. This means in all cases where the majority of the division is employed, the division commander on the spot directs the coordination of the weapons during the entire battle. If forced by conditions, as it was during the battles between the Don and Volga when several widely separated **Kampfgruppe** had to be assembled out of the available infantry, Panzers, and artillery, it is necessary that each of these **Kampfgruppen** be led by a "neutral" commander who in no case also directly commands the Panzers or infantry in the **Kampfgruppe** at the same time.

The means of command for the commander is the 10-Watt radio set built into the Panzers. With this device the commander is connected to the Panzer leader and also with the leader of the infantry group to which one Panzer with the desired radio set is attached. The "neutral" commander with his **S.P.W.** is connected with **Kampfgruppen** dispatched outside the **Schwerpunkt** and with his operations officer working farther back in the rear. In accordance with the usual rules of command, the commander of the artillery group finds himself by the force commander. As already explained above, he is capable of effectively supporting the Panzer attack only as commander of a artillery group consisting of self-propelled batteries. If he doesn't have mobile batteries, the danger remains that the commander of the Panzer group will be restricted in his mobility, remaining bound to the less mobile artillery that supports him.

The position of the commander during a battle is so far forward that he can easily observe and direct the Panzer battle. He is at a sufficient distance from the forward Panzer wave that he does not become entangled in the tank versus tank or tank versus anti-tank gun action. These battles absorb the attention of those Panzers fighting in the forward line to such an extent that the embroiled commander can no longer grasp the tactical decisions which apply to coordination of the other weapons. Usually the commander's position cannot be selected so that it is outside of the range of enemy artillery fire. However, due to the special means of command through the radio set, he can remain mobile. He will be positioned as far forward in an attacking wave of Panzers as he is allowed while still maintaining contact with the infantry group. From this location, the commander is in a position to reorganize the individual Panzer groups in the battle as the situation develops and the requirements for coordination of the various weapons evolve.

Cooperation of individual Panzer groups with infantry groups is possible if the "neutral" commander remains in contact with the specific Panzer groups through his radio set. Subordination of Panzer groups under infantry groups is rejected on principle. The infantry commander is not capable of coordinating the infantry, heavy infantry weapons, and artillery as well as the Panzers because he is already completely burdened in directing the battle for these other weapons. For this reason, subordination of Panzers under **Infanterie-Divisions** which were not trained in the coordination of the three weapons branches is rejected on principle.

The requirement to achieve success by the coordination of all three weapons does not exclude consolidation of all Panzers for a unified attack. This should be strived for more often. However, concentration of the Panzer forces in the **Schwerpunkt** will not be attempted prior to the beginning of a rigid set-piece battle, but by reorganizing the individual Panzer groups through flexible battle command and building the **Schwerpunkt** during the battle by the "neutral" commander himself.

5. The specifications for the design of Panzers are also to be drawn from the described tactics and command techniques for a **Panzer-Division**. The main emphasis in Panzer design must be based on mobility and firepower, because in the competition between Panzers and anti-tank defenses an indestructible Panzer can be obtained only by increasingly heavier types, which still can't be guaranteed. Cooperation of the weapons branches can never be too close. The anti-tank defense front must be shaken by artillery fire and the attack of the infantry to such an extent that the Panzer attack can quickly overrun the position. More importantly, the Panzers must be in a position to wipe out anti-tank defense

fronts at increased ranges with their own fire or so cripple them that it is possible for the attack to advance. Panzers are in a position to do this only if they possess weapons of such a caliber that with a combination of fire and movement, they can achieve fire superiority over the stationary anti-tank defensive weapons. The requirements for increased firepower, increased mobility, and at the same time relatively higher invulnerability are not compatible with each other. This doesn't need to be explained in any further detail.

The arrival of the self-propelled artillery batteries is awaited with great expectation. With longer firing ranges than the Panzers themselves, they will be capable of achieving the fire superiority that is needed to again win back supremacy over anti-tank defenses.

During battles this Winter, excellent experiences were obtained with **Sturmgeschuetz-Abteilungen**. Because of their high mobility and firepower, they were employed and directed utilizing the same principles used for Panzers. They were superior to the Panzers with regard to mobility. Using these same principles, **Pak Sfl.** (self-propelled anti-tank guns) were also employed with success in supplementing the Panzer and Sturmgeschuetz troops, especially with their firepower.

Employment of Tigers proved contrary to this. All three basic design requirements should have been fulfilled in the Tigers, namely firepower, mobility and strong armor protection. Fewer positive results were achieved with Tigers because their mobility isn't sufficient for the flexible battle tactics sketched out above. It should be taken under consideration that this experience was obtained with new units that were thrown into battle without proficiency in command by radio. However, the impression of their lack of mobility, especially in rolling terrain with hard frozen ground, remains unchanged even if training of the personnel is achieved.

In response to questions posed on how to deal with **Pak-Fronts** (massed anti-tank gun positions), the commander of the **6.Panzer-Division** sent the following reply to the **XXXXVIII.Panzer-Korps** on 19 April 1943:

When encountering a **Pak-Front** that can't be enveloped, at first lay down concentrated artillery fire on the chosen breakthrough position and then onto the flanks of the breakthrough position. The Panzer units attack during the concentrated artillery barrage and break into the position directly after the last concentrated barrage. The formation of the entire **Panzer-Abteilung** should be two companies in the front line and one echeloned company on each wing. When available, **Sturmgeschuetze** should be included within the companies as the first wave. When **Sturmgeschuetze** aren't available, use **Pz.Kpfw.IVs**. During the breakthrough, companies in the forward wave charge through to the depth of the position. The companies echeloned to the right and left widen the point of penetration to both sides and then follow after the forward companies.

When encountering a mutually supporting front of numerous **Pak-Stuetzpunkten**, based on the terrain, attack the **Stuetzpunkt** that is the easiest to attack while suppressing the **Stuetzpunkte** to its right and left. Start out with concentrated artillery fire on the **Stuetzpunkt** to be attacked directly. At the same time, the complete **Panzer-Abteilung** advances against the middle **Stuetzpunkt** with one company in the lead and one company on each flank to envelop the **Stuetzpunkt**. Half of the fourth company is used to cover each of the two neighboring **Stuetzpunkte**.

Directly before the penetrating into the enemy position, artillery fire is turned onto the neighboring **Stuetzpunkte**. The formation within the **Panzer-Kompanien** is the same as above. The follow-up after destroying the enemy **Pak-Stuetzpunkt** is the same as above. Within the **Panzer-Kompanie**, the company commander as a rule directs concentrated fire on identified and especially important targets by platoon.

If the enemy front can be enveloped, the method of attack remains the same as attacking enemy **Pak-Stuetzpunkte**.

Simultaneous support from aircraft assists in the approach and penetration into enemy defensive positions.

Attacks can be laid on in favorable terrain on not too dark a night, preferably in the last dark hour of the night. Exact scouting on the previous day is a preliminary requirement for this.

Woods in which the trees are not too thick are suitable for approaching the defensive position. The movements will be considerably slowed down, breakdowns caused by forcing tracks through the woods are not preventable, and fuel consumption is very high. But the attack frequently succeeds without any total losses, surprising the enemy by breaking into the position from an unexpected location.

Panzers with thicker armor and longer range weapons should be in the front wave. Position a **Panzer-Gruppe** of two **Pz.Kpfw.III** in front and on the flanks for reconnaissance. As a rule, **Pz.Kpfw.IIs** are used only for messenger tasks.

Generally an attack in several stages comes into play if more than one complete **Panzer-Abteilung** is available.

At least one armored **Pionier-Zug** should be permanently assigned to each **Panzer-Abteilung** to take care of the numerous Pionier tasks that are continuously encountered and to destroy captured weapons.

Reorganization of the Panzertruppen - October 1942 through December 1943

No additional **Heeres Panzer-Divisions** were formed in 1943. With the exception of the political orders to create **SS** and **Luftwaffe** units, the expansion program for the **Panzertruppen** was all but finished. Only a few scattered **Heeres Panzer-Abteilungen** were newly created and sent to plug holes. Due to losses on all fronts, the reorganization program for the **Heeres Panzertruppen** consisted mainly in attempting to outfit a complete **Panzer-Abteilung** for each **Panzer-Division** on the Eastern Front, converting existing units into **Tiger-Abteilungen** and **Panther-Abteilungen**, and re-creating units that had been wiped out at Stalingrad and in Tunisia.

Panzer-Verband 700 - On 16 October 1942, **OKH/GenStdH/Organisations-Abteilung** ordered **Heeresgruppe B** to create **Panzer-Verband 700** consisting of three **leichte Panzer-Kompanie (t)** and one **mittlere Panzer-Kompanie** as soon as possible and assign it to the **16.Infanterie-Division (mot)**. The **Pz.Kpfw.38(t)** were to be provided from excess by the **22.Panzer-Division**, and the **Pz.Kpfw.IV** for the **4.mittlere Panzer-Kompanie** were to be issued from new production. At the same time, **Panzer-Regiment 2, 24,** and **36** (of the **16., 24.,** and **14.Panzer-Divisions**, respectively) were to be reorganized into two **Panzer-Abteilungen** each with three **leichte Panzer-Kompanien** and one **mittlere Panzer-Kompanie.**

SS-Panzer-Regiments - On 14 October 1942, orders were cut to immediately create the following additional Panzer units for each of three new **SS-Panzer-Regiments (SS-Panzer-Regiment 1** for **SS-Division LSSAH, SS-Panzer-Regiment 2** for **SS-Division Das Reich,** and **SS-Panzer-Regiment 3** for **SS Totenkopf Division):**

Number	K.St.N.	Date	Unit Name
1	1103	1Nov41	**Stab Panzer-Regiment**
1	SS	13Oct42	**Panzer-Pionier-Kompanie (mot)**
1	1107	1Nov41	**Stab Panzer-Abteilung**
1	1150	1Nov41	**Stabs-Kompanie Panzer-Abteilung**
2*	1171	1Nov41	**leichte Panzer-Kompanie**
1*	1175	1Nov41	**mittlere Panzer-Kompanie**
1	1187	1Jun42	**Panzer-Werkstatt-Kompanie**

*Instead of two **leichte** and one **mittlere Panzer-Kompanien**, **SS-Panzer-Regiment 1** was authorized three **mittlere Panzer-Kompanien**.

The first **Panzer-Abteilung** had already been created for these three **SS-Divisions** in the spring and summer of 1942. On 15 November 1942, a **schwere Panzer-Kompanie d** was created for each of the three **SS-Panzer-Regiments.**

On 14 November 1942, **SS-Division "Das Reich"** was renamed as **SS-Panzer-Grenadier-Division "Das Reich."** On 16 November 1942, the **SS-Totenkopf Division** was renamed **SS-Panzer-Grenadier-Division "Totenkopf."** On 24 November 1942, the **SS-Division LSSAH** was renamed **SS-Panzer-Grenadier-Division LSSAH.**

Panzer-Abteilung 138 - On 30 November 1942, the independent **Panzer-Abteilung 138** was created with three **mittlere Panzer-Kompanien**, quickly outfitted with eight **Pz.Kpfw.III** and 30 **Pz.Kpfw.IV**, and sent to **Heeresgruppe B/Don** to help try to stabilize the crumbling front.

Panzer-Regiment Hermann-Goering - On 19 September 1942, the **Chef des OKW** recorded that Hitler had ordered **Division Goering** to be outfitted with Panzers and **Sturmgeschuetze** in the same way as the **Panzer-Divisions** in the West. On 9 October 1942, the **Reichsmarschall des Grossdeutschen Reiches und Oberbefehlshaber der Luftwaffe** ordered the immediate creation of **Division Hermann Goering** out of **Brigade Hermann Goering**. The **I.** and **II.Abteilung/Panzer-Regiment Hermann Goering** were to be created with three **leichte** and two **mittlere Panzer-Kompanien** on 1 December 1942. The **Stab Panzer-Regi-**

ment **Hermann Goering** was to be created at a later date. The **3.Kompanie** for the **I.Abteilung** had already been created for **Brigade "Hermann-Goering"** in the Spring of 1942.

Panzer-Regiment 9 - On 25 November 1942, the **Stab Panzer-Regiment 18** was assigned to the **25.Panzer-Division** in Norway and renamed **Stab Panzer-Regiment 9** on 4 December 1942. **Panzer-Abteilung z.b.V.40** was renamed **II.Abteilung/Panzer-Regiment 9** on 5 December and **Panzer-Abteilung 214** was renamed **I.Abteilung Panzer-Regiment 9** on 16 December 1942.

Panzer-Regiment 26 - **Panzer-Regiment 202** assigned to the **26.Panzer-Division** was renamed **Panzer-Regiment 26** on 5 January 1943. The **II.Abteilung/Panzer-Regiment 202** was renamed **II.Abteilung/Panzer-Regiment 26** and the **III.Abteilung/Panzer-Regiment 202** was renamed **I.Abteilung/Panzer-Regiment 26**. At the same time, the **I.Abteilung/Panzer-Regiment 202**, which had been sent to the Balkans to fight partisans, was renamed **Panzer-Abteilung 202**.

Panzer-Regiment "Grossdeutschland" - **Panzer-Regiment 203**, which had fought under **Heeresgruppe Nord** as an independent unit, was pulled out and sent back to Germany. On 13 January 1943, the **II.Abteilung/Panzer-Regiment 203** was renamed **II.Abteilung/Panzer-Regiment "Grossdeutschland"** and converted to three **mittlere Panzer-Kompanien**. At the same time, on 13 January 1943, the **13.schwere Panzer-Kompanie/Panzer-Regiment "Grossdeutschland"** was created from the renamed **3.Kompanie/Panzer-Regiment 203**. **Panzer-Abteilung "Grossdeutschland"** was renamed **I.Abteilung/Panzer-Regiment "Grossdeutschland"** on 1 March 1943 after the rest of the **Panzer-Regiment** had joined it at the front.

Panzer-Regiment 1 - The **1.Panzer-Division** along with the remnants of **Panzer-Regiment 1** were pulled out of the front in December 1942 and sent back to Germany for rest and refitting. On 15 January 1943, the **II.Abteilung/Panzer-Regiment 1** was renamed **I.Abteilung/Panzer-Regiment 1**. A new **II.Abteilung/Panzer-Regiment 1** was created from the **I.Abteilung/Panzer-Regiment 203** on 27 January 1943, and **Panzer-Regiment 1** was expanded to a total of eight **Panzer-Kompanien**.

New Organization for Panzer-Abteilungen - The following new set of **K.St.N./K.A.N.**, reflecting the increase in **Pz.Kpfw.IV** production, was used to create new or refurbish existing **Panzer-Abteilungen** when authorized by specific orders:

K.St.N.	Date	Unit Name
1103	1Nov41	**Stab Panzer-Regiment**
1107	1Nov41	**Stab Panzer-Abteilung**
1150b	25Jan43	**Stabs-Kompanie b einer Panzer-Abteilung**
1190	25Jan43	**Panzer-Flamm-Zug**
1175a	25Jan43	**mittlere Panzer-Kompanie a**
1185	1Jun42	**Panzer-Werkstatt-Zug**

The **Stabskompanie b einer Panzerabteilung**, organized in accordance with K.St.N.1150b dated 25 January 1943, contained an **Aufklaerungszug** with five **Panzerkampfwagen IV (7,5 cm L/43) (Sd.Kfz.161)** and a **Nachrichtenzug** with three **Panzerkampfwagen III (5 cm) (Sd.Kfz.141)** of which two were **Panzerbefehlswagen**. The **Panzer-Flamm-Zug**, organized in accordance with K.St.N.1190 dated 25 January 1943, was to have seven **Panzerflammwagen (Sd.Kfz.141)**. The **mittlere Panzer-Kompanie a**, organized in accordance with K.St.N.1175a dated 25 January 1943, contained a **Kompanie Trupp** with two **Panzerkampfwagen IV (7,5 cm L/43) (Sd.Kfz.161)** and four **Zuege** each with five **Panzerkampfwagen IV (7,5 cm L/43) (Sd.Kfz.161)**.

Only 100 **Panzerflammwagen (Sd.Kfz.141)** were produced and issued as follows:

28 to **Panzer-Regiment "Grossdeutschland"**
15 to **Panzer-Regiment 11**
14 to **Panzer-Regiment 1**
14 to **Panzer-Regiment 24**
14 to **Panzer-Regiment 26**
7 to **Panzer-Regiment 14**
7 to **Panzer-Regiment 16**
1 to **Panzer-Schule Wunsdorf**

Later, **Panzer-Regiment "Grossdeutschland"** transferred 13 of its **Panzerflammwagen** to **Panzer-Regiment 15**. These were the only units that were authorized by orders to use K.ST.N.1190 for the **Panzer-Flamm-Zug** which was intended for incorporation into the **Stabskompanie** of a **Panzer-Abteilung**.

Re-creating Panzer-Units Wiped Out in Stalingrad - **Panzer-Regiment 2, 24,** and **36** (with **Panzer-Divisions 16, 24,** and **14**, respectively) had been wiped out in Stalingrad. On 17 February 1943, all three **Panzer-Regiments** were re-created with two **Panzer-Abteilungen** each with four **Panzer-Kompanien**. Implementing General Guderian's directive to reestablish the strength of a **Panzer-Brigade** with four **Panzer-Abteilungen** within each **Panzer-Division**, orders were cut on 3 March 1943 to add a **III.(Tiger) Abteilung** with three **schwere Panzer-Kompanie d** along with the independent **Sturmgeschuetz-Abteilung** with three **Sturmgeschuetz-Batterien** to the **14., 16.,** and **24.Panzer-Division**. The **III.(Tiger) Abteilung** and the independent **Sturmgeschuetz-Abteilung** were dropped and replaced by a **III.(Sturmgeschuetz) Abteilung** in each **Panzer-Regiment** by orders dated 20 March 1943. This **III.(Sturmgeschuetz)**

Abteilung was to consist of a **Stab**, **Stabskompanie**, four **Kompanien** each with 22 **Sturmgeschuetz**, and a **Werkstatt-Zug**.

Panzer-Abteilung 103, 129, and 160 (with the 3., 29., and 60.Infanterie-Division (mot), respectively) had also been wiped out on the Eastern Front. **Panzer-Abteilung 103** and **129** were both re-created with four **Panzer-Kompanien** on 11 February 1943. **Panzer-Abteilung 160** was re-created with four **Panzer-Kompanien** on 17 February 1943 and renamed **Panzer-Abteilung "Feldherrnhalle"** on 20 June 1943.

Disbanding/Integrating Panzer-Units on the Eastern Front

- On 1 February 1943, **Panzer-Verband 700** was ordered to be disbanded, with the remnants incorporated into **Panzer-Regiment 35**. On 10 February 1943, **Panzer-Regiment 204** of the **22.Panzer-Division** was ordered to be disbanded and the remnants incorporated into **Panzer-Regiment 11**. On 15 February 1943, **Panzer-Abteilung 127** of the **27.Panzer-Division** was ordered to be disbanded and the remnants incorporated into the **7.Panzer-Division**. On 27 March 1943, **Panzer-Abteilung 138** was incorporated into the **19.Panzer-Division** and renamed **II.Abteilung/Panzer-Regiment 27**.

On 15 March 1943, **Pz.A.O.K.2** was contacted by OKH to determine the status of the Panzer units and disposition of excess Panzer crews as follows:

If possible, complete units were to return to Germany to be rested and refitted. The integrity of these units was to be maintained. Intentions were to return these units to their parent Regiments as complete new Panzer-Abteilungen, and everything would be done to achieve this. Naturally, other necessities could occur. Any excess Panzers above the authorized establishment of one Panzer-Abteilung per Panzer-Regiment were to remain with the Panzer-Division as a reserve. Additional new Panzers from Germany were to be provided to those units below authorized strength based on the urgency of the need. The authorized strength established by the Armee was 85 Panzers based on:

Regiment-Stab	*7 Pz.Kpfw.II, 1 Pz.Kpfw.III, 2 Pz.Bef.Wg.*
Abteilung-Stabskp.	*7 Pz.Kpfw.II, 1 Pz.Kpfw.III, 2 Pz.Bef.Wg.*
3 le.Pz.Kp.	*each with 17 Panzers**
1 m.Pz.Kp.	*14 Panzers**

An authorized strength of 22 Panzers in each Kompanie was planned for newly created/recreated units.

*The type of Panzer was not designated.

When initially sent to the Front, all Panzer units were outfitted in accordance with the applicable K.St.N./K.A.N. as specified and modified by specific orders. Once they were in action, however, the only purpose the K.St.N./K.A.N. served was in status reports stating the number/percentage of Panzers that were operational or required repair in compari-

son to the authorized strength specified in the K.St.N. The K.St.N. was not used as a basis for tactical formations or in determining where in a unit replacement Panzers fit in. The organization table dated 19 April 1943 for **Panzer-Regiment 11** of the **6.Panzer-Division** is an example of mixing **Pz.Kpfw.IVs** into each **Zug** of all the **Panzer-Kompanien**, regardless of whether it was officially a **leichte** or **mittlere Panzer-Kompanie**. This was the practice of many of the **Panzer-Divisions** on the Eastern Front during the Spring of 1943, as most of the replacement Panzers were **Pz.Kpfw.IVs** during the buildup for Operation "**Zitadelle**."

Reorganization of Panzer Units in Tunisia

- On 17 January 1943, **II.Abteilung/Panzer-Regiment 5** with all the Panzers in **Panzer-Regiment 5** was transferred to **Panzer-Regiment 8** and renamed **II.Abteilung/Panzer-Regiment 8**. A new **I.Abteilung/Panzer-Regiment 5** (initially named **Panzer-Abteilung Grün**) was created and issued all new Panzers (13 Pz.Kpfw.III lang, 8 Pz.Kpfw.III 7.5, and 17 Pz.Kpfw.IV lang) in Tunis by 15 January 1943. With the exception of two **Panzerbefehlswagen**, **Panzer-Abteilung 190** with all its Panzers had been incorporated into **Panzer-Regiment 5** as its **II.Abteilung** by 6 February 1943.

Orders were cut on 26 February 1943 reorganizing the **Panzer-Regiments** of all three **Panzer-Divisions** in Tunisia. **Panzer-Regiment 5** of the **21.Panzer-Division** was authorized to have four **mittlere Panzer-Kompanien** each with 22 **Pz.Kpfw.IV** in both the **I.** and **II.Abteilung**. **Panzer-Regiment 7** of the **10.Panzer-Division** was authorized four **mittlere Panzer-Kompanien** each with 22 **Pz.Kpfw.IV** in both the **I.** and **II.Abteilung** and incorporated the **schwere Panzer-Abteilung 501** with its two **schwere Panzer-Kompanie d** as the **III.Abteilung**. **Panzer-Regiment 8** of the **15.Panzer-Division** was authorized four **mittlere Panzer-Kompanien** each with 22 **Pz.Kpfw.IV** in both the **I.** and **II.Abteilung** and incorporated the **schwere Panzer-Abteilung 504** with its two **schwere Panzer-Kompanie d** as the **III.Abteilung**.

New Panzer-Abteilungen for Defense of Mediterranean Islands

- On 13 April 1943, **Panzer-Abteilung 215** was created as an independent **Heerestruppen** unit with three **mittlere Panzer-Kompanien** and stationed on Sicily. On 6 July 1943, it was assigned to the **15.Panzer-Grenadier-Division** and the **2.Kompanie/schwere Panzer-Abteilung 504** was incorporated as the **4.schwere Panzer-Kompanie**. **Panzer-Abteilung 215** was renamed **Panzer-Abteilung 115** on 30 September 1943.

On 22 May 1943, **Panzer-Abteilung Rhodos** was created for the defense of the island of Rhodes with the **1.Kompanie** from **Sturmgeschuetz-Batterie 92** and the newly created **2.Kompanie** as a **mittlere Panzer-Kompanie** organized under K.St.N.1175 dated 25 January 1943 with two **Pz.Kpfw.IV** in the **Kompanie Trupp**, four **Pz.Kpfw.IV** in each of three **Zuge**, and one **Pz.Kpfw.IV** as a reserve. **Panzer-Abteilung Sardinien** was established on

Stabskompanie b einer Panzerabteilung

K.St.N.1150b v. 25.1.1943

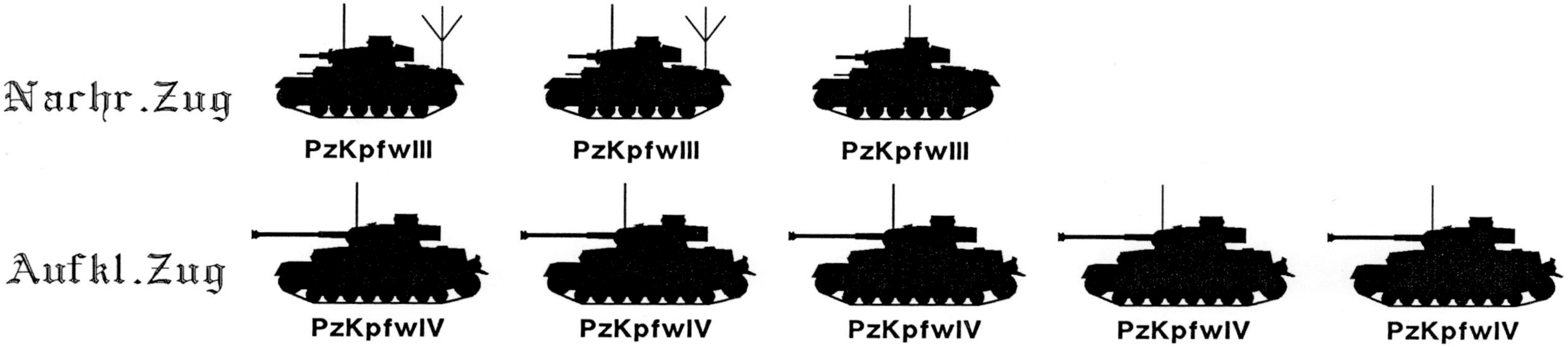

PzKpfwIV

PzKpfwIV

PzKpfwIII

PzKpfwIV

PzKpfwIII

PzKpfwIV

PzKpfwIII

PzKpfwIV

Nachr.Zug

Aufkl.Zug

Panzer–Flamm–Zug

K.St.N.1190 v. 25.1.1943

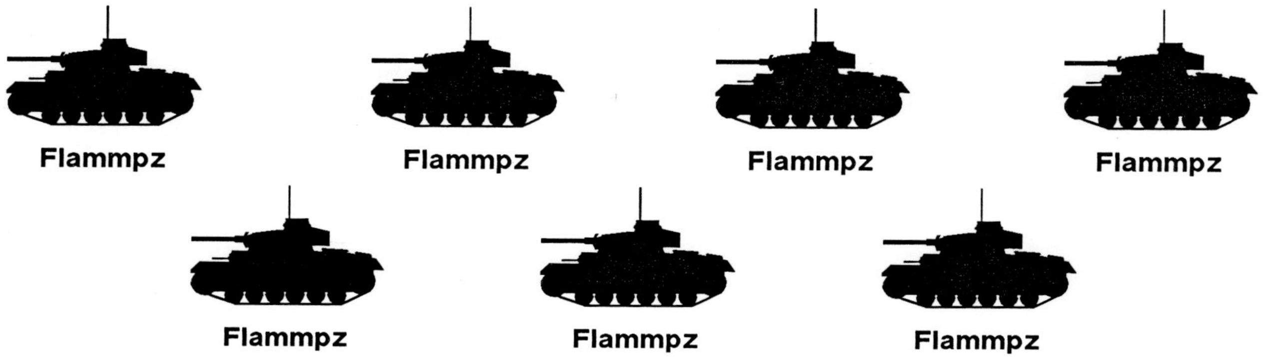

Flammpz

Flammpz

Flammpz

Flammpz

Flammpz

Flammpz

Flammpz

Flammpz

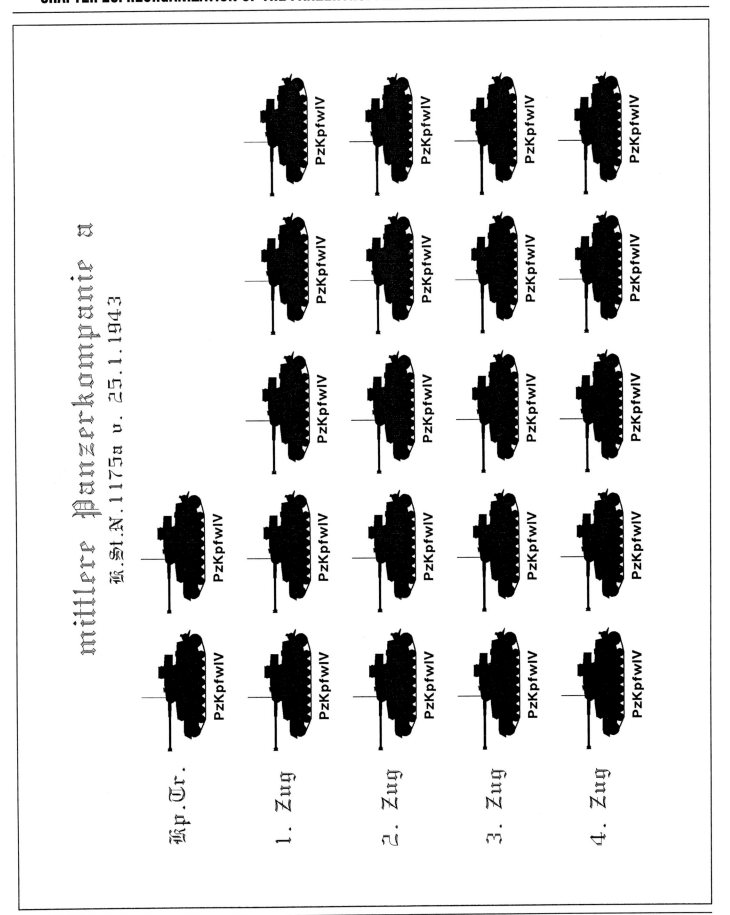

Sardinia with 14 **Pz.Kpfw.III** and 10 **Pz.Kpfw.IV** in early May 1943. On 6 July 1943, **Panzer-Abteilung 190** was recreated from **Panzer-Abteilung Sardinien**, expanded to three **Panzer-Kompanien**, and assigned to the **90.Panzer-Grenadier-Division**.

Reorganization of the SS-Panzer-Regiments on the Eastern Front

On 1 May 1943, the **Panzer-Regiments** of **SS-Panzer-Grenadier-Divisions LSSAH**, **Das Reich**, and **Totenkopf** were ordered to reorganize. Personnel from one **Abteilung** from both **SS-Panzer-Regiment 1** and **2** were to be sent back to Germany to create two **Panther-Abteilungen**. The remaining elements of the **Panzer-Regiments** were to be reorganized and filled with 75 newly issued **Pz.Kpfw.IV**, so that: **Totenkopf** would have a **Panzer-Regiment** with two **Abteilungen** each with two **mittlere** and one **leichte Panzer-Kompanien**, **LSSAH** would have a reinforced **Panzer-Abteilung** with four **mittlere Panzer-Kompanien**, and **Das Reich** would have one **Panzer-Abteilung** with two **mittlere** and two **leichte Panzer-Kompanien** and one **Abteilung** with two **T34-Kompanien** and one **leichte Panzer-Kompanie**. Issued 20 new Tigers, the single **schwere Panzer-Kompanien** in each of the three **Panzer-Regiments** was to have an authorized strength of 15 Panzers, including one **Panzerbefehlswagen**.

Organization of Panzer-Regiment 11 on 17 April 1943								
	PzII	PzIII lg.	PzIII 7.5	PzIV lg.	PzBef	Flamm Pz	Sub Total	Grand Total
Rgts.Stab								
le.Pz.Zug	6						6	
Nachr.Zug			1		3		4	10
St.Kp.II/11								
le.Pz.Zug	7						7	
Nachr.Zug			1		2		3	
Flamm Zug						7	7	
Flamm Zug						7	7	24
5.Kompanie								
Kp.-Trupp		1		1			2	
1.Zug		4	1	1			6	
2.Zug		3	1	2			6	
3.Zug		2	1	2			5	19
6.Kompanie								
Kp.-Trupp		1		1			2	
1.Zug		3	1	2			6	
2.Zug		3	1	1			5	
3.Zug		3		2			5	18
7.Kompanie								
Kp.-Trupp		1		1			2	
1.Zug		3	1	1			5	
2.Zug		3	1	1			5	
3.Zug		3		2			5	17
8.Kompanie								
Kp.-Trupp		1		1			2	
1.Zug		4	1	1			6	
2.Zug		3	1	2			6	
3.Zug		2	1	2			5	19
Total	13	40	12	23	5	14		107

Orders to Reorganize the Panzer-Divisions on the Eastern Front

On 14 June 1943, the OKH GenStdH/Org.Abt. ordered the reorganization of the **Panzer-Regiments** and **Panzer-Abteilungen** of the **Ostheeres** as follows: *It is expected that it will be possible to fill every **Panzer-Abteilung** in all **Panzer-Divisions** in the **Ost-Heeres** with 96 Panzers (mostly **Pz.Kpfw.IV**, several **Pz.Kpfw.III lang**) by December 1943. In addition, it is intended that a **Panther-Abteilung** be created in Germany for the majority of the **Panzer-Divisions**. Therefore, it is necessary to reorganize the **Panzer-Abteilungen** in the **Ost-Heeres**.*

*All **Panzer-Regiments** or **Panzer-Abteilungen** in the **Ost-Heeres** are to be reorganized or builtup to the following organization:*

K.St.N.	Date	Unit
1103	1Nov41	*Panzer-Regiment Stab (if still available)*
1107	1Apr43	*Panzer-Abteilung Stab*
1150b	25Jan43	*Stabs-Kompanie Panzer-Abteilung*
1190	25Jan43	*Panzer-Flamm-Zug under the Stabs-Kompanie (Created only by specific orders)*
1175a	25Jan43	*4 Panzer-Kompanien*
1187b	25Apr42	*Panzer-Werkstatt-Kompanie*

Reserve Panzer-Divisions

Starting in the Summer of 1943, the following units were activated from the **Ersatzheer** and transferred to **Ob.West** as **Reserve-Panzer-Divisions**:

155.Reserve-Panzer-Division from **Pz.Div.Nr.155** on 4 August 1943 with **Reserve-Panzer-Abteilung 7**

179.Reserve-Panzer-Division from **Pz.Div.Nr.179** on 30 July 1943 with **Reserve-Panzer-Abteilung 1**

233.Reserve-Panzer-Division on 10 August 1943 (to Denmark) with **Reserve-Panzer-Abteilung 5**

273.Reserve-Panzer-Division newly created on 25 October 1943 with **Reserve-Panzer-Abteilungen 25 und 35**.

Panzer-Division Norwegen

In August 1943, the **25.Panzer-Division** was transferred from Norway to France to get ready to be sent to the Eastern Front. The remnants left behind in Norway were then reformed into a brigade-size unit named **Panzer-Division Norwegen**. On 6 September 1943, the **I.Abteilung/Panzer-Regiment 9** was renamed **Panzer-Abteilung Norwegen**. On 22 September 1943, **Panzer-Brigade Stab 21** was renamed the **Stab Panzer-Division Norwegen**, retaining its **K.St.N.** as a **Brigade Stab**.

21.Panzer-Division (neu)

The **21.Panzer-Division**, which had been wiped out in Tunisia, was reestablished on 15 July 1943 and named **21.Panzer-Division (neu)**. On 15 July 1943, **Panzer-Regiment 100** was assigned to **21.Panzer-Division (neu)**, expanded to eight **Panzer-Kompanien**, and gradually began to convert from **Beute-Panzer** to **Pz.Kpfw.IVs**.

Uniform Organization for the Panzer-Division 1943 and Panzer-Grenadier-Division 1943

On 24 September 1943, the **OKH/GenStdH/Org.Abt.** ordered:

*The attached organization is hereby universally ordered for all **Panzer- und Panzer-Grenadier-Divisions** of the*

Panzer-Division 43

Anl. 1 zu OKH/Gen.St.d.H./Org. Abt.
Nr. I/4430/43 g.Kdos. v. 24.9.43.

Panzertruppen

Vorläufiges Soll: je. Kp.: 17 Pz. Kfwg.
z.Zt. noch fehlende Pz. Rgts. Stäbe werden
mit der Panther-Abt. zugeführt.

⊗) Eingliederung in den Rgts.-Verband
erst nach Herstellung der vollen
Einsatzfähigkeit.

▽) Aufstellung nur auf besonderen
Befehl.

II. St.

I. St.

ohne 2. Zug

z.Zt. im Heimatkriegsgebiet
zur Umbewaffn. auf Panther.

Panz. Gren. Rgt.

×) Aufstellung wird im Rahmen
der materiellen Möglichkeiten
jeweils befohlen.

gp.

II. I. II. I.

Pz. Jäg. Abt.

Spätere Verwend.
bleibt vorbehalten.

×) Pz. II oder 38t

St.

○) Aufstellung nur auf besond. Befehl.

○○) Ausstattung m. Pz. Spähwgn. „Luchs" auf
besond. Befehl.

○○○) je nach Fahrzeuglage: Krad, Kettenkrad
oder Volkswagen, später wie 3. Kp.

Pz. Aufkl. Abt.

H. Flak-Art. Abt.

○) Von Pz. Jäg. Abt. eingegliedert
△) oder Sf.

mit
Scheinw.-Staff.

×) Wenn III. Abt. Sf. le. F.H. statt s. F.H.

××) Umgl. auf 3 Battr. s. F.H. (Sf) vorgesehen.
10cm Kan. Battr. wird dann als 10. Battr.
dem Rgts. Stab unmittelbar unterstellt.

Artillerie

St.

××) III. II. I.

St. St. St.

Pz.-Felders.-Btl.

Waffenaust.
wird in neuer
KStN festgelegt.

Pz. Nachr.-Tr.

□) Nur nach Eingliederung
einer Panther Abt. ab 1944.

Pz.-Pioniere

St.

Verw.-Tr. | *Feldpost* | *Ordn.-Tr.*

DVA

San.-Tr.

Kf. Park-Tr.

Höchstaust.: Jeweilige Zahl der
Kf. Kp. wird Divisionsweise
befohlen.

Nachsch.-Tr.

Ers.

Panzer-Grenadier-Div. 43

Anl. 2 zu OKH/Gen.St.d.H./Org. Abt.
Nr. I/4430/43 g.Kdos. v. 24.9.43.

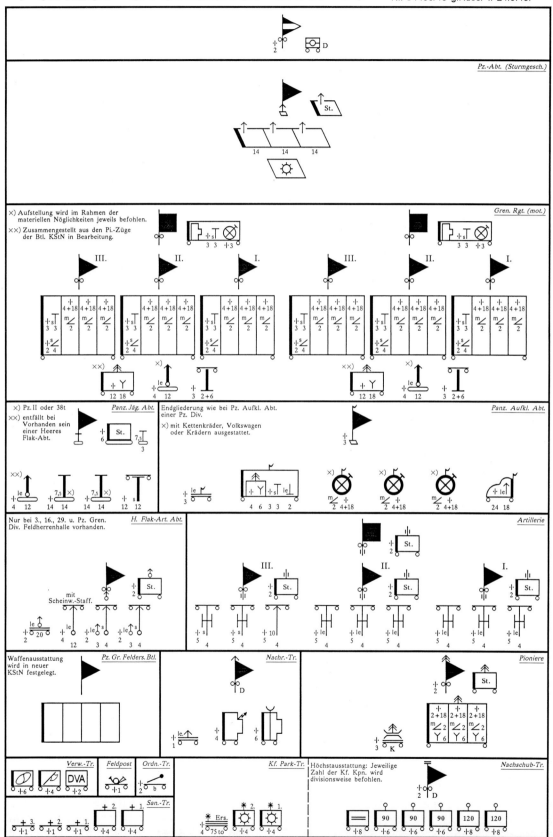

*Heeres (with the exception of **Panzer-Grenadier-Division "Grossdeutschland"**, **21.Panzer-Division**, and **Panzer-Division Norwegen**). These new organizations are entitled "Gliederung Panzer-Division 1943" and "Gliederung Panzer-Grenadier-Division 1943."*

*After a **Panther-Abteilung** is sent back to its parent **Panzer-Regiment**, specific orders will be issued to re-create a **Panzer-Regiment Stab**, if this **Stab** is not already on hand. Incorporation of the **Panther-Abteilung** will first occur when the Panther is technically operational.*

*The provisional strength authorized for every **Panzer-Kompanie** is 17 Panzers. In the meantime, the **Panzer-Regiment** of the **16.Panzer-Division** will remain organized with three **Abteilungen**.*

<u>Renaming and Reorganizing the SS-Divisions</u> - On 22 October 1943, the **SS-FHA Org.Abt.** ordered that the **SS-Divisions** be renamed as follows:

From	To
SS-Pz.Gren.Div. LSSAH	1.SS-Pz.Div. LSSAH
SS-Pz.Gren.Div. Das Reich	2.SS-Pz.Div. Das Reich
SS-Pz.Gren.Div. Totenkopf	3.SS-Pz.Div. Totenkopf
SS-Pz.Gren.Div. Wiking	5.SS-Pz.Div. Wiking
SS-Pz.Gren.Div. Hohenstaufen	9.SS-Pz.Div. Hohenstaufen
10.SS-Pz.Gren.Div.	10.SS-Pz.Div. Frundsberg
SS-Pz.Gren.Freiw.Div.Nordland	11.SS-Freiw.Pz.Gren.Div. Nordland
SS-Pz.Gren.Div. Hitlerjugend	12.SS-Pz.Div. Hitlerjugend
SS-Pz.Gren.Div."RF-SS"	16.SS-Pz.Gren.Div. Reichsfuehrer SS
SS-Pz.Gren.Div."G.v.B."	17.SS-Pz.Gren.Div.Götz von Berlichingen

The **9.**, **10.**, and **12.SS-Panzer-Divisions** were still in the process of formation. They were each authorized to have a complete **Panzer-Regiment** with a **Panther-Abteilung** of four **Kompanien** and a **Pz.Kpfw.IV-Abteilung** of four **Kompanien**. Also in the process of formation, the **11.**, **16.**, and **17.SS-Panzer-Grenadier-Divisionen** were each authorized to have a **Panzer-Abteilung** with four **Kompanien**. In addition, each of these **SS-Divisions** was authorized to have a **Sturmgeschuetz-Abteilung** with three **Batterien**. Later, prior to being sent to the Front, (with the exception of the **11.SS**) this **Sturmgeschuetz-Abteilung** was completely dropped or integrated into the **Panzer-Abteilung**. **II.Abteilung/SS-Panzer-Regiments 9** and **10** were both reorganized into two **Panzer-Kompanien** each with 22 **Pz.Kpfw.IV** and two **Panzer-Sturmgeschuetz-Kompanien** each with 22 **Sturmgeschuetze**. As requested by the **11.SS-Panzer-Grenadier-Division**, without any Panzers the personnel of **Panzer-Abteilung 11 "Hermann von Salza"** rejoined its parent division in **Heeresgruppe Nord** on 30 December 1943 to help crew some of the **Sturmgeschuetze** that had been issued to **SS-Sturmgeschuetz-Abteilung 11**.

The organization of **SS-Panzer-Abteilung 16** and **17** was revised to three **Panzer-Sturmgeschuetz-Kompanien** each with 14 **Sturmgeschuetze**.

<u>New K.St.N. Dated 1Nov43</u> - The following new set of K.St.N./K.A.N. dated 1 November 1943 was used to create new or refurbish existing Panzer-Regiments when authorized by specific orders:

K.St.N.	Date	Unit Name
1103	1Nov43	**Stab und Stabskompanie eines Panzer-Regiments**
1150b	1Nov43	**Stabs-Kompanie b einer Panzer-Abteilung**
1175a	1Nov43	**mittlere Panzer-Kompanie a**

The **Stab und Stabskompanie eines Panzer-Regiments**, organized in accordance with K.St.N.1103 dated 1 November 1943, contained a **Nachrichtenzug** with three **Panzerkampfwagen "Panther" (7,5 cm 42 (L/70)) (Sd.Kfz.171)** as **Panzerbefehlswagen** and an **Aufklaerungszug** with either five **Panzerkampfwagen IV (7,5 cm 40 (L/43)) (Sd.Kfz.161/1)** or five **Panzerkampfwagen IV (7,5 cm 40 (L/48)) (Sd.Kfz.161/2)**. The **Stabskompanie b einer Panzerabteilung**, organized in accordance with K.St.N.1150b dated 1 November 1943, contained an **Aufklaerungszug** with five **Panzerkampfwagen IV (7,5 cm 40 L/43) (Sd.Kfz.161/1)** and a **Nachrichtenzug** with three **Panzerkampfwagen III (5 cm L42) (Sd.Kfz.141)** of which two were Panzerbefehlswagen. The **mittlere Panzer-Kompanie a**, organized in accordance with K.St.N.1175a dated 1 November 1943, consisted of a **Gruppe Fuehrer** with two **Panzerkampfwagen IV (7,5 cm 40 L/43) (Sd.Kfz.161/1)** and four **Zuege** each with five **Panzerkampfwagen IV (7,5 cm 40 L/43) (Sd.Kfz.161/1)**. A **Panzer-Regiment** with its **Stab und Stabs-Kompanie** and a single **Panzer-Abteilung** with four **mittlere Panzer-Kompanie a**, when ordered to use the K.St.N. dated 1 November 1943, had a total authorized strength of three **Panzerkampfwagen "Panther"**, 98 **Panzerkampfwagen IV**, and three **Panzerkampfwagen III**.

PANTHER-ABTEILUNGEN

The first **Panther-Abteilung** was established on 9 January 1943 when the **II.Abteilung/Panzer-Regiment 33** was renamed **Panzer-Abteilung 51**. As specified in orders dated 17 January, **Panzer-Abteilung 51** was to be organized in accordance with:

K.St.N.	Date	Unit Name
1107	1Nov41	**Stab Panzer-Abteilung**
1150a	10Jan43	**Stabs-Kompanie Panzer-Abteilung "Panther"**
1177	10Jan43	**mittlere Panzer-Kompanie "Panther"**
1185a	10Jan43	**Panzer-Werkstatt-Zug "Panther"**

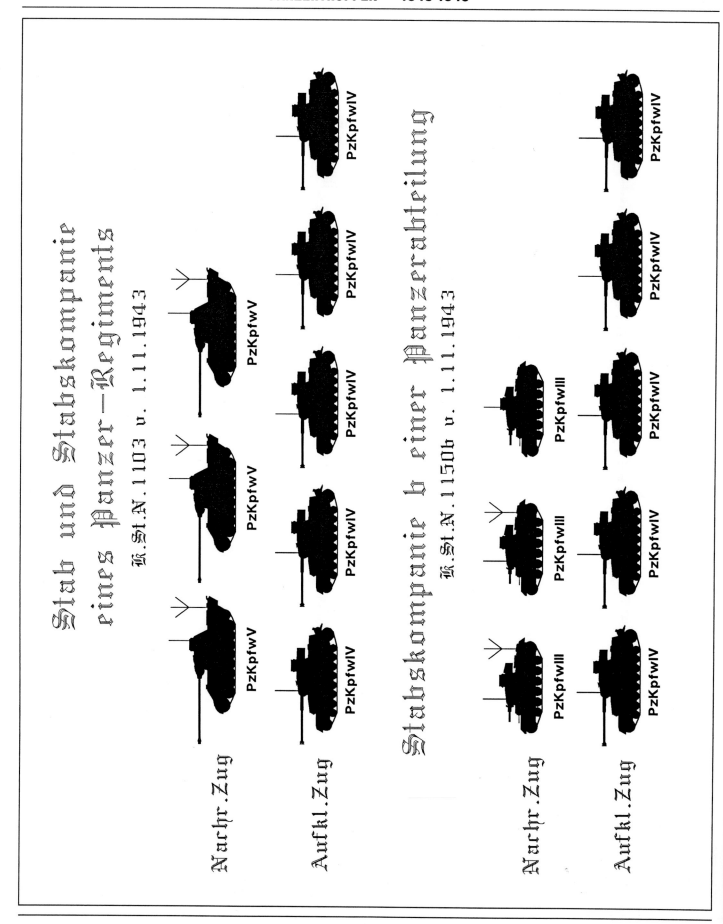

Stab und Stabskompanie
eines Panzer—Regiments

R.St.N. 1103 v. 1.11.1943

Nachr.Zug

PzKpfwV   PzKpfwV   PzKpfwV

Aufkl.Zug

PzKpfwIV   PzKpfwIV   PzKpfwIV   PzKpfwIV   PzKpfwIV

Stabskompanie b einer Panzerabteilung

R.St.N. 1150b v. 1.11.1943

Nachr.Zug

PzKpfwIII   PzKpfwIII   PzKpfwIII

Aufkl.Zug

PzKpfwIV   PzKpfwIV   PzKpfwIV   PzKpfwIV

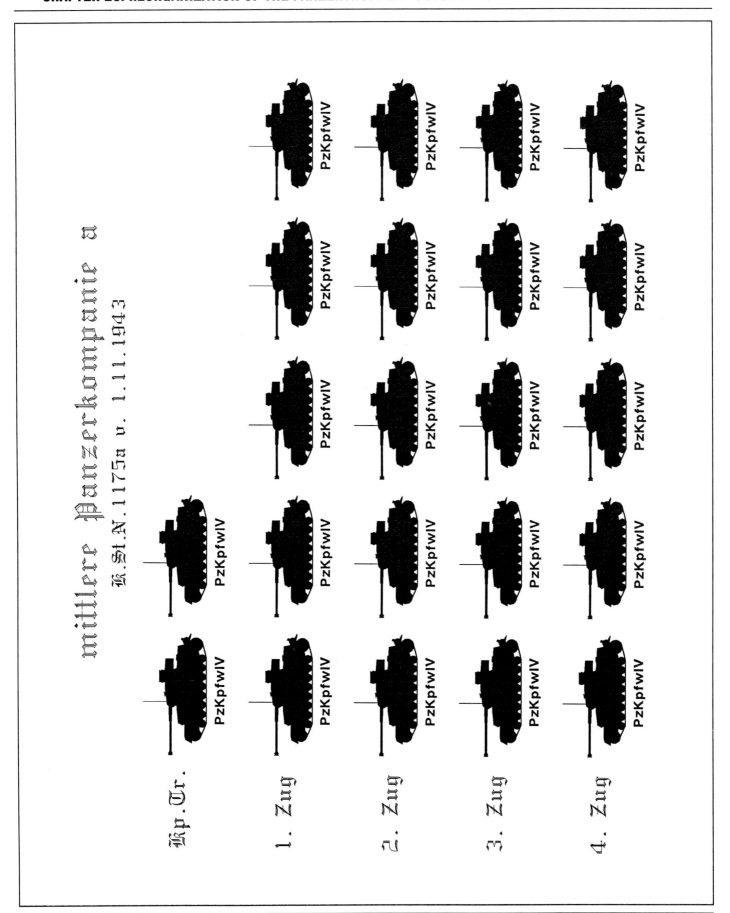

The **Stabskompanie einer Panzerabteilung "Panther"**, organized in accordance with K.St.N.1150a dated 10 January 1943, contained an **Aufklaerungszug** with five **Panzerkampfwagen "Panther" (7,5 cm L/70) (Sd.Kfz.171)** and a **Nachrichtenzug** with three **Panzerkampfwagen "Panther" (7,5 cm L/70) (Sd.Kfz.171)** (of which two where **Panzerbefehlswagen**). The **mittlere Panzer-Kompanie "Panther"**, organized in accordance with K.St.N.1177 dated 10 January 1943, contained a **Kompanie Trupp** with two **Panzerkampfwagen "Panther" (7,5 cm L/70) (Sd.Kfz.171)** and four **Zuege** each with five **Panzerkampfwagen "Panther" (7,5 cm L/70) (Sd.Kfz.171)**. The total authorized strength for a **Panzer-Abteilung "Panther"**, organized in accordance with the K.St.N. dated 10 January 1943, was 96 **Panzerkampfwagen "Panther."**

<u>**Conversion of Additional Panther-Abteilungen**</u> - The second unit authorized to convert to Panthers was the **I.Abteilung/Panzer-Regiment 15**, renamed **Panzer-Abteilung 52** on 6 February 1943. **Panzer-Lehrgaenge Panther**, formed for training the Panther crews, began to assemble in Erlangen on 1 March 1943. Two **Panzer-Kompanien** from the **I.Abteilung/Panzer-Regiment 1** were sent to Grafenwoehr to begin training on Panthers on 5 March 1943. The **II.Abteilung/Panzer-Regiment 201** (renamed **II.Abteilung/Panzer-Regiment 23** in August 1943) began to convert in mid-April, followed on 5 May 1943 by the **I.Abteilung/Panzer-Regiment 31**, **I.Abteilung/Panzer-Regiment 11**, and **III.Abteilung/Panzer-Regiment 4** (renamed **I.Abteilung/Panzer-Regiment 4** on 19 October 1943). On 1 May 1943, personnel from one **Abteilung** out of **SS-Panzer-Regiment 1** and **2** were ordered to return to Germany to create two **Panther-Abteilungen**. The **I.Abteilung/Panzer-Regiment 2** was converted to a **Panther-Abteilung** on 25 August 1943.

<u>**Modified Organizations**</u> - K.St.N.1150a for the **Stabskompanie einer Panzerabteilung "Panther"**, revised on 1 June 1943, still maintained five **Panzerkampfwagen "Panther" (7,5 cm L/70) (Sd.Kfz.171)** in the **Aufklaerungszug**, but instead of the former two, all three **Panzerkampfwagen "Panther" (7,5 cm L/70) (Sd.Kfz.171)** in the **Nachrichtenzug** were **Panzerbefehlswagen**.

Many of the **Panther-Abteilungen** were not authorized by orders to be issued a full complement of 96 Panthers. A **Panther-Abteilung** with 76 Panthers was authorized to have only 17 Panthers in each **Kompanie** (minus the **4.Zug**). A **Panther-Abteilung** with only 71 Panthers was also missing the **Aufklaerungszug** in the **Stabskompanie**.

<u>**Panther-Abteilungen Sent to Eastern Front**</u> - In 1943, Panther units were sent to the Eastern Front in the following order:

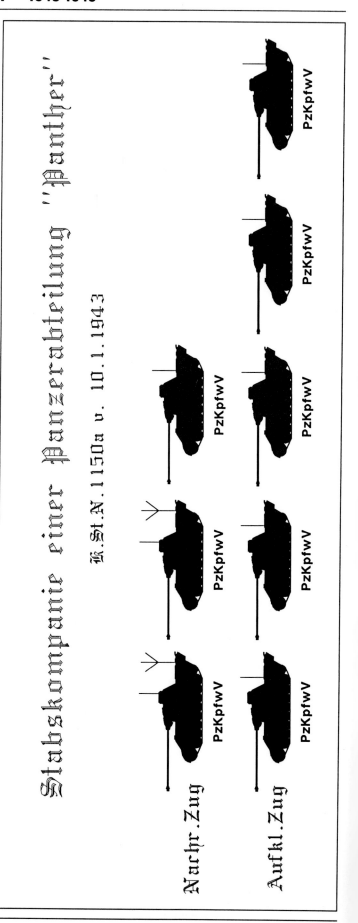

Stabskompanie einer Panzerabteilung "Panther"

K.St.N. 1150a v. 10.1.1943

PzKpfwV

PzKpfwV

PzKpfwV

PzKpfwV

PzKpfwV

PzKpfwV

PzKpfwV

PzKpfwV

Nachr.Zug

Aufkl.Zug

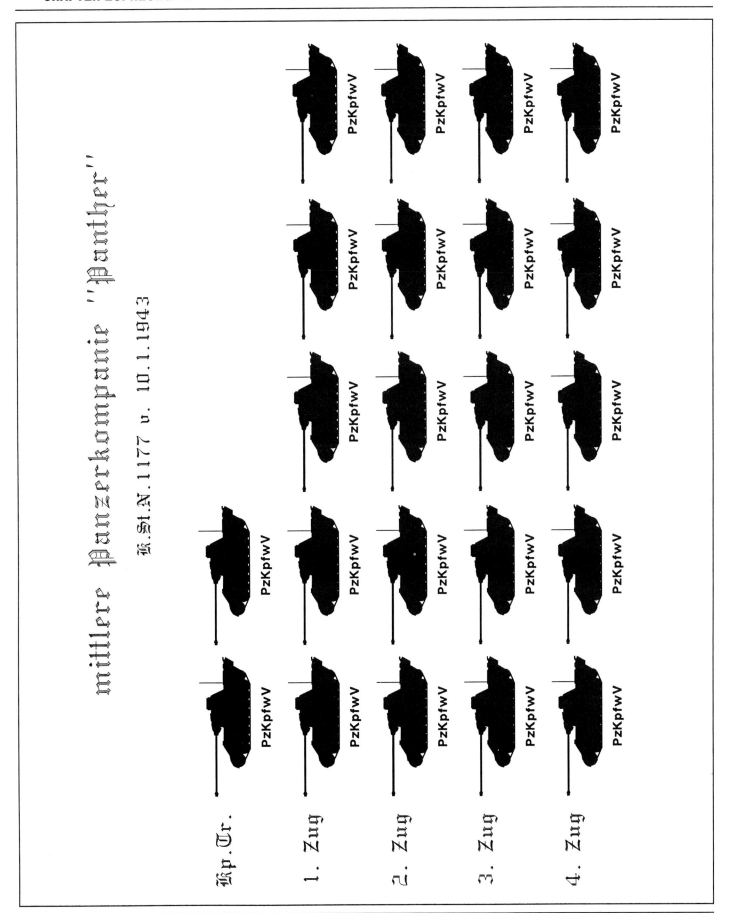

mittlere Panzerkompanie "Panther"

K.St.N. 1177 v. 10.1.1943

Kp.Tr. — PzKpfwV, PzKpfwV

1. Zug — PzKpfwV, PzKpfwV, PzKpfwV, PzKpfwV, PzKpfwV

2. Zug — PzKpfwV, PzKpfwV, PzKpfwV, PzKpfwV, PzKpfwV

3. Zug — PzKpfwV, PzKpfwV, PzKpfwV, PzKpfwV, PzKpfwV

4. Zug — PzKpfwV, PzKpfwV, PzKpfwV, PzKpfwV, PzKpfwV

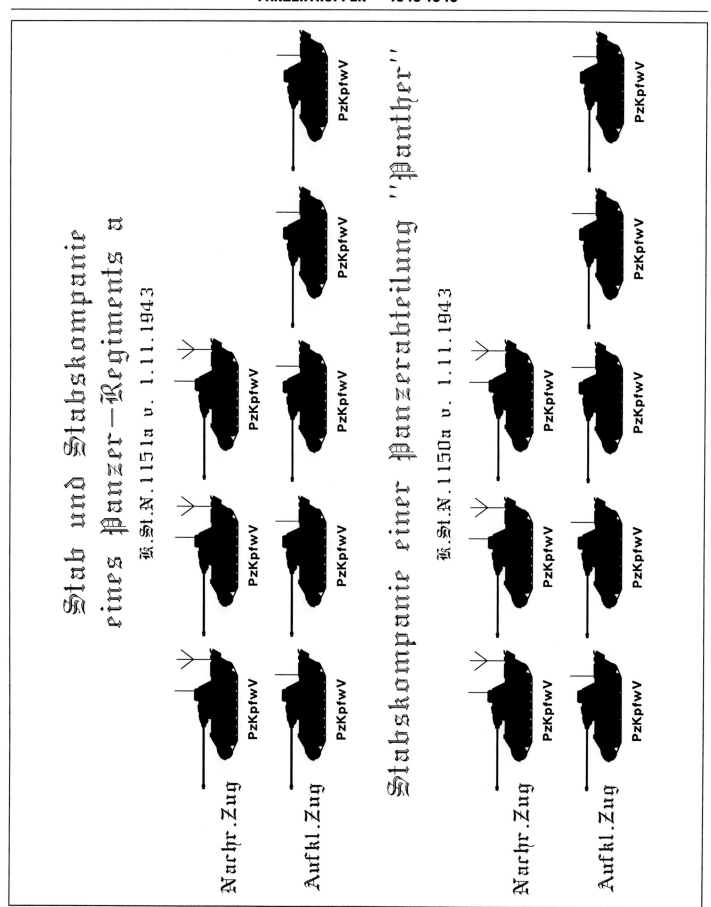

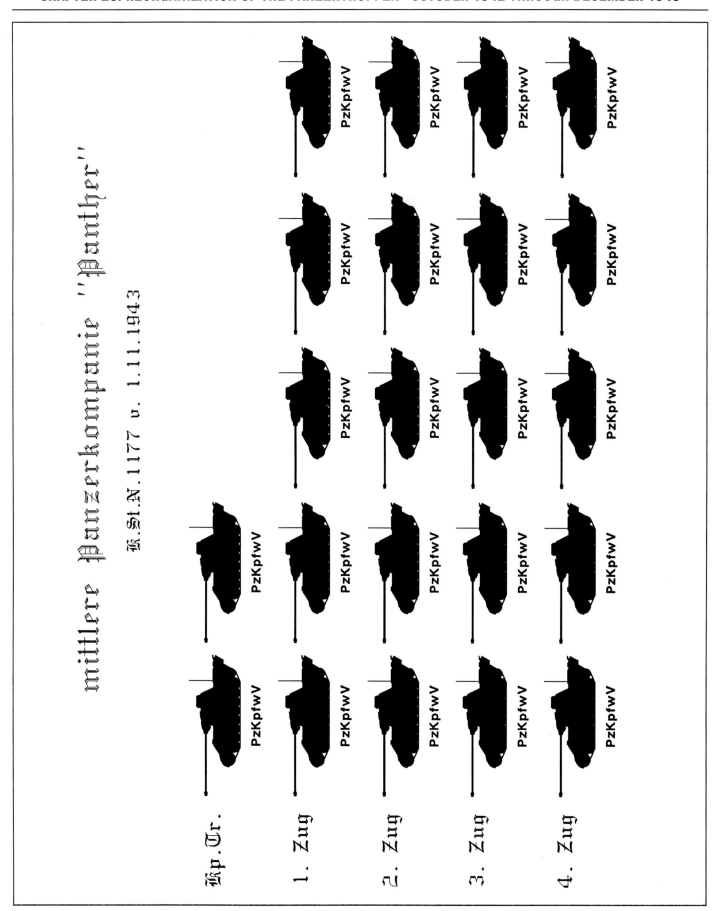

Unit Name	Month	No.of Panthers
Panzer-Abteilung 51	July	96
Panzer-Abteilung 52	July	96
Panzer-Regiment Stab 39	July	8
I.Abteilung/SS-Panzer-Regiment 2	August	71
II.Abteilung/Panzer-Regiment 23	September	96
I.Abteilung/Panzer-Regiment 2	October	71
I.Abteilung/Panzer-Regiment 1	November	76
I.Abteilung/SS-Panzer-Regiment 1	November	96
I.Abteilung/Panzer-Regiment 31	December	76

Following their baptism to fire in Operation **"Zitadelle"** in July 1943, the surviving Panthers were consolidated into **Panzer-Abteilung 52**, renamed **I.Abteilung/Panzer-Regiment 15** on 24 August 1943. **Panzer-Abteilung 51** received a complete new allotment of 96 Panthers as replacements in early August and remained in action with **Panzer-Grenadier-Division "Grossdeutschland."**

New K.St.N. Dated 1Nov43 - A new set of K.St.N./K.A.N. dated 1 November 1943 were published for reorganization of units with Panthers as follows:

K.St.N.	Date	Unit Name
1151a	1Nov43	**Stab und Stabskompanie Panzer-Regiments a**
1150a	1Nov43	**Stabs-Kompanie Panzer-Abteilung "Panther"**
1177	1Nov43	**mittlere Panzer-Kompanie "Panther"**

The **Stab und Stabskompanie eines Panzer-Regiments a**, organized in accordance with K.St.N.1151a dated 1 November 1943, contained a **Nachrichtenzug** with three **Panzerkampfwagen "Panther" (7,5 cm 42 (L/70)) (Sd.Kfz.171)** as **Panzerbefehlswagen** and an **Aufklaerungszug** with five **Panzerkampfwagen "Panther" (7,5 cm 42 (L/70)) (Sd.Kfz.171)**. The **Stabskompanie einer Panzerabteilung "Panther"**, organized in accordance with K.St.N.1150a dated 1 November 1943, still had eight **Panzerkampfwagen "Panther" (7,5 cm 42 L/70) (Sd.Kfz.171)** of which three were **Panzerbefehlswagen**, and the **mittlere Panzer-Kompanie "Panther"**, organized in accordance with K.St.N.1177 dated 1 November 1943, still had 22 **Panzerkampfwagen "Panther" (7,5 cm 42 L/70) (Sd.Kfz.171)**. A complete **Panzer-Regiments a**, outfitted in accordance with the K.St.N. dated 1 November 1943, would have had a total complement of 104 **Panzerkampfwagen "Panther."**

TIGER-KOMPANIEN UND ABTEILUNGEN

The next step in establishing Tiger units after the formation of the first three **schwere Heeres Panzer-Abteilungen** in the Spring of 1942 was to assign a **Tiger-Kompanien** as an integral part of **Panzer-Regiments**. There was a phase from

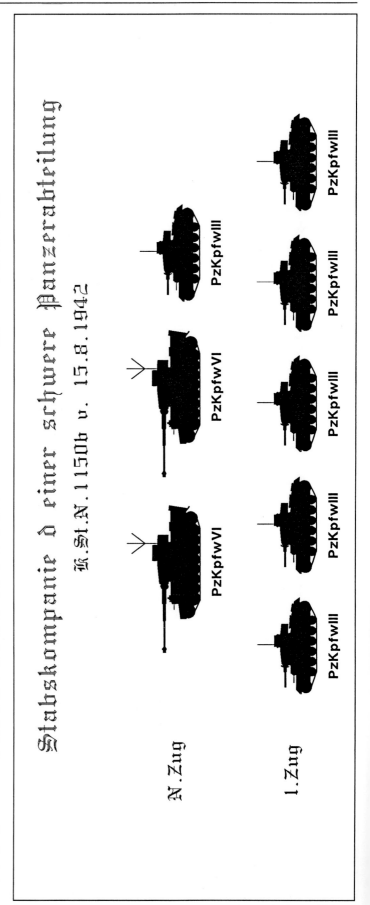

Stabskompanie à einer schwere Panzerabteilung

K.St.N.1150b v. 15.8.1942

PzKpfwVIII

PzKpfwVIII

PzKpfwVI

PzKpfwVIII

PzKpfwVI

PzKpfwVIII

PzKpfwVIII

N.Zug

1.Zug

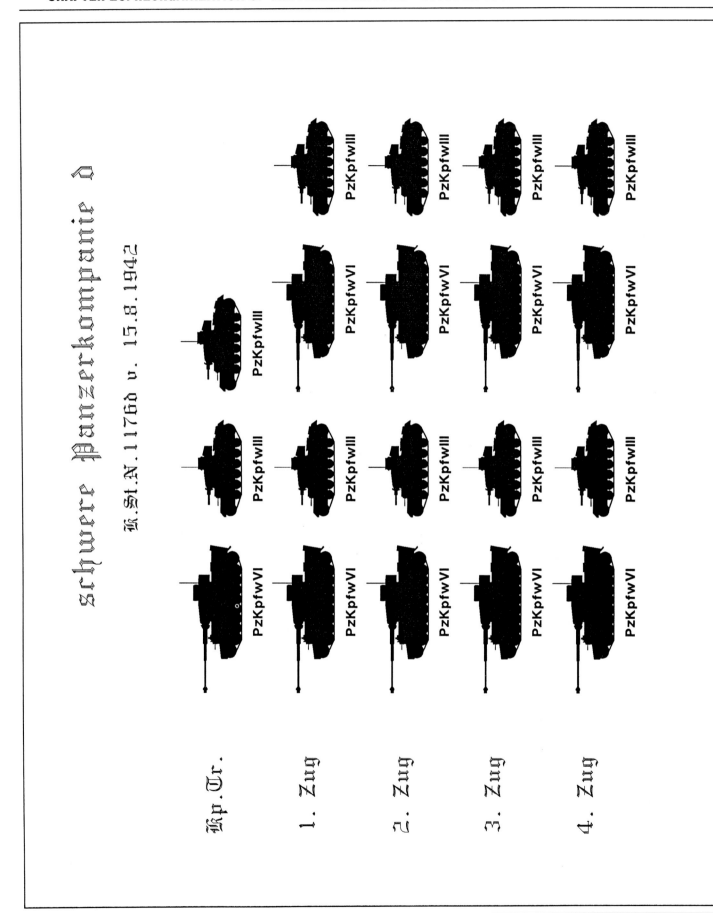

schwere Panzerkompanie d

K.St.N.1176b v. 15.8.1942

Kp.Tr.

1. Zug

2. Zug

3. Zug

4. Zug

January through February 1943 when **schwere Panzer-Abteilungen** were assigned as the **III.Abteilungen** integral to **Panzer-Regiments** within **Panzer-Divisions**. Only after obtaining the opinions of the commanders of the first three **schwere Heeres Panzer-Abteilungen** in the field was the organization changed to create independent units with only Tigers in each of the three **schwere Panzer-Kompanien** of a **schwere Panzer-Abteilungen**.

Schwere Panzer-Kompanien for the SS - On 13 November 1942, orders were cut to create, effective 15 November 1942, three **schwere Panzer-Kompanien**, one for each of the **SS-Panzer-Regiments 1, 2,** and **3**, in accordance with K.St.N.1176d dated 15 August 1942 for a **schwere Panzer-Kompanie d** with nine **Pz.Kpfw.VIH (Sd.Kfz.182)** and ten **Pz.Kpfw.III (5 cm) (Sd.Kfz.141)**.

Schwere Heeres-Panzer-Abteilung 504 - In December 1942, orders were cut to create **schwere Panzer-Abteilung 504** by 18 January 1943 with the following organization:

K.St.N.	Date	Unit Name
1107	1Nov41	**Stab Panzer-Abteilung**
1150b	25Apr42	**Stabskompanie**
1176d	15Aug42	**schwere Panzer-Kompanie**
1187b	25Apr42	**Panzer-Werkstatt-Kompanie**

By 17 January 1943 the applicable K.St.N. for the organization of **schwere Panzer-Abteilung 504** had been revised to K.St.N.1150 dated 15 August 1942 for the **Stabskompanie d schwere Panzer-Abteilung**, and K.St.N.1176d Ausf.A dated 15 December 1942 for the **schwere Panzer-Kompanie d**. Schwere Panzer-Abteilung 504 was converted to "Tropen" and outfitted with 20 **Pz.Kpfw.VIH (Sd.Kfz.182)** and 25 **Pz.Kpfw.III (5 cm) (Sd.Kfz.141)**, with orders to be transferred to Tunisia.

Schwere Panzer-Kompanie for Grossdeutschland - On 13 January 1943, the **13.schwere Panzer-Kompanie/Panzer-Regiment "Grossdeutschland"** was created from the renamed **3.Kompanie/Panzer-Regiment 203**. It was organized in accordance with K.St.N.1176 Ausf.B dated 15 December 1942 with 9 **Pz.Kpfw.VI(H) (Sd.Kfz.182)** and 10 **Pz.Kpfw.III (5 cm) (Sd.Kfz.141)**.

Schwere Heeres-Panzer-Abteilung 505 - On 24 January 1943, orders were cut to create **schwere Panzer-Abteilung 505** by 18 February 1943 in accordance with the following organization:

K.St.N.	Date	Unit Name
1107	1Nov41	**Stab Panzer-Abteilung**
1150d	15Aug42	**Stabskompanie d schwere Panzer-Abteilung**
1176d Ausf.B	15Dec42	**schwere Panzer-Kompanie d**
1187b Ausf.B	25Apr42	**Panzer-Werkstatt-Kompanie b**

Schwere Panzer-Abteilung 505 was outfitted with 20 **Pz.Kpfw.Tiger (8,8 cm L/56) (Sd.Kfz.181)** and 25 **Pz.Kpfw.III (5 cm) (Sd.Kfz.141)** and sent to the Eastern Front in April 1943.

New Organization Authorizing 45 Tigers in a schwere Panzer-Abteilung - The following new set of K.St.N./K.A.N. dated 5 March 1943 was used to create new or refurbish existing Tiger units when authorized by specific orders:

K.St.N.	Date	Unit Name
1150e	5Mar43	**Stabskompanie schweren Panzer-Abteilung "Tiger"**
1176e	5Mar43	**schwere Panzer-Kompanie e**

The **Stabskompanie einer schweren Panzerabteilung "Tiger"**, organized in accordance with K.St.N.1150e dated 5 March 1943, contained a **Nachrichtenzug** with either three **Panzerkampfwagen "Tiger" (8,8 cm L/56) (Sd.Kfz.181)** of which two were **Panzerbefehlswagen**, or three **Panzerkampfwagen "Tiger" (8,8 cm L/71) (Sd.Kfz.182)** of which two were **Panzerbefehlswagen**. The **schwere Panzer-Kompanie e**, organized in accordance with K.St.N.1176e dated 5 March 1943, contained a **Kompanie Trupp** with either two **Panzerkampfwagen "Tiger" (8,8 cm L/56) (Sd.Kfz.181)** or two **Panzerkampfwagen "Tiger" (8,8 cm 43 L/71) (Sd.Kfz.182)**, as well as three **Zuege** each with either four **Panzerkampfwagen "Tiger" (8,8 cm L/56) (Sd.Kfz.181)** or four **Panzerkampfwagen "Tiger" (8,8 cm 43 L/71) (Sd.Kfz.182)**. A complete **schwere Panzer-Abteilung**, organized under the K.St.N. dated 5 March 1943, was authorized to have 45 **Panzerkampfwagen "Tiger."**

Expansion to Three Kompanien in each schwere Panzer-Abteilung - A **3.Kompanie** was created for **schwere Panzer-Regiment 501** on 6 March 1943, for **schwere Panzer-Regiment 504** on 20 March 1943, and for **schwere Panzer-Abteilung 505** on 3 April 1943. The **2.Kompanie/schwere Panzer-Abteilung 502** had been renamed **3.Kompanie/schwere Panzer-Abteilung 503** on 10 February 1943. A new **2.Kompanie** and **3.Kompanie** were created for **schwere Panzer-Abteilung 502** on 1 April 1943. The **III.schwere Abteilung/Panzer-Regiment "Grossdeutschland"** was created on 1 July 1943 with the incorporation of the **13.schwere Panzer-Kompanie/Panzer-Regiment "Grossdeutschland"** as the new **9.Kompanie**, the **3.Kompanie/schwere Panzer-Abteilung 501** as the new **10.Kompanie**, and the **3.Kompanie/schwere Panzer-Abteilung 504** as the new **11.Kompanie**.

The elements of **schwere Panzer-Abteilungen 502, 503,** and **505** on the Eastern Front were authorized by specific orders to adopt the new K.St.N. dated 5 March 1943 and were issued new Tigers to fill them to their authorized strength of three Tigers in each **Stabskompanie** and 14 Tigers in each **schwere Panzer-Kompanie**.

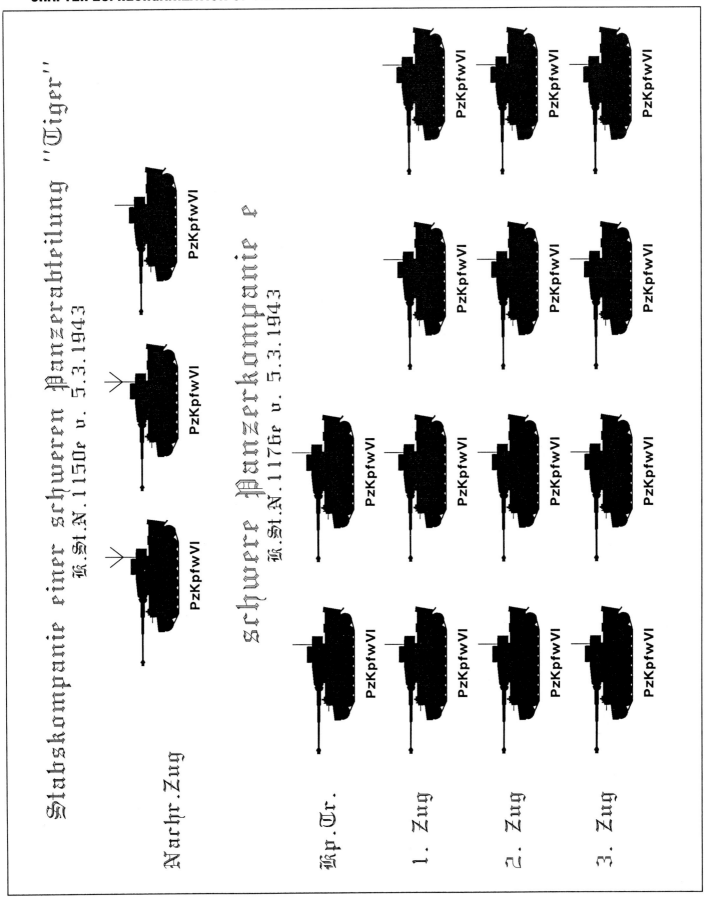

Stabskompanie einer schweren Panzerabteilung "Tiger"
K.St.N.1150b v. 5.3.1943

Nachr.Zug

PzKpfwVI

PzKpfwVI

PzKpfwVI

schwere Panzerkompanie e
K.St.N.1176b v. 5.3.1943

Kp.Tr.

PzKpfwVI

1. Zug

PzKpfwVI PzKpfwVI PzKpfwVI

2. Zug

PzKpfwVI PzKpfwVI PzKpfwVI

3. Zug

PzKpfwVI PzKpfwVI PzKpfwVI

Additional **schwere Heeres Panzer-Abteilungen** were created in 1943 with three **schwere Panzer-Kompanien** as follows:

Unit	Date	Note
s.H.Pz.Abt.506	8May43	from **III.Abt./Pz.Rgt.33**
s.H.Pz.Abt.509	9Sep43	
s.H.Pz.Abt.501	9Sep43	re-created from remnants of original
s.H.Pz.Abt.507	23Sep43	from **I.Abt./Pz.Rgt.4**
s.H.Pz.Abt.508	25Sep43	from remnants of **Pz.Rgt.8**
s.H.Pz.Abt.504	18Nov43	re-created using **Pz.Abt.18**

Schwere Heeres Panzer-Abteilung 506 was outfitted with 45 Tigers and shipped to the Eastern Front in September 1943. **Schwere Heeres Panzer-Abteilung 508**, also outfitted with 45 Tigers, arrived on the Eastern Front in early November 1943.

Schwere SS-Panzer-Abteilungen

On 22 April 1943, the **SS-FHA** ordered the creation of a **Tiger-Abteilung** for the **I.SS-Panzer-Korps**. A **Stab** for the new **schwere SS-Panzer-Abteilung** was to be raised in Germany. Its three **schwere Panzer-Kompanie**, previously created on 15 November 1942, were to remain on the Eastern Front with **SS-Panzer-Regiment 1**, **2** and **3**, authorized to be reorganized under **K.St.N.1176e**, and sent 17 new Tigers in April and May 1943.

The **I.SS-Panzer-Korps** was renamed **II.SS-Panzer-Korps** effective 1 June 1943. On 27 July 1943, the **SS-FHA Org.Abt.** ordered the creation of the **Korps-Stab** and **Korps-Truppen** for a new **I.SS-Panzer-Korps "LSSAH."** Its new **schwere SS-Panzer-Abteilung** had already been ordered to be created at the Sennelager training area by orders from **SS-FHA Org.Abt.** dated 19 July 1943 with the following organization:

K.St.N.	Date	Unit Name
1107	1Apr43	**Stab Panzer-Abteilung**
1150e	5Mar43	**Stabs-Kompanie schwere-Panzer-Abteilung**
1176e	5Mar43	**schwere Panzer-Kompanie**
1187b	25Apr42	**Panzer-Werkstatt-Kompanie**

The **schwere Panzer-Kompanie** that had been assigned to **SS-Panzer-Grenadier-Division "LSSAH"** from **schwere Panzer-Abteilung Gen.Kdo.II.SS-Panzer-Korps** was reassigned as the third **schwere Panzer-Kompanie** in the new **schwere Panzer-Abteilung Gen.Kdo.I.SS-Panzer-Korps "Leibstandarte."** This same order authorized the creation of a new **schwere Panzer-Kompanie** to replace it.

On 22 October 1943, **SS-Korps-Truppen** were renamed by adding 100 to the **SS-Korps** number, resulting in **schwere SS-Panzer-Abteilung 101** and **schwere SS-Panzer-Abteilung 102**. On 28 October 1943, the operational **1.** and

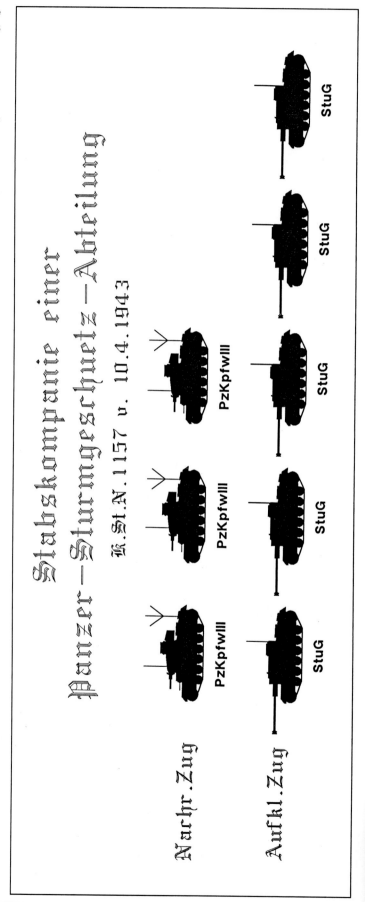

Stabskompanie einer
Panzer-Sturmgeschütz-Abteilung
K.St.N.1157 v. 10.4.1943

StuG
StuG
PzKpfwIII
StuG
PzKpfwIII
StuG
PzKpfwIII
StuG

Nachr.Zug
Aufkl.Zug

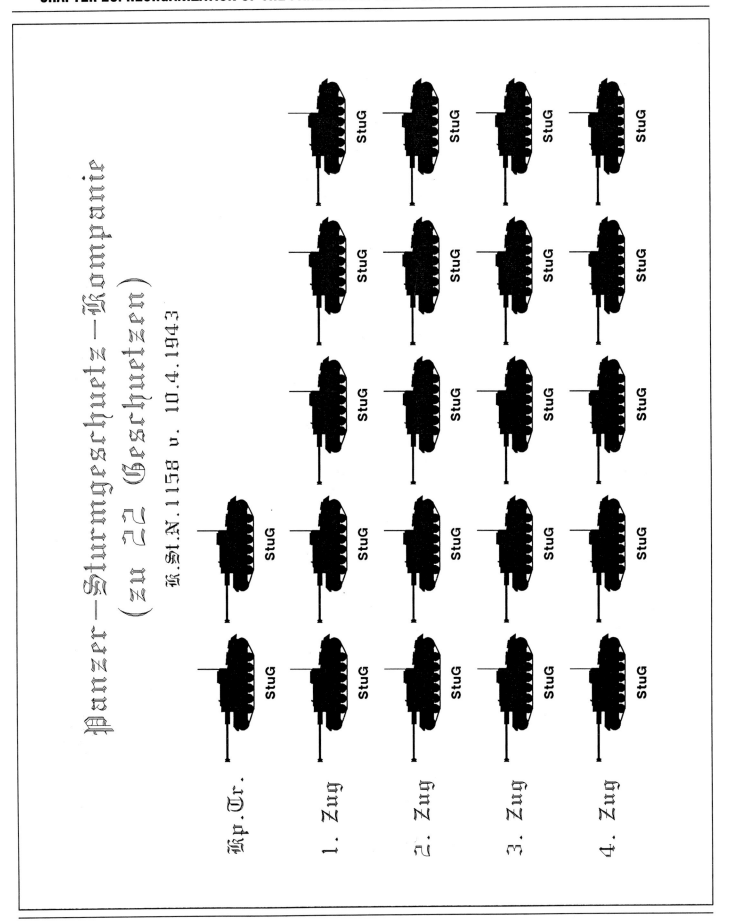

Panzer—Sturmgeschuetz—Kompanie
(zu 22 Geschuetzen)
K.St.N.1158 v. 10.4.1943

Kp.Tr.

1. Zug

2. Zug

3. Zug

4. Zug

StuG

2.Kompanien/schwere-SS-Panzer-Abteilung 101 were attached to **SS-Pz.Div."LSSAH"** and shipped to the Eastern Front with 27 Tigers. The **Stab** and **3.Kompanie/schwere-SS-Panzer-Abteilung 101** remained behind in the West.

As related in its status report on 8 January 1944, the **schwere SS-Panzer Abteilung 103** was originally created on 1 July 1943 as the **II.Abteilung/SS-Panzer-Regiment 11** in Grafenwoehr. It was employed as infantry in Yugoslavia from the end of August 1943 until early January 1944 when it moved to Holland. The order dated 1 November 1943 to convert the **II.Abteilung/Panzer-Regiment 11** to the **schwere SS-Panzer-Abteilung 103** wasn't accomplished until the end of November.

<u>New K.St.N. Dated 1Nov43</u> - The following new set of K.St.N./K.A.N. dated 1 November 1943 was used to create new or refurbish existing Tiger units when authorized by specific orders:

K.St.N.	Date	Unit Name
1150e	1Nov43	**Stabskompanie schweren Panzer-Abteilung "Tiger"**
1176e	1Nov43	**schwere Panzer-Kompanie e**

The **Stabskompanie einer schweren Panzer-Abteilung "Tiger"**, organized in accordance with K.St.N.1150e dated 1 November 1943, contained a **Nachrichtenzug** with either three **Panzerkampfwagen "Tiger" (8,8 cm 36 L/56) (Sd.Kfz.181)** as **Panzerbefehlswagen** or three **Panzerkampfwagen "Tiger" (8,8 cm 43 L/71) (Sd.Kfz.182)** as **Panzerbefehlswagen**. The **schwere Panzer-Kompanie e**, organized in accordance with K.St.N.1176e dated 1 November 1943, still had 14 **Panzerkampfwagen "Tiger"**, but it had the option of **Panzerkampfwagen "Tiger" (8,8 cm L/56) (Sd.Kfz.181)** or **Panzerkampfwagen "Tiger" (8,8 cm 43 L/71) (Sd.Kfz.182)**.

PANZER-STURMGESCHUETZ-ABTEILUNGEN FOR PANZER-DIVISIONS

In order to increase the operational strength of **Panzer-Divisions**, General Guderian requested that **Sturmgeschuetz-Abteilungen** be created for the **III.Abteilung** of a **Panzer-Regiment**. These were established for the three **Panzer-Divisions** (14., 16., and 24.) that had been wiped out in Stalingrad. The **III.Abteilung/Panzer-Regiment 2** was created on 31 March 1943 with four **Kompanien**, the **III.Abteilung/Panzer-Regiment 24** was created with four **Kompanien** from **Panzer-Abteilung 127** on 5 April 1943, and the **III.Abteilung/Panzer-Regiment 36** was created with four **Kompanien** on 25 April 1943.

The applicable K.St.N. created for a **Panzer-Sturmgeschuetz-Abteilung** were:

K.St.N.	Date	Unit Name
1107	1Apr43	**Stab Panzer-Abteilung (Sturmgeschuetz)**
1157	10Apr43	**Stabskompanie einer Panzer-Sturmgeschuetz-Abteilung**
1158	10Apr43	**Panzer-Sturmgeschuetz-Kompanie (zu 22 Geschuetzen)**

The **Stabskompanie einer Panzer-Sturmgeschuetz-Abteilung**, organized in accordance with K.St.N.1157 dated 10 April 1943, contained an **Aufklaerungszug** with five **gp.Selbstfahrlafette fuer Sturmgeschuetze 7,5 cm (Sd.Kfz.142)** and a **Nachrichtenzug** with three **Panzerkampfwagen III (5 cm) (Sd.Kfz.141)** as **Panzerbefehlswagen**. The **Panzer-Sturmgeschuetz-Kompanie (zu 22 Geschuetzen)**, organized in accordance with K.St.N.1158 dated 10 April 1943, contained a **Kompanie Trupp** with two **gp.Selbstfahrlafette fuer Sturmgeschuetze 7,5 cm (Sd.Kfz.142)** and four **Zuege** each with five **gp.Selbstfahrlafette fuer Sturmgeschuetze 7,5 cm (Sd.Kfz.142)**. The complete **Panzer-Sturmgeschuetz-Abteilung** established in accordance with the K.St.N. dated 10 April 1943 had an authorized strength of three **Panzerkampfwagen III** and 93 **Sturmgeschuetz**.

In July 1943, **III.Abteilung/Panzer-Regiment 24** and 36 were both reorganized into **Panzer-Sturmgeschuetz-Abteilungen** with two **Panzer-Sturmgeschuetz-Kompanien** and two **Panzer-Kompanie a**. In July 1943, **Panzer-Abteilung 215** was given a single **Panzer-Sturmgeschuetz-Kompanie (zu 22 Geschuetzen)**. On 6 November 1943, the **Panzer-Abteilung** of **Panzer-Grenadier-Division "Feldherrnhalle"** was reorganized as a **gemischte Panzer-Abteilung** with two **Panzer-Sturmgeschuetz-Kompanien** and two **Panzer-Kompanie a**.

The revised K.St.N.1157 dated 1 November 1943 for the **Stabskompanie einer Panzer-Sturmgeschuetz-Abteilung** still called for an **Aufklaerungszug** with five **Sturmgeschuetze** and a **Nachrichtenzug** with three **Panzerkampfwagen III (5 cm L/42) (Sd.Kfz.141)** as **Panzerbefehlswagen**. The revised K.St.N.1158 dated 1 November 1943 for the **Panzer-Sturmgeschuetz-Kompanie (zu 22 Geschuetzen)** still called for 22 **Sturmgeschuetze**.

PANZER-STURMGESCHUETZ-ABTEILUNGEN FOR PANZER-GRENADIER-DIVISIONS

A new organization was created on 20 June 1943 for **Panzer-Sturmgeschuetz-Abteilung zu 45 Geschuetzen** with three **Kompanien**, intended for use in the organization of **Panzer-Abteilungen** in **Panzer-Grenadier-Divisions** outfitted with **Sturmgeschuetz**, as follows:

K.St.N.	Date	Unit Name
1107	1Apr43	**Stab Panzer-Abteilung (Sturmgeschuetz)**

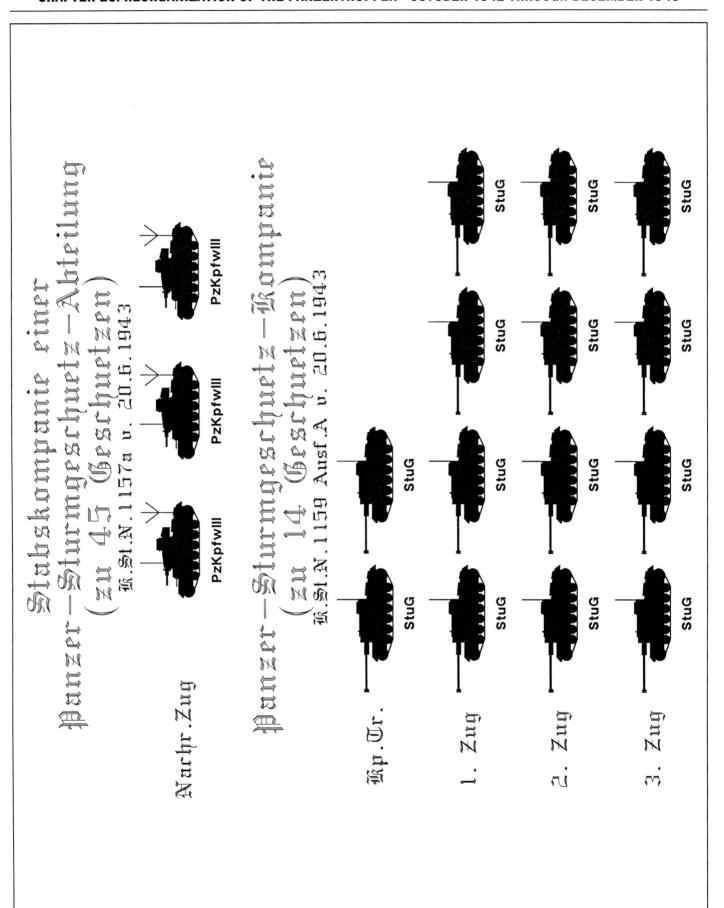

Stabskompanie einer
Panzer-Sturmgeschuetz-Abteilung
(zu 45 Geschuetzen)
K.St.N.1157a v. 20.6.1943

Nachr.Zug

PzKpfwIII PzKpfwIII PzKpfwIII

Panzer-Sturmgeschuetz-Kompanie
(zu 14 Geschuetzen)
K.St.N.1159 Ausf.A v. 20.6.1943

Kp.Tr.

StuG StuG

1. Zug

StuG StuG StuG StuG StuG

2. Zug

StuG StuG StuG StuG StuG

3. Zug

StuG StuG StuG StuG StuG

1157a	20Jun43	**Stabskompanie einer Panzer-Sturmgeschuetz-Abteilung zu 45 Geschuetzen**
1159 Ausf.A	20Jun43	**3 Panzer-Sturmgeschuetz-Kompanie (zu 14 Geschuetzen)**

In accordance with K.St.N.1157a dated 20 June 1943, the **Stabskompanie einer Panzer-Sturmgeschuetz-Abteilung zu 45 Geschuetzen** was to have a **Nachrichtenzug** with three **Panzerkampfwagen III (5 cm) (Sd.Kfz.141)** as **Panzerbefehlswagen**. The three **Panzer-Sturmgeschuetz-Kompanie (zu 14 Geschuetzen)**, organized in accordance with K.St.N.1159 Ausf.A dated 20 June 1943, were to have a **Kompanie Trupp** with two **gp.Selbstfahrlafette fuer Sturmgeschuetze 7,5 cm (Sd.Kfz.142)** and three **Zuege** each with four **gp.Selbstfahrlafette fuer Sturmgeschuetze 7,5 cm (Sd.Kfz.142)**.

This **Panzer-Sturmgeschuetz-Abteilung zu 45 Geschuetzen** organization applied to:

Panzer-Abteilung 103	converted on 21 July 1943
Panzer-Abteilung 129	converted on 21 July 1943
Panzer-Abteilung 5	created on 25 August 1943
Panzer-Abteilung 7	created on 25 August 1943
Panzer-Abteilung 8	created on 25 August 1943
Panzer-Abteilung 118	created on 23 September 1943
Panzer-Abteilung 190	ordered to convert on 9 October 1943
III.Abteilung/Panzer-Regiment 2	converted on 12 November 1943

Panzer-Abteilung 5, **7**, and **8** were created from the surviving remnants of **Panzer-Regiments 5**, **7**, and **8** (lost in Tunisia) and were later assigned to the **25.**, **10.**, and **20.Panzer-Grenadier-Divisions**, respectively. **Panzer-Abteilung 118** was created for the **18.Panzer-Grenadier-Division**. **Panzer-Abteilung 190** was authorized to retain its **Pz.Kpfw.IVs** until it received 42 **Sturmgeschuetz IV** in February 1944.

The revised K.St.N.1157a dated 1 November 1943 for the **Stabskompanie einer Panzer-Sturmgeschuetz-Abteilung (zu 45 Geschuetzen)** still called for three **Panzerkampfwagen III (5 cm) (L/42) (Sd.Kfz.141)** as **Panzerbefehlswagen**, and K.St.N.1159 Ausf.A dated 1 November 1943 for the **Panzer-Sturmgeschuetz-Kompanie (zu 14 Geschuetzen)** still called for 14 **Sturmgeschuetze**.

FUNKLENK-PANZER UNITS

On 25 January 1943, with all elements having returned from the Eastern Front, the **Funklenk-Panzer** units were completely reorganized as follows:

Panzer-Abteilung (Fkl) 301	expanded into four **Kompanien** by absorbing the disbanded **Panzer-Abteilung (Fkl) 302**
Panzer-Kompanie (Fkl) 311	created from old **2.Kp./Pz.Abt.301**
Panzer-Kompanie (Fkl) 312	created from **1.le.Pz.Kp.f**
Panzer-Kompanie (Fkl) 313	created from **3.Kp./Pz.Abt.302**
Panzer-Kompanie (Fkl) 314	created from **2.le.Pz.Kp.f**

The revised K.St.N. for the **Funklenk-Panzer** units were:

K.St.N.	Date	Unit Name
1150f	1Feb43	**Stabskompanie einer Panzerabteilung f**
1171f	1Jan43	**leichte Panzer-Kompanie f**

The **Stabskompanie einer Panzerabteilung f**, organized under K.St.N.1150f dated 1 February 1943, contained a **Nachrichtenzug** with one **Panzerbefehlswagen (Sd.Kfz.267)** and one **Panzerkampfwagen III (5 cm) (Sd.Kfz.141)** as a **Panzerbefehlswagen (Sd.Kfz.268)**.

The **leichte Panzer-Kompanie f**, organized under K.St.N.1171f dated 1 January 1943, had a **Kompanie Trupp** with two **Panzerkampfwagen III (5 cm) (Sd.Kfz.141)** and two **Zuege** each with four **Panzerkampfwagen III (5 cm) (Sd.Kfz.141)** and 12 **Sprengstofftraeger (Sd.Kfz.301)**.

Panzer-Kompanie (Fkl) 315 was created by renaming the **1.Kompanie/Panzer-Abteilung (Fkl) 301** on 6 July 1943. **Panzer-Kompanie (Fkl) 316** was created as a new unit on 15 August 1943.

STURMPANZER-ABTEILUNG

On 19 April 1943, orders were cut to create **Sturmpanzer-Abteilung 216** by 20 May 1943. The **Stabs-Kompanie** was to be organized under K.St.N.1150 dated 1 November 1941 with two **Panzerbefehlswagen**. Each of the three **Sturmpanzer-Kompanie (zu 13 Sturmpanzer)** was to be organized under K.St.N.1175 dated 1 November 1941 with one **Sturmpanzer** in the **Kompanie-Trupp** and four **Sturmpanzer** in each of the three **Zuege**.

The order for the number of **Sturmpanzer** to be produced was increased from 40 to 60, was reflected in the following K.St.N. series specifically created for a **Sturmpanzer-Abteilung**:

K.St.N.	Date	Unit Name
1156	5May43	**Stabskompanie einer Sturmpanzer-Abteilung**
1160	5May43	**Sturmpanzer-Kompanie (14 Geschuetze)**
1164	5May43	**Staffel einer Sturmpanzer-Abteilung**

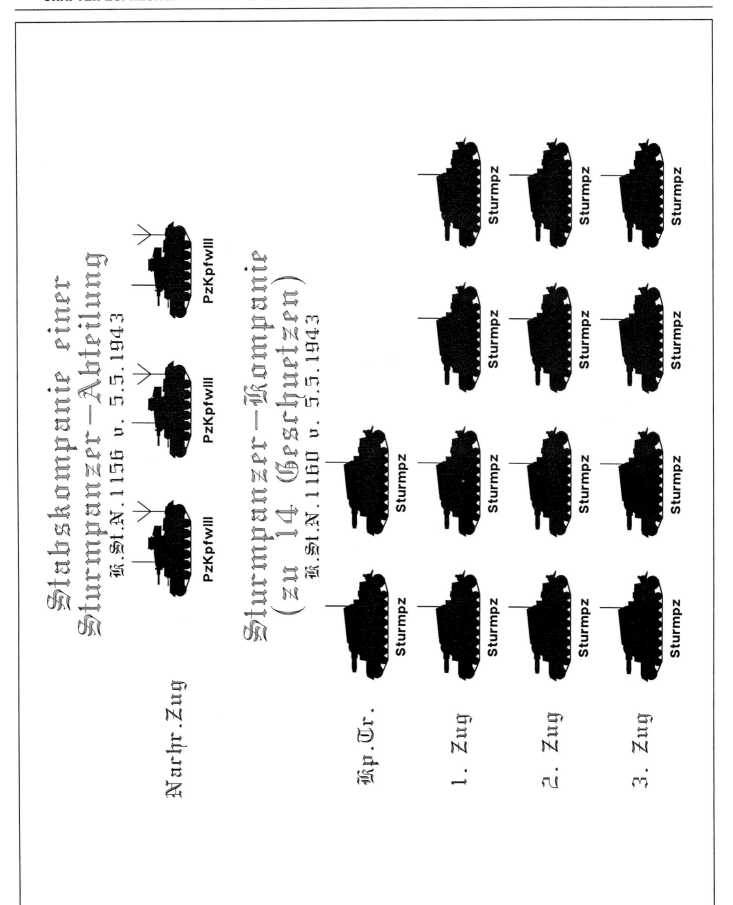

Stabskompanie einer
Sturmpanzer–Abteilung
K.St.N.1156 v. 5.5.1943

Nachr.Zug

PzKpfwIII   PzKpfwIII   PzKpfwIII

Sturmpanzer–Kompanie
(zu 14 Geschuetzen)
K.St.N.1160 v. 5.5.1943

Kp.Tr.

1. Zug

2. Zug

3. Zug

Sturmpz   Sturmpz   Sturmpz   Sturmpz
Sturmpz   Sturmpz   Sturmpz   Sturmpz
Sturmpz   Sturmpz   Sturmpz   Sturmpz
Sturmpz   Sturmpz

In accordance with K.St.N.1156 dated 5 May 1943, the **Stabskompanie einer Sturmpanzer-Abteilung** contained a **Nachrichtenzug** of three **Panzerkampfwagen III (5 cm) (Sd.Kfz.141)** as **Panzerbefehlswagen**. The **Sturmpanzer-Kompanie (14 Geschuetze)**, organized under K.St.N.1160 dated 5 May 1943, contained a **Kompanie Trupp** with two **Sturmgeschuetze IV (Sd.Kfz.166)** and three **Zuege** each with four **Sturmgeschuetze IV (Sd.Kfz.166)**. The **Staffel einer Sturmpanzer-Abteilung**, organized under K.St.N.1164 dated 5 May 1943, was to have 18 **Sturmgeschuetze IV (Sd.Kfz.166)**.

The revised K.St.N.1156 dated 1 November 1943 for the **Stabskompanie einer Sturmpanzer-Abteilung** still called for a **Nachrichtenzug** with three **Panzerkampfwagen III (5 cm L/42) (Sd.Kfz.141)** as **Panzerbefehlswagen**. The revised K.St.N.1160 dated 1 November 1943 for the **Sturmpanzer-Kompanie (14 Geschuetze)** called for 14 **Sturmgeschuetze IV fuer 15 cm Stu.Haub.43 (Sd.Kfz.166)**.

BEUTE-PANZER UNITS

On 20 October 1942, an order was cut in order to gather all of the scattered elements of **Beute-Panzer** units together under one command (**Panzer-Brigade Stab 100, Panzer-Kompanie 100, Stab Panzer-Abteilung 223, schwere Panzer-Kompanie 223(f), Panzer-Kompanie 81, Panzer-Kompanie Niederlande**, and the **1. und 2.Kompanien/ Panzer-Ersatz-Abteilung 100**). It was entirely outfitted with French **Beute-Panzer**. On 8 December 1942, **Stab Panzer-Regiment Stab 100** was created from **Stab Panzer-Brigade 100**. On 8 January 1943, the **II.Abteilung/Panzer-Regiment 100** was created with three **Panzer-Kompanien** from **Panzer-Kompanie 81** and **Panzer-Kompanie Paris**. On 10 January 1943, the **I.Abteilung/Panzer-Regiment 100** was created with three **Panzer-Kompanien** from the **2.Kompanie** and **Stab Panzer-Abteilung 223**. A **4.** and **8.Panzer-Kompanie** were added on 15 July 1943, and **Panzer-Regiment 100** was assigned to the newly re-created **21.Panzer-Division (neu)**.

On 19 October 1943, plans were made to distribute Panzers that had been taken over from the Italians. These were to be used to outfit the following Panzer units that had been previously issued French **Beute-Panzer**: **Panzer-Kompanie z.b.V.12** (by expansion into a **Panzer-Abteilung**), **Panzer-Abteilung 202**, and **Panzer-Abteilung V.SS-Gebirgs-Korps Prinz Eugen**. A total of 150 Italian **Beute-Panzer** were needed.

On 29 October 1943, **Sicherungs-Regiment (mot) 100** was ordered to be formed in France with a **Panzer-Sicherungs-Kompanie** with 17 **Beutepanzer**, organized in accordance with K.St.N.1171c dated 1 April 1941.

On 29 November 1943, **Panzer-Abteilung 205** and **206** were created in the West, each with two **Beute-Panzer-**

Kompanien. The **Stabskompanie einer Panzer-Abteilung c** organized under K.St.N.1150c dated 1 February 1941 was altered by ordering that the **leichte Zug** be replaced with a **schwere Zug** with five **Pz.Kpfw.B2(f)**. It still contained a **Nachrichtenzug** with two **Pz.Kpfw.S35(f)**. Each of the **Panzer-Kompanie c** organized under K.St.N.1171c dated 1 April 1941 was to have four **Pz.Kpfw.S35(f)** and 14 **Pz.Kpfw.H38(f)**.

MISCELLANEOUS PANZER UNITS

On 22 November 1942, the **Panzer-Sicherungs-Kompanie z.b.V.** was created from elements of **Panzer-Abteilung z.b.V.40** for the **20.Armee**. This **leichte Panzer-Sicherungs-Kompanie** organized in accordance with K.St.N.1171a dated 5.1.43 had a **Kompanie Trupp** with one **Panzerkampfwagen I (M.G.) (Sd.Kfz.101)** and three **Zuege** each with five **Panzerkampfwagen I (M.G.) (Sd.Kfz.101)** and one **Panzerkampfwagen III (3,7 cm) (Sd.Kfz.141)**. It was renamed **Panzer-Kompanie 40** on 21 January 1943 and disbanded on 15 July 1943.

On 6 January 1943, a **mittlere Panzer-Kompanie** of the **Panzer-Lehr-Regiment** was ordered to be prepared for employment on the Eastern Front and ready to be loaded on railcars by 1200 hours on 8 January. Named **Panzer-Lehr-Kompanie 233**, it was organized in accordance with K.St.N.1175 dated 1 November 1941 and outfitted with four **Pz.Kpfw.III lang**, eight **Pz.Kpfw.IV kurz**, and two **Pz.Kpfw.IV lang**. It was incorporated into **Panzer-Regiment "Grossdeutschland"** as the new **1.Kompanie** on 4 March 1943.

Before the loss of Sicily, eight Tigers were shipped from the ordnance depot on 28 July 1943 to outfit an independent unit destined for Italy. Known as **Tigergruppe Meyer**, this small unit with its eight Tigers was attached to **Panzer-Jaeger-Abteilung 46** from August through November 1943. By 4 February 1944, **Tigergruppe Schwebbach** (formerly known as **Tigergruppe Meyer**) was attached to the **LXXVI.Panzer-Korps** to attack the bridgehead created by the Allied landing at Anzio. On 11 March 1944, the surviving crews and Tigers of **Tigergruppe Schwebbach** were incorporated into **schwere Heeres Panzer-Abteilung 508**.

In the late Summer of 1943, three **Panzer-Sicherungs-Kompanien** were created to perform security tasks in Italy. These were the **Panzer-Einsatz-Kompanie 35**, created on 25 August 1943, the **2.Panzer-Sicherungs-Kompanie** on 28 August 1943, and the **3.Panzer-Sicherungs-Kompanie** on 9 September 1943. The **3.Panzer-Sicherungs-Kompanie** was ordered to be organized in accordance with K.St.N.1175 dated 1 November 1941 without the **leichte Zug** with 15 **Pz.Kpfw.IV lang**, one as a reserve.

STRENGTH OF PANZER UNITS IN THE WEST ON 31 DECEMBER 1943

Name of Unit	Pz.Kpfw.III			Pz.Kpfw.IV		Pz.Kpfw.		StuG	
	kz	lg	75	kz	lg	V	VI	kz	lg
21.Pz.Div.				10	57				
9.SS-Pz.Div.	5				49	4		1	42
10.SS-Pz.Div.	5				49				42
12.SS-Pz.Div.				4	73	3			
I./Pz.Rgt.3	17					3			
I./Pz.Rgt.4						38			
I./Pz.Rgt.6						76			
I./Pz.Rgt.11						4			
I./Pz.Rgt.24						4			
I./Pz.Rgt.25						4			
I./Pz.Rgt.27						4			
I./Pz.Rgt.35						4			
I./Pz.Rgt.36						3			
I./Pz.Rgt.G.D.						4			
I./SS-Pz.Rgt.3						4			
s.Pz.Abt.507							19		
s.Pz.Abt.508							19		
FKL Abt.301									31
FKL Kp.312									2
FKL Kp.313			10						
FKL Kp.314									4
FKL Kp.315									10
Pz.Abt.118									45
155.Res.Pz.Div.	8	10	13	5	15				
179.Res.Pz.Div.	10	17	13	6	15				
273.Res.Pz.Div.	10	12	14	7	23				
Total:	55	39	50	32	281	155	38	1	176

24
Operation Zitadelle

During the Spring of 1943 in the build-up for Operation Zitadelle, over 1000 Panzers were sent to the Eastern Front as reinforcements and replacements. New units included the **schwere Panzer-Abteilung 505**, **Sturmpanzer-Abteilung 216**, and **Panzer-Abteilung (Fkl) 316** for **Heeresgruppe Mitte** and **Panzer-Abteilung 51** and **52** with the **Stab-Panzer-Regiment 39** for **Heeresgruppe Sued**. The replacements were mainly used to refit each **Panzer-Division** that was to take part in the upcoming offensive with a complete **Panzer-Abteilung** of four **gemischte Panzer-Kompanien**. There were exceptions to this general rule as shown in the charts on the Organization and Strength of Panzer Units before Operation Zitadelle on 1 July 1943.

At the start of the offensive the **Panzertruppen** on the Eastern Front were organized as shown in the Order of Battle dated 7 July 1943. **Heeresgruppe Mitte** on the north side of the Kursk salient had eight **Panzer-Divisions** under its command with a total of 747 Panzers, along with 31 Tigers in the **schwere Panzer-Abteilung 505**, 45 **Sturmpanzer** in **Sturmpanzer-Abteilung 216** and 89 Ferdinand in **schwere Panzer-Jaeger-Abteilung 656**. In addition, 141 replacement Panzers arrived during July for units under **Heeresgruppe Mitte** including 98 **Pz.Kpfw.IV L/48**, 14 Tigers, and 10 Sturmpanzer.

Heeresgruppe Mitte didn't commit the **Panzer-Divisions** in the lead attack at dawn on 5 July 1943. They relied on the heavy armor in **schwere Panzer-Abteilung 505** and schwere **Panzer-Jaeger-Abteilung 656** to create gaps in the Russian defensive belts for the **Panzer-Divisions** to exploit. Just how well this worked out is related by the following excerpts

A **Sturmgeschuetz** used for radio control of the **BIV Sprengstofftraeger** with the **Panzer-Kompanie (Fkl) 314** in training prior to being sent to **Heeresgruppe Mitte**. The BIVs were used in an attempt to clear gaps in the minefields for the heavy armor of **schwere Panzer-Abteilung 505** and **schwere Panzer-Jaeger-Regiment 656** at the start of Operation **Zitadelle** on 5 July 1943. (MJ)

Two **Sturmpanzers** from **Sturmpanzer-Abteilung 216** loading ammunition. The troops complained that the method of fastening the **Schuerzen** (side skirts) to the rails and fenders was inadequate to prevent their loss. (KHM)

from the war diary of **Panzer-Abteilung 21** in the **20.Panzer-Division**:

4 July 1943 - At 2100 hours, **Panzer-Abteilung 21** began moving to the assembly area. To the clanging of parade music, the **Panzer-Kompanien** headed south past the commander. The **Abteilung** arrived complete at the assembly area, a depression north of Lebedicha, and had taken up positions by 2400 hours.

5 July 1943 - Wake-up call at 0400 hours. The vehicles were inspected again for the smallest details by the maintenance section and crews to determine operational readiness. At 0430 hours, the major battle in the Kursk salient began at the left-hand neighbor. Uncountable shots fired by artillery could be heard in the distance. Bomber squadrons carried their loads over the **Abteilung**. It still remained quiet in front of our sector. Only now and then did the Russians send a pair of shells over. Then at 0530 hours, the artillery fire hammered down in the division's sector. Hundreds of shells blanket the Russian positions, while bombs dropped by the Stuka and bomber squadrons create giant smoke and dust clouds on the horizon.

About 0800 hours, the **Abteilung** started to advance without encountering any enemy activity, moved past Wech-Tagino, arrived at Point 218.2, and halted there for a long time. The first Russian bombers attacked and in aerial combat the first enemy machines fell to the ground. To our front the Tigers had pounded the first gaps in the enemy positions which the **Abteilung** then charged through.

Without encountering any further enemy activity, the advance went up to the cherry orchard north of Podoljan. Enemy tanks that had pulled back out of Gnilez were taken under fire and driven off. In the interim, a ford was prepared in Podoljan and the **Abteilung** started their advance toward

Bobrik where within a short time our **Pioniere** prepared a crossing. Point 224.5 was reached, where a long halt occurred.

About 1800 hours, the **Abteilung** with the **Panzer-Grenadiere** started to attack toward Ssaborowka. The **1.Kompanie** was on the right for flank security, then the **4.Kompanie, Stab, 3.Kompanie**, and the **2.Kompanie** on the left. Shortly after starting, the commander's Panzer and another Panzer drove onto mines, resulting in a short delay. The attack rapidly advanced on the right wing, but here also one Panzer of the **1.Kompanie** was damaged by a mine. After a short firefight, effectively supported by combat aircraft, the **Abteilung** entered Ssaborowka and crossed the Ssopa. Five T34 tanks that stood well camouflaged within the Ssopa depression on the far side were destroyed by the **4.Kompanie**. The **2.Kompanie** was on guard south of the totally destroyed Ssaborowka, while the rest of the **Abteilung** took up positions north of the village with flank security toward the right. During the night, Russian bombers attacked our positions several times without success. The supply vehicles arrived about midnight. Vehicles were refueled, ammo loaded, and the first meal of the day consumed.

6 July 1943 - Resupply of the **Abteilung** was hardly completed when the Russian counterstrike began at 0200 hours. Thirty enemy tanks were reported in the southeast and 50 in the southwest. The **3.** and **4.Kompanien** moved to the south side of the villages and took up defensive positions. Our own attack was carried farther to the south with the objective of gaining the high road south of Point 230.4. Strong anti-tank gun and anti-tank rifle fire struck the **Abteilung**. The Russians stubbornly defended so that the **Panzer-Grenadiere** could only follow the Panzers slowly. Again Panzer losses

(text continues on page 83)

ORDER OF BATTLE - 7 JULY 1943

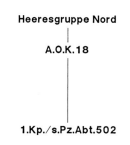

Heeresgruppe Nord

A.O.K.18

1.Kp./s.Pz.Abt.502

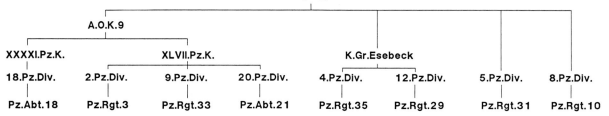

Heeresgruppe Mitte

A.O.K.9

XXXXI.Pz.K.	XLVII.Pz.K.			K.Gr.Esebeck			
18.Pz.Div.	2.Pz.Div.	9.Pz.Div.	20.Pz.Div.	4.Pz.Div.	12.Pz.Div.	5.Pz.Div.	8.Pz.Div.
Pz.Abt.18	Pz.Rgt.3	Pz.Rgt.33	Pz.Abt.21	Pz.Rgt.35	Pz.Rgt.29	Pz.Rgt.31	Pz.Rgt.10

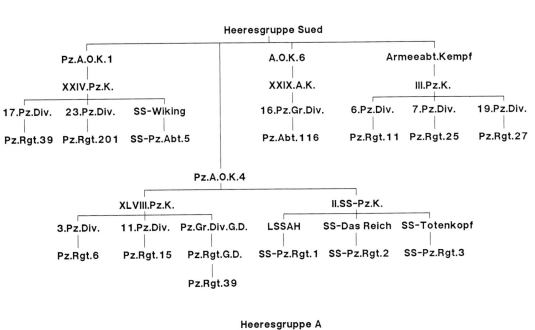

Heeresgruppe Sued

Pz.A.O.K.1   A.O.K.6   Armeeabt.Kempf

XXIV.Pz.K.			XXIX.A.K.	III.Pz.K.		
17.Pz.Div.	23.Pz.Div.	SS-Wiking	16.Pz.Gr.Div.	6.Pz.Div.	7.Pz.Div.	19.Pz.Div.
Pz.Rgt.39	Pz.Rgt.201	SS-Pz.Abt.5	Pz.Abt.116	Pz.Rgt.11	Pz.Rgt.25	Pz.Rgt.27

Pz.A.O.K.4

XLVIII.Pz.K.			II.SS-Pz.K.		
3.Pz.Div.	11.Pz.Div.	Pz.Gr.Div.G.D.	LSSAH	SS-Das Reich	SS-Totenkopf
Pz.Rgt.6	Pz.Rgt.15	Pz.Rgt.G.D.	SS-Pz.Rgt.1	SS-Pz.Rgt.2	SS-Pz.Rgt.3
		Pz.Rgt.39			

Heeresgruppe A

A.O.K.17

XLIX.Geb.K.

13.Pz.Div.

Pz.Rgt.4

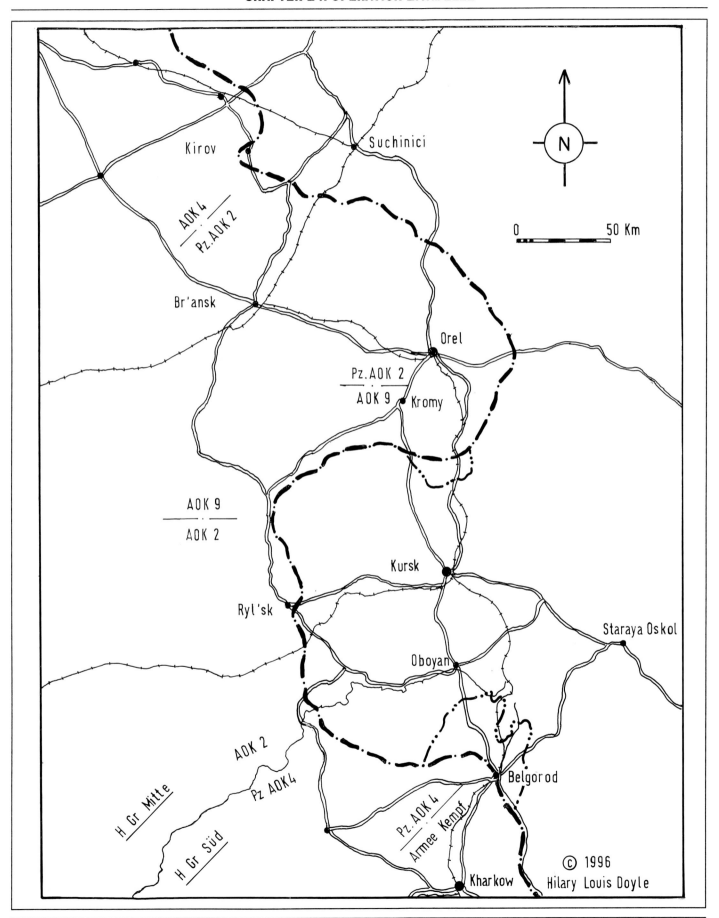

ORGANIZATION AND STRENGTH OF PANZER UNITS
BEFORE OPERATION ZITADELLE - 1 JULY 1943

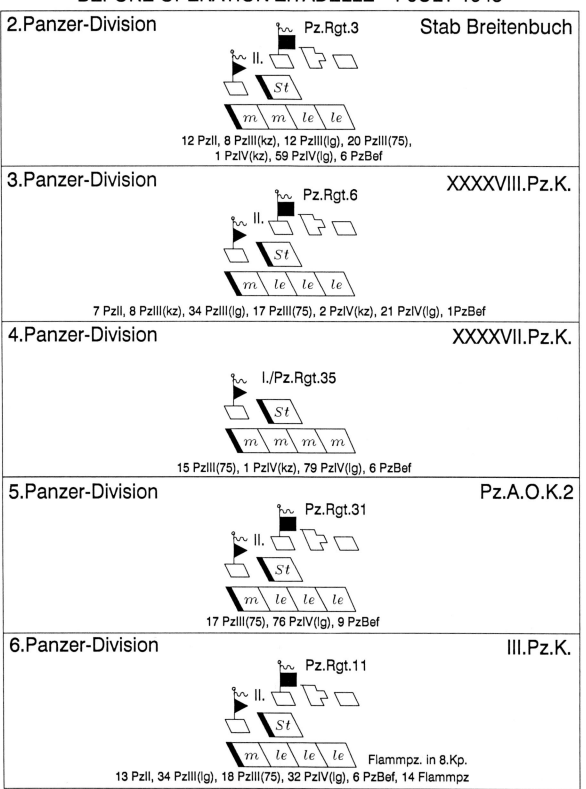

2.Panzer-Division — Pz.Rgt.3 — Stab Breitenbuch

12 PzII, 8 PzIII(kz), 12 PzIII(lg), 20 PzIII(75),
1 PzIV(kz), 59 PzIV(lg), 6 PzBef

3.Panzer-Division — Pz.Rgt.6 — XXXXVIII.Pz.K.

7 PzII, 8 PzIII(kz), 34 PzIII(lg), 17 PzIII(75), 2 PzIV(kz), 21 PzIV(lg), 1PzBef

4.Panzer-Division — I./Pz.Rgt.35 — XXXXVII.Pz.K.

15 PzIII(75), 1 PzIV(kz), 79 PzIV(lg), 6 PzBef

5.Panzer-Division — Pz.Rgt.31 — Pz.A.O.K.2

17 PzIII(75), 76 PzIV(lg), 9 PzBef

6.Panzer-Division — Pz.Rgt.11 — III.Pz.K.

Flammpz. in 8.Kp.
13 PzII, 34 PzIII(lg), 18 PzIII(75), 32 PzIV(lg), 6 PzBef, 14 Flammpz

ORGANIZATION AND STRENGTH OF PANZER UNITS BEFORE OPERATION ZITADELLE - 1 JULY 1943

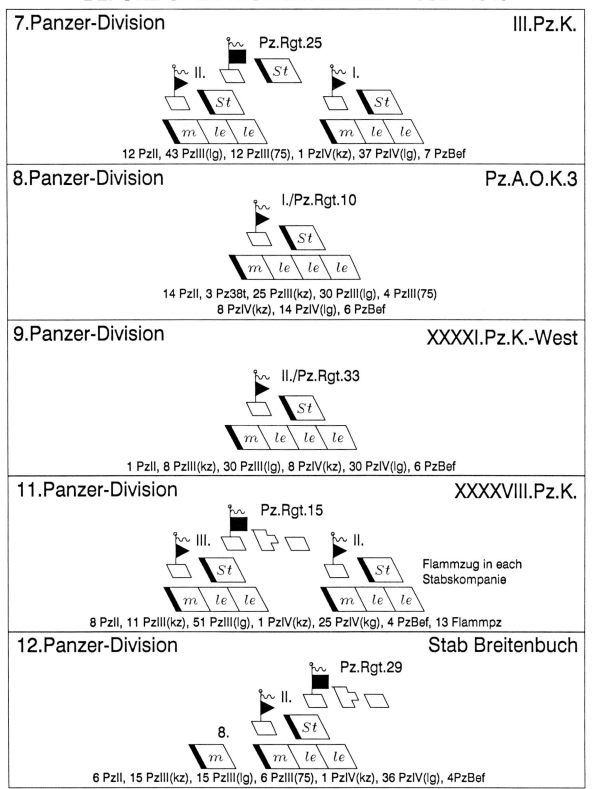

7.Panzer-Division — III.Pz.K.

Pz.Rgt.25

12 PzII, 43 PzIII(lg), 12 PzIII(75), 1 PzIV(kz), 37 PzIV(lg), 7 PzBef

8.Panzer-Division — Pz.A.O.K.3

I./Pz.Rgt.10

14 PzII, 3 Pz38t, 25 PzIII(kz), 30 PzIII(lg), 4 PzIII(75)
8 PzIV(kz), 14 PzIV(lg), 6 PzBef

9.Panzer-Division — XXXXI.Pz.K.-West

II./Pz.Rgt.33

1 PzII, 8 PzIII(kz), 30 PzIII(lg), 8 PzIV(kz), 30 PzIV(lg), 6 PzBef

11.Panzer-Division — XXXXVIII.Pz.K.

Pz.Rgt.15

Flammzug in each Stabskompanie

8 PzII, 11 PzIII(kz), 51 PzIII(lg), 1 PzIV(kz), 25 PzIV(kg), 4 PzBef, 13 Flammpz

12.Panzer-Division — Stab Breitenbuch

Pz.Rgt.29

6 PzII, 15 PzIII(kz), 15 PzIII(lg), 6 PzIII(75), 1 PzIV(kz), 36 PzIV(lg), 4PzBef

ORGANIZATION AND STRENGTH OF PANZER UNITS
BEFORE OPERATION ZITADELLE - 1 JULY 1943

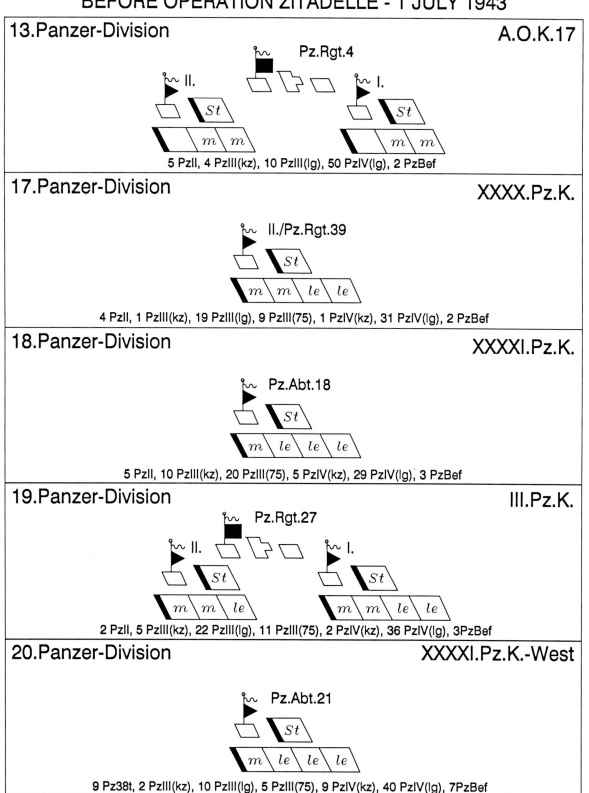

13.Panzer-Division — A.O.K.17

Pz.Rgt.4 — II. — I.

5 PzII, 4 PzIII(kz), 10 PzIII(lg), 50 PzIV(lg), 2 PzBef

17.Panzer-Division — XXXX.Pz.K.

II./Pz.Rgt.39

4 PzII, 1 PzIII(kz), 19 PzIII(lg), 9 PzIII(75), 1 PzIV(kz), 31 PzIV(lg), 2 PzBef

18.Panzer-Division — XXXXI.Pz.K.

Pz.Abt.18

5 PzII, 10 PzIII(kz), 20 PzIII(75), 5 PzIV(kz), 29 PzIV(lg), 3 PzBef

19.Panzer-Division — III.Pz.K.

Pz.Rgt.27 — II. — I.

2 PzII, 5 PzIII(kz), 22 PzIII(lg), 11 PzIII(75), 2 PzIV(kz), 36 PzIV(lg), 3PzBef

20.Panzer-Division — XXXXI.Pz.K.-West

Pz.Abt.21

9 Pz38t, 2 PzIII(kz), 10 PzIII(lg), 5 PzIII(75), 9 PzIV(kz), 40 PzIV(lg), 7PzBef

ORGANIZATION AND STRENGTH OF PANZER UNITS BEFORE OPERATION ZITADELLE - 1 JULY 1943

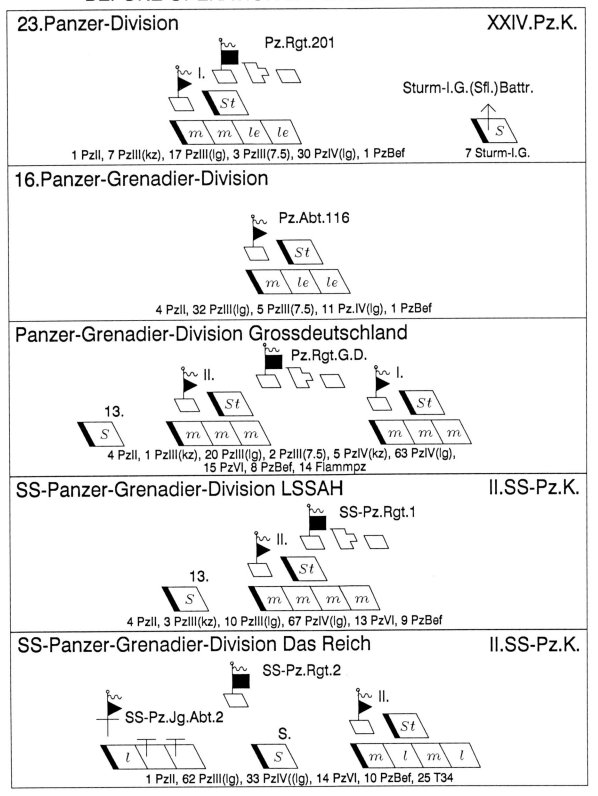

23.Panzer-Division   XXIV.Pz.K.

Pz.Rgt.201

Sturm-I.G.(Sfl.)Battr.

1 PzII, 7 PzIII(kz), 17 PzIII(lg), 3 PzIII(7.5), 30 PzIV(lg), 1 PzBef

7 Sturm-I.G.

16.Panzer-Grenadier-Division

Pz.Abt.116

4 PzII, 32 PzIII(lg), 5 PzIII(7.5), 11 Pz.IV(lg), 1 PzBef

Panzer-Grenadier-Division Grossdeutschland

Pz.Rgt.G.D.

4 PzII, 1 PzIII(kz), 20 PzIII(lg), 2 PzIII(7.5), 5 PzIV(kz), 63 PzIV(lg),
15 PzVI, 8 PzBef, 14 Flammpz

SS-Panzer-Grenadier-Division LSSAH   II.SS-Pz.K.

SS-Pz.Rgt.1

4 PzII, 3 PzIII(kz), 10 PzIII(lg), 67 PzIV(lg), 13 PzVI, 9 PzBef

SS-Panzer-Grenadier-Division Das Reich   II.SS-Pz.K.

SS-Pz.Rgt.2

SS-Pz.Jg.Abt.2

1 PzII, 62 PzIII(lg), 33 PzIV((lg), 14 PzVI, 10 PzBef, 25 T34

ORGANIZATION AND STRENGTH OF PANZER UNITS
BEFORE OPERATION ZITADELLE - 1 JULY 1943

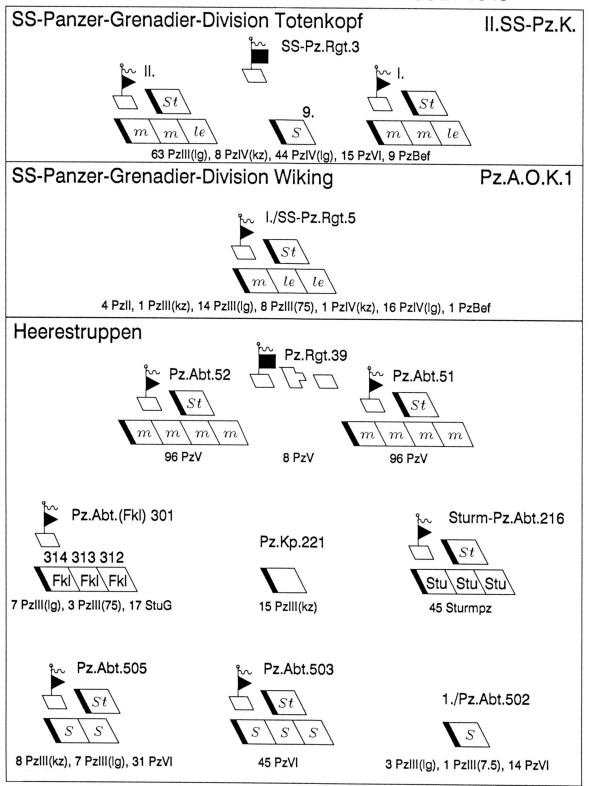

SS-Panzer-Grenadier-Division Totenkopf   II.SS-Pz.K.

SS-Pz.Rgt.3

II.

St

m m le

9.

S

I.

St

m m le

63 PzIII(lg), 8 PzIV(kz), 44 PzIV(lg), 15 PzVI, 9 PzBef

SS-Panzer-Grenadier-Division Wiking   Pz.A.O.K.1

I./SS-Pz.Rgt.5

St

m le le

4 PzII, 1 PzIII(kz), 14 PzIII(lg), 8 PzIII(75), 1 PzIV(kz), 16 PzIV(lg), 1 PzBef

Heerestruppen

Pz.Rgt.39

Pz.Abt.52

St

m m m m

96 PzV

8 PzV

Pz.Abt.51

St

m m m m

96 PzV

Pz.Abt.(Fkl) 301

314 313 312

Fkl Fkl Fkl

7 PzIII(lg), 3 PzIII(75), 17 StuG

Pz.Kp.221

15 PzIII(kz)

Sturm-Pz.Abt.216

St

Stu Stu Stu

45 Sturmpz

Pz.Abt.505

St

S S

8 PzIII(kz), 7 PzIII(lg), 31 PzVI

Pz.Abt.503

St

S S S

45 PzVI

1./Pz.Abt.502

S

3 PzIII(lg), 1 PzIII(7.5), 14 PzVI

A **Kompanie** of **Pz.Kpfw.IV Ausf.G**s advancing across a wheat field at the start of Operation **Zitadelle**. The last **Pz.Kpfw.IV** had not been outfitted with **Schuerzen**, although others in the lead have the additional protection against Russian anti-tank rifles. (BA)

occurred due to mines. After reaching the high road, the **Panzer-Grenadiere** dug in on line with the Panzers.

Then, the Russian counterstrike set in with strong forces. Flashes from many artillery batteries could be seen far off on the horizon laying down heavy fire on the **Abteilung**. At the same time, several waves of enemy tanks, with infantry riding on them, charged toward our attack point. An extremely heavy tank battle ensued. Hauptmann Mueller was severely wounded and Leutnant Arnold fell. Losses caused by mines and hits from tank guns increased. Oberleutnant Dr. Glauner took over the **4.Kompanie**. The **Abteilung** was also quite successful. Over 20 enemy tanks already stood in flames and the enemy infantry had taken large losses. Our Stukas and combat aircraft brought relief. The Russians also attacked the **Abteilung** with heavy bombers several times but were unsuccessful. Several Panzers ran out of ammunition and turned back to Ssaborowka, where in the interim the supply vehicles had arrived.

The intensity of the battle continued to increase. The first reserve, the **1.Kompanie**, had long since been thrown into the battle, while the Russians continued to throw new masses of tanks and infantry into the battle and blanketed our posi-

tions with strong artillery fire and rocket salvoes. About 1600 hours, the division commander arrived at the forward command post of **Grenadier-Regiment 59** commanded by Oberst Demme, where a short commanders' conference occurred. Surprisingly, eight T34 tanks suddenly emerged on the right flank and entered the western part of the village. Damaged Panzers and those that were reloading ammunition quickly repulsed the attack. Oberleutnant Dr. Glauner received the Iron Cross First Class and two members of the **4.Kompanie** were awarded the Iron Cross Second Class by the division commander because they knocked out six of the attacking tanks with their Panzers. Oberleutnant Harmann, Oberarzt Micus, Leutnant Hoffmann were wounded. Leutnant Guenther took over command of the **2.Kompanie**. About 1700 hours, the attack could be proven to be repulsed. Over 30 enemy T34 tanks and one assault gun were destroyed in addition to several anti-tank guns, anti-tank rifles, and machine guns. The **Abteilung** had endured one of its hardest days in battle in which officers and men excelled at staying in action. Several crews had their Panzers knocked out three times and then drove a fourth time against the numerically superior enemy.

About 1815, another warning of enemy tanks. Over 50 enemy tanks rolled forward from the southwest and broke through the right flank, while a further 30 were thrown back that attacked the **Abteilung** from the front. The right flank of the division was endangered. A reserve group from the **Abteilung** under Oberfeldwebel Kohla caught up with the enemy tanks near Bobrik while **Sturmgeschuetze** and **Pak Sfl.** struck the enemy in the flank. The battle continued until after dark. Then the enemy tanks pulled back after several losses. As they pulled out, several more enemy tanks were knocked out by the **Abteilung**.

7 July 1943 - The attack to reach the Sswopa sector started on the right wing. The **Abteilung** arrived about 1000 hours. Shortly before, a Russian air attack had occurred without causing serious damage. With **Aufklaerungs-Abteilung 20**, the attack was carried forward toward the west to Points 234.1 and 228.9 south and southwest of Gnilez. The Russians struck back against the **Abteilung** with about 30 tanks out of the woods southwest of Gnilez. The main body of Russians pulled back after a short time. Five enemy tanks were shot up, and all weapons engaged enemy infantry. The Russians built up in Krassawka and pulled back toward the west. The **Abteilung** turned off toward the south, whereupon several Panzers ran onto mines. Well-emplaced field positions were taken. Then the **Abteilung** pulled out, turned back toward Ssaborowka, and met up with the supply vehicles.

8 July 1943 - About 0830, the **Abteilung** set off toward Bobruk, where they moved into an assembly area in a ravine that ran toward the west.

At 1030 hours, new orders came in from the division: "**Abteilung** immediately return to Ssaborowka and stand ready. At 1400 hours use two **Panzer-Kompanien** to support the attack of **Panzer-Grenadier-Regiment** on Ssamodurowka." At about 1130 hours, the **Abteilung** started back from Bobruk toward Ssaborowka under the command of Oberleutnant Winter because the **Abteilung** commander had driven to the division. The **2.Kompanie** reinforced by the **10.Zug** from the **3.Kompanie** was ordered to support the planned action.

At 1325 hours, Leutnant Reckel brought over the following order from the division: "Entire **Abteilung** immediately take up defensive positions facing Point 225.4 west of the ravine running toward the northwest of Point 219.0. Ssopatal is to be closely observed because the Russian elements have already moved into the valley west of there." Because the **Bataillon** defending the ravine was to be pulled out for the planned attack on Ssamodurowka and Krassawka, the **Abteilung** had to cover the gap and repulse enemy attacks. About 1400 hours, the **Abteilung** set off to the ordered defense line.

While the **Abteilung** was still moving toward the defense line, about 1530 hours a message came in from the division: "Hauptmann Darius, report immediately to Oberst Braun and there conduct a Panzer attack." The commander immediately drove to Braun's command post in Sswopatal near Point

204.8. The **Abteilung** crossed through a quickly improved ford and started the ordered attack with the infantry on the western part of Ssamodurowka at about 1600 hours. Alone, the **1.Kompanie** remained in the defensive line west of Point 219.0. At first the attack advanced smoothly through the high grain fields. The **Abteilung** drove in the **Breitkeil** formation. **4.Kompanie** right, **3.Kompanie** left, **2.Kompanie** behind in the middle. The **2.Kompanie** was later pulled out to the right and took over flank protection. Enemy resistance stiffened near Point 200. Anti-tank gun and anti-tank rifle fire struck the **Abteilung**. At the same time, several enemy tanks appeared on the right flank and fired at the **Abteilung**.

The **Grenadiere** advanced slowly because the enemy nests of resistance were difficult to spot in the tall grain field. The **2.Kompanie** commander's Panzer was knocked out of action by bundled explosives. The attack was halted. Only the **3.Kompanie** rolled to the left over the ridge toward the village. The **Abteilung** turned toward the right and took up the firefight with enemy tanks, but the range was too long to effectively engage them. Several of our own Panzers were hit and fell out.

In the interim, the **1.Kompanie** had advanced farther, had taken the 30-ton bridge 800 meters east of Krassawka, and was in position directly east of Krassawka. At the same time, the **3.Kompanie** quickly pushed forward into Ssamodurowka almost without encountering any enemy activity, and the **Grenadiere** occupied the village. The **Panzerbefehlswagen** ran onto mines while transporting wounded back.

At 1839 hours, an order came in from division: "**Abteilung** support Demme at Line 220.5 and the Tjeploje school. Immediately contact Demme." The **Abteilung** with three **Kompanien** immediately advanced to the ordered line. Four Panzers of the **3.Kompanie** ran onto mines during this move. The commander's Panzer hit a mine while crossing the ford in the east side of Ssamodurowka causing Leutnant Tempeler to be severely wounded and resulting in his death the same day.

As of 1928 hours, a message arrived from the division: "With all means support Braun in taking Ssamodurowka and repulsing enemy counterattacks. Then support Demme." The **Abteilung** immediately turned about and drove back to Braun. Nightfall and great danger from mines prohibited any further movement, so the **Abteilung** took up a position near the school. The commander got in contact with the division and received the order: "At first light start off to support Demme."

9 July 1943 - In the sector of the **II./113** northeast of Ssamodurowka, in defensive positions the **Abteilung** was hit by strong artillery and heavy infantry weapon fire, resulting in several crew members being wounded. Enemy movements and infantry targets in Krassawka and on the heights to the northwest were taken under well-placed fire. The **1.Kompanie** attacked the north end of Krassawka and suppressed enemy infantry who had numerous anti-tank rifles. One **Pz.Kpfw.IV lang** was knocked out of action by mine

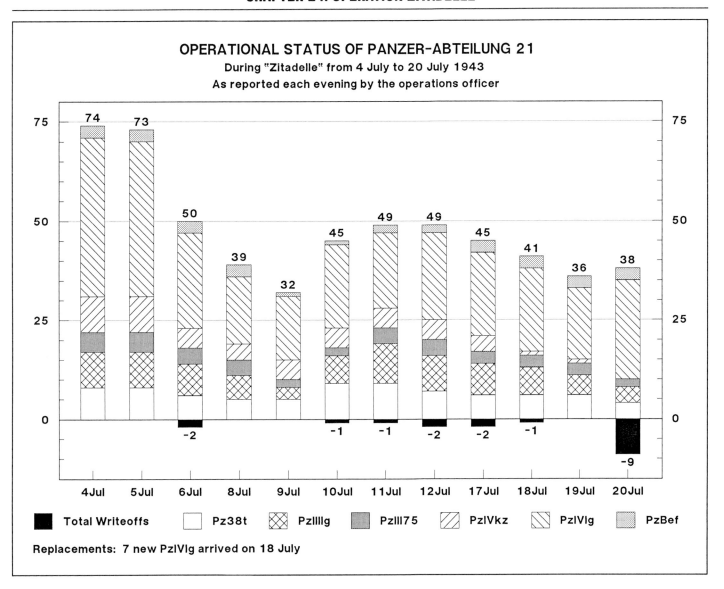

OPERATIONAL STATUS OF PANZER-ABTEILUNG 21
During "Zitadelle" from 4 July to 20 July 1943
As reported each evening by the operations officer

Legend: Total Writeoffs, Pz38t, PzIIIg, PzIII75, PzIVkz, PzIVlg, PzBef

Replacements: 7 new PzIVlg arrived on 18 July

damage. Oberleutnant Winter and Leutnant Lauterberg were wounded by shell fragments. During the night the **1.Kompanie** advanced to Ssamodurowka. Several bombs dropped by Russian light night bombers in the **Abteilung** area did not damage anything.

The attack of **Heeresgruppe Mitte** had stalled out after a shallow penetration into the Russian defensive positions. Their offensive ended on 12 July when the Russians attacked toward Orel, forcing them to commit two Panzer-Divisions to meet this new threat. Details on the engagements fought in this period were recorded by Hauptmann Schultz, commander of the **I.Abteilung/Panzer-Regiment 35** of the **4.Panzer-Division** in his following observations on Russian tank tactics for the period from 8 July through 21 August 1943:

Defensive Tactics: The Russians had prepared defensive positions on all commanding and tactically important terrain features which tanks only had to be driven into in order to be used as armored machine gun and cannon nests. The **Panzer-Abteilung** *encountered one such position when they attacked Point 274.5 southeast of Teploje. Our attack was stopped. Silencing the dug-in tanks was difficult because they were very well camouflaged and their guns were very close to the ground. The long width of the position didn't allow it to be enveloped and attacked from the rear with the available forces.*

The Russian tanks, especially the T34, KW-1 and KW-II, are very well suited for such employment because of their thick armor and good weapons. When it isn't possible to attack from the rear, they can be destroyed only with the cooperation of heavy artillery and Stukas. In addition to these tanks, which are supposedly assigned tactically to the local infantry commander, the Russians still have sufficient additional armored forces that they can employ in a mobile counterattack. Only because of this can they afford from the start to tie down a large number of tanks to one specific location.

Offensive Tactics: The Russians started to counterattack after the German offensive was brought to a halt. They searched out -assisted by the numerical superiority of their equipment - the weakest locations on the front and first attacked near Trossna with a few tanks. The **Panzer-Abteilung** arrived after they had already achieved a breakthrough there. In spite of their being in a tactically superior situation, we managed to tie them down in the front and take them out with a pincers attack. This maneuver was not clearly recognized by them, so they were beaten in a mobile tank-versus-tank battle. The Russians immediately shifted their main point of attack farther to the west and concentrated about 200 tanks at Tschern. With 100 of these tanks, they initiated an attack in the direction of Gostoml. In the interim, the **Panzer-Abteilung** had been transferred to Lonowez. The Russian attack broke down because their right flank ran directly past the front of the **Panzer-Abteilung**; they didn't employ tanks correctly using overwhelming fire and movement, and five of the lead enemy tanks were knocked out by one of our own **Panzer-Kompanien** sent out on the right wing at Point 261.0 south of Krasnikowo.

During the further course of the defensive battle, the **Panzer-Abteilung** was always moved into hull-down positions at the right time. The Russians attacked in various strengths of up to 60 tanks and were always beaten back.

Continuous losses caused the opponents to change their tactics to halting at long range in open terrain. They only advanced to the attack accompanied by infantry, up ravines and through villages, and were successful against our infantry. But then their tanks were knocked out by our Panzers positioned in hull-down, reverse slope positions. They lost the flexibility to search out a favorable position to attack. They continued to run straight at positions, even where several tanks were already knocked out there.

In addition to employing their tanks to support infantry, the Russians attempted to employ the German tactic of sending in concentrated tank brigades to penetrate into a position. But the Russian tank commanders were not sufficiently trained to continue attacking with their tanks after they had broken into the infantry positions. Their tanks stand around and look about for a long time until they are finally knocked out.

The Russians are hardly capable of achieving any success with relatively the same size force sent against a Panzer force of at least company strength led by a German commander employing mobile defensive tactics.

For the month of July, units under **Heeresgruppe Mitte** had lost 304 Panzers as total write-offs (37 percent of the strength at the start of the offensive) and were down to 371 operational Panzers on 31 July (compared to 746 operational on 30 June). The cause of the losses were reported as 69% hit by AP and artillery shells, 3% by mines, 13% stuck in mud and ravines, 11% mechanical failure and track breakage, and 4% not specified.

For Operation Zitadelle, **Heeresgruppe Sued** on the south side of the Kursk salient utilized five **Panzer-Divisions** and four reinforced **Panzer-Grenadier-Divisions** under its command with a total of 1035 Panzers along with 45 Tigers

A mixed column of **Pz.Kpfw.IIIs** and **Pz.Kpfw.IVs** advancing across a field. The commanders went into action with the cupola hatches open. (BA)

A **Pz.Kpfw.III Ausf.M** of the **3.Kompanie/SS-Panzer-Regiment 3** shortly before moving to the assembly area in preparation for Operation **Zitadelle**. (WS)

in the **schwere Panzer-Abteilung 503** and 200 Panthers in **Stab Panzer-Regiment 39** and **Panzer-Abteilung 51** and **52**. In addition, 80 replacement Panzers arrived during July for the units committed to the offensive under **Heeresgruppe Sued**, including 44 **Pz.Kpfw.IV L/48**, 12 Panthers, and 5 Tigers.

The nine **Panzer** and **Panzer-Grenadier-Divisions** were organized into three **Panzer-Korps**, each with an allotment of heavy armor. The **III.Panzer-Korps** was given **schwere Panzer-Abteilung 503**. Under the **XLVIII.Panzer-Korps**, the 200 Panthers were attached to **Panzer-Grenadier-Division "Grossdeutschland"** in addition to its organic **schwere Panzer-Kompanie** with 15 Tigers. Each of the **SS-Panzer-Grenadier-Divisions** in the **II.SS-Panzer-Korps** had an organic **schwere Panzer-Kompanie** with a total of 42 Tigers.

Panzer tactics employed in penetrating the Russian defense in depth and the subsequent withdrawal are related in the following excerpts from the war diary of **Panzer-Regiment 11** of the **6.Panzer-Division**:

4 July 1943 - At Bolchowez

*X-1 day had arrived. At 2000 hours, the combat elements moved out from quarters in the following order: **Regiments-Stab, 6., 8., 5., 7.Kompanie**. Following **6.Kompanie** were the **leichter Zug/ II./Pz.Rgt.11**, **Nachrichtenzug**, messengers, and **Stab II./Pz.Rgt.11**. The march route of about 30 kilometers went through Ugrim-Generalowka, southeast of Almasnoje, Krasnoja, to Bolchowez. The last elements of the **Panzer-Regiment** arrived at about 0230 hours.*

*With the exception of enemy aircraft activity, the night passed quietly up to 0200 hours. Towards 0200 hours, heavy enemy artillery harassing fire started. In addition to **Panzer-Regiment 11**, other elements of **Kampfgruppe von Oppeln**, the **II./Panzer-Grenadier-Regiment 114** and the **3.Kompanie/Panzer-Pionier-Battalion 57** were quartered in Bolchowez.*

5 July 1943 - At Bolchowez, later in the Michailowka bridgehead

*About 0200 hours, the **Kampfgruppe** commander's orders were read to the troops. A large offensive battle loomed* ahead. About 0225 hours, the strong artillery barrage began. The artillery from our division fired from over 80 tubes. About 0600 hours, a conference was held by the **Kampfgruppen** commander, Oberst von Oppeln. The 24-ton bridge that the **Kampfgruppe** planned to use had been destroyed by a direct hit from artillery fire. The **Kampfgruppe** was to cross over a different bridge in Michailowka. At 1030 hours, the **Kampfgruppe** set off in the direction of Michailowka in the following order: **Panzer-Regiment 11** with the armored **Pionier-Zug**, the **II./Panzer-Grenadier-Regiment 114**, and the remainder of the **3.Kompanie/Panzer-Pionier-Bataillon 57**. The column stopped before reaching the bridge in Michailowka. Enemy resistance in Stary Gorod was very strong. **Kampfgruppe von Bieberstein** could not make headway there. In addition, the difficulty in advancing was increased by very heavily mined roads leading out of the bridgehead and strong enemy air attacks that were directed mainly at the 24-ton bridge in Michailowka. The **Kampfgruppe** waited until 1700 hours. Then new orders came from the division: "**Kampfgruppe von Oppeln** will be sent in along the attack routes of the **7.Panzer-Division**."

About 2000 hours, the **Kampfgruppe** left Michailowka, moving through Bjelgorod to the new assembly area south of Kolonoje-Dubowoje. All of the elements of the **Kampfgruppe** arrived in the ordered assembly area by about 0200 hours. The **I./Panzer-Artillerie-Regiment 76** and a **Tiger-Kompanie** were attached to the **Kampfgruppe**.

6 July 1943 - In a forest south of Kolonoje-Dubowoje

The night passed quietly except for enemy air activity. About 1100 hours, a conference was held by the **Kampfgruppen** commander, Oberst von Oppeln. Orders to attack were given. About 1200 hours, the **Kampfgruppe** set out in the following order: **Tiger-Kompanie, Panzer-Regiment 11**, and **II./Panzer-Grenadier-Regiment 114**. About 1300 hours, the 60-ton bridge was reached. Oberst von Oppeln drove ahead to get in contact with the bridgehead commander from the **7.Panzer-Division**. About 1430 hours, the **Kampfgruppe** formed up in depth and started to attack in the direction of Generalowka. The **Tiger-Kompanie** drove at the point, followed by the **Regiments-Stab** with Oberst von Oppeln, **5.Kompanie, 7.Kompanie** echeloned toward the right rear, and **8.Kompanie** echeloned toward the left rear. **II./Panzer-Grenadier-Regiment 114** followed at an interval. Subjected to the heaviest enemy artillery and tank gun fire, the **Kampfgruppe** reached Point 216.1 and Height 207.9. The **6.** and the **8.Kompanien** supported by Tigers were sent toward collective farm Ssolojew and encountered strong enemy resistance. Both **Kompanien** suffered losses. About 2000 hours, contact was made on the right with the advancing **Panzer-Regiment 25** of the **7.Panzer-Division**. During the night, **Kampfgruppe von Oppeln** pulled into a hedgehog formation on Height 207.9. The objective for the day was reached.

Results: 7 enemy tanks (of which 6 T34 and 1 T70), 10 anti-tank guns, 1 infantry gun, 3 17.2 cm guns, 1 anti-aircraft

battery of 4 7.62 cm guns, and approximately 120 enemy dead.

Losses: 8 Panzers from hits, 3 by mines.

7 July 1943 - At Sewrikowo

The night passed quietly. About 0430 hours, Oberst von Oppeln gave the orders for further attacks on Jastrebowo and Sewrikowo. At 0730 hours, the **Kampfgruppe** started to attack. **7.Kompanie/Panzer-Regiment 11** and the **Tiger-Kompanie** drove at the point. After a Stuka attack, the **Kampfgruppe** reached Jastrebowo in a quick bound. A large minefield was spotted and the **3.Kompanie/Panzer-Pionier-Bataillon 57** cleared a gap. The **Kampfgruppe** had to pass through the minefield in single file. Heavy anti-tank and tank gun fire struck the **Kampfgruppe** from Ssewrikowo and the right flank. In spite of this, with **7.Kompanie** in the lead, Ssewrikowo was reached at about 1100 hours. Both bridges over the Rasumnaja River were destroyed and there wasn't a ford available. The **Pioniere** pulled forward the equipment needed to build a 24-ton bridge. Russian heavy artillery and rocket salvoes interfered with the **Pioniere** building the bridge. **II./Panzer-Grenadier-Regiment 114** dismounted and built an infantry bridgehead over the Rasumnaha. The 24-ton bridge was completed at about 2000 hours. The **Kampfgruppe** remained in Ssewrikowo in order to start an attack across the Rasumnaja early the next day.

Results: 1 T34, 8 7.62 cm anti-tank guns, 3 17.2 cm guns with towing vehicles, 12 trucks destroyed or captured.

8 July 1943 - At Ssewrikowo

At 0200 hours, Kampfgruppe von Oppeln set off over the completed 24 ton bridge toward Kampfgruppe Unrein in the following order: **7., 5., 8.,** and **6.Kompanien/Panzer-Regiment 11** followed by **Artillerie-Abteilung Jahn** and **Sturmgeschuetze**. The **Flammpanzer** and the **leichter Zug** remained behind on guard. The assembly area was on Height 212.1. About 0730 hours, **Kampfgruppe von Oppeln** set off to attack Melichowo with the **7.Kompanie/Panzer-Regiment 11** at the point. At first the attack went smoothly forward. Heavy artillery and rocket salvo fire along with threats to the flanks from Postnikoff and Kalinina significantly hindered the attack. An anti-tank trench was encountered 4 kilometers in front of Melichowo. **Pioniere** were sent to use explosives to create a crossing point. The anti-tank trench could be crossed at about 1300 hours. The area behind the anti-tank trench was heavily mined. **Pioniere** cleared a gap. The **Panzer-Grenadiere** dismounted and fought on foot through terrain that was heavily occupied by the enemy. Crossing the anti-tank trench with Panzers went very slowly. Several Panzers ran onto mines. At Point 218.3, strong enemy anti-tank and tank gun fire was encountered out of the northwest. Then a short assembly was made to prepare for the attack on Melichowo. The **8.** and **5.Kompanien/Panzer-Regiment 11** were assigned to the point. Strong enemy resistance, encountered in

OPPOSITE: Two **Pz.Kpfw.IV Ausf.Gs** of the **6.Kompanie/Panzer-Regiment 11** pulling out of a ravine. (BA)

Melichowo, was very quickly broken by a rapid charge. Here, the Tigers shot up six T34 tanks.

Melichowo was taken at 1600 hours. The attack continued toward Schlachowoje after a short halt. The Tigers and **6.Kompanie/Panzer-Regiment 11** were sent in frontally to tie down the opponent. Strong tank gun fire came out of Schachowoje. The 5., 7., and 8.**Kompanien/Panzer-Regiment 11** attacked Schlachowoje from the west, striking from the northwest side of Melichowo over the road from Dalnaja Igumenka to Schlachowoje toward Point 220. The **5.Kompanie/Panzer-Regiment 11** was sent to screen the left flank. The commander decided to pull into the woods west of Melichowo for the night.

Results: 6 tanks shot up, 19 anti-tank guns destroyed, 2 trucks and 11 towing vehicles captured or destroyed, about 100 enemy dead and 130 prisoners.

<u>9 July 1943 - In woods west of Melichowo</u>

About 0700 hours, Staffel Mueller joined up. Due to the heavy vehicle traffic, the Kampfgruppe received heavy artillery fire. The stationary Panzers of the 6. and **8.Kompanien** were spotted in their positions by enemy anti-tank guns and artillery. Several Panzers were hit and set on fire. Several members of the **Kampfgruppe** were killed or wounded. Due to this unfavorable position, the commander decided to pull back to the forest southwest of Melichowo, leaving behind a **Panzer-Zug** under Leutnant A____r and two Kompanien of the **II./Panzer-Grenadier-Regiment 114**. This reorganization occurred after nightfall.

<u>10 July 1943 - In forest southwest of Melichowo</u>

The **Kampfgruppe** remained in a reserve position because it had reached its initial objective and the neighboring division hung back a bit. Only scattered harassing artillery fire.

<u>11 July 1943 - In forest southwest of Melichowo</u>

The planned attack on Olchowatka was delayed because of unfavorable weather. The **Tiger-Abteilung** under the command of Hauptmann von Kageneck was attached to the **Kampfgruppe** and the **Kampfgruppe** was reorganized. Due to the high number of Panzers lost, the **II./Panzer-Regiment 11** was consolidated into two **Kompanien** commanded by Oberleutnant Spiekermann and Oberleutnant Reutemann.

The attack on Olchowatka began at 0300 hours. The **Tiger-Abteilung** in the lead (which had increased again to 19 operational Tigers), followed by the 8. and **7.Kompanien/Panzer-Regiment 11**. After crossing the Dalnaja Iumenka to Schlachowoje road, the **Abteilung** came under strong anti-tank gun fire from Points 220 and 230.3. The **Kampfgruppe** could only advance very slowly due to the heavily mined area. After reaching Point 230.3, the **8.Kompanie/Panzer-Regiment 11** turned east, drove around the wood lot north of Schlachowoje, and charged toward the northeast into Schlachowoje. Strong enemy resistance was met within Schlachowoje, which was destroyed by energetic blows from the **8.Kompanie/Panzer-Regiment 11** commanded by Oberleutnant Spiekermann.

The **Tiger-Abteilung** and **7.Kompanie/Panzer-Regiment 11** struck farther toward Olchowatka. The opponent attempted to break up the attack with strong artillery and rocket salvo fire. Except for one delay, the attack went forward smoothly. Heavy enemy resistance was not encountered in Olchowatka itself. After Olchowatka was taken, the **Kampfgruppe** continued to attack, took Point 224.4, and struck further toward Snamenka. Little enemy resistance was encountered in Snamenka. On Point 223.3, the **Kampfgruppe** was hit by enemy artillery and rocket salvos. The **Kampfgruppe** pushed east past Werchne Oljohanen and with the **8.Kompanie/Panzer-Regiment 11** in the lead broke into Worchne Oljchanez out of the northeast. The village was lightly occupied by the enemy. The **7.Kompanie/Panzer-Regiment 11** reached Point 234.3 and the lead elements encountered an anti-tank trench south of Kasatschje.

A crossing over the anti-tank ditch was scouted by **7.Kompanie/Panzer-Regiment 11** at dusk. Afterward, the **Kampfgruppe** arrived in Kasatschje toward 2200 hours. The village was lightly occupied by the enemy. It was decided to spend the night in Kasatschje. Oberst von Oppeln gave the order to strike forward toward Rschawez in order to build a bridgehead over the Ssewernjy Donets. The **7.Kompanie/Panzer-Regiment 11** took the point, followed by the **7.Kompanie/Panzer-Grenadier-Regiment 114**, **8.Kompanie/Panzer-Regiment 11**, the rest of the **II./Panzer-Grenadier-Regiment 114** and the Tigers. The **Kampfgruppe** rolled through Kurakowka at 0030 hours without encountering enemy activity. A Russian truck convoy was passed without recognizing their enemy. At 0040 hours, the point, under the command of Leutnant Huchtmann, arrived at the east entrance of Rshawez. In spite of numerous guards, moving convoys, and horse-drawn vehicles, the point passed through Rshawez unrecognized and advanced to the bridge. The integrity of the column was broken when a vehicle broke down. The point led by Leutnant Huchtmann met a column of T34 tanks carrying infantry. An attempt was made to get past the tank column without being recognized. The rest of the **Kampfgruppe** arrived resulting in a short confusion. A firefight started with the T34 tanks. Five T34 tanks were destroyed in close combat by Major Dr. Baeke and Leutnant Zobel. Altogether, 10 T34 and 1 T70 tanks were destroyed. Further along, four anti-tank gun positions were rolled over, and two rocket launchers and several towing vehicles were destroyed. Rshawez itself was taken. The **II./Panzer-Grenadier-Regiment 114** crossed over the destroyed bridge and built a bridgehead on the far bank of the Donets.

The **I./Panzer-Grenadier-Regiment 114** arrived in Rshawez at about 0500 hours and reinforced the bridgehead.

<u>12 July 1943 - In Rshawez</u>

The 7. and **8.Kompanien/Panzer-Regiment 11** took over the defense of Rshewez. A **Panzer-Zug**, under Oberfeldwebel Parhofer from the **7.Kompanie/Panzer-Regiment**, was sent on reconnaissance through Kurakowka toward Point 214 and reported that strong enemy tank forces were in Alexandrowka.

The Russians attempted to attack Rshewez at about 1800 hours. After three T34 tanks were shot up, the Russians pulled back again.

13 July 1943 - In Rshawez

Elements of the **Kampfgruppe** remained on guard. The opponent tried to attack the Rschawez bridgehead. Three T34 tanks were shot up. In unsuitable positions, four Panzers were hit and knocked out of action. Heavy losses occurred when our own bombers dropped bombs on **Kampfgruppe** positions. The **Regiment** and **Kampfgruppe** commander Oberst von Oppeln Bronikowski and his adjutant Oberleutnant Guckel were wounded. 13 July was not only a black day for **Panzer-Regiment 11** but also for the entire division. After already having been wounded once in the morning, in the forward line Generalmajor von Huenersdorff was again severely wounded when hit in the head. He later died as a result of this severe wound.

Major Dr. Baeke took over command of the **Regiment** for Oberst von Oppeln and Hauptmann Scheibert took over the **Abteilung**. About 1800 hours, the **Regiment** pulled out and moved to a new assembly area near Kurakowka to attack Alexandrowka.

14 July 1943 - At Kurakowka

The attack began at 0700 hours. **Sturmgeschuetze** and Tigers were attached. The Panzers of the **Kampfgruppe** were consolidated into one **Kompanie**.

Alexandrowka was taken after the anti-tank ditch was crossed. Strong tank forces and numerous enemy infantry were there. A large number of prisoners were captured. Six T34 and five T60 tanks were destroyed during the battle in addition to numerous infantry weapons. In the evening, the **Kampfgruppe** took up a defensive line that ran directly west of Alexandrowka.

15 July 1943

On orders from the division, the **Kampfgruppe** was left to rest and held in reserve for counterstrikes.

16 July 1943

The **Kampfgruppe** pulled into an assembly area near Point 240, with **II./Panzer-Grenadier-Regiment 114** to strike forward at about 1700 hours toward Point 222.1 to help the

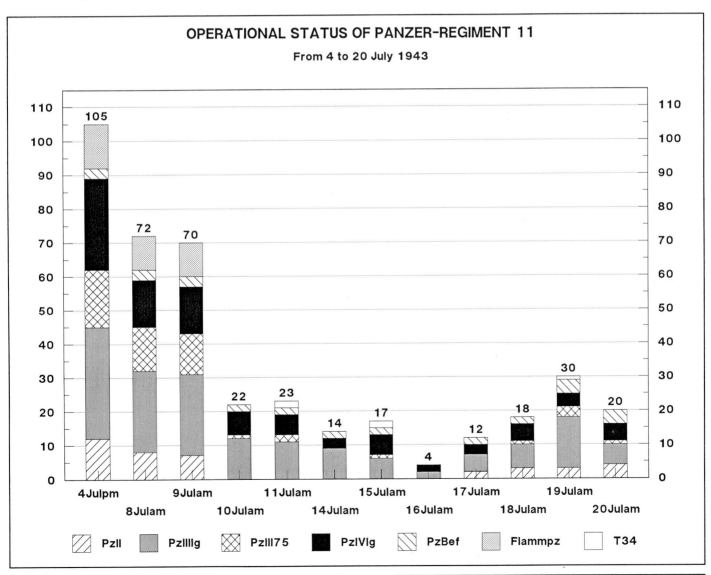

OPERATIONAL STATUS OF PANZER-REGIMENT 11

From 4 to 20 July 1943

Legend: PzII, PzIIIlg, PzIII75, PzIVlg, PzBef, Flammpz, T34

I./Panzer-Grenadier-Regiment 4 to advance. **Kompanie Spiekermann** encountered strong enemy tank forces on Point 222.1. Two of our own Panzers fell out due to hits. Three Panzers under Leutnant Glosemeyer remained on guard through the night at Point 222.1. All of the wounded found on Point 222.1 were rescued during the night.

17 July 1943
The Russians broke into our positions on Point 241.5. At 0310 hours, **Kompanie Schoener** started to counterattack accompanied by **Sturmgeschuetze** and **II./Panzer-Grenadier-Regiment 4**. After a short, hard battle, the height was taken by the **Sturmgeschuetze** and **II./Panzer-Grenadier-Regiment 4**. Oberleutnant Schoener remained in reserve and defended toward the east. The **Regiment** returned to the old assembly area southwest of Point 240, leaving behind a **Panzer-Zug** on guard at Point 241.5.

An alarm call at 1745 hours. The enemy were reported to be attacking Point 222.1 with tanks.

By 1800 hours, the attack had already been repulsed by the infantry. One **Panzer-Zug** remained south of Point 222.1 on guard. The rest pulled into an assembly area by the anti-tank ditch 1 kilometer southwest of Point 240.

At 1830 hours, Generalmajor von Huenersdorff died of his wounds. The **Regiment** was immediately given the name **Panzer-Regiment 11 "von Huenersdorff."**

18 July 1943 - At Nowo Oskotschnoje
The situation remained unchanged.

The **Regiments** command post was moved to the southeast exit of Nowo Oskotschnoje. Major Baeke had the task of overseeing the quick repair of the Panzers located in the **Werkstaetten**. During the night of 18/19 July 1943, at 0200 hours, two companies of Russians attacked Point 222.1. They were thrown back after a short battle and the area of the breakthrough was mopped up.

Results: 1 T34 shot up, about 100 enemy killed.

19 July 1943 - At Kurakowka
Hauptmann Scheibert took over command of the **Kampfgruppe** consisting of **Panzer-Regiment 11, II./Panzer-Grenadier-Regiment 114**, and the armored elements of **Panzer-Pionier-Bataillon 57**.

At 0930 hours, a messenger sent to the division received the verbal order to pull back and pull into the new main defense line, a line from Olchanez to the north edge of Nowo Oskotschnoje to Schalokowo to 2 kilometers north of Heimenoje. **Infanterie-Regiment 168** was on the right, **Infanterie-Regiment 315** on the left.

The Russians strengthened their attacks on the new defense line during the day, sometimes only with infantry forces; sometimes a few tanks also appeared. The hot points in the defense were by the **II./Panzer-Grenadier-Regiment 4** north of Alexanjewka, Points 241.4 and 231.5, as well as Points 222.1 and 224.3 by the **I./Panzer-Grenadier-Regiment 4**. The occupiers of these points changed frequently. The counterattacks to regain these heights, conducted by **Panzer-Zuege** of the consolidated **Kompanie Reutemann**, resulted in high losses for the opponent. The opponent finally managed to occupy Points 231.4 and 241.5 after a strong attack supported by 14 T34 tanks and a large number of anti-tank guns in the evening. At the same time, **Panzer-Zug Krautwurst (5.Kompanie/Panzer-Regiment 11)** shot up a T34 tank at Point 222.1.

In spite of further enemy penetrations threatening to disrupt the planned retirement of the entire division, all available Panzers (except **Panzer-Zug Krautwurst** and the **S.P.W.** of the **2./Panzer-Aufklaerung-Abteilung 6**) were sent in to build up a defense line at Point 2 directly west of Alexejewka. After briefly testing this line, the Russians broke off their advance. About 2100 hours, under cover of this defense line, the **II./Panzer-Grenadier-Regiment 4** broke off contact with the enemy.

At 2115 hours, the rear guard under Hauptmann Scheibert pulled back to the crossroads 1 kilometer west of Kasatschje. Because elements of the division, including **Panzer-Zug Krautwurst**, were still in contact with the opponent and at night the terrain, cut by numerous ravines presented no possibility for finding ones way back, the rear guard remained at the crossroads by Point 240 until first light.

20 July 1943 - At Kriwzowo
At 0430 hours, the **Kampfgruppe** under the command of Hauptmann Scheibert arrived in Kriwzowo. The day was occupied in repairing vehicles. About 1700 hours, the command post was moved to the north exit of Sabynio. Here they awaited the return of Major Baeke.

The night passed quietly with the exception of light harassing fire by enemy artillery.

Results: 2 antitank guns, 1 T34 tank, and 2 anti-aircraft guns destroyed and about 150 enemy killed.

In spite of General Guderian's advice that Tigers should be employed concentrated in a **schwere Panzer-Abteilung**, on 4 July 1943, one **schwere Panzer-Kompanie** from the **schwere Panzer-Abteilung 503** was attached to each of the **6., 7.**, and **9.Panzer-Divisions**. On 6 July 1943, the commander of **schwere Panzer-Abteilung 503**, Hauptmann Graf Kageneck, reported the problems with mines and poor tactical handling that his scattered unit was encountering:

III.Panzer-Korps reported the loss of 13 Tigers in one **Kompanie** that had started out with 14 Tigers on the morning of 5 July 1943. Nine Tigers fell out due to mine damage. It would take two or three days to repair each one of them.

The reasons for this extraordinarily high loss rate from mines was:

1. From the start, there wasn't a single map available showing the location of mines that had been laid by the German units in front of the bridgehead. Two completely contradictory mine plans were available, and both were incorrect. Therefore, two Tigers ran onto our own mines directly after setting off. Another two Tigers hit mines during further ad-

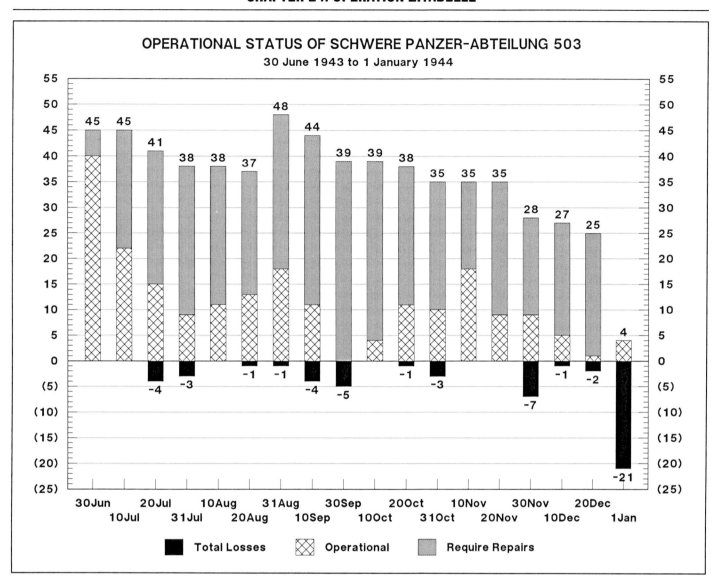

OPERATIONAL STATUS OF SCHWERE PANZER-ABTEILUNG 503
30 June 1943 to 1 January 1944

Total Losses — **Operational** — **Require Repairs**

vances across terrain that was shown on the map to be free of mines.

2. Mine clearing was sloppily conducted, so that three additional Tigers fell out due to mines after being shown supposedly mine-free gaps.

And yet again on the morning of 5 July, two trucks from **Panzer-Grenadier-Regiment 74** hit mines on a road declared to be clear of mines. After this, 120 mines were lifted from an area shown on the map to be free of mines.

3. The eighth Tiger drove onto enemy mines directly in front of the enemy positions even though he was directed by **Pioniere** that had already gone ahead.

The ninth Tiger ran onto mines when it attempted to move into position against an enemy tank attack reported on the left flank.

Counter to the original plan, in which the Tigers were to advance in direct contact with **Panzer-Grenadiere** and directly behind the mine-detecting sections of **Pioniere**, the Tigers were actually sent out in front of the **Grenadiere** and **Pioniere**. By the evening of 5 July, four Tigers stood 50 to 80 meters in front of the infantry elements.

Eight Tigers fell out for two or three days as a result of carelessness or tactically incorrect employment. Therefore, during this period they were not available for their actual purpose, fighting enemy tanks and heavy weapons.

The cause of losses during their first three days in action were reported by **schwere Panzer-Abteilung 503** on 8 July 1943 as follows:

39 Tigers started out on 5 July. An additional 5 Tigers were operational by 6 July. During the period from 5 through 8 July, a total of 34 Tigers fell out, requiring repairs that would take over eight hours (7 were hit, 16 were damaged by mines, and 9 broke down mechanically). Two burned-out Tigers were total write-offs. Up to now, 22 Tigers have been repaired. At 1200 hours on 8 July 1943 the Tiger situation was: 33 operational, 8 requiring short-term (up to 8 days) repairs, 2 requiring long term (over 8 days) repairs, and 2 written off as total losses.

Tigers from the **2.Kompanie/schwere Panzer-Abteilung 503** advancing up an unsurfaced road during Operation **Zitadelle**. (BA)

Dissatisfied with how the Tigers had been tactically employed by the units to which they were attached, General der Panzertruppe Breith, commander of the **III.Panzer-Korps**, issued the following directive on 21 July 1943:

Based on experience in the recent battles, I issue the following instructions for the cooperation of Tigers with other weapons:

1. As a result of its high performance weapon and strong armor, the Tiger should be used primarily against enemy tanks and anti-tank weapons and secondarily - and then only as a complete exception - against infantry targets. As experience has shown, its weapons allow the Tiger to fight enemy tanks at ranges of 2000 meters and longer, which has especially worked on the morale of the opponent. As a result of the strong armor, it is possible to close to short range with the enemy tanks without being seriously damaged from hits. Still, the Tiger should attempt to start engaging enemy tanks at ranges over 1000 meters.

As often as the situation allows - which was possible very often during the recent battles - prior to employment of Tigers the terrain should be scouted with the primary purpose

*of determining the possibility of crossing rivers and streams, bridges, and marshlands. **Kompanie** and **Zug** leaders and also Panzer commanders may not shy from dismounting and performing scouting patrols on foot in order to prevent the entire unit from getting stuck in difficult terrain. In connection with this, unnecessary losses of Tigers on mines often could have been prevented. The same applies to the other types of Panzers.*

A known weakness of the Tiger is caused by the location of the commander's cupola on the left side of the turret. The commander can't see an extensive area close to the right side of the Tiger, which presents a threat from the opponent's tank-hunter teams. Therefore, it is well known that it is necessary for other troops to protect the Tiger from this threat.

***S.P.W., Sturmgeschuetze, leichte** and **mittlere Panzers** must follow closely behind when Tigers attack in order to screen the Tigers' flanks and to exploit the Tigers' success. But above all, during battles in areas occupied by infantry in the main battlefield, the escorting armored vehicles are to eliminate the tank-hunter teams that may endanger the Tigers. The **Grenadiere** must take advantage of the high morale and actual effect caused by Tigers breaking into the en-*

emy main battle line in order to immediately advance and sweep through the defensive system. Otherwise, the danger exists that when the Panzers drive away, the enemy infantry resistance will again come to life and cause unnecessary losses to the **Grenadiere**.

It is not only the task of the **S.P.W.**, **Sturmgeschuetze**, **leichte** and **mittlere Panzers** to automatically protect the Tigers from tank-hunter teams, but in addition the task of all weapons, especially **Grenadiere** and **Pioniere**, is to support the Tigers. Tigers are usually knocked out in close terrain (forest, villages, ravines, sunken lanes), but less often in open terrain.

3. During the attack on 5 July in a sector of the **Korps** front, lack of knowledge about our own minefields worked out to be detrimental to our Tigers. Many Tigers ran onto mines as a result. Later as a result of incomplete mine clearing by **Pioniere**, additional Tigers hit mines, so that the **Tiger-Kompanie** sent in there was almost completely immobilized during the first stage of the battle. The loss of the **Tiger-Kompanie**, which was the **Schwerpunkt** of the attacking division, was very detrimental to directing the battle during the first two days of the offensive. Special value is to be placed on training the **Pioniere** in careful mine clearing and exactly marking gaps in the minefields. The forward **Kampfgruppen**

should plan to constantly have sufficient **Pioniere** not only to clear away obstacles but also to clear minefields, because from experience the anti-tank ditches, villages, narrow passages in the depth of the defensive zone are always protected by mines.

4. I forbid employment of Panzers including Tigers under **Kompanie** strength. For defense, Panzers are to be consolidated into attack groups that are to be sent in as planned counterstrikes. After completing a counterstrike, these Panzer groups are to be immediately pulled back to return to the disposal of the sector or division commander. Dispersal of Panzers in the main battle line or guarding other weapons by day and by night must not occur.

5. After reading, destroy this order and report its destruction.

Panthers were first sent into combat during Operation Zitadelle. The 200 Panthers under **Panther-Regiment von Lauchert** were assigned to the XLVIII.Panzer-Korps of the **4.Panzer-Armee** under Heeresgruppe Sued. **Panzer-Abteilung 52** with Panzer-Regiment **Stab 39** arrived by rail on 1 July and moved into their assigned assembly area at Kosatschek on 2 July 1943. Ten trains carrying **Panther-Abteilung 52** arrived on 3 July, with the rest expected on the

This **Panther Ausf.D** from the **1.Kompanie/Panzer-Abteilung 51** was first committed into action during Operation **Zitadelle**. (BA)

morning of 4 July, only one day before the start of the offensive. During the approach march, motor fires resulted in two Panthers being destroyed and written off as total losses.

On 2 July, the **XLVIII.Panzer-Korps** war diary remarks that deficiencies existed in the Panther units. They hadn't conducted tactical training as a complete **Abteilung** and radio sets hadn't been tested. Since their assembly areas were so close to the front, permission couldn't be given for them to test and practice with the radio sets.

On 4 July, the entire **Panther-Regiment**, including both **Abteilungen**, had arrived and advanced into a valley north of Maschtschenoje. **Brigade-Stab 10**, commanded by Oberst Decker, was assigned to **Panzer-Grenadier-Division "Grossdeutschland"** to take command of both the **Panther-Regiment** and **Panzer-Regiment "Grossdeutschland."** On the morning of the offensive at 0640 on 5 July, the **Panther-Regiment** was attached to **Panzer-Grenadier-Division "Grossdeutschland"** under the command of **Brigade-Stab 10**. After refueling the **Panther-Regiment** started to advance in the direction of the crossing point by Beresowyj at 0800 hours. What happened next is described in the following letter written on 17 July 1943 by the commander of **Stab Panzer-Brigade 10**, Oberst Decker:

Dear General!

As requested, after the first combat operation was over for us, I am reporting on my activities here. I succeeded in arriving on schedule with my adjutants. My staff arrived on 11 July. I was happy to have them since permission for their requisition was downright deplorable.

*The **Panzer-Brigade** was attached to the "Grossdeutschland" Division. The second regiment under command was **Panzer-Regiment "Grossdeutschland"** with its eight **Pz.Kpfw.IV Kompanien** and a **Tiger-Kompanie**. The commander of **Panzer-Regiment "Grossdeutschland"** was Graf Strachwitz, the "**Panzer-Loewe**" (Tank Lion). Working with him was very unpleasant. During the attack, he simply did not come on the radio and operated independently. This went on so far that I was ordered to appear before General von Knobelsdorff (commanding general of the **XLVIII.Panzer-Korps**) to answer for the brigade headquarters not functioning. In the interim, Strachwitz directed the **Panzer-Brigade** and employed the Panthers outright crazily. This resulted in continuous mine damage and flank protection was never built up. Therefore, the Panthers, whose sides are vulnerable, were shot up.*

*On 5 July, I started a major attack with the **Panzer-Brigade** but got no farther than to a ravine. In ignorance of our outstanding main gun, eight "General Lee" tanks approached to within 2200 meters. With a few shots they were set on fire and burned like Christmas tree sparklers. My gunner, who was my adjutant, shot up one of these eight. Next day, in an attack with 300 Panzers, I charged up to the second defensive position. After very successfully completing this attack with few losses, I was ordered to report to General von Knobelsdorff.*

*When I returned after four days, in comparison to the 200 with which we started, the number of operational Panthers had shrunk to 12 due to idiotic tactical employment. Major von Lauchert was desperate and welcomed my return. Personnel losses were also very high. The **Panther-Regiment** had lost 9 officers killed and 19 wounded officers.*

*I then created two **Abteilungen** from the remainder of both **Panzer-Regiments**. On the very first day after my return, 58 enemy tanks (mostly T34) and over 30 anti-tank guns were destroyed, with a loss of 2 out of 23 of our Panthers in the action. We always accomplished the tasks that we received.*

"Grossdeutschland" is very reasonable, which can't be said about the commanding general. Oberstleutnant Koehn, who commanded a battalion here, will have made a corresponding report.

I am slowly working in with my headquarters. We suffer due to the lack of both tents and mobile homes. Therefore we are living in the Panzers, in the open, or in the ruins of pony sheds.

In general, it can be said that the Panther is a very good vehicle in spite of several startup illnesses and the motor is still too vulnerable. Unlike the Tiger, the sides are not invulnerable to 76 mm anti-tank guns. The main gun is exceptional. Up to now, the regiment has knocked out 263 tanks. Russian KW-I tanks were knocked out at ranges up to 3000 meters and almost all of the Russian T34 tanks at ranges from 1500 to 2000 meters.

A note for the war diary made by the operations officer of the 4.Panzer-Armee revealed the status on the morning of 7 July: The **Panther-Regiment** started with 184 operational Panthers. There are now still 166 operational Panthers, 32 in need of repair and 4 total write-offs. A second note recorded after midday on 7 July: "Grossdeutschland" reported that only about 80 are still operational of the approximately 300 Panzers with which they started the offensive on 4 July.

Tactical mistakes made during the first engagements with Panthers as well as other observations were recorded and used in lessons by the commander of the **Panzer-Lehrgaenge "Panther"**, Major Streit, as follows:

1. Due to bunching up, the firepower from our Panthers couldn't be employed, the enemy succeeded in knocking out a high number, and very many Panthers were lost on mines.

*2. **Pioniere** were not available for mine clearing. Time was not allowed to search for gaps. The exact opposite was ordered. In spite of the mine fields, the order was given to immediately continue to advance.*

*3. Attacks were conducted without issuing situational orders. The companies knew absolutely nothing about the attack plans. Confusion set in from the start, since neither objectives, formation, or direction were ordered. Panthers being thickly bunched up directly in front of the enemy defensive positions led to unnecessarily high losses. The **Abteilung** commander must firmly lead his companies in the attack with*

A **Panther Ausf.D** from the **2.Kompanie/Panzer-Abteilung 52** moving forward to an assembly area. While the launchers are still mounted on the turret side, there aren't any **Nebelkerzen** (smoke candles) in them. Use of this device had been discontinued following reports of crews being incapacitated when the **Nebelkerzen** were set off by hits from small-arms fire. (KHM)

clear orders. Unfortunately, the companies were often self-dependent. As an example, sudden changes in direction could be recognized only after it was noticed that several Panthers had turned.

4. When confronted with obstacles, only the number of Panthers that are absolutely needed to subdue the enemy are to advance in the forward line.

5. Appropriate flank protection was never established during the first attacks. This led to unbearably high losses. If they already receive flanking fire during an attack, companies must first build up flank protection. Also, the company commander must know the objective and attack direction.

6. Later, when attacks were made with flank protection and broad formations, the losses were noticeably small. Therefore, space and intervals within combat formations should be longer than the standard 50 meters, but in no case shorter.

7. Tactical training as a unit didn't occur. This made itself very unpleasantly noticeable indeed.

8. Defense against close attack and envelopment from tank hunter teams are always difficult to repulse with the Panther's weapons.

9. The Panther does not possess the ability to lay a smoke screen which proved to be tactically disadvantageous. An effective smoke screen device is urgently requested by the troops.

10. At the start, problems with the radio sets and intercom made command difficult. The problems were solved in the interim, and communications improved sufficiently to meet the troops' specifications.

11. Additional tank recovery services must be provided at the right time, especially when high losses occur when breaking off action or retreating. Recovery units attached to the army are to be utilized.

13. The Panther is clearly superior in tank-versus-tank combat.

14. Combating anti-tank guns is still difficult. In most cases anti-tank guns are difficult to spot (small targets) and are well dug-in. In many cases it is difficult to destroy the entire crew. Therefore, survivors reman the gun. In comparison, the Panther presents a very large target that is easily recognized.

15. In general, Russian employment of anti-tank guns is approximately as follows: They set up a very strong anti-tank defense in favorable terrain, mostly along the edge of woods. The 76 mm guns are the lighter anti-tank weapon. These positions are supported by concentrated artillery and mortars that are placed farther back. The infantry is positioned in hiding, ready to attack with tank support. If he receives ener-

getic defensive fire, he quickly pulls out and tries to lure our forces into counterattacking. Counterattacks then are almost always repulsed with heavy losses, since they collide with the overwhelming defense.

A **Pak-Front** in the area of Parchomowka was built up with 18 anti-tank guns in an area only about 400 meters wide. Still stronger flank support was provided by heavy anti-tank guns, T 34 and KW I tanks. A heavy concentration of artillery was located about 3000 meters in the rear of the enemy flank.

High explosive shells fired by Russian anti-tank guns are greatly feared by our infantry. It was only possible to carry an attack forward again with very strong artillery support and air strikes by Stukas, in spite of the fact that our troops were an elite unit (**"Grossdeutschland" Division**).

Having visited the front on 10 July 1943, the **General-inspekteur der Panzertruppen**, General Guderian, sent copies of his analysis in the following report sent on 17 July to General Zeitzler, **Chef des Stabes/OKH**:

<u>Report on the Operations of **Panzer-Regiment (Panther) von Lauchert**</u>

<u>Tactical Experience</u>: The tactical employment of a new type of Panzer does not release the commander from using

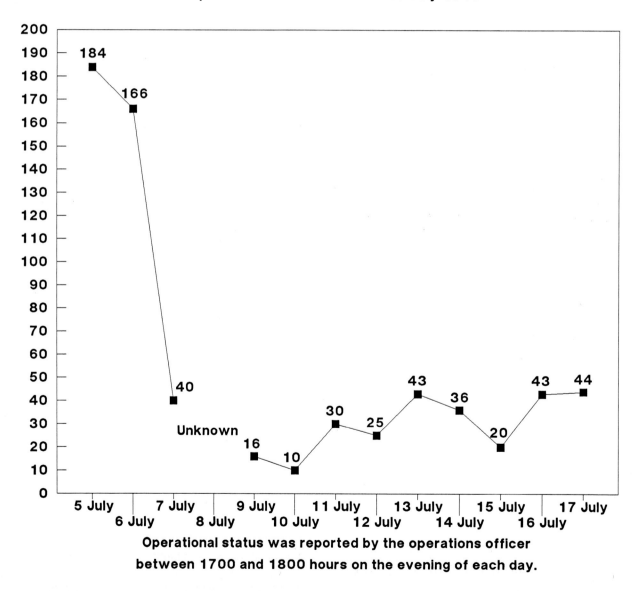

STATUS OF OPERATIONAL PANTHERS
Operation Zitadelle from 5 to 17 July 1943

Operational status was reported by the operations officer between 1700 and 1800 hours on the evening of each day.

the proven principles of Panzer tactics. This especially applies to cooperation with other weapons and employment of concentrated Panzer units.

The **Generalinspekteur der Panzertruppen** created a **Panzer-Brigade Stab** to ensure control over the 300 Panzers in the reinforced **"Grossdeutschland" Division**. Because of friction between personnel, this **Brigade Stab** did not function at the start. Personal considerations should not be allowed to play a role when the future of the Reich is being gambled.

It is wrong to pull out other heavy weapons where Panthers were employed, only because Panthers are there. It is correct to create a **Schwerpunkt**, concentrating the other weapons (**Artillerie, Pioniere, Luftwaffe, Panzer-Grenadiere**) with the Panthers in order to quickly succeed with minimal losses.

The attack is to quickly penetrate into the depth of the opponent's defensive system, take out the enemy artillery and ensure that armored infantry and infantry are accompanied forward.

Following the high losses during the first few days, further losses were even higher. The number of Panthers that started into battle each day was very small (at times only 10 Panthers). Therefore, the defenders could easily repulse the attacks.

The enemy defense consisting of 7,62 cm anti-tank and tank guns succeeded in knocking out Panthers only with flank shots. Penetration of the frontal armor was never achieved.

Close attention must be paid to guarding the flanks of the Panther attack! All the other available weapons must be employed in this effort. Panthers need to attack utilizing an especially wide formation to prevent the enemy from flanking the core of the attacking unit.

When firing, individual Panthers should be brought into position with their front facing the enemy fire.

For breaking through a strongly defended and mined main battle zone, a **Panzer-Funklenk-Kompanie** (radio-controlled mine clearing company) should be attached in the future.

In all cases, cooperation with combat engineers should be assured. Materials needed for crossing bogland should be prepared in advance and carried along to prevent delays during an attack.

Organization: The organization of the combat elements of the **Panther-Regiment** was proven successful. In no case should the platoons, companies or battalion be weakened. The number of wheeled vehicles could be somewhat reduced. Especially due to steady losses, supplying all of the Panthers is practically never necessary.

Training: The time allotted for training was too short. Therefore, the drivers did not achieve the necessary proficiency. The maintenance personnel were not sufficiently trained. The gunners and commanders did not receive the necessary tactical training.

Because of the necessary rebuild work at Grafenwoehr, training exercises were accomplished only at the platoon level.

The missing training was very noticeable indeed. A large part of the technical and tactical losses are traceable to this cause.

Situation of the Regiment after Seven Days in Action: Due to enemy action and mechanical breakdowns the combat strength sank rapidly during the first few days. By the evening of 10 July there were only 10 operational Panthers in the front line. Twenty-five Panthers had been lost as total write-offs (23 were hit and burnt and two had caught fire during the approach march). One hundred Panthers were in need of repair (56 were damaged by hits and mines and 44 by mechanical breakdown). Sixty percent of the mechanical breakdowns could be easily repaired. Approximately 40 Panthers had already been repaired and were on the way to the front. About 25 still had not been recovered by the repair service.

On the evening of 11 July, 38 Panthers were operational, 31 were total write-offs and 131 were in need of repair. A slow increase in combat strength is observable. The large number of losses by hits (81 Panthers up to 10 July) attests to the heavy fighting.

The deep, heavily mined, main battlefield of the Russians must result in above average losses of materiel through hits and mines. The fact that the Panther appeared for the first time on the battlefield focused general interest. Comparisons against losses of other Panzer units were not made. Therefore the high command and troops quickly jumped to the conclusion: The Panther is worthless!

In closing, it should be remarked that the Panther has been proven successful in combat. The high number of mechanical breakdowns that occurred should have been expected since lengthy troop trials have still not been accomplished. The curve of operational Panthers is on the rise. After the deficiencies in the fuel pumps and the motors are corrected, the mechanical breakdowns should remain within normal limits. Without consideration of our own mistakes, the disproportionately high number of losses through enemy action attests to especially heavy combat.

An attachment to the report contained detailed remarks on the adequacy of components as experienced on Panthers in action:

Main Gun: The accuracy and penetrating ability are good. As of 10 July, 140 enemy tanks had been shot up. The average range was 1500 to 2000 meters. Also, one T34 tank was destroyed at a range of 3000 meters. After the third shot, the commander's vision was hindered by burned propellant fumes causing the eyes to tear. The **Sehstab** (observation periscope) was still not available!

Several weapons became unserviceable as a result of anti-tank rifle hits on the gun tubes (bulges on the inside). Replacement of damaged gun tubes with gun mantlets can not be covered by cannibalizing other total write-offs.

Machine guns: In general, the machine guns fired very well. Stoppages sometimes occurred due to the cables stretching. Possibly the cable material is poor quality. The belt feed made from sheet metal bent.

Smoke candle dischargers turned out to be unusable, since they were very quickly destroyed by enemy fire. Development of a usable self-enveloping smoke device must be hastened.

Armor: Enemy weapons did not penetrate through the frontal armor of the Panther. Even direct hits from straight on fired from 76 mm anti-tank and tank guns did not penetrate through the gun mantlet. However, the sides of the Panther were penetrated at ranges exceeding 1000 meters. The 76 mm anti-tank and tank rounds broke cleanly through the turret sides and both the sloped and vertical hull sides. In most cases, the Panther immediately caught on fire. This was possibly due to the large amount of propellant in the ammunition that is carried.

The Panther is basically invulnerable to artillery fire. However, direct hits by calibers of over 150 mm on the roof of the hull and turret had the effect of deforming the armor and causing internal damage. Hits by lighter caliber shells hitting the commander's cupola and the roof armor showed no effect.

Weak Spots: Pistol port plugs were hit (possibly by 45 mm armor piercing shells) and shot into the inside of the turret. A loader and a commander were killed. The rim of the pistol port plugs should be reinforced. The communications hatch on the left turret wall was cracked by a direct hit (possibly by a 76.2 mm armor-piercing shell), incapacitating the turret crew.

There is concern that rounds hitting the lower half of the gun mantlet will be deflected downward and penetrate through the roof of the crew compartment.

Effects of Mines: About 40 Panthers fell out during the first few days due to enemy mines. In general, only 4 to 6 track links and 2 to 4 roadwheels were damaged. On several Panthers the roadwheel support arms were also bent. Occasionally, damage occurred to the drive sprocket and idler wheel. In several cases the ammunition stored under the turret platform ignited and the Panthers burned out.

Turret: It is difficult to operate the hatch for the commander's cupola when the Panther is standing on a slope or when the Panther is on fire. Hatches for the driver and radio operator have jammed so that evacuation was not possible.

In general the brackets for the gunsight have held up. In only one case was it reported that the bracket was bent. A wiper for the front optics is absolutely necessary, since it takes too long to retract the gunsight during combat.

Mechanical Deficiencies in the Chassis: Most mechanical failures were defective fuel pumps (20 in **Panzer-Abteilung 52** by 8 July). Fuel collected on the floor due to fuel pump leaks, resulting in the total write-off of three Panthers due to fires. When on a steep side slope, the Panther easily catches on fire. In most cases, the motor fires were extinguished by the crew or the automatic fire extinguisher system activated.

Motor Failure: During this period, motor failures were abnormally high. **Panzer-Abteilung 52** already had 12 defective motors by 8 July. After several days, the number of breakdowns decreased. Therefore it is speculated that the motors were not sufficiently run in.

Transmissions: Transmissions didn't experience a high number of breakdowns. The transmission modification at Grafenwoehr were apparently successful. By 8 July, **Panzer-Abteilung 52** had experienced 5 transmission failures.

The numbers used by General Guderian in his report, showing the status of the Panthers on 10 July, were initial estimates. The data were corrected by the report dated 11 July which was compiled to show the status as of 2400 hours on 10 July. The detailed report lists the problems with the Panthers needing repair and reveals the cause of breakdowns. Many more Panthers were rendered inoperable due to damage from hits and mines than from mechanical breakdowns, as shown in the detailed lists from 10 and 12 July 1943:

Repair Needed:	10 July	12 July
Suspension	70*	38
Motor	23	25
Turret	19	31
Hull	15	5
Radio Set	12	10
Transmission	4	3
Gun	0	4
Total:	131	116

* Of which 12 are both suspension and radio sets.

On 26 July 1943, Oberstleutnant Reinhold attached to the **4.Panzer-Armee** during Operation Zitadelle reported on the **_"Pz.Kpfw.V (Panther)"_**:

The weapons functioned free of problems. The Panther often succeeded in killing T34 tanks at ranges over 3000 meters.

A large number of Panther losses occurred as a result of:

Hits: The frontal armor is sufficient but not the 40 mm thick side armor, which was cleanly penetrated. This caused very many total write-offs, since Panthers burned out when the ammunition or fuel ignited.

Also, the roof armor is too weak. Armor-piercing rounds that hit the lower half of the gun mantlet were deflected and penetrated the roof plate. This resulted in driver and radio operator casualties. Strengthening the armor is not possible, since the suspension is not adequate for a larger load.

The new hatch design caused problems, especially for the driver and radio operator. When hit, the hatch cover jams and can't be opened. If the Panther was to catch on fire, in many cases the driver and radio operator couldn't evacuate. In action crews don't close the hatches, and accept the loss of protection so that they can still quickly evacuate if a fire occurs.

Mechanical Deficiencies: The cause for motor failures is still not known. It is possibly traceable to the short run-in time and unskilled drivers. Motors were overrevved. This caused overheating and broken connecting rods. In many cases fuel pumps failed. The pump seals leaked and pump membranes were defective. Leaks in oil line and fuel line connections increased the danger of fire.

Mine Damage: Detonating mines caused damage to the suspension.

Report from the Maintenance Engineer on 19 July 1943:
Situation report at 1600 hours on 18 July 1943:
Pz.Abt.51: 33 operational, 32 in need of repair, 31 total write-offs
Pz.Abt.52: 28 operational, 40 in need of repair, 4 returned to Germany for major overhaul, 24 total write-offs

The repair services for both **Panther-Abteilungen** work very well. About 25 Panthers are repaired daily. There is a shortage of repair parts caused by the high number of losses. Air transport from Germany was of great help, especially motors and fuel pumps. The situation has now improved due to the arrival of repair parts by express train. Parts are now available for most of the Panthers in need of repair.

As a result of the order to immediately retreat, broken-down Panthers that haven't been towed can't be recovered. It is estimated that the following Panthers will have to be destroyed with explosive charges: 3 Panthers from **Panzer-Regiment Stab 39**, 29 Panthers from **Panzer-Abteilung 51** of which about nine are still repairable, and 24 Panthers from **Panzer-Abteilung 52**, for a total of 56 (including 40 already reported as total write-offs).

This report is somewhat misleading since it infers that many Panthers that could have been repaired were left behind or destroyed when the units pulled back. As reported by the **4.Panzer-Armee Oberquartiermeister Abteilung V** on 20 July 1943 all but 7 of the 56 burned-out Panthers that were left behind were loaded with explosives and blown up. Following orders to retire from the salient, repairable Panthers were towed back behind the lines. Starting on 18 July, all 14 **Zugkraftwagen 18t** from **Panzer-Berge-Kompanie 3** were made available along with the 19 **Zugkraftwagen 18t** that belonged to **Panzer-Regiment 39**. There was no shortage of recovery vehicles for retrieving the Panthers. Due to

heavy rainfall on 18 July that turned the trails to bottomless mud, three **Zugkraftwagen 18t** were required to tow each Panther.

The status of the 200 Panthers on 20 July 1943 was reported as:

- 41 Panthers were operational
- 85 Panthers were repairable by the regimental maintenance units
- 16 Panthers had been damaged to the extent that they needed to be returned to the ordnance depot in Germany for major overhaul
- 56 Panthers had burned out (Of these, 49 were filled with explosives and blown up. Seven Panthers that had burned out but due to enemy action could not be blown up fell into enemy hands on 19 July 1943)
- 2 Panthers with motor fires were already total write-offs before the campaign began.

The number of operational Panthers in the **O.Qu.Abt.V** reports was frequently different from those reported by the operations officer. Each evening the operations officer reported the number of operational Panthers with forward combat echelons that should be available for action the next day. Every ten days the **O.Qu.Abt.V** reported the status of all Panthers in the inventory irrespective of location. Between 21 and 31 July 1943, **Panzer-Regiment 39** received 12 replacement Panthers shipped from Germany. The following **O.Qu.Abt.V** reports on the status of the Panthers belonging to **Panzer-Regiment 39** reveals that most of their permanent losses didn't occur until after the general retreat of **Heeresgruppe Sued** that was forced by the Russian Summer offensive:

Date	Operational	In Need of Repair	Total Write-Offs	Total
10 July	38	131	31	200
20 July	41	101	58	200
31 July	20	108	84	212
11 August	9	47	156	212

For the month of July, the other units that had been utilized by **Heeresgruppe Sued** in Operation Zitadelle had lost 175 Panzers as total write-offs (14 percent of the strength at the start of the offensive) and were down to 472 operational Panzers on 31 July (compared to 947 operational on 30 June).

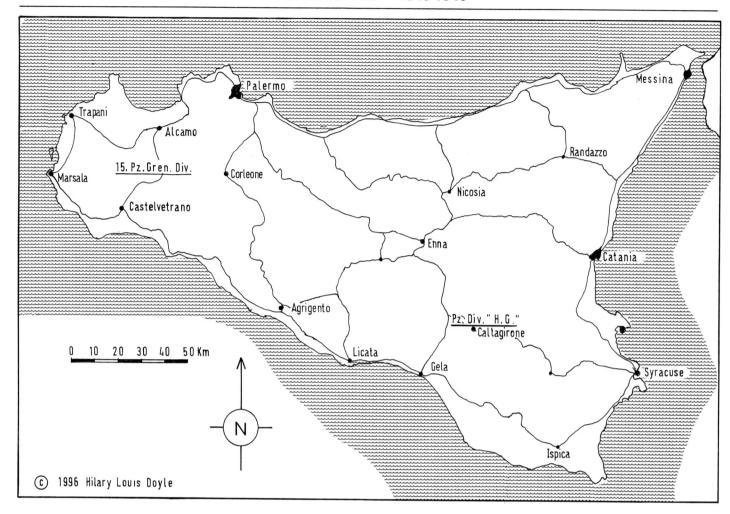

© 1996 Hilary Louis Doyle

at Niscemi. During the afternoon, the **II.Abteilung** continued moving away from the pursuing enemy and went over to defense on rear slopes. Breaking contact was achieved in an orderly manner; nothing fell into the enemy's hands. Oberleutnant Schoenhess was severely wounded in addition to losses of non-commissioned officers and men. The strong enemy air force activity made itself very unpleasantly felt.

Losses: 1 **Pz.Kpfw.IV** hit by naval guns, 1 **Pz.Kpfw.III** caught fire by itself.

13 July 1943

During the day, the **II.Abteilung** with the main body of **Kampfgruppe Hahm** moved to positions on reverse slopes southwest of Grammichele. The newly consolidated **Kompanie Haen**, created from elements of the **5.** and **6.Kompanie** along with four Tigers, defended Height 398 south of the Caltagirone barracks.

Losses: 1 **Pz.Kpfw.III** destroyed in close combat, 1 **Pz.Kpfw.III** blown up to prevent capture.

14 July 1943

With the exception of decreased enemy artillery activity, the day passed quietly. An enemy forward observation post was destroyed.

Losses: 2 **Pz.Kpfw.IV** lost to anti-tank guns.

15 July 1943 - Defense near Grammichele

The **7.Kompanie** with an infantry company counterattacked Height 398 and threw back the opponent. A renewed enemy attack with artillery and tank support occurred in the afternoon. This attack was also beaten off.

Results: 12 Lee and Sherman tanks, 3 armored cars, 2 anti-tank guns and many trucks were destroyed.

Losses: Oberleutnant Haen wounded, Leutnant Goetze missing, plus crew losses. 1 **Pz.Kpfw.IV** and 1 **Pz.Kpfw.III** blown up to prevent capture.

16 July 1943

During the day, the **II.Abteilung** broke off contact from the opponent and moved through Palagonie and Ramacca to Sferro. Oberleutnant Dreher of the **7.Kompanie** was in charge of a **Kampfgruppe** that took over the rear guard, closed off side valleys, blew up bridges, and harassed the slowly pursuing enemy. As soon as American infantry were fired on, they take cover and remain lying. They immediately requested artillery fire that pummeled our nests of resistance. The opponent lost 3 tanks, 3 armored half-tracks, and 2 anti-tank guns.

Losses: 2 **Pz.Kpfw.III** were blown up to prevent capture.

17 July 1943 - On road from Catania to Enna

The new main battle line was established alone the rail

line from Catania to Enna. Little combat activity; four trucks destroyed.

Losses: 1 **Pz.Kpfw.III** knocked out by an enemy tank.

18 July 1943 - north of Misterbianco

The **II.Abteilung** was employed in mobile anti-tank defense in the main battle line. The **Panzer-Zuege** were dispersed to individual **Kampfgruppen**. Five armored cars were destroyed.

19 July 1943

Major Preuss took over command of the **Kampfgruppen von Rahenow** and **Rebholz**. The commander of the **II.Abteilung** was assigned to the headquarters of **Kampfgruppe Preuss**. On orders from the division, an infantry company was created from elements of the **II.Abteilung** and dug in between Sferro and Gerbini.

20 July 1943

Localized combat activity along the rail line. Two enemy anti-tank guns and many vehicles were destroyed.

21 July 1943

The front line was secured after a mop-up of several areas where the enemy had penetrated. Four enemy tanks, two armored cars, and several trucks were destroyed during several counterattacks. The troops located opposite our positions were mainly British, including divisions that had previously fought in France and Africa.

22 July 1943

Localized combat activity.

23 July 1943 - Abteilung command post in Simeto

The main battle line was pulled back somewhat near Catenanuova, where **Panzer-Zug Hoffmann** was attached to a **Fallschirmjaeger-Bataillon**.

24 to 26 July 1943

Nothing of significance occurred.

27 July 1943

Two Sherman tanks were knocked out by the **7.Kompanie** during a short fight near Gerbini.

28 July 1943

Strong artillery fire near Catenanouva.

During the night, **Panzer-Zug Hoffman** and one **Fallschirmjaeger-Zug** conducted a counterattack.

Malaria causes daily losses in the **Kompanien**.

Losses: 1 **Pz.Kpfw.III** received a direct hit from artillery fire and was a total write-off.

29 July 1943

Nothing of significance occurred.

30 July 1943

After the usual artillery preparation, the opponent began an attack on Regalbuto. Our own infantry were beaten back; the Panzers were bypassed.

31 July 1943

In the early morning hours, Oberleutnant Dreher led a counterattack and reoccupied the old positions. However, at first light, it was revealed that the opponent occupied the flanks. A renewed attack by the superior opponent threw back the infantry in the village. Without infantry, the Panzers fought at close range between the houses. The opponent lost many anti-tank guns, mortars, and trucks.

1 August 1943

A counterattack again threw the enemy out of the northern end of Regalbute. Two Sherman tanks were knocked out. On the same day, the newly organized **Kompanie Ludwig** conducted a very successful counterattack near Sferro. In total, eight tanks and several trucks were knocked out, many infantry killed.

Losses: 1 **Pz.Kpfw.IV** lost to an anti-tank gun.

2 August 1943

During the night of 1/2 August, the entire division broke off contact with the enemy because the pressure on the right wing was too strong. Previously prepared new positions were occupied as planned.

Losses: 1 **Pz.Kpfw.III** detonated.

3 August 1943 - At Biancavilla

The opponent renewed attacks on Gerbini from Sferro. **Panzer-Zug Hoffman** pulled back, fighting to the main defense line.

4 August 1943

In positions near Paterno and Adrano.

5 August 1943

A planned counterattack of **Kompanie Dreher** was called off because the terrain was unfavorable for Panzers.

6 August 1943

The **Kampfgruppe** were employed east and west of Aetna. Therefore, the **Panzer-Zuege** were now completely scattered apart from each other. The **II.Abteilung** command post was moved to Francavilla. The unfavorable climate caused further losses through illness.

7 August 1943

One enemy tank was knocked out by **Kompanie Haeussner** during a defensive battle near Nicolosi.

8 August 1943

Rear guard battles at Maletto and Fleri.

9 August 1943

No unusual combat activity.

10 August 1943

Kompanie Haeussner counterattacked at Milo south of St.Michele.

11 August 1943

Heavy enemy artillery fire.

12 August 1943

Kompanie Dreher repulsed a strong enemy attack. One enemy tank was knocked out of action and one anti-tank gun was destroyed.

13 August 1943

Kompanie Dreher was pulled out and sent toward Messina.

Losses: 2 **Pz.Kpfw.IIIs** broke down mechanically and had to be blown up.

14 August 1943

Kompanie Haeussner on guard near Baracca.

A Tiger from the **2.Kompanie/schwere Panzer-Abteilung 504** abandoned in Sicily after apparently losing the right track after hitting a mine. (TTM)

15 August 1943 - At Messina
A new infantry advance was repulsed.
16 August 1943
The last defenders by Messina pulled back during the evening. The enemy laid artillery fire on the city.
17 August 1943 - At Messina
The last three Panzers of the **II.Abteilung** under the com-

mand of Leutnant Thatenhorst were transported across the straits to the mainland. The campaign in Sicily has ended.
18 August 1943
The **II.Abteilung** assembled in the Gambati area. For the first time it could be observed just how weak the individual **Kompanien** were. Most of the losses were caused by illness. The cooler climate in the mountains was noticeably

more pleasant. We were astounded that the Panzers could drive so high into the mountains.

The fate of the 17 Tigers on Sicily was reported by Major Gierga, commander of **Panzer-Abteilung 215**, in the following report to the **Generalinspekteur der Panzertruppen** dated 28 August 1943:

*On orders from the division, at the start of July, I transferred the 17 Tigers from the **Abteilung** to **Panzer-Regiment "Hermann Goering."***

*Before the transfer, I proposed to the commander, Oberstleutnant Urban, as well as the division supply and technical officers, to give them a complete **Werkstatt-Zug** that was already entrusted with repair of Tigers along with elements of the **Bergezug** in exchange for one of their **Werkstatt-Zuege**. Successful recovery and repair of the new Tigers would be questionable without this exchange. The proposal was rejected by **Panzer-Division "Hermann Goering"** with the excuse that an exchange was out of the question; instead, only transfers from my **Abteilung** were to occur. I reported this to my division commander. After telephone calls between General Rodt and General von Senger, I was ordered to give up the 10 special mechanics, all of the special tools, all replacement parts, as well as the portal crane along with the 17 Tigers.*

*Because of transport difficulties, **Panzer-Regiment "Hermann Goering"** did not pick up all these replacement parts, so that part of them (rubber tires, roadwheels and more) in addition to about 80 tons of 8.8 cm ammunition were left lying and fell into enemy hands.*

*Based on the after-action report from the **Tiger-Kompanie** and the report from Leutnant Goldschmidt, the last commander of the **Tiger-Kompanie**, at the beginning of the campaign the **Tiger-Kompanie** was assigned to **Panzer-Grenadier-Regiment "Henrice."** The **Panzer-Grenadiere** interfered with the employment of the **Tiger-Kompanie** and the terrain was insufficiently scouted, so that several Tigers*

became bogged in the mud. The Tigers became separated from our own infantry, so they were cut off, making recovery or repair impossible.

*Ten Tigers had already been lost during the first three days when they were blown up to prevent capture. Of the remaining seven Tigers, three more were lost by 20 July when they caught fire or were blown up to prevent capture. The excess Tiger crews were employed as infantry at the Gerbini airfield despite the strongest arguments from the **Tiger-Kompanie** commander. During the further retreat employed as rearguard, three of the last four Tigers broke down and were blown up to prevent capture. The last Tiger was transported across the straits to the mainland.*

*Based on statements made by Leutnant Goldschmidt, a large portion of the Tigers could have been repaired and saved by well-prepared recovery and maintenance work if they had been guarded by adequate infantry support. In no way were the **Werkstatt** and the recovery service of **Panzer-Regiment "Hermann Goering"** up to this task. In addition, during the retreat the portal crane, so important for repairing Tigers, was blown up by the **Werkstatt-Kompanie**.*

The German units gradually retreated across Sicily toward the northeast to Messina for evacuation to the mainland. During the nights of 10/11 and 11/12 August 1943, 34 Panzers and 44 **Sturmgeschuetze** were transported by ferry from Sicily to Italy. The rest, employed as rearguard, had been transferred by the morning of 17 August. Panzers lost as total write-offs in the defense of Sicily were:

Unit	Pz.III	Pz.IV	Pz.VI	Pz.Bef.	StuG	StuH
Pz.Abt.215	5	31		1		
Pz.Rgt.H.G.	28	21		4	4	3
Pz.Abt.129					5	
2./s.Pz.Abt.504			16			

A total of 118 out of 217 Panzers and **Sturmgeschuetze** that had been committed to the defense of Sicily were lost.

26

The Third Year on the Eastern Front

Taking advantage of the German forces being weakened by their failed attempt to capture the Kursk salient, the Russians launched major offensives against both **Heeresgruppe Mitte** and **Heeresgruppe Sued**. The German forces were now forced to continuously react to their opponents move's. The following combat reports reveal the tactics used by all the different types of **Panzer-Abteilungen** (Tiger, Panther, mixed **Sturmgeschuetz/Pz.Kpfw.IV**, and **Panzer-Sturmgeschuetz**) that were thrown in to stop the Russians advance. In their desperation, most of these new replacement units were sent in piecemeal as they unloaded from the trains. Invariably their operational strength plummeted after a few days in combat, resulting in weakened units that were capable only of localized defensive counterstrikes instead of concentrated powerful counteroffensives.

In mid-August, the **Stab, 10.,** and **11.Kompanie** of the **III.(Tiger) Abteilung/Panzer-Regiment Grossdeutschland** joined the division at the Front. On 31 August 1943, Major Gomille, commander of the **III.(Tiger) Abteilung/Panzer-Regiment Grossdeutschland**, wrote the following report on how they were greatly hampered by not having their **Werkstatt-Kompanie** and other necessary services:

14 August 1943 - **Abteilung** command post in the forest 2 kilometers southeast of Jassenowoje.

About midday, the columns from the last transport arrived at the command post. The trains were unloaded at Nisch.Ssirowatka, causing a road march of 110 kilometers. The general condition of the **Abteilung** was:

Stab:	3 **Tiger-Befehlswagen**
	7 **S.P.W.** of the **Aufklaerungs-Zug** without weapons
10.Kp.:	Complete (except for one Tiger still in Germany)
11.Kp.:	4 Tigers and most of the equipment for the maintenance group burned out during transport

9.Kp.:	Not a single operational Tiger (this was formerly the **13.Kp./Pz.Rgt.G.D.**)
Missing:	The entire **Stabs-Kompanie** and **Werkstatt-Kompanie** (minus one Zug), and all wheeled vehicles for the **Stab**.

Three **Tiger-Befehlswagen** and 13 Tigers from the **10.** and **11.Kompanien** were operational on the evening of 14 August 1943. Ten Tigers had fallen out due to major and minor mechanical problems during the march from Nisch.Ssirowatka to the **Abteilung** command post. The first major effects were already appearing that were caused by the **Abteilung** having to go into action without any supply, repair services, **Bergezug** (recovery platoon) and repair parts. The lack of any services necessary for maintaining a Panzer unit became increasingly critical during the following days in action.

Orders came in from the **Regiment** at 1200 hours for the **Abteilung** to be prepared for action by 0300 hours the next day. They were to go into action toward Belsk (30 kilometers south-southwest of Akhtyrka), where the Russians had already crossed the Vorskla with weak forces. It was thought that the enemy would reinforce this bridgehead with stronger forces and advance toward the north in order to envelop our own bridgehead at Akhtyrka from the west.

Leutnant Janetzke (leader of the **Abteilung Aufklaerungs-Zug**) was sent out on a scouting patrol to determine the condition of the roads and bridges as well as the terrain in the entire sector up to Belsk. About 1830 hours, the **Abteilung** moved out of the assembly area toward the southwest with an assignment that Grun was to be held, no matter what. However, the enemy had already taken Grun and had sent out his reconnaissance patrols further toward the north. By nightfall, the **Abteilung** had arrived at Persche Trawnja (5 kilometers northeast of Grun), where the **Abteilung** and other elements of the division prepared to attack the next day.

ORGANIZATION AND STRENGTH OF PANZER UNITS
REPLACEMENT UNITS SENT TO EASTERN FRONT

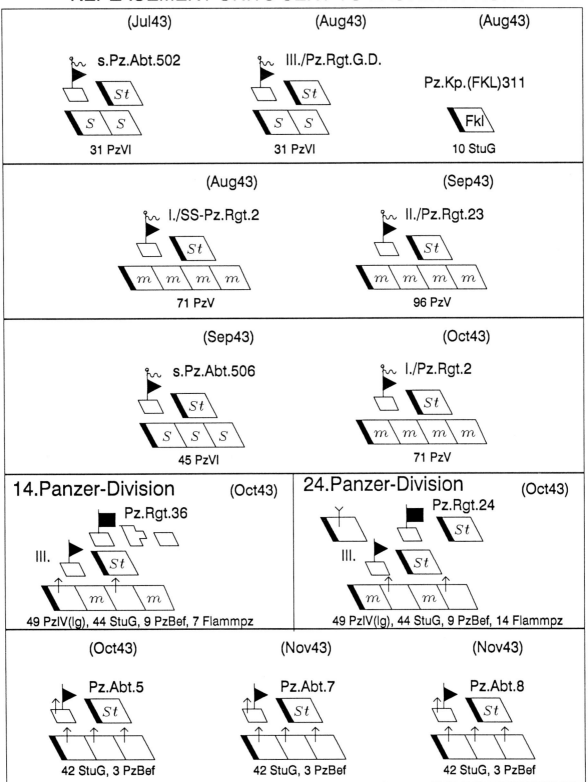

15 August 1943 - At 0400 hours, commander conference at the southwest exit from Jassenowoje. The operations officer of the division, Oberst von Natzmer, commanded a **Kampfgruppe** consisting of **Panzer-Regiment Grossdeutschland (Tiger Abteilung, I.Abteilung,** and a **Panther-Kompanie), Aufklaerungs-Abteilung (mot)** and **II.Sf./ Artillerie-Regiment Grossdeutschland,** which was ordered to advance through Grun and Budy to Belsk and destroy the enemy that had broken through the front.

At 0530 hours, the **Kampfgruppe** set off in the following formation: **Tiger-Abteilung** in the lead, followed by the **I.Abteilung** and **Panther-Kompanie,** who were to provide flank protection for the leading **Tiger-Abteilung.** The **Panzer-Regiment** was escorted by the **Sf. Artillerie-Abteilung.**

The **Abteilung** advanced toward Grun along both sides of the road. About 1 kilometer north of Grun, the **Abteilung** came under heavy anti-tank gunfire from the ridgeline east of

the north edge of the village. These enemy anti-tank guns were destroyed during a short fight. Shortly thereafter, directly in front of the edge of the village, the lead Tiger ran onto mines which caused only light damage. The **Abteilung** then received an order to attack along the edge of the village of Grun. The **Abteilung** turned to the left and gained the ridgeline. From here two deep ravines, very difficult to negotiate and running across the direction of attack, had to be crossed. For this purpose, the main body of the **10.Kompanie** was assigned to provide covering fire while the **11.Kompanie** immediately continued to attack. When crossing both ravines, the **Abteilung** was subjected to raging fire out of the right flank from the edge of the village from numerous, excellently camouflaged heavy anti-tank guns and several assault guns on T34 chassis. This enemy force wasn't completely silenced until after a lengthy firefight.

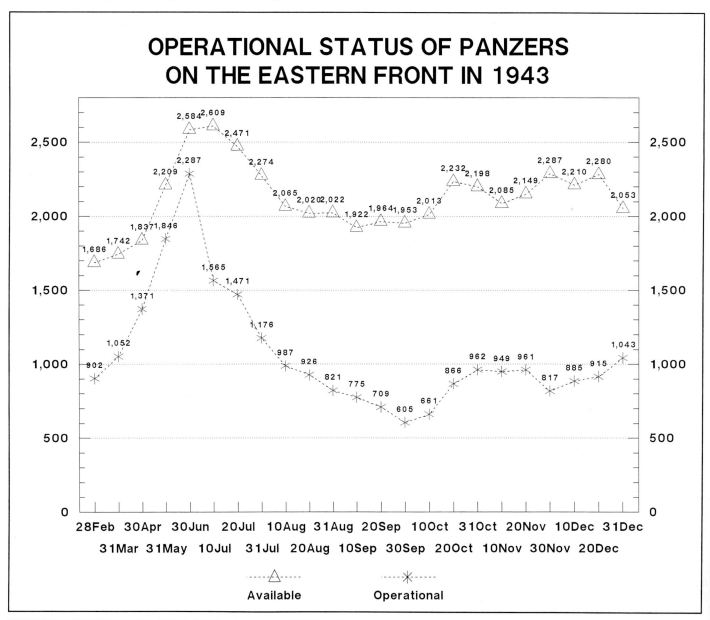

OPERATIONAL STATUS OF PANZERS ON THE EASTERN FRONT IN 1943

Available — △ —   Operational — ✱ —

Hauptmann von Villebois, commander of the **10.Kompanie**, *was severely wounded during this action. His Tiger was hit eight times by 12.2 cm shells from the assault guns on T34 chassis. One hit penetrated the hull side. The turret was hit six times, three of which resulted only in small dents, while two hits caused fractures and small pieces to break off. The sixth hit broke out a large piece (about two hand widths) from the turret armor that flew into the fighting compartment. The entire electrical firing circuit for the main gun was knocked out by the hits and several vision blocks were destroyed or broke out of the weak holders. The weld seam on the hull was sprung open for about 50 cm from the location of the penetration, so that it wasn't possible for the* **Werkstatt** *to repair it.*

After reaching the cemetery, the **Abteilung** turned toward the right and entered the village, destroyed two assault guns on T34 chassis in a short fight, and advanced up to the south edge of Grun without encountering any enemy resistance worth mentioning.

Now the **Abteilung** still had six operational Tigers, of which two were **Befehlswagen**. Five Tigers had fallen out due to damage caused by hits, one Tiger from mines, and the rest from mechanical failure. Driving in the lead, the **Abteilung** continued the attack toward the southeast, turned at the road from Grun to Budy, and continued to advance with the right wing along the road. The north edge of Budy was stubbornly defended by Russian anti-tank and anti-aircraft guns. The enemy was destroyed without a single loss. After filling up with ammunition and fuel, about 1900 hours the **Abteilung** started off again toward Belsk, driving in the lead with the last three Tigers that were still combat operational. The middle of Belsk was reached at about 0100 hours after destroying additional anti-tank guns and clearing a mine barrier without suffering any further losses. The Panzer attacks had been excellently supported by the **II.(Sf.)/Artillerie-Regiment Grossdeutschland**.

Personnel Losses:	One man killed, one officer severely wounded, and three officers and three men lightly wounded.
Equipment Losses:	Six Tigers damaged by enemy action (five by hits and one by mines) Seven Tigers fell out due to mechanical failures (engine, transmission, and gun)
Results:	21 anti-tank guns, anti-aircraft guns and artillery pieces; eight tanks and assault guns; and one armored car destroyed.

<u>16 August 1943</u> - March from Belsk through Grun to the forest 2 kilometers southwest of Akhtyrka. Five operational Tigers.

<u>17 August 1943</u> - 10 operational Tigers.

<u>18 August 1943</u> - The division was supposed to advance from Akhtyrka toward the southwest through Kaplunowka and Parchomowka in order to gain contact with the SS units advancing south of the Merla. Elements of the **10.Panzer-Grenadier-Division** on the right and elements of the **7.Panzer-Division** on the left provided flank protection for **Grossdeutschland**. On the previous day, the **Abteilung** commander had personally scouted the assembly area and the terrain over which the attack was to occur. The terrain was very suitable for a Panzer attack due to very rolling hills. **FKL-Kompanie 311**, attached to the **Abteilung**, was sent by the division to another location to provide security. Mines were not expected in the first sector to be attacked, because on the previous days the enemy had continuously pulled in new forces and had attacked with tanks and infantry almost without interruption.

For this attack, the **I.(SPW) Bataillon/Panzer-Grenadier-Regiment Grossdeutschland** and the **II.(Sf.)/Artillerie-Regiment Grossdeutschland** were attached to the **Panzer-Regiment (Tiger-Abteilung, I.Abteilung, 2.Panther-Kompanie)** The **Tiger-Abteilung** had orders to drive in the front line on a wide front along the right side of the road from Akhtryka to Micheilowka to break through the first Russian position and gain the important heights by Point 171.1 (3 kilometers northeast of Michailowka) as quickly as possible. The **I.Abteilung** was assigned the task of screening the right and left flanks of the **Tiger-Abteilung** while the Panthers had orders to provide covering fire for the Tigers from favorable firing positions overlooking the rolling terrain.

In order to deceive the enemy about our intentions, about 0800 hours, after a short barrage from the artillery, the **Fuesilier-Regiment Grossdeutschland** attacked the enemy-occupied village of Bolch.-Osero. About 0830 hours, the **Panzer-Regiment** started their own attack. After leaving the city of Achtyrka, the **Abteilung** received anti-tank fire from the west and southwest edge of Bolch.-Osero. While going into firing positions, eight Tigers hit mines simultaneously. These were all German wooden box mines under which the enemy had sometimes laid one or two heavy shells (apparently 21 cm) to increase the explosive effect. The minefield was so thick that most of the Panzers hit three or four mines at the same time. While the simple wooden box mines caused only superficial damage, the mines coupled with shells resulted in heavy damage. Five Tigers were lightly damaged, while three Tigers were immobilized with major damage to the tracks and suspension. The **Abteilung** did not get into further action on this day because of the mine damage.

Personnel Losses:	One man wounded (bomb fragment)
Equipment Losses:	Eight Tigers on mines
Results:	Five anti-tank guns destroyed.

Four Tigers were operational in the evening.

<u>19 August 1943</u> - The four operational Tigers of the **Abteilung**, under the command of Oberleutnant Arnold, joined up with the **Regiment**. These four Tigers were employed at the left front of the formation during the attack on Parchomowka. In this battle against a strong Russian anti-tank front, one Tiger was knocked out by a hit from an assault gun on a T34 chassis. The round cleanly penetrated

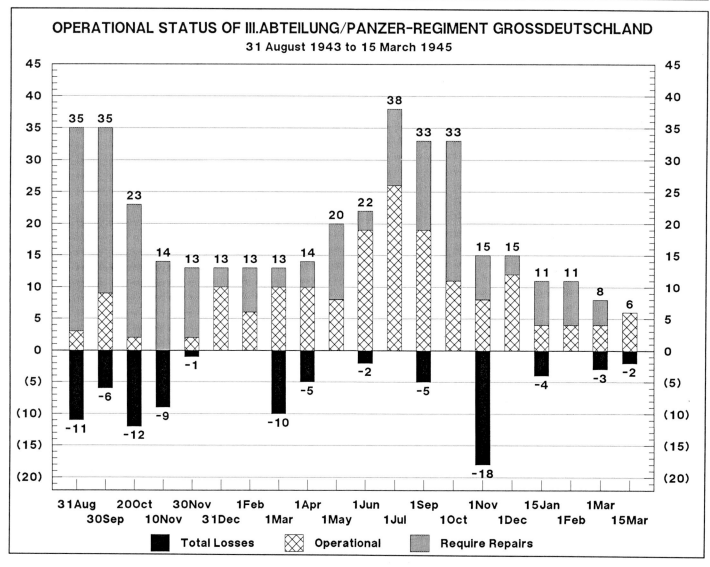

OPERATIONAL STATUS OF III.ABTEILUNG/PANZER-REGIMENT GROSSDEUTSCHLAND
31 August 1943 to 15 March 1945

Legend: ■ Total Losses ⊠ Operational ▨ Require Repairs

the left side of the superstructure by the driver. After destroying this strong anti-tank gun position, the attack advanced toward Parchomowka, where the enemy quite stubbornly defended the edge of the village with anti-tank guns and T34 and KW-I tanks.

Personnel Losses: Three men dead, one wounded.
Equipment Losses: One Tiger heavily damaged (super structure side penetrated), the guns on two Tigers damaged
Results: 12 tanks, 12 heavy anti-tank guns, and six light anti-tank guns destroyed.
Five Tigers were operational in the evening.

20 August 1943 - During late afternoon, the unit moved south from Parchomowka and gained contact with **SS-Division Totenkopf**. Five enemy tanks were knocked out by the two remaining operational Tigers. Three Tigers had suffered mechanical breakdowns; two of them had problems with their transmissions and electrical generators.

22 August 1943 - During a localized counterattack directly

northeast of Parchomowka, one Tiger was sent in and destroyed six heavy anti-tank guns and numerous anti-tank rifles.

23 August 1943 - On this day, the **Abteilung** commander took over the **Panzergruppe** (two Tigers, nine Panthers, three **Pz.Kpfw.IV lang**, three **Pz.Kpfw.IV kurz**, three **Pz.Kpfw.III lang**, three **Flammpanzer**, and one **Pz.Bef.Wg.**) in the sector of the **Grenadier-Regiment**, east and northeast of Michailowka (12 kilometers southeast of Akhtyrka). This was almost all of the operational Panzers in the **Regiment**. Operations were restricted to repulsing several enemy tank attacks.

Equipment Losses: One Tiger hit on the gun
Results: 25 tanks and 7 guns destroyed.

24 August 1943 - During the night of 24/25 August, the division moved to the west and southwest and prepared to defend an area in the general line about 2 to 4 kilometers west of the Parchomowka to Bugrowatij road. At the same time, all the operational Panzers from the **Regiment** arrived under the command of Major Gomille. While one group of four Panzers was positioned in an especially threatened sector of the **Fuesilier-** and **Grenadier-Regiments**, the **Abteilung** commander held back all of the rest of the Panzers near his command post, ready to attack at any time. During the afternoon, on orders from the division, any Panzers that were not fully operational had to be sent off to Kotelwa in order to ensure that all Panzers could be pulled back behind the new main defense line during the maneuvers planned for that evening to break off contact with the enemy.

Only two Tigers and five Panthers were left with the **Abteilung** commander. About 1700 hours, the enemy started to attack our weak lines with several tanks and very strong infantry. While the enemy penetration by the **Grenadier-Regiment** was brought to a halt by an immediate counterattack in which four enemy tanks were knocked out, the enemy broke through the **7.Panzer-Division** to the left of **Grossdeutschland**. However, no enemy tanks were located there when our own Panzers attacked to relieve the left-hand neighbor.

About 2300 hours, the maneuvers to break contact were initiated. Only two Tigers were still operational, the rest having fallen out from hits or mechanical breakdown. With the aid of these two Tigers, after intensive effort lasting until dawn, the other damaged Panzers were able to be towed behind the new main defense line by Kotelwa.

26 August 1943 - After giving up the five Panthers, the **Abteilung** commander on the morning of 26 August remained in possession of only two conditionally operational Tigers, which had arrived in the new bivouac area for the **Regiment** at Budischtscha at about 1100 hours. About 1300 hours, both of these Tigers had to be sent farther toward Kotelwa because the enemy had broken through directly east of Kotelwa with tanks and infantry. One of the Tigers broke down from engine and transmission failure in Kotelwa. After knocking out two T34 tanks, the other Tiger was hit in the suspension, sight, and gun by 7.62 cm rounds so that it was no longer combat operational. Both Tigers were recovered.

Having been sent to the front to determine the status of the **II.Abteilung/Panzer-Regiment 23** sent in with 96 Panthers, Oberstleutnant Mildebrath wrote the following report for the **Generalinspekteur der Panzertruppen** on 9 September 1943:

With the Fieseler-Storch placed at my service I searched for the headquarters of 6.Armee, reputed to be in Bassan, 8 km southwest of Pologi. Since the headquarters were not found either in Bassan or in Pologi, I began the search for the **XVII.Armee-Korps** in the area east of Konstantinopol on the

Two Tigers of the **1.Kompanie/schwere Panzer-Abteilung 503** give their escorting infantry a ride as they prepare to counterattack on 11 December 1943. (BA)

track from Saporosche to Stalino. Numerous columns, cattle herds, and fleeing civilians were found moving to the west along this track. Vision was hampered, since all of the barns had been set on fire. The airfield at Konstantinopol had already been abandoned.

By landing east of Ulakti, contact was made with the crews of two broken-down Panthers. They stated that the supply and maintenance services of the **II.Abteilung/Panzer-Regiment 23** were set up west of Pokrowskoje and broken down Panthers were collected there. A military police officer reported that he had heard on the radio that the enemy had cut and occupied the main route by Malajamichaelowka during the morning of 9 September.

After a long search north and south of the area around Pokrowskoje, the maintenance company was found in Terstianka and the supply unit in Ssamoilowska. During the flight, 15 Panthers were observed moving to the west. Oberleutnant Klemm, commander of the **6.Kompanie/ Panzer-Regiment 23**, and several other officers found with the supply unit reported the following: The battalion was unloaded in Makejewka and immediately gathered in an assembly area by Mospino, from which an attack was made to release encircled infantry. Then, every day without a break they were sent into action and made long marches every night. The same as in the beginning, the vulnerabilities of the Panther appeared in spite of good training of the maintenance personnel. Fifty percent of the Panthers had already broken down at the first assembly area, two-thirds with motor damage and one-third with broken final drives or hydraulic turret drives. This ratio applied to almost all breakdowns. As a result of continuous action, no time remained for the troops to care for the vehicles.

Very soon the **Abteilung** was split into several groups. The first train with six Panthers and several supply vehicles remained with the **23.Panzer-Division**. Three Panthers were guarding two division headquarters in Krasnogorowka. Major Fechner had eight Panthers in the area 5 kilometers to the north. A further eight Panthers were located 5 kilometers north-northeastward of Fechner. These were tactically employed as firefighters, the same as the rest of the groups. Five Panthers were total write-offs and 54 were not operational due to major or minor problems and are moving or being towed to the west.

Fourteen heavily damaged Panthers from the **Abteilung** were ready to be loaded at the train station in Stalino-West. Since the water supply for steam locomotives was the first thing blown up at the train station, plans to ship the Panthers by rail fell through. In spite of this, most of the Panthers were towed back. However, three of the Panthers had to be blown up. Since there was still hope that locomotives from other train stations could be obtained, the Panthers weren't blown up until the moment that Russian infantry successfully attacked the train station.

Reports from **Heeresgruppe Sued** stated that there were 87 Panthers. For 9 September, the **Abteilung** reported only

84 Panthers, of which 25 were operational, 5 were total write-offs and 54 were in need of repair. The difference between the numbers is not resolvable, since the **Abteilung** can't be successfully assembled due to continuous action in the various locations.

In addition, other Panthers were diverted for combating Partisans, for reconnaissance, to liberate encircled artillery and infantry, and to guard against being blown up. In any case, an overview of all vehicles in the **Abteilung** was not possible.

As a result of much too small an allotment of only four **Zugkraftwagen 18t**, towing could occur only by sector or by using repaired Panthers. The number of operational Panthers could significantly increase if additional **Zugkraftwagen 18t** were issued. Most of the Panthers that had been used for towing were very heavily damaged (failure of the motor, final drives, drive shaft and hydraulic pump).

The **Abteilung** reported that the extraordinary capability of the main gun and armor were especially enjoyable. Fires in the Panthers did not occur after penetration by anti-tank rounds. Losses due to enemy action are only about 10 percent of the breakdowns.

Since the **Abteilung** was tactically employed attached to an **Armee**, close cooperation with an armored infantry or artillery unit for support was lacking. For a period, Major Fechner had fed and employed 200 leaderless infantry in his leaguer. The combat morale of our infantry has seriously declined due to the shortage of officers and supplies. Therefore, enemy attacks easily succeed when the Panthers are pulled out for other tasks or for resupply.

The armor steel of the opponent was stated to be very much poorer. Possibly the troops were deceived by the outstanding effect of the **7.5 cm Kw.K.42 L/70** gun.

In spite of the continuous action and retreat, the morale and capability of the **Abteilung** are excellent. Personnel losses are negligibly small, only three dead.

As before, the troops are still excited about the tactical capabilities of the Panther, but deeply disappointed that the majority of the Panthers can't engage in combat due to a miserable motor and other mechanical weaknesses. They would gladly give up some speed, if automotive reliability could be gained.

Until the same automotive reliability as the **Pz.Kpfw.III** and **IV** is achieved, the **Abteilung** must be provided with extra repair parts, especially motors and final drives, and the necessary equipment and personnel to perform maintenance and repairs.

Since the **Abteilung** consists of very good, older **Panzertruppen** and sufficient time was available for individual training, all problems can be traced to design and production mistakes. Training cannot be used as an excuse in any case. During the allotted time planned for training, 592 modifications were made to their Panthers, with almost no time left for unit tactical training in the **Abteilung**.

Since the part of the **Abteilung** with the commander was

A **Panther Ausf.A** of the **7.Kompanie/Panzer-Regiment 23** moving across the open terrain of southern Russia. (BA)

rumored to be on the move or in action against an enemy force that had broken through farther to the west, direct contact could not be achieved due to the schedule.

To prevent their loss in the event that the enemy advanced farther from the north, immediate employment of at least ten *Zugkraftwagen 18t* was requested from the **Heeresgruppe** for recovering broken down Panthers found on the main route.

On 20 September 1943, the **II.Abteilung/Panzer-Regiment 23** reported their status as follows:

The **Abteilung** was unloaded east of Stalino and immediately sent into action by the **6.Armee**. Instead of the **18 Zugkraftwagen 18t** that had been requested, only four were issued. Large problems immediately occurred in recovering combat and mechanical breakdowns. The front continuously pulled back. Recovery of a Panther was possible only by using two *Zugkraftwagen 18t*.

From the original 96 Panthers that belonged to the **Abteilung**, 28 had to be blown up as a result of enemy action or enemy tanks attacking broken-down Panthers being towed along the main route. Of the remaining 68 Panthers, 8

are operational with **Kampfgruppe Sander** and 3 are operational with the **Abteilung** in Nowij Swet.

A further 11 Panthers should be repaired by 23 September. The Panthers that aren't expected to be repaired by 23 September are located as follows: 13 in the **Abteilung Werkstatt** in Zaporoshye, 24 at a collection point east of the Dnepr, 4 in the **Regiment Werkstatt**, 4 loaded on railcars, and 1 guarding the dam in Zaporoshye.

The following status report, dated 16 November 1943, reveals how the **I.Abteilung/SS-Panzer-Regiment 1** of the **1.SS-Panzer-Division** fared directly after its arrival at the front:

Panther-Abteilung Kuhlmann was unloaded in the area Shitomir - Berditschew - Kasatin on 7 and 8 November. On orders of the commander of the **XXXIX.Panzer-Korps**, the **Abteilung** assembled in the area east of Berditschew during the night of 8/9 November. On 8 November 1943, the corps commander ordered **Panther-Abteilung Kuhlmann** to advance toward the northwest along the rail line from Kasatin.

Without maintenance and in continuous action, within six

days the **Abteilung** had advanced 210 kilometers and shot up 40 enemy tanks. Resupply of fuel was possible only by an armored train. The Panther was known by the entire **Abteilung** to be an excellent weapon.

Summary of losses: Seven total write-offs caused by hits on the sides and rear. Mechanical breakdowns consisted of 4 clutches, 38 motors, 1 starter, 1 hydraulic pump, 5 final drives, 1 magneto, 1 suspension, 1 fan drive, 1 turret traverse drive, and 1 radiator. Of these it was estimated that 22 could be repaired within six days and 32 needed over six days. 35 operational Panthers were available on 14 November.

During the attack on Ssolowjewka on 15 November, 5 Panthers were lost through enemy action (it was not yet known if they were total write-offs) plus 9 temporary losses from mechanical breakdowns.

Hauptmann Hans-Joachim Schwaner, commander of the **III./Panzer-Regiment 36**, wrote the following combat report for their actions on 1 November 1943:

Organization of **Kampfgruppe Langkeit**: Stab/Panzer-Regiment 36, **III.Abteilung/Panzer-Regiment 36** (minus the **12.(Sturmgeschuetz) Kompanie**), **I./Panzer-Grenadier-Regiment 103**, **I./Panzer-Artillerie-Regiment 4**, and **1./Panzer-Pionier-Bataillon 13**.

Orders: The same assignment as the previous day. Attack from Nowo-Iwanowka farther toward the northeast through Wolnaja-Dolina, crossing the rail line from Kriwoi-Rog to Pjatischatki, past Wassiljewka and Wesselaja-Dolina, penetrate to Ssaxagen in order to destroy the forces which have recently gathered there.

Assembly point: Defensive positions around Nowo-Iwanowka during the night of 31 October/1 November.

March order: Start out of the assembly area at 0515 hours in the following formation: **11.Kompanie** to the right front, **9.Kompanie** to the left front, **Stab** in the center, followed by the **10.(Sturmgeschuetz) Kompanie**.

Attack up to the ridgeline south of Sarje: The first stage, out of the assembly area up to the line of a 1500-meter-long hedgerow, passed without any enemy activity. Movement and

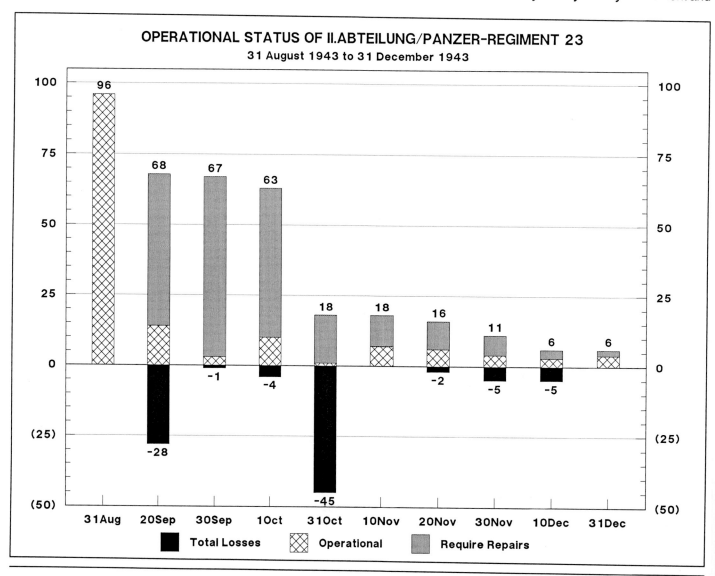

OPERATIONAL STATUS OF II.ABTEILUNG/PANZER-REGIMENT 23
31 August 1943 to 31 December 1943

Legend: ■ Total Losses ▨ Operational ▨ Require Repairs

ORGANIZATION AND STRENGTH OF PANZER UNITS
REPLACEMENT UNITS SENT TO EASTERN FRONT

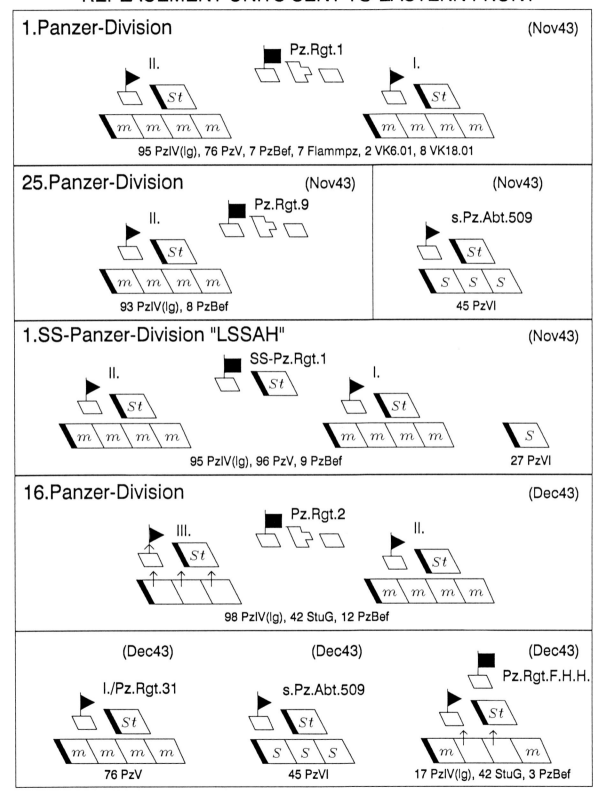

1.Panzer-Division (Nov43)

II. Pz.Rgt.1 I.

95 PzIV(lg), 76 PzV, 7 PzBef, 7 Flammpz, 2 VK6.01, 8 VK18.01

25.Panzer-Division (Nov43) (Nov43)

II. Pz.Rgt.9

s.Pz.Abt.509

93 PzIV(lg), 8 PzBef

45 PzVI

1.SS-Panzer-Division "LSSAH" (Nov43)

II. SS-Pz.Rgt.1 I.

95 PzIV(lg), 96 PzV, 9 PzBef

27 PzVI

16.Panzer-Division (Dec43)

III. Pz.Rgt.2 II.

98 PzIV(lg), 42 StuG, 12 PzBef

(Dec43) (Dec43) (Dec43)

I./Pz.Rgt.31   s.Pz.Abt.509   Pz.Rgt.F.H.H.

76 PzV   45 PzVI   17 PzIV(lg), 42 StuG, 3 PzBef

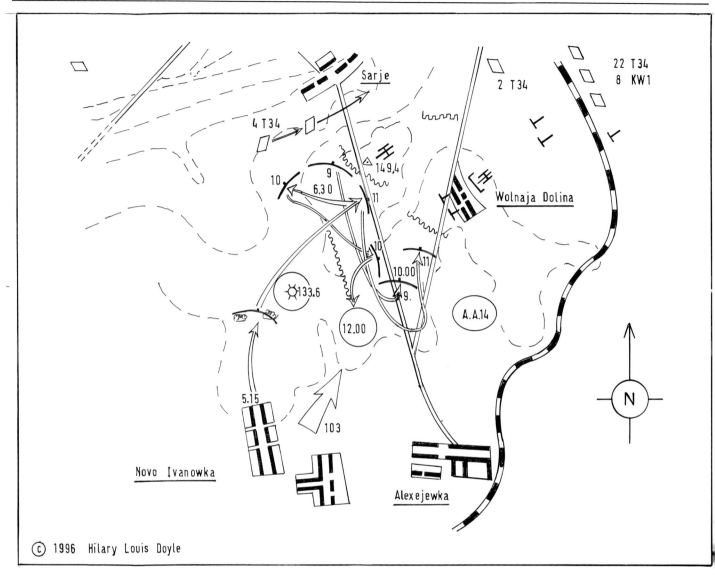

Sarje

4 T34

2 T34

22 T34
8 KW1

149,4

10   9
6.30   11

Wolnaja Dolina

10

11

10.00

133.6

9.

12.00

A.A.14

5.15

103

Novo Ivanowka

N

Alexejewka

artillery arriving were spotted on the heights south of Sarje. These were destroyed without any loss to us by rapidly charging the enemy infantry and artillery observers attempting to take up positions. The **S.P.W.-Bataillon** only hesitatingly followed the attack of the **Panzer-Abteilung**. It then received an assignment to advance to the south of the **Panzer-Abteilung**.

Battle on the heights: At first, the **Panzer-Abteilung** was subjected to well-directed artillery fire from Sarje. A **Pz.Kpfw.IV** of the **Stab** was hit in the suspension and immobilized. In addition, heavy anti-tank guns and two anti-aircraft batteries were spotted taking up positions north of Sarje. This gave the left-hand neighbor, the armored elements of the **24.Panzer-Division** advancing toward the northeast through Ternowatka, a lot to achieve. We observed more than five of their Panzers knocked out, one after the other, within a short time. We engaged the enemy forces in front of the **24.Panzer-Division** who were within our effective range of fire (2000 to 2500 meters). The **9.** and **10.Kompanie** destroyed three heavy anti-tank guns and knocked out the crews of several

anti-aircraft guns. During this time, additional artillery and anti-aircraft gun fire was directed at us. A Panzer of the **9.Kompanie** was knocked out. During the further battle on the heights, first six T34 tanks and then four T34 tanks and assault guns that wanted to disappear to the east toward Sarje were effectively engaged. Altogether, six T34 tanks were knocked out by the **9.** and **10.Kompanien**. In the interim, the **11.Kompanie** felt their way forward over the ridgeline toward the northeast and engaged in a firefight with anti-tank and artillery guns that had been spotted on the road embankment about 1500 to 2000 meters east of our point. The enemy anti-tank guns were well camouflaged and often changed position. In spite of the fact that they were difficult to target, the **11.Kompanie** destroyed four anti-tank guns and two artillery pieces. On orders from the **Regiment**, further advances were temporarily delayed while waiting for the advancing **24.Panzer-Division**. The resistance increased in front of both divisions, so that we had the impression that the opponent had erected a solid defensive front around Sarje and east up to the rail line. The **S.P.W.-Bataillon** was also hit by strong fire while advancing south of the **Panzer-Abteilung**. They dismounted and made only slow forward progress fighting through enemy infantry positions.

Attempt to attack from further south with the S.P.W.-Bataillon: On orders from the **Regiment**, the **Panzer-Abteilung** broke off contact, leaving behind elements of the **10.Kompanie** to secure the heights and, utilizing the cover of a ridgeline to the east, drove south to the **Panzer-Grenadiere** positions, turned back to the northeast, and supported them in their attack. The unit was exposed to the enemy during the turn. The **9.** and **11.Kompanien** were hit by strong fire from enemy T34 and KW-I tanks as well as by anti-tank and artillery fire located in good positions in the area of the rail line embankment at a range of about 2000 meters. We counted or spotted 22 T34 and 8 KW-I tanks as well as innumerable anti-tank and artillery guns that took us under direct fire.

An attack by Stukas and bombers on the rail line embankment and along the road appeared to have effectively destroyed the enemy positions. The **9.** and **11.Kompanie** exploited these bombing attacks to continue their advance. The **10.Kompanie**, after repulsing an attack by a regiment of enemy infantry from their defensive position on the heights, received orders to follow our advance or to provide covering fire from favorable positions. Even while the last Stuka bombs were falling, the resistance of the enemy tanks came back to life. They didn't let themselves be distracted by the bombs and opened up a murderous fire. Two **Pz.Kpfw.IVs** of the **9.Kompanie** were knocked out and their advance was halted. The **11.Kompanie** managed to rush forward another 400 meters under strong tank and anti-tank fire. There they reached a depression from which they could effectively engage anti-tank guns that just appeared on the southwest edge of the village of Wolnaja-Dolina; they hadn't been previously spotted. The **11.Kompanie** destroyed three anti-tanks guns and two T34 tanks. They also supported the advance of the forward elements of the **Grenadiere** in their fight against enemy infantry. When they regained contact with the **Abteilung**, the **10.Kompanie** also ran into strong enemy fire. On orders from the **Regiment**, the attack was called off. The **Aufklaerungs-Abteilung** of the division that had been sent east of the **Kampfgruppe** was also stopped by the same anti-tank, artillery, and tank fire and halted east of the road on line with the **Abteilung**. Concentrated artillery fire by the division as well as further Stuka attacks were not capable of shaking up the strong enemy positions. So, the line that had been reached by the afternoon was defended, and further attacks ceased.

Firefight on line that had been reached, and assembling the Abteilung: As far as the strong artillery and anti-tank gun fire allowed, recognized enemy targets were still taken under fire. During the previous combat day, only weak enemy air force activity occurred. During the afternoon several Russian bombing and strafing aircraft attacks occurred as well as rocket barrages. Especially the artillery and **Grenadiers**, but also the Panzers were attacked several times by strafing aircraft. But this resulted in only very few losses to the **Artillerie** and **Grenadiere**. An order came from the **Regiment** to retire behind the next ridgeline in order to prevent losses. The **11.Kompanie** lost two **Pz.Kpfw.IVs** knocked out by heavy anti-tank guns when they pulled out of their advance positions and had to travel across the enemy front. Thereby, the

Escorting infantry climbing aboard a **Pz.Kpfw.IV Ausf.H** in preparation for an attack across open country. (BA)

Abteilung's losses increased to six, three of which could be recovered late in the afternoon and after nightfall.

Before nightfall, the **Regiment** ordered that a **Kompanie** was to be sent to provide fire support for an attack by **Panzer-Grenadier-Regiment 108** on the village of Alexejewka. The **10.Kompanie** was sent and advanced to within 1500 meters of the village when they recognized that the **Grenadier-Regiment**, supported by **Sturmgeschuetz** from the **12.Kompanie**, had already entered the village and that their fire support was no longer needed.

<u>Withdrawal of the **Abteilung** and return to the starting position</u>: In carrying out orders from the division, at about 1600 hours, the **Abteilung** drove back to Nowo-Iwanowka and went into defensive positions for the night facing toward the north and northeast. During the night, an order was received that the entire **Kampfgruppe** was to be transferred to an area 60 kilometers southeast of Kriwoi-Rog for a new assignment.

Results for 1.11.43: 16 anti-tank guns, 14 tanks, 2 assault guns, and 12 artillery pieces destroyed.

Operational Panzer strength: 9 **Pz.Kpfw.IV**, 9 **StuG**, 1 **Pz.Bef.Wg.**

Losses: 6 men wounded.

The following extracts are from a report written on 4 November 1943 by Hauptmann Markowsky of the **III./Panzer-Regiment 24** of the **24.Panzer-Division** on the first days in action north of Kriwoi-Rog:

My **Abteilung** consisted of two **Pz.Kpfw.IV-Schwadronen** and two **Sturmgeschuetz-Schwadronen**, each with 22 armored vehicles. The **Stab** has only two **Panzerbefehlswagen (5 cm Kw.K. lang)**. Unfortunately an **Aufklaerungs-Zug** was not available. I could have often used one. The mixture of **Sturmgeschuetze** and **Pz.Kpfw.IVs** has proven itself to be useful. The **Sturmgeschuetze** are employed very much like Panzers often without any special protection against attack from close combat troops. This was okay because the local Russian infantry didn't attempt to attack in this way. Sometimes a **Sturmgeschuetz-Schwadron** was detached for another assignment. The **24.Panzer-Division** doesn't have a **Panzer-Jaeger-Abteilung**, but the **III.Abteilung** was still often employed together, which was always best for us.

The **Abteilung** now has nine days of heavy combat behind it. During this period it knocked out 184 enemy tanks, 87 anti-tank guns, and 26 artillery pieces with only four of our own lost as total write-offs. The enemy tanks were almost exclusively T34 with a few heavy 15 cm assault guns. The superiority over the Russian tanks isn't due very much to the equipment as, primarily, to the training of the crews and the leadership within the **Schwadronen**, and secondarily, to the concentrated employment of the **Abteilung**. Support from the other weapons, such as artillery and aircraft, has not yet been smoothly worked out for several different reasons. We are especially lacking good radio communication. That will be corrected and work itself out. But this is necessary so that our attacks won't fail, as has recently occurred twice when we encountered massive anti-tank and anti-aircraft gun fronts that we couldn't envelop because of the terrain and we were too weak.

We now count on an average operational combat strength of 10 to 15 Panzers per **Schwadron**. Most of the losses are caused by mechanical breakdowns. I consider it to be very good that the number of Panzers in each **Schwadron** was increased to 22. This saves lives and increases the combat power. One thing has become very clear to me: we can win the war here only with massed Panzers and with nothing else.

Therefore the cry: Give us Panzers and more Panzers! But give us personnel that are trained and not new recruits! So long as our Panzers are everything but foolproof, this is idiocy, which unfortunately is always repeated.

Will we again experience in this war that continuous supplies of Panzers and trained crews are received to replace the losses as they occur and thereby maintain a combat-tested unit that remains operational instead of first being totally wiped out and then refurbished again?

Not only the actual but also the psychological advantages would be enormous. But after what I have already seen, I do not have much more hope. The **Panzer-Waffe** is the weapon that will decide the war, nothing more and nothing less! I have now seen the truth of this statement with my own eyes.

The following excerpts are from a report written on 9 November 1943 by an unidentified Hauptmann from the same unit:

I can briefly report to the Oberst after the first combat actions are behind us:

1. On the question of whether Panzers and **Sturmgeschuetze** are to be mixed together in the same unit, I remain of the opinion that in no case should they be mixed within units. Another solution would be overly complicated.

2. How well has it worked out? Both **Pz.Kpfw.IV lang** and **Sturmgeschuetze** have worked out well. The advantage of the **Sturmgeschuetz** is that its low profile makes it easier to sneak up on tanks. The disadvantage of the **Sturmgeschuetz** is the lack of a machine gun. The **Sturmgeschuetz** is the ideal weapon for engaging enemy tanks (at least in the terrain in southern Russia). But it can never fully replace the Panzers. I consider it bearable that up to half of the allotment of armored vehicles in a **Panzer-Abteilung** are **Sturmgeschuetze**.

3. The battle here is conducted with Panzers, **Pak**, **Artillerie**, and the **Luftwaffe**. The other weapons branches are of lower importance. The infantry has the least importance because it is so poor. From my view, after such a long war it is no longer possible to restore the fought-out infantry to a decisive weapons branch. Therefore, in my opinion we should produce Panzers, **Pak** and **Artillerie** using all the means available.

A row of **Pz.Kpfw.IV Ausf.H**s on alert. The **Schuerzen** fasteners had been improved to prevent their being lost when encountering brush. (BA)

To the question of the value of these weapons in comparison to each other, I have the following view:

*a. The **Pak**, **Sturmgeschuetz** and **Artillerie** serve to strengthen the defense.*

*b. We need Panzers, Panzers, and more Panzers (including **Sturmgeschuetze**) to increase the offensive power. We need Panzers when we want to be successful in attacking and breaking through, but they must actually be employed in mass and in depth. I am convinced that we can cleanly penetrate any position where we actually concentrate massed Panzers.*

*4. Value of the Russians here: The infantry are mostly poor but numerous because the Russians immediately drafted the Ukrainians from the territory they regained. We have taken prisoners who were working in Germany three months ago. The Russians have very many anti-tank guns, which are our most bothersome opponent. His Panzers are poorly led tactically and are poor shots. We don't view them as dangerous opponents. During the period from 24 October to 1 November 1943 in the area north of Kriwoi-Rog, my **Panzer-Regiment** knocked out 181 enemy tanks and lost only four of our Panzers as total write-offs. In comparison, I have now lost six*

additional Panzers during a few days in combat against anti-tank guns. Up to now, I have seldom been subjected to Russian artillery fire. The Russians fire a lot from their tanks, anti-tank guns, heavy assault guns, and light artillery pieces; that is quite bothersome, as they shoot up the area with a very large expenditure of ammunition.

5. In closing, up to now my strongest impression of our combat action is that we absolutely must have numerically superior, really strong Panzer units if we want to achieve offensive victories. And, this we must do.

On 7 December 1943, the Oberstleutnant commanding **Panzer-Regiment 36** wrote the following experience report on the employment of **Sturmgeschuetze** within a **Panzer-Abteilung**:

*The **III./Panzer-Regiment 36** was outfitted as follows for employment on the Eastern Front: two **Kompanien** and an **Aufklaerungs-Zug** with 49 **Pz.Kpfw.IV lang** and two **Kompanien** with 44 **Sturmgeschuetz**.*

*The **Abteilung** first went into battle on 28 October 1943 and had been in combat for 16 days by 1 December 1943.*

Employment of **Sturmgeschuetze** within the **Panzer-Abteilung** and together with **Panzer-Grenadiere** has occurred in four different combat scenarios:

1. **Sturmgeschuetze** attacking in the first wave.

2. **Sturmgeschuetze** providing flank protection in the second wave.

3. **Sturmgeschuetze** cooperating with the **Panzer-Grenadiere**.

4. **Sturmgeschuetze** in defense.

All four possibilities were tested in practice during the six weeks in action, resulting in the following experiences:

1. The only advantage of using **Sturmgeschuetze** to attack in the first wave is that they present a somewhat smaller target than the **Pz.Kpfw.IV**. The disadvantages are the following: A Panzer can maintain the direction of attack while utilizing its traversable turret even when it must engage targets that appear to the left or right side. The **Sturmgeschuetz** must always turn its front toward the enemy. For example, it must first turn half left in order to engage an enemy target located toward the left front. These turns delay the engagement of enemy targets and slow down the assault of the **Panzergruppe**. It is especially difficult and restrictive to engage enemy targets in heavy ground during the rainy season. The driver must often steer by repeatedly driving forward and backward in order to bring the gun into the necessary field of fire. The many steering maneuvers overtax the transmission and especially the brakes. In a few cases things have gone so far that the tracks have been thrown in heavy ground.

During attacks through enemy infantry positions, which are usually very strongly occupied with anti-tank rifles, the lack of a machine gun protected by armor makes itself very negatively felt. The armor shield for the machine gun mounted on the roof of the **Sturmgeschuetz** does not protect against anti-tank rifle fire from the front or against infantry weapons fired from the side.

2. It is somewhat better to employ the **Sturmgeschuetz** in the second wave and to cover the flanks, because in covered positions it can let an approaching enemy tank attack close the range. The same weaknesses described for their employment in the first wave are apparent when **Sturmgeschuetze** are used in an attack to eliminate a threat to the flank. The **Sturmgeschuetz** only needs to turn to the right or left, but then again it has more difficulty than a **Pz.Kpfw.IV** in engaging enemy tanks advancing from several directions.

3. The employment of **Sturmgeschuetze** together with **Panzer-Grenadiere** has worked out to be the best. The **Sturmgeschuetze** provide the **Panzer-Grenadiere** with strong morale support, especially during an enemy tank attack. When attacking with **Panzer-Grenadiere**, the **Sturmgeschuetz** can engage the enemy's heavy weapons such as the anti-tank guns, tanks, artillery pieces, and heavy machine guns while the enemy infantry and anti-tank rifles can be held off from the **Sturmgeschuetze** by the **Panzer-Grenadiere**.

4. **Sturmgeschuetze** have proven themselves to be very good in defense. As a mobile anti-tank defense, **Sturmgeschuetze** can effectively engage the enemy from previously scouted positions behind our own main battle line. They were shown to be very useful for scouting the firing positions in advance on foot.

In closing, it can be said that in a mixed **Panzer-Abteilung**, the **Pz.Kpfw.IV** has been shown to be superior to the **Sturmgeschuetz**, especially in offensive actions. This is proven by the following overview of the results and losses of the mixed **Panzer-Abteilung** for the period from 28 October to 1 December 1943:

Average Number of Panzers Employed	Enemy Weapons Destroyed by the Panzers		
	Tanks	_Anti-Tank Guns_	_Artillery Pieces_
17	136	117	20

Average Number of **Sturmgeschutz** Employed	Enemy Weapons Destroyed by the **Sturmgeschuetz**		
	Tanks	_Anti-Tank Guns_	_Artillery Pieces_
13	5	59	34

The ratio of kills by the Sturmgeschuetz in comparison to the Pz.Kpfw.IV was about 70 percent. The losses as total write-offs from 16 days in combat were 20 **Pz.Kpfw.IV** and 16 **Sturmgeschuetze**. In 35 working days, 52 **Pz.Kpfw.IV** and 74 **Sturmgeschuetze** were repaired by the **Werkstatt-Zug**. During the period from 28 October to 1 December 1943, the mixed **Panzer-Abteilung** destroyed 211 tanks, 176 anti-tank guns, 54 artillery pieces, 41 motor vehicles, and 101 anti-tank rifles along with 1700 enemy killed.

Report on the total write-off of Panzers and **Sturmgeschutz**:

	Pz.Kpfw.IV	_StuG_	_Flammpz_
1. Total write-offs from hits (burned out, etc.)	9	12	0
2. Total write-offs from hits (for example turret blown off, ruptured weld seams, etc.) that were recovered and butchered by the Werkstatt	6	1	0
3. Total write-offs that occurred by Panzers lost and left lying in enemy held territory:			
a. mechanical breakdown	6	4	0
b. damaged by hits	5	6	2
4. Total write-offs because there was insufficient towing capability available to recover the scattered broken down Panzers caused by continuous moves:	_7_	_2_	_1_
Total:	33	25	3

Current Panzer Status:	**Pz.Kpfw.IV**	**StuG**	**Flammpz**	**Pz.Bef.**
Operational	8	6	2	4
Require repairs <14 days	8	8	2	4
Require repairs >14 days	4	5	0	1
Total Write-offs	33	25	3	0
Total:	53*	44	7	9

* Received 4 newly issued Pz.Kpfw.IV

At the present time, there are only 18 Panzers in the _Werkstatt_. For the last 14 days, the other five Panzers are located in Kriwoj Rog where they were towed. In spite of large efforts to induce the rail personnel, the Panzers could not yet be transported from there. At the present time, sections of the rail line and **Rollbahn** from Kriwoj Rog to Kirowograd have been captured by the Russians, so that it is only possible to transport the Panzers south. One time a train was assigned for the Panzers but then it was taken back. The **Regiment** is still attempting to get these Panzers returned.

As further explanation for the statistics, the **Regiment** reports that the many total write-offs were caused mainly by the fact that the terrain across which the Panzers attacked could not be held due to a lack of **Panzer-Grenadiere**. Dif-

ferent attempts to recover broken-down Panzers by having another Panzer tow them, ended with the second Panzer also being lost by being knocked out or by mechanical failure.

Transferring the **Regiment** along a front sector of about 150 to 200 kilometers made Panzer recovery considerably more difficult. The recovery equipment must be utilized in different sectors, because the Russians pressed everywhere and any immobilized Panzer that couldn't be immediately recovered was in danger of falling into enemy hands by the next day. An increase in recovery vehicles was not achieved in spite of a major effort. A **Zugmaschine** promised from the **Armee** didn't appear and **Zugmaschinen** were not to be obtained from the **Panzer-Instandsetzungs-Abteilungen** because their **Bergezuege** were employed mainly in the areas around Shitomir and Kiev.

Report on the combat actions of the **Panzer-Abteilung 7** outfitted with three **Panzer-Sturmgeschuetz-Kompanien** during the period from 30 November to 4 December 1943:

30 November 1943 - Unloaded the **Stabs-Kompanie**, **3.Kompanie**, and **Werkstatt-Zug** in Bobinskaja.

A **Pz.Bef.Wg. Ausf.K** assigned to the **Nachrichten-Zug** of **Panzer-Regiment 2** of the **16.Panzer-Division**. (BA)

1 December 1943 - In cooperation with **Panzer-Grenadiere** and the **Panzer-Aufklaerungs-Abteilung** and attached to the **3.Panzer-Division**, the **3.Kompanie** attacked west of the **Rollbahn** toward Tscherkassy-West. During the attack, they crossed an anti-tank trench and several trench systems.

One **Pz.Bef.Wg.**, sent by the commanding general on reconnaissance to Tscherkassy, was knocked out by an enemy anti-tank gun. One man was wounded and two killed.

Results: 6 anti-tank guns and 3 trucks.

2 December 1943 - After unloading the **1.** and **2.Kompanien**, the **Abteilung** (minus the **3.Kompanie**, which remained attached to the **3.Panzer-Division**) went into action with 24 **Sturmgeschuetze** by the **72.Infanterie-Division**. Enemy positions were attacked at Dolgaja-Grab and Bliznezy-Grab on the northern edge of Kirilowka. Directly north of Kirilowka, a farmstead was captured after destroying several anti-tank guns. Our very weak infantry force (100 men with two light machine guns, young recruits and German-Rumanians) couldn't be moved farther forward from there.

Because of ammunition shortage and strong enemy resistance (anti-tank guns along the edge of the villages and in the right flank, and anti-tank rifles in large numbers and from all directions), after consulting with the infantry commander, the **Abteilung** pulled back 2 kilometers. After resupplying, a second attack couldn't be conducted because of nightfall.

The unsuccessful attack was due to insufficient preparation, rash orders, and infantry support from troops whose combat experience was too weak.

The **3.Kompanie** under the **3.Panzer-Division** was sent in to free the south side of Tscherkassy and the **Rollbahn**.

*Losses: 2 **Sturmgeschuetze** total write-offs from hits from anti-tank guns, 11 **Sturmgeschuetze** temporarily out of action due to hits and mechanical breakdowns. 6 men killed and 11 wounded.*

Results: 6 anti-tank guns and 2 infantry guns.

3 December 1943 - The **Abteilung** with the **1.** and **2.Kompanie** was attached to the **3.Panzer-Division** and as a result of a night march reached an area 3 kilometers south of Kurgan-Grab. At 0830 hours, the **Abteilung** pulled forward along the mine barrier. The operational elements of the **Abteilung** were concentrated into one **Kompanie** of 13 **Sturmgeschuetze** under the command of Oberleutnant Schoenhaar.

At 1100 hours, closely following the infantry, the **Abteilung** attacked southwest toward Kirilowka. The south side of Kirilowka was taken. Infantry pulled back out of the village without offering any resistance to a counterattack by Russian infantry with five T34 tanks. After knocking out three T34 tanks, **Kompanie Schoenhaar** pulled back about 300 meters from the village, and then after regrouping, again attacked, pulling the infantry forward and by evening had taken the entire villages of Kirilowka and Ternowka. During the night, the **Abteilung** defended the village and was resupplied.

*Losses: 2 **Sturmgeschuetze** from the **3.Kompanie** total write-offs (1 knocked out by a tank, 1 by an anti-tank gun), 7 **Sturmgeschuetze** temporarily out of action from hits. Two men killed and four wounded.*

Results: 7 tanks and 5 anti-tank guns destroyed, and 2 tanks immobilized.

4 December 1943 - In the morning, together with **Regiment List**, seven **Sturmgeschuetze** under the command of Leutnant Marre started to attack toward the north and crossed the rail line after silencing enemy anti-tank guns. They knocked out three tanks and broke into the enemy positions before nightfall. A further advance was made about 2 kilometers to the north in which an additional two tanks were knocked out. The **3.Kompanie** was employed on the south edge of Tscherkassy.

*Losses: 2 **Sturmgeschuetze** total write-offs (knocked out by anti-tank guns), 9 **Sturmgeschuetze** damaged by hits or temporarily out of service due to mechanical breakdowns. 3 men killed and 5 wounded.*

Results: 5 tanks (of which 3 T34, 1 Sherman, and 1 unknown type), 2 anti-tank guns, and 3 mortars destroyed.

5 December 1943 - The forward elements were pulled out and loaded on trains for transport to the area north of Kirolograd.

The I.(Panther) Abteilung/Panzer-Regiment 31 was outfitted with 76 Panthers and sent to Heeresgruppe Sued instead of back to the 5.Panzer-Division. Again, instead of being sent in as a consolidated unit, it was committed piecemeal directly from the trains as revealed by the combat report of **Kampfgruppe Kretschmer** (**7.Transport**) of the **2.Kompanie/Panzer-Regiment 31** written by the **Kompanie** commander, Hauptmann Graf Rothkirch, on 5 December 1943:

On 5 December 1943 at 0800 hours, the vehicles (six Panthers and three **Zugmaschinen** with trailers) off the seventh transport train left the unloading station at Schirowka and drove to Snamenka. Already while on this road, the vehicles were engaged by very heavy mortar fire from the forest north of the rail line. Heavy artillery, mortar and tank gun fire was hitting the west side of the village as the vehicles entered Snamenka-West.

In Snamenka-West it was reported that enemy tanks were to the northwest. Leutnant Kretschmer diverted from his orders to join up with the **Abteilung** and drove into position on the northwest edge of the village. In driving snow, four T34 tanks were spotted on the railway embankment and engaged at a range of 2 kilometers. The effect of the rounds couldn't be seen because of the increasing intensity of the snowstorm.

Leutnant Kretschmer drove into the village with his Panther to search for the **Abteilung**. As soon as he received a message from an infantry officer that tanks were attacking Snamenka-West from a depression west of the village, he immediately turned around and returned to the edge of the village. Ten T34 tanks carrying and followed by about 150 infantry charged out of the depression toward the village. The Panthers immediately opened fire and within minutes had knocked out six T34 tanks that went up in flames (three by Leutnant Kretschmer, two by Feldwebel Buss, and one by Unteroffizier Grundmann). One T34 tank that got into the village and attempted to depart over the railway embankment north of Snamenka-West, but it immediately went up in flames when it was knocked out by Unteroffizier Moritz before it reached the rail line.

After this success, about 1030 hours the **Kampfgruppe** immediately started to chase the retreating opponent. The three remaining T34 tanks fled over the railway embankment. In a firefight, one of the T34 tanks was knocked out by Leutnant Klepper. The retreating infantry were engaged with machine guns and **Sprenggranaten** (high explosive shells). The enemy was followed up to the rail line and driven back to the forest beyond. Because infantry did not come up to secure the area, about 1200 hours Leutnant Kretschmer allowed the **Kampfgruppe** to pull back and drive back to Snamenka-West.

Another report on the combat activities of the **2.Kompanie/Panzer-Regiment 31** for the period from 5 to 8 December 1943 was written to justify the award of the **Deutsches Kreuz in Gold** for the commander, Hauptmann Graf Rothkirch:

The **Kompanie**, with five Panthers and an additional six Panthers from the **3.Kompanie** under Leutnant Pakosch, was employed to defend the north side of the city of Snamonka on 5 December 1943. Feldwebel Buebscher of the **3.Kompanie** knocked out three T34 tanks. At 0200 hours on 6 December, an order was received for Hauptmann Graf Rothkirch to return to the **Abteilung** command post with his five Panthers. There the **Kompanie** received orders to drive to the **Panzer-Regiment 15** command post in Petrowo along with an additional six Panthers from Leutnant Kretschner. Hauptmann Graf Rothkirch went ahead in the **Kuebel** to obtain instructions.

At 0345 hours, the **Kompanie** received an order to attack at 0600 hours for about 5 kilometers along the rail line east of Snamenka, then turn south and attack the village of Schkijarewitscha with an attached **SPW-Kompanie** and clear out the enemy. The Russians were supposed to have broken through there with 12 tanks carrying infantry. Afterward, the **Kompanie** was to reconnoiter to the south up to the village of Stari Alexandrowka. After completing this assignment, the **Kompanie** was to push northeast to Dikowka to meet up with **Panzer-Regiment 15** for a further attack on Dikowka. A **gepanzerte Panzer-Grenadier-Bataillon** mounted on **SPW** was attached to **Panzer-Regiment 15**. In the interim Leutnant Kretschmer had directed the **Kompanie** to the east side of Snamenka and prepared for combat.

Unfortunately, the **Panzer-Grenadiere** didn't arrive until 0710 hours. On 0715 hours, the **Kompanie** started to attack, turned south after traveling the ordered 5 kilometers, and because of a vague map arrived on the north side of Stari Alexandrowka. Four enemy trucks were destroyed and enemy infantry successfully engaged as the **Kompanie** turned around. The **Kompanie** attacked toward Stari Alexandrowka along the slopes of a deep ravine and came within 300 meters of the village without noticeable enemy activity. When rolling into position, Kretschmer's **Zug** on the right side of the ravine came under heavy fire from tanks and artillery but managed to knock out two T34 tanks. The **Panzer-Grenadiere** followed up the ravine at an interval of 200 meters but remained pinned down because effective fire from the enemy was too strong and their own effect was too little. Kretschmer was ordered to tie down the enemy defenses in the north while Siefarth's **Zug** detoured to the west in order to flank the position. But here the **Zug** ran into heavy defensive fire without being able to effectively engage the strong anti-tank gun defenses that were excellent and very well covered by ground cover and the rolling terrain. Just four T34 tanks and a 12.2 cm assault gun were knocked out. After Kretschmer's **Zug** managed to destroy three anti-tank guns, three of his Panthers were suddenly knocked out. Two of them could be driven back personally by Leutnant Kretschmer and Feldwebel Lambeck, while the third remained stationary with its engine compartment on fire. It is worth noting that the drivers of all three Panthers were wounded. The **Kompanie** commander and Siefarth's **Zug** came within 150 meters of the village but a further advance was not thinkable because the enemy fired smoke. In light of this situation, plus the fact that about 400 to 500 Russians had dug in in the village with a significant number of anti-tank guns, further reinforced by strong tank forces and anti-aircraft guns, and after considering that instead of a complete **SPW-Kompanie**, only three **SPW** with altogether 15 infantry were available, the **Kompanie** pulled back in order to eventually attempt to attack the village from the northwest. **Panzer-Regiment 15** approved this decision.

One Panther was knocked out when hit by an anti-tank gun during the first attack. The damage could be quickly repaired, so that the next day it reappeared with the **Kompanie** in operational condition.

About 1515 hours, an attack led by Leutnant Pakosch advanced from a wooded lot south of Orlowka Balka toward the west side of Stari Alexandrowka. Because the **Kompanie** commander knew exactly the enemy situation in this village and foresaw the coming misfortune, in order to split the defense the **Kompanie** again attacked this village from the north to support the attack led by Leutnant Pakosch. The **Kompanie**'s attack toward the village went well but because of the failing light couldn't start to be effective. In the meantime, three Panthers under Leutnant Pakosch were knocked out when hit from the front at a range of about 1500 meters and Leutnant Pakosch was killed.

On 7 December 1943 at 0130 hours, an order arrived for the **Kompanie** to report at 0530 hours to the **Kampfgruppe Lauchert** command post 4 kilometers west of Dikowka for a new assignment. They remained there as an attack reserve for the **Regiment** commander. An attack that was to start at 0600 hours from Dikowka along the rail line toward Pantajowka with the **Aufklaerungs-Abteilung 11** and **Abteilung von Sievers** didn't start at the ordered time because of fog, and the plan was completely abandoned because the Russians had broken through 10 kilometers east of Snamenka with infantry and strong tank forces. The **Kompanie** knocked out three T34 tanks close to the **Regiment** command post. The **Kompanie** remained to guard the **Regiment** command post in the **Kussel** in positions south and north of the rail line. In the meantime, the strong Russian forces had occupied the village of Konstantinowka. Reconnaissance of the wooded lot to the south of this village by Oberfeldwebel Seifarth revealed that this was also dotted with Russian infantry and anti-tank guns. Oberfeldwebel Seifarth's Panther was knocked out and burned out. Another Panther was hit by anti-tank gunfire, and all were hit by heavy anti-tank rifle fire. The Russian infantry were effectively engaged with high explosive shells and a T34 tank was knocked out. In the interim, a strong Russian attack came out of the north. One of our Panthers was lost by a direct hit from 17.2 cm artillery. Up to now, in most cases the radio operators and drivers were severely wounded in all of our Panther losses.

In accordance with an orientation about 1700 hours, all elements to the east of us were pulled back in the evening on line with the Regiment command post in order to establish a hedgehog position to protect the retiring movement from Snamenka. A **Panzer-Grenadier-Bataillon**, the 1. and 2.Kompanie/Panzer-Regiment 31, and four **Pz.Kpfw.IV lang** from **Panzer-Regiment 15** were available. Local command of the Panzer elements was taken over by Hauptmann Graf Rothkirch. This order was changed at 1900 hours by an order that all elements were to be pulled back immediately on line with Orlowa Balka. All Panzers that had mechanical problems were to be driven to the rear immediately. The two Panthers still remaining with the **2.Kompanie** were to break through to **Panzer-Regiment 15** at Patrowe.

On 8 December 1942 at 0230 hours, the **Regiment** marched off to catch the Russians that had broken through near Sarudnyj Bairak about 16 kilometers south of Snamenka. The Panzer elements of the **Regiment** moved south of the **Rollbahn** toward Nowaja Praga. The planned action didn't occur because the Russians hadn't advanced far enough. The **2.Kompanie** was released to return to their **Abteilung** in Sarudnyj Bairuk.

Achievements of the **2.Kompanie** during the period from 5 to 8 December 1943:

Name	T34 Tanks	Assault Guns	AT Guns	AA Guns	Mortars	Trucks
Hauptmann Graf Rothkirch	5					
Leutnant Kretschmer	4		2		1	1
Leutnant Klepper	1		2			
Oberfeldwebel Seifarth	3	1				
Feldwebel Buss	3					
Feldwebel Ruppe	1					1
Unteroffizier Grundmann	2		1			
Unteroffizier Moritz	2		1	1	1	2
Total:	21	1	6	1	2	4

The following report by the Abteilung commander, Major Gierga, on the combat actions of **schwere Panzer-Abteilung 509** from 19 December to 31 December 1943 reveals the problems faced in fighting with Tigers without adequate logistical and tactical support:

Part I - At midday on 18 December, the **Abteilung** received orders to join **Kampfgruppe Schulz** and to advance from Jasowka (about 40 kilometers southeast of Korosten), through Fortunatowka, east past Ustinowka toward Ssloboda on the Irscha River to relieve both of the divisions attacking eastward toward Tschepowitschi.

On orders from the **7.Panzer-Division**, the **Kampfgruppe** started off from the assembly area north of Janowka at about 0800 hours and encountered a strong anti-tank defense and mines in the south side of Fortunatowka. Three of the Tigers attacking in the front line ran onto mines.

Leaving elements to provide protective fire in the south side of Fortunatowka, the **Abteilung** then attacked the village from the east and captured it. After a mop-up of the village with infantry supported by Panzers, the attack continued toward the north. Ustinowka was strongly occupied by the enemy and was bypassed on the left. Also, the forest east of Ustinowka was so strongly occupied by the enemy that the attack was brought to a halt in the evening hours. During the night, the infantry were supposed to build a bridgehead over the Sdriwlja east of Ustinowka, and then in the morning the attack was to be renewed in accordance with the previous orders.

Achievements: Six tanks, five anti-tank guns, and about 100 Russians destroyed.

Our losses: Seven Panzers temporarily out of action due to damage from mines and hits. Two officers and three men wounded.

During the night, the infantry reported that the bridgehead had been created, whereupon the attack of the armored **Kampfgruppe** was ordered for the morning of 20 December.

The **Kampfgruppe** was already subjected to heavy anti-tank gun fire as they approached the bridge. Because of the forest the field of fire was hardly 100 meters. The ordered attack was started. After crossing the bridge, the Tigers received such heavy defensive fire from close range (about 50 to 200 meters) that at this location four Tiger were already temporarily out of action due to hits on the gun and running gear as well as two clean penetrations of the front and side. Our own infantry (**Kampfgruppe Wischeropp**) followed the Panzer attack extremely slowly and combed through the patch of woods so poorly that the Russians there were not eliminated at all.

Therefore, the **Kampfgruppe** received continuous heavy defensive fire in the left flank and front as they continued advancing north to the east of this patch of woods. During the further advance, six additional Tigers fell out due to the heavy fire from anti-tank guns and tanks. Then the **Kampfgruppe** commander, Oberst Schultz, halted any further advance in this terrain, which was totally unsuitable for Panzers. At nightfall, the **Abteilung** was pulled back to the area east of Fortunatowka.

Achievement: Six tanks and 12 anti-tank guns destroyed.

Our losses: Ten Tigers temporarily out of action due to heavy damage from hits. One officer and eight men wounded.

Recovery of all of the Tigers, which in part were immobilized from hits, was accomplished with the greatest difficulty.

On the morning of 23 December, four Tigers were detached to **Kampfgruppe Knoblauch** to gain a defensive line for the infantry. The **Kampfgruppe** accomplished their task without noticeable enemy resistance.

At 1100 hours on 24 December, the **Abteilung** received orders that they were attached to the **8.Panzer-Division** and were to move immediately to Kotscherowo east of Shitomir (about 90 kilometers). Seventeen Tigers were operational. The **Abteilung** arrived in Shitomir during the night and worked through the entire night on maintenance. At dawn they started the move to Kotscherowo. As the commander, driving in the lead, arrived near Kotscherowo there was still only one **Kampfgruppe** from the **8.Panzer-Division** in action, under the command of Major von Mitzlaff. Nothing could be learned about the location of the division headquarters. Through getting in contact with the division supply officer, who was found in Korostyschew, the **Abteilung** commander learned that in the interim the **Korps** had ordered that **Panzer-Abteilung 509** be attached to the **1.Panzer-Division**.

This was confirmed when the commander got in contact with the commander of the **1.Panzer-Division** in Korostychew, and the **Tiger-Abteilung** was attached to **Kampfgruppe Neumeister**. They were ordered for the time being to remain in Krostyschew at the disposal of the **Kampfgruppe**. About 1300 hours, the **Abteilung** received an order from **Kampfgruppe** commander Neumeister to advance and join **Kampfgruppe Mitzlaf** of the **8.Panzer-Division** and under all circumstances to hold the area on the **Rollbahn** from Shitomir to Kiev about 9 kilometers west of Kotscherowo. The **Tiger-Abteilung** pulled forward to **Kampfgruppe von Mitzlaff** and went into position on both sides of the **Rollbahn** so that any enemy attack from the east could be repulsed. **Kampfgruppe Mitzlaff**, which had suffered heavy casualties for a few days and was missing almost all of their heavy weapons, still only possessed abnormally weak combat strength.

During the night of 25 and 26 December, the infantry guards in front of the Tigers fled back into the woods when a few enemy tanks appeared; thus the **Tiger-Abteilung** had to move forward and remain stationary without any infantry defenders. Some of the crews dismounted and took over the

infantry defense and fired at the Russians who came within short range (20 to 50 meters). The defensive line was held. It was very difficult to bring up our own infantry to positions on line with the Tigers during the night. The enemy occupants on the edge of the forest opposite were noticeably reinforced. Now and then, the enemy felt their way forward along the road with several tanks.

At 0600 hours on 26 December, the **Tiger-Abteilung** received orders from **Kampfgruppe** commander Oberstleutnant Neumeister (commander of a **Panzer-Grenadier-Regiment** in the **1.Panzer-Division**) for the main part of the **Abteilung** (7 Tigers) and a **Bataillon** mounted on **S.P.W.** (14 **S.P.W.**) to start north from their present positions, moving through Foschtschewka, north around the patch of woods lying to the north of it, then advance southwest along the Dudowik and fall on the rear of the enemy. At the same time, **Kampfgruppe Mitzlaff** and a **Bataillon** from **Regiment Neumeister** was to attack frontally and then occupy the new position on the Dudowik. On orders from the **Kampfgruppe** commander, three Tigers had to remain with the frontally attacking elements. The commander of the **Tiger-Abteilung** informed the **Kampfgruppe** commander of the difficulty of this undertaking, because from a review of maps it was apparent that the terrain was totally unsuitable for Panzers. The reply was that it was an order from above that had to be followed.

About 0900 hours, the **Tiger-Abteilung** started off and reached the river bank without encountering any substantial enemy resistance. During the further advance along the bank, the **Abteilung** received intensely heavy defensive fire from tanks, assault guns, and anti-tank guns from close range (300 to 1000 meters). Because the field of view and field of fire were extraordinarily poor, it was possible for the **Abteilung** to return the fire only after some of the defenders weapons were spotted by their muzzle flashes. Two Tigers became stuck in the rough terrain and were also immobilized by hits. The **Abteilung** managed to knock out four tanks, three anti-tank guns, and two assault guns. The **Abteilung** reported the strong defense to the **Kampfgruppe** commander and asked how far forward the frontally attacking infantry had come and, based on the development of the situation, if the original task was to be held, too. The **Abteilung** received the reply that the **Kampfgruppe** commander wasn't aware of how far the infantry had advanced because at the moment he wasn't in contact with them, and that the original orders stood. Somewhat later, the **Abteilung** received the news that our own infantry had not even left their starting positions because of the heavy defensive fire. Because under these conditions the **Tiger-Abteilung** was attracting the entire defensive fire, the commander declined to advance any farther and reported this to the **Kampfgruppe** commander, who was far behind (about 1000 meters) our own infantry who were to have attacked. At the same time, an alarm call came in to the **Abteilung** to immediately turn back to the starting point because the **Rollbahn** between us and Korostyschew had just been cut. The **Abteilung** failed in their attempt to recover the

Tigers that were stuck and immobilized by hits because the running gear was too heavily damaged and the Tigers lay under continuous heavy fire from artillery and anti-tank guns. As a result, parts that were still usable were retrieved from inside the Tigers, which were blown up under orders from the *Abteilung* commander.

The *Abteilung* turned back to the starting position and received orders to break through to the west along with the infantry advancing through the woods on both sides of the *Rollbahn* to regain control of the *Rollbahn*. In the interim, the Russians pushed westward along the *Rollbahn* with strong tank and infantry forces. During the day, one of the three Tigers that had remained behind on the *Rollbahn* was immobilized by a hit. However, these three Tigers remained in their positions and continued to fight bitterly until the last German unit had retreated to the west. During this fight, the immobilized Tiger received such heavy fire that it was totally destroyed. Even though heavily damaged, both of the other Tigers could follow the *Abteilung* under their own power. After arriving at Korostyschew, the *Abteilung* was attached to **Panzer-Regiment 1** under the command of Major Phillipp.

Achievement: Four tanks, three anti-tank guns, and two assault guns knocked out.

Our losses: Four Tigers lost as total write-offs, four additional Tigers heavily damaged. One officer and seven men killed. Six men wounded.

At 1030 hours on 27 December, the *Abteilung* received orders that they were directly attached to the **Armee Oberkommando** and all operational elements were to move to Berditschew. The *Abteilung* had seven operational Tigers, and an additional seven were on the way from Shitomir. As a result of completely blocked roads, the *Abteilung* arrived in Berditschew at 0800 hours on 28 December with eight Tigers. The others had broken down from mechanical failures along the march. With these eight Tigers the *Abteilung* was ordered to advance against an enemy tank attack on Berbitschew from the east. The *Abteilung* reached the area of Ssadzi, about 10 kilometers east of Berditschew. However, the enemy tanks that had been moving toward Berditschew had turned off toward the southeast. As a result, the *Abteilung* remained near Ssadzi on guard and reported the situation to the **Armee Oberkommando**.

About 1700 hours, the *Abteilung* received orders that they were attached to the **1.Panzer-Division** and were to pull back to the southeast sector of Berditschew. The assignment for the next day was to advance southeast with **Kampfgruppe Losch** and capture the village of Pusyrki-Gurowez. The remaining operational elements of the *Abteilung*, four Tigers, started off with the **Kampfgruppe** at about 0800 hours and encountered strong enemy tank forces in Pusyrki. Nineteen T34 tanks and six trucks were destroyed, four mortars were captured and given to the infantry along with 60 prisoners, and over 100 enemy were killed in Pusyrki by the four operational Tigers.

During the night of 29/30 December, the *Abteilung* was ordered to be combat ready the next morning in the area of Brodezkoje with Panzer elements of **1.Panzer-Division** who were attached to the *Abteilung* in order to build a defensive front with the **1.Panzer-Division** from the crossroads 1 kilometer southeast of Medwedowka to the north up to Berditschew, conduct a Panzer attack to the east at Pljachowa and gain contact with the **18.Artillerie-Division** located there. The *Abteilung* conducted this attack about 1500 hours but encountered only weak enemy resistance. However, the enemy attacked from Kasatin in a northeasterly direction. As a result, a defensive front was established east of Pljachowa with the four Tigers. Because the **Artillerie** cleared out of Pljachowa and pulled back to the south, and the **Flak** at the crossroads also packed up and pulled back south, the Panzer elements were pulled back to the right wing of the **1.Panzer-Division** on the crossroads southeast of Medwedowka and left to reinforce the defenses against the strong enemy forces located to the southeast. The other elements of the **Panzergruppe** remained in the area of Ziegelei east of Brodezkoje because a strong enemy tank force had also been reported in Gluchowzy and in the patch of woods south of there. During the night of 30/31 December, the enemy occupied the village and strong enemy forces advanced to the east toward the crossroads. A section of the Panzers located there was sent out about 800 meters against the enemy and encountered strong enemy anti-tank defenders that had taken up positions east of the village and about 150 infantry advancing along the road. The Panthers destroyed eight anti-tank guns and killed about 100 Russians, following which the Russians pulled back into the village and dug in. Further advance was not possible because the necessary infantry forces to support it were not available.

During the afternoon a strong enemy infantry and tank group of about two regiments of infantry and 32 counted tanks moved southeast of Gluchowz. As a result, the right wing of the **1.Panzer-Division** was left strongly defended by Panzers and after a conference with the commander of the **Kampfgruppe** farthest to the south, a strong defensive position was abandoned on the crossroads west of Wowtschinez on the right wing of the division.

Part II - During the continuous employment of the *Abteilung*, attacking during the day and on guard at night, at times it became necessary to supply the crews with medication to prevent them from falling asleep at night. At the present time, there are very few **Panzer-Grenadier** units, who, unless they know there are Panzers behind them, will not hold and defend captured positions or hold out to defend their ordered defensive sectors during enemy attacks. During the last 14 days, the *Abteilung* had to use elements to stand guard every night (usually everything that was operational) and in addition had to take over the local defense of the Tigers during the night by the **8.Panzer-Division**. Every unit, which spots a Tiger, cries out for it to hold the defense. The commanders of the **Kampfgruppen** and divisions are largely in agreement with them. Their few defensive weapons often *makes it necessary to reinforce them with Tigers. Still, in most cases, the Tigers were held ready for action close behind the infantry and were not employed continuously in the foremost defensive line.*

*Also, if it is not possible to pull the **Tiger-Abteilung** out of action for a short period for maintenance, an attempt must be made on the part of higher commanders to give the **Abteilung** a chance to accomplish repair work directly behind the front line.*

*Frequently changing the higher command to which the **Abteilung** was assigned has worked out to be especially disadvantageous to the **Abteilung**. The divisions to which the **Abteilung** was attached know that this is only for a short time and therefore do not have the same interest in the **Abteilung** as in their own units.*

*In no way is the recovery service in the **Abteilung** adequate, especially during battles while retreating. As an example, 12 Tigers requiring short-term repairs were located with the **Werkstatt** in Gorbulew when this village suddenly had to be evacuated. The four operational **Zugmaschinen** were just enough to tow one Tiger. All the other Tigers had to be towed by other Tigers. Tigers are unsuitable for this and as a result weren't available for combat. The other point is that towing other Tigers led to major damage to their engines, clutches, and transmissions. After our own infantry had already pulled out, only through a major effort did the **Abteilung** succeed in towing all of the Tigers with the exception of the two Tigers that had been burned out. Both of the burned-out Tigers were completely cannibalized and destroyed. Just when these Tigers were towed into Shitomir, at the last moment orders were received to evacuate Shitomir and pull back farther to the west. In part, this evacuation had to be conducted under enemy action because there were now 20 Tigers that needed to be towed. Up to now, this evacuation has succeeded to the west of Berditschew. But two Tigers were lost as a result of damage from hits and couldn't be recovered. If the commander of the **Abteilung**, who should and must constantly be found with the elements employed forward, is not oriented on the overall situation that makes an evacuation of the **Werkstatt** necessary, and this evacuation can not be started until as late as in both the Shitomir and Gorbulew cases, the **Abteilung** commander must decline responsibility for evacuation of Tigers that can't be towed because of enemy activity. Even so, as far as possible, elements of the **Bergezuege** of the **Korps** and the **Armee** must be placed at their disposal because the recovery services available within the **Abteilung** aren't even sufficient to recover those Tigers that are knocked out in action.*

*During the tactical employment of the **Tiger-Abteilung**, the **Kampfgruppe** commander must be found frequently forward with the Tigers and lead based on what he personally sees. It is impossible to correctly employ this important weapon if the commander is located far behind the last element of the **Kampfgruppe**, as was Oberstleutnant Neumeister on 26 December. It is impossible to lead by radio.*

The final report from **Panzer-Abteilung 116** in the **16.Panzer-Grenadier-Division** for the period from 1 July 1943 to 31 January 1944 reveals that a normal **Panzer-Abteilung** outfitted mainly with **Pz.Kpfw.IIIs** and a few **Pz.Kpfw.IVs** handled by experienced crews was tactically superior to the Russian tank brigades outfitted with T34 tanks. They achieved a very high kill ratio for each Panzer lost, as shown in the following statistics:

*During the period from 1 July 1943 to 31 January 1944, the combat elements of **Panzer-Abteilung 116** fought 76 battles along a stretch of 3020 kilometers. They managed to destroy:*

2 J.B.2 aircraft	
251 enemy tanks	(2 KW-I, 12 12.2 cm assault guns, 227 T34, 1 General Lee, 1 T60, and 8 T70)
245 guns	(12 12.2 cm guns, 40 7.62 cm guns, 147 7.62 cm anti-tank guns, 43 4.5 cm anti-tank guns, and 10 7.62 cm anti-aircraft guns)
87 mortars	
164 anti-tank rifles	
34 trucks	

4,680 enemy killed and 435 captured very many uncounted pony carts, horses, and infantry weapons.

Our losses:

Personnel:	Officers	Men
killed	4	39
wounded	16	176
missing	0	14

*Equipment: 37 Panzers (1 **Pz.Kpfw.II**, 26 **Pz.Kpfw.III**, 7 **Pz.Kpfw.IV**, 2 **Pz.Bef.Wg.**, 1 **Pz.Kpfw.III 7.5 cm kurz**) of which 21 were destroyed by hits, 2 were knocked out by hits and fell into enemy hands because of a shortage of recovery vehicles, 8 broke down mechanically and were destroyed with explosive charges, and 6 broke down mechanically but were not destroyed.*

Fuel consumption:	357,850	liters
Ammunition expenditure:	4,687	**Sprgr.Patr. 7.5 cm (lang)**
	1,798	**Pzgr.Patr. 7.5 cm (lang)**
	1,237	**Hl/B 7.5 cm (lang)**
	99	**HL/B 7.5 cm (kurz)**
	39	**Pzgr.Patr. 7.5 cm (kurz)**
	5,700	**Sprgr.Patr 5 cm (lang)**
	2,845	**Pzgr.Patr. 5 cm (lang)**
	219,140	**Schuss M.G.-Munition**

In the March issue of "**Notizen fuer Panzertruppen**" (Notes for the Panzer Troops), the **Generalinspekteur der Panzertruppen**, General Guderian, included the following combat report from an unidentified **Panther-Abteilung** (which may have been the **I.Abteilung/Panzer-Regiment 1**):

The last operation of the **Abteilung**, during which 30 Panthers were continuously in action for six consecutive days, confirmed the excellent performance of the **Pz.Kpfw.V** (Panther). A very great deal can be done with a well-trained crew, careful maintenance and tactically correct employment. During these six days, the battalion destroyed 89 tanks and assault guns, 150 guns, etc.

In spite of massed enemy defenses there were only six "total write-offs" due to enemy fire. The following lessons were learned from these operations:

The great range of the gun must be exploited under all circumstances. Fire can be opened at a range of 2000 meters. Almost all the targets destroyed (heavy weapons and tanks) were engaged at ranges from 1500 to 2000 meters. Ammunition expenditure was relatively low. Every fourth or fifth round was a hit, even with high explosive rounds.

The hitherto accepted attack formations (arrowhead, broad arrowhead) with their normal distances and intervals should not be employed with Panthers. Intervals and distances for these formations must be at least doubled. At the same time, there must be closer teamwork.

Exposing the Panther to enemy fire at close range must be avoided at all costs. To this end, battle reconnaissance must be pushed forward. One useful method was to send one Panther troop about 1000 to 2000 meters ahead in order to draw enemy fire, thus giving the main body a chance to open up at its effective range.

Flank protection is vitally necessary for the Panther, which is vulnerable from the sides. The unit commander must always have a reserve of Panthers on which he can call for immediate neutralization of any flank threat. Pulling back elements from the leading tanks is always too late for a task of this kind. Normally, the reserve moves forward some 1000 meters to the rear of the main body.

During employment as a complete regiment, a tactic found to be very successful was for the Pz.Kpfw.IVs to take over flank protection while the Panthers drove on ahead with undiminished speed as the spearhead.

Massed employment (which was generally possible for the **Abteilung** in fighting east of A) clearly had a shattering effect on the enemy's morale. Concentrated fire on inhabited localities was frequently practiced, leading to the Russians'

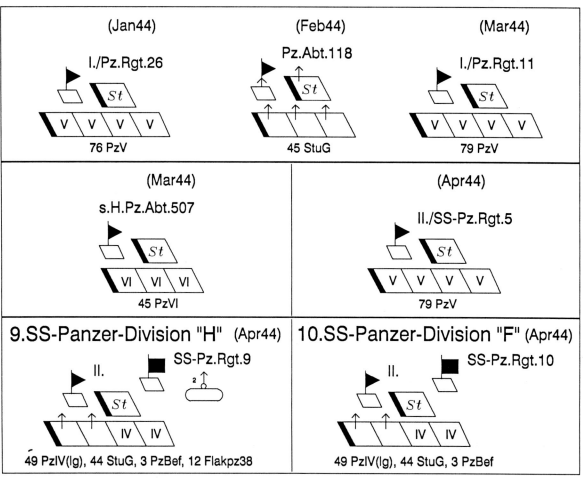

ORGANIZATION AND STRENGTH OF PANZER UNITS
REPLACEMENT UNITS SENT TO EASTERN FRONT

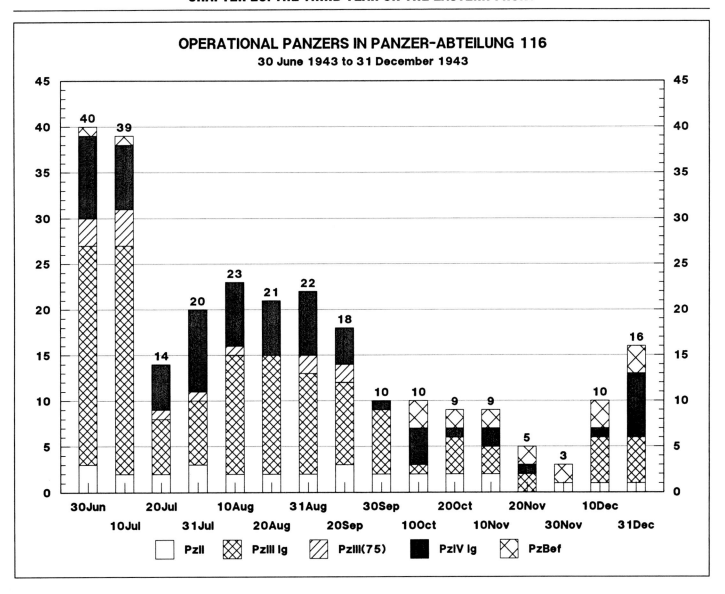

OPERATIONAL PANZERS IN PANZER-ABTEILUNG 116
30 June 1943 to 31 December 1943

hastily abandoning their heavy weapons. Tank crews caught in this way sometimes abandoned their T34s before the tanks were hit! Concentrations of this type should include both high explosive and armor-piercing shells. The number of rounds to be fired by each Panther should be ordered by the commander over the radio net. Interrogations of prisoners of war show that the Russian is extremely impressed by the trajectory of the **7,5 cm Kw.K.42** gun. The Russians avoid an open clash with Panthers unless he has superiority in numbers.

In spite of improved engine performance (the **Abteilung** traveled an average of 700 kilometers per Panther with only 11 engines being replaced), for marches of more than 100 kilometers, the Panthers should be transported by rail, because the track is considerably strained especially in winter.

Remarks by the **Generalinspekteur der Panzertruppen**: The report is approved in its entirety. It contains a number of essential principles for the successful employment of Panther formations, particularly the following:

1. Extended formations in attack. The report emphasizes that normal intervals should be doubled.

2. Panthers can stop the enemy from getting too close in. Their strength is long-range firing (up to 2500 meters and above). Hence, battle reconnaissance should be pushed forward early. In tank formations this is too often neglected. However, it can be decisive. This holds true for all tanks.

3. Flank protection for Panthers should be established by other tanks, self-propelled guns and **Panzer-Grenadiere**.

4. Contrary to the established practice, at last this **Abteilung** was employed as a body. This consolidated formation is the reason for its special success. By itself, this method guarantees rapid and decisive results.

5. Concentrating fire on important targets is the principle laid down in the new gunnery manual for the Panther. It has been infrequently applied up to now, but it will clearly be very successful.

6. Rail transport should be used at every opportunity in view of the present short lifespan of the tank engine.

A **Befehls-Panther Ausf.A** approaching a burning village. (BA)

Tigers of the **schwere Panzer-Abteilung 507** in an assembly area preparing for an attack on Tarnopol in April 1944. (BA)

The following report was written by the **20.Panzer-Division** on 8 March 1944 on their combat experience during recent defensive battles:

Detailed scouting of the terrain is necessary for both offensive and defense operations. Panzer crews may not be asked to attack when it is already known in advance that they will soon be bogged down in a marsh. Even if the **Panzer-Grenadier** attack is stopped, Panzers may not be sent ahead when the terrain isn't suitable. This invariably leads to losses.

Often the statement is made: "But T34 tanks drive through!" We can't accomplish this with the few available Panzers, or at the very start of an attack most of the Panzers would be stuck in the marshy ground and be shot up.

An attack against enemy positions prepared for defense cannot be conducted with the Panzers in the lead. The **Panzer-Grenadiere** carry this battle, and Panzers support them by providing covering fire. If it is necessary to drive forward during the attack, sufficient Panzers are to be employed to cover and guard the advancing Panzers. It is especially important to provide them with mine-detecting troops.

If the **Panzer-Grenadier** attack is pinned down by heavy artillery fire, in most cases it will not be possible to succeed even with Panzers, because where Russians have organized a defense, they always have many anti-tank weapons.

In addition, don't ask for the impossible from the Panzers!

The statement: "You are armored; therefore drive forward" is ridiculous. The Panzers quickly attract enemy fire onto themselves and fall out quicker than the **Panzer-Grenadier**, who utilizes the terrain for cover and camouflage.

In the preparations for an attack, every detail should be discussed with the **Panzer-Grenadiere**. Success always occurred in situations when both the Panzer and **Panzer-Grenadier** units clearly understood each other and were in agreement. Good camaraderie between the Panzer crews and the **Panzer-Grenadiere** (as well as the **Artillerie**) is by itself a prerequisite for success.

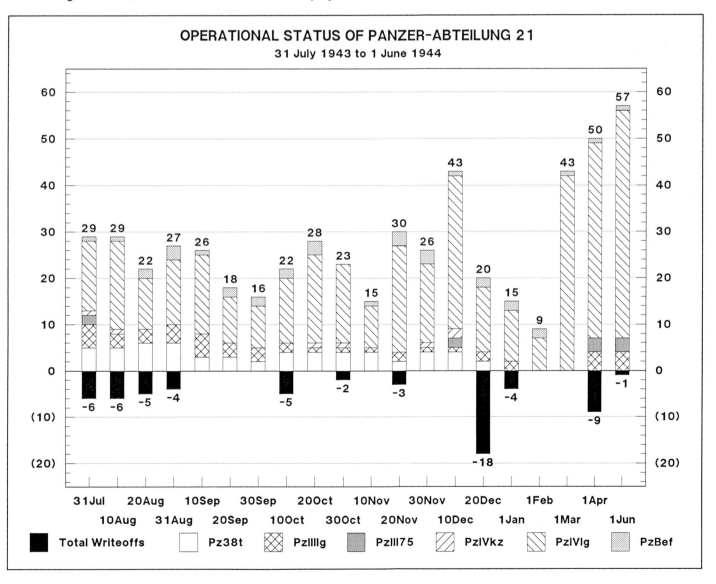

After reaching the objective, the Panzers should not remain up front but should be pulled back to stand ready for concentrated counterattacks. This is not always possible! After a difficult attack, our mostly weak battalions are in danger of being beaten back by counterattacks from the opponent, who is always far superior in number.

After reaching the objective, organization of the defense always takes a certain amount of time. Immediate counterattacks by the enemy are therefore extremely dangerous. The Panzers must remain forward in defensive **Schwerpunkten** in order to provide the backstop for the tired **Panzer-Grenadiere** and to immediately counterattack and defeat any enemy penetration.

Only after the defense is basically organized, anti-tank weapons and artillery completely prepared for defense, can the Panzers be pulled back to their assembly areas.

In many cases during recent battles, Panzers were used to compensate for the low infantry strength and the shortage of maneuverable self-propelled anti-tank guns. Therefore they were inevitably split up into small groups of three or four Panzers. It was shown that such small groups, correctly employed, can be thoroughly effective on defense. But they must not be asked to conduct absurd attacks. This type of demand must be decisively objected to. Massive employment, firepower, and shock value are not present!

When there were favorable ground conditions, several times a Panzer attack at night was shown to be completely successful. The Russians were especially allergic to the sound of Panzers at night. With his numerous anti-tank rifles and guns, the enemy defense is less effective when the targets can't be seen. Usually, the Panzers and **Panzer-Grenadiere** had hardly any losses.

During enemy attacks supported by tanks, the **Infanterie** and the **Artillerie** defense must be directed against the enemy infantry. The **Pak** and Panzers deal with the enemy tanks by themselves.

It has continuously been shown that when they are correctly employed tactically, even when fewer in number, German Panzers are superior to the Russian tanks. The Russians frequently still blindly charge. For example, they attack with infantry riding on the tanks across open terrain against a position from which they have already been repulsed many times. However, on repeated occasions the Russians have also shown organized tank attacks using fire and movement tactics!

27

Defense of Italy

Southern Italy was defended by the **10.Armee** with **Panzer-Division Hermann Goering**, the **15.Panzer-Grenadier-Division**, and the **29.Panzer-Grenadier-Division**, which had returned from Sicily, as well as the **16.** and **26.Panzer-Divisions**. The other divisions located in central and northern Italy, including the **3.Panzer-Grenadier-Division**, **24.Panzer-Division**, and **SS-Panzer-Grenadier-Division "LSSAH"**, were subsequently involved with the disarmament of the Italian army. Both the **24.Panzer-Division** and the **SS-Panzer-Grenadier-Division "LSSAH"** were transferred to the Eastern Front in the Fall of 1943 and did not engage the Allied armies in Italy. The **90.Panzer-Grenadier-Division**, which had been formed on Sardinia, was transferred to Corsica and only later to mainland Italy in September 1943.

Pursuing the retreat out of Sicily, the Allies crossed into Italy at the straits of Messina and then landed at Salerno in early September 1943. After successfully capturing Naples, the Allied forces moved northward, conquering all of southern Italy. The style that the Panzer tactics evolved in the rugged terrain of southern Italy are revealed in the following combat reports from the **III.Abteilung/Panzer-Regiment Hermann Goering** and **Panzer-Kompanien** in the **II.Abteilung/Panzer-Regiment 26**.

The **III.Abteilung/Panzer-Regiment Hermann Goering** outfitted with **Sturmgeschuetze** had been very successful in knocking out tanks in Sicily, claiming to have destroyed 56 tanks as compared to a loss of four **Sturmgeschuetze** and three **Sturmhaubitze** from all causes. However, they ran into difficulties in applying the tactics necessary to successfully combat enemy tanks, as related by the following report from the **11.(Sturmgeschuetz) Batterie/Panzer-Regiment Hermann Goering**:

*On 2 October 1943, the **11.Batterie** was attached to **Abteilung Rossmann** and employed in the Cardito area. Two **Sturmgeschuetz** stood as an advanced **Stuetzpunkt** under*

A **Pz.Kpfw.IV Ausf.H** of the **7.Kompanie/Panzer-Regiment Hermann Goering** moving through an Italian village in October 1943. (BA)

ORGANIZATION AND STRENGTH OF PANZER UNITS FOR DEFENSE OF ITALY ON 20 AUGUST 1943

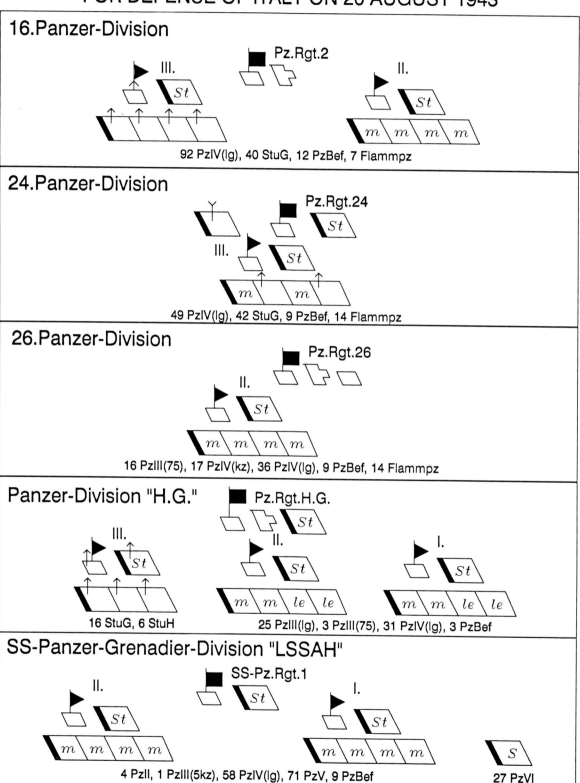

16.Panzer-Division

Pz.Rgt.2

92 PzIV(lg), 40 StuG, 12 PzBef, 7 Flammpz

24.Panzer-Division

Pz.Rgt.24

49 PzIV(lg), 42 StuG, 9 PzBef, 14 Flammpz

26.Panzer-Division

Pz.Rgt.26

16 PzIII(75), 17 PzIV(kz), 36 PzIV(lg), 9 PzBef, 14 Flammpz

Panzer-Division "H.G."

Pz.Rgt.H.G.

16 StuG, 6 StuH   25 PzIII(lg), 3 PzIII(75), 31 PzIV(lg), 3 PzBef

SS-Panzer-Grenadier-Division "LSSAH"

SS-Pz.Rgt.1

4 PzII, 1 PzIII(5kz), 58 PzIV(lg), 71 PzV, 9 PzBef   27 PzVI

ORGANIZATION AND STRENGTH OF PANZER UNITS FOR DEFENSE OF ITALY ON 20 AUGUST 1943

3.Panzer-Grenadier-Division

Pz.Abt.103

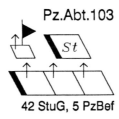

42 StuG, 5 PzBef

15.Panzer-Grenadier-Division

Pz.Abt.215

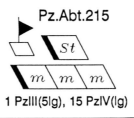

1 PzIII(5lg), 15 PzIV(lg)

29.Panzer-Grenadier-Division

Pz.Abt.129

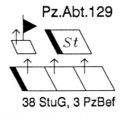

38 StuG, 3 PzBef

90.Panzer-Grenadier-Division

Pz.Abt.190

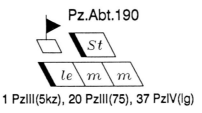

1 PzIII(5kz), 20 PzIII(75), 37 PzIV(lg)

the command of Wn. Boerner at the road fork for Cardito-Aftragola-Cosovia. The **Zug** under Stwn. Schulze-Ostwald stood with two **Sturmgeschuetz** on the south edge of Cardito. **Zug Wallhaeusser** with two **Sturmgeschuetz** was on guard 2 kilometers east of Carditio. The **Sturmgeschuetz** commanded by Schulte was positioned 1 kilometer east of Cardito on guard toward the southeast.

Up to 1745 hours, no combat activity occurred near the **Batterie**. At 1745 hours, Leutnant Winkler of the **Aufklaer-ungs-Abteilung** reported the approach of enemy tanks from the direction of Afragola. About 1800 hours, Oberleutnant

Jekosch and Leutnant Roebig rode forward on a motorcycle with sidecar to establish contact with **Zug Boerner**, which had become surrounded. Six kilometers south of Carditio, enemy tanks fired at the motorcycle, killing Leutnant Roebig and wounding Oberleutnant Jekosch and the motorcycle driver.

After knocking out two enemy tanks, **Zug Boerner** slugged its way through to Cardito. **Sturmgeschuetz** Schulze-Oswald shot up the Sherman tank that had fired at the **Batterie** commander's motorcycle. After Oberleutnant Jekosch was wounded, Stwn. Schulze-Oswald took over command of **Zug**

Schulze-Ostwald and *Zug Boerner* and ordered the consolidation of these *Sturmgeschuetz* on the south side of Cardito.

Sounds from tracked vehicles were heard continuously from 1900 to 2100 hours, apparently from enemy tanks. The approach of 25 to 30 tanks was suspected.

Two scouting patrols requested by Hauptmann Luebke from Stwn. Schulze-Ostwald brought back no additional information. Two further scouting patrols sent out by Stwm. Schultz-Ostwald himself were also unsuccessful. It was conjectured that the scouting patrols had not gone out far enough.

Results: 3 Sherman heavy tanks knocked out, two trucks carrying infantry destroyed, pursuing infantry repulsed with machine gun fire.

Losses: No equipment losses.

On 3 October 1943, the **11.Batterie** was attached to **Abteilung Rosmann** and still located in yesterday's sector. In the early morning hours, the enemy attempted to break through our forward line near Caivano. The *Sturmgeschuetz* of Leutnant Wallhaeusser hit and set on fire a Sherman advancing from the flank and knocked out a heavy armored car that came up the road. After this, the enemy ceased attacking in this sector. Further noise from tracked vehicles was heard in the southeast and faded out as they moved north.

About 1600 hours, strong enemy infantry and tank forces broke through near Cardito. The two *Sturmgeschuetz* in advanced positions pulled back a piece after some of the crew members were wounded during the heavy rolling artillery barrages.

On orders from Hauptmann Luebke, all troops were pulled back to the north edge of Caivano in order to prepare for a counterattack. The counterattack reached its intended objective, the south side of Caivano. During a continued advance toward the north side of Cardito, on orders from Hauptmann Luebke, two *Sturmgeschuetz* had to pull into an unfavorable firing position. Before they could take up usable firing positions, they were knocked out at short range by enemy tanks that could aim at them undisturbed. The *Sturmgeschuetz* of Leutnant Wallhaeusser was totally destroyed by three direct hits. The second *Sturmgeschuetz* received two direct hits but managed to pull back under its own power. The third *Sturmgeschuetz* that had been sent in guarded the south side of Caivano from the road to Cardito and made the retreat of the *Zug* on the left possible. The *Sturmgeschuetz* held its position 2 kilometers east of Cardito until nightfall and pulled back to Caivano at about 2115 hours. Another *Sturmgeschuetz* was positioned 700 meters southeast of Cardito to secure a farm path.

During the night, the four *Sturmgeschuetz* moved through Caserta and pulled into a rest area on the Caserta to S.Maria road. At dawn on 4 October, the *Sturmgeschuetz* moved across the Volturno and arrived at the ordered assembly area by Pontelatone-Formicola during the morning.

Results: One Sherman tank hit and set on fire, one heavy armored car knocked out.

Personnel losses: 1 killed, 1 missing, 6 wounded
Equipment losses: 1 **Sturmhaubitze 42** total write-off, 1 **Sturmkanone 40** can't be repaired within 14 days, 1 **Sturmhaubitze 42** can be repaired within 14 days.

Details on the loss of the **Sturmhaubitze 42** were reported by Leutnant Wallhaeusser:

About 1600 hours, after the successful break-in of strong infantry and tank forces near Cardito, on the north side of Caivano, I met Hauptmann Luebke, commander of the **Panzer-Aufklaerungs-Abteilung**, and received orders to lead a counterattack with the available *Sturmgeschuetz*. Two *Sturmgeschuetz*, in which some of the crew members had been wounded, were manned by the crew members of a *Sturmhaubitze* that was out of action because of repeated failure to eject burst shell casings. I climbed into the lead *Sturmgeschuetz* and undertook the ordered counterattack with the other two *Sturmgeschuetz*.

At my request for infantry support, Hauptmann Luecke replied: "On the way, attempt to gather together all available personnel and accomplish the counterattack with these." I rolled slowly through the village with my *Sturmgeschuetz* and reached the south side of Caivano as ordered. On the way, I had collected about 30 infantry, among them a Leutnant from the **3.Kompanie**. I told him that I had orders from Hauptmann Luebke to gather all available personnel together and to hold the south side of Caivano with these and my three *Sturmgeschuetz*. The infantry took up their positions. The enemy blanketed us with heavy mortar fire. After about 10 minutes, the Leutnant from the **3.Kompanie** came and told me that on orders from Hauptmann Luebke we should pull back to the middle of the village. Thereupon I pulled my *Sturmgeschuetz* back about 200 meters to the ordered position.

A short time later, Hauptmann Luebke came and again ordered a counterattack. Now, he himself went along. We advanced past the south edge of Caivano. Shortly before the S-curve between Caivano and Cardito where the view was restricted because of a 2-meter-high wall, I informed Hauptmann Luebke that I must remain here for the interim because I didn't have any field of fire in the S-curve. I received orders to immediately drive through. About 10 meters before the second turn in the S-curve, I halted and sent infantry forward to scout out the area that couldn't be observed from my position. In a short time they came back and reported that several Sherman tanks were standing on the road. Hauptmann Luebke ordered that we should drive out into the field on the right in order to take the enemy tanks under fire. I told Hauptmann Luebke that this was an impossible position because we were hardly 200 meters away from the enemy and would show our flanks while attempting to get into a firing position. Hauptmann Luebke countered: "Immediately drive there. There is only one possibility here, either the Sherman tanks or yours". I drove to the ordered position. The *Sturmgeschuetz* could only pull very slowly through the wet

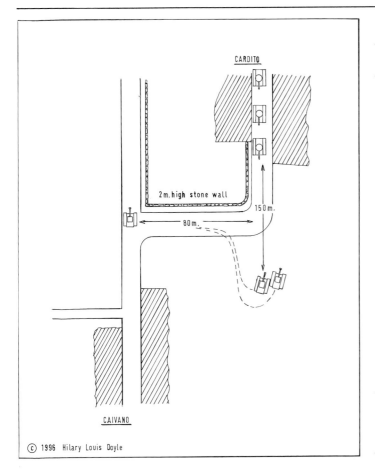

CARDITO

2m.high stone wall

150 m.

80 m.

CAIVANO

© 1996 Hilary Louis Doyle

The **9.Sturmgeschuetz-Kompanie** of **Panzer-Division Hermann Goering** was guarding the roads in the area of Capua. The **Sturmgeschuetz** were already in position for many hours without a single Brit letting himself be spotted. The tank alarm was suddenly given in the afternoon. Four Sherman tanks were reported by the **Grenadiere**. The crews feverishly made everything combat ready for going into action. Soon the sounds of a tank were heard. As the four tanks came closer, the first **Sturmgeschuetz** went onto the attack. The bushes behind which it had stood parted as the **Sturmgeschuetz** drove into firing position in spite of mortar fire attempting to lay down a ring of steel and iron. And finally, one after another, **Panzergranate** left the gun. The first tank was already burning from the second hit. The second tank was immobilized by hits so that the crew abandoned the tank. The third Sherman was hit twice but managed to get away. The fourth Sherman retreated immediately after the first shot was fired. Upset about the failed attack, for about an hour the British artillery pounded the area where the **Sturmgeschuetz** had been located without causing the slightest damage.

Only a little over half of the gun-armed Panzers with the **II.Abteilung/Panzer-Regiment 26** were **Pz.Kpfw.IVs** with 7.5 cm Kw.K. L/48 guns. It still had a significant contingent of **Pz.Kpfw.IIIs** and **Pz.Kpfw.IVs** with the shorter barrelled 7.5 cm Kw.K. L/24 guns. The commander of the **5.Kompanie/ Panzer-Regiment 26** wrote the following after-action report for the period from 30 November to 2 December 1943:

*During the night of 30 November/1 December, five **Pz.Kpfw.IV (L48)** of the **1.Zug** were on guard on the south side of Lanciano. The Panzers remained there for the entire day without any enemy activity. About 1600 hours, these Panzers were sent forward to reconnoiter in the direction of Castelfrentano. Again it didn't result in any enemy activity. During the night of 1/2 December, an additional four **Pz.Kpfw.IV (L48)** and three **Pz.Kpfw.III (L24)** from the **5.Kompanie** pulled forward to Lanciano. During the night, **Grenadiere** in position on the eastern edge of Lanciano were thrown out of their positions by Indian scouting patrols. In combination with our Panzers, they retook their old positions at dawn. Three **Pz.Kpfw.IV (L48)** pulled into hull-down positions in the **Grenadiere** front line. When enemy tanks attacked and three **Pz.Kpfw.III (L24)** and two **Pz.Kpfw.IV (L48)** counterattacked at about 1000 hours, two Panzers in hull-down positions knocked out a Sherman tank at a range of 1200 meters and a Churchill tank at a range of 600 meters.*

*Tendrils of smoke emanated from both tanks at the very first shot. Both of the second shots set the enemy tanks on fire. Heavy clouds of smoke revealed that the tanks were completely destroyed. A few further shots increased the strength of the fire. An hour later the tanks still burned brightly. At the start of the counterattack by the two **Pz.Kpfw.IV (L48)** and three **Pz.Kpfw.III (L24)**, another Churchill was set on fire by a **Pz.Kpfw.III (L24)** firing six **HI-Granate**.*

*and loose soil and hardly made any progress. About five minutes elapsed before we stood in the right place. The enemy tanks, which had shut off their engines, clearly saw our final movements and aimed at us completely undisturbed. In spite of this, I fired the first shot. I was then hit by their first shot not a second later. The engine quit immediately. I wanted to throw out a smoke canister when we were hit a second time. It must have hit on the sloped plate above the driver. The blast caused the roof plate above the gunner to fly off. This shell, which must have been deflected, hit the cupola, bent this inward, and then slowly skidded over my shoulder and hand into the fighting compartment and lay there hissing. I immediately yelled "Raus!". In the same moment, we were hit a third time. I was tossed out by the blast from this hit. I came to again in a roadside ditch about 40 meters away. Two passing infantry soldiers bound my wounds. I don't remember how I got into the roadside ditch. A short time later the second **Sturmgeschuetz** came past; it also had received direct hits but could still move under its own power. I rode back with this **Sturmgeschuetz**.*

But not all defensive actions were as unsuccessful or hampered by tactically incompetent orders. On 28 October 1943, the commander of the **9.(Sturmgeschuetz) Kompanie/ Panzer-Regiment Hermann Goering** reported:

The counterattack was carried forward for a further 10 kilometers, bothered only by enemy artillery fire. Upon arriving at the objective, the lead Panzer reported a large assembly of various types of enemy tanks at a range of 1500 meters at 1400 hours. Our Panzers were hit by heavy fire from enemy artillery, tanks, and anti-tank guns as they took up firing positions. The lead Panzer was hit several times in the right side and immediately went up in flames. The crew managed to get out, with only one man slightly burned. A **Pz.Kpfw.III (L24)** was hit in the running gear twice in rapid succession and was immobilized with only one track. Under covering fire from the other two **Pz.Kpfw.III (L24)** and a **Pz.Kpfw.IV (L48)**, the commander and the radio operator climbed out and freed the tow cable under heavy enemy fire. A **Pz.Kpfw.III (L24)** pulled up to tow the immobilized Panzer. Directly after moving several meters, this Panzer lost a track, and the tow cable parted and had to be replaced. Enemy artillery, tanks, and anti-tank guns continued to fire at us. With the exception of damage to the side **Schuerzen**, antenna, etc., no heavy damage occurred.

After the immobilized Panzer was towed back to the road out of sight of the opponent, both of the Panzers that had provided covering fire left their positions. From then on we were subjected to heavy artillery fire on the entire return trip. Not far from the starting point at a hairpin curve, an enemy anti-tank gun had taken up a position on a ridge and rapidly fired at us as we drove around the curve. The running gear of a **Pz.Kpfw.III (L24)** was damaged, and hits on the armor caused deep dents that pushed in the ammunition racks and ammunition. However, this Panzer could continue under its own power. We again received very heavy barrages from enemy artillery along further stretches. A ricocheting round knocked a head-size hole in the belly of the hull and damaged the fuel pump of the **Pz.Kpfw.III (L24)** being towed. This action came to an end at about 1330 hours.

Around this time, a British armored car, entering the city from the south, ran into the position of an additional **Zug** of four **Pz.Kpfw.IV (L48)**. The enemy armored car was knocked out with three shots.

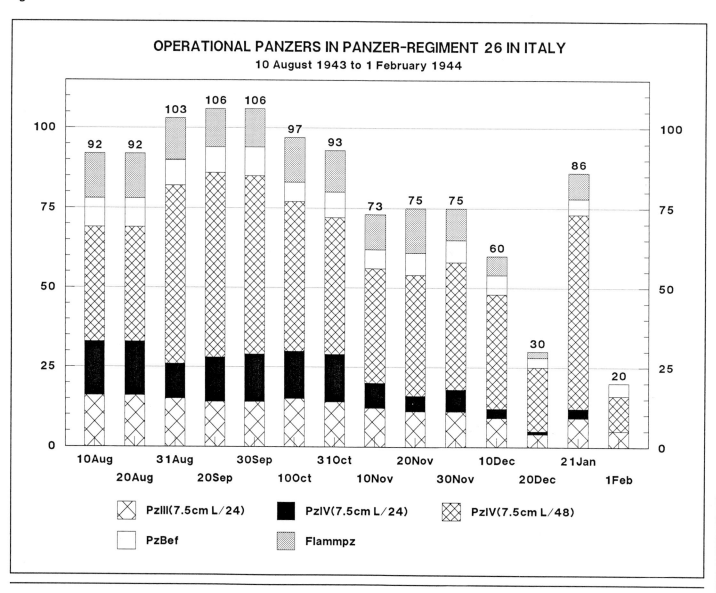

A **Pz.Kpfw.IV Ausf.H** of the **8.Kompanie/Panzer-Regiment 26** with the accompanying infantry riding on the rear deck. (CHY)

The Panzers on the east edge of Lanciano remained in their positions until nightfall. They used their pistols and machine pistols to shoot up several Brits who were creeping forward and took a Brit prisoner after his motorcycle was destroyed. From 1715 to 2345 hours, these Panzers remained in position as the rear guard for the **Grenadiere** who were pulling out. About 1630 hours, a British towing vehicle, wanting to recover the knocked-out armored car on the south side of Lanciano, was halted and captured. Two prisoners were taken, one severely wounded cared for and turned over to the Italians. At X-hour, this **Zug** pulled out of this position.

During the morning of 1 December, we looked into a bunker that had previously been occupied by infantry and was again occupied by the **I./Grenadier-Regiment 67** and found

M.G.42s, anti-tank guns, mortars, machine pistols, carbines, and pistols along with a large amount of ammunition for these weapons, mines, field kitchens, food, clothing, packs, and written messages. This all pointed to an extraordinarily disorderly retreat without cause. One of our Panzers had been blown up in Lanciano during this panic.

The commander of the **7.Kompanie/Panzer-Regiment 26**, Oberleutnant Ruckdeschel, reported on their attack on Ruatti on 6 December 1943:

About 0920 hours on 6 December 1943, the **Kompanie** was alerted to throw out the enemy with tanks who had entered Ruatti. Our combat strength was seven **Pz.Kpfw.IV 7.5** *cm Kw.K. lang* and two *Pz.Kpfw.III 7.5 cm Kw.K. kurz*. The *Kompanie* left their quarters at about 0940 and reached the area north of Point 155, 2 kilometers southwest of Ruatti. Here the situation was discussed with the commander of *Grenadier-Regiments 200* who occupied this sector. However, I couldn't obtain a clear picture of the enemy strength in Ruatti. It then took a long time before the *Grenadiere* who were to accompany our attack arrived. The earliest we could start to attack was at about 1400 hours.

The *Kompanie* drove along the road up to the trail that led northeastward toward Ruatti. From here on, the *Kompanie* fanned out to a wide formation along the left side of the trail and rolled toward Ruatti with one *Zug* echeloned back and one *Zug* echeloned to the side. Even though the ground was level, because of the heavy mud we could advance only in first gear. The olive trees and relatively high grapevines deprived the commanders of any field of view. In addition, we encountered relatively thick fog at times, so that at times one could see less than 100 meters. The *Grenadiere* followed well and conducted themselves splendidly.

The *Kompanie* had approached within about 200 meters of Ruatti when suddenly a hellish fire struck us. *Panzer 724* was hit, apparently in the fuel tank, and immediately burned. The *Kompanie* returned fire from all weapons. Naturally, we could shoot only in the direction of spotted muzzle flashes, because nothing could be recognized due to the dense trees. The enemy initiated massive defensive fire. In addition, we were subjected to well-placed heavy artillery fire. *Panzer 725* was immobilized by hits (right track off), immediately followed by the turret being hit. *Panzer 733* fell out almost at the same time due to a hit in the gearbox. The six Panzers still remaining in the *Kompanie* rolled toward the village using fire and movement tactics, while keeping up a lively fire in the direction of the muzzle flashes because one still could not recognize anything else. A house in the village started to burn. *Panzer 722*, which had driven out to the right over the trail, spotted and fired at 30 enemy infantry clustered together. They may have been wounded for the most part. After turning onto the trail, the commander spotted an enemy tank on the edge of the village which he knocked out with three shots.

While keeping up a lively rate of fire, the rest of the *Kompanie* had worked forward by rushes up to about 50 meters from the village. They fired at houses occupied by enemy infantry. *Panzer 721* was hit several times on the turret, causing the gun to fly back into the fighting compartment. Directly in front of the village, we spotted another enemy tank standing broadside to us with its gun aimed at us; however, he wasn't firing anymore. It is presumed that he was knocked out by us. Driving on the left wing, *Panzer 734* silenced two weapons in separate positions that had been recognized by their muzzle flashes. It could not be seen whether the weapons were destroyed. About 30 meters before Ruatti, Panzer 734 was hit in the engine and then hit several more times shortly thereafter.

Enemy defensive and artillery fire continued unabated. The *Grenadiere*, which had reached the first houses along the trail, were forced to pull back. Under these conditions and to prevent the loss of more Panzers, I considered that it was better for me to see to the wounded and the dismounted crews. Assisted by my loader, I helped a severely wounded radio operator from *Panzer 721* into my Panzer. The same with Leutnant Menzer, who had been wounded by a shell fragment while outside his Panzer. After the rest of the lightly wounded crew of *Panzer 721* and another commander climbed on, I brought them back to the point where we had started and turned them over to the medics. In the interim, *Panzer 712* helped another Panzer that was stuck. An attempt to tow back *Panzers 725* and *733* miscarried. I therefore ordered that everything usable be retrieved out of these Panzers and then to destroy them with explosive charges.

With two other Panzers, I stood on guard on the road in the area north of Point 155 until 0330 hours.

Personnel losses: Three killed who haven't been able to be recovered yet. Five wounded of which two remained with the unit. No trace has been found of five crew members.

Equipment losses: Five Panzers totally destroyed, four *Pz.Kpfw.IV 7.5 cm Kw.K. lang* and one *Pz.Kpfw.IV 7.5 cm Kw.K. kurz*. Two additional Panzers damaged and only two Panzers remaining operational.

The commander of the **6.Kompanie/Panzer-Regiment 26**, Oberleutnant Schaft, reported on their actions for the period of 14 to 16 December 1943:

On 14 December 1943, the *Kompanie* was ordered to advance on the road from Orsogna to Ortona to Point 155 together with the *I./9* and seal off the enemy breakthrough. Along with the *Kampfgruppe* belonging to the *Abteilung* under Major Brandt, we started out from Point 280 at about 2330 hours and without encountering any enemy resistance to speak of reached the group of houses 500 meters south of Point 155 about 0215 hours. Here the *Kampfgruppe* was halted by a radio call from Major Brandt because both of the *Pionier-Kompanien* that had attacked by way of Point 181 to envelop the enemy still lay too far back. *Kampfgruppe Schaft* sent a reconnaissance patrol forward that reported Point 155 free of the enemy. Then at about 0345 hours, Point 155 was occupied by one *Zug 1./9* and four *Pz.Kpfw.IV 7.5 cm Kw.K. lang* from the *6.Kompanie*. The gap on both sides of Point 155 was closed after the *Pionier-Kompanien* arrived at 0520 hours. About 0720 hours, two enemy tanks attacked the lead *Pz.Kpfw.IV* from the southeast supported by heavy artillery preparation. One enemy Sherman tank was hit three times, turned back, and remained stationary after moving about 1200 meters. The second enemy tank damaged the *Pz.Kpfw.IV 7.5 cm Kw.K. lang* by two hits on the gun mantlet and on the commander's cupola, and turned back before a second of our Panzers could be pulled forward for support.

ORGANIZATION AND STRENGTH OF PANZER UNITS SENT AS REINFORCEMENTS TO ITALY

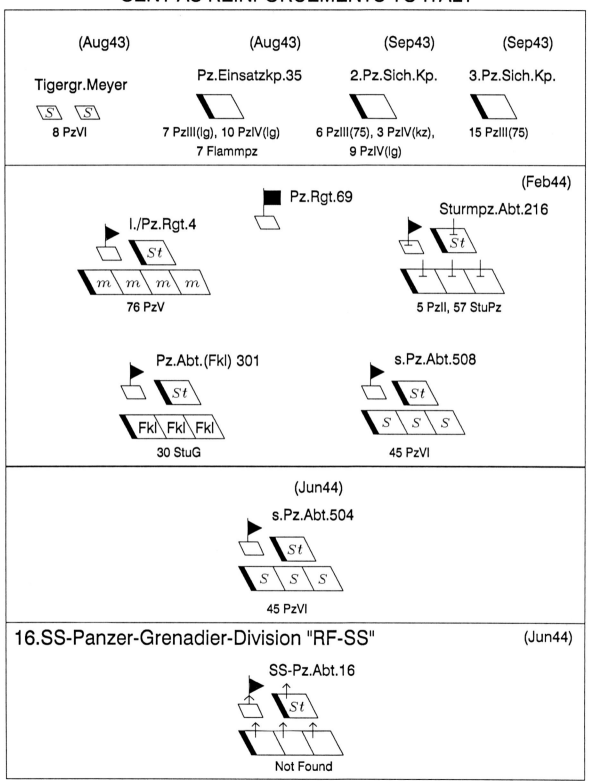

The area on and around Point 155 lay under heavy artillery fire throughout the day. Our own Panzers remained in position while the infantry pulled back about 400 meters because of heavy losses.

*During the early morning hours of 16 December, the infantry in **Kampfgruppe Brandt** were pulled out for a new assignment, while the **6.Kompanie** remained in the old location. About 0500 hours, after heavy artillery preparation, the opponent again attempted to advance on Point 155. The attack was repulsed and the enemy tanks turned back after they laid down a smoke screen on the area. At 1030 hours, a new artillery barrage suddenly hit Point 155. The renewed attempt by the opponents to advance with infantry and tanks was thwarted. One enemy Churchill tank was destroyed by a*

*direct hit. The enemy infantry were driven back by machine gun fire that caused heavy losses. One of our **Pz.Kpfw.IV** was destroyed by a direct hit (one dead, two wounded). Because of renewed artillery fire, the Panzers were pulled back 400 meters. At 1600 hours, the **Kompanie** received an order to pull back past Point 181 in the direction of Tollo. With all of the Panzers that were still operational and without being noticed by the opponent, the **6.Kompanie** moved across country and arrived at the new area about 0030 hours.*

The Allied drive stalled out by January 1944 on the Axis defensive line that included Monte Cassino. At this time the strength of the Panzer units in Italy was:

STRENGTH OF PANZER UNITS IN ITALY ON 21 JANUARY 1944

Name of Unit	Pz.Kpfw.III			Pz.Kpfw.IV		Pz.Kpfw.		Pz.	StuG
	Fl	lg	75	kz	lg	V	VI	Bef.	
26.Pz.Div.	11		12	11	80				14
Pz.Div.H.G.		21	14		27				14
3.Pz.Gren.Div.								4	44
15.Pz.Gren.Div.					22			1	21
29.Pz.Gren.Div.								1	41
90.Pz.Gren.Div.		2	14		26				4
Tigergr.Meyer							8		
2.Sich.Eins.Kp.	3		6		5				
31.Inf.Div.		23							
Total:	14	46	45	11	160	0	8	6	138

The **16.Panzer-Division** had been pulled out of Italy in November 1943, refitted, and sent to the Eastern Front. Twenty-five **Pz.Kpfw.IVs** were shipped from the **Heereszeugamt** in late January 1944 as replacements for **Panzer-Regiment Hermann Goering** and the **26.Panzer-Division**. **Panzer-Abteilung 190** was refitted with 42 **Sturmgeschuetz IV** in February 1944, giving up its Panzers to other units in Italy.

The Allies attempted to bypass the defensive line by landing at Anzio-Nettuno but failed to penetrate inland. In response, the **OKH** organized and sent a special force of armor consisting of 45 Tigers in **schwere Panzer-Abteilung 508**, 76 Panthers with the **I.Abteilung/Panzer-Abteilung 4**, 11 Ferdinands with the **1.Kompanie/schwere Panzer-Jaeger-Abteilung 653**, 57 **Sturmpanzer** with **Sturmpanzer-Abteilung 216**, and 30 **Sturmgeschuetze** with **Panzer-Abteilung (Fkl) 301** to drive the Allies back into the sea.

A trip report to the landing site in Italy written by Oberstleutnant d.G. Rohrbeck on 27 February 1944 reveals why this assembled force of "superior" German armor wasn't able to wipe out the beachhead:

North of Aprilia the enemy have positioned Sherman tanks under cover of the railway embankment in mutually protective flanking positions. The terrain south of Aprilia is not suitable for Panzers.

*The long approach march along mountain roads and then the employment of Panzers in deep mud have resulted in especially high equipment losses through breakdowns. The Panzers are scattered around the rear area with track, steering brakes, and transmission problems. They are blocking the roads because towing equipment is seldom available. A Panzer is hardly ever seen in the front lines. When this does occur, it is only a short time before the Panzers are shot up. As an example, out of only five Panthers that made it into action in the **3.Panzer-Grenadier-Division** sector on 17 February, within 3 hours, four of the Panthers were shot up or broke down.*

There are many problems with the terrain and visibility. The enemy has spread out from both landing sites and has firm roads in his sector. Our own observation positions in the overlooking heights are countered by the unfavorable position of the sun and by artillery spotter aircraft which continuously relieve each other. Combating enemy artillery spotter

A **Sturmpanzer** from **Sturmpanzer-Abteilung 216** with a Panther from the **I.Abteilung/Panzer-Regiment 4**. Both units were sent down to Italy to attempt to wipe out the bridgehead at Anzio-Nettuno. (BA)

A **BIV Sprengstofftraeger** from **Panzer-Abteilung (Fkl) 301** at the head of a column of Panthers from the **I.Abteilung/Panzer-Regiment 4** preparing to attack the bridgehead at Anzio-Nettuno. (BA)

aircraft with our own fighters is impossible because their air-craft remain within the effective range of their light anti-air-craft units.

A natural haze covers the enemy zone during the morning up to 1100 hours. And, during the afternoon after 1600 hours, the enemy lays down a manmade smoke screen. Observations can't be made between 1100 and 1600 hours because of the angle of the sun. An exact view of the harbor and the unloading ships occurred only on 17 and 23 February because of strong winds.

A manmade smoke screen in no man's land is constantly renewed by the enemy firing phosphorus shells. In low wind conditions, a bell shaped cloud remains hanging over the battlefield that significantly disturbs the work of our flash spotters.

The difficulty of the terrain (soft ground, cratered fields, steep ravines cutting across the path of advances) forces the Panzers to remain on the hard-surface roads. This channels every movement and results in high equipment losses when attempting to engage the enemy in his superior position.

Having failed in several attempts to retake the bridgehead, the specialized Panzer units were pulled back to the area of Rome to recuperate. The Allies, after finally managing to capture Monte Cassino, started a major offensive on 22 May 1944. How the **4.Kompanie/Panzer-Regiment 4** with their Panthers fared when sent in to stop the Allied drive is related by the following excerpts from their war diary:

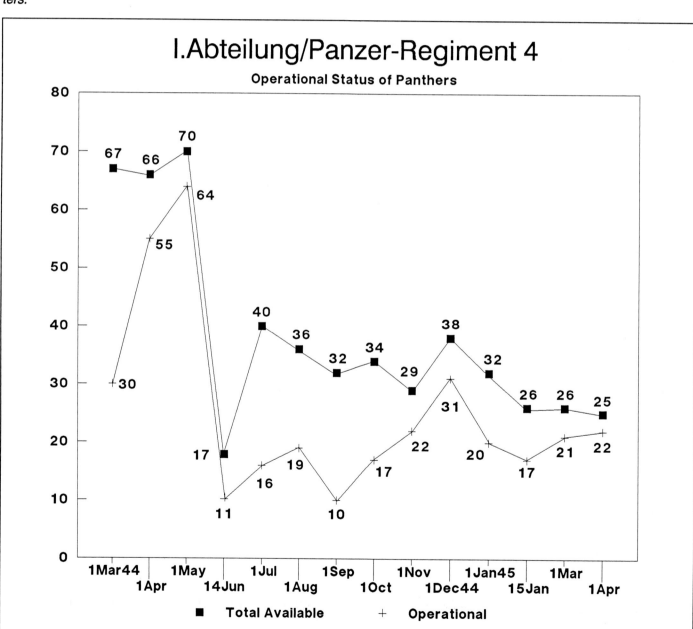

At 0355 hours on 23 May 1944, the combat elements were alerted by the commander of the 4.Kompanie. At 0445, three Panthers (401, 414 and 431) left the assembly area. The other four Panthers (421, 422, 423, and 433) were to follow as soon as they finished refueling. This hadn't been completed because the gasoline had been delivered in 200-liter drums with only one pump. At 0515, due to heavy artillery fire, the three advance Panthers were forced to immediately change position.

Enemy tanks and infantry started to attack at 1030. A decision was made to attack the enemy in the flank. The route was subjected to heavy artillery barrages. Finding the way was almost impossible because of the powder fumes and artificial smoke. Bypassing the various barrage zones, five Panthers managed to attack the enemy in the flank without loss due to enemy fire. Panthers 423 and 431 had remained behind due to mechanical problems. The opponent fled the battlefield, pulling back to the east, leaving all his weapons and equipment behind. An immediate enemy tank counterattack was repulsed. Panther 433 was knocked out in this last action. The commander was killed and the gunner and loader wounded. A short time later the gunner in Panther 423 was wounded.

All of the enemy tank attacks were beaten back. Altogether 28 enemy tanks were destroyed. Nine were claimed by Panther 433, six by Panther 422, five each by Panthers 415 and 414, and three by Panther 401. All 28 of these enemy tanks burned immediately. Three additional enemy tanks were knocked out but didn't burn and were not claimed as kills.

By firing ***Sprenggranaten*** *(high explosive shells) with and without fuzes set on delay into the woods opposite, as later related by a prisoner, three enemy infantry companies preparing to counterattack were completely decimated so that they couldn't initiate their attack.*

At 2040, out of fuel, Panther 411 was damaged by artillery fire. One crew member was wounded. At 2300 on 23 May, Panther 415 arrived at the repair group.

At 0430 on 24 May 1944, an order was received to return to the old assembly area immediately. There, after refueling, all Panthers were to defend against enemy tanks attacking from the east and southeast.

At 1030, the ordnance officer of ***Panzer-Grenadier-Regiment 163*** *reported that four enemy tanks had broken through at Regno. The company was alerted and immediately advanced across the ford at Melfa with four operational Panthers. The* ***Kompanie*** *commander in Panther 401 drove to the commander of* ***Panzer-Grenadier-Regiment 163*** *to obtain additional information. In the interim the rest of the company attacked. Four enemy tanks were destroyed (two by Panther 414 and one each by Panther 415 and 421). Two Panthers (414 and 415) were knocked out with one man wounded. The other two Panthers (421 and 423) were no longer operational.*

The ***Kompanie*** *commander intended to defend the ford at Melfa by taking up a hull-down position. Instead, at 1030, he was ordered by the* ***Abteilung*** *commander to attack in the direction of the ford by Roccasecca. During this time, the road was already blocked by enemy tanks standing at a range of 50 to 80 meters off the side of the road. While driving along the road toward Roccasecca, Panther 401 was knocked out and burned (two of the crew wounded). This took the last Panther out of action.*

Since they couldn't take part in this last attack, Panthers 421 and 423 were ordered to immediately pull back through the ford. Panther 421 made it without incident. Panther 423 was attacked by an enemy tank while crossing the ford at Melfa. Since the gunsight had been blinded by a hit, rough aim was taken at a range of 80 to 100 meters and the enemy tank shot up. This ended combat east of the Melfa sector. No operational Panthers remained.

During combat on 23 and 24 May 1944, the company lost six Panthers as total write-offs in exchange for destroying a total of 33 enemy tanks. Five Panthers (401, 411, 414, 415, and 422) burned out due to fire from enemy tanks. After running out of fuel, and already damaged by hits from enemy tank fire, Panther 433 burned out when hit by artillery fire.

The **3.Kompanie/schwere Panzer-Abteilung 508** was also committed to stopping the Allied drive. They lost almost all of their Tigers, as related in the following report on their activities between 23 and 25 May 1944 in the general area of Cisternia:

The ***3.Kompanie****, which had brought down 14 Tigers from France, lost two burned out at the end of February 1944 - one through carelessness on the part of the crew and another by Allied anti-tank action. A driver had not paid attention to the tightness of fuel line joints, and fuel leaking onto the floor of the Tiger was ignited by a discarded cigarette butt. The crew got out unharmed, but the Tiger was a total write-off. The incident was glossed over but would have had serious consequences on home service, for crews were strictly warned not to smoke inside a Panzer, and drivers in particular are told, "Be careful, you've got a million marks and three and a half million working hours under your ass."*

The ***3.Kompanie*** *received four of the latest pattern Tigers during May 1944 and was two tanks over the authorized* ***K.St.N.*** *strength on 23 May 1944, i.e., 16 instead of 14.*

The order was given to move without speed restrictions to counterattack American forces advancing from the beachhead and seeking to join up with troops pushing toward Rome from the south.

The ***3.Kompanie*** *formed up behind the railway embankment between the Mussolini Canal (Point 43) and the level crossing and engaged troop concentrations with* ***Sprenggranaten****. It then crossed the embankment. Three Tigers broke down in the attempt (one with transmission trouble and two with tracks riding over the sprocket teeth).*

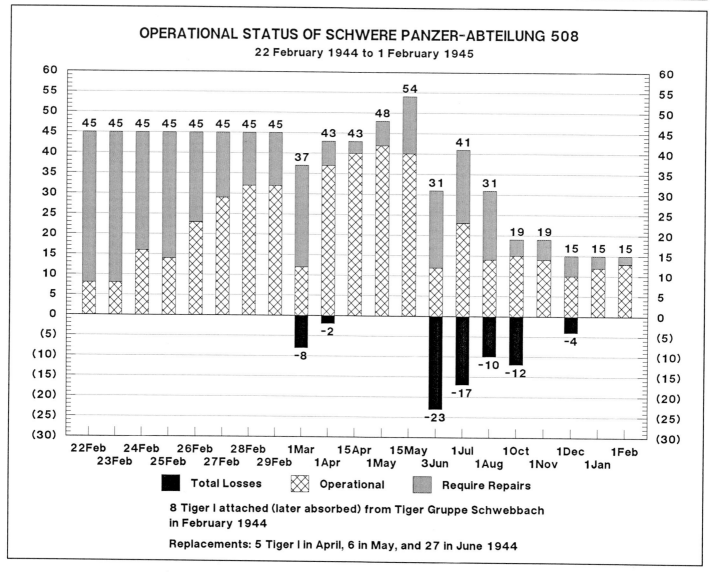

OPERATIONAL STATUS OF SCHWERE PANZER-ABTEILUNG 508
22 February 1944 to 1 February 1945

Total Losses — **Operational** — **Require Repairs**

8 Tiger I attached (later absorbed) from Tiger Gruppe Schwebbach in February 1944

Replacements: 5 Tiger I in April, 6 in May, and 27 in June 1944

The remaining 13 crews all had to stop on open ground because their guns had dug into the ground when the Tigers descended the steep embankment, and needed to be cleaned out.

The Allied troops were driven back about 3 kilometers and a number of Sherman tanks were surprised and knocked out.

The first loss sustained in action was a Tiger which had one radiator destroyed by an artillery round and had to limp back toward Cori in stages. Twelve Tigers were thus left in action during the night of 23/24 May 1944.

On the morning of 24 May 1944, to everyone's surprise a retreat was ordered and anti-tank fire accounted for one Tiger (hit on the right final drive and subsequently blown up by its crew).

Eleven Tigers withdrew to the embankment and the **3.Kompanie** commander ordered five Tigers to continue to hold the enemy while six were used to tow away the three Tigers which originally had failed to cross. Four of the six towing Tigers experienced transmission trouble, and the com-

mander then ordered the three towed Tigers to be destroyed. Two of the five operational Tigers assisted in towing away the new breakdowns.

These eight Tigers got back to an assembly point near Ouri, leaving only four Tigers in fighting order. Of these four, one was hit by anti-tank fire and two more experienced transmission trouble (all three were blown up), so that only one operational Tiger was left.

Two converted Sherman tanks came down from Rome during the night of 24/25 May 1944 and extricated the last operational Tiger, which had also broken down in the meantime, by towing it in tandem along the railway track.

By 24 May 1944, the situation had deteriorated so much that it was manifestly impossible to get towing vehicles through, and the **3.Kompanie** commander ordered that the nine Tigers which had reached the assembly area be blown up.

Although a good many of the crews had gone back to Rome with the one operational Tiger, the commander and about 45 men were left near Cori. They had to march back to

Rome and came under fire several times in the process, surviving in an exhausted condition.

The Panzer units took a severe beating during the Allied offensive which succeeded in capturing Rome. Twenty-seven Tigers and 38 Panthers were shipped from the Heereszeugamt as replacements between 27 May and 4 June 1944. In addition, **schwere Panzer-Abteilung 504**, already under orders to move to the Eastern Front, had its orders rescinded and was shipped by rail to Italy in June 1944.

Panzer-Division Hermann Goering was pulled out of Italy in July 1944 leaving its Panzers behind, refitted, and sent to the Eastern Front. In late August 1944, the **3.** and **15.Panzer-Grenadier-Divisions** were pulled out of Italy and sent to the Western Front. This left the **26.Panzer-Division** and the **29.** and **90.Panzer-Grenadier-Divisions**, which remained in Italy to the end of the war. The **16.SS-Panzer-Grenadier-Division "Reichsfuehrer-SS"**, transferred to Italy by June 1944 to rest and refit, was sent to **Heeresgruppe Sued** in February 1945.

In the August 1944 edition of the **Nachrichtenblatt der Panzertruppen**, an article dealt with recent experiences related to Panzer unit command and combat on the Southwest Front, as Italy was known:

Experiences similar to those on the Western Front have occurred in Italy. The enemy air power superiority is present in the same way as well as his heavy artillery concentrations.

In detail, the following experiences have been noted:

1. During enemy breakthroughs with tanks, the infantry follow up mounted in armored carriers and occupy the terrain so fast and so strong that counterattacks are usually unsuccessful.

Countermeasure: Only an immediate counterstrike with small groups that are positioned ready to attack behind the main battle line promises success and disrupts the opponents attempts to set up a defense.

2. When enemy tanks don't succeed in breaking through, they pull back and fire light signals. This is followed directly by concentrated artillery fire.

This **Sturmgeschuetz** of the **2.Kompanie/Panzer-Abteilung 103** was knocked out in Cori during the major Allied offensive in May 1944. (NA)

A Tiger of the **3.Kompanie/schwere Panzer-Abteilung 504** sent down to Italy in early June 1944 to halt the Allied drive. (MJ)

Countermeasure: Alternative positions are required to be prepared for all anti-tank and heavy weapons. As soon as the enemy tanks pull back out of effective range of our weapons, the guns must change position and the crews disappear into prepared covered holes.

*3. Enemy tanks don't come closer than 50 meters when they spot our **Panzer-Vernichtungstrupps** (tank destroying squad).*

*Countermeasure: Carefully camouflage the **Panzer-Vernichtungstrupps**. In addition a cold blooded leader is needed who has the nerve to let the tanks advance close enough. Cooperation between the anti-tank weapons and the **Panzer-Vernichtungstrupps** must be ensured.*

4. In order to combat Panzers at night, the opponent couples mortars firing flares with his anti-tank guns. Flares shot from the mortars light up the Panzer long enough for the anti-tank gun to aim. The anti-tank gun opens fire after the flare goes out. For the target to be sufficiently illuminated, the flare must come within 130 meters. The maximum range for firing at a Panzer is given as 300 meters (extract from a British division order).

Countermeasure: Panzers that are illuminated by these flares must immediately move to a new position to the side, at the latest by the time the flare goes out. Because the British give the maximum range as 300 meters, the illumination of their own weapons can't be prevented. These weapons can be engaged and destroyed by concentrated fire from the Panzers or our other weapons that are in the immediate area.

Experiences of American tankers

A captured American after-action report, which doesn't reveal anything new to us, states the following:

*1. Concentration and cooperation of tanks and infantry. Infantry should stay close to the tanks. Advancing in the tank tracks reduces losses from **S-Minen**. Carrying infantry on the tanks is useful.*

Separation of tanks and infantry, especially directly before nightfall, must be prevented.

*2. Tanks can be used to clear areas sown with **S-Minen** and to clear out barbed wire barriers.*

3. Tank assembly points must be protected by infantry at night.

4. Tanks sent into combat in cities promise little success.

The preferences of the crews for lighter, more maneuverable Panzers was recorded in a report written on 1 November 1944 by Albert Speer on his trip to Italy during 19 to 25 October 1944:

On the Southwest Front, opinions are in favor of the Sherman tank and its cross-country ability. The Sherman tank climbs mountains that our Panzer crews consider impassable. This is accomplished by the especially powerful engine in the Sherman in comparison to its weight. Also, according to reports from the **26.Panzer-Division**, *the terrain-crossing ability on level ground (in the Po valley) is completely superior to our Panzers. The Sherman tanks drive freely cross-country, while our Panzers must remain on trails and narrow roads and therefore are very restricted in their ability to fight.*

All Panzer crews want to receive lighter Panzers, which are more maneuverable, possess increased ability to cross terrain, and guarantee the necessary combat power just with a superior gun.

This desire by the troops corresponds with conditions that will develop in the future as a result of the drop in production capacity and of the fact that, because of a shortage of chrome, sufficient armor plate can't be produced to meet the increased production plans. Therefore, either the number of Panzers produced must be reduced or it will be necessary to reduce the thickness of the armor plate. In that case, the troops will unequivocally ask for a reduction of the armor thickness in order to increase the total number of Panzers produced.

28

Reorganizing and Rebuilding the Panzertruppen in 1944

One of the main goals of the reorganization programs in 1944 was to outfit every **Panzer-Division** with a **Panther-Abteilung** in addition to the normal **Panzer-Abteilung** with **Pz.Kpfw.IVs**. Due to shortages in wheeled vehicles, a new organizational scheme known as "**freie Gliederung**" was introduced which "freed" the motor transport from each **Panzer-Kompanie** and consolidated the baggage and supply vehicles into a **Versorgungs-Kompanien** (supply companies) within each **Panzer-Abteilung**.

Only two new **Heeres Panzer-Divisions** were formed. Forced by circumstances, the major effort went into rebuilding **Panzer-Divisions** and **Panzer-Grenadier-Divisions** that had been decimated at the Front. Based on Hitler's suggestion, independent **Heeres Panzer-Brigades** were formed starting in July 1944. With only two exceptions these independent **Heeres Panzer-Brigades** had been absorbed into normal **Panzer-Divisions** and **Panzer-Grenadier-Divisions** by the end of November 1944.

Panzer-Lehr-Division - Ordered to be created on 30 December 1943, the **Panzer-Lehr-Division** was assembled in early January 1944 from already existing elements, including the **Panzer-Lehr-Abteilung**. The **Panzer-Lehr-Abteilung** was renamed the **II.Abteilung/Panzer-Lehr-Regiment** and was to have four **Panzer-Kompanien**, each with 22 **Pz.Kpfw.IVs**. On 20 January 1944, the organization of the **I.Abteilung/Panzer-Lehr-Regiment** was shown as three **Panzer-Kompanien** each with 22 Panthers and a **Panzer-Jaeger-Kompanie** with 22 Jagdpanthers. **Panzer-Kompanie (Fkl) 316** was incorporated into the unit, reporting directly to the **Panzer-Regiment Stab**. On 3 February 1944, clarifying orders called for the **Panzer-Lehr-Division** to convert **Panzer-Kompanie (FKL) 316** into a **Panzer-Kompanie (Tiger II)** with 14 Tiger II in accordance with K.St.N.1176c dated 1 November 1943. Orders dated 21 January 1944 stated that units in **Panzer-Lehr-Division** were to be converted to "**freie Gliederung**." The list of applicable K.St.N. dated 1 March

1944 had the following special K.St.N. for the units in the **Panzer-Lehr-Regiment**:

K.St.N.	Date	Unit Name
1103	1Nov43	**Stab und Stabs-Kompanie Panzer-Regiment**
f.G.	1Nov43	**Stab Panzer-Abteilung IV**
f.G.	1Nov43	**Stabskompanie Panzer-Abteilung IV**
f.G.	1Nov43	**Panzer-Kompanie IV**
f.G.	1Nov43	**Versorgungs-Kompanie Freie Panzer-Abteilung**
f.G.	1Nov43	**Stab Panzer-Abteilung "Panther"**
f.G.	1Nov43	**Stabs-Kompanie Panzer-Abteilung "Panther"**
f.G.	1Nov43	**Panzer-Kompanie "Panther"**
f.G.	1Nov43	**Versorgungs-Kompanie Panzer-Abteilung "Panther"**
1187	1Jun42	**Panzer-Werkstatt-Kompanie**
1176c	1Nov43	**Fkl.Kompanie (Tiger)**

The **I.(Panther) Abteilung/Panzer-Regiment 6** was assigned as the **I.Abteilung/Panzer-Lehr-Regiment** and remained with the **Panzer-Lehr-Division**. A **Panther-Abteilung** wasn't created as the **I.Abteilung/Panzer-Lehr-Regiment 130** until 7 August 1944. On 8 November 1944, the **I.Abteilung/Panzer-Regiment 6** was renamed **I.Abteilung/Panzer-Lehr-Regiment 130** and vice versa.

2.Panzer-Division - The **2.Panzer-Division** was pulled out of the Eastern Front and had been resting and refitting in the **Ob.West** area since 15 January 1944. On 18 January 1944, the **I.Abteilung/Panzer-Regiment 3** was re-created and ordered to convert to a **Panther-Abteilung** with the following organization:

1107	1Nov43	**Stab Panzer-Abteilung**
1150a	1Nov43	**Stabs-Kompanie Panzer-Abteilung "Panther"**

1177   1Nov43   4 **Panzer-Kompanie "Panther"**

The complete **Panzer-Regiment 3** was to be outfitted with 79 Panthers and 101 **Pz.Kpfw.IVs.**

Reserve-Panzer-Divisions Used to Refit Three Panzer-Divisions - On 15 March 1944, Hitler ordered that three **Panzer-Divisions** be refitted/created in the West by using the three **Reserve-Panzer-Divisions** (**155.**, **179.**, and **273.**). The three divisions initially selected were the **9.Panzer-Division**, **10.Panzer-Grenadier-Division**, and **16.Panzer-Grenadier-Division**. On 2 May 1944, the order was revised with the **11.Panzer-Division** replacing the **10.Panzer-Grenadier-Division**. The **16.Panzer-Grenadier-Division** was reorganized and renamed the **116.Panzer-Division**. Each of these three **Panzer-Divisions** was to have a complete **Panzer-Regiment** with a **Panther-Abteilung** consisting of four **Panzer-Kompanien** each with 17 Panthers and a **Panzer-Abteilung** of four **Panzer-Kompanien** each with 22 **Pz.Kpfw.IVs.**

The **Reserve-Panzer-Abteilung 1** was used to create the **II.Abteilung/Panzer-Regiment 116** on 1 May 1944. The existing **Panzer-Abteilung 116** was renamed **I.Abteilung/Panzer-Regiment 116**, and the **Stab** for **Panzer-Regiment 116** was created from the renamed **Stab Panzer-Regiment 69** on 5 May 1944. **Panzer-Regiment 116** was renamed **Panzer-Regiment 16** on 23 May 1944. On 3 July 1944, the **I.Abteilung/Panzer-Regiment 16** of the **116.Panzer-Division** was ordered to convert to a **Panther-Abteilung "freie Gliederung"** and organized as follows:

K.St.N.	Date	Unit Name
1107a(f.G.)	1Apr44	**Stab Panzer-Abteilung (frei)**
1150(f.G.)	1Apr44	**Stabs-Kompanie Panzer-Abteilung (frei)**
1177(f.G.)	1Apr44	**4 Panzer-Kompanie (Panther) (frei)**
1151a(f.G.)	1Apr44	**Versorgungs-Kompanie (frei)**
1185a	10Jan43	**Panzer-Werkstatt-Zug**

Lacking its own **Panther-Abteilung**, the **I.Abteilung/Panzer-Regiment "Grossdeutschland"** had been attached to the **116.Panzer-Division** on 6 May 1944. It was shipped to the Eastern Front in early June and replaced by the **I.Abteilung/Panzer-Regiment 24** on 19 June 1944.

Refitting Two SS-Panzer-Divisions - On 4 December 1943, orders were issued to reorganize the debilitated **2.SS-Panzer-Division** into a **Kampfgruppe** that was to remain on the Eastern Front. **SS-Panzer-Regiment 2** was reduced to a **Panzer-Abteilung** consisting of three **Panzer-Kompanien** (one **Kompanie** each of **Pz.Kpfw.IVs**, Panthers, and Tigers). The remainder of the **2.SS-Panzer-Division** returned to the West to rest and refit. On 11 April 1944, the **Kampfgruppen** of the **1.** and **2.SS-Panzer-Division** were ordered to pull out of the Front as soon as the situation allowed and were trans-

ferred to **Ob.West** to complete the rebuilding of both divisions. **SS-Panzer-Regiment 1** was organized with the **I.Abteilung** of four **Panther-Kompanien**, each with 17 Panthers, and the **II.Abteilung** with four **Panzer-Kompanien**, each with 22 **Pz.Kpfw.IVs**. **SS-Panzer-Regiment 2** was organized with a **I.Abteilung** of four **Panther-Kompanien**, each with 17 Panthers, and a **II.gemischte Abteilung** with two **Panzer-Kompanien** each with 22 **Pz.Kpfw.IVs** and two **Panzer-Sturmgeschuetz-Kompanien** each with 22 **Sturmgeschuetze**. During June 1944, the **II.Abteilung/SS-Panzer-Regiment 2** was reorganized so that it only had one **Panzer-Sturmgeschuetz-Kompanie** and three normal **Panzer-Kompanien** with **Pz.Kpfw.IVs**.

Reorganizing Panzer-Regiment Hermann Goering - On 4 May 1944, **Panzer-Regiment Hermann Goering** was reorganized. Its **II.Abteilung** was to have four **Panzer-Kompanien** with 17 **Pz.Kpfw.IV** each. The **III.Abteilung** was to be converted to a **Panzer-Jaeger-Abteilung** organized in accordance with the following K.St.N.:

K.St.N	Date	Unit Name
1106d	1Nov43	**Stab Panzer-Jaeger-Abteilung**
1155d	1Nov43	**Stabs-Kompanie Panzer-Jaeger-Abteilung**
1149 Ausf.A	1Feb44	**2 Sturmgeschuetz Abteilung (in Panzer-Jaeger-Abteilung)**

The **3.Panzer-Jaeger-Kompanie (mot)** was to be outfitted with towed **Pak**. The 21 **Panzerjaeger IV (7,5 cm Pak 39 (L/48)) (Sd.Kfz.162)** (later renamed **Jagdpanzer IV**) had already been shipped by rail from the **Heeres-Zeugamt** to the **III.Abteilung/Panzer-Regiment Hermann-Goering** on 25 April 1944. Outfitting an **Abteilung** with Panthers for **Panzer-Regiment Hermann Goering** was not planned to begin until July 1944.

Reorganization to Freie Gliederung - The following new set of K.St.N. dated 1 April 1944 were established for organizing **Panzer-Regiments** in a **"freie Gliederung."** In this new organization the supply and baggage vehicles were taken away from each **Kompanie** and concentrated into a **Versorgungs-Kompanie**.

K.St.N.	Date	Unit Name
1103	1Apr44	**Stab und Stabskompanie eines Panzer-Regiments**
1196	1Apr44	**Panzer-Fliegerabwehrzug (3,7 cm Flak 43)**
1107a(fG)	1Apr44	**Stab einer Panzer-Abteilung (freie Gliederung)**
1150(fG)	1Apr44	**Stabskompanie einer Panzer-Abteilung (freie Gliederung)**

(text continues on page 158)

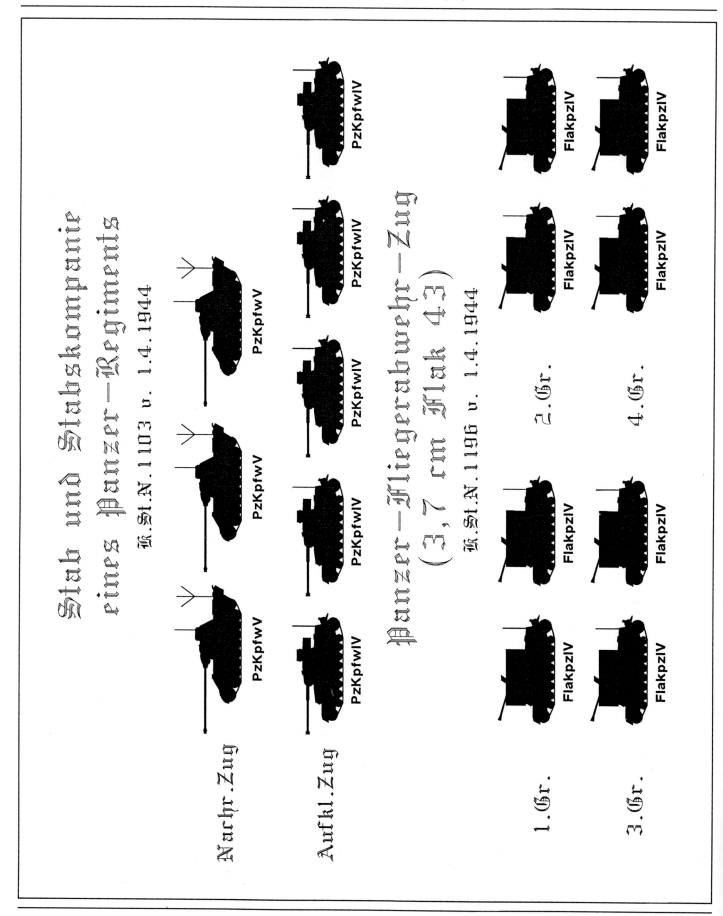

Stab und Stabskompanie
eines Panzer–Regiments

K.St.N.1103 v. 1.4.1944

Nachr.Zug — PzKpfwV, PzKpfwV, PzKpfwV

Aufkl.Zug — PzKpfwIV, PzKpfwIV, PzKpfwIV, PzKpfwIV, PzKpfwIV

Panzer–Fliegerabwehr–Zug
(3,7 cm Flak 43)

K.St.N.1196 v. 1.4.1944

1.Gr. — FlakpzIV, FlakpzIV
2.Gr. — FlakpzIV, FlakpzIV
3.Gr. — FlakpzIV, FlakpzIV
4.Gr. — FlakpzIV, FlakpzIV

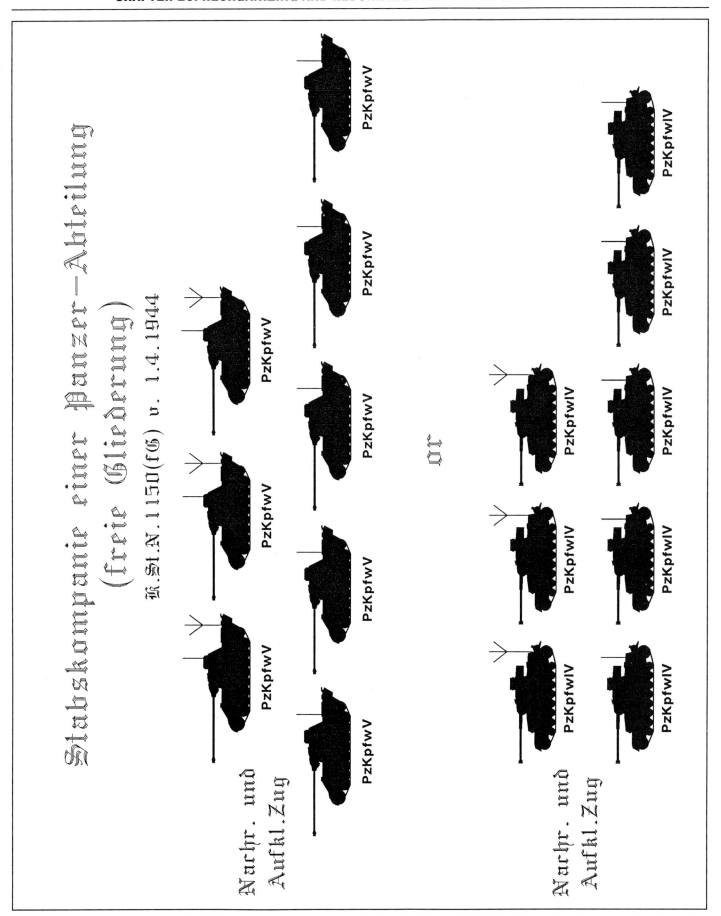

Stabskompanie einer Panzer–Abteilung
(freie Gliederung)
K.St.N.1150(fG) v. 1.4.1944

Nachr. und Aufkl.Zug

PzKpfwV
PzKpfwV
PzKpfwV
PzKpfwV
PzKpfwV
PzKpfwV
PzKpfwV
PzKpfwV
PzKpfwV
PzKpfwV

or

Nachr. und Aufkl.Zug

PzKpfwIV
PzKpfwIV
PzKpfwIV
PzKpfwIV
PzKpfwIV
PzKpfwIV
PzKpfwIV
PzKpfwIV
PzKpfwIV
PzKpfwIV

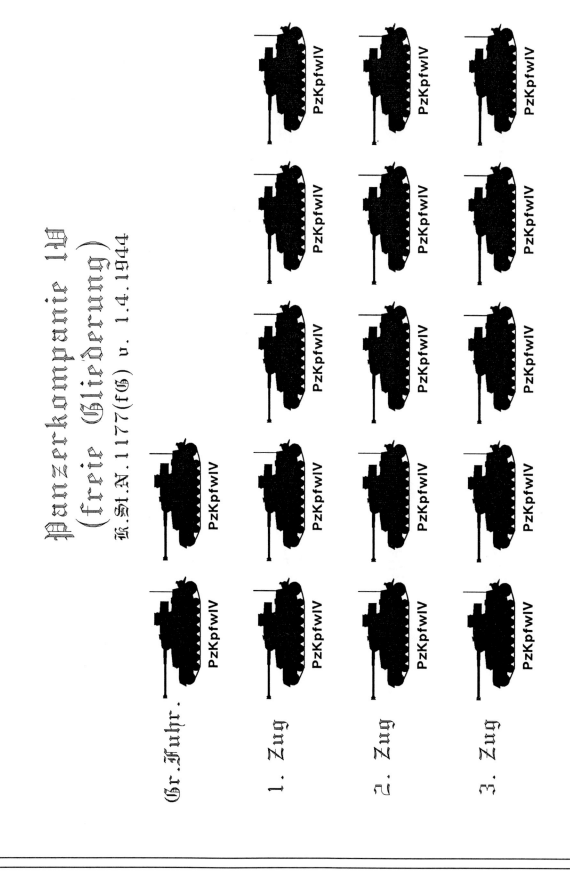

Panzerkompanie 1d
(freie Gliederung)
K.St.N.1177(fG) v. 1.4.1944

Kr.Fuhr.   PzKpfwIV

1. Zug   PzKpfwIV   PzKpfwIV   PzKpfwIV   PzKpfwIV

2. Zug   PzKpfwIV   PzKpfwIV   PzKpfwIV   PzKpfwIV

3. Zug   PzKpfwIV   PzKpfwIV   PzKpfwIV   PzKpfwIV

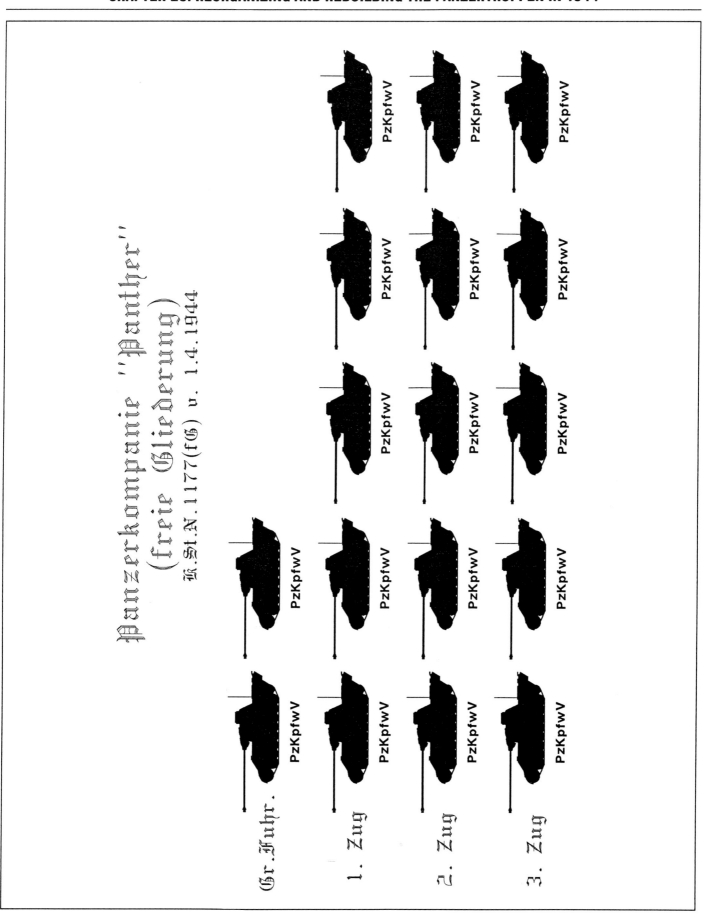

| 1177(fG) | 1Apr44 | Panzer-Kompanie "Panther" oder Panzer-Kompanie IV (freie Gliederung) |
| 1151(fG) | 1Apr44 | Versorgungs-Kompanie Panzer-Abteilung (freie Gliederung) |

The **Stab und Stabskompanie eines Panzer-Regiments**, organized in accordance with K.St.N.1103 dated 1 April 1944, contained a **Nachrichten-Zug** with three **Panzerkampfwagen "Panther" (7,5 cm 42 (L/70)) (Sd.Kfz.171)** as **Panzerbefehlswagen** and an **Aufklaerungs-Zug** with five **Panzerkampfwagen IV (7,5 cm 40 (L/48)) (Sd.Kfz.161/1)** or five **Panzerkampfwagen IV (7,5 cm 40 L/48) (Sd.Kfz.161/2)**. The **Panzer-Fliegerabwehr-Zug (3.7 cm Flak 43)**, organized in accordance with K.St.N.1196 dated 1 April 1944, was a **"Teil-Einheit"** attached to the **Panzer-Regiment Stabs-Kompanie** and was to have four **Gruppen** each with two **Flakpanzerkampfwagen IV (3,7 cm Flak 43) (Sd.Kfz.161/3)**. The **Stabskompanie einer Panzer-Abteilung (freie Gliederung)**, organized in accordance with K.St.N.1150(f.G.) dated 1 April 1944, contained a **Nachrichten und Aufklaerungs-Zug** with three **Panzerkampfwagen "Panther" (7,5 cm 42 L/70) (Sd.Kfz.171)** as **Panzerbefehlswagen** or three **Panzerkampfwagen IV (7,5 cm 40 L/48) (Sd.Kfz.161/2)** as **Panzerbefehlswagen**, and five **Panzerkampfwagen "Panther" (7,5 cm 42 L/70) (Sd.Kfz.171)** or five **Panzerkampfwagen IV (7,5 cm 40 L/48) (Sd.Kfz.161/2)**. The **Panzer-Kompanie "Panther" oder Panzer-Kompanie IV (freie Gliederung)**, organized in accordance with K.St.N.1177(fG) dated 1 April 1944, had a **Gruppe Fuehrer** with two **Panzerkampfwagen "Panther" (7,5 cm 42 L/70) (Sd.Kfz.171)** or two **Panzerkampfwagen IV (7,5 cm 40 L/48) (Sd.Kfz.161/2)** and three **Zuege** each with five **Panzerkampfwagen "Panther" (7,5 cm 42 L/70) (Sd.Kfz.171)** or five **Panzerkampfwagen IV (7,5 cm 40 L/48) (Sd.Kfz.161/2)**.

Elements of **Panzer-Lehr-Division** including the **Panzer-Lehr-Regiment** were ordered to reorganize to the **"freie Gliederung"** on 6 May 1944. On 20 May 1944, **Panzer-Regiment 100** of the **21.Panzer-Division** was ordered to reorganize to the **"freie Gliederung"** and was renamed **Panzer-Regiment 22** effective immediately. The **I.Abteilung/Panzer-Regiment 22** was to be outfitted with 17 **Pz.Kpfw.IVs** in each of its four **Panzer-Kompanien** and the **II.Abteilung** still in possession of **Beute-Panzers** was to be outfitted with 14 **Pz.Kpfw.IVs** in each of its four **Panzer-Kompanien**. Also on 20 May 1944, the **2.Panzer-Division** was ordered to reorganize to the **"freie Gliederung."**

It wasn't until 3 August 1944, that the **OKH/Gen.Insp.d.Pz.Tr./GenStdH/Org.Abt.** issued the following order for the **Heeres Panzer-Divisions** to reorganize in accordance with the standardized **"Gliederung Panzer-Division 44"**:

1. The *"Gliederung Panzer-Division 44"* goes into effect immediately for all **Panzer-Divisions**.
2. Within the bounds of their available personnel and material, the **Panzer-Divisions** are to convert to this organization. The status of their reorganization is to be reported in the monthly operational status reports. **Panzer-Lehr-Division** and the **21.Panzer-Division** are exceptions. A special organization applies to these two divisions.
3. The list of application K.St.N. for **Panzer-Division 44** is included as an Appendix 2.

The **Panzer-Regiments** were to be organized in accordance with the following K.St.N.:

K.St.N.	Date	Unit Name
1103	1Apr44	Stab und Stabs-Kompanie Panzer-Regiment
1196	1Apr44	(T.E.) Panzer-Fla-Zug (3,7 cm Fla 43)
1107a(fG)	1Apr44	Stab Panzer-Abteilung (f.G.)
1150(fG)	1Apr44	Stabs-Kompanie Panzer-Abteilung (f.G.)
1177(fG)	1Apr44	Panzer-Kompanie "Panther" or Panzer-Kompanie IV (f.G.)
1151(fG)	1Apr44	Versorgungs-Kompanie Panzer-Abteilung IV (f.G.)
1151a(fG)	1Apr44	Versorgungs-Kompanie Panzer-Abteilung "Panther" (f.G.)
1187(fG)	1Apr44	Panzer-Werkstatt-Kompanie Panzer-Regiment

The organization chart stated that provisionally each **Panzer-Kompanie** was to be outfitted only with 17 **Pz.Kpfw.IVs** or Panthers.

Refitting Decimated Panzer-Divisions - The **6., 19.,** and **25.Panzer-Divisions** had already been decimated by the Spring of 1944. They were transferred back to home bases in Germany to rest and refit starting in May 1944. Because of other priorities, their rebuilding hadn't been completed by the end of June 1944. After the start of the major Russian summer offensive, orders were issued to quickly outfit the **Panzer-Regiments** for both the **6.** and **19.Panzer-Divisions** and return them to the Eastern Front.

On 12 July 1944, orders were issued to quickly pull **Fallschirm-Panzer-Division Hermann-Goering** out of Italy and sent it to the Eastern Front. It was to leave all of its Panzers behind in Italy and be refitted with 64 **Pz.Kpfw.IVs** for the **II.Abteilung** (14 per **Panzer-Kompanie**) and 31 **Jagdpanzer IVs** for the **III.Abteilung/Panzer-Regiment Hermann Goering**.

Elements of the **25.Panzer-Division** were used to create independent **Heeres Panzer-Brigaden**. On 5 August 1944, orders were issued to create **Kampfgruppe 25.Panzer-Division** from the remnants and send it to the Eastern Front. Initially, the only Panzer unit with **Kampfgruppe 25.Panzer-**

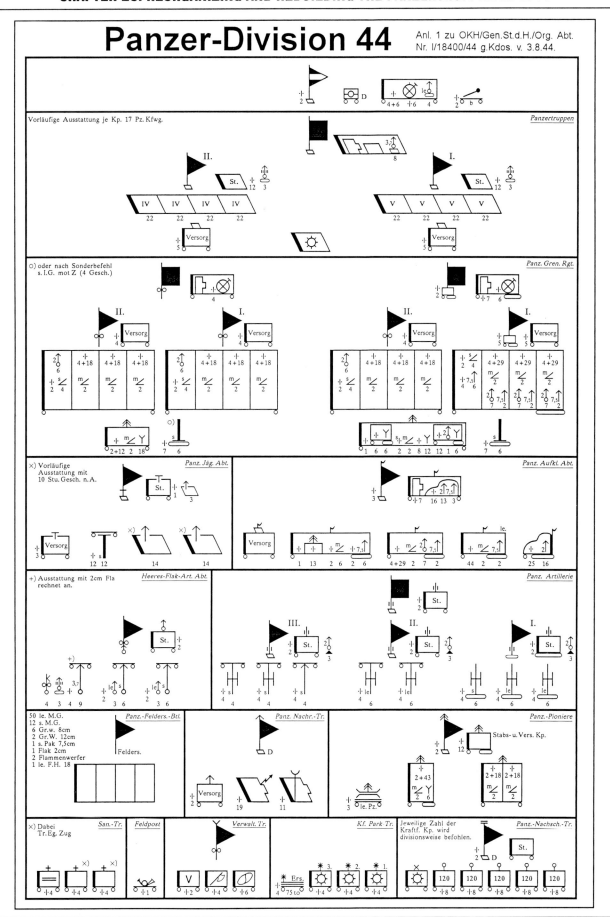

Panzer-Division 44

Anl. 1 zu OKH/Gen.St.d.H./Org. Abt.
Nr. I/18400/44 g.Kdos. v. 3.8.44.

PANZERTRUPPEN • 1943-1945

Division was a single **Panzer-Kompanie** with 14 Pz.Kpfw.IVs assigned to the **Panzer-Jaeger-Abteilung.**

Formation of Independent Heeres Panzer-Brigades - The incident that initiated the formation of independent **Heeres Panzer-Brigades** was a meeting with Hitler recorded by the **Chef des Heeresstabes beim Chef OKW** as follows:

*1. On 2 July, while considering the **Heeresgruppe Mitte** situation, Hitler stated that it would be useful to have small, mobile, fast, armored **Kampfgruppe** available during this type of situation which could quickly be brought into action to surprise and destroy the attacking enemy armored spearheads.*

*2. Hitler thinks that the approximate organization for these **Kampfgruppe** should be one **gepanzerte SPW-Bataillon**, one **Panzer-Gruppe** with a strength of 30 to 40 Panzers (including **leichte Panzer-Jaeger IV**), one **Pak-Kompanie** or **Pak 37** towed by SPW, and several **2 cm** or **3.7 cm Flak-Wagen.***

*3. Hitler requested about 12 of these **Kampfgruppen**, which he wanted to be named **Brigaden.***

*4. For complete mobility of these **Kampfgruppen**, which could be achieved even in the coming Winter, Hitler implied that it would be necessary to outfit the new **Sturmgeschuetz 38t** with wider tracks.*

*5. Hitler is waiting for a proposal on the organization of these **Kampfgruppen.***

On 3 July 1944, the **OKH/GenstdH/Org.Abt.** proposed that the 12 **Kampfgruppen** could be created by converting elements of the six **Panzer-Divisions** (6., 9., 11., 19., 25., and 116.) that were currently being refitted. This proposal wasn't accepted. A new order from **OKH/GenStdH/Org.Abt.** dated 11 July 1944 called for the creation of ten **Panzer-Brigaden**, designated **Panzer-Brigade 101 to 110**, in accordance with the attached organization chart. Each **Panzer-Brigade** was to have a **Panzer-Abteilung** with three **Panzer-Kompanien** each with 11 Panthers and a **Panzer-Jaeger-Kompanie** with 11 Pz.IV/70(V). In addition, there were three Panthers and four **Flakpanzer** in the **Panzer-Abteilung Stab**.

The original order dated 11 July was modified on 24 July 1944 to include the following details:

*The ten **Panzer-Brigaden** were to be ready for combat as follows: 101 to 104 by 15 August, 105 and 106 by 31 August, 107 and 108 by 15 September, and 109 and 110 by 25 September.*

Panzer-Brigaden 106** and **110** were to be named **Panzer-Brigade 106 (Feldherrnhalle)** and **Panzer-Brigade 110 (Feldherrnhalle).

*Personnel for **Panzer-Brigaden 101** to **104, 108,** and **109** were to come from elements of the **Ersatz-Heeres** primarily from the **233.Reserve-Panzer-Division** and also from the **25.Panzer-Division**. Personnel for **Panzer-Brigade 110** were to come from **Ersatz-Brigade "Feldherrnhalle."***

Panzer-Brigade 105** and **107** were to be created from the useful elements of the remnants of the **18.** and **25.Panzer-Grenadier-Divisions**, and **Panzer-Brigade 107** from the remnants of **Panzer-Grenadier-Division "Feldherrnhalle."

There was no consistency in the specification for the K.St.N. for these **Panzer-Brigades**. On 24 July 1944, the K.St.N. for **Panzer-Brigades** were identified as K.St.N.X dated 15 July 1944 for the **Stab Panzer-Abteilung (f.G.)** and K.St.N.XI dated 15 July 1944 for the **Panzer-Kompanie Panther (f.G.)**. On 26 July 1944, the K.St.N. for creating **Panzer-Brigade 109** and **110** were identified as:

K.St.N.	Date	Unit Name
1107a(fG)	1Apr44	**Stab Panzer-Abteilung (frei)** reinforced with a **Gruppe Fuehrer** (K.St.N.1150(fG) dated 1Apr44) with changes and the **1.&.2.Gruppe** from a **Panzer-Fla-Zug** (K.St.N.1196(f.G.) v.1.4.44)
1177(fG)	1Apr44	**Panzer-Kompanie "Panther" (frei)** with changes
1149(fG)	1Apr44	**Panzer-Jaeger (Sturmgeschuetz) Kompanie (frei)**

However, no matter what K.St.N. designations were noted, the authorized strength for the **Panzer-Abteilung** remained at 36 Panthers, 11 **Pz.IV/70(V)**, and 4 **Flakpanzer**.

On 6 August 1944, the **OKH/GenStdH/Org.Abt.** cut orders for a new organization for **Panzer-Brigaden 105** to **110** as shown in the attached organization chart. This did not affect the organization of the **Panzer-Abteilungen**. Reorganization of **Panzer-Brigade 101** to **104** was planned to occur at a later time.

On 10 August 1944, orders were issued to create the "**Fuehrer-Grenadier-Brigade.**" The **III.Abteilung** of this **Fuehrer-Grenadier-Brigade** was to be organized in accordance with the following K.St.N.:

K.St.N.	Date	Unit Name
1107i(fG)	*	**Stab Panzer-Abteilung (f.G.)**
1177i(fG)	*	**Panzer-Kompanie "Panther" (f.G.)**
1149i(fG)	*	**Panzer-Jaeger (Sturmgeschuetz) Kompanie (f.G.)**
1151i(fG)	*	**Versorgungs-Kompanie Panzer-Abteilung "Panther"**

* The date of the issue for the K.St.N. hadn't been established. Again, these K.St.N. still reflected the same organization and authorized strength for the **Panzer-Abteilung** of 36 Panthers, 11 **Pz.IV/70(V)**, and 4 **Flakpanzer**.

Three additional independent **Heeres Panzer-Brigaden**, numbered **111, 112,** and **113**, were created in early September 1944 from the "**Walkuere**" draft. One **Panzer-Abteilung** each (numbered **2111, 2112,** and **2113**) was formed on 1

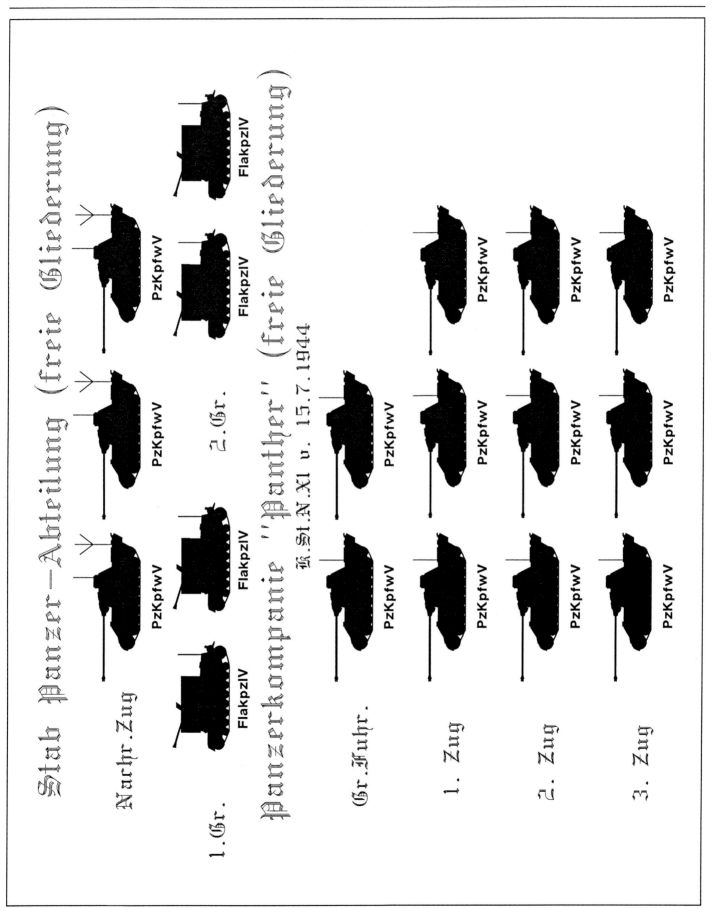

Nr. I/18056/44 g. Kdos. v 11.7. 44

Panzer-Brigade

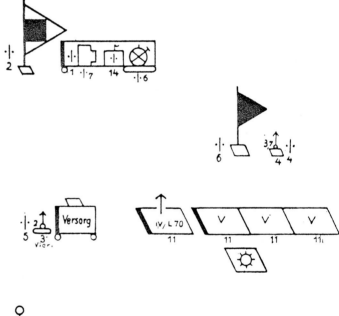

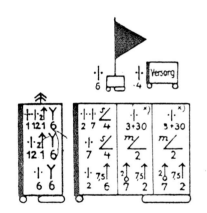

x) davon 2 Züge m. je 28 M.Pi. 44

Anl. zu OKH/Gen.StdH/Org.Abt.
Nr.I 18050/44 g Kdos. v. 6.8.44 I Angel.

Panzer-Brigade

(Endgliederung)

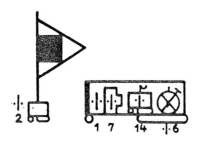

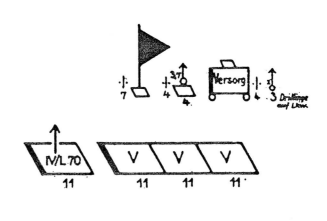

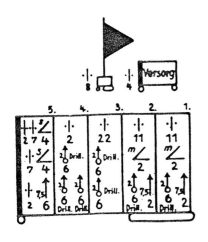

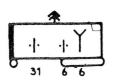

September 1944 for these **Panzer-Brigaden**. Each of the **Panzer-Abteilung** was to be outfitted with 45 **Pz.Kpfw.IVs**, three **Pz.Kpfw.IVs** in the **Abteilung Stab**, and 14 **Pz.Kpfw.IVs** in each of the three **Panzer-Kompanien**. The strength of these **Panzer-Brigaden** was further increased by assigning a **Panther-Abteilung** which had been previously created for a **Panzer-Division**. The **I.Abteilung/Panzer-Regiment 16** was assigned to **Panzer-Brigade 111**, **I.Abteilung/Panzer-Regiment 29** to **Panzer-Brigade 112**, and **I.Abteilung/Panzer-Regiment 130** to **Panzer-Brigade 113**. Each of these **Panther-Abteilungen** were to be outfitted with 3 Panthers for the **Abteilung Stab** and 14 Panthers in each of three **Panzer-Kompanien**.

With the exception of the **Panzer-Brigade 106 (FHH)** and the **Fuehrer-Grenadier-Brigade**, the independent **Heeres Panzer-Brigaden** were only short-lived. They were disbanded by absorbing their elements into the already existing **Panzer-Divisions** and **Panzer-Grenadier-Divisions** as follows:

In September 1944:

> **Pz.Brig.105** in **9.Pz.Div.**
> **Pz.Brig.111** in **11.Pz.Div.**
> > (except **I./Pz.Rgt.16** sent to **116.Pz.Div.**)
> **Pz.Brig.112** in **21.Pz.Div.**
> > (except **I./Pz.Rgt.29** to Grafenwoehr)
> **Pz.Brig.113** in **15.Pz.Gr.Div.**
> > (except **I./Pz.Rgt.130** to Bergen)

In October 1944:

> **Pz.Brig.101** in **20.Pz.Div.**
> **Pz.Brig.108** in **116.Pz.Div.**
> **Pz.Brig.109** in **Pz.Gr.Div.FHH**

In November 1944:

> **Pz.Brig.102** in **7.Pz.Div.**
> **Pz.Brig.103** in **5.Pz.Div.**
> **Pz.Brig.104** in **25.Pz.Div.**
> **Pz.Brig.107** in **25.Pz.Gr.Div.**
> **Pz.Brig.110** in **13.Pz.Div.**

In all cases, the Panzers from these **Panzer-Brigades** were taken over by the recipient divisions. In some cases, the **Panzer-Abteilungen** (numbered **2101** to **2113**) that had belonged to the **Panzer-Brigades** were renamed as **Panzer-Abteilungen** organic to their assigned divisions. In other cases, cadres of personnel retained their unit designation and were returned to the training grounds.

On 4 November 1944, orders were issued to create **Panzer-Brigade 150 ("Rabenhuegel")**. It was to be outfitted with captured equipment, disguised to fool American troops into believing it was a friendly unit, and therefore facilitate capturing important bridges and crossroads during the planned Winter offensive. It was not organized in the same way as the previous independent **Heeres Panzer-Brigaden**.

Its only Panzer unit was a single **Panzer-Kompanie** from the **I.Abteilung/Panzer-Regiment 11** which was issued five Panthers that were disguised as American M10 tank destroyers.

Refitting Units Decimated in the West - After the Panzer units in the West were severely mauled in the Falaise pocket and the ensuing drive to the Seine River, the decimated remnants were gradually pulled out of the Front to rest and refit. The **Panzer-Lehr-Division** was the first unit to be pulled out and sent back to refit by orders dated 20 August 1944. This was followed by orders on 3 September 944 to pull out the **1.SS**, **2.SS**, and **12.SS-Panzer-Divisions** for complete refitting. Elements of the **2.**, **9.**, **11.**, **21.**, **116.**, **9.SS**, and **10.SS-Panzer-Divisions** were reorganized into **Kampfgruppen** and remained in action at the Front, gradually being pulled out as the situation allowed to refit for the planned major offensive.

Following the decline in production as the Allied strategic bombing campaign began to have an impact, an insufficient number of Panzers were available to refit **Panzer-Regiments** with 79 Panthers and 81 **Pz.Kpfw.IV**, as called for by the normal **Gliederung Panzer-Division 44**. Therefore, orders were issued revising the **Panzer-Regiment's** organization and lowering the number of Panzers authorized for each unit.

The **11.Panzer-Division** was the only unit left in the West with a **Panzer-Regiment** with two **Panzer-Abteilungen** each with four **Panzer-Kompanien**. But each **Panzer-Kompanie** was authorized to possess only 14 **Pz.Kpfw.IVs** or 14 Panthers, and each **Abteilung** and **Regiment Stab** was authorized to possess only two **Panzerbefehlswagen**.

The **2.Panzer-Division**, **2.SS-Panzer-Division**, and **9.SS-Panzer-Division** each had a **Panzer-Regiment** with two **Panzer-Abteilungen** each with four **Panzer-Kompanien**. Their **Panther-Abteilung** was authorized to possess 14 Panthers in each **Panzer-Kompanie**. Their **gemischte Panzer-Abteilung** was authorized to possess two **Panzer-Kompanien** with 14 **Pz.Kpfw.IVs** each and two **Panzer-Sturmgeschuetz-Kompanien** with 14 **Sturmgeschuetze** each.

The **9.Panzer-Division** and **116.Panzer-Division** had a similar organization with a **Panther-Abteilung** of four **Panzer-Kompanien** each with 14 Panthers, but their **gemischte Panzer-Abteilung** only had one **Panzer-Sturmgeschuetze-Kompanie** with 14 Sturmgeschuetz along with the two **Panzer-Kompanien** with 14 **Pz.Kpfw.IVs** each.

The **21.Panzer-Division**, **Panzer-Lehr-Division**, **1.SS-Panzer-Division**, **10.SS-Panzer-Division**, and **12.SS-Panzer-Division** were all reduced to a **Panzer-Regiment** with a single **Panzer-Abteilung** of four **Panzer-Kompanien** (two **Panzer-Kompanien** with 17 Panthers each, and two **Panzer-Kompanien** with 17 **Pz.Kpfw.IVs** each) plus four Panthers as **Panzerbefehlswagen** for the **Regiment** and **Abteilung Stab**.

Status of Refitting the Panzer-Divisions in the West on 3 November 1944

Pz.Div.	Pz.Rgt.	StuG	Pz.IV	Pz.V
2	3	28 (0)*	30 (41)	60 (8)
9.	33	14 (0)	30 (0)	60 (41)
11.	15		58 (43)	60 (57)
21.	22		34 (29)	38 (8)
116.	16	14 (0)	30 (16)	60 (41)
Lehr	130		34 (34)	38 (38)
1.SS	SS-1		34 (34)	38 (38)
2.SS	SS-2	28 (28)	30 (34)	60 (25)
9.SS	SS-9	28 (0)	30 (32)	60 (2)
10.SS	SS-10		34 (0)	38 (13)
12.SS	SS-12		34 (37)	38 (41)

*The first number is the authorized strength. The number in parentheses is the total of those on hand plus those issued.

New K.St.N. Dated 1Nov44 - The following new set of K.St.N. dated 1 November 1944 was used to create new or refurbish existing Panzer-Regiments "freie Gliederung" when authorized by specific orders:

K.St.N.	Date	Unit Name
1103	1Nov44	**Stab und Stabskompanie eines Panzer-Regiments**
1107(fG) Ausf.A	1Nov44	**Stab und Stabskompanie (fG) einer Panzer-Abteilung "IV"**
1107(fG) Ausf.B	1Nov44	**Stab und Stabskompanie (fG) einer Panzer-Abteilung "Panther"**
1177(fG) Ausf.A	1Nov44	**Panzer-Kompanie "Panther" oder "IV" (17 Pz.Kpfw.)(fG)**
1177(fG) Ausf.B	1Nov44	**Panzer-Kompanie "Panther" oder "IV" (14 Pz.Kpfw.)(fG)**
1177a(fG)	1Nov44	**Panzer-Kompanie "Panther" oder "IV" (10 Pz.Kpfw.)(fG)**

The **Stab und Stabskompanie eines Panzer-Regiments**, organized in accordance with K.St.N.1103 dated 1 November 1944, contained a **Stabskompanie-Gruppe Fuehrer** with three **Panzerkampfwagen "Panther" (7,5 cm 42 (L/70)) (Sd.Kfz.171)** as **Panzerbefehlswagen** and an **Aufklaerungs-Zug** with five **Panzerkampfwagen "IV" (7,5 cm 40 (L/48)) (Sd.Kfz.161/2)**. The **Stab und Stabskompanie (fG) einer Panzer-Abteilung "IV"**, organized in accordance with K.St.N.1107(fG) Ausf.A dated 1 November 1944, contained a **Stabskompanie - Gruppe Fuehrer** with three **Panzerkampfwagen IV (7,5 cm 40 (L/48)) (Sd.Kfz.161/2)** as **Panzerbefehlswagen** and an **Aufklaerungs-Zug** with five **Panzerkampfwagen IV (7,5 cm 40 (L/48)) (Sd.Kfz.161/2)**. The Ausf.B of K.St.N.1107(fG) dated 1 November 1944 for a

(text continues on page 170)

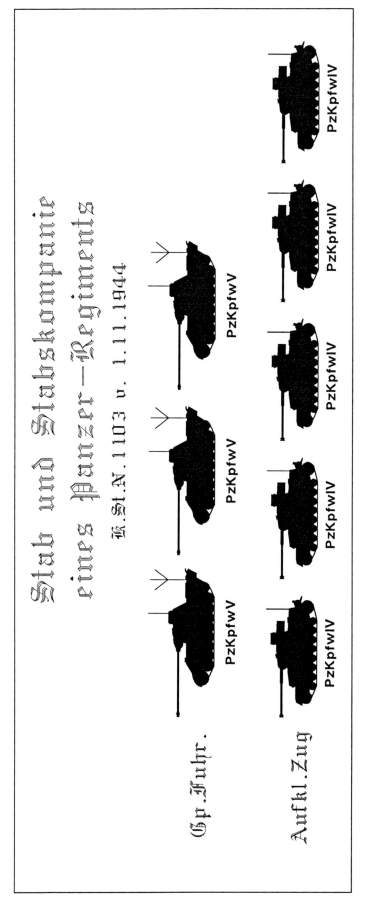

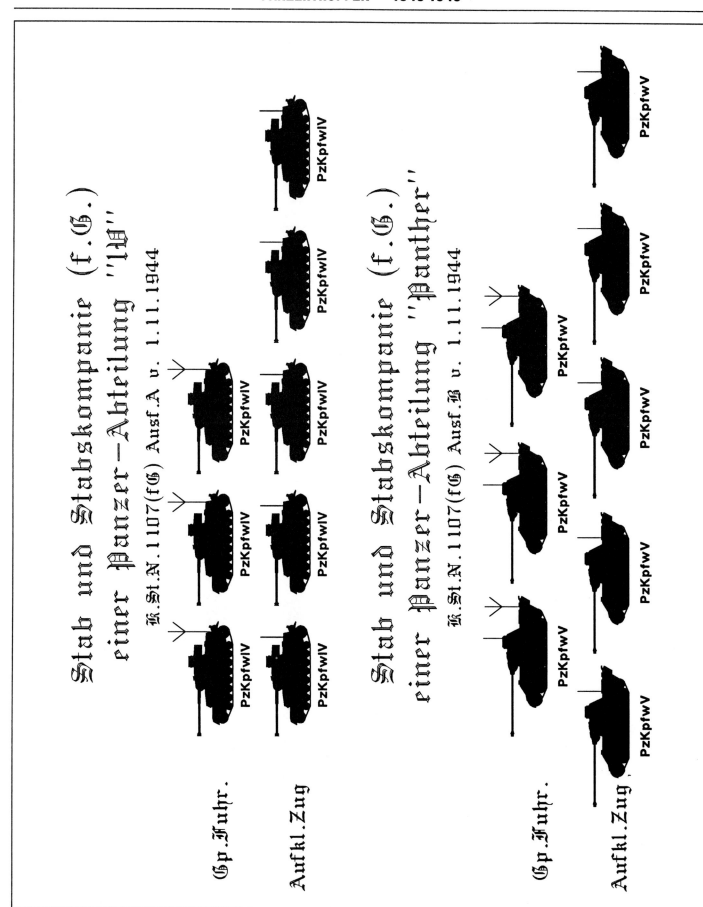

Stab und Stabskompanie (f.G.) einer Panzer–Abteilung "IV"

K.St.N.1107(fG) Ausf.A u. 1.11.1944

Gp.Fuhr.

Aufkl.Zug

PzKpfwIV

Stab und Stabskompanie (f.G.) einer Panzer–Abteilung "Panther"

K.St.N.1107(fG) Ausf.B u. 1.11.1944

Gp.Fuhr.

Aufkl.Zug

PzKpfwV

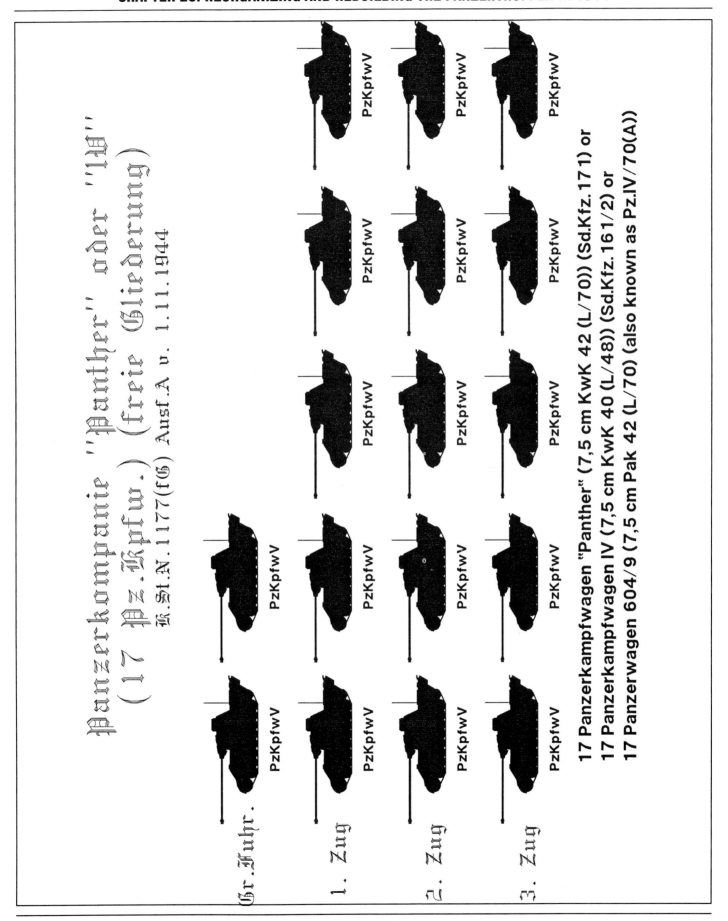

Panzerkompanie "Panther" oder "IV"
(17 Pz.Kpfw.) (freie Gliederung)
K.St.N.1177(fG) Ausf.A u. 1.11.1944

17 Panzerkampfwagen "Panther" (7,5 cm KwK 42 (L/70)) (Sd.Kfz.171) or
17 Panzerkampfwagen IV (7,5 cm KwK 40 (L/48)) (Sd.Kfz.161/2) or
17 Panzerwagen 604/9 (7,5 cm Pak 42 (L/70) (also known as Pz.IV/70(A))

Gr.Fhr.

1. Zug

2. Zug

3. Zug

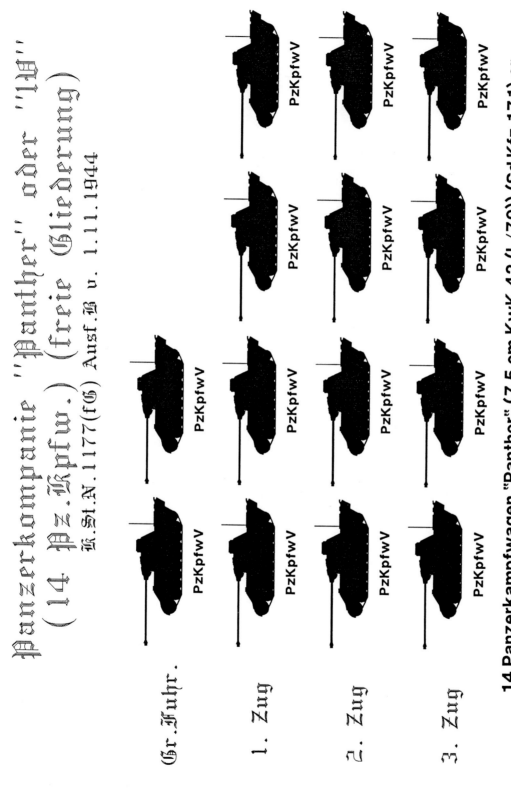

Panzerkompanie "Panther" oder "IV" (14 Pz.Kpfw.) (freie Gliederung) K.St.N.1177(fG) Ausf.B u. 1.11.1944

Gr.Fuhr.

1. Zug

2. Zug

3. Zug

14 Panzerkampfwagen "Panther" (7,5 cm KwK 42 (L/70)) (Sd.Kfz. 171) or
14 Panzerkampfwagen IV (7,5 cm KwK 40 (L/48)) (Sd.Kfz. 161/2) or
14 Panzerwagen 604/9 (7,5 cm Pak 42 (L/70)) (also known as Pz.IV/70(A))

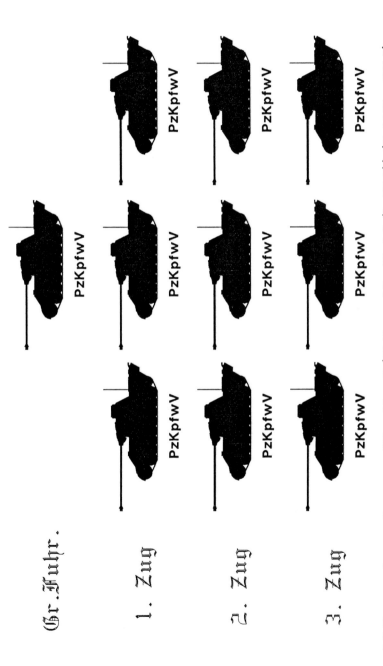

Panzerkompanie "Panther" oder "IV"
(10 Pz.Kpfw.) (freie Gliederung)
K.St.N.1177A(fG) v. 1.11.1944

Gr.Fuhr.

1. Zug

2. Zug

3. Zug

PzKpfwV

10 Panzerkampfwagen "Panther" (7,5 cm KwK 42 (L/70)) (Sd.Kfz.171) or
10 Panzerkampfwagen IV (7,5 cm KwK 40 (L/48)) (Sd.Kfz.161/2) or
10 Panzerwagen 604/9 (7,5 cm Pak 42 (L/70)) (also known as Pz.IV/70(A))

Stab und Stabskompanie (fG) einer Panzer-Abteilung "Panther" was the same as Ausf.A with the exception that the **Pz.Kpfw.IVs** were replaced by eight **Panzerkampfwagen "Panther" (7,5 cm KwK 42 (L/70)) (Sd.Kfz.171)**. The **Panzer-Kompanie "Panther" oder "IV" (17 Pz.Kpfw.)(fG)**, organized in accordance with K.St.N.1177(fG) Ausf.A dated 1 November 1944, contained a **Gruppe Fuehrer** with a choice of two **Panzerkampfwagen "Panther" (7,5 cm 42 (L/70)) (Sd.Kfz.171)**, two **Panzerkampfwagen IV (7,5 cm 40 (L/48)) (Sd.Kfz.161/2)**, or two **Panzerwagen 604/9 (7,5 cm Pak 42 (L/70))**, and each of the three **Zuege** had five **Panzerkampfwagen "Panther" (7,5 cm 42 (L/70)) (Sd.Kfz.171)**, five **Panzerkampfwagen IV (7,5 cm 40 (L/48)) (Sd.Kfz.161/2)**, or five **Panzerwagen 604/9 (7,5 cm Pak 42 (L/70))**.

In the Ausf.B of K.St.N.1177(fG) dated 1 November 1944 for a **Panzer-Kompanie "Panther" oder "IV" (14 Pz.Kpfw.)(fG)**, the **Gruppe Fuehrer** still had two Panzers but each of the three **Zuege** was reduced to four Panzers. The **Panzer-Kompanie "Panther"/IV (10 Pz.Kpfw.)(fG)**, organized in accordance with K.St.N.1177a(fG) dated 1 November 1944, was authorized one **Panzerkampfwagen "Panther"** or one **Panzerkampfwagen IV** with the **Gruppe Fuehrer** and three **Panzerkampfwagen "Panther"** or three **Panzerkampfwagen IV** in each of the three **Zuege**.

Kampfgruppe Fuehrer-Begleit-Brigade

Kampfgruppe Fuehrer-Begleit-Brigade - To support planned offensives, the **Fuehrer-Begleit-Brigade** was reinforced with additional Panzer units that had been sent back by other divisions to rest and refit. On 28 November 1944, the status report for the **Kampfgruppe Fuehrer-Begleit-Brigade** included the **5.Kompanie/I./Fuehrer-Begleit-Bataillon "Grossdeutschland"** with 17 **Pz.Kpfw.IV** and 5 **Pz.IV/70(A)**, the **Stab Panzer-Brigade 103** with the **II.Abteilung/Panzer-Regiment 2** with one **Panzer-Kompanie** (6 **Pz.Kpfw.IV** and 11 **Pz.IV/70(A)**), and the **II.Abteilung/Panzer-Regiment "Grossdeutschland"** with three **Panzer-Kompanien** (7 **Pz.Kpfw.IV** and 38 **Pz.IV/70(V)**).

TIGER UNITS

Five **Tiger-Abteilungen** that had been created or re-created in 1943 were outfitted with their full complement of 45 Tiger I and sent into action as follows:

Month	Unit	Front
February	**s.H.Pz.Abt.508**	Italy
March	**s.H.Pz.Abt.507**	East
June	**s.H.Pz.Abt.504**	Italy
June	**s.SS-Pz.Abt.101**	West
June	**s.SS-Pz.Abt.102**	West

The **schwere Heeres Panzer-Abteilung 503** was ordered to return from the Eastern Front to rest and refit on 25 May 1944. It was outfitted with 12 Tiger II and 33 Tiger I to fill its authorized strength of 45 Tigers in June 1944. It was transferred to the Western Front and loaded on trains starting on 27 June, not getting into action until 11 July due to transport delays.

The last of the ten **schwere Heeres Panzer-Abteilungen**, the **510**, was formed on 6 June 1944, the same date as the Allied invasion of Normandy. Outfitted with 45 Tiger I shipped from the **Heeres-Zeugamt** between 20 June and 7 July 1944, the **schwere Heeres Panzer-Abteilung 510** was sent to **Heeresgruppe Mitte** on the Eastern Front by orders dated 19 July 1944.

New K.St.N. Dated 1 Jun44 - The following new set of K.St.N. dated 1 June 1944 was used to create new or refurbish existing Tiger units to **"freie Gliederung"** when authorized by specific orders:

K.St.N.	Date	Unit Name
1107b(fG)	1 Jun 44	**Stab und Stabskompanie schweren Panzer-Abteilung "Tiger" (freie Gliederung)**
1176(fG)	1 Jun 44	**schwere Panzer-Kompanie "Tiger" (freie Gliederung)**

The **Stab und Stabskompanie schweren Panzer-Abteilung "Tiger" (freie Gliederung)**, organized in accordance with K.St.N.1107b(f.G.) dated 1 June 1944, contained a **Gruppe Fuehrer** with three **Panzerkampfwagen "Tiger" (8,8 cm 36 L/56) (Sd.Kfz.181)** as **Panzerbefehlswagen** or three **Panzerkampfwagen "Tiger" (8,8 cm 43 L/71) (Sd.Kfz.182)** as **Panzerbefehlswagen**. The Ausf.A version of the **schwere Panzer-Kompanie "Tiger" (freie Gliederung)**, organized in accordance with K.St.N.1176(f.G.) Ausf.A dated 1 June 1944, contained a **Gruppe Fuehrer** with two **Panzerkampfwagen "Tiger" (8,8 cm 36 L/56) (Sd.Kfz.181)** or two **Panzerkampfwagen "Tiger" (8,8 cm 43 L/71) (Sd.Kfz.182)**, and three **Zuege** each with four **Panzerkampfwagen "Tiger" (8,8 cm 36 L/56) (Sd.Kfz.181)** or four **Panzerkampfwagen "Tiger" (8,8 cm 43 L/71) (Sd.Kfz.182)**. The Ausf.B version was for the **schwere Panzer-Kompanie "Tiger" (FKL) (freie Gliederung)**. It was to be outfitted with 36 **Sprengstofftraeger (Sd.Kfz.301)** in addition to its 14 Tigers.

Refitting Complete Units with Tiger II - Decimated by the Russian Summer offensive, the **schwere Heeres Panzer-Abteilung 501** was pulled out to refit in early July 1944. It was reorganized under the new **"freie Gliederung"** K.St.N.1107b and 1176 dated 1 June 1944 and outfitted with 45 Tiger II. On 6 August 1944, the **schwere Heeres Panzer-Abteilung 501** was ordered to return to the Eastern Front to join **Heeresgruppe Nordukraine**.

Both the **3.Kompanie/schwere Heeres Panzer-Abteilung 503** and the **1.Kompanie/schwere SS-Panzer-Abteilung 101** were pulled out of the West and refitted with

14 Tiger II in late July 1944, and sent back to the West in early August 1944.

The **schwere Heeres Panzer-Abteilung 505** was ordered out of the Eastern Front on 7 July 1944 to rest and reorganize at the troop training grounds at Ohrdruf. Outfitted with 45 Tiger II in July and August, it was loaded on trains on 9 September and arrived on the Eastern Front at Nasielsk on 11 September 1944.

On 15 August 1944, the **schwere Heeres-Panzer-Abteilung 506** was ordered to return from the Eastern Front to reorganize and rebuild at Paderborn. Its 45 Tiger IIs were shipped from the **Heeres-Zeugamt** in August and September. Loaded on trains on 22 September, **schwere Heeres Panzer-Abteilung 506** was sent to Holland to help repulse the British spearhead at Arnhem, Holland. **Schwere Panzer-Kompanie Hummel** was incorporated into the **schwere Heeres Panzer-Abteilung 506** as the **4.Kompanie** by orders dated 8 December 1944.

On 9 September 1944, the **schwere Heeres Panzer-Abteilung 503** was ordered out of the West to rest and refit at Sennelager by Paderborn. It was outfitted with 45 Tiger IIs in September, loaded on trains on 12 October, and unloaded in Budapest, Hungary on 14 October 1944.

The **schwere SS-Panzer-Abteilung 101** (later renamed **501**) was ordered on 9 September 1944, to transfer to Sennelager to rest and refit. Outfitted with 45 Tiger II, the **schwere SS-Panzer-Abteilung 501** was shipped back to the Western Front on 5 December 1944.

New K.St.N. Dated 1Nov44 - The following new set of K.St.N. dated 1 November 1944 was used to create new or refurbish existing Tiger units when authorized by specific orders:

K.St.N.	Date	Unit Name
1107(fG) Ausf.D	1Nov44	**Stab und Stabskompanie (fG) einer schwere Panzer-Abteilung "Tiger"**
1176(fG)	1Nov44	**schwere Panzer-Kompanie "Tiger" (fG)**

The **Stab und Stabskompanie (fG) einer schweren Panzer-Abteilung "Tiger"**, organized in accordance with K.St.N.1107(fG) Ausf.D dated 1 November 1944, contained a **Stabskompanie - Gruppe Fuehrer** with three **Panzerkampfwagen "Tiger" (8,8 cm KwK 36 (L/56)) (Sd.Kfz.181)** or **Panzerkampfwagen "Tiger" (8,8 cm KwK 43 (L/71)) (Sd.Kfz.182)** as **Panzerbefehlswagen**. The **schwere Panzer-Kompanie "Tiger"(fG)** organized in accordance with K.St.N.1176(fG) dated 1 November 1944 had a **Gruppe Fuehrer** with two **Panzerkampfwagen "Tiger" (8,8 cm 36 L/56) (Sd.Kfz.181)** or two **Panzerkampfwagen "Tiger" (8,8 cm 43 L/71) (Sd.Kfz.182)**, and three **Zuege**, each with four **Panzerkampfwagen "Tiger" (8,8 cm 36 L/56) (Sd.Kfz.181)** or four **Panzerkampfwagen "Tiger" (8,8 cm 43 L/71) (Sd.Kfz.182)**.

Renaming Three schwere Heeres Panzer-Abteilungen - To avoid confusion in identification with the three **SS-Panzer-Abteilungen** that had been renumbered from **101**, **102**, and **103** to **501**, **502**, and **503**, the three **schwere Heeres Panzer-Abteilungen** were subsequently renamed as follows:

> **s.H.Pz.Abt.501** to **s.H.Pz.Abt.424** on 27 November 1944
> **s.H.Pz.Abt.502** to **s.H.Pz.Abt.511** on 5 January 1945
> **s.H.Pz.Abt.503** to **s.H.Pz.Abt.FHH** on 21 December 1944

PANZER-STURMGESCHUETZ-ABTEILUNGEN FOR PANZER-GRENADIER-DIVISIONS

On 3 May 1944, orders were issued to refit **Panzer-Grenadier-Division Feldherrnhalle** by 1 June 1944. Its **Panzer-Sturmgeschuetz-Abteilung** was to be reorganized into a **Panzer-Abteilung** with three **Panzer-Kompanien**, each with 14 **Pz.Kpfw.IVs**.

New K.St.N. to convert the **Panzer-Grenadier-Divisions** to **"freie Gliederung"** were established on 1 May 1944. The new organization for the **Panzer-Sturmgeschuetz-Abteilung** within the **Panzer-Grenadier-Division** was reorganized as follows:

K.St.N.	Date	Unit Name
1107c(fG)	1May44	**Stab und Stabs-Kompanie Panzer-Sturmgeschuetz-Abteilung (f.G.)**
1159(fG)	1May44	**Panzer-Sturmgeschuetz-Kompanie (f.G.)**
1151c(fG)	1May44	**Versorgungs-Kompanie Panzer-Sturmgeschuetz-Abteilung (f.G.)**

The **Stab und Stabs-Kompanie einer Panzer-Sturmgeschuetz-Abteilung (freie Gliederung)**, organized in accordance with K.St.N.1107c(fG) dated 1 May 1944, contained a **Gruppe Fuehrer** with three **Panzerkampfwagen III (5 cm (L/42)) (Sd.Kfz.141)** as **Panzerbefehlswagen**. The **Panzer-Sturmgeschuetz-Kompanie (f.G.)**, organized in accordance with K.St.N.1159(fG) dated 1 May 1944, had a **Gruppe Fuehrer** with two **Sturmgeschuetze III fuer 7.5 cm Stu.Kan.40 (L/48) (Sd.Kfz.142/1)** and three **Zuege**, each with four **Sturmgeschuetze III fuer 7.5 cm Stu.Kan.40 (L/48) (Sd.Kfz.142/1)**.

It wasn't until 20 August 1944, that the **OKH/Gen.Insp.d.Pz.Tr./GenStdH/Org.Abt.** issued the following order for the **Heeres Panzer-Grenadier-Divisions** to reorganize in accordance with the standardized **"Gliederung Panzer-Grenadier-Division 44"**:

1. The "Gliederung Panzer-Grenadier-Division 44" goes into immediate effect for all Panzer-Grenadier-Divisions.

2. Within the bounds of their available personnel and material, the Panzer-Grenadier-Divisions are to convert to this organization. The status of their reorganization is to be

Panzer-Grenadier-Div. 44

Anl. 1 zu OKH/Gen.Insp.d.Pz.Tr./Org. Abt.
Nr. I/2278/44 g.Kdos. v. 13.8.44.

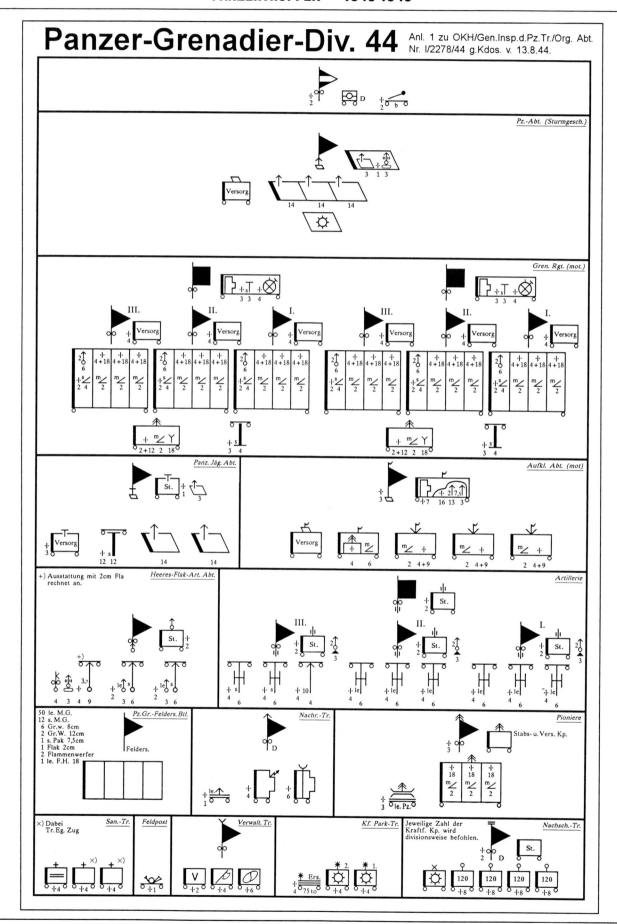

reported in the monthly operational status reports. **Panzer-Grenadier-Division "Grossdeutschland"** *and* **Panzer-Grenadier-Division "Feldherrnhalle"** *are exceptions. A special organization applies to these two divisions.*

3. The list of applicable K.St.N. for **Panzer-Grenadier-Division 44** *is included as an Appendix.*

The **Panzer-Sturmgeschuetz-Abteilung** in each **Panzer-Grenadier-Division** was to be organized in accordance with the following K.St.N.:

K.St.N.	Date	Unit Name
1107c(fG)	1May44	**Stab und Stabs-Kompanie Panzer-Sturmgeschuetz-Abteilung (f.G.)**
1159(fG)	1May44	**Panzer-Sturmgeschuetz-Kompanie (f.G.)**
1151c(fG)	1May44	**Versorgungs-Kompanie Panzer-Sturmgeschuetz-Abteilung (f.G.)**
1185	1Jun42	**Panzer-Werkstatt-Zug**

The entire **Panzer-Sturmgeschuetz-Abteilung** was authorized to possess 45 **Sturmgeschuetze**.

On 1 June 1944, four **SS-Panzer-Grenadier-Divisions** (4., 16., 17., and 18.) were in the process of being refitted. They each had an **SS-Panzer-Abteilung** of three **Panzer-Sturmgeschuetz-Kompanien**, with each **Kompanie** authorized to have 14 **Sturmgeschuetze**.

As a result of the major Russian Summer offensive, the 18. and 25.**Panzer-Grenadier-Divisions** as well as the **Panzer-Grenadier-Division Feldherrnhalle** were wiped out on the Eastern Front in July 1944. Surviving remnants of these divisions were utilized to create independent **Heeres-Panzer-Brigaden**.

Panzer-Grenadier-Division FHH was rebuilt by absorbing **Panzer-Brigade 109** in October 1944. The 25.**Panzer-Grenadier-Division** was rebuilt in November 1944 by incorporating **Panzer-Brigade 107**. Both of their **Panzer-Abteilungen** retained the organization of the **Panzer-Abteilungen** taken over from the **Panzer-Brigades**, with three **Panther-Kompanien**. **Panzer-Abteilung 118** of the 18.**Panzer-Grenadier-Division** retained its previous organization and was refitted with 45 **Sturmgeschuetze**.

<u>New K.St.N. Dated 1Nov44</u> - The following new set of K.St.N. dated 1 November 1944 was used to create new or refurbish existing **Panzer-Sturmgeschuetz-Abteilungen** when authorized by specific orders:

K.St.N.	Date	Unit Name
1107(fG) Ausf.C	1Nov44	**Stab und Stabskompanie (fG) einer Panzer-Sturmgeschuetz-Abteilung**
1159(fG) Ausf.A	1Nov44	**Panzer-Sturmgeschuetz-Kompanie (fG)**

The **Stab und Stabskompanie (fG) Panzer-Sturmgeschuetz-Abteilung**, organized in accordance with K.St.N.1107(fG) Ausf.C dated 1 November 1944, contained a **Stabskompanie - Gruppe Fuehrer** with three **Sturmgeschuetze III 7,5 cm StuK 40 (L/48) (Sd.Kfz.142/1)** as **Panzerbefehlswagen**. The **Panzer-Sturmgeschuetz-Kompanie (fG)**, organized in accordance with K.St.N.1159(fG) dated 1 November 1944, had a **Gruppe Fuehrer** with two **Sturmgeschuetze III fuer 7.5 cm Stu.Kan.40 (L/48) (Sd.Kfz.142/1)** and three **Zuege**, each with four **Sturmgeschuetze III fuer 7.5 cm Stu.Kan.40 (L/48) (Sd.Kfz.142/1)**.

STURMPANZER UNITS

After being pulled out of the Eastern Front in December 1943, **Sturmpanzer-Abteilung 216** on 22 January 1944 was ordered to quickly refit in accordance with the following organization:

K.St.N.	Date	Unit Name
1107	1Nov43	**Stab einer Panzer-Abteilung**
1156	1Nov43	**Stabs-Kompanie einer Sturmpanzer-Abteilung**
1160	1Nov43	3 **Sturmpanzer-Kompanie (14 Geschuetze)**

On 31 January/1 February 1944, orders were issued to reinforce each **Sturmpanzer-Kompanie** with a fourth **Zug** of four **Sturmpanzer**. **Sturmpanzer-Abteilung 216** was sent to Italy in February 1944 with 18 **Sturmpanzer** in each of the three **Sturmpanzer-Kompanien** as well as three **Sturmpanzer** for the **Abteilung Stab** and a **leichte Zug** of five **Pz.Kpfw.II**.

On 26 February 1944, orders were issued to create a **4.Kompanie/Sturmpanzer-Abteilung 216** by 20 March 1944 with 14 **Sturmpanzer** in accordance with K.St.N.1160 dated 1 November 1943.

The second **Sturmpanzer-Abteilung** (number 217) was created on 7 April 1944. **Sturmpanzer-Abteilung 217** was issued 45 **Sturmpanzer** for its **Abteilung Stab** and three **Sturmpanzer-Kompanien** and sent to the Western Front in July 1944.

On 4 August 1944, **Sturmpanzer-Abteilung 218** was to be created by 20 August 1944 utilizing **Sturmgeschuetz-Brigade 914**. In reality only two new **Sturmpanzer-Kompanien** were created and outfitted at this time. **Sturmpanzer-Kompanie z.b.V.218** was created in August 1944 and the **2.Kompanie/Sturmpanzer-Abteilung 218** on 16 August 1944. **Sturmpanzer-Kompanie z.b.V.218** with 10 **Sturmpanzer** was sent to the Eastern Front to **Heeresgruppe Mitte** in mid-August 1944, and the **2.Kompanie/Sturmpanzer-Abteilung 218** with 10 **Sturmpanzer** was shipped to the Western Front in late August 1944.

<u>**Reorganization to Freie Gliederung**</u> - The following new set of K.St.N. dated 1 September 1944 was established for organizing **Sturmpanzer-Abteilung** in a **"freie Gliederung."** In this new organization the supply and baggage vehicles were taken away from each **Kompanie** and concentrated into a **Versorgungs-Kompanie.**

K.St.N.	Date	Unit Name
1107d(fG)	1Sep44	**Stab und Stabskompanie einer Sturmpanzer-Abteilung (freie Gliederung)**
1160(fG)	1Sep44	**Sturmpanzer-Kompanie (freie Gliederung)**

The **Stab und Stabskompanie einer Sturmpanzer-Abteilung (freie Gliederung)**, organized in accordance with K.St.N.1107d(f.G.) dated 1 September 1944, contained a **Gruppe Fuehrer** with three **Sturmpanzer IV fuer 15 cm Sturm-Haub.43 (Sd.Kfz.166)** as **Panzerbefehlswagen**. The **Sturmpanzer-Kompanie (freie Gliederung)**, organized in accordance with K.St.N.1160(f.G.) dated 1 September 1944, consisted of a **Gruppe Fuehrer** with two **Sturmpanzer IV fuer 15 cm Stu.Haub.43 (Sd.Kfz.166)** and three **Zuge**, each with four **Sturmpanzer IV fuer 15 cm Stu.Haub.43 (Sd.Kfz.166).**

The last **Sturmpanzer-Abteilung** (number **219**) was created on 30 September 1944 by utilizing the **Sturmgeschuetz-Brigade 237** and the **4.Kompanie/Sturmpanzer-Abteilung 216. Sturmpanzer-Abteilung 219** was outfitted with 28 **Sturmpanzer** and sent to **Heeresgruppe Sued** on the Eastern Front in November 1944.

<u>**New K.St.N. Dated 1Nov44**</u> - The following new set of K.St.N. dated 1 November 1944 was to be used to create new or refurbish existing **Sturmpanzer** units when authorized by specific orders:

K.St.N.	Date	Unit Name
1107(fG) Ausf.C	1Nov44	**Stab und Stabskompanie (fG) einer Sturmpanzer-Abteilung**
1159(fG) Ausf.B	1Nov44	**Sturmpanzer-Kompanie (fG)**

The **Stab und Stabskompanie (fG) einer Sturmpanzer-Abteilung**, organized in accordance with K.St.N.1107(fG) Ausf.C dated 1 November 1944, contained a **Stabskompanie - Gruppe Fuehrer** with three **Sturmgeschuetze IV fuer 15 cm Stu.Haub.43 (L/12) (Sd.Kfz.166)** as **Panzerbefehls-wagen**. The **Sturmpanzer-Kompanie (fG)**, organized in accordance with K.St.N.1159(fG) Ausf.B dated 1 November 1944, had a **Gruppe Fuehrer** with two **Sturmgeschuetze IV fuer 15 cm Stu.Haub.43 (L/12) (Sd.Kfz.166)** and three **Zuge** each with four **Sturmgeschuetze IV fuer 15 cm Stu.Haub.43 (L/12) (Sd.Kfz.166).**

STURM-MOERSER UNITS

Orders to form the first **Sturm-Moerser-Kompanie** were issued on 13 August 1944. Still manned by factory personnel from the assembly firm of Alkett, two **Sturmmoerser** were shipped to Warsaw with this first unit, **Sturm-Moerser-Kompanie 1000**, arriving 15 to 18 August 1944. A **Zug** from **Sturm-Moerser-Kompanie 1000** was sent to the Western Front and unloaded in Meaux on 25 August 1944.

The official organization for the **Panzer-Sturm-Moerser-Kompanie "Tiger"** was published as K.St.N.1161 dated 15 September 1944. The **Gruppe Fuehrer** was to be outfitted with a **mittlere Beobachtungs-Panzerwagen (Sd.Kfz.251/18)** and each of the two **Zuege** with two **Panzersturm-moerser 38 cm "Tiger."**

Sturm-Moerser-Kompanie 1001 with four **Sturm-moerser** was ordered to be created on 23 September 1944, and **Sturm-Moerser-Kompanie 1002** with four **Sturmmoerser** was ordered to be created on 22 October 1944. Also on 22 October 1944, **Sturm-Moerser-Kompanie 1000** was ordered to return from the Front to rest and refit. Both **Sturm-Moerser-Kompanien 1000** and **1001** were sent to the Western Front in December 1944 to participate in the Ardennes offensive.

FUNKLENK-PANZER UNITS

In late 1943/early 1944, three **Funklenk-Panzer-Kompanien** were outfitted with Tigers to serve as radio control vehicles for the **BIV Sprengstofftraeger. Panzer-Kompanie (FKL) 316** was assigned to the **Panzer-Lehr-Regiment, Panzer-Kompanie (FKL) 314** was incorporated into and renamed **3.Kompanie/schwere Heeres Panzer-Abteilung 504**, and **Panzer-Kompanie (FKL) 313** was incorporated into and renamed **3.Kompanie/schwere Heeres Panzer-Abteilung 508**. These **schwere Panzer-Kompanie "Tiger" (F.K.L.)** were organized in accordance with K.St.N.1176f dated 1 February 1944, with a **Gruppe Fuehrer** with two **Panzer-kampfwagen "Tiger" (8,8 cm 36 L/56) (Sd.Kfz.181)** or two **Panzerkampfwagen "Tiger" (8,8 cm 43 L/71) (Sd.Kfz.182)**, three **Zuege** each with four **Panzerkampfwagen "Tiger" (8,8 cm 36 L/56) (Sd.Kfz.181)** or four **Panzerkampfwagen "Tiger" (8,8 cm 43 L/71) (Sd.Kfz.182)** and nine **Sprengstofftraeger (Sd.Kfz.301)**, and the **Gefechts-tross - Sondergeraet-Reserve** with nine **Sprengstofftraeger (Sd.Kfz.301).**

On 7 April 1944, the **Panzer-Kompanie (FKL) 312** was renamed **1.Kompanie/Panzer-Abteilung (FKL) 301**. On 5 June 1944, **Panzer-Abteilung (FKL) 301** with three **Kompanien** was sent to **Heeresgruppe Nordukraine** on the Eastern Front. The **4.Kompanie/Panzer-Abteilung (FKL) 301** remained behind in the West, attached to the **2.Panzer-Division.**

New K.St.N. Dated 1 Jun44 - The following new set of K.St.N. dated 1 June 1944 were to be used to create new or refurbish existing **Funklenk-Panzer** units when authorized by specific orders:

K.St.N.	Date	Unit Name
1107f	1 Jun44	**Stab einer Panzer-Abteilung f**
1150f	1 Jun44	**Stabs-Kompanie einer Panzer-Abteilung f**
1171f	1 Jun44	**leichte Panzer-Kompanie f**

The **Stabs-Kompanie einer Panzer-Abteilung f**, organized in accordance with K.St.N.1150 f dated 1 June 1944, contained a **Nachrichten-Zug** with three **Panzerkampfwagen III (5 cm L/42) (Sd.Kfz.141)** as **Panzerbefehlswagen**. The **leichte Panzer-Kompanie f**, organized in accordance with K.St.N.1171f dated 1 June 1944, consisted of a **Gruppe Fuehrer** with two **Sturmgeschuetz III fuer 7,5 cm Stu.Kan.40 (L/48) (Sd.Kfz.142/1)**, two **Zuege** each with four **Sturmgeschuetz III fuer 7,5 cm Stu.Kan.40 (L/48) (Sd.Kfz.142/1)** and 12 **Sprengstofftraeger (Sd.Kfz.301)**, and a **Gefechtstross - Sondergeraet-Reserve** with 12 **Sprengstofftraeger (Sd.Kfz.301)**.

On 22 June 1944, orders were issued to recreate **Panzer-Abteilung (FKL) 302** utilizing the **4.Kp./Pz.Abt.(FKL) 301**, **Pz.Kp.(FKL) 315**, and **Pz.Kp.(FKL) 317** to create the **1.**, **2.**, and **3.Kompanie** organized in accordance with the following K.St.N.:

K.St.N.	Date	Unit Name
1107f	1 Jun44	**Stab einer Panzer-Abteilung f**
1150f	1 Jun44	**Stabs-Kompanie einer Panzer-Abteilung f**
1171f	1 Jun44	**3 leichte Panzer-Kompanie f**

On 2 July 1944, the **4.Kp./Pz.Abt.(FKL)301** was ordered to remain with the **2.Panzer-Division** and be replaced by **Pz.Kp.(FKL) 316** from the **Panzer-Lehr-Division** for conversion to the **1.Kp./Pz.Abt.(FKL) 302**. On 25 July 1944, **Panzer-Kompanie (FKL) 311** was ordered to reorganize in accordance with K.St.N.1171f dated 1 June 1944 and at the same time was renamed **4.Kp./Pz.Abt.(FKL) 302**. **Panzer-Abteilung (FKL) 302** with all four **Kompanien** was sent to Warsaw in mid-August 1944.

On 19 August 1944, **Panzer-Abteilung (FKL) 301** was ordered to return from the Eastern Front and convert to Tigers as radio control vehicles for the **BIV Sprengstofftraeger**. **Panzer-Abteilung (FKL) 301** was outfitted with 31 Tigers and sent to the Western Front.

Panzer-Kompanie (FKL) 319 was created in September 1944, outfitted with 10 **Sturmgeschuetze** and 36 **BIV Sprengstofftraeger**, and sent to the Western Front.

New K.St.N. Dated 1 Oct44 - A new K.St.N. dated 1 October 1944 was used to convert existing **Funklenk-Panzer** units to the **"freie Gliederung"** when authorized by specific orders. The **leichte Panzer-Kompanie f (freie Gliederung)**, organized in accordance with K.St.N.1171f dated 1 October 1944, consisted of a **Gruppe Fuehrer** with two **Sturmgeschuetz III fuer 7,5 cm Stu.Kan.40 (L/48) (Sd.Kfz.142/1)** and two **Zuege** each with four **Sturmgeschuetz III fuer 7,5 cm Stu.Kan.40 (L/48) (Sd.Kfz.142/1)** and nine **Sprengstofftraeger (Sd.Kfz.301)** or **(Sd.Kfz.304)**.

MISCELLANEOUS PANZER UNITS

On 26 January 1944, orders were issued to create two **Panzer-Fliegerabwehr-Zuege** every 10 days starting on 1 February for incorporation into the **Panzer-Regiments** of the following Divisions: **2.Pz.Div.**, **9.Pz.Div.**, **90.Pz.Gren.Div.**, **Pz.Lehr-Div.**, **Pz.Div.H.G.**, **9.SS-Pz.Div.**, **10.SS-Pz.Div.**, and **12.SS-Pz.Div.** The **Panzer-Fliegerabwehr-Zug (2 cm Flak 38)**, organized in accordance with K.St.N.1195 dated 1 February 1944, consisted of three **Gruppe** each with four **Panzerkampfwagen 38 fuer 2 cm Flak 38 (Sd.Kfz.140)**. A total of 11 of these **Panzer-Fla-Zuege** were created and supplied to the **21.Pz.Div.**, **26.Pz.Div.**, **29.Pz.Gren.Div.**, and **17.SS-Pz.Gren.Div.** as well as the divisions named in the above order with the exception of the **9.Pz.Div.**

On 25 February 1944, orders were issued to consolidate the three **Panzer-Sicherungs-Kompanien** into one **Panzer-Abteilung** organized in accordance with the following K.St.N.:

K.St.N.	Date	Unit Name
1107	1 Apr43	**Stab einer Panzer-Abteilung**
1157	1 Nov43	**Stabs-Kompanie einer Panzer-Abteilung** with changes (3 **Pz.Kpfw.III** as **Pz.Bef.Wg.**)
1159 Ausf.A	1 Nov43	**3 mittlere Panzer-Kompanie**

Based on these orders the **Stabs-Kompanie/Panzer-Abteilung 208** was created on 18 March 1944. On 1 April 1944, the **2.Panzer-Sicherungs-Kompanie** was redesignated as the **1.Kompanie/Panzer-Abteilung 208**, the **3.Panzer-Sicherungs-Kompanie** as the **2.Kompanie**, and **Panzer-Sicherungs-Kompanie 35** as the **3.Kompanie**.

On 4 July 1944, orders were issued to create **Kampfgruppe Panzer-Grenadier-Brigade "v.Werthern"** utilizing elements of the **Fuehrer-Grenadier-Bataillon** with one **Panzer-Kompanie** with 12 **Pz.Kpfw.IV** and 5 **Sturmgeschuetze**.

The **schwere Panzer Kompanie "Einsatz Dunkirchen"** was hastily formed by the **schwere Panzer Ersatz und Ausbildungs Abteilung 500** at the training grounds near Paderborn. This unit with 14 Tiger I (renamed **schwere Panzer-Kompanie Hummel** on 20 September 1944) was sent west on 19 September to stop the British at Arnhem in Holland. Continuing to fight on the Western Front, **schwere**

Panzer-Kompanie Hummel was incorporated into **schwere Heeres Panzer-Abteilung 506** as the **4.Kompanie** by order dated 8 December 1944.

On 27 November 1944, Hitler ordered that in a special action a large number of **Flammpanzer** (at least 20 to 30) were to be completed. The next day, Hitler ordered an immediate determination of how many **Flammenwerferwagen** could be completed from available **Panzer** or **Sturmgeschuetz** chassis in the next three days. On 3 December, Hitler received a report that the ordered **Flammenwerfer** action was on schedule, with an expected total of 35 **Flammpanzer**. Along with the refurbishing of at least 10 **Pz.Kpfw.III (Fl)**, 20 **Jagdpanzer 38** were selected for conversion to **Flamm-Panzer 38**. Ten **Panzerflammwagen III** were issued to the newly created **Panzer-Flamm-Kompanie 351** and sent to **Heeresgruppe Sued** on the Eastern Front. The 20 **Flamm-Panzer 38** were issued, 10 each, to the newly created **Panzer-Flamm-Kompanie 352** and **353** and sent to **Heeresgruppe G** on the Western Front.

On 8 December 1944, orders were issued to outfit **Panzer-Abteilung 208** with effective Panzers and send it to **Heeresgruppe Sued** on the Eastern Front. Panzers were shipped from the **Heeres-Zeugamt** as follows: 31 **Pz.Kpfw.IV** on 8 December and 14 **Pz.IV/70(A)** on 19 December 1944. On 11 December 1944, **Panzer-Abteilung 212** was ordered to take over the **Pz.Kpfw.IIIs** from **Panzer-Abteilung 208**.

29

Invasion of Normandy to the Battle of the Bulge

Nine **Panzer-Divisions** and an **SS-Panzer-Grenadier-Division** were stationed in the West when the Allies landed in Normandy on 6 June 1944. Only three of these divisions were available to repulse the landing. The other divisions, scattered throughout France in various states of combat readiness, were being refitted after their surviving cadres had been pulled out of the Eastern Front during the Spring of 1944. The **Generalinspekteur der Panzertruppen** compiled a strength report to present to Hitler dated 10 June 1944 on the available Panzers in the West. In most cases this is not the strength of the divisions and **Panzer-Abteilungen** when they were sent into combat on the Western Front. Many of these Panzer units were still refitting and were issued and received additional Panzers before being sent into combat. The total strength (operational and in repair) of the Panzer units when they were actually committed into action is shown on the charts for the <u>Organization and Strength of Panzer Units Employed on the Western Front</u>.

The following tactical analysis of the situation in Normandy dated 19 June 1944 was reported by General Guderian to Hitler on 20 June 1944:

I. <u>Employment of Panzer Units on the Invasion Front up to 10 June</u>.

1. The enemy fights by completely exploiting his air supremacy and his material superiority. He is aggressive, but not so aggressive that it is costly.

The British follow attrition tactics similar to those used in Africa and strangle supply lines. This does not guarantee a decisive battle.

2. The 21.Panzer-Division started a penetrating attack on 7 June which struck into the 6th British Airborne Division.

3. Panzer-Lehr-Division started next, and by and by elements of the 12.SS-Panzer-Division "Hitler Jugend" entered the battlefield severely hindered by the enemy air force. As they arrived, elements of these divisions immediately attacked the enemy spearheads that were advancing at nu-

STRENGTH OF PANZER UNITS IN THE WEST ON 10 JUNE 1944

Name of Unit	III	Pz.Kpfw. IV	V	VI	StuG	Beute Pz.
2.Pz.Div.		98	79			
9.Pz.Div.		78	40		5	
11.Pz.Div.	26	89			8	
21.Pz.Div.		112				
116.Pz.Div.	13	86			6	
Pz.Lehr-Div.		98	88		.	
1.SS-Pz.Div.		45	54		45	
2.SS-Pz.Div.		54	78		42	
12.SS-Pz.Div.		98	66			
17.SS-Pz.Gr.Div.					42	
I./Pz.Rgt.15			4			
I./Pz.Rgt.24			9			
I./Pz.Rgt.25			11			
I./Pz.Rgt.27			79			
I./Pz.Rgt.29			8			
I./Pz.Rgt.36			10			
I./Pz.Rgt.GD			79			
I./SS-Pz.Rgt.3			6			
I./SS-Pz.Rgt.9			40			
I./SS-Pz.Rgt.10			4			
s.H.Pz.Abt.510				6		
s.SS-Pz.Abt.101				45		
s.SS-Pz.Abt.102				45		
s.SS-Pz.Abt.103				6		
Pz.Abt.205						51
Pz.Abt.206						46
Pz.Abt.213						36
Pz.Abt.(Fkl)302					10	
Pz.E.u.A.Abt.100						46
Total:	**39**	**758**	**655**	**102**	**158**	**179**

ORGANIZATION AND STRENGTH OF PANZER UNITS EMPLOYED ON THE WESTERN FRONT

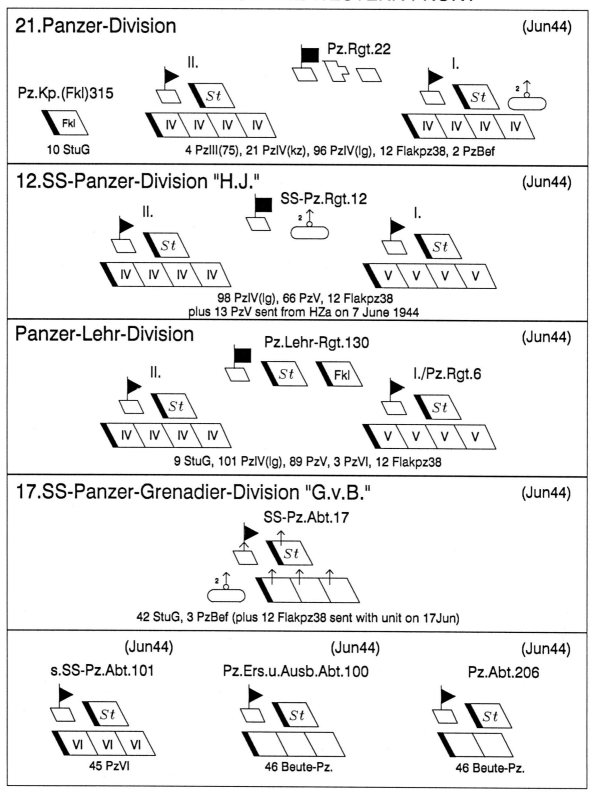

21.Panzer-Division (Jun44)

Pz.Kp.(Fkl)315

II.

Pz.Rgt.22

I.

10 StuG

4 PzIII(75), 21 PzIV(kz), 96 PzIV(lg), 12 Flakpz38, 2 PzBef

12.SS-Panzer-Division "H.J." (Jun44)

II.

SS-Pz.Rgt.12

I.

98 PzIV(lg), 66 PzV, 12 Flakpz38
plus 13 PzV sent from HZa on 7 June 1944

Panzer-Lehr-Division (Jun44)

Pz.Lehr-Rgt.130

II.

I./Pz.Rgt.6

9 StuG, 101 PzIV(lg), 89 PzV, 3 PzVI, 12 Flakpz38

17.SS-Panzer-Grenadier-Division "G.v.B." (Jun44)

SS-Pz.Abt.17

42 StuG, 3 PzBef (plus 12 Flakpz38 sent with unit on 17Jun)

(Jun44)

(Jun44)

(Jun44)

s.SS-Pz.Abt.101

Pz.Ers.u.Ausb.Abt.100

Pz.Abt.206

45 PzVI

46 Beute-Pz.

46 Beute-Pz.

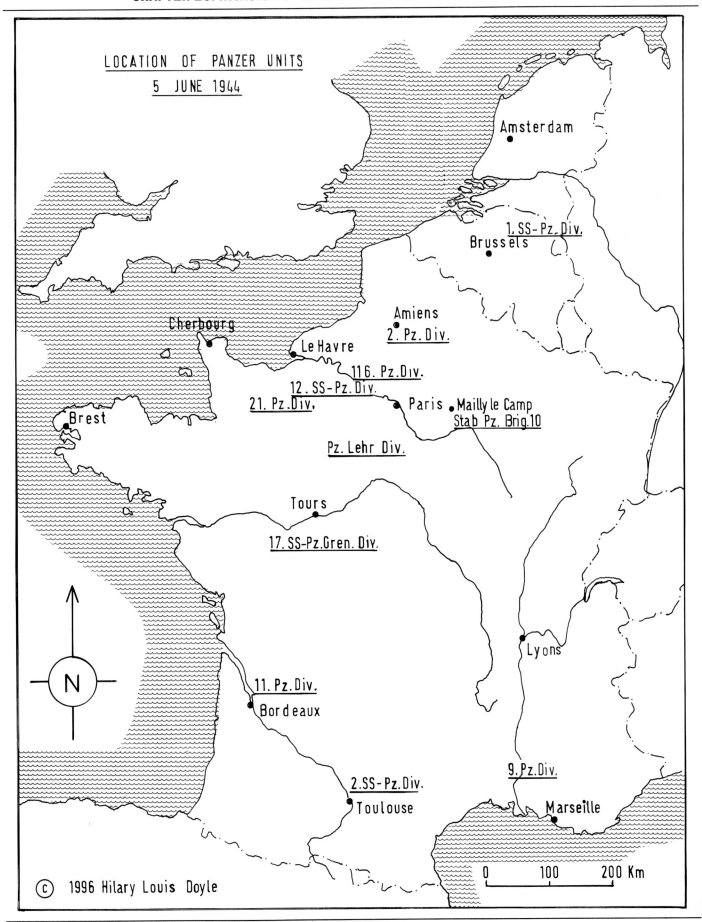

LOCATION OF PANZER UNITS
5 JUNE 1944

Amsterdam

1. SS-Pz. Div.

Brussels

Amiens
2. Pz. Div.

Cherbourg

Le Havre

116. Pz. Div.

12. SS-Pz. Div.

21. Pz. Div.

Paris   Mailly le Camp
Stab Pz. Brig. 10

Pz. Lehr Div.

Brest

Tours

17. SS-Pz. Gren. Div.

Lyons

N

11. Pz. Div.
Bordeaux

9. Pz. Div.

2. SS-Pz. Div.
Toulouse

Marseille

0   100   200 Km

ⓒ 1996 Hilary Louis Doyle

merous locations supported by tanks. In these battles on a wide front, a concentrated single assault group has to be limited to a combat strength of about one and one-half divisions.

4. Because of the enemy command of the skies, Panzer units arriving by road marches are especially short of fuel. After the initial battles, they also have ammunition shortages.

5. Arrival of the **Tiger-Abteilung** of the **I.SS-Panzer-Korps** was first expected at noon on 10 June. It was delayed because of the enemy command of the air. Every attempt to march during the day turned out to be useless. Attempts to move during the day resulted in numerous burned-out vehicles on the roads.

II. Possibility of eliminating the enemy beachhead with the available Panzer forces.

1. It doesn't appear to be possible to throw the Anglo-Americans back into the sea with their present forces and equipment as long as:

a. the guns from about 60 to 70 warships can fire undisturbed with aircraft spotters, and

b. the effect of the Anglo-American air force can be concentrated unhindered on this limited space.

2. **By itself, the highest bravery of the Panzertruppe cannot make up for the loss of two branches of the Wehrmacht.**

III. No more Panzer units may be sent into combat against the beachhead than can be resupplied at any given time.

Supplies still have not been guaranteed for the three **Panzer-Divisions** that have already been committed. In view of the concentrated effect of the enemy air forces on the narrow area opposite the beachhead, don't send in more **Panzer-Divisions**. Instead, supply personnel and material to fill the **Panzer-Divisions** in order to maintain their high combat power.

IV. Securing supply lines to the forward units is decisive.
It is possible to send in supplies only at night.

Proposed solution: a. Comb through the operational area, b. Secure the supply routes, c. Guard the ammunition and fuel dumps of the **Panzertruppe**. Send forces from the **Ersatzheer** to accomplish this.

A **Pz.Kpfw.IV Ausf.H** of the **8.Kompanie/Panzer-Regiment 3** moving through a French village. (BA)

The frontal armor of this Tiger of the **schwere SS-Panzer-Abteilung 101** successfully held up to the punishment from the opponent's anti-tank guns. (NA)

V. Tactics of the Panzer-Divisions already committed, considering the present enemy air force and navy situation.

Conduct an aggressive defense that will preserve the strength of our own forces. Offensive thrusts with limited objectives.

VI. Assemble new Panzer forces as an operational reserve.

1. Place the newly sent combat-ready Panzer forces in a central location as the decisive weight on the scale. No premature employment, not even by elements.

2. It is decisive that these reinforcements arrive soon and, above all else, undisturbed by the enemy air force.

3. Inform the commanders of the newly arrived units of the important lessons that have been learned:

a. Only night marches, between 2230 and 0530 hours.

b. Camouflage and dig in the command posts. Dig in the vehicles.

c. Separate the radio location from the command posts.

d. Camouflage the officers' uniforms, especially generals and general staff officers.

e. Employ commando guides and shield the supplies by night.

VII. Create a barrier line at a distance of about 100 kilometers from the front. This line may be crossed after 0530 hours and before 2230 hours only in exceptional cases with special permission from the traffic control organization.

VIII. Immediately send a general staff officer who has experience in combat against the Allies as the supply commander with authority to intercede on the spot.

IX. Improve the supply situation by seizing civilian vehicles.

As an example, the **17.SS-Panzer-Grenadier-Division** took the vehicles that they needed and successfully resisted all bureaucratic attempts to take them away. Only the **SS** can do this! Part of the vehicles commandeered by the **11.Panzer-Division** were taken away by bureaucratic authorities.

Proposed solution: Immediately permit units to seize vehicles from specified areas. Otherwise the danger exists that the vehicles will wander off into southern France and be seized by the British.

*X. There still aren't any exact reports on personnel. The Panzer situation is still not clear, because significant numbers of Panzers from both the **12.SS-Panzer-Division** and the **Panzer-Lehr-Division** that suffered mechanical breakdowns during the approach march still haven't arrived in maintenance.*

*XII. **Schwere Panzer-Abteilung (Tiger) 503** can't be made ready for combat before 2400 hours on 23 June because most of the wheeled vehicles and the repair services have not yet arrived and only 50 percent of the replacement parts - without spare engines, final drives, or transmissions - are available with the unit.*

*XIV. The **Panther-Abteilung** of the **9.SS-Panzer-Division "Hohenstaufen"** isn't ready for combat because it lacks the repair services and maintenance platoon. It is expected to be ready for combat after 20 June.*

Schwere SS-Panzer-Abteilung 101 had suffered a large number of mechanical breakdowns on the long road marches and arrived piecemeal at the front with less than half of their Tigers operational. The following account of one of their initial engagements in the West was written as justification for awarding SS-Obersturmfuehrer Wittmann, **Kompanie** commander in **schwere SS-Panzer-Abteilung 101**, the swords to the **Ritterkreuz**:

*On 12 June 1944, SS-Obersturmfuehrer Wittmann was ordered to secure the left flank of the Korps by Villers-Bocage because it was expected that the British armored forces who had broken through would strike toward the south and southeast. **Panzer-Grenadiere** were not available. Wittmann arrived at the ordered time with six **Panzerkampfwagen VI**.*

*During the night of 12/13 June, **Kompanie-Wittmann** had to change position three times because of the very heavy artillery fire. In the early morning hours of 13 June, they were located near Point 213 northeast of Villers-Bocage with five operational **Panzerkampfwagen VI**.*

About 0800 hours, the guard post reported to SS-Obersturmfuehrer Wittmann that a strong column of enemy tanks was advancing along the Caen to Villers-Bocage road. Wittmann, who was under cover with his Tiger 200 meters south of the road, recognized a British armored battalion, followed by a British armored infantry battalion.

The situation required quick action. Wittmann couldn't give orders to his men, who were some distance away. Instead, firing on the move, he immediately charged with his Panzer into the British column. This rash attack split the enemy column. Wittmann destroyed four Sherman tanks at a range of 80 meters, positioned himself with his Tiger in and alongside the column, and drove alongside the column at a range of 10 to 30 meters, firing in the direction he was driving. Within a short time he knocked out 15 enemy heavy tanks. Another six tanks were knocked out and the crews forced to abandon them. The escorting battalion mounted on armored half-tracks was almost totally destroyed. The four Panzers from

*Wittmann's **Kompanie** that were following behind took about 230 prisoners from here.*

*Well in advance of his **Kompanie**, Wittmann charged ahead into the village of Villers-Bocage. An enemy heavy anti-tank gun immobilized his Panzer in the middle of the village. In spite of this, he still destroyed all of the vehicles within range and scattered the enemy unit. Afterward, Wittmann and his crew dismounted the Panzer, slugged through on foot to the **Panzer-Lehr-Division** about 15 kilometers to the north, reported to the operations officer, immediately turned back with 15 **Pz.Kpfw.IVs** from the **Panzer-Lehr-Division**, and again struck toward Villers-Bocage. With his **Schwimm-Volkswagen**, which in the interim had rejoined him, Wittmann slugged through to the **1.Kompanie**, which had been employed along the main road toward Villers-Bocage. After orienting them on his impression of the combat situation, Wittmann sent the **1.Kompanie** against the enemy tanks and anti-tank guns that were still in the village.*

*Through his resolute actions, Wittmann destroyed a large part of the strong enemy spearhead (the British 22nd Armoured Brigade) that was already advancing deep in the rear of our front and, by immediate decisiveness with the highest personal bravery, averted the strong danger threatening the entire front of the **I.SS-Panzer-Korps**. The **Korps** did not have any other reserves available at this time.*

Including the battle today, Wittmann has knocked out a total of 138 enemy tanks and 132 anti-tank guns with his Panzer.

In a departure from his maxim of concentrated Panzer forces, General Guderian recommended a change of tactics in his presentation of the situation report to Hitler on 28 June 1944:

*The **Panzer-Divisions** have fought exceptionally well. After 21 days in action, the **Panzertruppen** find themselves in an extraordinarily fresh condition and want to attack.*

<u>*Employment of the **Panzertruppen** in Normandy*</u> *- The hedges and cut-up terrain of Normandy forces increased employment of infantry. Immediately sending in **Infanterie-Divisions**, in combination with the available Panzer forces, promises that our attempts to build **Schwerpunkte** will succeed.*

*Wherever **Panzertruppe** go into action on the Invasion Front, the **Panzer-Kampf-Trupp-Taktik** is to be used instead of the previous tactic of employing concentrated forces. (The latter tactics are still to be used in most other circumstances.) The **Panzer-Kampf-Trupp-Taktik** consists of close cooperation of small Panzer units combined with **Panzer-Grenadiere** or **Infanterie** units.*

*With concentrated forces, closely held **Panzer-Abteilungen** with a mounted **SPW-Bataillon** have to attack immediately at high speed to reach the ordered objective. This is the best way to neutralize the effect of enemy anti-tank guns and mines.*

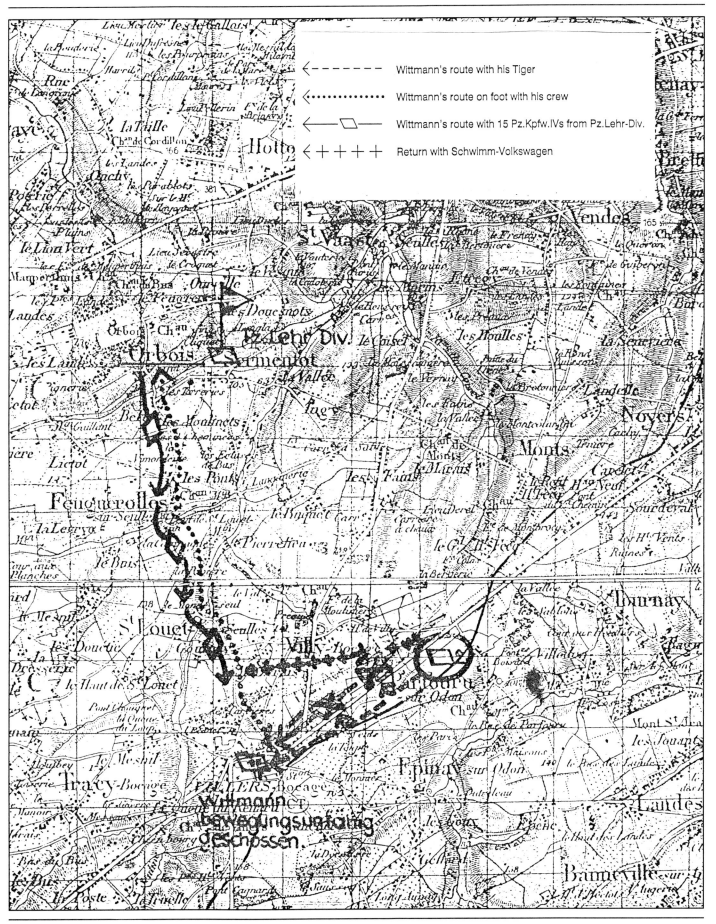

← — — — —	Wittmann's route with his Tiger
← • • • • • • • • •	Wittmann's route on foot with his crew
← —▱—	Wittmann's route with 15 Pz.Kpfw.IVs from Pz.Lehr-Div.
← + + + +	Return with Schwimm-Volkswagen

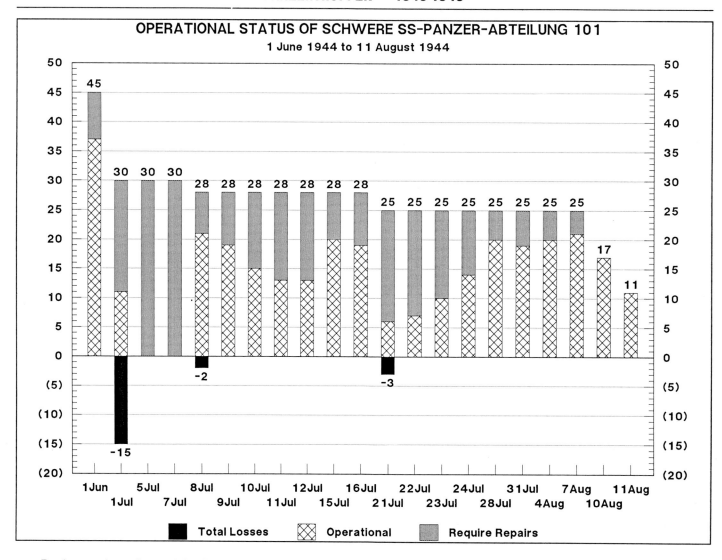

OPERATIONAL STATUS OF SCHWERE SS-PANZER-ABTEILUNG 101
1 June 1944 to 11 August 1944

Legend: ■ Total Losses ▨ Operational ▦ Require Repairs

Begin attacks only at night. Poor weather is also to be exploited for reducing the effect of enemy air supremacy.

*Technical Details - The **Pz.Kpfw.IV**, **V**, and **VI** have proven themselves to be good. However, the Panther burns astonishingly quickly. The lifespan of the Panther's engine (1400 to 1500 kilometers) is considerably higher than that of the Panther's final drives. A solution is urgently needed!*

*Mountings for the **Schuerzen** (side skirts) on the Panzers must be strengthened because of the hedgerows in Normandy.*

The troops will soon request spaced armor on the rear deck because of the success of strafing aircraft. A disadvantage is that it would further increase the weight of German Panzers, which are already too heavy.

While there are reports that **Sturmgeschuetze** were having difficulties in engaging targets in the hedgerow country of the Bocage in Normandy, this was not true of the Panzers which General Guderian again advocated in his memorandum for a report to Hitler on 29 June 1944 on conversion of **Pz.Kpfw.IV** to **Sturmgeschuetz** with L/48 or L/70 guns:

*At the average range in combat of 600 to 1200 meters, the **7.5 cm Kw.K. L/48** firing **Panzergranate 39** ammunition is adequate for engaging all British, American, and Russian tanks (including the British Cromwell tank) that have appeared to date.*

*Experience reports from Sicily, Italy, and Normandy comparing the **Pz.Kpfw.IV** to the **Sturmgeschuetz** unanimously state that when employed on coastal roads, in mountainous terrain, and in the sunken lanes and hedges of Normandy, the **Sturmgeschuetz** is both tactically and technically considerably less favored than the **Pz.Kpfw.IV**. The terrain makes impossible or at least severely limits aiming the **Sturmgeschuetz** to the sides.*

*Based on the latest observations reported by General Thomale in Paris and reports from the **Panzer-Offizier Ob.West**, employment of **Sturmgeschuetz** in the sunken lanes and the hedges of Normandy is difficult because the gun is mounted too low. In contrast, the **Panzerkampfwagen** can fire out of the sunken lanes and also over the hedges because of the height of the gun and traversable turret.*

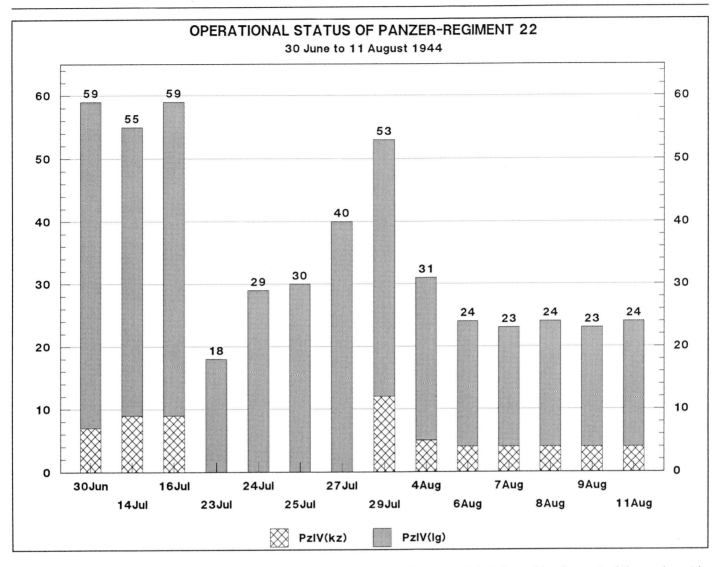

OPERATIONAL STATUS OF PANZER-REGIMENT 22
30 June to 11 August 1944

Legend: PzIV(kz), PzIV(lg)

On 3 July 1944, a list of the number of enemy tanks claimed to have been knocked out on the Invasion Front was compiled by division and type of weapon:

Type of Weapon	17.SS	2.Pz	Lehr	12.SS	21.Pz	Total
Pz.Kpfw.	-	-	85	105	37	227
StuG & Pak-Sf.	7	15	18	-	15	61
Pak & Flak (mot)	5	4	7	16	41	105
Artillerie	-	-	4	-	3	36
Nahkampfwaffen	5	5	40	23	5	108
Grand Total	17	24	154	144	101	537

In June 1944, the **9.SS-Panzer-Division "Hohenstaufen"** and the **10.SS-Panzer-Division "Frundsberg"** were pulled out of the Eastern Front and transferred to the Western Front. The **II.Abteilung** of both **SS-Panzer-Regiments** were assembled behind the front and ready to go into action on 29 June 1944. The lead **Kompanie** of **SS-Panzer-Regiment 1** of the **1.SS-Panzer-Division "LSSAH"** was sent into action on 2 July followed by the rest of the regiment in early July. The **2.SS-Panzer-Division**, held in reserve during late June, also went into action in early July.

The Panzer units reported the following losses as total write-offs during the period from 6 June to 8 July 1944:

Unit Name	StuG	PzIV	PzV	PzVI	Total
2.Pz.Div.		3	20		23
21.Pz.Div.		54			54
Pz.Lehr-Div.	3	41	36		80
1.SS-Pz.Div.			1		1
2.SS-Pz.Div.		28	3		31
9.SS-Pz.Div.	9	18	12		39
10.SS-Pz.Div.	4	6	3		13
12.SS-Pz.Div.		47	37		84
17.SS-Pz.Gren.Div.	9				9
s.SS-Pz.Abt.101				15	15
Grand Total	25	197	112	15	349

The only replacements that had arrived between 6 June and 8 July were 17 **Pz.Kpfw.IV (L/48)** for the **21.Panzer-Division**.

The following preparation order from the commander of the **SS-Panzer-Regiment 2** of the **2.SS-Panzer-Division "Das Reich"** covered details on tactics that were to be employed by Panzers in the Normandy Bocage:

A. General

Here on the Invasion Front we are facing an enemy superior to us in equipment but not in fighting spirit. We shall also emerge victorious in this struggle because fighting spirit is the deciding factor in battle. I wish to see this continuously brought home to the men in talks and lectures. I expect my **Kompanie** *commanders to be able to rouse their men, filling them with a fanatical elan. Every man must be convinced of our ability to cancel out enemy air and material superiority. We shall exploit the inferior quality of the enemy soldier as a fighting man. The enemy tanks are timid. If we tackle them energetically, we shall make them run and soon destroy them.*

B. Battle Tactics

1. Here there will be none of the tank fighting that we dream about. The close country compels us to fight with small battle or assault groups with close cooperation between Panzers, **Panzer-Grenadiere, Pioniere,** *and* **Artillerie.**

2. The most trouble to all the units will be caused by the enemy artillery. Artillery must be the first objective, and it must be destroyed at all costs. Each commander must bear this in mind when left without orders. Once the attack is started there must be no halting, for that only means our death and destruction. The enemy will begin to falter when his artillery position has been occupied. Then we must exploit his weakness and push on without regard to maintaining contact with flanking or following units. During the attack we should not adhere strictly to the allotted boundaries and objectives, but must exploit the terrain and signs of enemy weakness in order to penetrate into the depth of the enemy position. Gaps can easily be closed and flanks easily protected because the attack will be echeloned in great depth.

3. The main burden of fighting in this close country will be borne by **Panzer-Grenadiere**. *The task of the Panzer crews is to support them to the utmost and to exploit every opportunity to independently push forward.*

4. The intention is to mount a divisional attack against the new fortified enemy line with the two **Panzer-Grenadier-Regiments** *leading, supported by the* **Sturmgeschuetz-Batterie** *and the* **Artillerie-Regiment**. *I have offered two* **Panzer-Kompanien** *to support the* **Grenadiere**, *with the intention that they will follow the attacking* **Grenadiere** *in the role of* **Sturmgeschuetze**. *They will have the additional task of reconnoitering and marking routes forward for the following* **Panzer-Kampfgruppe** *and for exploiting every opportunity for a tank thrust.*

The commanders of both **Panzer-Kampfgruppen** *will follow with their* **Stabs-Kompanien** *some distance to the rear of their two leading* **Panzer-Kompanien.** *The* **Stabs-Kompanien** *will be further reinforced by one* **Pionier-Zug** *each.*

The tasks assigned to the **Panzer-Kampfgruppen** *commanders are:*

a. Close liaison with the **Panzer-Grenadier-Kampfgruppen**.

b. Early ground and situation reconnaissance.

c. Reconnaissance of approach routes for the **Panzer-Kampfgruppen** *to follow, employing the* **Pioniere** *to effect any necessary repairs and improvements.*

d. Exploitation of every opportunity for an armored thrust, making ruthless penetrations with the forces at their disposal.

5. The **Panzer-Kampfgruppen**, *under the two* **Abteilung** *commanders, will organize themselves into two independent waves:*

First Wave: In the first group the commander of the armored **Panzer-Grenadier-Bataillon**; *in the other group the commander of the* **Aufklaerungs-Abteilung**. *It will be seen that I have made the first wave strong in* **Grenadiere** *and weak in Panzers. The* **Grenadiere** *will attack on foot, using some of their* **S.P.W.** *as ammunition carriers, and parking the majority in the rear. On the invasion front there will be no chance of this wave fighting mounted. The task of this wave will be to get the enemy moving, thus starting the ball rolling for the fully armored elements.*

The first wave will move by bounds, almost, one might say, from hedge to hedge. It would be absurd to lay down hard and fast rules for this wave, as the ground varies so much that only flexible tactics, changing with each situation, are likely to have any success. Where the closeness of the country precludes unified command of the wave, it should be divided into two independent **Kampfgruppen** *(reinforced* **Kompanien**). *The* **Grenadier-Kompanien** *will take the main responsibility for the fighting. The* **Panzer-Kompanien** *will be split up and put in support of the* **Grenadiere**.

Second Wave: The second wave contains the completely armored elements, held ready to take up the pursuit of the shaken enemy who has been forced into movement. They will also be employed if the first wave has got stuck and there is a better chance of success on other sectors or in another direction. Local thrusts in the open flanks will be necessary for their protection. The **Panzer-Kompanien** *will take the main responsibility for the fighting in this wave.* **Grenadiere** *and* **Pioniere** *come under their command.*

6. The **Panzer-Kompanien** *will consist of 8 to 12 Panzers. All Panzers in excess of this number will be combined as a regimental reserve where, together with the regimental* **Aufklaerungs-Zug** *and the armored* **Flak-Kompanie**, *they will comprise a further reserve assault group.*

C. Training and Preparation

The few remaining days at our disposal will be spent in intensive training. The men must be toughened. The following are the detailed guiding principles:

ORGANIZATION AND STRENGTH OF PANZER UNITS EMPLOYED ON THE WESTERN FRONT

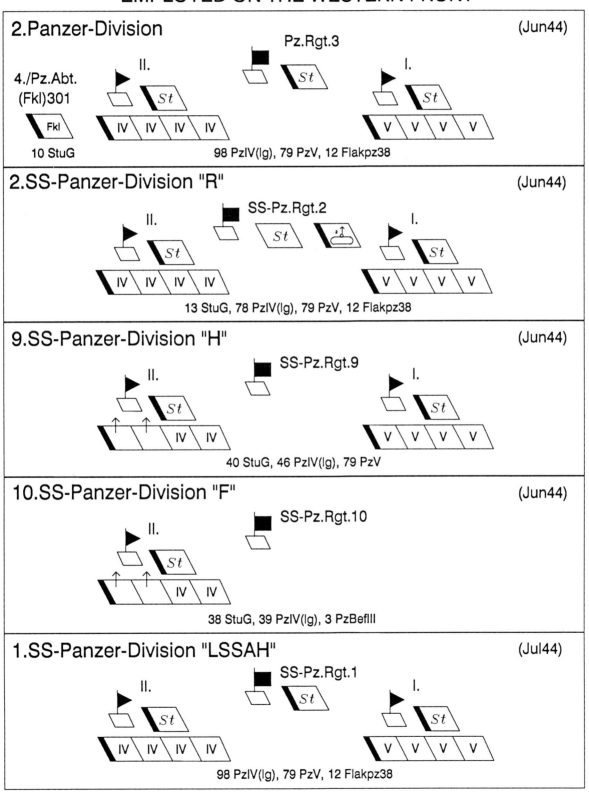

2.Panzer-Division (Jun44)

Pz.Rgt.3

4./Pz.Abt. (Fkl)301

II.

I.

10 StuG

98 PzIV(lg), 79 PzV, 12 Flakpz38

2.SS-Panzer-Division "R" (Jun44)

SS-Pz.Rgt.2

II.

I.

13 StuG, 78 PzIV(lg), 79 PzV, 12 Flakpz38

9.SS-Panzer-Division "H" (Jun44)

SS-Pz.Rgt.9

II.

I.

40 StuG, 46 PzIV(lg), 79 PzV

10.SS-Panzer-Division "F" (Jun44)

SS-Pz.Rgt.10

II.

38 StuG, 39 PzIV(lg), 3 PzBefIII

1.SS-Panzer-Division "LSSAH" (Jul44)

SS-Pz.Rgt.1

II.

I.

98 PzIV(lg), 79 PzV, 12 Flakpz38

1. Night Training:

a. Close cooperation of Panzers, **Pioniere**, and motor-cyclists. This must ensure that the Panzers can, whatever the terrain, follow up and give flexible support to the attacking **Panzer-Grenadiere**. I know that Panzers can't fight independently in forward areas at night, but they must exploit every possible opportunity and, if possible, even push forward alone.

b. At night, alternative means of communication with **Grenadiere** and **Pioniere** is important. It is necessary to have one or two runners riding on every commander's Panzer.

c. As many Panzers as possible, especially the commander's Panzer, must be outfitted with headlights. These are to be used only on orders from the **Kompanie** commander or the independent **Zug** leader. Short flashes are sufficient to spot the enemy, after which there must be a change of position. Designation of target and fire commands will occur before the headlights are turned on. All Panzers are to open fire when the headlights are turned on, including those that have not clearly spotted a target. As soon as the Panzers cease firing, the attack will go in with the Panzers alongside the **Grenadiere**.

d. As far as possible, light signals should not be fired from the Panzers. **Grenadiere** should be detailed for this task and pushed forward to fire the signals from under suitable cover without compromising the Panzers. If fired from Panzers, they should be fired obliquely to the target and only on an officer's orders.

e. Using binoculars, Panzer commanders are to observe continuously from their open hatches.

f. Movement by leapfrogging bounds providing mutually supporting fire is not feasible in this terrain. The danger of shooting each other up is too great. Therefore, the attack will be conducted with the **Zuege** in line abreast. The remainder of the **Kompanie** will follow in line ahead to cover the flanks.

2. There must be small-scale daytime exercises, including the following:

a. All Panzers will be camouflaged. Flat surfaces will be covered with wire netting on which foliage will be interlaced. The **Schuerzen** (side skirts) will also be camouflaged in this manner.

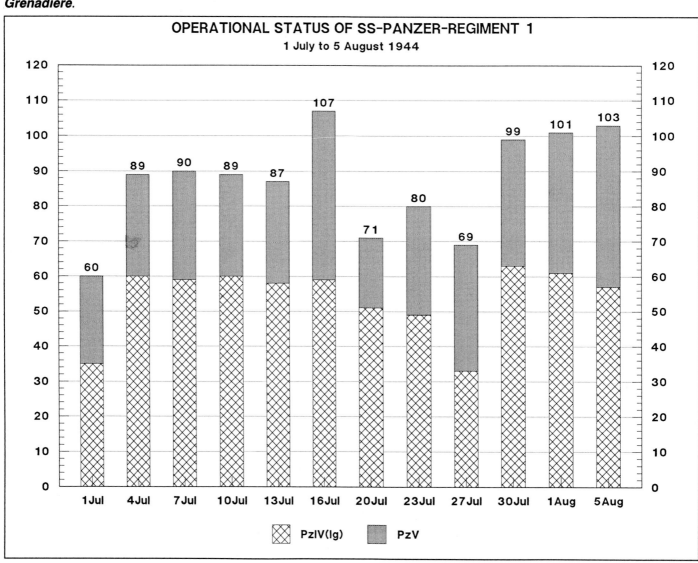

b. During the day, the Panzers are to move by short bounds from cover to cover. All firing positions must also afford cover. Loose formations are necessary. Under these conditions the Panzers may even, as an exception, operate by **Halb-Zuege** *(sections).*

c. Firing from hedges must be practiced. If necessary, loaders should dismount and make a field of fire. Hedgecutters should be organized. If defensive fire is very heavy, fire should be opened at any suspected source.

d. The principal weapon in this terrain is the machine gun. All Panzers will therefore be issued with at least 5500 rounds of machine gun ammunition. Each Panzer will also be issued 20 hand grenades for the engagement of enemy infantry.

3. Feint attacks are easy to simulate in this terrain and are most useful because they disperse the enemy artillery and air effort. They will be planned and rehearsed now.

Up to 27 July 1944, the number of Panzers lost as total write-offs was reported as 60 **StuG**, 224 **Pz.Kpfw.IV**, 131 **Pz.Kpfw.V**, 23 **Pz.Kpfw.IV**, and 12 **Flakpz.38t** for a total of 450. This was not a substantial increase over the 349 reported as lost by 8 July 1944.

The British analyzed Panzers captured in Normandy from 6 June to 7 August 1944 to determine how they had become casualties. Of 110 Panzers examined, 53 were caused by armor-piercing shot, 8 by hollow charge projectiles, 9 by artillery high explosive shells, 1 by mines, 7 by rocket projectiles from aircraft, 3 by cannon from aircraft, 7 were destroyed by crew, 4 were abandoned and 18 were due to unknown causes.

An article in the August 1944 issue of the **Nachrichtenblatt der Panzertruppen** published by the **Generalinspekteur der Panzertruppen** covered the experience in Panzer combat as follows:

The following experiences on the **Western Front**, *related to command and combat of Panzer units, have occurred recently during the last few weeks:*

Combat on the Invasion Front is known for the opponent's air supremacy, heaviest artillery concentrations, and intensive air, ground, and radio reconnaissance, and for terrain in Normandy that is unsuitable for Panzers. These conditions affect:

I. Marches

1. It is impossible to conduct marches without enemy aerial observation. Therefore, marches can be conducted only at night. Pulling into cover must be completed by dawn, especially if the day's objective has not been reached. Never use lights during night marches.

2. Conduct marches only in small groups. Maintain air defense intervals within the groups, even at night. The enemy fighters illuminate the road with searchlights.

3. The prerequisite for a smoothly flowing march is well-organized route scouting and guiding. When halts occur, the vehicles must be prevented from closing up.

4. When enemy aircraft attack, each vehicle is to independently drive into cover. The entire march movement halts.

5. Single vehicles must halt from time to time, turn off the engine, and listen. Aircraft are often heard at longer range than they can be seen.

6. Fighters continue to attack until there are signs that the vehicles are burning. In such attacks, which are also directed against single vehicles, the opponent can be successfully fooled by throwing out smoke pots or grenades.

II. Bivouacs

1. Avoid towns, because they are increasingly selected for aircraft attack, and the bivouacked units (headquarters) are reported to the enemy by the civilians.

2. Move into woods, maintaining large intervals, and prohibit civilians from entering the bivouac areas.

3. Dig in wheeled vehicles. Wheels and engines must be protected against fragments.

4. In all cases, forbid the use of radio communication even for tuning in. This also applies to assembly areas. Several times units behind the front were covered by carpet bombing after sending a few radio messages. Directional signals!

III. Combat

1. The terrain is unsuitable for Panzers, so the forces must deviate from the otherwise successful concentrated employment of Panzers. Therefore, organize as **Panzer-Jagd-Kommandos** *or so-called* **Panzerkampftrupps**.

2. These **Panzerkampftrupps** *consist of a few Panzers and stand ready directly behind the front line. Their tasks are to immediately counterstrike and destroy enemy tanks that have broken through.*

3. The **Panzerkampftrupps** *are to cooperate closely with and be directed by the* **Panzer-Grenadiere** *and* **Grenadiere**.

4. The deployment will be conducted so that ground observation is taken away from the opponent. Camouflaging the vehicles until they are not recognizable protects them against attacks from the air. Commanders and gunners are to predetermine the primary ranges and make sketches of the ranges for themselves.

5. Alternate positions are to be prepared in advance for the Panzers that will also serve as **Auflaufstellungen** *(defensive positions with cover from which to ambush an enemy force allowed to close to short range). From these* **Auflaufstellungen**, *it must be possible to effectively engage the flanks of enemy tanks that have broken through.*

6. The sensitivity of the opponent in close combat and in flanking attacks will be exploited by a quick counterstrike immediately after the artillery fire is lifted from the main battle line.

7. At the start of such a counterstrike, the **Grenadiere** *protect the flanks of the Panzers and fight directly with them.*

Summary: For all units, maximum use of the terrain, camouflage, digging in, and strict security during radio and telephone communication are the highest commandments. Civilians must be constantly hindered from informing the enemy.

From previous experience it has been confirmed:

1. The combat spirit of our Panzer crews and their training in Panzers are far superior to those of the enemy tank forces. The enemy's superiority derives only from the number of his tanks.

2. The combat spirit of British infantry is poor. Therefore, British tank-hunting teams have very rarely appeared.

3. In spite of their heavy armor, the Tigers are also forced by the enemy's air supremacy, very well directed artillery fire on point targets, and 9.2 cm anti-aircraft/tank guns to follow the basic tactical principles that apply to the **leichte Panzer-Kompanie**: *camouflage, terrain exploitation, and hidden firing positions!*

Reinforcements in the form of the **116.Panzer-Division** and the **9.Panzer-Division** were committed in late July/early August in an attempt to stop the American breakout from Normandy. The **116.Panzer-Division** had been given the **I.Abteilung/Panzer-Regiment 24** as its **Panther-Abteilung**. An example of the problems encountered in stopping the Allied spearheads was written on 18 September 1944 by Wachtmeister Mueller of the **2.Schwadron/Panzer-Regiment 24** for an action that had occurred in early August 1944:

The **Abteilung** *was moving south to cover approaches that could be taken by the pursuing enemy. We met the opponents in the morning hours on a summer day. There were only four Panthers under the leadership of Leutnant Stetzka. I myself was the driver of his Panther. With his calm demeanor, he described the situation and then gave orders to advance. Following the direction of my commander, I brought the Panther into position on the left side of the road. The immediate area was completely open and presented absolutely no cover. Several* **Grenadiere** *were positioned around the Panther for close defense. There were no other friendly units to our left. No sooner had we taken up our position than enemy artillery spotter aircraft arrived. After several minutes the first rounds burst around us and the other Panthers. To our left, a sunken lane ran parallel to the road. I noticed Americans coming out of the sunken lane 800 to 1000 meters away. Before I could inform the commander of this target, they quickly turned and disappeared as soon as they had spotted the Panthers.*

Twenty minutes later the artillery fire suddenly stopped. Twelve to 15 young men in civilian clothes came out of the same sunken lane. When they spotted the Panthers they totally panicked and ran around for close to half an hour at a range of 800 meters in front of our gun. Then they disappeared again the way they came.

Shortly thereafter, the artillery fire started again. The hits came close to the Panther. Only by continuously changing position were we able to prevent the artillery fire from having any effect.

Then I heard the Leutnant telling the gunner about enemy tanks and immediately spotted two Shermans on the ridge 1200 meters from us. Hardly had the fire command been given than the commander spotted additional tanks pushing out of the sunken lane to our left. The first shot landed close in front of the first enemy tank. The second shot hit. The crew bailed out.

Then I heard in the earphones, "Mueller, reverse." The Leutnant wanted to cancel the threat to our flank. From orders to the gunner, I knew that we were surrounded by at least eight Shermans. Still totally calm, the commander gave orders to turn and engage the tanks that had cut us off. Three tanks were taken under fire. No hits were observed.

Then the order: "Retire down the road." At the same moment a stunning noise inside the Panther. A hit. This time us. The motor still ran, and I tried to bring the Panther out of enemy fire. I still drove 300 meters before the heat from the burning tank caused me to bail out. I dove under the Panther for cover and saw the radio operator jump out and run away. Then I heard the voice of my commander beside the Panther. I crawled over and saw that both of his lower legs were missing below the knee. No cries of pain came from his lips. He immediately determined what had happened to the crew. I tried to bind the wounds, but he refused, saying: "Leave it, Mueller; it is pointless." I couldn't carry him away from the burning tank, since heavy machine gun fire hit all round us. Then I proposed: "Herr Leutnant, we should give up as prisoners and I will get medical help immediately." He declined, stating: "Mueller, take my identification tag and my pay book. I order you to take these back to the squadron." He then asked me to greet his parents, said farewell, and again ordered me to break through to the squadron.

After the Allied breakout from Normandy, an enveloping attack trapped most of the **Panzer-Divisions** in the Falaise pocket from which very few Panzers escaped. The shape that the **Panzer-Divisions** were in was reflected in the Panzer operational status report for the evening of 21 August 1944: **10.SS-Pz.Div.** - No Panzers, **12.SS-Pz.Div.** - 10 Panzers, **1.SS-Pz.Div.** - No report, **2.Pz.Div.** - No Panzers, **2.SS-Pz.Div.** - 15 Panzers, **9.SS-Pz.Div.** - 20 to 25 Panzers, **116.Pz.Div.** - 12 Panzers, **21.Pz.Div.** - Still in combat.

British examination of 223 Panzers captured from 8 to 31 August 1944 revealed the cause of their loss as 24 by armor-piercing shot, 1 by hollow charge projectiles, 4 by artillery high explosive shells, 7 by rocket projectiles from aircraft, 1 by cannon from aircraft, 2 by bombs, 108 destroyed by crew, 63 abandoned, and 13 due to unknown causes.

In late August/early September 1944, the **3.** and **15.Panzer-Grenadier-Divisions** were pulled out of Italy and sent to France in an attempt to avoid a complete disaster.

In an attempt to stem the Allied advances through France, in September seven of the 14 **Panzer-Brigades**, hastily created to plug the gaping hole in the Eastern Front, were sent to plug the gaping hole in the Western Front. The combat experience of several of these **Panzer-Brigades** is recorded in the following reports:

ORGANIZATION AND STRENGTH OF PANZER UNITS EMPLOYED ON THE WESTERN FRONT

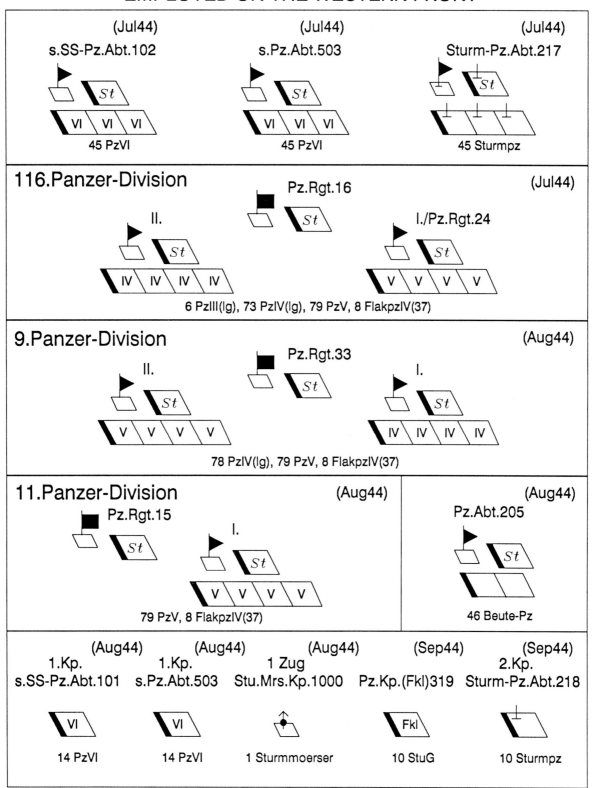

(Jul44)
s.SS-Pz.Abt.102

45 PzVI

(Jul44)
s.Pz.Abt.503

45 PzVI

(Jul44)
Sturm-Pz.Abt.217

45 Sturmpz

116.Panzer-Division

(Jul44)

II.

Pz.Rgt.16

I./Pz.Rgt.24

6 PzIII(lg), 73 PzIV(lg), 79 PzV, 8 FlakpzIV(37)

9.Panzer-Division

(Aug44)

II.

Pz.Rgt.33

I.

78 PzIV(lg), 79 PzV, 8 FlakpzIV(37)

11.Panzer-Division

(Aug44)

Pz.Rgt.15

I.

79 PzV, 8 FlakpzIV(37)

(Aug44)
Pz.Abt.205

46 Beute-Pz

(Aug44)
1.Kp.
s.SS-Pz.Abt.101

14 PzVI

(Aug44)
1.Kp.
s.Pz.Abt.503

14 PzVI

(Aug44)
1 Zug
Stu.Mrs.Kp.1000

1 Sturmmoerser

(Sep44)
Pz.Kp.(Fkl)319

10 StuG

(Sep44)
2.Kp.
Sturm-Pz.Abt.218

10 Sturmpz

Starting in September 1944, four of the eight **Flakpanzer IV** in the **Fliegerabwehr-Zug** were **"Wirbelwind"** and four were **"Moebelwagen."** (NA)

Report by Hauptmann Hanemann commander of **Panzer-Abteilung 2105** for the period from 3 to 17 September 1944:

The **Abteilung** assembled in the area of Tirlemont. From there, two companies advanced against the enemy main route from Loewen to Diest. No losses occurred.

A **Panzer-Kompanie** with five Panthers, a **Sturmgeschuetz-Kompanie** with nine **PanzerIV/70(V)** and a **Panzer-Grenadier-Kompanie** were in action west of Theuz attached to the **89.Infanterie-Division**. This battle group had to pull back due to enemy pressure and because they were bypassed. Two Panthers and two **PanzerIV/70(V)** had to be blown up because of the fuel shortage. The **89.Infanterie-Division** had supplied only 100 liters.

Since then the **Abteilung** has been deployed only in groups of one to four Panthers together with **Panzer-Grenadiere** in the defensive line.

OPPOSITE: **Pioniere** with mine-detecting equipment climb aboard this **Panther Ausf.G.** (BA)

By Limbourg, the **Abteilung** was scattered over an 8-kilometer-wide area in groups of one to four Panthers separated from each other by about a kilometer. On orders from the **9.Panzer-Division**, the **Brigade** was employed to defend a sector on a wide front. Command of the **Abteilung** by radio was not possible. Singly or in pairs, the Panthers were shot up by the **"Jabos"** (fighter-bombers) or enemy tank groups. The **Abteilung** withdrew to Eynatten with three Panthers after the loss of nine Panthers by Limbourg. This surely would not have happened if, instead of being ordered to remain in the front line, the Panthers had been positioned further back and held ready in reserve to attack.

On 12 September, a strong enemy tank group attacked Eynatten. One Panther broke down mechanically and another Panther was shot up. After the **Panzer-Grenadiere** retreated, the remaining Panther retired to the Westwall.

On 13 September, the last two operational Panthers **(Befehls-Panthers)** of the **Abteilung** were defending in the "Hoecker" Line. Then they counterattacked near Rott. Both **Befehls-Panthers** were lost after shooting up eight Sherman

ORGANIZATION AND STRENGTH OF PANZER UNITS EMPLOYED ON THE WESTERN FRONT

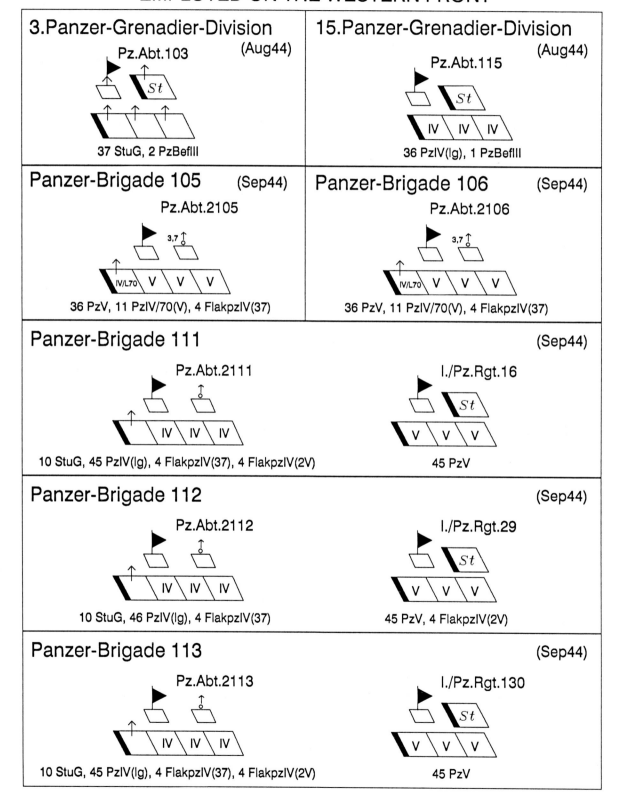

3.Panzer-Grenadier-Division (Aug44)
Pz.Abt.103

37 StuG, 2 PzBefIII

15.Panzer-Grenadier-Division (Aug44)
Pz.Abt.115

36 PzIV(lg), 1 PzBefIII

Panzer-Brigade 105 (Sep44)
Pz.Abt.2105

36 PzV, 11 PzIV/70(V), 4 FlakpzIV(37)

Panzer-Brigade 106 (Sep44)
Pz.Abt.2106

36 PzV, 11 PzIV/70(V), 4 FlakpzIV(37)

Panzer-Brigade 111 (Sep44)
Pz.Abt.2111   I./Pz.Rgt.16

10 StuG, 45 PzIV(lg), 4 FlakpzIV(37), 4 FlakpzIV(2V)   45 PzV

Panzer-Brigade 112 (Sep44)
Pz.Abt.2112   I./Pz.Rgt.29

10 StuG, 46 PzIV(lg), 4 FlakpzIV(37)   45 PzV, 4 FlakpzIV(2V)

Panzer-Brigade 113 (Sep44)
Pz.Abt.2113   I./Pz.Rgt.130

10 StuG, 45 PzIV(lg), 4 FlakpzIV(37), 4 FlakpzIV(2V)   45 PzV

tanks. An **8.8 cm Pak/Flak** gun was found unmanned in Rott. The crew had run away prior to the first round landing and weren't to be found.

On 14 September, four Panthers and three **PanzerIV/70(V)** that had been repaired were deployed in small groups as mobile anti-tank guns along a 3-kilometer-wide stretch of the bunker line. At the same time, the **9.Panzer-Division** ordered that the damaged Panzers undergoing repair be towed to defend the road toward the southwest of Dueren.

These false tactical directions were repeatedly given by all higher commands with the excuse that the especially pressing situation made this employment necessary. The basis for this situation appears to be that the **Brigade** commander was employed by the **9.Panzer-Division** as a stationary sector commander with attached **Infanterie** and **Luftwaffe** elements. Therefore, he was no longer in a position to command the remainder of **Panzer-Brigade 105** in accordance with accepted tactical doctrine.

Even though as a result of mechanical failures the companies were not up to strength, it would have been possible to employ the **Abteilung** in the form of a Panzer assault group, held ready to attack about 1 to 3 kilometers behind the front line.

Up to now, 43 Sherman tanks have been shot up by the **Abteilung**. At this time there are six Panthers, one **PanzerIV/70(V)**, and one **Flakpanzer IV** operational. Eight Panthers and five **PanzerIV/70(V)** are in need of repair. Two **Befehls-Panthers** are urgently needed.

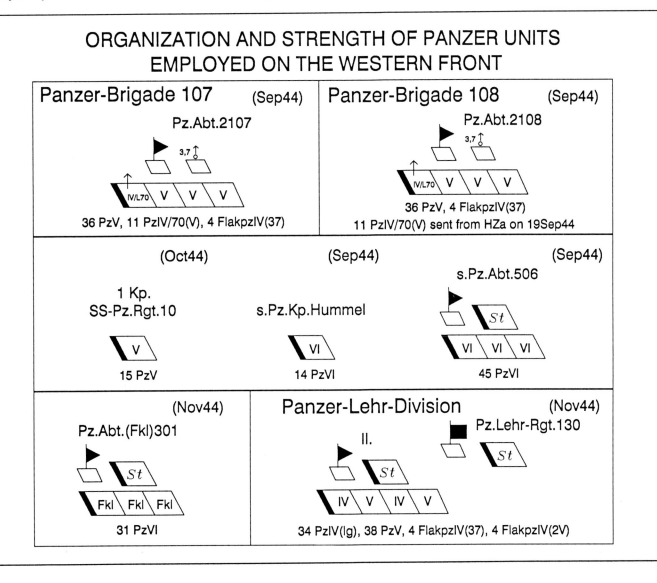

ORGANIZATION AND STRENGTH OF PANZER UNITS EMPLOYED ON THE WESTERN FRONT

Panzer-Brigade 107 (Sep44)

Pz.Abt.2107

36 PzV, 11 PzIV/70(V), 4 FlakpzIV(37)

Panzer-Brigade 108 (Sep44)

Pz.Abt.2108

36 PzV, 4 FlakpzIV(37)
11 PzIV/70(V) sent from HZa on 19Sep44

(Oct44)

1 Kp.
SS-Pz.Rgt.10

15 PzV

(Sep44)

s.Pz.Kp.Hummel

14 PzVI

(Sep44)

s.Pz.Abt.506

45 PzVI

(Nov44)

Pz.Abt.(Fkl)301

31 PzVI

Panzer-Lehr-Division (Nov44)

II.

Pz.Lehr-Rgt.130

34 PzIV(lg), 38 PzV, 4 FlakpzIV(37), 4 FlakpzIV(2V)

ABOVE: A **Panther Ausf.G** covered with branches in an attempt at breaking up the silhouette. This doesn't appear to be very effective in open country. (BA) BELOW: Tiger IIs of the **schwere Panzer-Abteilung 506** concealed in a fruit orchard in the Aachen area in October 1944. (BA)

Report by Leutnant Schreiber on the first action of **Panzer-Abteilung 2108** with **Panzer-Brigade 108**:

After an approach march of 40 kilometers during the night of 18/19 September, **Panzer-Brigade 108** prepared for action in the area of Halsdorf, 10 kilometers southwest of Bitburg. The assembly area was on a height in plain view of the opponent and probably was also observed. The attack was launched without artillery preparation. The Panthers attacked over a small ridge into the opponent's position. The Panthers received well-aimed anti-tank and tank gun fire from a range of 10 to 20 meters. Ten Panthers were total write-offs, and several others require extensive repairs. The **Abteilung** commander, signals officer and two platoon leaders were killed. The **Abteilung** adjutant and two company commanders were severely wounded. A company commander and four platoon leaders were lightly wounded. Due to anti-tank and tank gun fire, the **Panzer-Grenadiere** that were following the Panthers had heavy losses in **S.P.W.** (Sd.Kfz.251 armored halftracks) and personnel.

Excerpts from a report dated 16 September 1944 by Oberst Schanze on the fate of **Panzer-Brigade 112**:

Panzer-Brigade 112 was sent into action on 12/13 September against the American breakthrough southwest of Epinal. During this necessary action, the **Brigade** lost almost all of its Panthers and half of its **Pz.Kpfw.IVs** to fighter-bomber attacks, artillery fire, and tanks. The **I.(Panther) Abteilung/Panzer-Regiment 29** was practically destroyed. They still possess four operational Panthers. A further three Panthers and a **Befehls-Panther** are in need of repair.

Thirty-four Panthers are total write-offs. During this action, practically no mechanical breakdowns occurred. The exclusive cause of the total write-offs was attacks from behind by 16 to 20 **"Jabos"** (fighter-bombers) with rocket bombs and phosphorus shells fired from mounted weapons. A considerable number of crew members were casualties. The **Abteilung** commander was severely wounded and his adjutant was killed.

(text continues on page 201)

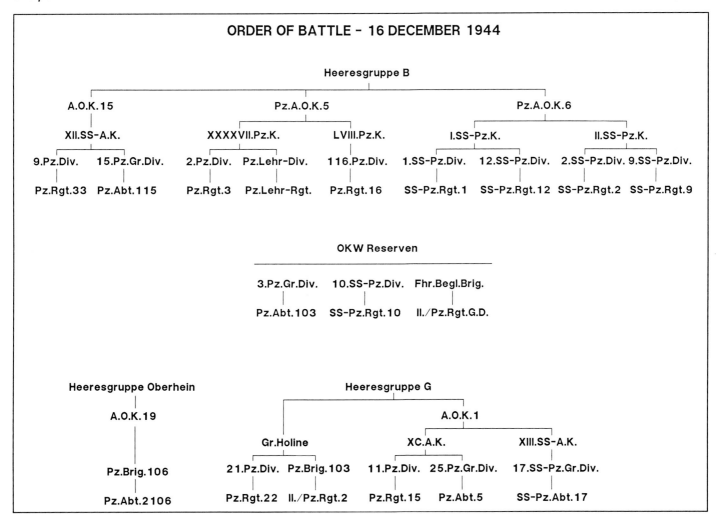

ORDER OF BATTLE – 16 DECEMBER 1944

Heeresgruppe B

A.O.K.15 — Pz.A.O.K.5 — Pz.A.O.K.6

A.O.K.15
XII.SS-A.K.
9.Pz.Div.   15.Pz.Gr.Div.
Pz.Rgt.33   Pz.Abt.115

Pz.A.O.K.5
XXXXVII.Pz.K.   LVIII.Pz.K.
2.Pz.Div.   Pz.Lehr-Div.   116.Pz.Div.
Pz.Rgt.3   Pz.Lehr-Rgt.   Pz.Rgt.16

Pz.A.O.K.6
I.SS-Pz.K.   II.SS-Pz.K.
1.SS-Pz.Div.   12.SS-Pz.Div.   2.SS-Pz.Div.   9.SS-Pz.Div.
SS-Pz.Rgt.1   SS-Pz.Rgt.12   SS-Pz.Rgt.2   SS-Pz.Rgt.9

OKW Reserven

3.Pz.Gr.Div.   10.SS-Pz.Div.   Fhr.Begl.Brig.
Pz.Abt.103   SS-Pz.Rgt.10   II./Pz.Rgt.G.D.

Heeresgruppe Oberhein
A.O.K.19
Pz.Brig.106
Pz.Abt.2106

Heeresgruppe G
A.O.K.1
Gr.Holine   XC.A.K.   XIII.SS-A.K.
21.Pz.Div.   Pz.Brig.103   11.Pz.Div.   25.Pz.Gr.Div.   17.SS-Pz.Gr.Div.
Pz.Rgt.22   II./Pz.Rgt.2   Pz.Rgt.15   Pz.Abt.5   SS-Pz.Abt.17

ORGANIZATION AND STRENGTH OF PANZER UNITS
FOR OPERATIONS 'WACHT AM RHEIN' AND 'NORDWIND'

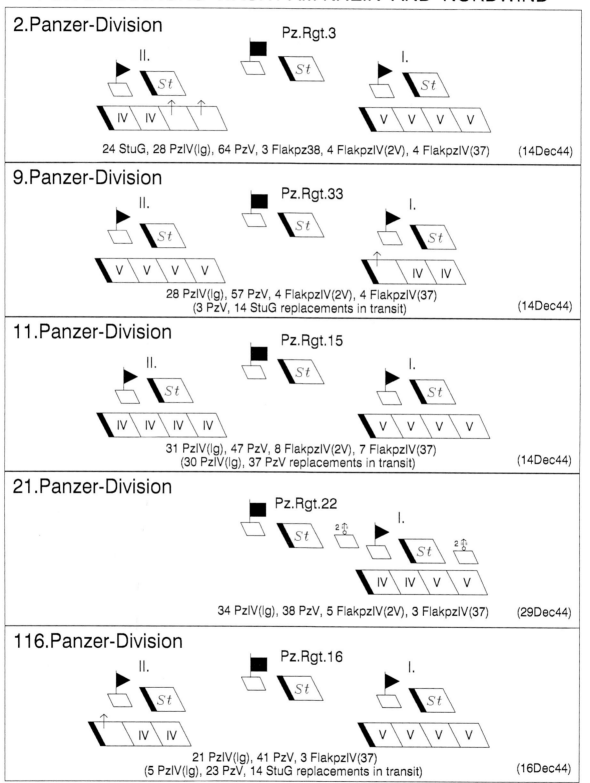

2.Panzer-Division

Pz.Rgt.3

24 StuG, 28 PzIV(lg), 64 PzV, 3 Flakpz38, 4 FlakpzIV(2V), 4 FlakpzIV(37) (14Dec44)

9.Panzer-Division

Pz.Rgt.33

28 PzIV(lg), 57 PzV, 4 FlakpzIV(2V), 4 FlakpzIV(37)
(3 PzV, 14 StuG replacements in transit) (14Dec44)

11.Panzer-Division

Pz.Rgt.15

31 PzIV(lg), 47 PzV, 8 FlakpzIV(2V), 7 FlakpzIV(37)
(30 PzIV(lg), 37 PzV replacements in transit) (14Dec44)

21.Panzer-Division

Pz.Rgt.22

34 PzIV(lg), 38 PzV, 5 FlakpzIV(2V), 3 FlakpzIV(37) (29Dec44)

116.Panzer-Division

Pz.Rgt.16

21 PzIV(lg), 41 PzV, 3 FlakpzIV(37)
(5 PzIV(lg), 23 PzV, 14 StuG replacements in transit) (16Dec44)

ORGANIZATION AND STRENGTH OF PANZER UNITS FOR OPERATIONS 'WACHT AM RHEIN' AND 'NORDWIND'

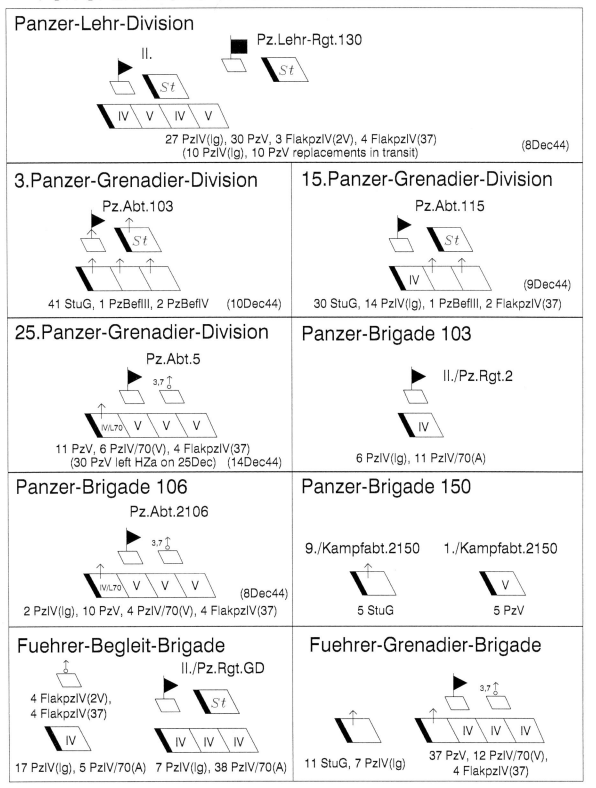

Panzer-Lehr-Division

Pz.Lehr-Rgt.130

27 PzIV(lg), 30 PzV, 3 FlakpzIV(2V), 4 FlakpzIV(37)
(10 PzIV(lg), 10 PzV replacements in transit)   (8Dec44)

3.Panzer-Grenadier-Division

Pz.Abt.103

41 StuG, 1 PzBefIII, 2 PzBefIV   (10Dec44)

15.Panzer-Grenadier-Division

Pz.Abt.115

30 StuG, 14 PzIV(lg), 1 PzBefIII, 2 FlakpzIV(37)   (9Dec44)

25.Panzer-Grenadier-Division

Pz.Abt.5

11 PzV, 6 PzIV/70(V), 4 FlakpzIV(37)
(30 PzV left HZa on 25Dec)   (14Dec44)

Panzer-Brigade 103

II./Pz.Rgt.2

6 PzIV(lg), 11 PzIV/70(A)

Panzer-Brigade 106

Pz.Abt.2106

2 PzIV(lg), 10 PzV, 4 PzIV/70(V), 4 FlakpzIV(37)   (8Dec44)

Panzer-Brigade 150

9./Kampfabt.2150   1./Kampfabt.2150

5 StuG   5 PzV

Fuehrer-Begleit-Brigade

4 FlakpzIV(2V),
4 FlakpzIV(37)

II./Pz.Rgt.GD

17 PzIV(lg), 5 PzIV/70(A)   7 PzIV(lg), 38 PzIV/70(A)

Fuehrer-Grenadier-Brigade

11 StuG, 7 PzIV(lg)

37 PzV, 12 PzIV/70(V),
4 FlakpzIV(37)

ORGANIZATION AND STRENGTH OF PANZER UNITS
FOR OPERATIONS 'WACHT AM RHEIN' AND 'NORDWIND'

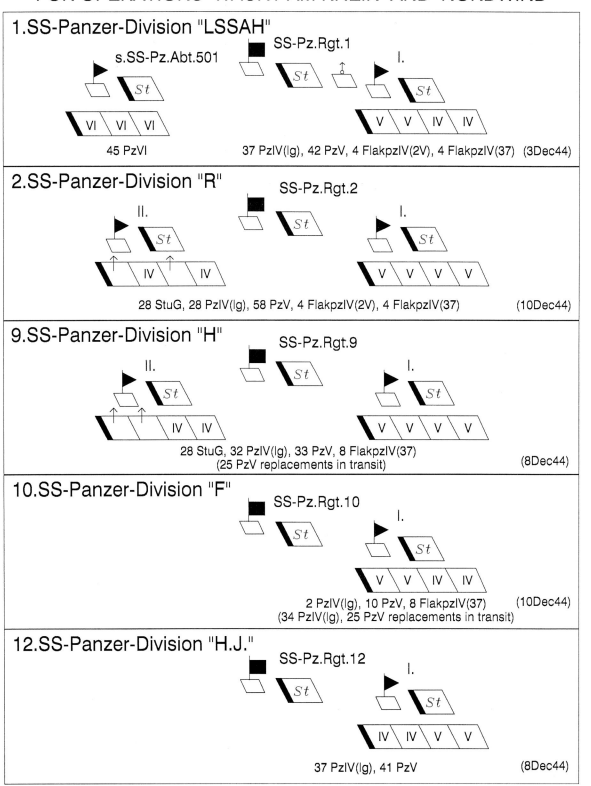

1.SS-Panzer-Division "LSSAH"

s.SS-Pz.Abt.501

SS-Pz.Rgt.1

I.

45 PzVI

37 PzIV(lg), 42 PzV, 4 FlakpzIV(2V), 4 FlakpzIV(37)   (3Dec44)

2.SS-Panzer-Division "R"

II.

SS-Pz.Rgt.2

I.

28 StuG, 28 PzIV(lg), 58 PzV, 4 FlakpzIV(2V), 4 FlakpzIV(37)   (10Dec44)

9.SS-Panzer-Division "H"

II.

SS-Pz.Rgt.9

I.

28 StuG, 32 PzIV(lg), 33 PzV, 8 FlakpzIV(37)
(25 PzV replacements in transit)   (8Dec44)

10.SS-Panzer-Division "F"

SS-Pz.Rgt.10

I.

2 PzIV(lg), 10 PzV, 8 FlakpzIV(37)   (10Dec44)
(34 PzIV(lg), 25 PzV replacements in transit)

12.SS-Panzer-Division "H.J."

SS-Pz.Rgt.12

I.

37 PzIV(lg), 41 PzV   (8Dec44)

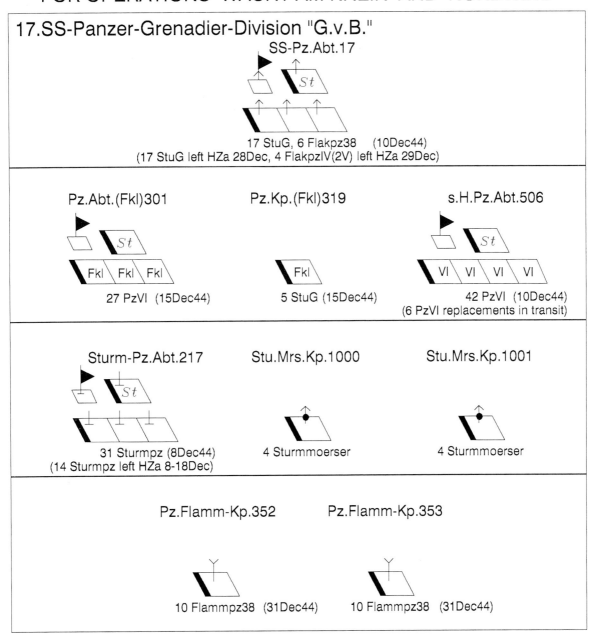

ORGANIZATION AND STRENGTH OF PANZER UNITS
FOR OPERATIONS 'WACHT AM RHEIN' AND 'NORDWIND'

17.SS-Panzer-Grenadier-Division "G.v.B."

SS-Pz.Abt.17

17 StuG, 6 Flakpz38   (10Dec44)
(17 StuG left HZa 28Dec, 4 FlakpzIV(2V) left HZa 29Dec)

Pz.Abt.(Fkl)301

27 PzVI (15Dec44)

Pz.Kp.(Fkl)319

5 StuG (15Dec44)

s.H.Pz.Abt.506

42 PzVI (10Dec44)
(6 PzVI replacements in transit)

Sturm-Pz.Abt.217

31 Sturmpz (8Dec44)
(14 Sturmpz left HZa 8-18Dec)

Stu.Mrs.Kp.1000

4 Sturmmoerser

Stu.Mrs.Kp.1001

4 Sturmmoerser

Pz.Flamm-Kp.352

10 Flammpz38 (31Dec44)

Pz.Flamm-Kp.353

10 Flammpz38 (31Dec44)

*Recovery of the total write-offs is not worthwhile. They are either totally burned out or destroyed by their own exploding ammunition. One of the 34 total write-offs is a **Befehls-Panther**. The second **Befehls-Panther** was hit in the turret and needs repair.*

With the exception of **Panzer-Brigade 106**, the other six **Panzer-Brigades** were disbanded and gave up their equipment to existing **Panzer** and **Panzer-Grenadier-Divisions**.

In some cases they were renamed to become new units in these older formations.

Preparations were initiated in October for a major offensive in the West. Due to disruptions in production and demands for replacements to cover losses, the number of Panzers authorized for each **Abteilung** was reduced. The organization and strength of the Panzer units used in Operations **"Wacht am Rhein"** and **"Nordwind"** are shown in the accompanying charts.

Operation **"Wacht am Rhein"** was the code name for the "Battle of the Bulge" which began on 16 December 1944. The operational status of the Panzers in all units in the West before, during, and following the offensives is shown in the following chart:

Status	StuG	Pz.IV	Pz.V	Pz.VI	Total
Available 15Dec	598	503	471	123	1695
(Operational)	(410)	(391)	(336)	(79)	(1216)
Available 30Dec	676	550	451	116	1793
(Operational)	(335)	(345)	(240)	(58)	(978)
Available 15Jan	716	594	487	110	1907
(Operational)	(340)	(330)	(221)	(64)	(955)

PanzerIV/70(V), **PanzerIV/70(A)**, **FlakpzIV**, and **Sturmpanzer** were all counted in the number for the **Pz.IV**. **Tiger I**, **Tiger II**, and **Sturmtiger** were all counted in the number for the **Pz.VI**. Only Panthers were counted in the number of **Pz.V**.

British examination of 57 Panzers that were captured in the period of 17 December 1944 to 16 January 1945 in the northern half of the Ardennes salient revealed the cause of the casualties as 1 by a bomb, 3 possibly by aircraft attack, 18 by armor-piercing shot, 3 by high explosive shell, 13 demolished, 11 abandoned, and 8 from unknown causes.

STATUS OF PANZERS ON WESTERN FRONT
31 May 1944 to 15 March 1945

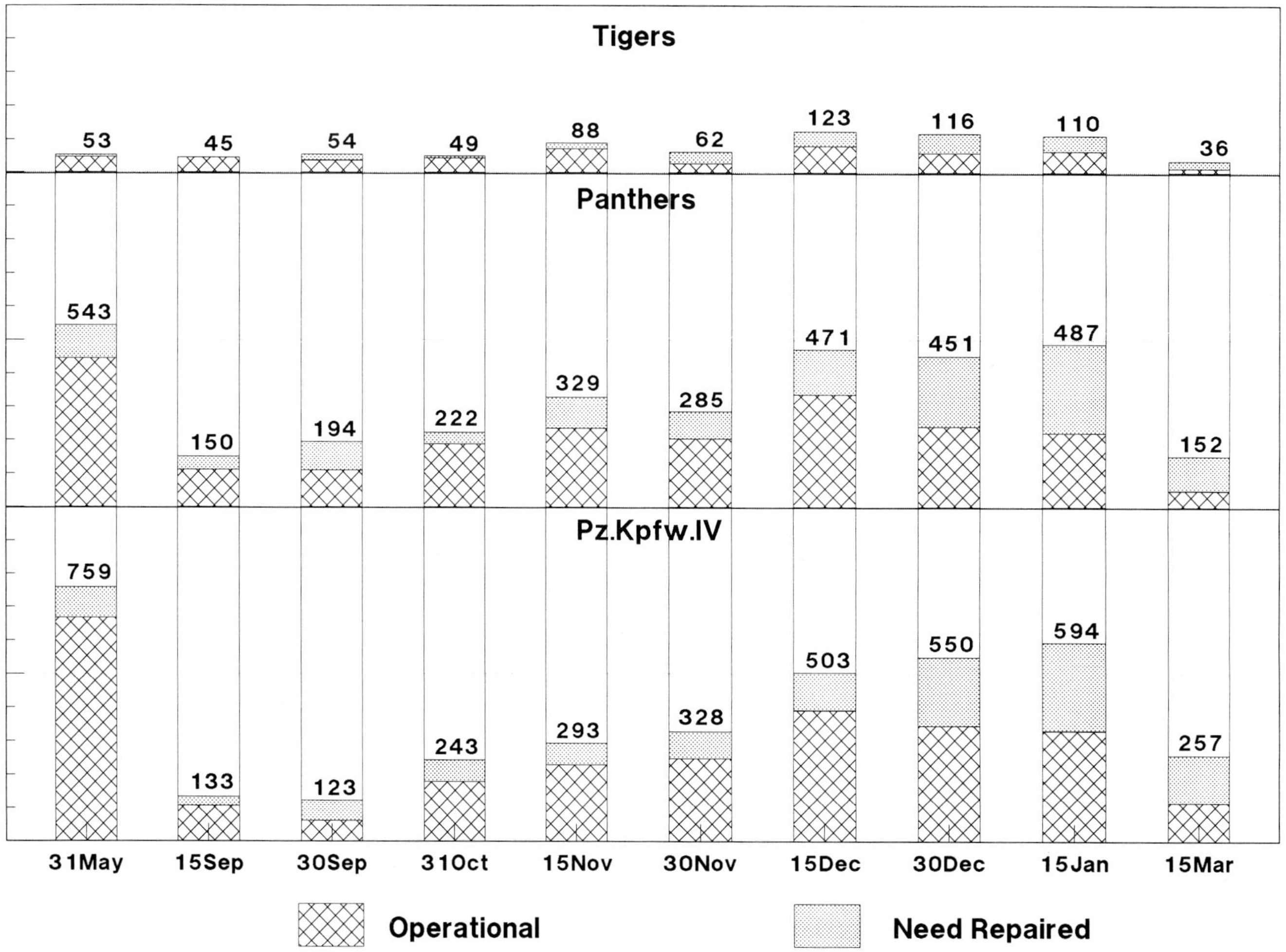

ABOVE: **Panther Ausf.G**s rolling forward to attack in the Hagenauer Forest on the lower Vogesen River on 3 January 1944. (BA) BELOW: A **Panther Ausf.G** passing through a gap in the "**Westwall**" defenses near Weissenburg on 6 January 1944. (BA)

30

The Last Year on the Eastern front

Following a relatively quiet Spring, 15 **Panzer-Divisions**, seven **Panzer-Grenadier-Divisions**, and six **schwere (Tiger) Panzer-Abteilungen** were on the Eastern Front awaiting the onslaught of the Russian summer offensive. As shown in the table on the Strength of Panzer Units in the East on 31 May 1944, some were **Panzer-Divisions** in name only because they possessed less than two full **Panzer-Kompanien**, with no replacements promised in the near future. Only six of the 15 **Panzer-Divisions** were in possession of a **Panther-Abteilung**. Two additional **Panther-Abteilungen** arrived before the start of the Russian offensive on 22 June 1944.

The Panzer forces had already become very proficient in the counterattack tactics needed to cope with overwhelming odds. No new tactics are revealed in the following reports on how the **Pz.Kpfw.IVs**, Panthers, Tigers, and **Sturmgeschuetze** were employed in combat on the Eastern Front during the last year of the war. But, many fundamental tactical principles laid down before the war are still stressed after five years in combat. One major point is the difficulty that some Panzer units encountered in fighting under the command of higher ranked infantry (**Grenadiere**) officers who still hadn't grasped the fundamentals of coordinated actions with Panzers. Not only did they have to fight against overwhelming odds but they were frequently handicapped by the incompetence of their own higher commanders.

Extracts from a translated Russian pamphlet entitled "Russian Tank Tactics" were included in the following article describing recent experience in Panzer combat on the Eastern Front published in the August 1944 issue of the **Nachrichtenblatt der Panzertruppen:**

Employment and Tactics of Russian Tank Units
The following quotations are from a translation of the Russian pamphlet entitled: "Russian Tank Tactics":

The importance of the tank units is related in the introduction. The conclusion drawn from experience in previous battles is that tank-versus-tank battles are unavoidable. The editor - a lieutenant colonel in command of a tank unit - emphasized that whenever possible the tanks of the enemy were to be destroyed as soon as possible by the air force, artillery, and anti-tank weapons, so that our tanks remained free to attack enemy infantry.

In his further discourse on tank battles he states:
"The commander must always cold-bloodedly and methodically consider which is more favorable: To immediately attack an enemy tank unit or to take up a defensive battle firing from stationary tanks. In the first case, he can suffer large losses. In the second case, he runs the danger of an enveloping attack resulting in being subjected to concentrated fire."

"Above all else, a tank battle is a firefight. Even though movement is important, the threat of enveloping the opponent should not necessarily force him to retreat. It is better to exploit the terrain for obtaining cover in order to open well-aimed rapid fire from favorable firing positions."

Our Position: The superiority of our Panzers clearly is proven by the intention of the enemy tank units to avoid tank-versus-tank combat. Our response is that we must seek to engage in tank-versus-tank actions at every opportunity, the prerequisite being that the destructive effects of the enemy air force and artillery against our units can be avoided so that movement or assembly by day can occur.

Aircraft attacks following the British pattern (carpet bombing) have already occurred in the East and will increase, so that the movement of Panzer units will be possible only at night, as is the case in the West and Italy. All commanders must reckon with this situation at the front and during training.

Recently, new Panzer units sent to the Eastern Front have again shown astounding thoughtlessness: Panzer units bivouac in villages. Panzers are parked by houses. Camouflage is only sketchy. Panzer convoys drive at peacetime intervals and when halted close up to intervals of five paces in bright

STRENGTH OF PANZER UNITS IN THE EAST ON 31 MAY 1944				
Unit Name	StuG	PzIV	PzV	PzVI
Heeresgruppe Suedukraine				
13.Pz.Div.		3 (2)		
10.Pz.Gr.Div.	10 (9)			
3.Pz.Div.		19(12) [17]		
23.Pz.Div.		10(10)	52(26) [24]	
24.Pz.Div.	16(15) [4]	40(36)		
Pz.Gr.Div.G.D. w/ I./26		14 (8)	55(30) [35]	20(12) [20] [4]
3.SS-Pz.Div."T"		28(23)		8 (2)
14.Pz.Div.	3 (2) [15]	35 (1)		
17.Pz.Div.		36(28) [1]		
Heeresgruppe Nordukraine				
7.Pz.Div.		47(34)		
s.Pz.Abt.509				46(37)
1.Pz.Div.		34(33)	26(23) [16]	
20.Pz.Gr.Div.	0 [42]			
8.Pz.Div. w/ I./11		11(10)	80(73)	
s.Pz.Abt.506				41(39) [5]
s.Pz.Abt.507				47(45)
4.Pz.Div.		70(68) [10]	0 [79]	
5.Pz.Div.		59(57) [20]	0 [79]	
s.Pz.Abt.505				42(36) [3]
5.SS-Pz.Div."W"	21(20)	27(27)	78(77)	
18.Pz.Gr.Div.	44(43)			
16.Pz.Div.	19(12) [17]	48(43)	10 (4) [32]	

STRENGTH OF PANZER UNITS IN THE EAST ON 31 MAY 1944				
Unit Name	StuG	PzIV	PzV	PzVI
Heeresgruppe Mitte				
20.Pz.Div.		56(49) [27]		
25.Pz.Gr.Div.	46(41)			
Pz.Gr.Div.FHH	17 (6) [14]	17 (8) [25]		
s.Pz.Abt.501				37(29)
Heeresgruppe Nord				
12.Pz.Div.		49(35) [23]		
s.Pz.Abt.502				57(33)
11.SS-Pz.Gr.Div."N"			12 (5)	
Total Available (Operational) [Replacements by 30Jun]	176 (148) [92]	603 (484) [123]	313 (238) [265]	298 (233) [32]

sunshine. Security during radio traffic was totally disregarded!

The Russian's view of the tank battle itself is largely the same as the German perception. The requirement for us to attempt tank-versus-tank battles may not lead to inferior and hasty attacks. The intellectual superiority of the responsible officer is decisive - choice of terrain, timing, and combat formation.

The article then deals with the recovery of damaged tanks: "In large battles, the problem of recovering and repairing dam-

aged tanks is of highest importance. Therefore, one must try to hold the battlefield in our own hands. Even when one is forced to pull back, one must hold the position until all of the damaged tanks can be towed away. Otherwise the combat unit will soon be reduced and used up."

Our Position: The importance of this problem must also be emphasized for us. The tactical orders must also consider the technical importance. It is incorrect to delay recovery of immobilized Panzers just because it is intended to hold the terrain for a longer time. Basically, recovery must begin immediately.

As a priority, it is the responsibility of all higher commanders to inform all Panzer units when they intend to pull back the main battle line. The number of Panzers that were left behind for the enemy as a result of sudden retreats last year, can't be further endured under any circumstances.

Flank Protection

"A special flanking tactic has been developed for simple infantry battles as well as tank battles. One constantly tries to outflank the enemy, to attack him in the flank, and to destroy him in this way. The conclusion is that we must also pay attention to our own flanks during defensive actions. Russians pay a lot of attention to the defense of their flanks. A Russian Generalmajor emphasizes that the outcome of every offensive will be decided on the flanks. The attention of the enemy (Germany) is directed from the beginning to the end as an operation against the flanks of the attacker. There he seeks decisive action and directs his counterattacks against them."

"At least one flanking battalion is contained within each division, supported by artillery and anti-tank weapons and if possible by light tanks. In addition, tank destroyer squads are positioned on the flanks."

Our Position: Flank defense is just as important in attacks as in defense. Nothing is achieved by speaking of dispositions and orders for flank defense when it is not accomplished in practice. A considerable number of German Panzer attacks are conducted without the necessary flank protection and therefore fail. The **Panzer-Jaeger-Abteilung** - in contact with the **Aufklaerungs-Abteilung**, and if occasion arises reinforced by the **Aufklaerungs-Zuege** from the **Panzer-Abteilungen** - is to be used for the same assignment as Russian flanking battalions.

Reconnaissance in the flanks is important for timely recognition of an enemy flank attack.

Using Panzers for Defense

"Tank units will also be employed for defense, especially if the opponent brings such units into play during his attack. A special backstop tactic was developed for this. It is conducted by locating tanks and anti-tank guns in well-protected rear positions, enticing the enemy tanks there, and then opposing them with concentrated fire."

Several examples of the backstop tactic were included to further explain the details of how it is practiced: "In another situation, a Major who was defending the approach to a defensive position erected a backstop position in the middle of the steppes. He positioned a light tank section with a front

ORGANIZATION AND STRENGTH OF PANZER UNITS
REPLACEMENT UNITS SENT TO EASTERN FRONT

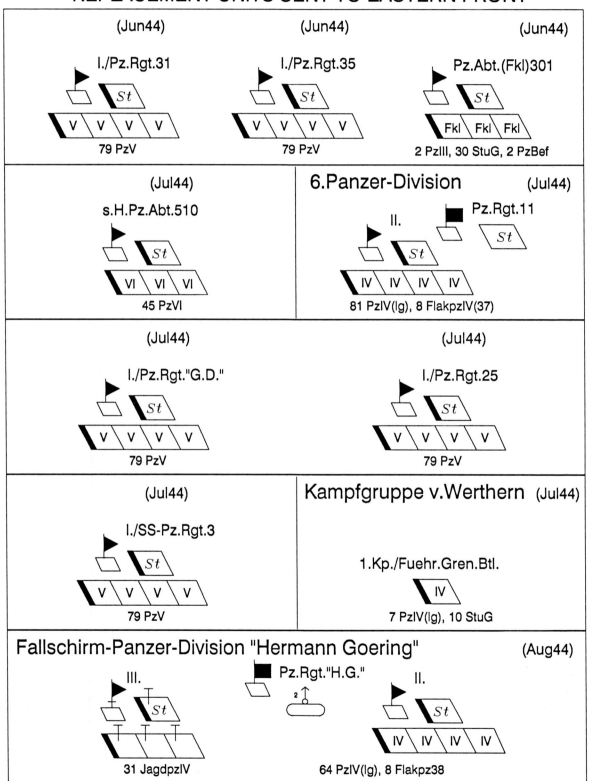

(Jun44)

I./Pz.Rgt.31

St

V V V V

79 PzV

(Jun44)

I./Pz.Rgt.35

St

V V V V

79 PzV

(Jun44)

Pz.Abt.(Fkl)301

St

Fkl Fkl Fkl

2 PzIII, 30 StuG, 2 PzBef

(Jul44)

s.H.Pz.Abt.510

St

VI VI VI

45 PzVI

6.Panzer-Division   (Jul44)

II.   Pz.Rgt.11

St   *St*

IV IV IV IV

81 PzIV(lg), 8 FlakpzIV(37)

(Jul44)

I./Pz.Rgt."G.D."

St

V V V V

79 PzV

(Jul44)

I./Pz.Rgt.25

St

V V V V

79 PzV

(Jul44)

I./SS-Pz.Rgt.3

St

V V V V

79 PzV

Kampfgruppe v.Werthern (Jul44)

1.Kp./Fuehr.Gren.Btl.

IV

7 PzIV(lg), 10 StuG

Fallschirm-Panzer-Division "Hermann Goering"   (Aug44)

III.   Pz.Rgt."H.G."   II.

St   2↑   *St*

                              IV IV IV IV

31 JagdpzIV   64 PzIV(lg), 8 Flakpz38

ORGANIZATION AND STRENGTH OF PANZER UNITS
REPLACEMENT UNITS SENT TO EASTERN FRONT

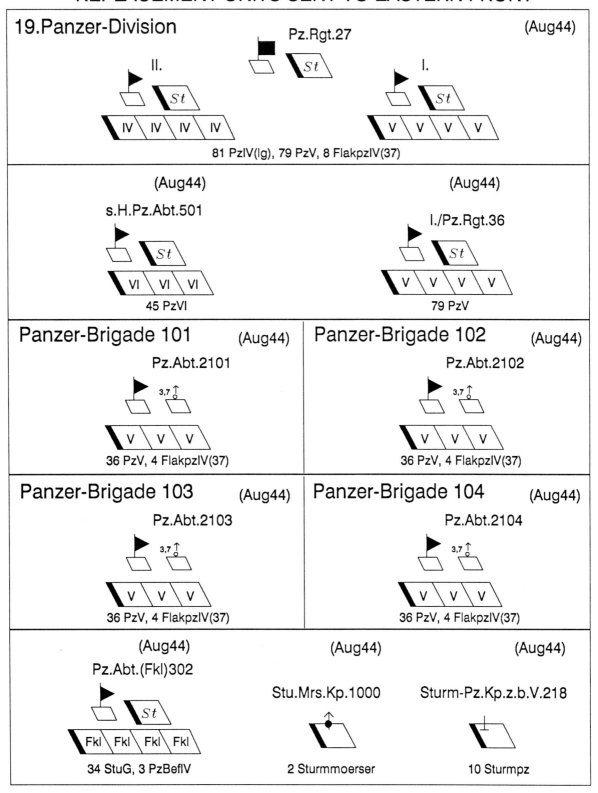

19.Panzer-Division (Aug44)

Pz.Rgt.27

II. St

I. St

IV IV IV IV

V V V V

81 PzIV(lg), 79 PzV, 8 FlakpzIV(37)

(Aug44)

s.H.Pz.Abt.501

St

VI VI VI

45 PzVI

(Aug44)

I./Pz.Rgt.36

St

V V V V

79 PzV

Panzer-Brigade 101 (Aug44)

Pz.Abt.2101

3,7

V V V

36 PzV, 4 FlakpzIV(37)

Panzer-Brigade 102 (Aug44)

Pz.Abt.2102

3,7

V V V

36 PzV, 4 FlakpzIV(37)

Panzer-Brigade 103 (Aug44)

Pz.Abt.2103

3,7

V V V

36 PzV, 4 FlakpzIV(37)

Panzer-Brigade 104 (Aug44)

Pz.Abt.2104

3,7

V V V

36 PzV, 4 FlakpzIV(37)

(Aug44)

Pz.Abt.(Fkl)302

St

Fkl Fkl Fkl Fkl

34 StuG, 3 PzBeflV

(Aug44)

Stu.Mrs.Kp.1000

2 Sturmmoerser

(Aug44)

Sturm-Pz.Kp.z.b.V.218

10 Sturmpz

and depth of two to three kilometers. Heavy tanks were positioned in a small wooded lot behind this backstop. They managed to hide all of the tanks and weapons by careful camouflage. The enemy Panzer unit drove up to within 2 or 3 kilometers of the position. Apparently, nothing could be spotted by the enemy, who started to approach. The Russians suddenly opened a cross-fire from a range of less than 1000 meters. The enemy was totally surprised and retreated."

The German Panzer losses in this action were stated to be three times as high as the Russian.

Our Position: The tactic known as "backstop" has already been used many times. Recently, it was more often employed using the numerous available anti-tank guns. If a Panzer unit winds up in the cross-fire of such a backstop, in no case may he abandon the firefight, because he then stands under concentrated fire while he himself can only work eccentrically. Also, this disadvantage cannot be equalized by a better rate of fire or better fighting spirit of our Panzer crews. It is therefore necessary for the commander to make a quick decision either to immediately start to attack in order to quickly cross the danger zone or to pull the unit back under cover of a smoke screen. In addition, the importance of combat reconnaissance is evident in preventing the unit from driving into such a backstop position.

<u>Anti-Tank Defense from Aircraft</u>

In addition to dropping bombs, aircraft are now increasingly firing automatic weapons and armor-piercing rounds. Fighter aircraft are used for this purpose, and so-called tank-hunting aircraft have been built specifically for this purpose.

*Our Position: Tank-hunting aircraft are continuously gaining more importance on every Front. It must continuously be reckoned with when the enemy has air superiority. They usually approach the Panzer unit from the rear. Until **Panzerfliegerabwehrzuegen** (armored anti-aircraft platoons) are provided to the Panzer units, the only effective possibility for defense is for the last wave of Panzers to fire every weapon at the attacking tank-hunting aircraft. This has frequently worked in the past because heavy fire prevents the aircraft from aiming or bombing - even when the aircraft are not hit.*

<u>Cooperation with Infantry</u>

The Russians often employ infantry riding on tanks which are outfitted solely with automatic weapons. Experience has shown that battalions that are thoroughly trained in cooperation with and support of tanks are very useful. They should help the tanks by pointing out enemy anti-tank weapons to the tank crews and deploy to silence these weapons. Also the importance of preparation for such an attack was emphasized: *"In one sector of the front, a unit consisting of 10 tanks and 60 infantry with automatic weapons were assigned to break through a German position. The infantry were volunteers and heavily outfitted with hand grenades and light mortars. The terrain through which they were to attack was scouted as thoroughly as possible. Every tank commander received a sketch of the enemy positions."*

Our Position: These statements relate known principles. A small unit is easier to lead and often has higher striking power than a larger unit. It is worth noting that volunteers were chosen who would increase the striking power. Terrain sketches for every commander are important because it must be repeatedly pointed out that thorough preparations are necessary for employment of Panzers, especially when cooperating directly with infantry.

The **19.Panzer-Division** was rested and refitted and was thrown back into the fray on the Eastern Front. The exploits of its **Panzer-Regiment 27** and one of its **Panzer-Grenadier-Regiments** were featured in the October issue of the <u>**Nachrichtenblatt der Panzertruppen**</u> in the following article on battles around villages:

A. <u>Attack</u>

<u>Objective</u>: Attack the fortified positions at Glowaczow with the entire **Panzer-Regiment** and **Panzer-Grenadier-Regiment** concentrated, take the position and break through to the north side of Lezenice.

<u>Battle Plan</u>: At 1900 hours, the **Panther-Abteilung** is to head east from Lipa advancing up to the road from Glowaczow to Barka, then turn south. The strong right wing is to attack toward the Glowaczow church, while the left wing, screening toward the north, is to attack the southwest side of Lezenice. At the same time, the **Panzer-Grenadier-Regiment** along with the **II.Abteilung/Panzer-Regiment 27** are to strike northeast and take Glowaczow and Lezenice.

<u>Execution</u>: The **Panther-Abteilung** started east at 1900 hours, supported by heavy covering fire from our own artillery, broke through the enemy main battle line, which was reinforced with numerous anti-tank guns, and crossed the road in a quick thrust.

At 1920 hours, the **Panther-Abteilung** turned southeast. Simultaneously, a heavy artillery barrage started, followed by an enemy tank attack in the depth of the **Panther-Abteilung's** flank. Under the protection of one **Panther-Kompanie**, which was employed for screening and forced the enemy tanks to turn away, the **Panther-Abteilung** continued to strike toward Glowaczow and Lezenice.

Toward 2000 hours, as the attack was effectively delivered on the heavily occupied northwest side of the village, the **Panzer-Grenadier-Regiment** and the **II.Abteilung/Panzer-Regiments 27**, which were already located on the southwest edge of Glowaczow, started to attack. The heavy clouds of dust and smoke as well as the failing light made it impossible to carry out a quick action and forced a tough and stubborn advance against the strongly occupied village of Glowaczow.

Glowaczow was in our hands at 2130 hours, with the exception of the high ground around the church. After destroying the remaining enemy, the units reached the north edge of Glowaczow at 2330 hours. After a break to reorganize the units, the attack on Lezenice was initiated at 0045

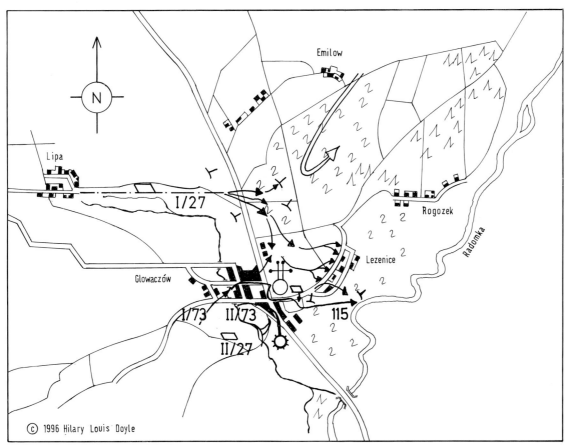

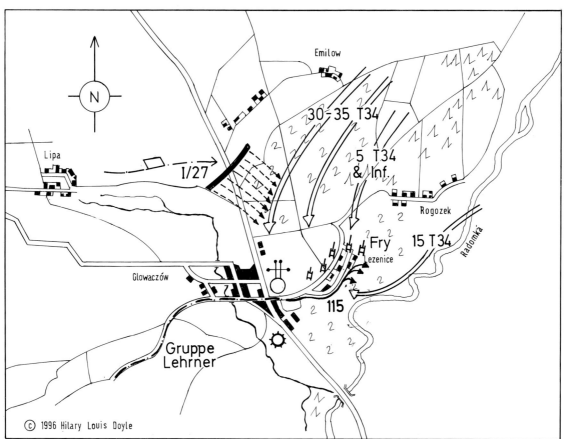

A **Pz.Kpfw.IV** of the **5.Kompanie/Panzer-Regiment 29** of the **12.Panzer-Division** in a Russian village in the Summer of 1944. (BA)

hours. Part of the **Panther-Abteilung** supported this attack by firing on the northwest edge of the village. Simultaneously, the **Panther-Abteilung** started an envelopment to the left toward the northeast side of Lezenice. In spite of bitter enemy resistance, Lezenice was also taken. Shortly after 0400 hours the units reached the northeast side of Lezenice. While the **Panther-Abteilung** was pulled back into the village of Lipa, the **II.Abteilung/Panzer-Regiment 27** and **Panzer-Grenadier-Regiment** built the newly ordered main battle line.

B. _Defense_

Based on the increasing preparatory artillery fire, a strong enemy attack was expected the next day. The **Panther-Abteilung** was ready in the village of Lipa, while the **II.Abteilung/Panzer-Regiment 27** was in defensive positions on the north edge of Lezenice. About 1400 hours, artillery preparation barrages started and the enemy started to attack from both sides of Rogozek. The **Panther-Abteilung** promptly drove east and took up scouted positions on both sides of the road facing southeast. The enemy attacked the northeast side of Lezenice with a strong infantry and tank force, to the right toward the Glowaczow church with a strong tank wedge, and to the left through Point 115 and the southwest side of Lezenice with a weaker assault wedge.

The left-hand enemy assault group, after bypassing our own right wing, struck toward Point 115 and were totally destroyed in short order by an awaiting group of Panzers. At the last moment, this prevented the enemy from rolling up our

own positions from the right wing, and all of the forces located in Lezenice could concentrate their fire on the main enemy forces attacking from the northeast. In spite of very heavy losses, the enemy managed to get into the village. However, he lost striking power because the tank unit advancing from the north toward the Glowaczow church ran into the flanking fire from the **Panther-Abteilung**.

After 15 enemy tanks were destroyed, the entire attack on the village was halted. An enemy group of infantry and tanks that were striking toward Lezenice were defeated by Panthers that were being repaired. Two additional enemy tanks were knocked out. The rest of the enemy tanks fled and pulled back into wooded lots northeast of Rogozek.

About 1530 hours, the enemy tank attack was completely defeated and two hours later the **Panzer-Grenadier-Regiment** and part of the **II.Abteilung/Panzer-Regiment 27** started to counterattack and cleaned out the enemy that had penetrated into the northeast side of Lezenice.

Results: 42 tanks, of which three were Josef Stalin heavy tanks, 38 guns, and uncounted light and heavy infantry weapons were destroyed in this battle. In addition, the enemy lost about 1000 men killed.

During the period from 5 January to 30 June 1944, the Panthers of the **I.Abteilung/Panzer-Regiment 26** had destroyed 211 enemy tanks and assault guns, 171 anti-tank guns and artillery pieces and 27 anti-tank rifles. In early August, it was sent to restore the situation on the border of East Prussia. Details on how Panthers fought are revealed in the following experience report from Obergefreiter Helmut Jurisch of the **3.Kompanie/Panzer-Regiment 26**:

We left our rest area in East Prussia on 8 August. Sitting on our Panthers, we rolled forward to attack the enemy positioned on the East Prussian border. The defense of Germany was at stake. As our Panthers rattled along the road, several "Marjelchen" on the roadside and in the fields waved to us. Soon we crossed the border as night closed in.

After a short halt in which the Panthers were refueled, we advanced to the assembly area. We were fed and lay down for a short sleep.

*About 0400 hours, the order "**Panzer, marsch!**" came. The Panthers advanced to attack. The first anti-tank guns sent us their morning greeting, which we successfully returned. Our Panthers' guns gained a strong respect from the anti-tank positions. Everything that hadn't already run away was swept away. The attack rolled smoothly forward. Soon we stood before the objective that still had to be taken, the city of Wilkowischken.*

The final attack zone lay before us. The right-hand neighbors were already ahead of us. An anti-tank ditch that had to be crossed lay in front of us. We advanced to the edge of the city. We couldn't advance farther since the houses were too close together. A small street snaked along the edge. It was the only way to enter the city.

At once the lead Panther was hit twice on the left side. The second hit penetrated. Commander and gunner sprang out. Driver and radio operator remained in the Panther and brought it back to safety. Nothing could be achieved other than to pull back to prevent further losses. The open flank was too poorly covered.

The lead Panthers, which had already crossed the bridge over the anti-tank ditch, had to pull back. The bridge collapsed under the next to last Panther. This Panther was lucky and managed to extricate itself under its own power. As the last Panther, we stood with our crate on the wrong side. We couldn't cross the destroyed bridge and had to search for another crossing. There wasn't much to consider. I quickly opened the hatch and was outside. I looked into the anti-tank ditch. Sharpshooters fired at everything that moved. There was a lot of water in the anti-tank ditch. Nothing for it; I must

Panther Ausf.As of the **I.Abteilung/Panzer-Regiment "Grossdeutschland"** loaded on rail cars for transfer to the Eastern Front. (JW)

go in. Better wet feet than a hole in the head. The water came up to my knees. It was really not so bad. I hadn't washed my legs during the last few days, anyway. It didn't take long to find a suitable crossing. In a short time the Panther was guided over. After the Panther had crossed over, a shell exploded close by and I received a small splinter in the lower right leg. I thought: "Na, that is not so bad! The brothers only want to tickle you a bit on the calf." Again, into the crate!

The Panthers gathered in a half circle. At first it was relatively quiet, but then came the blessing from above. We had just lit our cigarettes, when I heard the statement that our driver always said when something unpleasant was about to happen: "Ach, du Sch.....!" Then he slammed his hatch shut. Tank-hunting aircraft attacked. As always, they hit nothing again this time.

A **Panzer-Grenadier** reported to us that T34 tanks had broken through in our rear. We quickly took up positions. It didn't take long before the first one appeared. A short fire command - the T34 was halted. We waited. Another appeared. A burst of flame. He was burning! On the far right, two T34

tanks were already burning due to the fine work of our right-hand neighbor. The next T34 appeared at the corner of a house at a range of 500 meters. Comrade is becoming curious! Fire command. Shot. We wait. He's hit and on fire.

Nothing appeared for half an hour. Then they were again courageous. This time they came from the left. Two T34s at 2000 meters. We dispatched one with the second shot. The other was shot up by our neighbor. Tank-hunting aircraft returned a couple times without success.

We joined the rest of the Abteilung. Toward evening it was quieter and supplies were brought forward. The Panthers were refueled and filled with ammunition. Soon the cooking utensils rang. Never before had it tasted so good as on this evening!

Having been renamed the **II.Abteilung/Panzer-Regiment 36** on 1 September 1944, this **gemischte Panzer-Abteilung** was still successfully fighting with a mixture of **Pz.Kpfw.IVs** and **Sturmgeschuetze** in 1944. The following combat reports from September 1944 reveal details on their

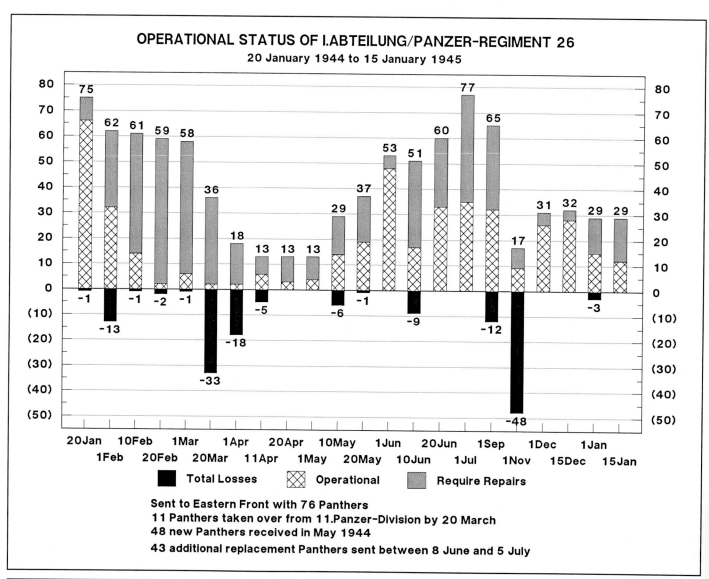

tactical employment and problems encountered in attempting to fight in difficult terrain.

Combat report from 16 September 1944 for the **II.Abteilung/Panzer-Regiment 36** attached to **Panzer-Grenadier-Regiment 108**

At 0030 hours, Hauptmann Neuendorff, the **Abteilung** commander, walked to the command post of **Panzer-Grenadier-Regiment 108** in Zagatani for a conference of all the commanders in the **Kampfgruppe**. There he received the orders from **Heeresgruppe Nord** that the objective for the previous day (advance to Ozolmuiza and clear out a enemy penetration in the Ozolmuiza sector, must be achieved without fail on 16 September 1944. At dawn, Hauptmann Neuendorff returned to Stukeni. In the **Panzerbefehlswagen** orders were immediately distributed to the **Kompanie** commanders. The **II.Abteilung/Panzer-Regiment 36** and the **II.Bataillon/Panzer-Grenadier-Regiment 108** were to assemble by the farmstead 1 kilometer southeast of Skukeni and be ready to attack at 0515 hours toward Liepkalne, the first objective that was to be reached during the morning. The **5. and 7.Kompanie/Panzer-Regiment 36** were in the lead, followed by the **Stab** with the **8.Kompanie** at the left rear and the **6.Kompanie** at the right rear. The intercom system in the commander's Panzer broke down when the attack started. The crew climbed into the second **Panzerbefehlswagen**.

At first, the **Abteilung** with **Grenadiere** riding on the Panzers moved through the woods and brushland northwest of Liepkalne to envelop the village from the right. They immediately received anti-tank gun and artillery fire from Liepkalne which increased in intensity as they reached the hollow between the wooded lots northwest of Liepkalne. The **Grenadiere** dismounted. The **Abteilung** commander ordered the **7.Kompanie** under Leutnant Kleinert to push forward up the hill to the first houses on the south edge of Liepkalne. When they reached the first farmstead, Leutnant Kleinert was subjected to heavy anti-tank fire from east of Liepkalne and infantry fire from the village itself. One Panzer was immobilized when the track was broken by a hit from an anti-tank gun. Another Panzer fell out from a anti-tank rifle hit penetrating into the engine compartment. Three anti-tank guns were knocked out by Leutnant Kleinert's **Kompanie**. To support Leutnant Kleinert, the **Abteilung** commander pulled the **6. and 8.Kompanie** on the right and left up to the edge of the village. The advance of the **8.Kompanie** was delayed an hour because the main part of their Panzers were stuck in the marshlands and had to be pulled out by Panzers that were still mobile. The **6.Kompanie** knocked out two enemy anti-tank guns on the right flank of the **Abteilung** and went into position next to Leutnant Kleinert on his right. At 1030 hours, the Panzer and **Grenadier** attack remained pinned down in the heavy anti-tank gun and mortar fire. Leutnant Kleinert reported that four enemy assault guns were approaching along the road from the east toward the crossroads in

Liepkalne. The shots fired by Leutnant Kleinert were ineffective because of the long range, and the assault guns managed to join up with the anti-tank gun front east of Liepkalne. One **Sturmgeschuetz** of the **8.Kompanie** that had reached the edge of the village was hit in the commander's cupola by fire from an anti-tank gun. The commander was killed. The **Abteilung** commander, adjutant, and the **Bataillon** commander of the **II./108** scouted on foot for a way to continue the attack and to detour around the enemy anti-tank gun front. All three were wounded by mortar fire during this scouting patrol. Before he was transported to the rear in the **Panzerbefehlspanzer** with the faulty intercom, the **Abteilung** commander radioed **Panzer-Grenadier-Regiment 108** that a further advance was impossible but that the line they had reached could be held.

Hauptmann Schurig took over command of the **Abteilung**. He positioned the **Abteilung** to defend the wooded lot southwest of Liepkalne as follows: The **6.Kompanie** defended toward the east at the edge of the woods, the **8.Kompanie** toward the north on the road from Zagateni to Liepkalne, and **Kompanie Kleinert** and the **Stab** toward the northeast on the edge of the village. About 1140 hours, Russian infantry attacked out of the village and were beaten back by the **II./108** supported by **Kompanie Kleinert**. Between 1200 and 1240 hours, enemy fire increased on the wooded lot occupied by the **Abteilung**. The **8.Kompanie** reported that the Russians were penetrating through the woods on the left flank of the **Abteilung** into our rear. Hauptmann Schurig sent two **Sturmgeschuetze** along with several **Grenadiere** to clear them out. But the **Sturmgeschuetze** couldn't move through the marshy area in front of the woods and returned to their previous positions.

During the afternoon, the heavy Russian anti-tank gun, artillery, mortar, rocket, and infantry fire on the woods continued. At 1300 hours, the Russians sent in JL2 and twin-engine bombers against our **Kampfgruppe**. The losses to the **Grenadiere** were extremely high. The **Grenadier's** ammunition situation forced extreme economy, so they could fire very little. Supplies and rations that were already brought into Skukeni the previous night couldn't get through to the **Abteilung**. A **Sanitaets-SPW**, which twice attempted to bring rations to the **Abteilung**, was knocked out both times and both drivers were killed.

Because of heavy radio traffic, the batteries in the **Panzerbefehlswagen** became weaker and weaker in spite of great care used in turning off the radio sets at times. After 1300 hours, the command post of the **Panzer-Grenadier-Regiment** couldn't be reached by medium-wave radio transmission. Therefore, after this the **Regiment** no longer had a clear picture of the situation of the **Abteilung** and **Grenadiere** that had been reported by our radio. Also the **Abteilung** didn't have any information about the situation to their right, left or rear. At 1600 hours, the radio set was turned on for a short time and contact was made with **Panzer-Regiment 36** on the ultra-short-wave set. **Panzer-Regiment 36** was located with the **I.Abteilung** about 3 kilometers north of Liepkalne on the **Rollbahn** from Barkaisi to Liepkalne. This **Kampfgruppe** appeared to have attracted the attention of a significant part of the enemy weapons onto itself because pressure on the **II.Abteilung** was reduced. Because there wasn't any contact with other units, Hauptmann Schurig requested further orders from the **Panzer-Regiment** commander. The **Panzer-Regiment** commander did not immediately reply to this request. When the **II.Abteilung** again turned on the radio sets at 1700 hours, they overheard the **Panzer-Regiment** commander ordering the **I.Abteilung/Panzer-Regiment 36** advancing toward Liepkalne to immediately break contact with the enemy, leaving behind all immobilized Panzers. The **Panzer-Regiment** commander replied that he wasn't responsible for the **II.Abteilung** and broke off radio contact with the **II.Abteilung**.

As night fell, the enemy pressure again increased. The Adjutant of the **II./108** managed to get through to Zagateni on foot under cover of darkness. There he received the order to immediately pull out the **II.Abteilung**, leaving behind part of the **Grenadiere** that were to be relieved by an **Infanterie-Division** the next day. The **II.Abteilung** left their positions about 2100 hours and were fired on by anti-tank guns that were ineffective at night. Driving back by way of Skukeni, Aizkarkli, Taktas, Torsteri, and Okle, the **II.Abteilung** arrived toward morning at the division command post, which was just pulling back on the **Rollbahn** from Okle to the railroad overpass in Ratlici. Here orders were received to pull into the area south of the rail station in Taurupe and prepare to load on railcars.

Daily Report:

Panzer Strength:	Pz.Kpfw.IV	StuG	Pz.Bef.Wg.
Operational:	9	9	1
Require Repairs:	23	11	1
Total Write-offs:	4	0	0

Personnel Losses: 1 killed, 5 wounded
Results: 9 anti-tank guns, 1 tank, 1 7.62 cm assault gun, and 2 mortars destroyed. About two companies of enemy killed.

Combat report from the 7.Kompanie/Panzer-Regiment 36 attached to **Aufklaerungs-Abteilung 14** on 18 September 1944

The **Pz.Kpfw.IVs** of the **II.Abteilung** returning from Taurube were concentrated as a **Kampfgruppe** under the command of Leutnant Kleinert. At 0700 hours on 18 September, **Kampfgruppe Kleinert** pulled into Lapsein with a strength of six **Pz.Kpfw.IV**. Here they received orders to join up with **Aufklaerungs-Abteilung 14**, attack and take Lafonteine. After leaving the woods north of Point 22.6, the **Kampfgruppe** drove into a marsh and got stuck. After destroying four anti-tank guns in Lafonteine, the Panzers pulled back to the woodline and then attacked from the south, driving along the road up to the crossroads 500 meters south of Lafonteine, and captured it after overrunning the infantry po-

sitions. Leaving the east side, the **Kampfgruppe** encountered an anti-tank gun front that was dug in in the area of Kipoli. One Panzer was hit and destroyed. The **Kampfgruppe** moved to the eastern edge of the village to guard toward the east, north, and south. About 1500 hours, the **Kampfgruppe** was pulled back to the crossroads to resupply. One Panzer broke down due to a mechanical failure. From there at 1700 hours, the **Kampfgruppe** started to attack the crossroads 1 kilometer south of Lomzi. While moving toward Plosi, the **Kampfgruppe** encountered heavy anti-tank gun fire in the left flank from the area of Pusbundes. The anti-tank guns were silenced after a 20-minute firefight. The results couldn't be determined because of the failing light. Fleeing infantry were engaged when the attack continued, and the crossroads was taken at 2000 hours. Six enemy tanks came out of the wooded lot 200 meters to the east of the crossroads. Four of them were destroyed in a battle lasting half an hour. The remaining tanks pulled back. The **Kampfgruppe** followed up to the edge of the small wooded lot and then took up defensive positions toward the north, east, and south at 2100 hours.

Daily Report: Four **Pz.Kpfw.IV** operational, one needing repairs, and one total write-off.

Results: Four tanks and four anti-tank guns destroyed.

Combat report of the 8.Kompanie/Panzer-Regiments 36 attached to the **II.Bataillon/Panzer-Grenadier-Regiment 108** on 18 and 19 September 1944:

At 1800 hours on 18 September 1944, Leutnant Siegert took command of three **Sturmgeschuetze** that he moved 200 meters north into positions on both sides of the road after he heard noise from enemy tanks on the road from Boldone to Klapi. At nightfall, the **Sturmgeschuetze** moved behind the hill 1 kilometer south of Ennes into defensive positions with a field of fire toward the **Rollbahn** running from Riga to Vecumi.

At 0730, the **Sturmgeschuetze** began to attack after the **Grenadiere** had moved into the wooded lot at the crossroads 200 meters north of Klape, moved through the wooded lot, and from the woodline fired at a farmstead full of Russians and set it on fire. Leutnant Siegert knocked out an anti-tank gun with his **Sturmgeschuetz**.

In the meantime, the other two **Sturmgeschuetze** had been sent to guard the eastern edge of the woods. During a counterattack by Russian tanks and infantry, they knocked out a T34 tank and halted Russian infantry.

Leutnant Siegert was wounded by fragments from anti-tank shells, the commander of the second **Sturmgeschuetz**, Feldwebel Bommert, was severely wounded, and the third **Sturmgeschuetz** was out of action due to damage to the gun, whereupon the **Sturmgeschuetze** pulled back to the starting point, a wooded lot 200 meters north of Sides. From there the **Sturmgeschuetz** with the damaged gun drove back to the repair section. The last **Sturmgeschuetz** was sent to guard the command post of the **II./108** in a house on the main

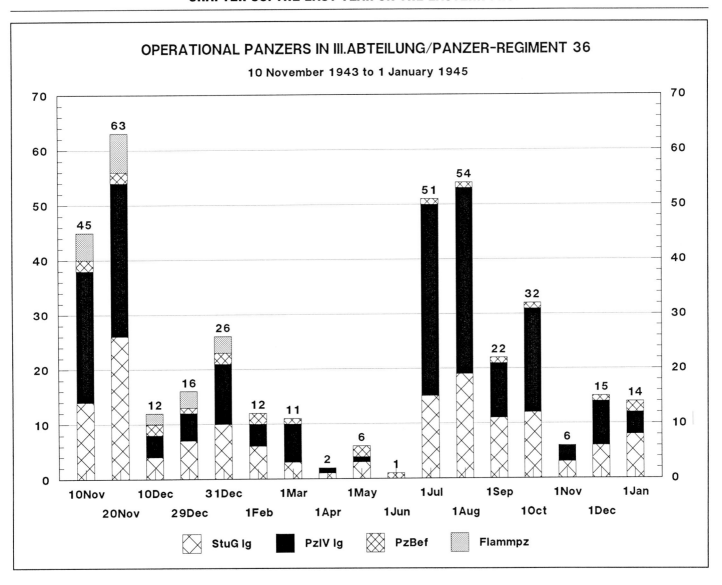

OPERATIONAL PANZERS IN III.ABTEILUNG/PANZER-REGIMENT 36

10 November 1943 to 1 January 1945

StuG lg   PzIV lg   PzBef   Flammpz

Rollbahn from Riga to Vecumi, 80 meters south of the Baldone to Klapi crossroads.

During the afternoon, two additional **Sturmgeschuetze**, which had been repaired, were pulled forward and also were positioned to guard the **Bataillon** command post. Leutnant Siegert, who could no longer command because of his wounds, passed on the command of the **Sturmgeschuetz** to the gunner.

When they pulled back, the **Sturmgeschuetz** got stuck in a marshy area at Point 17.1, 750 meters southeast of Sides. In spite of the attempts by the crew, it wasn't possible to recover the **Sturmgeschuetz**. This **Sturmgeschuetz** was not blown up, because it was located behind the newly gained main battle line. Radio equipment, machine guns, and handheld weapons were recovered. The breech block was removed from the gun.

After being treated by a doctor, Leutnant Siegert again took over command of the **Sturmgeschuetze**. During the evening of 19 September, enemy infantry trickled into the wooded lot 200 meters northwest of the Klapi crossroads.

Because of this, our main battle line had to be pulled back to the hill 200 meters south of the Vecumi to Baldone crossroads. The **Sturmgeschuetz** that had become stuck in the marshy area was now left in no man's land. It still wasn't blown up because the **Sturmgeschuetz** was supposed to be recovered with the help of a **Pionier-Zug**.

About 2200 hours, Russian infantry attacked our positions on the hill on both sides of the Vecumi to Riga road. The **Grenadiere** were thrown out of their positions. Leutnant Siegert decided to counterattack with both **Sturmgeschuetze**, which succeeded in returning the **Grenadiere** to their previous positions. He destroyed one anti-tank gun, two heavy machine guns and enemy infantry.

The **Sturmgeschuetze** then returned to guard the command post of the **II./108**.

The Russians again attacked with strong artillery and tank support. Two Russian 15 cm assault guns advanced to the anti-tank ditch south of the **Bataillon** command post. One Russian assault gun was knocked out by the two **Sturmgeschuetze** firing from ambush. The crew jumped out.

The **Panzer-Grenadiere** then fired **Faustpatronen** at the Russian assault gun. The **Sturmgeschuetze** moved off 200 meters up the road north of the **Bataillon** command post and fired at the second Russian assault gun which returned heavy fire. Behind the woods, the **Sturmgeschuetze** refueled and took on a full load of ammunition.

At 0300 hours in the morning, Leutnant Siegert decided to knock out the second Russian assault gun from ambush. He pulled both **Sturmgeschuetze** up to the woodline 200 meters north of Baldone, and fired at the Russian assault gun, which was illuminated by a burning house, setting it on fire and knocking it out. Then the **Sturmgeschuetze** returned to a position behind the wooded lot and pulled guard.

Results: Two anti-tank guns, one T34 tank, two 15 cm assault guns, one machine gun nest destroyed.

The September 1944 issue of the Nachrichtenblatt der Panzertruppen included a report from a Tiger-Kompanie that knocked out numerous Josef Stalin tanks in a short period:

The Tiger-Kompanie was ordered to throw out the enemy who had penetrated into a woods, and then continue to advance. About 1215 hours, together with an Infanterie-Bataillon, the Tiger-Kompanie started to attack. The thick forest caused extremely poor visibility (50 meters), and a narrow trail forced the **Tiger-Kompanie** to advance in single file. The Russian infantry fled their positions as soon as the Tigers appeared. The anti-tank guns, which were pulled forward into position by the opponent within three-quarters of an hour after entering the woods, were quickly destroyed in spite of the difficultly in seeing the targets. Some of the anti-tank guns were destroyed by hits and some were rolled over. Numerous undamaged anti-tank guns fell into our hands.

After the lead Zug of the **Tiger-Kompanie** advanced 2 kilometers through the forest, the **Zug** leader suddenly noticed knocked-down trees and saw a large muzzle brake (Josef Stalin) directly in front of him. He immediately gave the fire command: "**Panzergranate!** Cupola sight! Fire!" At the same time he was hit twice by 4.5 cm anti-tank gun shells that robbed him of his sight. In the interim, a second Tiger of the **Zug** driving through the woods pulled up on line with the **Zug** leader's Tiger. In spite of poor visibility, the **Zug** leader started the firefight at a range of 35 meters. In response, the Josef Stalin tank pulled back behind a small hill. In the meantime, the second Tiger had taken the lead and fired three shots at the enemy tank. When the third round was fired, the Tiger itself was hit by a 12.2 cm shell on the front below the radio operator's position. Apparently this armor-piercing shell didn't penetrate through because the Tiger was standing at an angle from the target. The enemy tank was knocked out of action by a shot which penetrated the gun. A second Josef Stalin tank attempted to cover the first as it pulled back. During a short firefight, one of these two Tigers hit the second tank under the gun. This round penetrated, immediately setting the enemy tank on fire. The rate of fire of the Josef Stalin tanks was comparatively slow.

The Kompanie commander made the following observations that were derived from their experience in fighting Josef Stalin tanks:

1. When a Tiger appears, most Josef Stalin tanks turn away and attempt to avoid a firefight.

2. In many cases, the Josef Stalin tanks let themselves engage in a firefight only at long range (over 2000 meters) and also only when they themselves are in favorable positions on the edge of a woods, village, or ridgeline.

3. The enemy crews lean toward evacuating their tank immediately after the first shot is fired at them.

4. In all cases the Russians strived to prevent a Josef Stalin tank from falling into our hands and with all means available attempted to tow the tank away or to blow it up.

Month	Days in Action	Knocked Out/Destroyed			Own Losses as Total Write-Offs		
		Tanks	Assault Guns	Anti-Tank Guns	PzIV	StuG	Bef
Jan44	17	105	7	45	3	6	
Feb44	7	3	10	16	1		
Mar44	4	4			3	2	
Apr44	2		5		1		
May44	6	1	2	17			
Jun44	2			1	2		
Jul44							
Aug44	5	3	2	23	4		
Sep44	8	21	3	27	9	6	1
Oct44	10	38	5	32	2		

Table title: **Claims and Losses of the III.Abteilung/Panzer-Regiment 36**

LEFT: The regiment commander's Panther of **Panzer-Regiment Hermann Goering** sent to the Eastern Front in the Fall of 1944. (JW)

5. The Josef Stalin can also be knocked out, even if a penetration of the frontal armor can't be achieved at long range. (A different **Tiger-Abteilung** reported that the front of a Josef Stalin can be penetrated by a Tiger only at ranges less than 500 meters.)

6. An attempt should be made to gain the flank or the rear of the Josef Stalin tank and destroy him with concentrated fire.

7. In addition, a firefight with Josef Stalin tanks should not be undertaken in less than **Zug** strength. Employment of single Tigers means their loss.

8. It has proven to be useful, after the first hits are registered, to blind the Josef Stalin by firing **Sprenggranaten** (high explosive shells).

Remarks by the **Generalinspekteur der Panzertruppen:**

1. These experiences agree with those of other Tiger units and are correct.

2. In regard to Point 4 - It would be desirable for the opponent to have observed the same attempt by all of our Tiger crews. "An undestroyed Tiger may never fall into enemy hands!" This principle must be achieved by every crew member by exemplary operational readiness.

BELOW: A Tiger II of the **3.Kompanie/schwere Panzer-Abteilung 501**, accompanied by two **Sturmgeschuetze**, engaged in mopping up a bridgehead in the Weichsel bend on 2 October 1944. (BA)

ORGANIZATION AND STRENGTH OF PANZER UNITS
REPLACEMENT UNITS SENT TO EASTERN FRONT

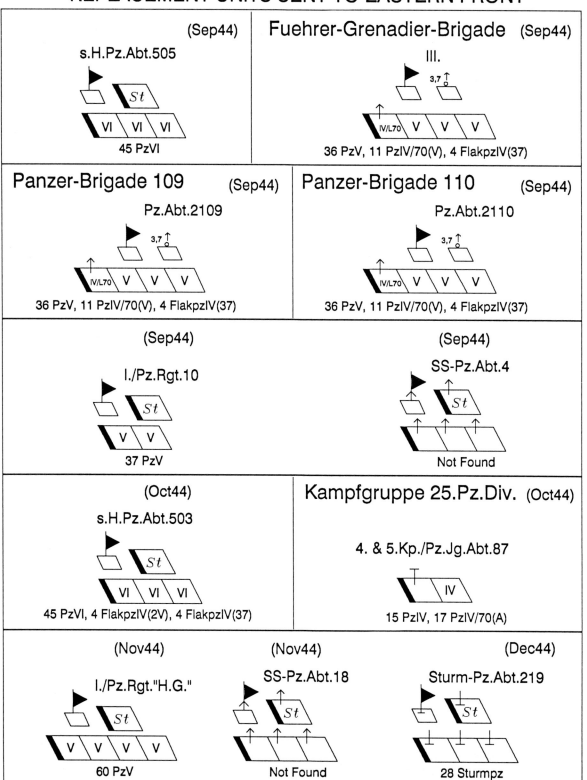

3. In regard to Points 5 and 6 - At a time when there are 12.2 cm tank guns and 5.7 cm anti-tank guns on the Eastern Front just like the 9.2 cm anti-tank/aircraft guns on the Western Front and in Italy, the Tiger can no longer disregard the tactical principles that apply to the other type of Panzers.

Also, just like other Panzers, a few Tigers can't drive up on a ridgeline to observe the terrain. In just such a situation, three Tigers received direct hits and were destroyed by 12.2 cm shells resulting in all but two of the crew members being killed.

The principles of Panzer tactics, that Panzers should only cross a ridgeline together, rapidly (leaf-frogging by bounds) and under covering fire, or else the Panzers must drive around the height - were definitely not unknown in this **Tiger-Abteilung**. Statements like "thick fur", "impregnable", and the "security" of the crews in the Tigers, which have become established phrases by other units and also partially within the **Panzertruppe**, must be wiped out and invalidated.

Instead, it is especially important for Tiger units to pay direct attention to the general combat principles applicable for tank-versus-tank combat.

4. In regard to Point 7 - This statement is correct; however, three Tigers should not flee from five Josef Stalin tanks only because they can't start the firefight at full **Zug** strength. Cases will also occur in which an entire **Zug** isn't always available. Many times tank-versus-tank combat will be directly decided, not by the number of tanks, but much more by superior combat tactics. Nothing is changed in the statement that "a single Panzer is lost."

5. In regard to Point 8 - In connection with this it may be stated that the Josef Stalin tanks can not only be penetrated from the flanks and rear by Tigers and Panthers but also by the **Pz.Kpfw.IV** and the **Sturmgeschuetz**.

The following article on tank-versus-tank combat in the October 1944 issue of the <u>Nachrichtenblatt der Panzertruppen</u> was surprising in that even on the Eastern Front the principles of concentrated employment had eroded into advocating the use of small groups of Panzers in certain circumstances:

Sometimes because of difficult terrain conditions, on the Eastern Front it has also been necessary to employ Panzers in small **Kampftrupps** in the same way that they have been reported on the Invasion Front. Also, on the defense Panzers have had to fight singly against enemy tanks. The following experience report from a **Panzer-Abteilung** elaborates on this method of combat:

Deeply cut terrain and our own weak **Panzertruppe** made it impossible for our own Panzers to counterattack. Because crossing ridges couldn't be prevented, the element of surprise was canceled from the start and our own Panzers had to drive across the enemy front, which caused us considerable losses from enemy tanks and especially from the numerous enemy anti-tank guns emplaced in the main battle-field. So almost without exception, the battle was conducted from a fire front established in commanding positions. These locations were laid out in the same way as close range positions by the **Panzer-Jaeger**, in that they were located with a field of fire of 100 to 200 meters directly in front of the Panzers hidden under full cover. Alarm posts were responsible for timely and rapid reports on the situation.

In this sector of the front, the enemy used his tanks only for local counterattacks in groups of five to six tanks. Attacks with concentrated forces rarely occurred.

The combat power of the Sherman tanks with Russian crews doesn't appear to be especially high, because the Russian tank crews have very little faith in this tank. Many times, crews abandoned Sherman tanks that were still serviceable after receiving the first hit. This Sherman tank, just like the T34 tank has not evolved to withstand the superior effectiveness of the **Pz.Kpfw.IV** and **Sturmgeschuetz** weapons. In general, firefights are conducted at ranges between 1200 and 2200 meters.

Our own artillery fire has often proven to be a handicap in fighting and destroying enemy tanks. Hardly had a Panzer ranged in on an enemy tank when it would be enveloped by a wide spreading cloud of dust and smoke which was immediately created every time the artillery fired. The enemy tank could pull back over the ridgeline under cover of this cloud of dust and smoke and take up a new position. After Panzers and **Panzer-Jaeger** open fire against enemy tanks, the artillery starts to fire even though they very seldom can obtain a hit on these small, individual targets. Therefore, artillery batteries must immediately cease firing when Panzers and **Panzer-Jaeger** start to engage enemy tanks.

Experiences in employing the Tiger II on the Eastern Front are revealed in the following report dated 25 November 1944 written by Hauptmann Fromme, commander of **schwere Panzer-Abteilung 503**:

The **Abteilung** was loaded to move to Hungary starting on 9 October 1944 in order to complete their reorganization in the area of Budapest. The government crises made it necessary to employ the **Abteilung** for the occupation of the castle on 16 October. This was almost exclusively a demonstration but was thoroughly successful.

Increased enemy activity east of the Theiss and near Debrecen required immediate employment. The Panzers were unloaded from rail transport in the Szelnok area but because of a shortage of **Ssyms-Wagen**, not all of them arrived on time in the assembly area. Those that were unloaded immediately marched off to the assembly area in order to start the attack several hours later. The Panzers that arrived the next day were also concentrated into a **Kampfgruppe** and attached to another division, so the **Abteilung** went into action in two **Kampfgruppen** with different divisions on different days with the intention of reassembling after successfully penetrating through the enemy defenses. Both **Kampfgruppen** were extraordinarily successful. From 19 October until the unit was reassembled on 23 October, 120 anti-tank guns and 19 artillery pieces were destroyed. The very tough and determined opponent (punitive battalion) was very shaken by an energetic charge. Rearward communications were brought into complete confusion by destroying convoys and a transport train, which caused the Russian 6th Army to pull out of the Debrecen area. The entire stretch covered in this action of about 250 kilometers was achieved without significant mechanical breakdowns. In these battles, the Tiger II proved itself in its armor protection as well as mechanical reliability. It was not exceptional that Tiger IIs that were hit up to 20 times without falling out.

The following action was limited to small tasks, especially counterthrusts with weak **Infanterie** forces against the enemy who crossed over the Theiss northeast of Szolnok. However, these caused the Russians to forbid their units from conducting any major combat actions where Tigers were located.

During this week, and continuing up to today, the **Abteilung** was not given time to perform maintenance in spite of urgent requests continuously being made. This was partially due to the situation, but also partially due to the lack of understanding of the higher command to which the unit was subordinated, who always asked two questions: "How many are operational?" and "How many will be repaired in the next few days?" In spite of this, up to 30 October on average 25 to 30 Tiger IIs were operational every day.

On 31 October, the **Abteilung** rolled to a new assignment under the **LVII.Panzer-Korps** in the Kecskomet area to catch the penetrating Russian wedges. In very difficult, partially swampy terrain that was unsuitable for Panzers, damage began to appear, especially to drive sprockets, tracks, track tension adjusters, and engine cooling fans. Within a few days, due to a shortage of replacement parts that were ordered on time but not delivered on time and then only partially, this led to most of the Tiger IIs breaking down.

As a result of the lack of towing capacity, the **Abteilung** was faced with the decision of either blowing up the broken-down Tigers beyond the main battle line or recovering them with Tigers that were still operational. Naturally, this resulted in mechanical breakdowns to Tigers used to tow other Tigers out. At the last minute, the **Abteilung** barely avoided losing a large number of Tigers through timely and advanced preparations that had been made for loading the Tigers on the rail cars.

The few operational Tigers that were left were shoved from division to division and, by inappropriate employment, given tasks that were not achievable and couldn't be carried out.

After 18 November, the **Abteilung** was in action in the Gyoengyoes. Continuous bad weather made it almost impossible to leave the roads. Because the **Panzer-Grenadier-Regiment** and **Grenadier-Regiment** are too weak, the Tigers and also the **Flak-Panzer** usually had to stand guard in

the main battle line without any sort of infantry close protection. Attacks in total darkness at night in unscouted terrain with infantry forces that were much too weak, capturing a city heavily occupied by enemy infantry and anti-tank guns by a night attack with 120 convalescents and a **SPW-Bataillon** with a strength of 40 men, were not unusual. These attacks were successful only if the **Grenadiere** actually accompanied the attack in front and to the side of the Tigers (to destroy the anti-tank guns that were frequently located in the doors of houses and gateways which couldn't be engaged by the Panzers) and if the infantry didn't crumble and desert the Tigers when they met the first resistance, so that it was easy for the enemy tank hunter teams to fight the Tigers.

The experience that Russians build up strong anti-tank gun positions directly behind his forward elements was proven again. Up to now, happily, the employment of American 9.2 cm and conical bore (7.5 cm reduced to 5.7 cm) anti-tank guns has led to only two Tigers lost as total write-offs. These weapons can also penetrate the gun mantlet at ranges under 600 meters. Penetrations of the rear of the turret cause the stowed ammunition to explode and usually result in the total destruction of the Tiger.

In tank-versus-tank combat, the **8.8 cm Kw.K.43** gun is effective in destroying all of the types of enemy tanks, including the Stalin, at ranges up to 1500 meters. Under favorable conditions, the T34 and T43 tanks can also be knocked out at ranges up to 3000 meters. As previously experienced in the West with Allied tanks, it was often observed that the Russian tanks declined to fight Tigers or turned and fled after their first tank was knocked out. The same thing applies to the Russian assault guns as to the Stalin tanks. Kills at over 1500 meters have not yet occurred.

In summary it can be said that the Tiger II has proven itself in every way and is a weapon that is feared by the enemy. The concentrated **Tiger-Abteilung** correctly employed tactically will always bring success. But most of the higher commands that were encountered did not perceive the technical and tactical importance of a **Tiger-Abteilung**.

Further details on the difficulties encountered are revealed in the following report dated 15 November 1944 from Oberleutnant Oemler, commander of **1.Kompanie/schwere Panzer-Abteilung 503**, on the action of **Kampfgruppe Oemler** with the **13.Panzer-Division** from 11 to 13 November 1944:

About 1430 hours, on 11 November 1944, the **Kampfgruppe Oelmer** received orders from the **13.Panzer-Division** to move to Tapiostentmarton. The **Kampfgruppe** arrived in Tapiostentmarton at 1500 hours and reported to the regimental command post. New orders from the division came in at 1530 hours: The **Kampfgruppe** attached to **Grenadier-Bataillon Seidel** was to drive through Point 108 to Farmos carrying the **2.Kompanie** of **Bataillon Seidel**. The **1.Kompanie** of **Bataillon Seidel** outfitted with **SPW** was to move through Nagykata to Farmos. From Farmos, they were to join up with the armored **Gruppe-Bataillon Gruen**, drive to Tapio Szele, and set up defenses south of the city.

They moved off directly after the **Grenadier-Kompanie** arrived. The commander of the **46.Infanterie-Division** informed the leader of the **Kampfgruppe** that the ordered route was easily passable for Tigers. However, this route couldn't be driven by Tigers and they detoured to the southeast to get to Farmos on a 2 kilometer route that ran parallel. Also this route was not passable because the bridge was too weak and the terrain was completely softened and marshy. The Tigers became stuck and had to turn back around.

About 1730 hours, the leader of the **Kampfgruppe** with Hauptmann Seidel and Hauptmann Gruen arrived by car in Farmos. Hauptmann Seidel didn't start the attack because in the meantime it had become totally dark, **Bataillon Seidel** and the Tigers hadn't arrived, Tapio Szele was occupied by the enemy, and the terrain couldn't even be crossed by **SPW**.

Because at night it wasn't possible to drive through on the route that the Tigers were supposed to take, Leutnant Fuerlingen immediately drove on the road through Nagykata to Tapiobiske in order to inform the division about the situation, to receive new orders, and to guide the Tigers through Nagykata. The division was completely unaware of the situation of the **Kampfgruppe**. The division had halted the Tigers and on orders from the **Korps** had ordered the Tigers to move to Nagykata, where they were to build a **Korps-Reserve** with armored **Bataillon Gruen** after 0430 hours on 12 November.

Leutnant Fuerlinger gave the situation report on **Kampfgruppe Seidel**, received new orders for armored **Bataillon Gruen**, and guided the Tigers after refueling to Tapiobiske.

On 12 November, the **Kampfgruppe** was located in Nagykata as **Korps-Reserve**. At 1230 hours, an order arrived by messenger from **Panzer-Regiment 23** that the **Tiger-Kampfgruppe** was attached to **Panzer-Regiment 23** and was to move through Jaszbereny to Jakohalma. The leader of the **Tiger-Kampfgruppe** immediately drove to the **13.Panzer-Division** for orientation on the situation. Here new orders were received: Tigers attached to **Bataillon Gruen** of the **13.Panzer-Division** were to clear the road of enemy from Nagykata to Jaszbereny and gain contact with the **23.Panzer-Division**. Carrying out the first order was not possible because the road was occupied by the enemy on a broad front.

About 1400 hours, the **Tiger-Kampfgruppe** started to move toward Jaszbereny, with the first objective the crossroads 2 kilometers southwest of Jaszbereny. Driving along the road, the lead Tigers encountered enemy tanks, assault guns, and very strong infantry forces 800 meters in front of the crossroads. One assault gun and three enemy tanks were knocked out. Further advance was impossible because **Bataillon Gruen**, attacking from the right flank, didn't come along and remained stationary 5 kilometers behind the Tigers. A battle by the Tigers alone on the road passing through the forest or leaving the road to move through marshy woods

and heather was not possible. In spite of heavy weapons support, the **SS-Bataillon** sent in to secure the woods couldn't halt the opponent's attack through thick undergrowth that closed in to close range, and the **SS** pulled out after blowing up the ammunition dump in the woods.

About 1500 hours, the **Bataillon** ordered the Tigers to pull back about 6 kilometers to on line with the **Bataillon** command post.

About 1900 hours, the **Tiger-Kampfgruppe** leader received orders to contact the commander of the **13.Panzer-Division** by telephone. About 1940 hours, the commander of the **13.Panzer-Division** telephoned the following order to the **Tiger-Kampfgruppe**: Three Tigers are to drive through the woods up to the edge about 800 meters from the crossroads, and three Tigers are to drive up to the start of the woods and stand guard 2 kilometers behind the first group of Tigers, and now and then, all night long, two Tigers are to drive between these two points in order to maintain contact. This is to prevent the Russian infantry from creeping through the woods. Each of these **Panzerstuetzpunkte** was to be guarded by 15 infantrymen.

The **Tiger-Kampfgruppe** leader immediately reported that:

1. The woods was heavily occupied by the enemy, especially in his eastern sector. It was not possible, even by day, to drive through with Tigers without the strongest infantry close defense.

2. The terrain was very marshy, and leaving the roads was not possible, especially at night.

3. Tigers on the road can't even traverse their guns because of the trees and if one Tiger was knocked out, it would not be possible for the rest to get past.

4. The Tigers can't drive around at night 5 kilometers in front of our own main battle line in terrain that can't be crossed by Panzers.

5. The forced march last night reduced the number of Tigers to six completely operational and one conditionally operational.

In spite of these objections, the division stood by its order, with the exception that two SPW instead of the Tigers were to maintain contact between the Tiger groups.

After the arrival of the first section of infantry at about 2200 hours, which had to first be hauled out of the main defense line, the first three Tigers under command of Leutnant Fuehrlinger set off with two Unteroffiziere, 12 men and two **SPW**. The start of the second group of three Tigers was delayed because the infantry were not yet on hand. The first group of three Tigers drove forward with four or five infantrymen riding on each Tiger. The night was pitch black. The sky covered by clouds. It was raining. You couldn't see anything.

The group stopped 200 meters in front of the position ordered by the division. The leader sent two infantrymen from his Tiger forward. They were fired on from all sides out of the woods and from the road when they had gotten only as far as 10 meters in front of the lead Tiger. The Tigers took up a hedgehog formation on the road. Slowly, the opponent crept past on the right and left. Several times, Russian close-combat troops were driven off when they came close to the Tigers. Since it was not possible to prevent the Russians from penetrating through the woods during the day, it was downright impossible at night. Only the fact that the opponent didn't know the Tiger group's strength can be thanked for the Russians not totally wiping them out.

One SPW had already broken down before they started. In the second group of Tigers, the lead Tiger broke a track 3 kilometers before the ordered position and the other two Tigers couldn't get past it because of the terrain.

As the enemy pressure became too strong, enemy tanks closed in on the **Kampfgruppe** from the south (apparently the T34 tanks also became stuck when they attempted to drive along the forest tracks), and the first group of Tigers slowly pulled back 400 meters. The **SPW** sent back to maintain communication was shot at and didn't drive any farther.

As the action progressed, Hauptmann Gruen was continuously informed by radio messages from the **Tiger-Kampfgruppe** leader. About 2300 hours, the **Tiger-Kampfgruppe** leader gave the operations officer of the **13.Panzer-Division** an exact description of the enemy situation by telephone from the command post of Hauptmann Gruen and asked if under these conditions the Tigers should hold their **Stuetzpunkt** in spite of the strong enemy pressure. There was the danger that the Russians would cut off the Tigers from resupply and would mine the road. In spite of this, the order was strictly maintained.

About 0200 hours, Hauptmann Gruen received an order to follow the Tigers and break through to Jaszbereny still at night. About 0500 hours, the **Bataillon**, which first had to be relieved in the main defense line, drove forward with the second group of three Tigers. After reaching the **Stuetzpunkt** with the first group of three Tigers, the **Kampfgruppe** started to attack. The lead Tiger immediately wiped out five 7.62 cm anti-tank guns in a stretch of 150 meters and advanced another 200 meters past the edge of the forest. Here the **Kampfgruppe** encountered a strong anti-tank gun front and well-camouflaged assault guns. Leutnant Bielefeld fell when hit from close range by an anti-tank gun while attempting to outflank the anti-tank guns by moving to the left over an open field.

Beside the road in the deserted Russian positions lay German **Faustpatronen**, explosives and other close-combat weapons. One Russian infantryman attempting to sneak up to the side of the Tiger with a **Faustpatrone** was shot up at a range of 20 meters. Because the **Infanterie** hadn't come along, the Tigers had to pull back after the opponents in the forest in battalion strength charged, yelling "Hurrah" and threw back the following **Infanterie** from the road to the left. The attack of the Russians was halted, and the **Kampfgruppe** took up a hedgehog defense.

The leader of the **Kampfgruppe** proposed to detour to the north and thereby gain contact with the **23.Panzer-Division**. The orders for this came in at about 1100 hours, and without encountering enemy activity, the **Kampfgruppe** arrived at the command post of the **II./SS-Regiment 40** at about

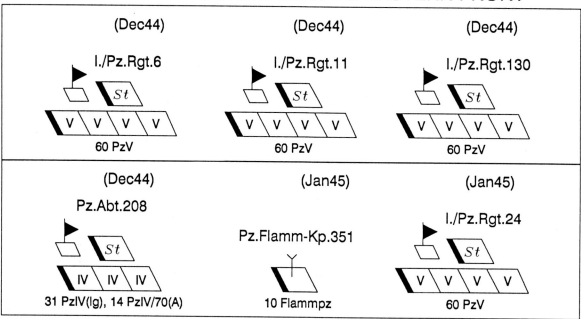

ORGANIZATION AND STRENGTH OF PANZER UNITS REPLACEMENT UNITS SENT TO EASTERN FRONT

(Dec44)	(Dec44)	(Dec44)
I./Pz.Rgt.6	I./Pz.Rgt.11	I./Pz.Rgt.130
60 PzV	60 PzV	60 PzV
(Dec44)	(Jan45)	(Jan45)
Pz.Abt.208	Pz.Flamm-Kp.351	I./Pz.Rgt.24
31 PzIV(lg), 14 PzIV/70(A)	10 Flammpz	60 PzV

A column of **Panther Ausf.G**s engaged in battles around the Russian bridgehead north of Kuestrin on 3 February 1945. (BA)

1500 hours. The Tigers then started south toward the crossroads and turned to the west south of the road from Jaszbereny to Nagykata, where the Tigers guarded the position as ordered. They returned toward the command post of Hauptmann Gruen at nightfall. One kilometer short of the command post, all of the Tigers became stuck in the road and with great difficulty were recovered by first light.

Through this totally inappropriate employment, four Tigers broke down due to track, drive-sprocket, and transmission damage. Working together with the division was extremely unenjoyable. Absolutely no attention was paid to the tactical principles for employing Tigers. Through reassignments and continuous changes in the unit assignments, it was not possible for supplies to reach the Tigers. As the messengers vehicle broke down, the request that another vehicle be loaned for a few hours in order to bring up the supply vehicles was declined by the Division **01** with the statement: "See to it how you bring up your fuel! I am not here for the purpose of getting your fuel!"

This last experience report is from the **I.Abteilung/ Panzer-Regiment 24**, which had been outfitted with 60 Panthers and sent to **Heeresgruppe Sued** on the Eastern Front in January 1945. During the period of this report the **Abteilung** was attached to one of four **Panzer-Divisions**, usually the **1.Panzer-Division**.

These experiences were gathered by one **Abteilung** which destroyed 110 tanks, 153 anti-tank guns, and 13 artillery pieces and captured 74 anti-tank guns during combat between 19 January and 15 February 1945.

The report should show the current difficulties with which the **Panzermann** has to fight and should counter the experience reports that have been written only from the **Grenadiere** perspective.

<u>The enemy weapons and their combat methods</u>

The anti-tank guns are the main opponent of Panzers in the Eastern Theater of War. The Russians use anti-tank guns en masse for defense or by cleverly towing them along behind an attack to swiftly bring them into action. The meaning of "**Pakfront**" does not totally describe the actual situations experienced in combat by the **Abteilung** because the opponent employs this weapon more concentrated in so called "**Paknest**" in an attempt to achieve a long range flanking effect. Sometimes the **Paknest** consist of 6 to 7 anti-tank guns in a circle of only 40 to 50 meters. Because of the excellent camouflage and use of terrain - sometimes the wheels are taken off to reduce the height - the Russians easily manage to open surprise fire at medium and close range. By allowing the lead vehicles to pass by, they attempt to open fire at our formation in the deep flank.

If the Russian anti-tank crews are spotted and taken under well-aimed fire, they quickly leave their weapon. However, they quickly reman the guns when not observed or when firing ceases and again take up the firefight.

The Russian tank forces are an opponent to be reckoned with only when they are in a situation to let our attack run onto them. We repeatedly offer the Russians opportunities through insufficient enemy reconnaissance and thereby attack with Panzers without advance clear orders and directions. In spite of its being tactically correct to let recognized enemy attacks close range, we are ordered to attack. Thus, the possibility of knocking out a large number of tanks is taken out of our hands.

On 3 February, during the battle around Stuhlweissenburg, it was expected that the Russians would mount a tank attack on the north side of the city, and this was mentioned several times by the Abteilung commander. In spite of this, together with Tigers from another unit, the **Abteilung** was ordered to start a counterattack farther north and hit the reported Russian tanks in the rear. The attack started out in fog with poor visibility. While our own Panzers prepared to attack further north, as expected the Russians started attacking south. A break-in into the city could be prevented only by pulling the Tigers back. Due to poor visibility the **Kampfgruppe** employed farther north ran onto an enemy defensive position reinforced with mines and the attack came to a halt.

The Russian tank forces are inferior in mobile battles, apparently due to the lack of strict command. The enemy is not in a situation to hold his forces together during an attack of long duration. Instead, he leans toward scattering. They try to make up for this weakness by swift but unplanned cross-country moves. The Russian tank forces are successful through mass employment and other factors such as our own weak defensive forces, exploiting surprises, and our own counterstrikes without clear advance orders.

The Russians understand defense of towns by clever use of anti-tank guns and tanks. The enemy toughly and bitterly awaits his chance and lets the opponent advance to close range in order to possibly shoot him up from the flank.

The Russian infantry is of little value and quickly leaves the battlefield as soon as Panzers appear. Only in street fighting and in close country are they tough fighting opponents, more so when they know they have been surrounded. Clever construction of field positions comes to their advantage. When we do not immediately counterstrike, the Russian infantry are quickly in position to start to swiftly build up a new defense.

Combat methods of our Panzers

The tasks assigned must be based on the available strength. The strained tactical situation in no way allows maintenance pauses so that the number of operational Panzers is significantly reduced during an action. All of the available Panzers should be concentrated to achieve a single combat task. Do not disperse! However, this mistake was repeatedly made. This resulted in three or four Panzers being halted and knocked out by the first Paknest that they encountered, sometimes by surprise, because of their numerically low strength. The other group of Panzers have to fight under the same conditions. As a result, both attacks are stopped due to our own losses.

On 10 February, while attacking south of Lepszeny, on orders from the **Kampfgruppe** commander three Panzers were ordered to drive past the town to take another village. As the battle progressed it turned out that the town was occupied only by weak enemy forces. Successful accomplishment of the assignment was lucky and in no way should be viewed as a measurement of the correctness of the tactics employed.

With smaller Panzer formations one should constantly attempt to tie down the enemy frontally with part of the force and attack the enemy in the flank with part of the force. The preparations must be fundamental, the orders clear, and necessary time allowed. Issuing orders at the command post should be done swiftly. If a Panzer formation attack covers a distance of over several kilometers, regrouping halts are absolutely necessary; otherwise the shock force is split up, the units become dispersed, and tactical command is impossible.

On 18 January, during an attack by the **Abteilung** southwest of a lake, the tempo of the attack was rushed by the **Kampfgruppe** commander in such a way that the Panzers of the entire **Abteilung** became scattered and mixed up as night fell. If they had suddenly encountered strong enemy resistance, control and command of the battle would not have been possible. If an attack advances smoothly because of weak enemy resistance, regrouping halts must occur, or else during the quickly changing situation in tank-versus-tank combat serious crises and preventable losses will occur.

A Panzer attack forced to take place in unfavorable weather conditions costs losses that in no way are offset by the achievements. In spite of repeated objections from the **Abteilung** commander, on 3 and 10 February the Panzers had to attack in fog with visibility sometimes down to 100 meters. In the first case, the front wave of an attack on the heights 3 kilometers north of Stuhlweissenburg ran into an alert enemy position ready to defend with anti-tank guns and tanks, took losses, and was halted. In the last case, during an attack on a village the enemy anti-tank guns weren't spotted until short range, costing the unnecessary loss of two Panzers.

The firing range is decisive for fighting with **Pakneste** that appear beside each other in a row as a **Pakfront**. If a Panzer formation is fired on surprisingly at short range, all weapons need to be employed immediately. If a Panzer formation encounters a strong anti-tank emplacement at long and medium ranges, they should break off the action and attack at a new location. The **Panzermann** must attempt to continuously utilize the long range of his weapon. However, this requires observation halts in order to spot the anti-tank guns in time.

Closely associated with this is the employment of our combat reconnaissance, which moves forward on a wide formation in front of the main body in order to find any **Paknest** that can be spotted only after they fire. During such a reconnaissance, with elan these Panzers must move at the highest possible speed from observation point to observation point, conduct detailed combat reconnaissance while halted, and cause the enemy to reveal himself by firing at suspicious terrain features. The combat reconnaissance can be thoughtfully and correctly handled only when they move far enough ahead of the main body that they are not pressured from behind. The successful battle with the anti-tank guns requires exacting reconnaissance, especially feeling one's way forward, quick decisions after spotting the target, clear and understandable orders, and swift implementation. In addition, the **Panzermann** has to suffer under the meager understanding of the **Grenadiere** commander, who can't comprehend how the Panzers must fight the enemy anti-tank guns.

The battlefield belongs to the **Panzermann** during tank versus tank combat. If dug-in enemy tanks are to be destroyed and this can't occur by a flank attack, the individual enemy tanks must be picked off singly by painstaking work employing scouting on foot and slowly advancing under cover. This requires time! Success is guaranteed by utilizing cunning, for example running the Panzers' motors to tie the opponent down frontally and slowly, centimeter by centimeter, sending in a Panzer that will fire from the flank. In this way on 2 February, within 20 minutes one **Schwadron** knocked out five Shermans and three T34 tanks that were exceptionally well camouflaged in a factory grounds on the north end of Stuhlweissenburg.

If I recognize an enemy tank attack in time, I basically let them advance. If I must attack an opponent in open terrain, the attack is conducted as a pincers movement simultaneously from two directions. This causes the enemy caught in the pincers to be shaken. In this way on 4 February, the **Abteilung** succeeded in knocking out 26 tanks and destroying 45 anti-tank guns north of Stuhlweissenburg. When a surprised enemy tank force that is not prepared for defense is encountered, a lightning swift engagement increases the panic of the opponent and guarantees success. Due to poor radio communications between enemy tanks, the Russians cannot improvise or quickly give out counterorders. Under these conditions, on 26 January during an advance by the **Abteilung** near Kajaszoszenipeter, one Panther knocked out three enemy tanks at a range of 20 meters.

Employment of Panzers in street fighting cannot be successfully conducted without the closest cooperation of **Grenadiere**. The limited ability to see out of the Panzer makes it easier for the enemy to fight it. The **Grenadiere** must help. Advancing by rushes from cover to cover under the protection of the Panzer's weapons, they spot anti-tank guns, tanks, and heavy infantry weapons and report them to the commanders. Mutual trust builds the basis for cooperation. Often the **Grenadiere** use the Panzers as cover and a shield against small arms fire and suffer losses from fire aimed at the Panzers. During the advance of our own Panzers on 1 February on the north side of Stuhlweissenburg, our own Panzer suffered losses from hidden anti-tank guns on the flank that could have been spotted in time and fought if escorting **Grenadiere** had advanced with the Panzers.

Night attacks were always successful with few losses when prepared according to plan, strictly led, and initiated using the element of surprise. Daring and resolute handling

are prerequisites. A night attack that fails leads to very high losses. A village that lay on a commanding sector of a riverbank, and occupied by anti-tank guns and tanks as well as numerous infantry, was captured by six Panthers and two **Befehls-Panthers** in a swift attack. With a low number of Panzers in the attacking force, the tempo of the attack can be freer than in larger formations of 30 Panzers where the individual combat movements must be well synchronized. Supplying the Panzers with a vast number of carbines with launching tubes for parachute flares is required. Other than special illumination devices, these are the only usable means of illuminating the battlefield during close combat without giving away our own positions.

It should be remarked on the effectiveness of the Panzer's weapons that in the big picture not enough firing occurs. Concentrated fire dealing heavy blows from over 10 guns works wonders even against toughly fighting Russians. If during an attack on a strongly fortified village, an **Abteilung** fires a concentrated barrage and then elements immediately charge, a break-in always is achieved and secured without loss. However, one repeatedly meets up with an incorrect concept of a proper barrage. If five Panzers fire five rounds at the target area, this is often called a barrage, but in reality for a Panther this is only skirmishing. The amount of ammunition to be expended must be in ratio with the number of Panzers used. Targets are to be designated in advance and may not be adjusted much during the actual barrage! The loader in the Panzer must achieve the firing rate of the loader of a Flak gun. Utilizing this effect, even today the Panthers breach the enemy defenses and pave the way for the attack! On 20 January, during a night attack on Kapolnas-Nyok, which was occupied by anti-tank guns and tanks that couldn't be made out in the darkness, the **Abteilung** with 20 Panzers fired a barrage of 15 rounds per Panzer at the edge of the village. The Russians fled from their positions and attempted to get away with tanks and anti-tank guns across the eastern tip of Veloence lake. At dawn, tanks that had broken through the ice and were abandoned by their crews revealed the effectiveness of the weapons.

The machine guns aren't fired enough! The turret machine gun is exceptionally effective against massed infantry targets. During a Panzer attack north of Stuhlweissenburg, a Russian counterattack in regimental strength ran into flanking machine gun fire from five Panthers. About 300 enemy dead were counted in a circle around a single Panzer.

During an attack on an anti-tank gun position, the main gun should be fired even when on the move. The defenders are pinned down and their will to resist is strongly shaken by the velocity of the weapon and the effect of shell fragments.

Relationship and Cooperation between Panzers and Grenadiere

Because of the large front-line sectors and the low combat strength of the **Grenadiere** caused by numerous losses, the Panzers are involved in all types of combat.

Successful cooperation with the **Grenadiere**, which saves the loss of Panzers, is dependent on the **Grenadiere**

ORGANIZATION AND STRENGTH OF PANZER UNITS
REPLACEMENT UNITS SENT TO EASTERN FRONT

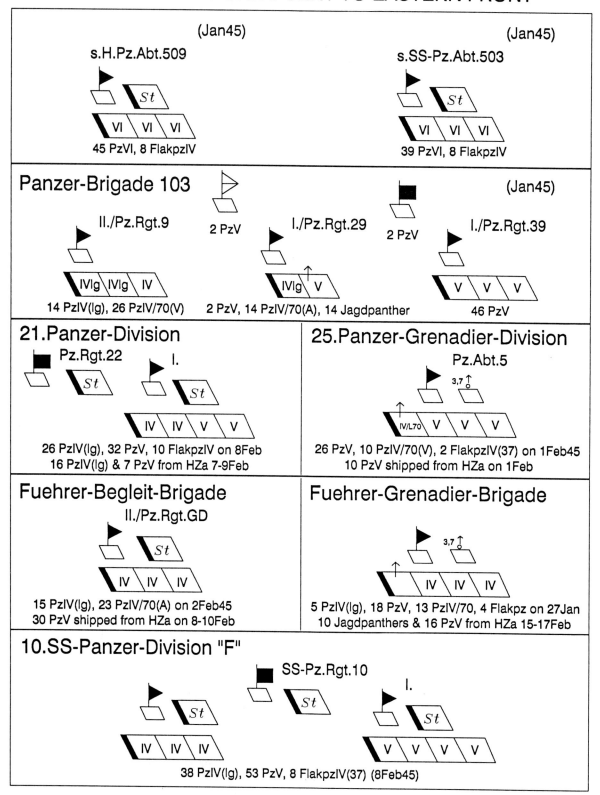

(Jan45)

s.H.Pz.Abt.509

45 PzVI, 8 FlakpzIV

(Jan45)

s.SS-Pz.Abt.503

39 PzVI, 8 FlakpzIV

Panzer-Brigade 103

II./Pz.Rgt.9

2 PzV

I./Pz.Rgt.29

2 PzV

I./Pz.Rgt.39

(Jan45)

14 PzIV(lg), 26 PzIV/70(V)

2 PzV, 14 PzIV/70(A), 14 Jagdpanther

46 PzV

21.Panzer-Division

Pz.Rgt.22

I.

26 PzIV(lg), 32 PzV, 10 FlakpzIV on 8Feb
16 PzIV(lg) & 7 PzV from HZa 7-9Feb

25.Panzer-Grenadier-Division

Pz.Abt.5

26 PzV, 10 PzIV/70(V), 2 FlakpzIV(37) on 1Feb45
10 PzV shipped from HZa on 1Feb

Fuehrer-Begleit-Brigade

II./Pz.Rgt.GD

15 PzIV(lg), 23 PzIV/70(A) on 2Feb45
30 PzV shipped from HZa on 8-10Feb

Fuehrer-Grenadier-Brigade

5 PzIV(lg), 18 PzV, 13 PzIV/70, 4 Flakpz on 27Jan
10 Jagdpanthers & 16 PzV from HZa 15-17Feb

10.SS-Panzer-Division "F"

SS-Pz.Rgt.10

I.

38 PzIV(lg), 53 PzV, 8 FlakpzIV(37) (8Feb45)

ORGANIZATION AND STRENGTH OF PANZER UNITS
REPLACEMENT UNITS SENT TO EASTERN FRONT

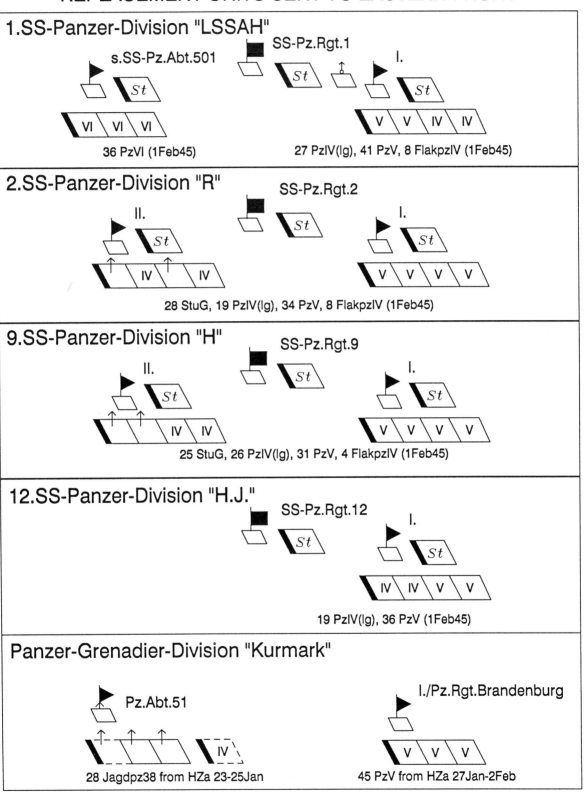

1.SS-Panzer-Division "LSSAH"

s.SS-Pz.Abt.501

SS-Pz.Rgt.1

I.

36 PzVI (1Feb45)

27 PzIV(lg), 41 PzV, 8 FlakpzIV (1Feb45)

2.SS-Panzer-Division "R"

II.

SS-Pz.Rgt.2

I.

28 StuG, 19 PzIV(lg), 34 PzV, 8 FlakpzIV (1Feb45)

9.SS-Panzer-Division "H"

II.

SS-Pz.Rgt.9

I.

25 StuG, 26 PzIV(lg), 31 PzV, 4 FlakpzIV (1Feb45)

12.SS-Panzer-Division "H.J."

SS-Pz.Rgt.12

I.

19 PzIV(lg), 36 PzV (1Feb45)

Panzer-Grenadier-Division "Kurmark"

Pz.Abt.51

I./Pz.Rgt.Brandenburg

28 Jagdpz38 from HZa 23-25Jan

45 PzV from HZa 27Jan-2Feb

ORGANIZATION AND STRENGTH OF PANZER UNITS
REPLACEMENT UNITS FOR THE EASTERN FRONT

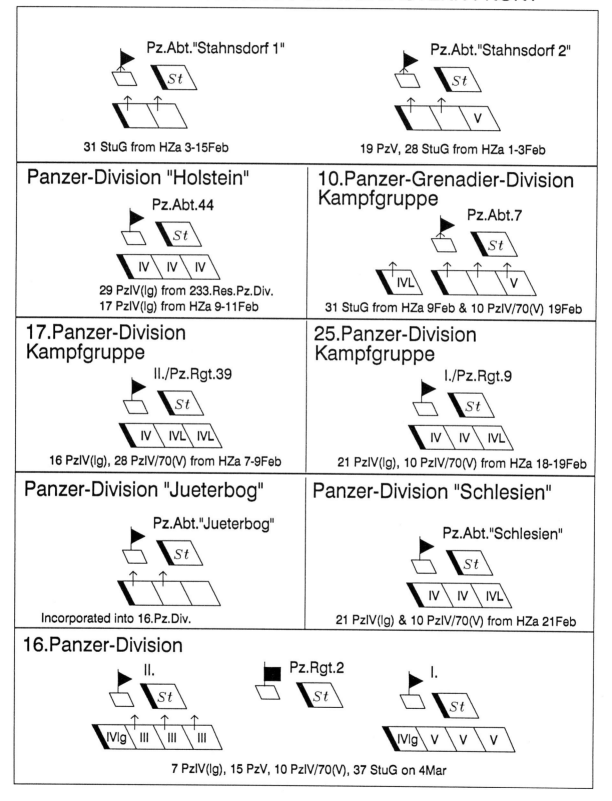

Pz.Abt."Stahnsdorf 1"

31 StuG from HZa 3-15Feb

Pz.Abt."Stahnsdorf 2"

19 PzV, 28 StuG from HZa 1-3Feb

Panzer-Division "Holstein"

Pz.Abt.44

29 PzIV(lg) from 233.Res.Pz.Div.
17 PzIV(lg) from HZa 9-11Feb

10.Panzer-Grenadier-Division Kampfgruppe

Pz.Abt.7

31 StuG from HZa 9Feb & 10 PzIV/70(V) 19Feb

17.Panzer-Division Kampfgruppe

II./Pz.Rgt.39

16 PzIV(lg), 28 PzIV/70(V) from HZa 7-9Feb

25.Panzer-Division Kampfgruppe

I./Pz.Rgt.9

21 PzIV(lg), 10 PzIV/70(V) from HZa 18-19Feb

Panzer-Division "Jueterbog"

Pz.Abt."Jueterbog"

Incorporated into 16.Pz.Div.

Panzer-Division "Schlesien"

Pz.Abt."Schlesien"

21 PzIV(lg) & 10 PzIV/70(V) from HZa 21Feb

16.Panzer-Division

II.

Pz.Rgt.2

I.

7 PzIV(lg), 15 PzV, 10 PzIV/70(V), 37 StuG on 4Mar

ORGANIZATION AND STRENGTH OF PANZER UNITS
REPLACEMENT UNITS FOR THE EASTERN FRONT

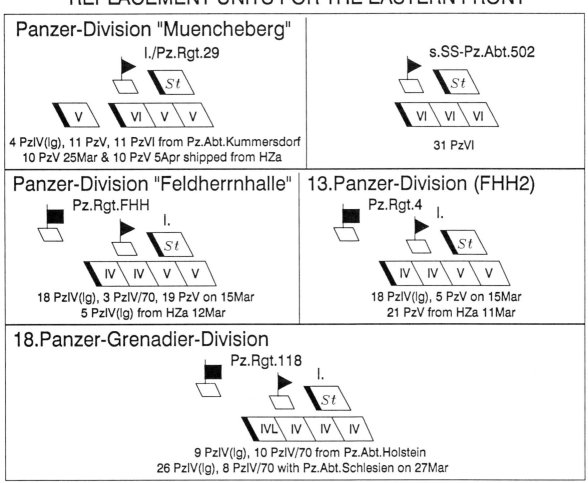

Panzer-Division "Muencheberg"
I./Pz.Rgt.29

4 PzIV(lg), 11 PzV, 11 PzVI from Pz.Abt.Kummersdorf
10 PzV 25Mar & 10 PzV 5Apr shipped from HZa

s.SS-Pz.Abt.502

31 PzVI

Panzer-Division "Feldherrnhalle"
Pz.Rgt.FHH

18 PzIV(lg), 3 PzIV/70, 19 PzV on 15Mar
5 PzIV(lg) from HZa 12Mar

13.Panzer-Division (FHH2)
Pz.Rgt.4

18 PzIV(lg), 5 PzV on 15Mar
21 PzV from HZa 11Mar

18.Panzer-Grenadier-Division
Pz.Rgt.118

9 PzIV(lg), 10 PzIV/70 from Pz.Abt.Holstein
26 PzIV(lg), 8 PzIV/70 with Pz.Abt.Schlesien on 27Mar

*commander's understanding of the needs and capabilities of the **Panzerwaffe** (the **Grenadier** commander is usually given command of the **Kampfgruppe**).*

*Unfortunately, however, a low point has been reached in this area which causes Panzer losses and high wear on the equipment. In part, the **Grenadiere** commander sees in the Panzer a cure for all of the difficult combat situations, because he doesn't know and can't recognize the weaknesses and limited capabilities of the Panzers. The **Grenadiere** commander sees in the Panzer a strong, armored, powerful monster with a giant gun without recognizing its disadvantages such as weak side armor, limited sight capability, and lower maneuverability in comparison to the **SPW**. The ease with which the Panzer can be damaged by weapons that are mostly aimed only at it is recognized by a **Grenadier** only from a distance. During combat with tanks and anti-tank guns, as a rule the **Grenadiere** are never by their own Panzers, because this is not their assignment and they don't have anything to search for there. However, hardly has the tank battle ended, when the **Grenadiere** commander comes forward to ask why*

the advance hasn't started again and why the battle lasted so long! And again overhurriedly, the Panzers are sent against the next objective. This creates an unfavorable situation for their next encounter with tanks.

*If the **Grenadiere** would ride along in the Panzer for one attack, they would very soon change their views! Even when the **Grenadiere** acknowledges that without Panzers he is not in a situation to accomplish any large combat assignments, he repeatedly sends the Panzers in based on his opinion, especially when it is a weak **Kampfgruppe** under the command of a young officer who doesn't like to listen to factual objections from the side of the **Panzerwaffe**. As a result, when after four days only five Panzers are still operational out of 20, the blame is directed at the "overrefined technique" or that the Panzer crews "don't want to remain in the front lines"!*

*There are **Grenadiere** that prefer to see the Panzers only advancing forward. Every warranted halt and observation based on Panzer tactics makes them impatient. When Panzers are halted somewhat longer in front of a village that has been reported to be heavily occupied by the enemy, in* order not to run into flanking fire from an enemy **Paknest** or dug-in enemy tanks, these actions are laid out as lack of zeal. An energetic attack is required after exact scouting and preparation as well as implementation in accordance with plans based on carefully considered employment, but not blindly driving into the enemy because time is burning under the fingernails. The view that "Panzers must again learn to drive forward" is sometimes voiced on the spot, where driving forward would mean massive destruction. If a **Panzermann** encountering mines remains stationary and scouts, pulls back in order to start to attack at another location, or with enemy tanks reported halts and observes, or in response to sudden flanking anti-tank or tank fire turns off to the right and takes up a firing position and doesn't continue to advance in the desired direction, this is not lack of zeal; instead it is correct tactical handling.

On 24 January, with and in front of the **Grenadiere**, 20 Panzers were ordered to attack the village of Baraczka that

was occupied by tanks and anti-tank guns. The **Grenadier** commander demanded an immediate start without issuing orders. "Anything further would come from the attack." That every Panzer attack must be talked through in advance, and once an attack starts it is difficult to redirect, were unimportant to this commander.

On 25 January at night, the **Abteilung** stood ready in Pottend. Because the relief of the Panzers by other units was delayed, they arrived at the assembly area later than planned. An exact orientation on the direction of attack and setting up the Panzers was rendered more difficult by the continuous pressure from the **Grenadier** commander. After the attack advanced 2 kilometers, a short halt to reorganize was interrupted by the **Kampfgruppen** commander. As a result the Panzers arrived at the first objective scattered and no longer under the control of the Panzer commander. Accomplishing the orders was made difficult because of poor visibility. Buildup of a new **Schwerpunkt** was delayed.

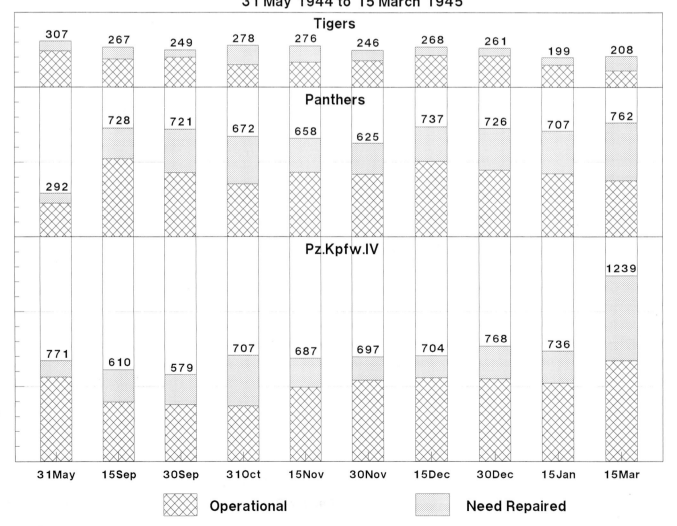

A column of **Pz.Kpfw.IV Ausf.J**s with wire mesh **Schuerzen** pass a trench that was part of the defensive system at Gran, Hungary In February 1945. (BA)

*On 10 February, our Panzers struck into the rear of the enemy south of Lepczeny. The Panzers turned away in the face of strong enemy resistance, and a new direction of attack was ordered. An immediate start in the new direction was demanded; issuing new orders and orientation were viewed as a waste of time. While the Panzers remained stationary to observe - our Panzers were being fired at from the flank by enemy tanks - the **Kampfgruppe** commander broke into the radio net and commanded "Panzers march", "Panzers advance" and thereby made it more difficult to direct the engagement of the armored group by radio.*

*On 26 January, our Panzers stood guard in a village on a sector of riverbank. We had to calculate that enemy tanks would appear at dawn on the opposite commanding height. Five Panzers were on guard with an open left flank that couldn't be sufficiently occupied because of the low **Grenadier** strength. Pulling back the Panzers and shortening the position were proposed but rejected by the **Grenadier** commander. During the day, as the Panzer moved in their positions to resupply, as expected, four Panzers were knocked out and were lost as total write-offs.*

On 3 February, a Panzer attack had to be conducted in the fog north of Stuhlweissenburg. Running into an enemy anti-tank gun position and tanks prepared for defense, and a loss of one Panzer as a total write-off, were the "achievements" of the day.

*On 14 February, our own Panzers were engaged in street fighting in the village of Croesz. Our own **Grenadiere** didn't close up with the Panzers, even though the toughly fighting Russian nests of resistance were pinned down by the effect of fire from the Panzers, so the Panzers had to be pulled back to the **Grenadiere** positions. In addition, two Panzers were lost as total write-offs due to their running onto mines.*

Many exorbitantly demanded tasks were consciously not carried out by the Panzer commanders, thereby preventing higher losses.

After the failure of the Winter offensives in the West, the main effort of the **Heeres** was again diverted to the East. Many of the mobile formations were pulled out of the Western Front and sent East to stabilize the Eastern Front and launch limited offensives. In late January/early February 1945 the **21.Panzer-Division, 25.Panzer-Grenadier-Division, Fuehrer-Begleit-Brigade, Fuehrer-Grenadier-Brigade, 1.SS-Panzer-Division, 2.SS-Panzer-Division, 9.SS-Panzer-Division, 10.SS-Panzer-Division,** and **12.SS-Panzer-Division** were transferred from the West to the Eastern Front. Additionally, in February and March 1945 several ad-hoc units were quickly assembled and shipped east, including the **Panzer-Grenadier-Division "Kurmark", Panzer-Division "Holstein", Panzer-Abteilung "Stahnsdorf 1", Panzer-Abteilung "Stahnsdorf 2", Panzer-Division "Jueterbog", Panzer-Division "Schlesien",** and **Panzer-Division "Muencheberg."**

31

Formation of
the Last Units

As one setback followed another, the **Heeres** was reduced to reacting to the next crisis. Old, played-out units were refitted at reduced strength and new formations were created from the remnants of totally decimated divisions or by activating training and reserve units without any combat experience. The newly created formations were **Panzer-Divisions** or **Panzer-Grenadier-Divisions** in name only. They were issued a mixture of whatever types of Panzers were available from the rapidly declining production base. These **Kampfgruppen** with the strength of weak brigades were sent into action as soon as they received their Panzers. At the end, the training units of the **Ersatzheer** were activated and sent into combat as a final futile gesture.

Panzer-Korps "Grossdeutschland" - On 14 December 1944, **Panzer-Korps "Grossdeutschland"** was ordered to be formed with **Panzer-Grenadier-Division "Grossdeutschland"** and **Panzer-Grenadier-Division "Brandenburg"** under its command. **Panzer-Regiment "Grossdeutschland"** was to be reorganized with the **I.Abteilung** consisting of three **Panther-Kompanien** each with 17 Panthers and a **II.Abteilung** of four **Panzer-Kompanien** each with 14 **Pz.Kpfw.IVs**. The **III.(Tiger) Abteilung/Panzer-Regiment "Grossdeutschland"** was renamed the **schwere Panzer-Abteilung "Grossdeutschland"** and placed directly under the **Korps** command. On 8 January 1945, **Panzer-Grenadier-Division "Grossdeutschland"** was ordered to reorganize as a **Panzer-Division** in accordance with the **"Gliederung Panzer-Division 44"** but without a **Pz.Kpfw.IV-Abteilung**. The **II.Abteilung/Panzer-Regiment "Grossdeutschland"** had already been detached and assigned to the **Fuehrer-Begleit-Brigade**.

As ordered on 14 December 1944, **Panzer-Regiment "Brandenburg"** was to be created with the **I.Abteilung** consisting of three **Panther-Kompanien** each with 17 Panthers and a **II.Abteilung** of four **Panzer-Kompanien** each with 14 **Pz.Kpfw.IVs**. On 17 January 1945, orders were cut to create

a **II.Abteilung/Panzer-Regiment "Brandenburg"** by 28 February with four **Pz.Kpfw.IV-Kompanien** in accordance with the K.St.N. listed for the **"Gliederung Panzer-Division 44."** Incorporation of the **Sturmgeschuetz-Brigade "Grossdeutschland"** as the **II.Abteilung/Panzer-Regiment "Brandenburg"** as ordered on 13 December 1944 had not worked out. **Sturmgeschuetz-Brigade "Grossdeutschland"** was to remain tactically subordinate to **Panzer-Grenadier-Division "Brandenburg"** until **Panzer-Regiment "Brandenburg"** was complete. On 18 January 1945, **Heeresgruppe Sued** was ordered to send the **I.Abteilung/Panzer-Regiment 26** to Breslau to be refurbished with three **Panther-Kompanien** (14 Panthers each) and three **Befehls-Panthers** by 27 January 1945 and renamed the **I.Abteilung/Panzer-Regiment "Brandenburg"** as the **Panther-Abteilung** for **Panzer-Grenadier-Division "Brandenburg."** Forty-five Panthers were shipped to the unit from the **Heeres-Zeugamt** in the period between 27 January and 2 February 1945. On 1 February 1945, orders were cut to create the **II.Abteilung/Panzer-Regiment "Brandenburg"** with four **Panzer-Kompanien** (14 **Pz.Kpfw.IV** each under K.St.N.1177(f.G.) dated 1Nov44) and four **Pz.Kpfw.IV** for the **Abteilung-Stab** for a total of 60 **Pz.Kpfw.IV** utilizing **Panzer-Abteilung z.b.V.12** and **Panzer-Kompanie "Gutschmidt."** On 2 February 1945, the **I.Abteilung/Panzer-Regiment "Brandenburg"** was ordered to join **Panzer-Grenadier-Division "Kurmark"** at Frankfurt am Oder.

10.SS-Panzer-Division "Frundsberg" - Orders were issued on 3 January 1945 for **Ob.West** to fill **SS-Panzer-Regiment 10** of the **10.SS-Panzer-Division "Frundsberg"** to complete their reorganization to a **Regiment Stab und Stabs-Kompanie** and a **Panther-Abteilung** with 60 Panthers and a **Panzer-Abteilung** with 45 **Pz.Kpfw.IV** by 8 January 1945. Panzers were shipped from the **Heeres-Zeugamt** to outfit the units as follows: 25 Panthers on 6-10 January and eight Pz.Kpfw.IV on 15 January.

Fuehrer-Begleit-Division- Orders were cut on 18 January 1945 to expand the **Fuehrer-Begleit-Brigade** into the **Fuehrer-Begleit-Division**. On 25 January a directive ordered that the **Stab Panzer-Regiment 102** be raised, with the **II.Abteilung/Panzer-Regiment "Grossdeutschland"** assigned as the **II.Abteilung/Panzer-Regiment 102**. Thirty Panthers were shipped from the **Heeres-Zeugamt** on 8-10 February. On 16 February 1945, orders were issued to form **Panzer-Regiment 102** with a **I.Abteilung** consisting of two **Panther-Kompanien** and two **Pz.Kpfw.IV-Kompanien** with 14 Panzers in each **Kompanie**. **Panzer-Jaeger-Abteilung 673** was assigned to the **Panzer-Regiment** in place of a second **Panzer-Abteilung**. On 2 March 1945, the **II.Abteilung/ Panzer-Regiment "Grossdeutschland"** was renamed **II.Abteilung/Fuehrer-Panzer-Regiment 1**.

Fuehrer-Grenadier-Division - Orders were cut on 18 January 1945 to expand the **Fuehrer-Grenadier-Brigade** into the **Fuehrer-Grenadier-Division**. On 25 January a directive ordered the creation of **Panzer-Regiment 101** with a **I.Abteilung/Panzer-Regiment 101**. On 16 February 1945, orders were issued to form **Panzer-Regiment 101** with a **I.Abteilung** consisting of two **Panther-Kompanien** and two **Pz.Kpfw.IV-Kompanien** with 14 Panzers in each Kompanie. Ten **Jagdpanthers** were shipped from the **Heeres-Zeugamt** on 15 February and 16 Panthers on 17 February. On 2 March 1945, the **Panzer-Regiment Stab Fuehrer-Grenadier-Brigade** was renamed **Stab Fuehrer-Panzer-Regiment 2**.

Stab Panzer-Brigade 103 - On 24 January 1945, the **Stab Panzer-Brigade 103** was assigned command over a **Panzer-Kampfgruppe** consisting of a **Panzer-Regiment Stab** with the **II./Panzer-Regiment 9**, **I.(Panther) Abteilung/Panzer-Regiment 29**, and **I.(Panther) Abteilung/Panzer-Regiment 39**. On 20 January 1945, orders were cut for the **II./Panzer-Regiment 9** requiring its employment outside of its parent division. It was to be organized with two **Panzer-Kompanien** each with 13 **Pz.IV/70** (K.St.N.1177(f.G.) dated 1Apr45) along with three **Pz.Bef.Wg.IV**. Fourteen **Pz.Kpfw.IV** were shipped from the **Heeres-Zeugamt** on 19 January and 26 **Pz.IV/70(V)** on 22 January 1945. Orders were cut on 21 January 1945 to prepare the **I.Abteilung/Panzer-Regiment 29** for combat with one **Kompanie** of 14 **Jagdpanther** (K.St.N.1149a(f.G.) dated 1Apr44) and one **Kompanie** of 14 **Pz.IV/70(A)** (K.St.N.1177(f.G.) dated 1Apr44). Fourteen **Jagdpanthers** were shipped from the **Heeres-Zeugamt** on 22 January, 14 **Pz.IV/70(A)** on 24 January, and 2 Panthers on 25 January 1945. On 15 January, the **I.Abteilung/Panzer-Regiment 39** was ordered to accelerate preparations for combat readiness, to be completed by 22 January 1945. It was to be organized with three Panthers for the **Abteilung-Stab** and 14 Panthers in each of three **Panzer-Kompanien** (K.St.N.1177 dated 1Apr44) for a total of 45 Panthers. Forty-six Panthers were shipped from the **Heeres-Zeugamt** to outfit the unit in the period between 16 and 22 January 1945.

Panzer-Brigade 103 was sent to **Heeresgruppe Mitte** in mid-January 1945. By 3 February 1945, **Panzer-Brigade 103** had managed to knock out 45 enemy tanks and had destroyed or captured 65 anti-tank guns. They had lost 35 Panthers as total write-offs, with an additional 15 Panzers surrounded in Steinau. **Panzer-Brigade 103** was ordered to be disbanded on 5 March 1945. On 9 March orders were issued for:

• **Panzer-Brigade Stab 103** to be used to create **Panzer-Division Stab "Muncheberg"**
• **I.Abteilung/Panzer-Regiment 29** to be sent to Muncheberg without Panzers. Four **Pz.Kpfw.IV** were to be given to the **17.Panzer-Division**, 12 **Pz.IV/70** to the **20.Panzer-Division**, and six **Jagdpanthers** to the **8.Panzer-Division**.

232.Panzer-Division - **Panzer-Feld-Ausbildungs Division "Tatra"** was created on 29 January 1945 in the rear area of **Heeresgruppe Sued**. It didn't have a **Panzer-Abteilung**. It was only promised a **Panzer-Jaeger-Ausbildungs-Abteilung** with two **Pak Sfl.-Kompanien**. On 21 February 1945, **Panzer-Feldausbildungs-Division "Tatra"**, still in the rear area, was renamed **232.Panzer-Division**. On 1 March 1945, it was reported that the **232.Panzer-Division "Tatra"** shouldn't be transferred to an area south of the Danube River because it was currently located in a very good training ground.

Panzer-Grenadier-Division "Kurmark" - Orders were issued on 30 January 1945 to create **Panzer-Grenadier-Division "Kurmark"** in accordance with the K.St.N. for the "Gliederung Panzer-Grenadier-Division 44" with a single **Panzer-Abteilung**. The **Panzer-Abteilung** was to consist of three **Jagdpz.38 Kompanien** and one **Pz.IV/70-Kompanie**. On 5 February 1945, the **Panzer-Abteilung** for **Panzer-Grenadier-Division "Kurmark"** was designated **Panzer-Abteilung 51**. Twenty-eight **Jagdpanzer 38** were shipped from the **Heeres-Zeugamt** during the period of 23 to 25 January 1945. On 2 February 1945, the **I.Abteilung/Panzer-Regiment "Brandenburg"** was ordered to join **Panzer-Grenadier-Division "Kurmark"** at Frankfurt am Oder. Forty-five Panthers were shipped to the **I.Abteilung/Panzer-Regiment "Brandenburg"** from the **Heeres-Zeugamt** during the period from 27 January to 2 February 1945.

Panzer-Division "Holstein" - Orders were issued on 1 February 1945 to immediately create **Panzer-Division "Holstein"** with a **Panzer-Abteilung** utilizing the **233.Reserve-Panzer-Division**. **Panzer-Abteilung 44** was created on 2 February 1944 with three **Pz.Kpfw.IV-Kompanien** and one **Panzer-Jaeger-Kompanie (Sf.)** and obtained 29 **Pz.Kpfw.IV** from the **233.Reserve-Panzer-Division.Panzer-Division "Holstein"** joined **Heeresgruppe Weichsel** on 12 February 1945. They took along 29 **Pz.Kpfw.IV** from Denmark. An additional

14 **Pz.Kpfw.IV** were transported from Stettin on 9 February and three **Pz.Bef.Wg.IV** from Linz on 11 February 1945. On 30 March 1945, orders were cut to re-create the **18.Panzer-Grenadier-Division** by consolidating **Panzer-Division "Holstein"** and **Panzer-Division "Schlesien."**

21.Panzer-Division - On 1 February 1945, the **21.Panzer-Division** was ordered to be transferred and started movement by rail out of the West to **Heeres-Gruppe Weichsel** in the area of Eberswalde. On 2 February 1945, it was requested that the **21.Panzer-Division** be filled to the organization authorized by **"Gliederung Panzer-Division 44."** On 5 February 1945, **Panzer-Regiment 22** was ordered to reorganize as a **Panzer-Regiment Stab mit Stabs-Kompanie und Fla-Zug** and a **gemischte Panzer-Abteilung** with **Stabs-Kompanie**, two **Pz.Kpfw.IV-Kompanien** (17 **Pz.Kpfw.IV** each), and two **Panther-Kompanien** (17 Panthers each). Sixteen **Pz.Kpfw.IVs** were shipped from the **Heeres-Zeugamt** on 7 February and seven Panthers on 9 February 1945.

25.Panzer-Grenadier-Division - On 1 February 1945, orders were cut to refurbish the **25.Panzer-Grenadier-Division** in the Kustrin area in accordance with the K.St.N. for the **"Panzer-Grenadier-Division 44 (freie Gliederung)"** with **Panzer-Abteilung 5**. Ten Panthers were shipped from the **Heeres-Zeugamt** on 1 February.

10.Panzer-Grenadier-Division (Kampfgruppe) - On 6 February 1945, **Heeresgruppe Mitte** was ordered to refurbish **10.Panzer-Grenadier-Division (Kampfgruppe)** with a **Panzer-Abteilung** to be outfitted with 21 **Sturmgeschuetz III** and 10 **Sturmgeschuetz IV**. A **4.Kompanie** for **Panzer-Abteilung 7** was formed from personnel from **Panzer-Jaeger-Kompanie 2110**. Panzers were shipped from the **Heeres-Zeugamt** to outfit the units as follows: 12 **StuGIV** and 19 **StuGIII** on 9 February, and 10 **PzIV/70(V)** on 19 February 1945.

17.Panzer-Division (Kampfgruppe) - On 6 February 1945, **Heeresgruppe Mitte** was ordered to refurbish the **17.Panzer-Division (Kampfgruppe)** with the **I.Abteilung/Panzer-Regiment 39** with one **Kompanie** outfitted with 17 **Pz.Kpfw.IV**, one **Kompanie** with 17 **Pz.IV/70**, and three **Panzerbefehlswagen** for the **Abteilung Stab**. Twenty-eight **Pz.IV/70(V)** were shipped from the **Heeres-Zeugamt** on 7 February and 16 **Pz.Kpfw.IV** on 9 February.

25.Panzer-Division - On 11 February 1945, **Heeresgruppe Mitte** was ordered to expeditiously refurbish the **25.Panzer-Division** as a **Kampfgruppe** with the **I.Abteilung/Panzer-Regiment 9** consisting of two **Pz.Kpfw.IV-Kompanien** (14 **Pz.Kpfw.IV** each), one **Panzer-Kompanie** with 14 **Pz.IV/70** and two **Pz.Bef.Wg.IV** for the **Abteilung Stab**. Twenty-one **Pz.Kpfw.IV** were shipped from the **Heeres-Zeugamt** on 18 February, 10 **PzIV/70(V)** on 19 February, 10 **Pz.Kpfw.IV** on 3 March, and 10 Panthers on 3 March 1945.

233.Panzer-Division - On 21 February 1944, the **233.Reserve-Panzer-Division** in Denmark was renamed **233.Panzer-Division**. At the same time, **Reserve-Panzer-Abteilung 5** was renamed **Panzer-Abteilung 55**. On 20 April, the **233.Panzer-Division** in Denmark reported the strength of **Panzer-Abteilung 55** as two **Pz.Kpfw.III kz**, 18 **Pz.Kpfw.III(75)**, three **Pz.Kpfw.IV kz**, two **Pz.Kpfw.IV (L/43)**, and four **Fla.Pz.3,7cm**.

Panzer-Division "Jueterbog" - On 21 February 1945, orders were issued to create **Panzer-Division "Jueterbog"** with one **Panzer-Abteilung** utilizing the **Division-Stab** from the **16.Panzer-Division**. Orders had already been cut on 20 February to create **Panzer-Abteilung "Jueterbog"** with one **Panzer-Kompanie** (with 10 Panzers using K.St.N.1177(f.G.) dated 1Nov44) and two **Panzer-Sturmgeschuetz-Kompanien** (each with 10 **Sturmgeschuetze** using K.St.N.1159(f.G.) dated 1Nov44) from **Panzer-Jaeger-Abteilung "Glienicke."** On 26 February, **Panzer-Division "Jueterbog"** was ordered to join **Heeresgruppe Mitte** in Bautzen. On the same day, orders were cut to incorporate **Panzer-Division "Jueterbog"** into the **16.Panzer-Division**.

Panzer-Division "Schlesien" - On 21 February 1945, orders were cut to create **Panzer-Divsion "Doeberitz"** with one **Panzer-Abteilung** using **Stab Panzer-Brigade 10** for the **Division Stab**. **Panzer-Abteilung "Doeberitz"** was to be created with three **Panzer-Kompanien** (each with 10 **Pz.Kpfw.IV** using K.St.N.1177(f.G.) dated 1.11.44) from **Panzer-Abteilung 303** by 24 February 1944. On 22 February 1945, **Panzer-Division "Doeberitz"** was renamed **Panzer-Division "Schlesien"** and **Panzer-Abteilung "Doeberitz"** renamed **Panzer-Abteilung "Schlesien."** Twenty-one **Pz.Kpfw.IV** were shipped from the **Heeres-Zeugamt** on 21 February, 10 **Pz.IV/70(V)** on 21 February, and 10 **Pz.Kpfw.IV** on 2 March 1945. On 26 February 1945, **Panzer-Division "Schlesien"** was ordered to be transferred to **Heeresgruppe Weichsel** near Frankfurt am Oder after 28 February 1945. A **4.Kompanie/Panzer-Abteilung "Schlesien"** was sent to join the unit by rail on 9 March 1945. On 30 March 1945, orders were cut to re-create the **18.Panzer-Grenadier-Division** by consolidating **Panzer-Division "Holstein"** and **Panzer-Division "Schlesien."**

16.Panzer-Division - On 26 February 1945, **Panzer-Division "Jueterbog"** was ordered to be incorporated into the **16.Panzer-Division**. The **16.Panzer-Division** was to reorganize with a **Panzer-Regiment** with two **Panzer-Abteilung**. Eight Panthers were shipped from the **Heeres-Zeugamt** on 18 February, 10 **Pz.IV/70(V)** on 23 February, 7 **Panthers** on 3 March, and 31 **StuGIII** on 4 March.

Panzer-Division "Muencheberg"- Orders were issued on 5 March 1945 to create **Panzer-Division "Muencheberg"** with **Panzer-Abteilung "Kummersdorf."** On 12 March 1945, **Panzer-Abteilung Kummersdorf** was ordered to hand over all their Panzers to the **I.Abteilung/Panzer-Regiment 29**, which had been assigned to **Panzer-Division "Muencheberg"** in their place. The **3.(Tiger)Kompanie/Panzer-Abteilung Kummersdorf** was renamed and incorporated into the **I.Abteilung/Panzer-Regiment 29** as the **3.Kompanie**. On 16 March 1945, it was requested that a **Panther-Kompanie** (K.St.N.1177(f.G.) dated 1Nov44) be formed by 20 March 1945 for **Panzer-Division "Muencheberg"** from a **Kompanie** of the **I.Abteilung/Panzer-Regiment 29** in Grafenwoehr. The **I.Abteilung** was to consist of four **Panzer-Kompanien** with the **1.** and **2.Kompanien** organized under K.St.N.1177, the **3.Kompanie** under K.St.N.1176 and the **4.Kompanie** under K.St.N.1177. In addition to those Panzers turned over by **Panzer-Abteilung "Kummersdorf"**, 10 Panthers were shipped from the **Heeres-Zeugamt** on 29 March and 10 Panthers on 5 April 1945. On 7 April 1945, orders were cut to transport one **Panther-Kompanie/I.Abteilung/Panzer-Regiment 29** and one **Kompanie/Panzer-Grenadier-Regiment 25**, both with infrared equipment, by rail from Wunsdorf to **Heeresgruppe Weichel** for incorporation into the **I.Abteilung/Panzer-Regiment 29** under **Panzer-Division "Muencheberg."**

Panzerkampfgruppe Nord - On 5 March 1945, a **Panzerkampfgruppe Nord** was formed with a **Panzer-Abteilung** of four **Panzer-Kompanien** from Bergen and **Schiesschule Putlos**. The **Stabskompanie Panzerkampfgruppe Nord** had a **Fla-Zug** with three **2 cm Flakvierling auf Pz.Kpfw.III Fahrgestell** and four **3,7 cm Flak auf Pz.Kpfw.III Fahrgestell** from Bergen. The **Abteilungs-Stab** was outfitted with two Panthers, the **gemischte Panzer-Kompanie** from Bergen with 10 Panthers and 6 Tigers, the **leichte Panzer-Kompanie** from Bergen with 22 **Pz.Kpfw.IV**, the **gemischte Panzer-Kompanie** from Putlos with 12 Panthers and two Tiger I, and the **leichte Panzer-Kompanie** from Putlos with seven **Pz.Kpfw.IV**. The two **Panzer-Kompanien** from Putlos were formed into **Panzer-Abteilung "Putlos"** and fought under **Panzer-Division "Clausewitz."**

Panzer-Division Feldherrnhalle - On 10 March 1945, **Heeresgruppe Sued** was ordered to create **Panzer-Korps Feldherrnhalle** and recreate/refurbish **Panzer-Division Feldherrnhalle** and the **13.Panzer-Division**. The **I.Abteilung/Panzer-Regiment Feldherrnhalle** for **Panzer-Division Feldherrnhalle** was created from **Panzer-Abteilung 208**. **Panzer-Regiment 4** was recreated for the **13.Panzer-Division**, which was renamed **Panzer-Division Feldherrnhalle 2**. Nineteen Panthers and 5 **Pz.Kpfw.IV** were shipped from the **Heeres-Zeugamt** to **Feldherrnhalle** in the period from 9 to 12 March. Twenty-one Panthers were shipped from the **Heeres-Zeugamt** to the **13.Panzer-Division** on 11 March and 20 **Pz.Kpfw.IV** on 12 March 1945.

Grundgliederung der Panzer-Division 45

On 25 March 1945, the following order for the "**Grundgliederung der Panzer-Division 45**" (basic organization for **Panzer-Divisions** in 1945) was issued from the office of the **Generalinspekteur der Panzertruppen** and **OKH/GenStdH/Org.Abt.** signed by Generaloberst Guderian as **Chef der GenStdH:**

*1. The **Grundgliederung der Panzer-Division 45** is to go into effect immediately for all **Panzer-Divisions** and **Panzer-Grenadier-Divisions** of the **Feldheeres** (in accordance with Attachment 1). The preliminary list of authorized personnel and equipment strengths for each unit is included as Attachment 2.*

*2. The **Panzer-Divisions** and **Panzer-Grenadier-Divisions** are to be reorganized to the **Gliederung der Panzer-Division 45** by utilizing their available personnel and equipment. Divisions for which personnel and equipment strengths are too low to reach the **Gliederung der Panzer-Division 45** are in the interim to reorganize as **Kampfgruppen** (in accordance with Attachment 3). The preliminary compilation of the authorized personnel and equipment strengths for each unit is included as Attachment 4.*

*Special orders will be issued for any excess units. The previous special organization remains in effect for the **232.Panzer-Division (Feld-Ausbildungs-Division)**.*

*3. The lists of applicable K.St.N.s, copies of new K.St.N., and final compilation of the authorized personnel and equipment strengths will be provided by the **Gen.Insp.d.Pz.Tr.***

*4. **Ob.West** and the **Heeresgruppen** are to report the reorganization of their assigned **Panzer-Divisions** and **Panzer-Grenadier-Divisions** to **OKH/GenStdH/Org.Abt.** on 1 May 1945.*

New K.St.N. Dated 1Apr45

As ordered on 25 March 1945 by Generaloberst Guderian, the following new set of K.St.N. dated 1 April 1945 were to be used to reorganize all of the existing **Panzer-Regiments** and **Panzer-Abteilungen** with the **Panzer-Divisions** and **Panzer-Grenadier-Divisions** in the **Feldheer:**

K.St.N.	Date	Unit Name
1103a	1Apr45	**Stab und Stabskompanie eines gemischten Panzer-Regiments**
1107(fG)	1Apr45	**Stab und Stabs-Kompanie Panzer-Abteilung "Panther"/IV (f.G.)**
1177a(fG)	1Apr45	**Panzerkompanie "Panther" oder "IV" (mit 10 Panzer) (f.G.)**
1192(fG)	1Apr45	**gemischte Panzer-Fliegerabwehr-Kompanie (3,7 cm Flak-Panzer IV und 2 cm Flak-4ling (Sf.) (f.G.)**

(text continues on page 241)

Panzer-Division 45

Anl. 1 zu OKH/Gen.St.d.H./Org. Abt.
Nr. I/1600/45 g.Kdos. v. 25.3.45.

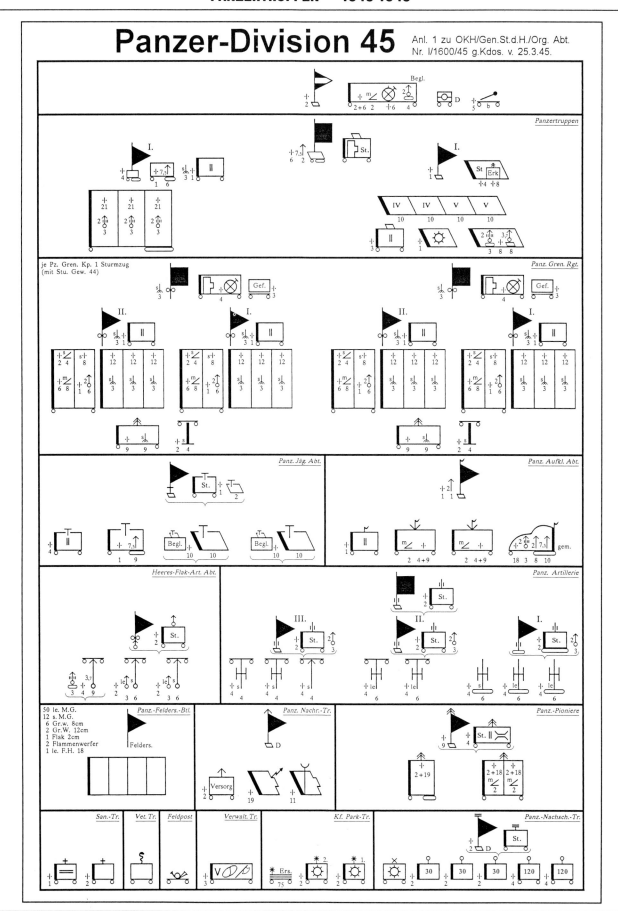

Kampfgruppe **Panzer-Div. 45**

Anl. 2 zu OKH/Gen.St.d.H./Org. Abt.
Nr. I/1600/45 g.Kdos. v. 25.3.45.

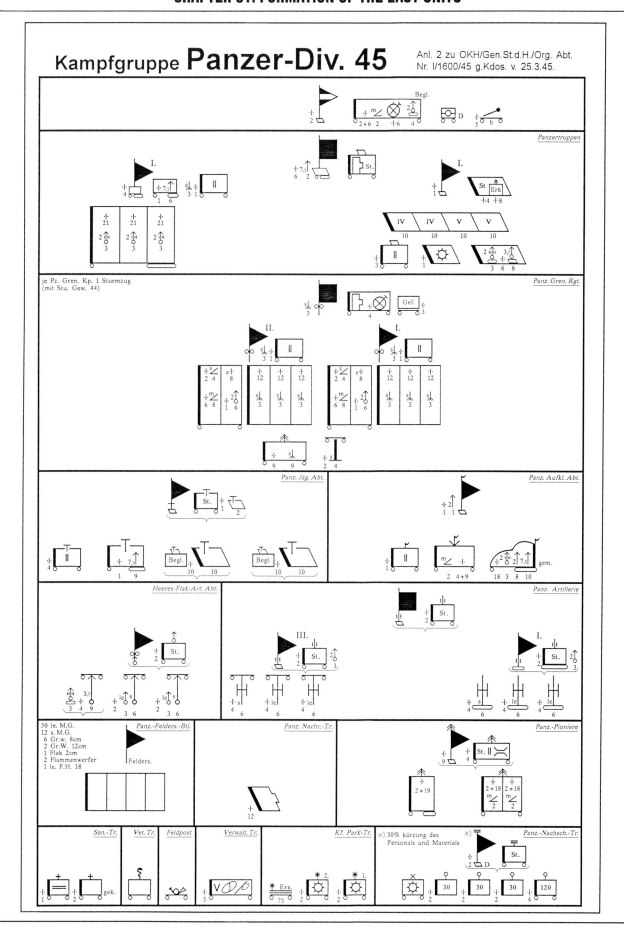

Stab und Stabskompanie

eines gemischten Panzer-Regiments

K.St.N.1103a v. 1.4.1945

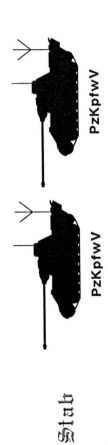

Stab

PzKpfwV   PzKpfwV

Stab und Stabskompanie

einer Panzerabteilung "Panther"/IV (f.G.)

K.St.N.1107(fG) u. 1.4.1945

Nachr.Zug

PzKpfwV   PzKpfwV

2 Panzerkampfwagen IV (7,5 cm KwK 40 (L/48) (Sd.Kfz.161/2) or
2 Panzerkampfwagen "Panther" (7,5 cm KwK 42 (L/70)) (Sd.Kfz.171)
as Panzerbefehlswagen

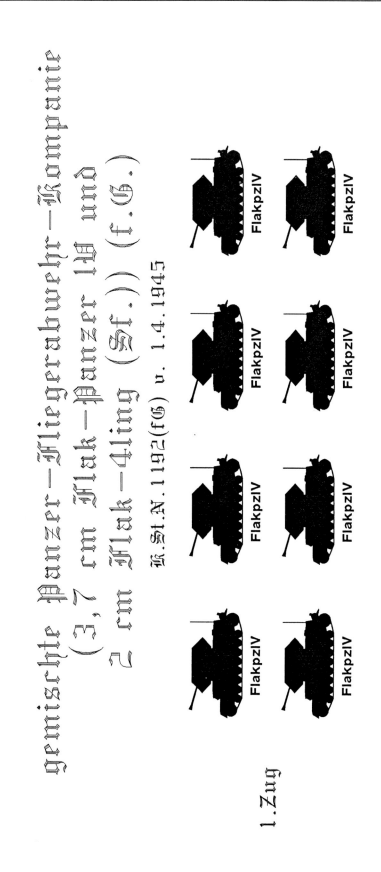

gemischte Panzer—Fliegerabwehr—Kompanie
(3,7 cm Flak—Panzer IV und
2 cm Flak—4ling (Sf.) (f.G.)

K.St.N.1192(fG) v. 1.4.1945

1.Zug

FlakpzIV FlakpzIV FlakpzIV FlakpzIV

FlakpzIV FlakpzIV FlakpzIV FlakpzIV

Panzerkompanie "Panther" oder "IV"
(10 Pz.Kpfw.) (freie Gliederung)
K.St.N. 1177a(fG) v. 1.4.1945

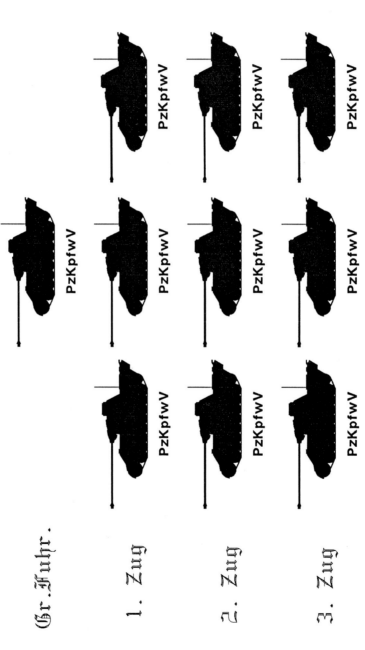

Gr.Fhr.

1. Zug

2. Zug

3. Zug

PzKpfwV

10 Panzerkampfwagen "Panther" (7,5 cm KwK 42 (L/70)) (Sd.Kfz. 171) or
10 Panzerkampfwagen IV (7,5 cm KwK 40 (L/48)) (Sd.Kfz. 161/2) or
10 Panzerwagen 604/9 (7,5 cm Pak 42 (L/70)) (also known as Pz.IV/70(A))

The **Stab und Stabskompanie eines gemischten Panzer-Regiments** organized in accordance with K.St.N.1103a dated 1 April 1943 contained a **Stab** with two **Panzerkampfwagen "Panther"** (7,5 cm 42 (L/70)) (Sd.Kfz.171) as **Panzerbefehlswagen**. The **Stab und Stabskompanie einer Panzerabteilung "Panther"/IV (f.G.)** organized in accordance with K.St.N.1107a(fG) dated 1 April 1945 contained a **Nachrichtenzug** with two **Panzerkampfwagen IV** (7,5 cm 40 (L/48)) (Sd.Kfz.161/2) as **Panzerbefehlswagen** or two **Panzerkampfwagen "Panther"** (7,5 cm 42 (L/70)) (Sd.Kfz.171) as **Panzerbefehlswagen**. The **Panzerkompanie "Panther" oder "IV" (mit 10 Panzer) (f.G.)** organized in accordance with K.St.N.1177a(fG) dated 1 April 1945 consisted of a **Kompanie Trupp** with one **Panzerkampfwagen "Panther"** (7,5 cm 42)(L/70) (Sd.Kfz.171) or one **Panzerkampfwagen IV** (7,5 cm 40 L/43) (Sd.Kfz.161/1) or one **Panzerwagen 604/9** (7,5 cm 42)(L/70) and three **Zuege** each with three **Panzerkampfwagen "Panther"** (7,5 cm 42)(L/70) (Sd.Kfz.171) or three **Panzerkampfwagen IV** (7,5 cm 40 L/43) (Sd.Kfz.161/1) or three **Panzerwagen 604/9** (7,5 cm 42)(L/70). The **gemischte Panzer-Fliegerabwehr-Kompanie (3,7 cm Flak-Panzer IV und 2 cm Flak-4ling (Sf.) (f.G.)** organized in accordance with K.St.N.1192(fG) dated 1 April 1945 was authorized eight **Flakpanzer IV** (3,7 cm Flak 43/1) in the **1.Zug**. The **gemischten Panzer-Regiment** with its **Stab und Stabs-Kompanie** and a single **Panzer-Abteilung** with four **Panzer-Kompanie** and a **gemischte Panzer-Fla-Kompanie** organized in accordance with K.St.N. dated 1 April 1945 was authorized to have 22 to 24 **Panzerkampfwagen "Panther"**, 20 to 22 **Panzerkampfwagen IV** and eight **Flakpanzer IV**.

18.Panzer-Grenadier-Division - Orders were cut on 30 March 1945 to recreate the **18.Panzer-Grenadier-Division** with a **gemischte Panzer-Regiment** consisting of one **Panzer-Abteilung** and one **Panzer-Grenadier-Bataillon** by consolidating **Panzer-Division "Holstein"** and **Panzer-Division "Schlesien."** The **I.Abteilung/Panzer-Regiment 18** was to have three **Panzer-Kompanien** with **Pz.Kpfw.IVs** and one **Panzer-Kompanie** with **Pz.IV/70**.

Panzer-Division "Clausewitz" - On 4 April 1945, a directive was issued to create **Panzer-Division "Clausewitz"** by utilizing **Panzer-Ausbildungs-Verband "Grossdeutschland."** This was revised on 6 April with directions to create **Panzer-Division "Clausewitz"** using the **Division-Stab mit Begleit-Kompanie "Holstein"**, **Panzer-Ausbildungs-Verband "Feldherrnhalle"**, and the remaining elements of **Panzer-Brigade 106** along with other remnants. On 7 April 1945 orders were issued to transport **Panzer-Jaeger-Abteilung "Grossdeutschland"** with two **Kompanien** and one **Kompanie** from **Panzer-Abteilung "Potsdam"** (total of 31 **Sturmgeschuetze**) by rail to **Ob.West** for **Panzer-Division "Clausewitz"** instead of the previous plans for three

Kompanien from **Panzer-Abteilung "Potsdam."** On 9 April, the remaining elements of **Panzer-Brigade 106** joined up with **Panzer-Division "Clausewitz."** Panzers were shipped from the **Heeres-Zeugamt** to outfit the units as follows: 31 **StuGIII** on 13 April, 10 Panthers on 14 April, 5 **Jagdpanther** on 14 April, and 10 **Pz.IV/70(V)** on 15 April 1945. On 13 April 1945, **Kampfgruppe Putlos** was ordered to join **Panzer-Division "Clausewitz."** Named as **Panzer-Abteilung "Putlos"** on 17 April, it was organized with an **Abteilung-Stab** outfitted with two Panthers, the **1.Kompanie** with two Tiger I and 10 Panthers, and the **2.Kompanie** with seven **Pz.Kpfw.IV**, one **Jagdpz.IV**, one **StuG**, and four **Pz.IV/70**. On the night of 17/18 April 1945, **Panzer-Abteilung "Putlos"** was in Uelzen under **Panzer-Division "Clausewitz."** Ten Panthers and five **Jagdpanthers** arrived in Buchen on 15 April and were given to the **Panther-Kompanie** of **Panzer-Abteilung 2106** under **Panzer-Brigade 106**. A second **Kompanie** with 10 **Pz.IV/70(V)** left Dresden on 15 April. The two operational **Jagdpanthers** and ten operational Panthers with **Panzer-Brigade 106** were ordered to go into action in the area east of Lueneburg on 16 April 1945.

9.Panzer-Division - On 7 April 1945, the **9.Panzer-Division** was ordered to create a **Kampfgruppe** with one **Panzer-Abteilung** consisting of two **Panther-Kompanien** (10 each), and one **Panzer-Kompanie** (10 **Pz.Kpfw.IV**) by 11 April 1945. On 9 April 1945 orders were issued to assemble new units from the remnants of decimated **Panzer** and **Sturmgeschuetz-Kompanien** under the **II.Abteilung/Panzer-Regiment 33** consisting of one **Panzer-Kompanie** from **Kampfgruppe 116**, one **Kompanie** with **Jagdpanzer 38**, one **Kompanie** with **Sturmgeschuetz III**, and one **Kompanie** with 10 **Pz.IV/70(V)**. On 17 April 1945, the **II.Abteilung/Panzer-Regiment 33** was transferred to Plauen to complete and take over 10 **Pz.IV/70(V)** at the Vomag assembly plant.

116.Panzer-Division - On orders from **Ob.West** dated 14 April 1945, a **Kampfgruppe** was to be created immediately from the remnants of the **116.Panzer-Division**. It was to have a **Panzer-Kompanie** with 14 Panthers and one **Zug** with four **Sturmtiger**.

7.Panzer-Division - On 14 April 1945, **Gen.Insp.d.Pz.Tr.** requested that the **7.Panzer-Division** be refurbished with 14 Panthers available from Wunsdorf and Grafenwoehr and the entire production of 20 **Pz.Kpfw.IVs** from Nibelungen-Werk. On 17 April 1945, the **4.Kompanie/Panzer-Regiment 11** with infrared equipment was ordered to be transported by rail from Wunsdorf to Neustrelitz and attached to **Panzer-Regiment 25** under the **7.Panzer-Division**. On 19 April 1945, the **7.Panzer-Division Kampfgruppe** possessed one mixed **Panzer-Abteilung** from **Panzer-Regiment 25** with 10 Panthers and 13 **Pz.Kpfw.IVs**.

TIGER UNITS

Schwere Heeres Panzer-Abteilung 509 - The **schwere Heeres Panzer-Abteilung 509** had already been pulled out of the Eastern Front to rest and refit in September 1944. In September, it had been issued 11 Tiger II which were subsequently turned over to the **schwere SS-Panzer-Abteilung 501**. After experiencing further delays in outfitting due to the severe interruptions in production at Henschel, **schwere Heeres Panzer-Abteilung 509** was sent 45 Tiger II from the **Heeres-Zeugamt** between 5 December 1944 and 1 January 1945. Loaded on trains on 12 January, **schwere Heeres Panzer-Abteilung 509** was sent to Hungary and went into action on 18 January 1945.

Schwere SS-Panzer-Abteilung 503 - Having previously received Tiger I that were then given away to other units, finally on 29 October 1944 **schwere SS-Panzer-Abteilung 503** was sent four Tiger II. This was later expanded by an additional six Tiger II acquired from the **schwere SS-Panzer-Abteilung 502**. Additional shipments of 29 new Tiger II were made from the **Heeres-Zeugamt** between 11 and 25 January 1945. With a total of 39 Tiger II (instead of the full complement of 45), the **schwere SS-Panzer-Abteilung 503** was loaded on trains on 27 January 1945 and sent to **Heeresgruppe Weichsel** on the Eastern Front.

Schwere SS-Panzer-Abteilung 502 - The **schwere SS-Panzer-Abteilung 102** (later renamed 502) was ordered on 9 September 1944 to transfer to Sennelager to rest and refit. Due to the shortage, the issue of the Tiger II was slow in coming. Six Tiger II sent to the unit from the ordnance depot on 27 December were passed along to the sister unit **schwere SS-Panzer-Abteilung 503**. Finally, 31 Tiger II were shipped from the ordnance depot between 14 February and 6 March 1945. **Schwere SS-Panzer-Abteilung 502** was transported to **Heeresgruppe Mitte** on the Eastern Front starting in mid-March, logging its first engagement in combat at Sachsendorf on 22 March.

Schwere Heeres Panzer-Abteilung 508 - On 4 February 1945, **schwere Heeres Panzer-Abteilung 508** in Italy turned its remaining 15 Tigers over to the **schwere Heeres Panzer-Abteilung 504** and returned to Germany to rest and be outfitted with Tiger II.

Schwere Heeres Panzer-Abteilung 507 - The **schwere Heeres Panzer-Abteilung 507** (minus one **Kompanie**) was ordered on 30 January 1945 to return from the Eastern Front to Sennelager to rebuild with Tiger II. On 20 February 1945, the **1.Kompanie/schwere Heeres Panzer-Abteilung 507** was ordered to return to its **Abteilung** in Sennelager for refitting. On 25 February 1945 orders were issued to refit **schwere Heeres Panzer-Abteilung 507** with 31 Tigers in Sennelager by 31 March 1945 with the following organization:

K.St.N.	Date	Unit Name
1107(fG)	1Nov44	**Stab und Stabskompanie Panzer-Abteilung**
1176(fG)	1Nov44	**schwere Panzer-Kompanie** (without 4 Tigers)
1151b(fG)	1Nov44	**Versorgungs-Kompanie**
1187b	1Nov44	**Panzer-Werkstatt-Kompanie**

The unit received four Tiger II on 19 March, 11 on 22 March, and the last six on 31 March 1945. They also acquired six Tiger II that had been issued previously to the **3.Kompanien** of **schwere Heeres Panzer-Abteilungen 510 und 511**. This brought their total strength up to 27 Tiger II. The Front came to the **schwere Heeres Panzer-Abteilung 507**, deployed in the defense of the local area.

3.Kompanien of **schwere Heeres Panzer-Abteilung 510 and 511** - The last 13 Tiger II produced by Henschel were picked up directly from the factory on 31 March by crews of the **3.Kompanie/schwere Heeres Panzer-Abteilung 510** and **3.Kompanie/schwere Heeres Panzer-Abteilung 511**. On 31 March, they reported that each **Kompanie** was in possession of eight Tiger II. Of these, 12 were brand-new production models from Henschel along with three older Tiger II from the **Waffenamt** at Sennelager and one older Tiger II from the **Waffenamt** at Northeim. On 1 April 1945, they engaged in combat in Kassel with seven Tiger II per **Kompanie**, reporting that three additional Tiger II had been lost due to bomb damage.

Schwere Heeres Panzer-Abteilung 507 - On 16 April 1945, **schwere Heeres Panzer-Abteilung 507** with the remaining elements of **schwere Heeres Panzer-Abteilung 508** (about 200 personnel) were transferred to the area west of Prague during the night of 16/17 April. On 17 April 1945, **schwere Heeres Panzer-Abteilung 507** was ordered to convert to a **Panzer-Jaeger-Abteilung** and renamed **Panzer-Abteilung 507**. It was to be outfitted with **Jagdpanzer 38** on 25 April 1945.

MISCELLAENEOUS UNITS

Panzer-Abteilung "Schlesien" - On 2 January 1945, a request was made to create **Panzer-Abteilung (Fkl) 303** with 45 **Sturmgeschuetze** using the **4.Kompanie/Panzer-Abteilung (Fkl) 301** and the **4.Kompanie/Panzer-Abteilung (Fkl) 302** by 31 January 1945. **Panzer-Kompanie (Fkl) 319** was also incorporated as the third **Kompanie**. On 16 February 1945, a directive was issued to quickly create **Panzer-Abteilung 303** with 31 **Sturmgeschuetze** without the **Funklenk** equipment for the defense of Berlin by converting **Panzer-Abteilung (Fkl) 303**. On 18 February 1945 orders were issued to create **Panzer-Abteilung 303** without **Funklenk** equipment with three **Panzer-Sturmgeschuetz-Kompanien** (each with 10 StuGIII under K.St.N.1159 dated 1Nov44). On 21 February 1945, orders were issued to re-

Panzer–Fliegerabwehr–Zug

(3,7 cm Flak 43/1 und 2 cm Flakvierling)

K.St.N.1196a Ausf.A v. 1.2.1945

1.Halbzug

2.Halbzug

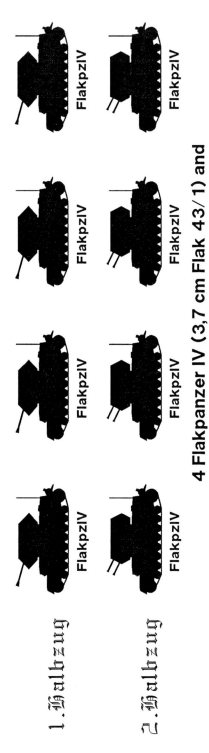

FlakpzIV · FlakpzIV · FlakpzIV · FlakpzIV
FlakpzIV · FlakpzIV · FlakpzIV · FlakpzIV

4 Flakpanzer IV (3,7 cm Flak 43/1) and

4 Flakpanzer IV (2 cm Flakvierling) (Sd.Kfz.161/4)

K.St.N.1196a Ausf.B v. 1.2.1945

8 Flakpanzer IV (2 cm Flakvierling) (Sd.Kfz.161/4)

K.St.N.1196a Ausf.C v. 1.2.1945

8 Flakpanzer IV (3,7 cm Flak 43/1)

name **Panzer-Abteilung 303** to **Panzer-Abteilung "Doeberitz."** The next day it was assigned to **Panzer-Division "Schlesien"** and ordered to be renamed **Panzer-Abteilung "Schlesien."**

Sturmpanzer-Abteilung 218 - Orders were issued on 6 January 1945 to create **Sturmpanzer-Abteilung 218** with **Stab und Stabskompanie** (K.St.N.1107d(f.G.) dated 1Sep44) and three **Sturmpanzer-Kompanien** (K.St.N.1160(f.G.) dated 1Sep44) utilizing the **1. and 2.Kompanie/Sturmpanzer-Abteilung 218** by 20 February 1945. The **1.Kompanie/Sturmpanzer-Abteilung 218** was to remain at the front by **Heeresgruppe Mitte** and first be assimilated after completion of the rest of the **Abteilung**. On 22 February 1945, plans were made to outfit **Sturmpanzer-Abteilung 218** with **Sturmgeschuetze** instead of **Sturmpanzer** in three **Panzer-Sturmgeschuetz-Kompanien** (K.St.N.1159(f.G.) dated 1Nov44). On 18 March 1945, **Sturmpanzer-Abteilung 218** was reported to have a strength of 43 **StuG III**. On 24 April 1945, **Sturmpanzer-Abteilung 218** was converted into a **Panzer-Jagd-Verband**.

Panzer-Kompanie (bo) "Berlin"- Orders were cut on 22 January 1945 to create **Panzer-Kompanie (bo) "Berlin"** with 10 **Pz.Kpfw.V** and 12 **Pz.Kpfw.IV** taken out of repair shops. Each of these immobile Panzers was to be manned by a crew of three ready to defend Berlin by 24 January.

Panzer-Fliegerabwehr-Zug (3,7 cm Flak 43/1 und 2 cm Flakvierling) - A new K.St.N.1196a dated 1 February 1945, contained three alternatives for the organization of the **Panzer-Fliegerabwehr-Zug (3,7 cm Flak 43/1 und 2 cm Flakvierling)**. **Ausfuehrung A** was organized with four **Flakpanzer IV (3,7 cm Flak 43/1)** in the **1.Halbzug** and four **Flakpanzer IV (2 cm Flakvierl.) (Sd.Kfz.161/4)** in the **2.Halbzug**. **Ausfuehrung B** was organized with four **Flakpanzer IV (2 cm Flakvierl.) (Sd.Kfz.161/4)** in both the **1. and 2.Halbzug**. **Ausfuehrung C** was organized with four **Flakpanzer IV (3,7 cm Flak 43/1)** in both the **1. and 2.Halbzug**.

Panzer-Abteilung "Stahnsdorf 1" - Orders were issued on 1 February 1945 to create **Panzer-Abteilung "Stahnsdorf 1"** with one **Panzer-Kompanie** (with 16 Panthers using K.St.N.1177 dated 1Nov43 as basis) and two **Panzer-Sturmgeschuetz-Kompanien** (with 14 **Sturmgeschuetze** each using K.St.N.1159 dated 1Nov43 as basis) by midnight on 1 February 1945. On 15 February 1945, orders were issued to transfer the **Panther-Kompanie** from **Panzer-Abteilung "Stahnsdorf 1"** to **Panzer-Abteilung "Kummersdorf."** Thirty-one **Sturmgeschuetz III** were shipped to **Panzer-Abteilung "Stahnsdorf 1"** from the **Heeres-Zeugamt** between 3 and 15 February 1944.

Panzer-Abteilung "Stahnsdorf 2" - Orders were issued on 1 February 1945 to create **Panzer-Abteilung "Stahnsdorf 2"** with one **Panzer-Kompanie** (with 16 Panthers using K.St.N.1177 dated 1Nov43 as basis) and two **Panzer-Sturmgeschuetz-Kompanien** (with 14 **Sturmgeschuetze** each using K.St.N.1159 dated 1Nov43 as basis) by midnight on 1 February 1945. Nineteen Panthers were shipped from the **Heeres-Zeugamt** on 1 February, followed by 28 **Sturmgeschuetz III** on 3 February. On 12 February 1945, a directive was issued to immediately send **Panzer-Abteilung "Stahnsdorf 2"** by rail to **Heeresgruppe Mitte**.

Panzer-Kompanie "Kummersdorf" - On 13 February 1945, orders were cut to create a mixed **Panzer-Kompanie "Kummersdorf"** (K.St.N.1175a dated 1Nov43 as basis) by 16 February from Panzers given up by **Versuchstelle Kummersdorf** including four **StuGIII**, three **Pz.Kpfw.IV**, three **Jagdpz.IV**, and three Panthers to be sent to **Panzer-Abteilung "Stahnsdorf 1."** **Versuchstelle Kummersdorf** reported the following operational Panzers on 13 February: four **StuGIII**, three Panthers, one **Pz.IV/70(A)**, one **Pz.IV/70(V)**, three **Pz.Kpfw.IV**, two **Jagdpz.IV**, one **Pz.Kpfw.III lg.**, one **Pz.Kpfw.IV kz.**, one **Jagdtiger**, and one **Bergepanther**.

Panzer-Abteilung "Kummersdorf"(bo) - Orders were issued on 16 February 1945 to create **Panzer-Abteilung "Kummersdorf"(bo)** with 31 Panzers in three **Panzer-Kompanien** (K.St.N.1177 dated 1Nov43 as basis) using the mixed **Panzer-Kompanie** from **Panzer-Abteilung "Stahnsdorf 1"** and the mixed **Panzer-Kompanie "Kummersdorf."** On 17 February 1945, the unit was renamed **Panzer-Abteilung "Kummersdorf."** On 12 March, **Panzer-Abteilung "Kummersdorf"** was ordered to hand over all its Panzers to the **I.Abteilung/Panzer-Regiment 29** attached to **Panzer-Division "Muencheberg."** Tiger-Kompanie/**Panzer-Abteilung "Kummersdorf"** was ordered to be incorporated into the **I.Abteilung/Panzer-Regiment 29** and renamed **3.Kompanie/Panzer-Regiment 29**.

SS-Panzer-Einsatz-Kompanie Ligurien - **SS-Panzer-Einsatz-Kompanie Ligurien** was created by **Armee-Gruppe Ligurien** on 13 February 1945 from the **14 Pz.Kpfw.III 7.5 cm L/24** left behind by the **1.Kompanie/Panzer-Abteilung 208**.

Panzer-Abteilung "Potsdam" - On 24 February 1945, orders were issued to create **Panzer-Abteilung "Potsdam"** with three **Panzer-Kompanien** (K.St.N.1159 dated 1Nov43) by 1 March 1945. On 7 April 1945, orders were issued to transport **Panzer-Jaeger-Abteilung "Grossdeutschland"** with two **Kompanien** and one **Kompanie** from **Panzer-Abteilung "Potsdam"** by rail to **Ob.West** for **Panzer-Division "Clausewitz"** instead of three **Kompanien** from **Panzer-Abteilung "Potsdam."** The remaining two **Kompanien** of **Panzer-Abteilung "Potsdam"** were placed at the disposal of the **OKH**.

Panzer-Kompanie Kummersdorf 2 (bo) - Orders to create **Panzer-Kompanie Kummersdorf 2 (bo)** (K.St.N.1177 dated 1Nov43 as basis) were issued on 2 April 1945. On 4 April, the **Kompanie** was ordered to be sent to **Ob.West** to reinforce the defenders of the city of Schweinfurt.

Sturmpanzer-Abteilung 219 - On 6 April 1945, **Heeresgruppe Sued** reported that **Sturmpanzer-Abteilung 219** was in the process of being outfitted with 30 **Beute-Panzer**, most of them T-34 tanks. Then they reported on 10 April 1945 that **Sturmpanzer-Abteilung 219** couldn't be out-fitted with **Beute-Panzer** because ammunition wasn't avail-able. It was suggested that **Sturmpanzer-Abteilung 219** be disbanded if **Sturmpanzer** weren't expected to be issued. On 26 April 1945, the **3.Kompanie/Sturmpanzer-Abteilung 219** was attached to **schwere Panzer-Abteilung "Feldherrnhalle."** The rest of **Sturmpanzer-Abteilung 219** was sent to **Panzer-Jagd-Brigade "Trumpa."**

Panzer-Abteilung "Putlos" - On 13 April 1945, **Kampf-gruppe "Putlos"** was ordered to join **Panzer-Division "Clausewitz."** Called **Panzer-Abteilung "Putlos"** on 17 April, it was organized with an **Abteilung-Stab** outfitted with two Panthers, the **1.Kompanie** with two Tiger I and 10 Panthers, and the **2.Kompanie** with seven **Pz.Kpfw.IV**, one **Jagdpz.IV**, one StuG, and four **Pz.IV/70**. On the night of 17/18 April 1945, **Panzer-Abteilung "Putlos"** was in Uelzen under **Panzer-Division "Clausewitz."**

ACTIVATION OF THE ERSATZ-HEERES

On 1 March 1945, the following inventory was reported for Panzers on hand with the training units in the **Ersatz-Heeres**: 328 **Pz.Kpfw.III**, 130 **Pz.Kpfw.IV**, 2 **Pz.IV/70(A)**, 2 **Pz.IV/70(V)**, 189 **Pz.Kpfw.V**, 38 & 17 **Pz.Kpfw.VI**, 3 **Fla.Pz.2 cm**, and 2 **Fla.Pz.3.7 cm** for a total of 711. However, most of these Panzers were not operational and were in very poor condi-tion.

The training units in the **Ersatz-Heeres** were activated for front-line service as one of the last desperate acts to stop the Allied advance from both East and West into Germany. The following list dated 24 March 1945 is only an example, because orders frequently changed as the situation contin-ued to deteriorate:

    Panzer-Ausbildungs-Verband "Ostsee"
        Pz.Brig.Stab 104
            Pz.Regt.Stab Coburg
                Pz.Ausb.Abt.13
                Pz.Ausb.Abt.5

    Panzer-Ausbildungs-Verband "Thueringen"
        Pz.Regt.Stab aus Pz.Tr.Schule Bergen
            Pz.Ausb.Abt.1
            Pz.Ausb.Abt.300
    Panzer-Ausbildungs-Verband "Westfalen"
            Pz.Ausb.Abt.11
            Pz.Ausb.Abt.500
    Panzer-Ausbildungs-Verband "Franken"
        Pz.Regt.Stab aus Pz.Jg.Schule Grafenwoehr
            Pz.Ausb.Abt.7
            Pz.Abt. aus Pz.Jg.Schule Grafenwoehr
    Panzer-Ausbildungs-Verband "Donau"
        Stab Pz.Div. Holstein
            Pz.Ausb.Abt.35
            Pz.Ausb.Abt.4
    Panzer-Ausbildungs-Verband "Boehmen"
        Stab Pz.Div. Schlesien
            Pz.Ausb.Abt.18
            Pz.Ausb.Abt.17
    Panzer-Ausbildungs-Verband "Grossdeutschland"
            Pz.Ausb.Abt.20
            Pz.Ausb.Abt."G.D."

These activated training units have frequently been misidentified as **Panzer-Divisions**. Some of these training units were absorbed into **Panzer-Divisions** and **Panzer-Grenadier-Divisions** that were being refitted at the end of the war. As examples of the operational Panzer strength on hand with these units:

• On 2 April 1945, **Panzer-Ausbildungs-Abteilung 300** had 2 Panthers, 1 **Pz.Kpfw.IV**, and 3 StuG.
• On 2 April 1945, under **Panzer-Ausbildungs-Verband "Westfalen"**, **Panzer-Ausbildungs-Abteilung 11** had 3 **Pz.Kpfw.II**, 4 **Pz.Kpfw.IV**, 3 Panthers, 2 StuG, and 1 **Jagdpz.38** and **Panzer-Ausbildungs-Abteilung 500** had 4 **Pz.Kpfw.III**, 5 Panthers, and 17 Tigers.
• On 2 April 1945, under **Panzer-Ausbildungs-Verband "Franken"**, **Panzer-Ausbildungs-Abteilung 7** had 1 **Pz.Kpfw.III**, 1 StuG, and 4 **Jagdpz.38** and **Panzer-Lehr-Abteilung Bergen** had 18 StuG, 2 **Pz.Kpfw.IV**, and 1 Panther.
• On 5 April 1945, **Panzer-Ausbildungs-Abteilung 5** under **Panzer-Ausbildungs-Verband "Ostsee"** had a single **Panzer-Zug** with two Panthers and a **Zug** with two **Jagdpanzer 38**.
• On 15 April 1945, **Panzer-Ausbildungs-Verband "Boehmen"** was in possession of 16 **Pz.Kpfw.IV**, 3 StuGIII, 12 **Jagdpanzer 38**, and 3 **Sturmpanzer**.

32

Defense of the Fatherland

Even though worn down from their continuous defensive struggle since July of 1943, most of the major **Panzertruppen** formations were still intact. The operational strength report for 15 March 1945 shows the order of battle and status of the **Panzertruppen** awaiting the Allied crossing of the Rhine and the Russian drives for Berlin and Vienna. Some of the **Sturmgeschuetze** and **Panzer IV/70** reported in these tables were in **Panzer-Jaeger-Abteilungen** as well as in the **Panzer-Abteilungen**. The original report did not specify associations within the divisions.

Reinforcements for the **Panzertruppen** arriving after 15 March 1945 consisted of 41 **Pz.Kpfw.IV**, 82 **Pz.Kpfw.V** and 31 **Pz.Kpfw.VI** for the Eastern Front and 66 **Pz.Kpfw.IV**, 61 **Pz.Kpfw.V**, and 34 **Pz.Kpfw.VI** for the Western Front.

In addition, the following Panzers were reported as on hand with the training units in the **Ersatz-Heeres** on 1 March 1945: 328 **Pz.Kpfw.III**, 130 **Pz.Kpfw.IV**, 2 **Pz.IV/70(A)**, 2 **Pz.IV/70(V)**, 189 **Pz.Kpfw.V**, 38 & 17 **Pz.Kpfw.VI**, 3 **Flakpz (2 cm)**, and 2 **Flakpz (3.7 cm)**, for a total of 711. However, most of these Panzers were not operational. After years of abuse, the few Panzers that were still operational were in very poor condition.

A **Panther Ausf.G** knocked out in Haiger, Germany by the 750th U.S. Tank Battalion in March 1945. (NA)

STRENGTH OF PANZER UNITS ON THE EASTERN FRONT ON 15 MARCH 1945						
Unit Name	StuG	PzIVlg	PzIV/70	Flakpz	PzV	PzVI
Heeresgruppe Sued						
1.Pz.Div.	2 (1)	5 (2)			59(10)	
3.Pz.Div.	7 (2)	14 (4)	11 (2)		39(13)	
6.Pz.Div.		22 (4)		5 (3)	68(19)	
13.Pz.Div.		18 (0)		1 (1)	5 (5)	
23.Pz.Div.	10 (7)	16 (6)	8 (0)	1 (0)	33 (7)	
232.Pz.Div.(Tatra)	1 (1)	1 (1)				
Pz.Div.FHH		18(16)	3 (2)		19(18)	
I./Pz.Rgt.24					32 (3)	
s.H.Pz.Abt.509				8 (2)		35 (8)
s.H.Pz.Abt.FHH				7 (2)		26(19)
1.SS-Pz.Div.LSSAH	7 (3)	29(14)	20 (2)	6 (3)	32(18)	
s.SS.Pz.Abt.501				8 (1)		32 (8)
2.SS-Pz.Div.R	26 (7)	22(14)	18 (7)	8 (4)	27(17)	
3.SS-Pz.Div.T	17(13)	17(16)			17 (8)	9 (7)
5.SS-Pz.Div.W	5 (4)	4 (3)			18(12)	
9.SS-Pz.Div.H	25(11)	20(11)	22(10)	5 (3)	35(12)	
12.SS-Pz.Div.HJ		23(10)	30(10)	8 (2)	24 (9)	
16.SS-Pz.Gr.Div.RF-SS	62(47)					
Heeresgruppe Mitte						
8.Pz.Div.		42(11)	30 (6)		10 (9)	
16.Pz.Div.	31 (8)	4 (0)	16 (8)		14(10)	
17.Pz.Div.		14(10)	19(18)	3 (3)		
19.Pz.Div.		20(20)	11 (9)		17(16)	
20.Pz.Div.	13 (6)	21(19)	10 (0)	2 (2)	9 (2)	
21.Pz.Div.	1 (1)	31(17)	16(14)	4 (4)	33(14)	
Fuehr.Begl.Div.	43(20)	10 (7)	20(12)	5 (2)	20(10)	
10.Pz.Gren.Div.	29(20)		9 (8)			
Pz.Gren.Div.Brandenburg	17 (9)	1 (0)				
I./Pz.Rgt.39					23 (4)	
Pz.Abt.1 Stahnsdorf	23(21)					
Pz.Abt.2 Stahnsdorf	18(14)				13 (9)	
Fallsch.Pz.Div.1		20(19)			20(12)	1 (0)
18.SS-Pz.Gr.Div.HW	19 (5)					
Heeresgruppe Weichsel						
25.Pz.Div.	1 (0)	31(11)	19(12)		10 (3)	
Pz.Div.Schlesien		30(20)	10 (3)			
Pz.Div.Muencheberg	4 (4)	4 (3)	1 (1)		11(10)	11 (8)
Fuehr.Gren.Div.	34(16)	3 (0)	7 (3)	3 (2)	26 (6)	
20.Pz.Gren.Div.		19 (0)	21(21)	3 (3)		
25.Pz.Gren.Div.	30(30)	1 (1)	20(19)	2 (2)	32(30)	
Pz.Gren.Div.Kurmark		3 (2)			38(26)	1 (1)
II./Pz.Rgt.9		17 (9)	13 (9)			
10.SS-Pz.Div.F		32(21)	8 (4)	8 (4)	50(23)	
11.SS-Pz.Gren.Div.N	26(13)				2 (0)	
s.SS.Pz.Abt.502						31(31)
s.SS.Pz.Abt.503				8 (5)		12 (1)
Heeresgruppe Nord						
4.Pz.Div.	3 (2)	5 (2)			15 (7)	
5.Pz.Div.	5 (3)	17(13)			14(11)	
7.Pz.Div.	8 (5)	2 (1)	10 (6)		9 (5)	
24.Pz.Div.	3 (0)	3 (2)	5 (3)			
Pz.Gren.Div.G.D.	1 (0)	1 (0)			5 (1)	6 (6)
s.H.Pz.Abt.505						13(12)
s.H.Pz.Abt.511						20(11)
4.SS-Pol.Pz.Gren.Div.	24 (7)			8 (5)	2 (0)	
Heeresgruppe Kurland						
12.Pz.Div.	5 (4)	63(56)				
14.Pz.Div.	17(15)			2 (2)	36(28)	
s.H.Pz.Abt.510						15(13)
Total Available (Operational)	545 (314)	603 (345)	357 (189)	97 (50)	776 (387)	212 (125)

STRENGTH OF PANZER UNITS ON THE WESTERN FRONT ON 15 MARCH 1945						
Unit Name	StuG	PzIVlg	PzIV/70	Flakpz	PzV	PzVI
Heeresgruppe H						
116.Pz.Div.	11 (2)	6 (2)	7 (4)	10 (5)	32 (8)	
15.Pz.Gren.Div.	14 (8)	3 (2)	21 (10)	2 (0)		
Heeresgruppe B						
2.Pz.Div.	22 (2)	16 (4)		5 (3)	35 (4)	
9.Pz.Div.	2 (2)	5 (1)	8 (3)	4 (0)	18 (10)	
11.Pz.Div.	6 (2)	17 (4)		11 (4)	33 (14)	
Pz.Lehr-Div.		6 (2)	14 (6)	2 (1)	29 (13)	
3.Pz.Gren.Div.	9 (4)	1 (1)	20 (6)			
Pz.Brig.106		3 (1)	7 (4)	3 (2)	5 (0)	
Pz.Abt.Fkl.301						13 (4)
s.H.Pz.Abt.506						15 (2)
Heeresgruppe G						
17.SS-Pz.Gren.Div.GvB	62 (47)	2 (2)		4 (4)		
Total Available (Operational)	126 (67)	59 (19)	77 (33)	41 (19)	152 (49)	28 (6)

STRENGTH OF PANZER UNITS IN ITALY ON 15 MARCH 1945						
Unit Name	StuG	PzIVlg	PzIV/70	Flakpz	PzV	PzVI
Heeresgruppe C						
26.Pz.Div.	8 (7)	84 (63)		6 (5)	26 (22)	
29.Pz.Gren.Div.	17 (12)	46 (44)		7 (7)		
90.Pz.Gren.Div.	42 (38)	1 (1)		8 (7)		
s.H.Pz.Abt.504						36 (32)
Total Available (Operational)	67 (57)	131 (108)	0	21 (19)	26 (22)	36 (32)

ORGANIZATION AND STRENGTH OF PANZER UNITS
THE LAST PANZER-DIVISION

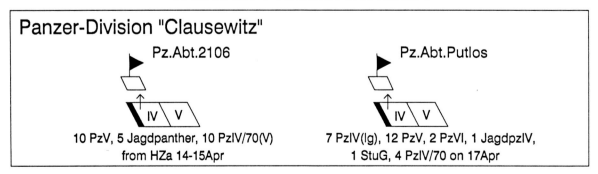

Panzer-Division "Clausewitz"

Pz.Abt.2106 — 10 PzV, 5 Jagdpanther, 10 PzIV/70(V) from HZa 14-15Apr

Pz.Abt.Putlos — 7 PzIV(lg), 12 PzV, 2 PzVI, 1 JagdpzIV, 1 StuG, 4 PzIV/70 on 17Apr

Appendices

APPENDIX A - FORMATION OF PANZER UNITS FOR THE HEER

Panzer-Division Stab	Created	Remarks
1.Panzer-Division	12Sep35	from Kdo.3.Kav.Div.
2.Panzer-Division	15Oct35	
3.Panzer-Division	15Oct35	
4.Panzer-Division	10Nov38	
5.Panzer-Division	24Nov38	
6.Panzer-Division	18Oct39	from 1.leichte Division
7.Panzer-Division	18Oct39	from 2.leichte Division
8.Panzer-Division	18Oct39	from 3.leichte Division
9.Panzer-Division	3Jan40	from 4.leichte Division
10.Panzer-Division	1Apr39	Surrendered in Tunisia in May43
11.Panzer-Division	1Aug40	from 11.Schuetzen Brigade
12.Panzer-Division	10Jan41	from 2.Infanterie Division (mot)
13.Panzer-Division	11Oct40 10Mar45	from 13.Infanterie Division (mot) Wiped out on Eastern Front in Jan45 Orders to re-create and rename Pz.Div.FHH2
14.Panzer-Division	15Aug40 Feb43	from 4.Infanterie Division Surrendered in Stalingrad in Feb43 Re-created
15.Panzer-Division	11Nov40	from 33.Infanterie Division Surrendered in Tunisia in May43
16.Panzer-Division	2Aug40 Feb43 4Mar45	from 16.Infanterie Division Surrendered in Stalingrad in Feb43 Re-created Incorporated Pz.Div.Jueterbog into 16.Pz.Div.
17.Panzer-Division	10Oct40	from 27.Infanterie Division
18.Panzer-Division	26Oct40	Converted to 18.Artillerie-Division on 19Oct43

Panzer-Division Stab	Created	Remarks
19.Panzer-Division	1Nov40	
20.Panzer-Division	15Oct40	
21.Panzer-Division	1Aug41	from 5.leichte Division
		Surrendered in Tunisia in May43
	15Jul43	Re-created as 21.Panzer-Division (new)
22.Panzer-Division	25Sep41	Disbanded on 6 April 1943
23.Panzer-Division	25Sep41	Div.Stab from Stab Pz.Brig.101
24.Panzer-Division	1Dec41	from 1.Kavallerie Division
		Surrendered in Stalingrad in Feb43
	Feb43	Re-created
25.Panzer-Division	28Feb42	
26.Panzer-Division	15Sep42	from 23.Infanterie Division
27.Panzer-Division	2Oct42	from part of 22.Pz.Div.
		Disbanded in February 1943
116.Panzer-Division	May44	Created from 116.Pz.Gren.Div. and 179.Res.Pz.Div.
155.Reserve-Panzer-Division	4Aug43	from Ersatzheer Pz.Div.Nr.155
		Used to rebuild 9.Pz.Div. in May44
178.Reserve-Panzer-Division		from Ersatzheer Pz.Div.Nr.178
179.Reserve-Panzer-Division	30Jul43	from Ersatzheer Pz.Div.Nr.179
		Used to create 116.Pz.Div. in May44
232.Panzer-Division	21Feb45	From renamed Panzer-Feldausbildungs-Division Tatra
233.Panzer-Division	21Feb45	from renamed 233.Res.Pz.Div.
233.Reserve-Panzer-Division	10Aug43	from Ersatzheer Pz.Div.Nr.233
		Elements used to create Pz.Div.Holstein as ordered on 1Feb45
		Renamed 233.Pz.Div. on 21Feb45
273.Reserve-Panzer-Division	25Oct43	Used to rebuild 11.Pz.Div. in May44
Panzer-Lehr Division	Jan44	Assembled from previously created Pz.Lehr units
Panzer-Division Clausewitz	6Apr45	from elements of Pz.Div.Holstein and others
Panzer-Division Doeberitz	21Feb45	from renamed Stab Pz.Brig.10
		Renamed Pz.Div.Schlesien on 22Feb45
Panzer-Division Feldherrnhalle	27Nov44	ordered renamed from Pz.Gren.Div.FHH
		Wiped out on Eastern Front in Jan45
	10Mar45	Orders to be re-created and renamed Pz.Div.FHH1

APPENDICES

Panzer-Division Stab	Created	Remarks
Panzer-Division Feldherrnhalle 2	10Mar45	from renamed 13.Pz.Div.
Panzer-Division Holstein	1Feb45	from elements of 233.Res.Pz.Div. Orders on 30Mar45 to use Pz.Div.Holstein to re-create the 18.Pz.Gren.Div.
Panzer-Division Jueterbog	21Feb45	from Stab 16.Pz.Div. Orders on 26Feb45 to incorporate Pz.Div.Jueterbog into 16.Pz.Div.
Panzer-Division Kempf	Aug39	4.Pz.Brig.Stab used as Div.Stab Renamed 4.Pz.Brig and assigned to 10.Pz.Div. on 1Nov39
Panzer-Division Muencheberg	5Mar45	Div.Stab from Pz.Brig.103 Stab
Panzer-Division-Norwegen	22Sep43	from elements of 25.Pz.Div. left behind in Norway Used to create Kampfgruppe 25.Pz.Div. in Aug44 Remnants reformed as Pz.Brig.Norwegen
Panzer-Division Schlesien	22Feb45	from renamed Pz.Div.Doeberitz Orders on 30Mar45 to use Pz.Div.Schlesien to re-create the 18.Pz.Gren.Div.

Panzer-Brigade Stab	Created	Remarks
1.Panzer-Brigade	15Oct35	Assigned to 1.Pz.Div. Reassigned to 18.Pz.Div. on 1Dec40 Renamed Pz.Brig.18 on 9Jan41
2.Panzer-Brigade	15Oct35	Assigned to 2.Pz.Div. Disbanded on 4Jul41
3.Panzer-Brigade	15Oct35	Assigned to 3.Pz.Div. Used to create 5.lei.Div. on 18Feb41
4.Panzer-Brigade	12Oct37	Created as independent Heerestruppe Employed as Stab Pz.Div.Kempf Aug39 Assigned to 10.Panzer-Division on 1Nov39 Disbanded on 13Nov41
5.Panzer-Brigade	10Nov38	Assigned to 4.Panzer-Division Disbanded 21Feb42
6.Panzer-Brigade	10Nov38	Created as independent Heerestruppe Assigned to 1.leichte Division Disbanded Oct39
8.Panzer-Brigade	10Nov38	Created as independent Heerestruppe Assigned to 5.Panzer-Division on 24Nov38 Renamed to Pz.Brig.100 Stab on 25Feb41

251

Panzer-Brigade Stab	Created	Remarks
Panzer-Brigade 10	27Jun43	Created from Stab Pz.Rgt.10 for Operation Zitadelle Transferred West as training command for Panther Abt. on 3Nov43 Stab Pz.Brig.10 renamed Stab Pz.Div.Doeberitz on 21Feb45
Panzer-Brigade 18	9Jan41	Renamed from Stab Pz.Brig.1 Disbanded on 30Jul41
Panzer-Brigade 21	25Jun43	Created from Stab Pz.Rgt.21 for Operation Zitadelle
Panzer-Brigade 100	1Mar41	Created from Stab Pz.Brig.8 as a Brigade Stab for Beute-Panzer-Regiments Stab Pz.Brig.100 renamed Rgt.Stab/Pz.Rgt.100 on 8Dec42
Panzer-Brigade 101	5Jul41	Created as Brigade Stab for Beute-Panzer-Regiments Used to create the Stab for 23.Pz.Div. on 21Sep41
Panzer-Brigade 101	21Jul44	Disbanded and integrated into 20.Pz.Div. in Oct44
Panzer-Brigade 102	20Jul44	Disbanded and integrated into 7.Pz.Div. in Nov44
Panzer-Brigade 103	26Jul44	Brig.Stab used to command a Panzer-Kampfgruppe from Jan to Mar45 Renamed as Stab Pz.Div.Muncheberg on 8Mar45
Panzer-Brigade 104	18Jul44	Disbanded and integrated into 25.Pz.Div.
Panzer-Brigade 105	28Jul44	Integrated into 9.Pz.Div. in Sep44
Panzer-Brigade 106	28Jul44	Assigned to Pz.Div.Clausewitz on 6Apr45
Panzer-Brigade 107	28Jul44	Disbanded and integrated into 25.Pz.Gr.Div. in Nov44
Panzer-Brigade 108	Jul44	Disbanded and integrated into 116.Pz.Div. in Oct44
Panzer-Brigade 109	19Jul44	Disbanded and integrated into Pz.Gr.Div.FHH in Oct44
Panzer-Brigade 110	19Jul44	Disbanded and integrated into 13.Pz.Div. in Nov44
Panzer-Brigade 111	4Sep44	Disbanded and integrated into 11.Pz.Div. as ordered 1Oct44
Panzer-Brigade 112	4Sep44	Disbanded and integrated into 21.Pz.Div. on 23Sep44
Panzer-Brigade 113	4Sep44	Disbanded and integrated into 15.Pz.Gr.Div. on 1Oct44
Panzer-Brigade 150	4Nov44	Orders to create as a unit disguised as American Disbanded 2Jan45
Panzer-Brigade Norwegen	Jul44	from remnants of Pz.Div.Norwegen after refurbishing the 25.Pz.Div.

APPENDICES

Panzer-Regiment	Created	Remarks
Panzer-Regiment 1	1Oct35	Created with two Abt. each with four Kp. and assigned to 1.Pz.Div. Activated with two Abt. each with two l.Kp. and one m.Kp. on 18Aug39 2.Kp./Pz.Rgt.1 renamed to 1./Pz.Abt.A on 25Jul40 5.Kp./Pz.Rgt.1 renamed to 3./Pz.Abt.A on 25Jul40 Pz.Abt.z.b.V.1 with 3 Kp. created for 1.Pz.Div. on 1Oct40 1. and 2.Kp./Pz.Abt.z.b.V.1 renamed 2. and 6.Kp./Pz.Rgt.1 on 15Oct40 I./Pz.Rgt.1 renamed Pz.Abt.116 on 19Jun42 II./Pz.Rgt.1 renamed I./Pz.Rgt.1 on 15Jan43 I./Pz.Rgt.203 renamed II./Pz.Rgt.1 on 27Jan43 Pz.Rgt.1 expanded to eight Kp. on 27Jan43 I./Pz.Rgt.1 converted to Panther Abt. on 1Nov43
Panzer-Regiment 2	1Oct35	Created with two Abt. each with four Kp. and assigned to 1.Pz.Div. Activated with two Abt. each with two l.Kp. and one m.Kp. on 20Aug39 2./Pz.Rgt.2 renamed 2./Pz.Abt.A on 25Jul40 Assigned to 16.Pz.Div.on 20Oct40 2.Kp./Pz.Rgt.2 created from renamed 3./Pz.Abt.z.b.V.1 on 20Oct40 III./Pz.Rgt.2 renamed from II./Pz.Rgt.10 on 28May42 Surrendered in Stalingrad in Feb43
	17Feb43	Re-created Pz.Rgt.2 with I. and II.Abt. each with four Kp. on 17Feb43 Re-created III./Pz.Rgt.2 with four Kp.on 31Mar43 I./Pz.Rgt.2 converted to Panther Abt.on 25Aug43 III./Pz.Rgt.2 converted to Pz-StuG-Abt with 3 Kp. on 12Nov43 II. and III./Pz.Rgt.2 refurbished and sent East in Nov43 Ordered on 26Feb45 to absorb Pz.Abt.Jueterbog and reorganize with two Pz.Abt. Pz.Abt.Jueterbog absorbed into Pz.Rgt.2 on 4Mar45
Panzer-Regiment 3	15Oct35	Created with two Abt. each with four Kp. and assigned to 2.Pz.Div. Activated with two Abt. each with two l.Kp. and one l.Kp.a on 1Sep39 Lost all Panzers when ships went down in May41 Expanded to eight Kp. on 5Sep41 I./Pz.Rgt.3 renamed to III./Pz.Rgt.33 on 10May42 II./Pz.Rgt.3 expanded to four Kp. on 1Feb43 Re-created I./Pz.Rgt.3 as a Panther Abt. with 4 Kp. on 5May43 Decimated in Falaise pocket Aug44 Rebuilt I./Pz.Rgt.3 with four Panther Kp. in Oct/Nov44 Rebuilt II./Pz.Rgt.3 with two Pz.IV and two StuG Kp. in Oct/Nov44
Panzer-Regiment 4	15Oct35	Created with two Abt. each with four Kp. and assigned to 2.Pz.Div. Activated with two Abt. each with two l.Kp. and one l.Kp.a on 1Sep39 Transferred to 13.Pz.Div. on 28Sep40 III./Pz.Rgt.4 created from renamed III./Pz.Rgt.29 on 15May42 I./Pz.Rgt.4 renamed to s.Pz.Abt.507 on 23Sep43 III./Pz.Rgt.4 converted to Panther Abt. with four Kp. on 5May43 III./Pz.Rgt.4 renamed I./Pz.Rgt.4 on 19Oct43 Incorporated Pz.Abt.2110 into II./Pz.Rgt.4 in Oct44 I./Pz.Rgt.4 renamed to I./Pz.Rgt.26 on 16Feb45 Wiped out on Eastern Front in Jan45

Panzer-Regiment	Created	Remarks
	10Mar45	Re-created with I.Abt. of four Kp. and the II.Abt. as a Pz.Gren.Btl. and renamed Pz.Rgt.FHH2
Panzer-Regiment 5	15Oct35	Created with two Abt. each with four Kp. and assigned to 3.Pz.Div. Activated with two Abt. each with two l.Kp. and one l.Kp.a on 15Aug39 Reassigned to 5.lei.Div. on 15Feb41 Expanded to eight Kp. by creating 3. and 7./Pz.Rgt.5 on 15Sep41 3. and 7./Pz.Rgt.5 sank on 19Dec41 Re-created 3. and 7./Pz.Rgt.5 on 6Jan42 New I./Pz.Rgt.5 created by 15Jan43 II./Pz.Rgt.5 renamed II./Pz.Rgt.8 on 17Jan43 Pz.Abt.190 incorporated into Pz.Rgt.5 and renamed II./Pz.Rgt.5 by 6Feb43 Surrendered in Tunisia in May43
Panzer-Regiment 6	15Oct35	Created with two Abt. each with four Kp. and assigned to 3.Pz.Div. Activated with two Abt. each with two l.Kp. and one l.Kp.a on 1Sep39 6./Pz.Rgt.6 renamed to 1./Pz.Abt.z.b.V.40 (4.Zug remained behind with 7.Kp./Pz.Rgt.6) on 8Mar40 5./Pz.Rgt.6 created to replace 6.Kp. on 20Mar40 2./Pz.Rgt.6 renamed to 2./Pz.Abt.C on 25Jul40 2./Pz.Rgt.6 re-created on 29Jul40 1. and 5./Pz.Rgt.6 renamed to 2. and 3./Pz.Abt.301 on 15Jan41 1. and 5./Pz.Rgt.6 re-created on 1Feb41 III./Pz.Rgt.6 from renamed I./Pz.Rgt.28 with three Tauch Kp. on 1Mar41 III./Pz.Rgt.6 disbanded on 15Mar43 II./Pz.Rgt.6 expanded to four Kp. in early 1943 I./Pz.Rgt.6 converted to Panther Abt. with four Kp. on 6Aug43 I./Pz.Rgt.6 assigned to Pz.Lehr-Div. in Jan44 I./Pz.Rgt.6 renamed to I./Pz.Rgt.130 and vice versa on 8Nov44
Panzer-Regiment 7	6Oct36	Created with two Abt. each with four Kp. and assigned to 1.Pz.Div. Assigned to 4.Pz.Brig. as independent Heerestruppen on 12Oct37 Activated with two Abt. each with two l.Kp. and one l.Kp.a assigned to Pz.Div.Kempf on 1Sep39 Reassigned to 10.Pz.Div. on 10Oct39 Expanded to eight Kp. by creating 3. and 7./Pz.Rgt.7 on 30May41 I./Pz.Rgt.7 renamed III./Pz.Rgt.36 on 2Jun42 I./Pz.Rgt.7 re-created in Jun42. Pz.Rgt.7 consisted of two Abt. each with three l.Kp. and one m.Kp. III./Pz.Rgt.7 from renamed s.Pz.Abt.501 on 26Feb43 Surrendered in Tunisia in May43
Panzer-Regiment 8	6Oct36	Created with two Abt. each with four Kp. and assigned to 3.Pz.Div. Assigned to 4.Pz.Brig. as independent Heerestruppen on 12Oct37 Activated with two Abt. each with two l.Kp. and one l.Kp.a under the 10.Pz.Div. on 1Sep39 Transferred to 15.Panzer-Division on 18Jan41 Expanded to eight Kp. by creating an additional two l.Kp. on 1Sep41 II./Pz.Rgt.5 renamed II./Pz.Rgt.8 on 17Jan43 Surrendered in Tunisia in May43

Panzer-Regiment	Created	Remarks
Panzer-Regiment 9	4Dec42	Stab/Pz.Rgt.9 renamed from Stab/Pz.Rgt.18 II./Pz.Rgt.9 renamed from Pz.Abt.z.b.V.40 on 5Dec42 I./Pz.Rgt.9 renamed from Pz.Abt.214 on 16Dec42 4.Kp. transferred to II./Pz.Rgt.9 on 24Aug43 I./Pz.Rgt.9 with 2.Kp. and 3.Kp. renamed Pz.Abt.Norwegen on 6Sep43 II./Pz.Rgt.9 used to create Pz.Abt.2103 and 2104 on 30Jun44 Pz.Abt.2104 renamed to I./Pz.Rgt.9 in 25.Pz.Div. on 5Nov44 Pz.Abt.2111 disbanded and remnants used to create II./Pz.Rgt.9 on 12Nov44 II./Pz.Rgt.9 with two Kp. assigned to Pz.Brig.103 on 20Jan45 I./Pz.Rgt.9 with three Kp. ordered on 11Feb45 to refurbish 25.Pz.Div.
Panzer-Regiment 10	12Oct37	I./Pz.Rgt.10 created with four Kp. as independent Heerestruppen I./Pz.Rgt.10 activated with two l.Kp. and one l.Kp.a and assigned to I.A.K. on 26Aug39 II./Pz.Rgt.10 created with two l.Kp. and one m.Kp. on 20Oct39 Rgt.Stab created and assigned to 8.Pz.Div. in Oct39 III./Pz.Rgt.10 created from renamed Pz.Abt.67 on 1Jan41 II./Pz.Rgt.10 renamed to III./Pz.Rgt.2 and assigned to 16.Pz.Div. on 28May42 III./Pz.Rgt.10 disbanded on 14Oct42 2. and 4./Pz.Rgt.10 equipped with Panthers in Sep44 Pz.Abt.2113 renamed to II./Pz.Rgt.10 on 12Dec44
Panzer-Regiment 11	12Oct37	Created with two Abt. each with three Kp. as independent Heerestruppen Expanded to eight Kp. on 10Nov38 Activated with two Abt. each with two l.Kp. and one m.Kp. assigned to 1.lei.Div. on 1Aug39 Pz.Abt.65 disbanded and used to form the 4. and 8.Kp./Pz.Rgt.11 on 3Jun42 I./Pz.Rgt.11 converted to Panther Abt. with four Kp. on 5May43 I./Pz.Rgt.11 sent to Eastern Front in 1944 as an independent unit initially attached to 8.Pz.Div. I./Pz.Rgt.11 returned to Regiment on 15Dec44
Panzer-Regiment 15	12Oct37	Created with two Abt. each with 3 Kp. as independent Heerestruppen Expanded by creating two new Kp. on 10Nov38 Assigned to the 5.Pz.Div. on 24Nov38 Activated with two Abt. each with two l.Kp. and one l.Kp.a on 26Aug39 5./Pz.Rgt.15 (without 4.Zug) renamed to 3./Pz.Abt.z.b.V.40 on 9Mar40 5./Pz.Rgt.15 re-created on 15Apr40 Assigned to the 11.Pz.Div. on 4Sep40 III./Pz.Rgt.15 from renamed II./Pz.Rgt.35 on 19Jun42 I./Pz.Rgt.15 renamed to Pz.Abt.52 on 6Feb43 Pz.Abt.52 renamed to I./Pz.Rgt.15 on 24Aug43 III./Pz.Rgt.15 renamed to I./Pz.Rgt.35 on 24Sep43 Expanded II.Abt. to four m.Kp. by creating the 8.Kp. on 7Oct43

Panzer-Regiment	Created	Remarks
		II./Pz.Rgt.15 ordered to Sagan to be rebuilt on 2Sep44 Pz.Abt.2111 disbanded and incorporated in Sep44
Panzer-Regiment 16	23May44	Renamed from Pz.Rgt.116 I./Pz.Rgt.16 converted to Panther-Abt. on 3Jul44 I./Pz.Rgt.16 assigned to Pz.Brig.111 in Sep44 I./Pz.Rgt.16 rejoined 116.Pz.Div. in Sep44 Pz.Rgt.16 rebuilt in Nov44 with a Panther-Abt. of four Kp. and a gem.Pz.Abt. with two Pz.IV and two StuG Kp.
Panzer-Regiment 18	6Dec40	Created Stab for Pz.Rgt.18 and assigned to 18.Pz.Div. I./Pz.Rgt.18 from Pz.Abt.A on 6Dec40 II./Pz.Rgt.18 from Pz.Abt.B on 1Dec40 III./Pz.Rgt.18 from II./Pz.Rgt.28 on 1Mar41 III./Pz.Rgt.18 renamed to Pz.Abt.103 on 5Apr42 II./Pz.Rgt.18 renamed to Pz.Abt.18 on 15May42 I./Pz.Rgt.18 renamed to Pz.Abt.160 on 15Jun42 Stab/Pz.Rgt.18 renamed Stab Pz.Rgt.9 on 4Dec42
Panzer-Regiment 21	1Oct40	Created with three Abt. each with two l.Kp. and one m.Kp. Assigned to 20.Pz.Div. on 1Dec40 I. and II./Pz.Rgt.21 disbanded on 29Apr42 III./Pz.Rgt.21 renamed to Pz.Abt.21 with four Kp. on 26Apr43 Stab/Pz.Rgt.21 renamed to Stab/Pz.Brig.21 on 18Jun43 Pz.Abt.2101 renamed to II./Pz.Rgt.21 in 20.Pz.Div. Stab/Pz.Rgt.21 formed from Stab/Pz.Brig.101 on 29Oct44 I./Pz.Rgt.21 renamed to II./Pz.Rgt.21 on 30Dec44
Panzer-Regiment 22	20May44	Renamed from Pz.Rgt.100 with two Abt. each with four Kp. by 21.Pz.Div. II./Pz.Rgt.22 converted to Panther Abt. with four Kp. on 7Aug44 I./Pz.Rgt.22 rebuilt in Dec44 with two Panther and two Pz.IV Kp. Orders on 5Feb45 to reorganize Pz.Rgt.22 with Stab and Stabs-Kp. and a gem.Pz.Abt. with two Pz.IV and two Panther Kp.
Panzer-Regiment 23	10Nov38	I./Pz.Rgt.23 created with four Kp. as independent Heerestruppen under Stab/Pz.Rgt.25 Activated with two l.Kp. and one l.Kp.a and assigned to 8.Armee on 25Aug39 Assigned to 7.Pz.Div. on 18Oct39 I./Pz.Rgt.23 renamed to II./Pz.Rgt.25 on 1Apr40
	16Aug43	Pz.Rgt.201 renamed to Pz.Rgt.23
Panzer-Regiment 24	3Dec41	Created Rgts.Stab from Rgts.Stab/Reiter Rgt.2 for 24.Pz.Div. Created with three Abt. each with two l.Kp. and one m.Kp. from Reiter Rgt.2 and 22 plus Pz.Abt.101 on 10Dec41 Surrendered at Stalingrad in Feb43
	17Feb43	Re-created with two Pz.Abt. each with four Kp. Re-created III./Pz.Rgt.24 with four Kp. from Pz.Abt.127 on 5Apr43 Converted III./Pz.Rgt.24 into a Pz.StuG Abt. with two StuG Kp. and two m.Kp. on 12Jul43 I./Pz.Rgt.24 converted to Panther Abt. with four Kp. then on 5Aug43

Panzer-Regiment	Created	Remarks
		ordered to the Reserves and assigned to the LVIII.Res.Pz.K. on 12Jul43 II./Pz.Rgt.24 renamed I./Pz.Rgt.24 on 25Jul43 I./Pz.Rgt.24 left Pz.Brig.10 to join Pz.Rgt.16 on 19Jun44
Panzer-Regiment 25	10Nov38	I./Pz.Rgt.25 created with four Kp. as independent Heerestruppen under Stab/Pz.Rgt.25 Activated with two l.Kp. and one l.Kp.a on 25Aug39 Assigned to 7.Pz.Div. on 18Oct39 II./Pz.Rgt.25 from renamed I./Pz.Rgt.23 on 1Apr40 III./Pz.Rgt.25 from renamed Pz.Abt.66 on 19Feb41 Expanded to a total of twelve Kp. by creating an additional three l.Kp., one for each Panzer-Abteilung on 10May41 III./Pz.Rgt.25 disbanded when Regiment reformed as two Abt. each with three Kp. on 15Mar42 Expanded to eight Kp. with recreation of 3. and 7.Kp. on 15Jun42 I./Pz.Rgt.25 converted to Panther Abt. with four Kp. on 15Oct43
Panzer-Regiment 26	5Jan43	Renamed from Pz.Rgt.202 by 26.Pz.Div. I./Pz.Rgt.26 converted to Panther Abt. on 31May43 I./Pz.Rgt.26 sent to Eastern Front in Jan44 I./Pz.Rgt.26 renamed I./Pz.Rgt.Brandenburg on 18Jan45 I./Pz.Rgt.4 renamed to I./Pz.Rgt.26 on 15Feb45
Panzer-Regiment 27	10Nov38 1Oct40	I./Pz.Rgt.27 with four Kp. created as independent Heerestruppen Renamed II./Pz.Rgt.31 and assigned to 5.Pz.Div. on 24Nov38 Created with three Abt. each with two l.Kp. and one m.Kp. Assigned to 19.Pz.Div. III./Pz.Rgt.27 disbanded on 10Aug41 I./Pz.Rgt.27 disbanded on 31Mar42 II./Pz.Rgt.27 renamed I./Pz.Rgt.27 on 1Apr42 II./Pz.Rgt.27 from renamed Pz.Abt.138 on 27Mar43 I./Pz.Rgt.27 re-created as Panther Abt. on 15Oct43
Panzer-Regiment 28	6Dec40	Created from Pz.Abt.C and D Rgt.Stab disbanded on 1Mar41, I./Pz.Rgt.28 renamed to III./Pz.Rgt.6 and II./Pz.Rgt.28 renamed to III./Pz.Rgt.18
Panzer-Regiment 29	1Oct40	Created with three Abteilung each with two l.Kp. and one m.Kp. Assigned to 12.Pz.Div. on 10Jan41 I. and II./Pz.Rgt.29 converted from Pz.38t to Pz.III in Jan42 III./Pz.Rgt.29 renamed to III./Pz.Rgt.4 on 15May42 8./Pz.Rgt.29 from renamed 1./Pz.Abt.z.b.V.66 on 2Oct42 I./Pz.Rgt.29 returned to Germany (before May43) Personnel from I./Pz.Rgt.29 sent to H.Gr.Nord to man dug in Panthers in Dec43 I./Pz.Rgt.29 turned Panthers over to SS-Pz.Abt.11 and returned to West in Feb44 I./Pz.Rgt.29 assigned to Pz.Brig.112 in Sep44 I./Pz.Rgt.29 turned equipment over to Pz.Rgt.22 and returned to refit in Sep44 I./Pz.Rgt.29 with two Kp. assigned to Pz.Brig.103 I./Pz.Rgt.29 assigned to Pz.Div.Muncheberg on 9Mar45

Panzer-Regiment	Created	Remarks
		Outfitted with Panzers from Pz.Abt.Kummersdorf and 3./Pz.Abt.Kummersdorf renamed 3./Pz.Abt.29 on 12Mar45
Panzer-Regiment 31	10Nov38	I./Pz.Rgt.31 with four Kp. created as independent Heerestruppen II./Pz.Rgt.31 renamed from I./Pz.Rgt.27 on 24Nov38 Pz.Rgt.31 assigned to 5.Pz.Div. on 24Nov38 Activated with two Abt. each with two l.Kp. and one l.Kp.a on 26Aug39 Re-created 5./Pz.Rgt.31 on 10Jul41. The previous 5.Kp. was to remain on Crete and was renamed 1./Pz.Abt.212 Expanded to eight Kp. by creating two new l.Kp. with 34 Pz.III and 6 Pz.II, one for each Abt. on 1Aug41 I./Pz.Rgt.31 converted to Panther Abt. with four Kp. on 5May43
Panzer-Regiment 33	2Feb40	Renamed from Pz.Rgt.Conze and assigned to 9.Pz.Div. III./Pz.Rgt.33 from renamed I./Pz.Rgt.3 on 10May42 II./Pz.Rgt.33 renamed to Pz.Abt.51(Panther) on 9Jan43 III./Pz.Rgt.33 renamed to s.Pz.Abt.506 on 8May43 II./Pz.Rgt.33 from renamed Pz.Abt.51 on 4Jan44 II./Pz.Rgt.33 under Pz.Brig.10 outfitting with Panthers in May44 II./Pz.Rgt.33 rejoined Regiment in Jul44 Absorbed Pz.Abt.2105 on 26Sep44 Pz.Rgt.33 rebuilt in Nov44 with a Panther-Abt. of four Kp. and a gem.Pz.Abt. with two Pz.IV and two StuG Kp.
Panzer-Regiment 35	10Nov38	Created with two Abt. each with four Kp. and assigned to 4.Pz.Div. Activated with two Abt. each with two l.Kp. and one l.Kp.a on 28Aug39 1./Pz.Rgt.35 renamed to 2./Pz.Abt.z.b.V.40 (4.Zug remained behind with 2.Kp./Pz.Rgt.35) on 9Mar40 Created 3./Pz.Rgt.35 to replace 1./Pz.Rgt.35 on 13Apr40 Expanded to seven Kp. with recreation of 1./Pz.Rgt.35 on 24Jan41 Expanded to eight Kp. with creation of 7./Pz.Rgt.35 on 17May41 II./Pz.Rgt.35 renamed III./Pz.Rgt.15 and assigned to 11.Pz.Div. on 19Jun42 Rgt.Stab renamed Pz.Jg.Rgt.656 on 24May43 III./Pz.Rgt.15 renamed to I./Pz.Rgt.35 and converted to Panther Abt. with four Kp. on 24Sep43 I./Pz.Rgt.35 renamed II./Pz.Rgt.35 on 8Jan44 Rgt.Stab re-created on 18May44 II./Pz.Rgt.35 renamed I./Pz.Rgt.35 on 26May44 7.Kp. disbanded, 8.Kp. outfitted with Jagdpz.IV from Pz.Jg.Abt.49 in Nov44 Left Panzers behind in Kurland, I./Pz.Rgt.35 reequipped with 2 Kp. with Pz.IV and 8.Kp. with StuG, and II./Pz.Rgt.35 reequipped with 3 Kp. with Panther and the 3.Kp. with Jagdpanthers in Jan45
Panzer-Regiment 36	10Nov38	Created with two Abt. each with four Kp. and assigned to 4.Pz.Div. Activated with two Abt. each with two l.Kp. and one l.Kp.a on 28Aug39 Transferred to 14.Pz.Div. on 11Oct40 II./Pz.Rgt.36 renamed to Pz.Abt.60 on 4Jan42 II./Pz.Rgt.36 from Pz.Abt.60 on 1May42

Panzer-Regiment	Created	Remarks
	17Feb43	III./Pz.Rgt.36 from II./Pz.Rgt.7 on 2Jun42 Surrendered Stalingrad in Feb43 Re-created with two Abteilungen each with four Kompanien III./Pz.Rgt.36 created with four Kp. on 25Apr43 I./Pz.Rgt.36 converted to Panther Abt. on 12Jul43 III./Pz.Rgt.36 as a Pz.StuG Abt. with two StuG Kp. and two m.Kp. on 24Jul43
Panzer-Regiment 39	1Oct40	Created for 17.Pz.Div. with two Abt. each with two l.Kp. and one m.Kp. I./Pz.Lehr Rgt. renamed III./Pz.Rgt.39 on 1Jun41 III./Pz.Rgt.39 renamed I./Pz.Lehr Rgt. which returned to Germany on 16Aug41 I./Pz.Rgt.39 renamed Pz.Abt.129 on 19Jun42 Rgt.Stab and I./Pz.Rgt.39 re-created on 27Nov44 I./Pz.Rgt.39 with three Panther Kp. assigned to Pz.Brig.103 on 22Jan45 I./Pz.Rgt.39 with two Kp. ordered on 6Feb45 to join 17.Pz.Div. I./Pz.Rgt.39 assigned to 17.Pz.Div. on 9Mar45
Panzer-Regiment 69	3Jan44	As Rgt.Stab for units in Italy from Rgt.Stab/Pz.Rgt.FHH Renamed Pz.Rgt.Stab 116 for 116.Pz.Div. on 5May44
Panzer-Regiment 100	22Dec41	I./Pz.Rgt.100 renamed from Pz.Abt.100 I./Pz.Rgt.100 renamed Pz.Abt.GD on 5Feb42
	8Dec42	Rgt.Stab from renamed Stab Pz.Brig.100 II./Pz.Rgt.100 with three Kompanien created from Pz.Kp.81, Pz.Kp.Paris and elements from Pz.Ers.Abt.100 on 8Jan43 I./Pz.Rgt.100 with three Kompanien created from 2.Kp. and Stab Pz.Abt.223 and elements from Pz.Ers.Abt.100 on 10Jan43 Added 4. and 8.Kompanien, 8.m.Kp. from Pz.Kp.100 on 15Jul43 Assigned to 21.Pz.Div.(neu) on 15Jul43 Renamed Pz.Rgt.22 on 20May44
Panzer-Regiment 101	25Jan45	Orders to create Pz.Rgt.101 with a I.Abt. for the Fuehrer-Grenadier-Division Orders on 16Feb45 to form I/Pz.Rgt.101 with two Panther and two Pz.IV Kp. from renamed III./Fuehrer-Gren.Brig. Orders on 2Mar45 to rename Pz.Rgt.Stab to Stab Fuehrer-Pz.Rgt.2
Panzer-Regiment 102	25Jan45	Orders to create Stab Pz.Rgt.102 for the Fuehrer-Begleit-Division with the II./Pz.Rgt.GD as the II./Pz.Rgt.102 Orders on 2Mar45 to rename II.Abt/Pz.Rgt.GD to II./Fuehrer-Pz.Rgt.1
Panzer-Regiment 116	1May44	II./Pz.Rgt.116 with four Kp. from Res.Pz.Abt.1 of 179.Res.Pz.Div. Rgt.Stab from renamed Stab Pz.Rgt.69 on 5May44 Pz.Abt.116 renamed I./Pz.Rgt.116 on 5May44 Renamed Pz.Rgt.16 on 23May44

Panzer-Regiment	Created	Remarks
Panzer-Regiment 118	30Mar45	Ordered to be created with the I.Abt. with four Kp. from Pz.Abt.Schlesien and the II.Abt. as a Pz.Gren.Btl. for the re-created 18.Pz.Gren.Div.
Panzer-Lehr-Regiment 130	4Jan43	Created as Rgt.Stab and assigned to Panzer-Lehr-Division I./Pz.Lehr-Rgt. renamed II./Pz.Lehr-Rgt. I./Pz.Rgt.6 assigned as Panther-Abt. to Pz.Lehr-Rgt. in Jan44 I./Pz.Rgt.130 created as Panther Abt. with four Kp. on 7Aug44 I./Pz.Rgt.130 assigned to Pz.Brig.113 in Sep44 I./Pz.Rgt.130 returned to refit in Sep44 II./Pz.Rgt.130 rebuilt with two Panther Kp. and two Pz.IV Kp. in Oct44 I./Pz.Rgt.130 renamed I./Pz.Rgt.6 and vise verse on 8Nov44
Panzer-Regiment 201	16Dec40	Created with two Abt. each with three Kp. with French Beute-Pz. II./Pz.Rgt.201 with 4. and 6.Kp. renamed to Pz.Abt.211 on 7Mar41 II./Pz.Rgt.201 from renamed Pz.Abt.301 on 22Mar41 Created a 7.s.Kp. on 1Apr41 7.s.Kp. transferred to Pz.Abt.(F)102 on 4Jun41 Created 7.Kp./Pz.Rgt.201 on 1Aug41 Assigned to 23.Pz.Div. effective 11Dec41 Order to convert from French to German Pz.Kpfw. for 23.Pz.Div. on 23Dec41 Created III./Pz.Rgt.201 on 2Feb42 Disbanded III./Pz.Rgt.201 on 5Mar43 II./Pz.Rgt.201 began converting to Panthers in Apr43 Renamed to Pz.Rgt.23 in Aug43
Panzer-Regiment 202	10Feb41	Created with two Abt. each with three Kp. with French Beute-Pz. Created a 7.s.Kp. on 1Apr41 7.s.Kp. transferred to Pz.Abt.(F)102 on 4Jun41 I./Pz.Rgt.201 sent to Yugoslavia on 18Sep41 Created III./Pz.Rgt.202 from elements of Pz.Rgt.11 on 10Jul42 II./Pz.Rgt.202 switched with and renamed Pz.Abt.190 on 4Sep42 Assigned to 26.Pz.Div. on 15Sep42 I./Pz.Rgt.202 with three Kp. renamed Pz.Abt.202 on 5Jan43 Renamed to Pz.Rgt.26, II./Pz.Rgt.202 renamed II./Pz.Rgt.26, III./Pz.Rgt.202 renamed I./Pz.Rgt.26 on 5Jan43
Panzer-Regiment 203	5Jul41	Created with two Abt. each with three Kp. with French Beute-Pz. Converted to German Pz.Kpfw. and sent to Eastern Front in Dec41 II./Pz.Rgt.203 renamed to II./Pz.Rgt.GD on 13Jan43 I./Pz.Rgt.203 renamed to II./Pz.Rgt.1 on 27Jan43
Panzer-Regiment 204	5Jul41	Created with two Abt. each with three Kp. with French Beute-Pz. Assigned to 22.Pz.Div. on 25Sep41 and converted to German Pz.Kpfw. Created III./Pz.Rgt.204 with two I.Kp. and one m.Kp. on 12Apr42 III./Pz.Rgt.204 renamed to Pz.Abt.127 on 1Oct42 Ordered disbanded and remnants incorporated into Pz.Rgt.11 on 10Feb43 Disbanded in Mar43

APPENDICES

Panzer-Regiment	Created	Remarks
Panzer-Regiment Brandenburg	14Dec44	Orders to create Pz.Rgt.Brandenburg for Pz.Gren.Div.Brandenburg I./Pz.Rgt.26 renamed I./Pz.Rgt.Brandenburg on 18Jan45 Orders on 1Feb45 to create II./Pz.Rgt.Brandenburg from Pz.Abt.z.b.V.12 I./Pz.Rgt.Brandenburg assigned to Pz.Gren.Div.Kurmark on 2Feb45
Panzer-Regiment Feldherrnhalle	Dec43	Ordered to be created for Pz.Gr.Div.FHH. Pz.Abt.FHH renamed I./Pz.Rgt.FHH Renamed Pz.Rgt.69 Stab on 3Jan44. I./Pz.Rgt.FHH renamed Pz.Abt.FHH
	27Nov44	Ordered to be created for Pz.Div.FHH. Pz.Abt.FHH renamed II./Pz.Rgt.FHH Wiped out on Eastern Front in Jan45
	10Mar45	Ordered to be created with the I.Abt. from Pz.Abt.208 and the II.Abt. as a Pz.Gren.Btl.
Panzer-Regiment Grossdeutschland	13Jan43	II./Pz.Rgt.GD from renamed II./Pz.Rgt.203 converted to 3 m.Kp. 13.s.Kp. created from 3.Kp./Pz.Rgt.203 on 13Jan43 Pz.Abt.GD renamed to I./Pz.Rgt.GD on 1Mar43 Created III.s./Pz.Rgt.GD from 13.s.Pz.Kp./Pz.Rgt.GD, 3./s.Pz.Abt.501, and 3./s.Pz.Abt.504 on 1Jul43 I./Pz.Rgt.GD converted to Panther Abt. with four Kp. on 15Oct43 I./Pz.Rgt.GD assigned to 116.Pz.Div. on 6May44 I./Pz.Rgt.GD assigned to 6.Pz.Div. in Jun44 II./Pz.Rgt.GD assigned to Fhr.Begl.Brig. in Nov44 III.s./Pz.Rgt.GD renamed to s.Pz.Abt.GD on 13Dec44 I./Pz.Rgt.GD under Pz.Gren.Div.GD on 13Dec44 II./Pz.Rgt.GD renamed II./Pz.Rgt.102 on 2Mar45

Panzer-Abteilung	Created	Remarks
Panzer-Abteilung 5	25Aug43	Created as Pz.StuG Abt. with three Kp. Assigned to 20.Pz.Gren.Div. on 21Sep43 Assigned to 25.Pz.Gren.Div. on 11Oct43
	5Nov44	Pz.Abt.2107 renamed to Pz.Abt.5 in 25.Pz.Gren.Div.
Panzer-Abteilung 7	25Aug43	Created as Pz.StuG Abt. with three Kp. Assigned to 10.Pz.Gren.Div. on 21Sep43 4./Pz.Abt.7 from Pz.Jg.Kp.2110 with 9 Pz.IV/70(V) on 1Mar45
Panzer-Abteilung 8	25Aug43	Created as Pz.StuG Abt. with three Kp. Assigned to 25.Pz.Gren.Div. on 21Sep43 Assigned to 20.Pz.Gren.Div. on 27Oct43 Joined 20.Pz.Gren.Div. at front in Jun44
Panzer-Abteilung z.b.V.12	15Apr44	Created from Pz.Kp.z.b.V.12 and expanded to three Kp. Ordered to create II./Pz.Rgt.Brandenburg from Pz.Abt.z.b.V.12 on 1Feb45
Armee Panzer-Abteilung 16 (Beute)	Mar45	Created in the field by H.Gr.Kurland from a Beute-Panzer-Kp. that had been formed in 1944

Panzer-Abteilung	Created	Remarks
Panzer-Abteilung 18	15May42	II./Pz.Rgt.18 renamed Pz.Abt.18 Pz.Abt.18 used to form s.Pz.Abt.504 on 18Nov43
Panzer-Abteilung 21	26Apr43	III./Pz.Rgt.21 with four Kp. renamed Pz.Abt.21 Pz.Abt.21 renamed I./Pz.Rgt.21 on 8Nov44
Panzer-Abteilung 33	1Jul38	Created from österr.Pz.Wg.Batl. and assigned to 4.lei.Div. Activated with three l.Kp.(verl.) on 1Sep39 Renamed to II./Pz.Abt.33 on 2Feb40
Panzer-Abteilung z.b.V.40	8Mar40	Created as independent Heerestruppen with three l.Kp. 4.Kp./Pz.Abt.z.b.V.40 formed from two independent platoons in Jul40 4.Kp. incorporated into new 3.Kp. on 7Nov40 Renamed to II./Pz.Rgt.9 on 5Dec42
Panzer-Abteilung 44	2Feb45	Created for Pz.Div.Holstein with three Pz.IV Kp. and one Pz.Jaeg.Kp.(Sf.)
Panzer-Abteilung 51	9Jan43	Created from II./Pz.Rgt.33 Renamed to II./Pz.Rgt.33 on 4Jan44
Panzer-Abteilung 51	5Feb45	Ordered to be created for Pz.Gren.Div.Kurmark with three Jagdpz.38 Kp. and one Pz.IV/70 Kp.
Panzer-Abteilung 52	6Feb43	Created from I./Pz.Rgt.15 Renamed to I./Pz.Rgt.15 on 24Aug43
Panzer-Abteilung 55	21Feb45	Res.Pz.Abt.5 renamed Pz.Abt.55 and assigned to 233.Pz.Div.
Panzer-Abteilung 60	4Jan42	Created from II./Pz.Rgt.36 Renamed to II./Pz.Rgt.36 on 1May42
Panzer-Abteilung 65	12Oct37	Created with four Kp. and assigned to 1.lei.Div. Activated with two l.Kp. and one m.Kp. on 1Aug39 Pz.Abt.65 disbanded and used to form the 4. and 8.Kp./Pz.Rgt.11 on 6Mar42
Panzer-Abteilung 66	10Nov38	Created with four l.Kp. and assigned to the 2.lei.Div. Activated with three l.Kp.(verl.) on 25Aug39 Attached to Pz.Rgt.25 and reorganized with two l.Kp. and one m.Kp. on 1Nov39 Renamed III./Pz.Rgt.25 on 19Feb41
Panzer-Abteilung z.b.V.66	30May42	Created with two Kompanien 1.Kp./Pz.Abt.z.b.V.66 renamed 8.Kp./Pz.Rgt.29 on 2Oct42 2.Kp./Pz.Abt.z.b.V.66 incorporated into s.Ski.Btl. on 18Mar44
Panzer-Abteilung 67	10Nov38	Created with 4 l.Kp. and assigned to the 3.lei.Div. Activated with 3 l.Kp.(verl.) on 26Aug39 Renamed III./Pz.Rgt.10 on 1Jan41

APPENDICES

Panzer-Abteilung	Created	Remarks
Panzer-Abteilung (F) 100	5Mar40	Created as a Flammpanzer Abt. with three Kp. Ordered to transfer remaining Pz.II and III to 18.Pz.Div. and return to Germany for refitting on 12Nov41 Renamed to I./Pz.Rgt.100 on 22Dec41 Renamed to Pz.Abt.GD on 5Feb42
Panzer-Abteilung (F) 101	4May40	Created as a Flammpanzer Abt. with three Kp. Disbanded and used to create Pz.Rgt.24 on 8Dec41
Panzer-Abteilung (F) 102	20Jun41	Created as a Beute-Flammpanzer Abt. with two Kp. from the 7.s.Kp. of Pz.Rgt.201 and 202 Disbanded on 8Aug41
Panzer-Abteilung 103	5Apr42 11Feb43	Created from III./Pz.Rgt.18 with two l.Kp. and one m.Kp. for the 3.Inf.Div.(mot) Surrendered at Stalingrad in Feb43 Re-created for 3.Inf.Div.(mot) with four Kp. Converted to Pz.StuG Abt. with three Kp. on 21Jul43
Panzer-Abteilung 115	20Sep43	Pz.Abt.215 with three Kp. renamed Pz.Abt.115
Panzer-Abteilung 116	19Jun42 28Mar43	Created from I./Pz.Rgt.1 with two l.Kp. and one m.Kp. for the 16.Inf.Div.(mot) Wiped out on Eastern Front in Feb43 Re-created with three Kp. Renamed I./Pz.Rgt.116 on 5May44
Panzer-Abteilung 118	23Sep43 16Nov44	Created with three StuG Kp. Re-created for 18.Pz.Gr.Div. with three StuG Kp.
Panzer-Abteilung 127	1Oct42	Created from III./Pz.Rgt.204 with three l.Kp. and one m.Kp. for the 27.Pz.Div. Orders for remnants to be assimilated into 7.Pz.Div. on 15Feb43 Used to create III./Pz.Rgt.24 on 5Apr43
Panzer-Abteilung 129	19Jun42 Feb43 11Feb43	Created from I./Pz.Rgt.39 with three l.Kp. and one m.Kp. for the 29.Inf.Div.(mot) Wiped out on Eastern Front in Feb43 Re-created with four Kp. Converted to three Pz.StuG Kp. on 21Jul43 Converted to Pz.Kpfw.III and Pz.Kpfw.IV in all three Kp. in Mar44
Panzer-Abteilung 138	30Nov42	Created with three m.Kp. as independent Heerestruppen Renamed to II./Pz.Rgt.27 and assigned to 19.Pz.Div. on 27Mar43
Panzer-Abteilung 160	15Jun42 17Feb43	Created from I./Pz.Rgt.18 with three Kp. for 60.Inf.Div.(mot) Wiped out on Eastern Front in Jan43 Re-created with four Kp. Renamed to Pz.Abt.FHH on 20Jun43
Panzer-Abteilung 190	1Aug42	Created for 90.leichte Division with three l.Kp. and one m.Kp. Pz.Abt.190 renamed to II./Pz.Rgt.202 and vise versa on 4Sep42 Pz.Abt.190 renamed to II./Pz.Rgt.5 by 6Feb43

Panzer-Abteilung	Created	Remarks
	6Jul43	Re-created from Pz.Abt.Sardinien with 1. and 2.Kp., expanded to three Kp., and assigned to 90.Pz.Gren.Div. Converted to StuG IV in Feb44
Panzer-Abteilung 202	5Jan43	Pz.Abt.202 with three Beutepanzer-Kp. renamed from I./Pz.Rgt.202 Ordered to convert to Ital.Pz.Kpfw. on 14Feb44
Panzer-Abteilung 205	29Nov43	Created with two Beutepanzer-Kp. in the West Ordered disbanded and used to create Pz.Jg.Abt.14 on 26Dec44
Panzer-Abteilung 206	29Nov43	Created with two Beutepanzer-Kp. in the West Disbanded 14Jul44
Panzer-Abteilung 208	1Apr44	Created by consolidating three Kp.; 1./Pz.Abt.208 from 2.Pz.Sich.Kp. 2./Pz.Abt.208 from 3.Pz.Sich.Kp., and 3./Pz.Abt.208 from Pz.Sich.Kp.35 Renamed I./Pz.Rgt.FHH on 10Mar45
Panzer-Abteilung 211	7Mar41	Created Pz.Abt.Wolf with two Kp. from II./Pz.Rgt.201 Pz.Abt.Wolf renamed Pz.Abt.211 on 24Mar41
Panzer-Abteilung 212	12Jul41	Created with two Kp. for defense of Crete. One Kp. from 5./Pz.Rgt.31, the second Kp. from six Beutepz.-Zuege Most of personnel transferred to the mainland in early Oct44 Ordered on 11Dec44 to outfit with Pz.IIIs from Pz.Abt.208 Formed Pz.Abt.Kreta on Crete with one Pz.Kp. with Panzers left behind by Pz.Abt.212 on 14Jan45
Panzer-Abteilung 213	17Nov41	Created with two schwere Beutepanzer-Kp.
Panzer-Abteilung 214	8Jan42	Created as independent Heerestruppen with three Kp. Expanded to four Kp. by creation of 4.m.Kp. on 3Mar42 Assigned to 25.Pz.Div. on 1Apr42 Renamed to I./Pz.Rgt.9 on 6Dec42
Panzer-Abteilung 215	13Apr43	Created as independent Heerestruppen with three m.Kp. Assigned to 15.Pz.Gr.Div. and 2./s.Pz.Abt.504 added as a 4.s.Kp. on 6Jul43 Created a Pz.StuG Kp. in Jul43 Renamed to Pz.Abt.115 on 30Sep43
Sturmpanzer-Abteilung 216	19Apr43	Created as independent Heerestruppen with three Sturmpz.Kp. 4./Sturmpz.Abt.216 created on 26Feb44 Used 4./Sturmpz.Abt.216 to create Sturmpz.Abt.219 on 30Sep44
Sturmpanzer-Abteilung 217	7Apr44	Created as independent Heerestruppen with three Sturmpz.Kp.
Sturmpanzer-Abteilung 218	4Aug44	Ordered to be created by 20Aug44 using StuG Brig.914 Sturmpz.Kp.z.b.V.218 created on 13Aug44 2./Sturmpz.Abt.218 created on 16Aug44
	6Jan45	Orders to create Sturmpz.Abt.218 with Stab and three Kp. utilizing the 1. and 2./Sturmpz.Abt.218

APPENDICES

Panzer-Abteilung	Created	Remarks
Sturmpanzer-Abteilung 219	30Sep44	Created as independent Heerestruppen using StuG Brig.237 and the 4./Sturmpz.Abt.216
Panzer-Abteilung 223	15Jul42	Created Abteilung-Stab Created 2.Kp./Pz.Abt.223 from 2.Kp./Pz.Rgt.202 on 15Jul42 Beute Pz.Kp.223 renamed 1.Kp./Pz.Abt.223 on 24Jun42 Stab and 2.Kp./Pz.Abt.223 used to create I./Pz.Rgt.100 on 10Jan43 Orders on 2Jan44 for 1./Pz.Abt.223 to be disbanded and integrated into 13.Pz.Div.
Panzer-Abteilung 300	15Sep41	Created from Minen-Räum Abt.1 Renamed to Pz.Abt.300(F.L.) and expanded by a third Kp. on 9Feb42 Renamed to Pz.Abt.301 on 9Sep42
Panzer-Abteilung 301	27Jan41	Created with three Beutepanzer-Kp. as independent Heerestruppen Renamed to II./Pz.Rgt.201 on 22Mar41
Panzer-Abteilung (Fkl) 301	9Sep42	Renamed from Pz.Abt.(F.L.) 300 3.Kp./Pz.Abt.302 transferred and renamed 2.Kp./Pz.Abt.301 on 20Oct42 Previous 2.Kp./Pz.Abt.301 transferred and renamed 3.Kp./Pz.Abt.302 on 1Nov42 Absorbed Pz.Abt.(Fkl) 302 and expanded into four Kp. on 25Jan43 1./Pz.Abt.(Fkl) 301 renamed Pz.Kp.(Fkl) 315 on 6Jul43 Pz.Kp.(Fkl) 312 renamed 1/Pz.Abt.(Fkl) 301 on 7Apr44 Ordered to convert to Tigers on 19Aug44 Renamed Panzer-Abteilung (Tiger/Fkl) 301 on 2Sep44 4./Pz.Abt.(Fkl) 301 renamed 3./Pz.Abt.(Fkl) 303 on 2Jan45
Panzer-Abteilung (Fkl) 302	15Oct42	Created from disbanded III./Pz.Rgt.10 with three Kp. 3.Kp./Pz.Abt.302 transferred and renamded 2.Kp./Pz.Abt.301 on 20Oct42 Previous 2.Kp./Pz.Abt.301 transferred and renamed 3.Kp./Pz.Abt.302 on 1Nov42 Stab disbanded with Kp. incorporated into Pz.Abt.301 on 25Jan43
	22Jun44	Order to re-create Pz.Abt.(Fkl) 302 using 4./Pz.Abt.(Fkl) 301, Pz.Kp.(Fkl) 315, and Pz.Kp.(Fkl) 317 as the 1., 2., and 3.Kp. 4./Pz.Abt.(Fkl) 301 replaced by Pz.Kp.(Fkl) 316 on 2Jul44 Pz.Kp.(Fkl) 311 renamed 4./Pz.Abt.(Fkl) 302 on 15Aug44
Panzer-Abteilung 303	2Jan45	Orders to create from 4./Pz.Abt.(Fkl) 301, 4./Pz.Abt.(Fkl) 302 and Pz.Kp.(Fkl) 319. Orders on 16Feb45 to create Pz.Abt.303 with three StuG Kp. without Funklenk equipment from Pz.Abt.(Fkl) 303 Orders on 21Feb45 to rename to Pz.Abt.Doeberitz and orders on 22Feb45 to rename to Pz.Abt.Schlesien
schwere Panzer-Abteilung 424	27Nov44	From renamed s.H.Pz.Abt.501 Disbanded to create s.Pz.Jg.Abt.512 on 11Feb45

PANZERTRUPPEN • 1943-1945

Panzer-Abteilung	Created	Remarks
schwere Panzer-Abteilung 501	10May42	Created Stab for s.Pz.Abt.501, s.Pz.Kp.501 renamed to 1./s.Pz.Abt., and s.Pz.Kp.502 renamed to 2./s.Pz.Abt. Incorporated into Pz.Rgt.7 as the III.Abt. on 26Feb43 Created 3./s.Pz.Abt.501 on 6Mar43 Stab, 1. and 2.Kp. surrendered in Tunisia in May43 3./s.Pz.Abt.501 renamed to 10./Pz.Rgt.GD on 1Jul43
	9Sep43	Re-created with three s.Kp. using remnants of original Renamed to s.Pz.Abt.424 on 27Nov44
schwere Panzer-Abteilung 502	25May42	Created as independent Heerestruppen with two s.Kp. 2./s.Pz.Abt.502 attached to s.Pz.Abt.503 on 24Dec42 2./s.Pz.Abt.502 renamed to 3./s.Pz.Abt.503 on 10Feb43 Created new 2. and 3.s.Kp. on 1Apr43 Renamed to s.Pz.Abt.511 on 5Jan45
schwere Panzer-Abteilung 503	5May42	Created as independent Heerestruppen with two s.Kp. 2./s.Pz.Abt.502 attached on 24Dec42 2./s.Pz.Abt.502 renamed to 3./s.Pz.Abt.503 on 10Feb43 Renamed to s.Pz.Abt.FHH on 21Dec44
schwere Panzer-Abteilung 504	8Jan43	Created as independent Heerestruppen with two s.Kp. Expanded by creation of 3.s.Kp. on 20Mar43 2./s.Pz.Abt.504 attached to Pz.Abt.215 on 13Apr43 Stab and 1.Kp. surrendered in Tunisia in May43 3./s.Pz.Abt.504 renamed to 11./Pz.Rgt.GD on 22Jun43 2./s.Pz.Abt.504 decimated in Sicily in Jul43
	18Nov43	Re-created from Pz.Abt.18 as independent Heerestruppen with three s.Kp. Pz.Kp.(Fkl) 314 incorporated into 3.s.Kp. on 10Mar44
schwere Panzer-Abteilung 505	12Feb43	Created as independent Heerestruppen with two s.Kp. Expanded by creation of 3.s.Kp on 3Apr43
schwere Panzer-Abteilung 506	20Jul43	Created from III./Pz.Rgt.33 as independent Heerestruppen with three s.Kp. s.Pz.Kp.Hummel renamed to 4.s.Kp./s.Pz.Abt.506 on 8Dec44
schwere Panzer-Abteilung 507	23Sep43	Created from I./Pz.Rgt.4 as independent Heerestruppen with three s.Kp. Ordered on 17Apr45 to convert to a Pz.Jaeg.Abt. and renamed Pz.Abt.507
schwere Panzer-Abteilung 508	25Sep43	Created from remnants of Pz.Rgt.8 as independent Heerestruppen with three s.Kp. Absorbed Tiger Gruppe Schwebbach (formerly Tiger Gruppe Meyer) in Mar44 Pz.Kp.(Fkl) 313 incorporated as 3.s.Kp. on 19Mar44
schwere Panzer-Abteilung 509	9Sep43	Created as independent Heerestruppen with three s.Kp.
schwere Panzer-Abteilung 510	6Jun44	Created as independent Heerestruppen with three s.Kp.
schwere Panzer-Abteilung 511	5Jan45	From renamed s.H.Pz.Abt.502

APPENDICES

Panzer-Abteilung	Created	Remarks
Panzer Verband 700	28Oct42	Created with three l.Kp. at the front with extra Pz.Kpfw.38(t) from 22.Pz.Div. Created 4.m.Kp. in Oct42 Ordered disbanded on 1Feb43, remnants incorporated into Pz.Rgt.35
Panzer-Abteilung 2101	21Jul44	Created for 101.Pz.Brig. with three Panther Kp. and a Jagdpz.Kp. Renamed to II./Pz.Rgt.21 in 20.Pz.Div. on 29Oct44
Panzer-Abteilung 2102	21Jul44	Created for 102.Pz.Brig. with three Panther Kp. and a Jagdpz.Kp. from elements of 233.Res.Pz.Div. Disbanded and equipment turned over to Pz.Rgt.25 in Nov44
Panzer-Abteilung 2103	21Jul44	Created for 103.Pz.Brig. with three Panther Kp. and a Jagdpz.Kp. from elements of Pz.Rgt.9 Disbanded and equipment turned over to Pz.Rgt.31 on 8Nov44
Panzer-Abteilung 2104	21Jul44	Created for 104.Pz.Brig. with three Panther Kp. and a Jagdpz.Kp. from elements of Pz.Rgt.9 Renamed to I./Pz.Rgt.9 in 25.Pz.Div. on 5Nov44
Panzer-Abteilung 2105	28Jul44	Created for 105.Pz.Brig. with three Panther Kp. and a Jagdpz.Kp. from remnants of 18.Pz.Gren.Div. Remaining equipment absorbed into II./Pz.Rgt.33 on 26Sep44 Personnel used to recreate elements of II./Pz.Rgt.10 on 10Dec44
Panzer-Abteilung 2106	28Jul44	Created for 106.Pz.Brig. with three Panther Kp. and a Jagdpz.Kp. from remnants of Pz.Gren.Div.FHH
Panzer-Abteilung 2107	28Jul44	Created for 107.Pz.Brig. with three Panther Kp. and a Jagdpz.Kp. from remnants of 25.Pz.Gren.Div. Renamed to Pz.Abt.5 in 25.Pz.Gren.Div. on 5Nov44
Panzer-Abteilung 2108	2Aug44	Created for 108.Pz.Brig. with three Panther Kp. and a Jagdpz.Kp. from remnants of 25.Pz.Gren.Div. Disbanded and incorporated into 116.Pz.Div. on 22Oct44
Panzer-Abteilung 2109	22Jul44	Created for 109.Pz.Brig. with three Panther Kp. and a Jagdpz.Kp. Renamed and incorporated into Pz.Gr.Div.FHH as Pz.Abt.FHH in Oct44
Panzer-Abteilung 2110	22Jul44	Created for 110.Pz.Brig. with three Panther Kp. and a Jagdpz.Kp. Incorporated into Pz.Rgt.4 of the 13.Pz.Div. in Nov44
Panzer-Abteilung 2111	1Sep44	Created for 111.Pz.Brig. with three Panther Kp. Equipment turned over to Pz.Rgt.15 in Sep44 Disbanded and remnants used to create II./Pz.Rgt.9 on 12Nov44
Panzer-Abteilung 2112	1Sep44	Created for 112.Pz.Brig. with three Panther Kp. Disbanded and equipment turned over to Pz.Rgt.22 on 27Sep44

PANZERTRUPPEN • 1943-1945

Panzer-Abteilung	Created	Remarks
Panzer-Abteilung 2113	1Sep44	Created for 113.Pz.Brig. with three Panther Kp. Equipment turned over to Pz.Abt.115 in Sep44 Renamed to II./Pz.Rgt.10 on 12Dec44
Beute-Panzer-Abteilung z.b.V. Afrika	12Feb42	Created in the field as a Beute-Panzer-Abteilung to be outfitted with captured British tanks Converted to the 2.Kp. of the Kampfstaffel for the commander of Pz.AOK Afrika effective 1Apr42
Panzer-Abteilung A	25Jul40	Created as a Tauchpanzer Abt. with three Kp. from elements of Pz.Rgt.1 and 2 Renamed to I./Pz.Rgt.18 on 6Dec40
Panzer-Abteilung B	24Jul40	Created as a Tauchpanzer Abt. with three Kp. from elements of Pz.Rgt.3 and 4 Renamed to I./Pz.Rgt.18 on 1Dec40
Panzer-Abteilung C	13Jul40	Created as Versuchstab U.K. Renamed to Pz.Abt.C as a Tauchpanzer Abt. with three Kp. on 24Jul40 Renamed to II./Pz.Rgt.28 on 6Dec40
Panzer-Abteilung D	23Jul40	Created as a Tauchpanzer Abt. with three Kp. Renamed to I./Pz.Rgt.28 on 6Dec40
III./Fuehrer Grenadier Brigade	1Sep44	Created with three Panther Kp. and a Jagdpz.Kp. Renamed I./Pz.Rgt.101 on 16Feb45
Panzer-Abteilung Doeberitz	21Feb45	Orders to create from renamed Pz.Abt.303 with three Kp. Renamed Pz.Abt.Schlesien on 22Feb45
Panzer-Abteilung Feldherrnhalle	20Jun43	Pz.Abt.160 renamed Pz.Abt.FHH Reorganized as a gem.Pz.Abt. with two StuG and two Pz.IV Kp. on 6Nov43 Renamed I./Pz.Rgt.FHH in Dec43 Renamed Pz.Abt.FHH on 3Jan44 Wiped out on Eastern Front in Jul44
	Oct44	Re-created from Pz.Abt.2109 Renamed II./Pz.Rgt.FHH on 27Nov44
s.Panzer-Abteilung Feldherrnhalle	21Dec44	s.Pz.Abt.503 renamed s.Pz.Abt.FHH
Panzer-Abteilung Grossdeutschland	5Feb42	Created from I./Pz.Rgt.100 with 3 m.Kp. Renamed to I./Pz.Rgt.GD on 1Mar43
s.Panzer-Abteilung Grossdeutschland	13Dec44	III.s./Pz.Rgt.GD renamed to s.Pz.Abt.GD
Panzer-Abteilung Jueterbog	20Feb45	Orders to create Pz.Abt.Jueterbog with three Kp. for Pz.Div.Jueterbog Pz.Abt.Jueterbog absorbed into Pz.Rgt.2 on 4Mar45
Panzer-Abteilung Kreta	14Jan45	Formed on Crete with one Pz.Kp. with Panzers left behind by Pz.Abt.212

APPENDICES

Panzer-Abteilung	Created	Remarks
Panzer-Abteilung Kummersdorf	16Feb45	Orders to create Pz.Abt.Kummersdorf(bo) with three Kp. Renamed Pz.Abt.Kummersdorf on 17Feb45 Ordered on 5Mar45 to join Pz.Div.Muencheberg Ordered to turn over all Panzers to I./Pz.Abt.29 and 3.Kp./Pz.Abt.Kummersdorf renamed 3./Pz.Rgt.29 on 12Mar45
Panzer-Abteilung Montfort	16Dec41	Created with one Kp each from Pz.Rgt.2, 4 and 36 Attached to A.O.K.6 on 5Jan42 Integrated into Pz.Rgt.6 in Apr42
Panzer-Abteilung Norwegen	6Sep43	I./Pz.Rgt.9 renamed to Pz.Abt.Norwegen
Panzer-Abteilung Potsdam	24Feb45	Orders to create with three Kp. Orders on 7Apr45 to transport one Kp. of Pz.Abt.Potsdam with Pz.Jaeg.Abt.Grossdeutschland to Pz.Div.Clausewitz
Panzer-Abteilung Putlos	17Apr45	Renamed from Kampfgruppe Putlos which had been ordered to join Pz.Div.Clausewitz on 13Apr45
Panzer-Abteilung Rhodos	22May43	Created for defense of Rhodes with 1.Kp. from StuG Battr.92 2.Kp. newly created as a m.Kp. with 15 Pz.IV (one as a reserve)
Panzer-Abteilung Sardinien	May43	Created with two Kp. for defense of Sardinia Renamed Pz.Abt.190 on 6Jul43
Panzer-Abteilung Schlesien	22Feb45	Pz.Abt.Doeberitz renamed Pz.Abt.Schlesien 4./Pz.Abt.Schlesien created in Mar45
Panzer-Abteilung Stahnsdorf 1	1Feb45	Orders to create with one Panther Kp. and two StuG Kp. Orders on 15Feb45 to transfer the Panther Kp. to Pz.Abt.Kummersdorf
Panzer-Abteilung Stahnsdorf 2	1Feb45	Orders to create with one Panther Kp. and two StuG Kp.
Panzer-Lehr-Abteilung	12Oct37	Created as independent unit Renamed to I./Pz.Lehr Rgt. on 15Apr39 Renamed to verst.Pz.Lehr Abt. and assigned as III./Pz.Rgt.5 to the 3.Pz.Div. on 1Aug39 Renamed to I./Pz.Rgt.Conze on 1Nov39 Renamed to I./Pz.Rgt.33 on 2Feb40

Panzer-Kompanie	Created	Remarks
2.Panzer-Sicherungs-Kompanie	28Aug43	Created as Pz.Sich.Kp. for Italy Renamed 1./Pz.Abt.208 on 1Apr44
3.Panzer-Sicherungs-Kompanie	9Sep43	Created as Pz.Sich.Kp. for Italy Renamed 2./Pz.Abt.208 on 1Apr44
Panzer-Kompanie z.b.V.12	22Jun41	Created as Pz.Kp.Führ.Gruppe z.b.V.12 for Beutepanzer-Zuege Reorganized and renamed Pz.Kp.z.b.V.12 on 1Apr42 Renamed to Pz.Abt.z.b.V.12 on 15Apr44

PANZERTRUPPEN • 1943-1945

Panzer-Kompanie	Created	Remarks
Panzer-Sicherungs-Kompanie 35	25Aug43	Created as Pz.Einsatz-Kp.35 as a Pz.Sicherungs-Kp. for Italy Renamed Pz.Sich.Kp.35 on 25Jan44 Renamed 3./Pz.Abt.208 on 1Apr44
Panzer-Kompanie 40	22Nov42	Pz.Sich.Kp.z.b.V. created from elements of Pz.Abt.z.b.V.40 for 20.Armee (3 Pz.III and 15 Pz.I) Renamed Pz.Kp.40 on 21Jan43 Disbanded Pz.Kp.40 on 15Jul43
Panzer-Kompanie 81	26Jun42	Created as a Beutepanzer-Kp. for the LXXXI.A.K. Elements used to create 5.Kp./Pz.Rgt.100 on 8Jan43
Panzer-Kompanie 100	2Jul42	from renamed Pz.Kp.Paris Renamed to 8.Kp./Pz.Rgt.100 on 15Jul43
Panzer-Kompanie 221	22Nov41	Created as the 3.Lehrgangs-Kp. of the Pz.Kpfw.-Lehrganges Krementschug Renamed to Pz.Kp.221 on 4Dec41 Ordered on 15Feb45 to be integrated into s.Kav.Abt.3
Beute Panzer-Kompanie 223	6Feb42	Created with three Beutepanzer-Zuegen Renamed 1./Pz.Abt.223 on 24Jun42
Panzer-Lehr-Kompanie 233	8Jan43	from one Kp. of Pz.Lehr-Rgt. ordered to Eastern Front Renamed 1./Pz.Rgt.GD on 4Mar43
Panzer-Kompanie (Fkl) 311	1Aug42	Created as 2.le.Pz.Kp.Z Renamed to 3./Pz.Abt.302 on 1Oct42 Renamed to 2./Pz.Abt.301 on 20Oct42 Renamed to Pz.Kp.(Fkl) 311 on 25Jan43 Renamed to 4./Pz.Abt.(Fkl) 302 on 15Aug44
Panzer-Kompanie (Fkl) 312	1Aug42	Created as 1.le.Pz.Kp.f Renamed to Pz.Kp.(Fkl) 312 on 25Jan43 Renamed to 1./Pz.Abt.(Fkl) 301 on 7Apr44
Panzer-Kompanie (Fkl) 313	25Jan43	From renamed 3./Pz.Abt.302 Pz.Kp.(Fkl) 313 incorporated into 3./s.Pz.Abt.508 on 19Feb44
Panzer-Kompanie (Fkl) 314	1Aug42	Created as 2.le.Pz.Kp.f Renamed to Pz.Kp.(Fkl) 314 on 25Jan43 Pz.Kp.(Fkl) 314 incorporated into 3./s.Pz.Abt.504 on 10Mar44
Panzer-Kompanie (Fkl) 315	6Jul43	From renamed 1./Pz.Abt.(Fkl) 301 Renamed to 2./Pz.Abt.(Fkl) 302 on 22Jun44
Panzer-Kompanie (Fkl) 316	15Aug43	Created as Pz.Kp.(Fkl) 316 Assigned to Pz.Lehr-Div. in Jan44 Renamed to 1./Pz.Abt.(Fkl) 302 on 2Jul44
Panzer-Kompanie (Fkl) 317	Jan44	Created as a Pz.Kp.(Fkl) Renamed to 3./Pz.Abt.(Fkl) 302 by orders dated 22Jun44

APPENDICES

Panzer-Kompanie	Created	Remarks
Panzer-Kompanie 318	22Nov41	Created by the Lehrgang for Pz.Kpfw.-Krementschug Assigned as Pz.Kp.318 to the 213.Sich.Div. from 4Dec41
Panzer-Kompanie (Fkl) 319	28Sep44	Created as a Pz.Kp.(Fkl) Renamed to 3./Pz.Abt.(Fkl) 303 on 15Jan45
Panzer-Flamm-Kompanie 351	10Dec44	Created with 10 Pz.Flamm-Wg.III
Panzer-Flamm-Kompanie 352	10Dec44	Created with 10 Flammpz.38
Panzer-Flamm-Kompanie 353	Dec44	Created with 10 Flammpz.38 Disbanded and incorporated into Pz.-Flamm-Kp.352 in Feb45
s.Panzer-Kompanie 501	16Feb42	Created as a s.Pz.Kp. Renamed to 1./s.Pz.Abt.501 on 10May42
s.Panzer-Kompanie 502	16Feb42	Created as a s.Pz.Kp. Renamed to 2./s.Pz.Abt.501 on 10May42
Sturm-Moerser-Kompanie 1000	13Aug44	Ordered to be created Transferred to Artillerie and renamed Sturm-Moerser-Batterie 1000 on 23Jan45
Sturm-Moerser-Kompanie 1001	23Sep44	Ordered to be created Transferred to Artillerie and renamed Sturm-Moerser-Batterie 1001 on 23Jan45
Sturm-Moerser-Kompanie 1002	22Oct44	Ordered to be created Transferred to Artillerie and renamed Sturm-Moerser-Batterie 1002 on 23Jan45
Panzer-Kompanie (bo) Berlin	22Jan45	Ordered to be created with immobile Panzers for defense of Berlin
Pz.Kp./Fuehrer-Begleit-Batallion	1Feb42	Created as a le.Pz.Kp. for the Fuehr.Begl.Btl. Sent to Eastern Front in Dec42
5./Fuehrer-Grenadier-Batallion	4Jul44 Dec44	Ordered to create a m.Kp. for Pz.Gr.Brig.v.Werthern Integrated into Fuehrer.Gren.Brig.
schwere Panzer-Kompanie Hummel	20Sep44	from renamed s.Pz.Kp.Einsatz Dunkirchen Renamed to 4.s.Kp./s.Pz.Abt.506 on 8Dec44
Panzer-Kompanie Kummersdorf	13Feb45	Orders to create from available Panzers at Versuchsstelle Kummersdorf Orders on 16Feb45 to be incorporated into Pz.Abt.Kummersdorf(bo)
Panzer-Kompanie Kummersdorf 2	2Apr45	Orders to create to defend Schweinfurt
Panzer-Kompanie Paris	8Jul41	Created as a Beutepz. Kp. Renamed to Pz.Kp.100 on 2Jul42

PANZERTRUPPEN • 1943-1945

In addition to "regular" Heeres units created by orders originating from the OKH Organization-Abteilung, a large number of Panzer-Kompanien and Panzer-Zuegen were created in the field and outfitted with captured equipment. The following list is limited to company sized units that have been identified in official records found to date and should not be considered as having identified every last Beute-Panzer-Kompanie that was formed. A thorough search through all of the surviving Armee, Korps, and Division records would very likely reveal additional units. Those interested in these Beute-Panzer units are advised to obtain publications written by Dr. Werner Regenberg who has specialized in detailed research on the operational use of captured tanks in the German Army.

Beute-Panzer-Kompanie	Created	Remarks
Pz.Kp./Sich.Rgt.3	by May42	Renamed 9.(Pz.)/Radf.Sich.Rgt.3 in Dec42
Beute-Pz.Kp.AOK 16	Dec41	outfitted with repaired Russian tanks
Pz.Sich.Kp./Sich.Rgt.(mot)100	29Oct43	
Pz.Kp./Bef.101	by May42	
Pz.Kp.207	by May42	
Pz.Kp.C(ND)224	1Jul43	
Pz.Kp./260.Inf.Div.	25Jan43	
Pz.Kp./281.Sich.Div.	by May42	Renamed Beute-Pz.Kp.281 on 29Sep42
Pz.Kp./285.Sich.Div.	by May42	Renamed Pz.Kp.285 on 16Oct42
Pz.Kp.445	26Nov41	
Pz.Sich.Kp./Sich.Rgt.1010	29Oct43	
Pz.Kp. Bergen	1945	
Pz.Kp.z.b.V./Geb.Korps.Norwegen	22May42	
le.Pz.Kp. Nieberlande	1945	
1.Ost Pz.Kp.Befh.Sued	4Apr43	
2.Ost Pz.Kp.Befh.Sued	4Apr43	
Pz.Kp. Stavanger	11Aug43	
le.Pz.Kp. Warschau	12Jun40	Outfitted with captured Polish tanks Renamed le.Pz.Kp.Ost on 3Sep40

FORMATION OF PANZER UNITS FOR THE LUFTWAFFE AND SS

Unit Name	Created	Remarks
Division Hermann Goering	9Oct42	Created from Brigade Hermann Goering
Panzer-Regiment Hermann Goering	1Dec42	Created two Abt. and five Kp. (3.Pz.Kp. previously created for Brigade HG) V./Artl.Rgt.HG renamed III./Pz.Rgt.HG in Jun43 8./Pz.Rgt.HG created in Jul43 Reorganized the II./Pz.Rgt.HG with four Pz.IV Kp. and the III./Pz.Rgt.HG as a Pz.Jaeg.Abt. on 4May44 On 3Jul44, Hitler ordered the formation of a Panther-Abt. for Pz.Rgt.HG
1.SS-Panzer-Division LSSAH	22Oct43	Renamed from SS-Pz.Gren.Div.LSSAH
2.SS-Panzer-Division Das Reich	22Oct43	Renamed from SS-Pz.Gren.Div.Das Reich
3.SS-Panzer-Division Totenkopf	22Oct43	Renamed from SS-Pz.Gren.Div.Totenkopf
5.SS-Panzer-Division Wiking	22Oct43	Renamed from SS-Pz.Gren.Div.Wiking
9.SS-Panzer-Division Hohenstaufen	22Oct43	Renamed from SS-Pz.Gren.Div.Hohenstaufen
10.SS-Panzer-Division Frundsberg	22Oct43	Renamed from SS-Pz.Gren.Div.Frundsberg
12.SS-Panzer-Division Hitlerjugend	22Oct43	Renamed from SS-Pz.Gren.Div.Hitlerjugend
SS-Panzer-Regiment 1	14Oct42	Created with Rgts.Stab and II.Abt. with three m.Kp. for SS-Div. LSSAH Created s.Pz.Kp. for SS-Pz.Rgt.1 on 15Nov42 SS-Pz.Abt.1 renamed I./SS-Pz.Abt.1 Orders on 1May43 for I./SS-Pz.Rgt.1 to convert to Panthers and II./SS-Pz.Rgt.1 reorganized with four m.Kp. Ordered on 22Oct43 to reorganize with a Panther-Abt with four Kp. and a Pz.IV Abt. with four Kp. Ordered on 11Apr44 to refit with two Abt each with four Kp. Decimated in Falaise pocket Aug44 Ordered in Sep44 to refit and reorganize with a single Pz.Abt. with two Panther and two Pz.IV Kp.
SS-Panzer-Regiment 2	14Oct42	Created with Rgts.Stab and II.Abt. with two l.Kp. and one m.Kp. for SS-Div. Das Reich Created s.Pz.Kp. for SS-Pz.Rgt.2 on 15Nov42 Ordered on 1May43 for I./SS-Pz.Rgt.2 to convert to Panthers and a III./SS-Pz.Rgt.1 created with two T34 Kp. and a l.Kp. Ordered on 22Oct43 to reorganize with a Panther-Abt with four Kp. and a Pz.IV Abt. with four Kp. Reduced to a Pz.Abt. with a Pz.IV Kp., a Panther Kp. and a Tiger Kp. by orders dated 4Dec43 Ordered on 11Apr44 to refit with two Abt each with four Kp. Decimated in Falaise pocket Aug44 Rebuilt I./SS-Pz.Rgt.w with four Panther Kp. in Nov44 Rebuilt II./SS-Pz.Rgt.2 with two Pz.IV and two StuG Kp. in Nov44

Unit Name	Created	Remarks
SS-Panzer-Regiment 3	14Oct42	Created with Rgts.Stab and II.Abt. with two l.Kp. and one m.Kp. for SS-Totenkopf Div. Created s.Pz.Kp. for SS-Pz.Rgt.3 on 15Nov42 Ordered on 1May43 to reorganize with two Abt. each with two m.Kp. and one l.Kp.
SS-Panzer-Regiment 5	28Feb43	Created Rgt.Stab and II./SS-Pz.Rgt.5 with four Kp. SS-Pz.Abt.5 renamed I./SS-Pz.Rgt.5 Began converting II./SS-Pz.Rgt.5 to a Panther-Abt. in Dec43
SS-Panzer-Regiment 9	1Feb43	Created for SS-Pz.Gr.Div.9 Ordered on 22Oct43 to reorganize with a Panther-Abt with four Kp. and a Pz.IV Abt. with four Kp. II.Abt. reorganized as a gem.Pz.Abt. with two Pz.IV Kp. and two StuG Kp. in Nov43 Rebuilt I./SS-Pz.Rgt.9 with four Panther Kp. in Nov44 Rebuilt II./SS-Pz.Rgt.9 with two Pz.IV and two StuG Kp. in Nov44
SS-Panzer-Regiment 10	1Feb43	Created for SS-Pz.Gr.Div.9 Ordered on 22Oct43 to reorganize with a Panther-Abt with four Kp. and a Pz.IV Abt. with four Kp. II.Abt. reorganized as a gem.Pz.Abt. with two Pz.IV Kp. and two StuG Kp. in Nov43 I./SS-Pz.Rgt.10 rebuilt in Dec44 with two Panther Kp. and two Pz.IV Kp. Orders on 3Jan45 for SS-Pz.Rgt.10 to expand to a Panther-Abt. with four Kp. and a Pz.Abt. with three Pz.IV Kp.
SS-Panzer-Regiment 11	1Jul43	Created for SS-Div.Nordland II./SS-Pz.Rgt.11 ordered to convert to s.SS-Pz.Abt.103 on 1Nov43 I./SS-Pz.Rgt.11 with four Kp. renamed SS-Pz.Abt.11 on 1Nov43
SS-Panzer-Regiment 12	3Nov43	Created for 12.SS-Pz.Div.HJ with a Panther-Abt with four Kp. and a Pz.IV Abt. with four Kp. Decimated in Falaise pocket Aug44 I./SS-Pz.Rgt.12 rebuilt in Nov44 with two Panther Kp. and two Pz.IV Kp.
SS-Panzer-Abteilung 1	1Feb42	Created with three m.Kp. for LSSAH Incorporated into SS-Pz.Rgt.1 as I.Abt. in Oct42
SS-Panzer-Abteilung 2	15Feb42	Created with two l.Kp. and one m.Kp. for SS-Div. Das Reich Renamed SS-Pz.Abt.5 on 18Apr42
	20Apr42	Created with two l.Kp. and one m.Kp. for SS-Div. Das Reich Incorporated into SS-Pz.Rgt.2 as I.Abt. in Oct42
SS-Panzer-Abteilung 3	1Jun42	Created with two l.Kp. and one m.Kp. for SS-Totenkopf Div. Incorporated into SS-Pz.Rgt.3 as I.Abt. in Oct42
SS-Panzer-Abteilung 4	May44	Created with three StuG Kp. for 4.SS-Pol.Pz.Gr.Div.

APPENDICES

Unit Name	Created	Remarks
SS-Panzer-Abteilung 5	18Apr42	Renamed from SS-Pz.Abt.2 and assigned to SS-Div. Wiking Created the 4.m.Kp. for SS-Pz.Abt.5 on 6Nov42 Renamed I./SS-Pz.Rgt.5 on 28Feb43
SS-Panzer-Abteilung 7	22Oct43	Renamed from SS-Pz.Abt."Prinz Eugen" which had originally been created as a Beute-Flammpanzer-Kp. on 1May42 Converted to SS-Pz.Jg.Abt.Skanderbeg on 17Jun44
SS-Panzer-Abteilung 11	1Nov43	Renamed from I./SS-Pz.Rgt.11 for 11.SS-Pz.Gr.Div. Nordland
SS-Panzer-Abteilung 16	Nov43	Created with three StuG Kp. for 16.SS-Pz.Gr.Div.RF-SS
SS-Panzer-Abteilung 17	15Nov43	Created with four m.Kp. for 17.SS-Pz.Gr.Div.G.v.B. Converted to three StuG Kp. in Apr44
SS-Panzer-Abteilung 18	15Jan44	Created from StuG-Battr.6 and expanded to three StuG Kp. for 18.SS-Pz.Gr.Div. Horst Wessel
schwere SS-Panzer-Abteilung 101	19Jul43	Orders to create the s.Pz.Abt.Gen.Kdo.I.SS-Pz.Korps with three s.Kp. Ordered on 22Oct43 to rename as s.SS-Pz.Abt.101 Renamed SS-Pz.Abt.501 in Sep44
schwere SS-Panzer-Abteilung 102	22Apr43	Orders to create a Stab for the three s.Pz.Kp. that had already been created for the SS on 15Nov42 Renamed s.SS-Pz.Abt.Gen.Kdo.II.SS-Pz.Korps on 1Jun43 Orders on 22Oct43 to rename as s.SS-Pz.Abt.102 Renamed SS-Pz.Abt.501 in Sep44
schwere SS-Panzer-Abteilung 103	1Nov43	Orders to convert II./Pz.Rgt.11 to s.SS-Pz.Abt.103 with three s.Kp. Renamed SS-Pz.Abt.501 in Sep44
SS-Panzer-Abteilung 105	22Oct43	Renamed from Pz.Abt./V.SS-Geb.Korps which had been created in the Summer of 1943
schwere SS-Panzer-Abteilung 501	Sep44	s.SS-Pz.Abt.101 renamed s.SS-Pz.Abt.501
schwere SS-Panzer-Abteilung 50	Sep44	s.SS-Pz.Abt.102 renamed s.SS-Pz.Abt.502
schwere SS-Panzer-Abteilung 503	Sep44	s.SS-Pz.Abt.103 renamed s.SS-Pz.Abt.503

APPENDIX B1 - PANZERKAMPFWAGEN II (2 cm Kw.K.) Sd.Kfz.121

	Produced During Month	Ready for Issue During Month		Losses During Month	Inventory on the 1st of the Month
		New	Rebuilt		
Jan43	0	0	2	49	997
Feb43			7	227	950
Mar43			22	61	730
Apr43			0	46	350*
May43			16	55	304
Jun43			9	38	265
Jul43			4	22	236
Aug43			11	12	218
Sep43			6	10	209
Oct43			2	8	433*
Nov43			2	13	419
Dec43			1	10	408
Jan44			1	4	399
Feb44			0	2	396
Mar44			23	4	394
Apr44			13	7	413
May44			10	3	419
Jun44			20	1	426
Jul44			1	61	445
Aug44			3	2	385
Sep44			0	0	386
Oct44		Not reported after October 1944			386
Nov44					
Dec44					
Jan45					
Feb45					
Mar45					
Apr45					

* Inventory adjusted on original report

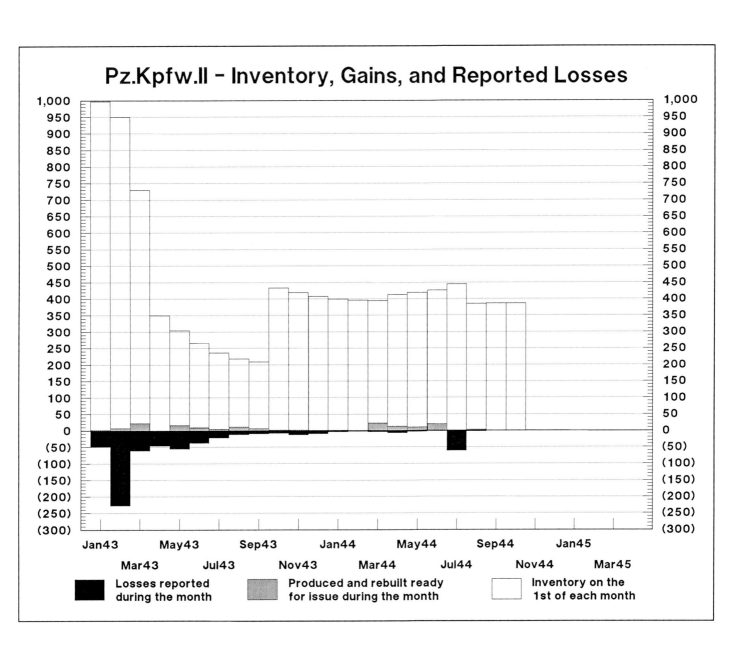

Pz.Kpfw.II – Inventory, Gains, and Reported Losses

Losses reported
during the month

Produced and rebuilt ready
for issue during the month

Inventory on the
1st of each month

APPENDIX B2 - PANZERKAMPFWAGEN 38(t) (3.7 cm Kw.K.)

	Produced During Month	Ready for Issue During Month		Losses During Month	Inventory on the 1st of the Month
		New	Rebuilt		
Jan43	0	0	5	40	287
Feb43			12	23	252
Mar43			52	111	242
Apr43			36	11	161*
May43			15	4	186
Jun43			7	0	197
Jul43			8	3	204
Aug43			12	3	212
Sep43			1	0	201
Oct43			8	3	255*
Nov43			3	14	260
Dec43			0	10	249
Jan44			0	0	227
Feb44			0	0	227
Mar44			0	0	227
Apr44			0	0	227
May44			2	0	227
Jun44			3	0	229
Jul44			2	0	232
Aug44			0	0	229
Sep44			0	0	229
Oct44	Not reported after October 1944				229
Nov44					
Dec44					
Jan45					
Feb45					
Mar45					
Apr45					

* Inventory adjusted on original report

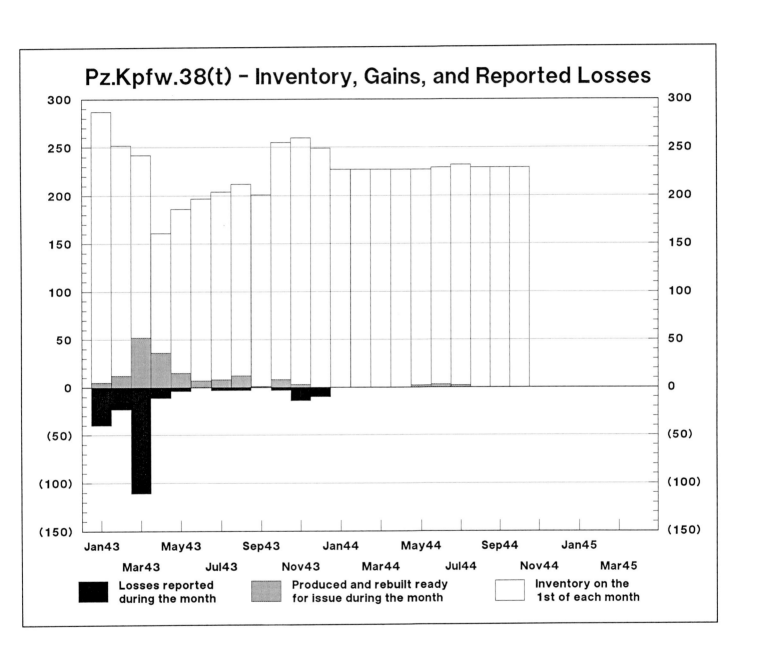

Pz.Kpfw.38(t) – Inventory, Gains, and Reported Losses

Losses reported during the month

Produced and rebuilt ready for issue during the month

Inventory on the 1st of each month

APPENDIX B3 - PANZERKAMPFWAGEN III (5 und 7.5 cm Kw.K.) Sd.Kfz.141

	Produced During Month	Ready for Issue During Month		Losses During Month	Inventory on the 1st of the Month
		New	Rebuilt		
Jan43	46	78	11	271	2944
Feb43	34	34	14	1053	2762
Mar43	35	19	9	242	1757
Apr43	46	43	5	249	1630*
May43	43	62	12	115	1429
Jun43	11	15	3	2	1370
Jul43	0	0	9	189	1276
Aug43	20	11	12	178	1077
Sep43	0	9	33	84	1006
Oct43		0	17	81	1131*
Nov43			12	119	1067
Dec43			10	50	960
Jan44			6	43	920
Feb44			5	38	883
Mar44			11	1	850
Apr44			27	52	860
May44			5	1	835
Jun44			6	41	839
Jul44			3	9	804
Aug44			5	2	798
Sep44			6	21	530*
Oct44			19	11	515
Nov44			10	0	523
Dec44			2	1	533
Jan45			0	0	534
Feb45			0	??	534
Mar45			??	??	??
Apr45			??	??	??

* Inventory adjusted on original report

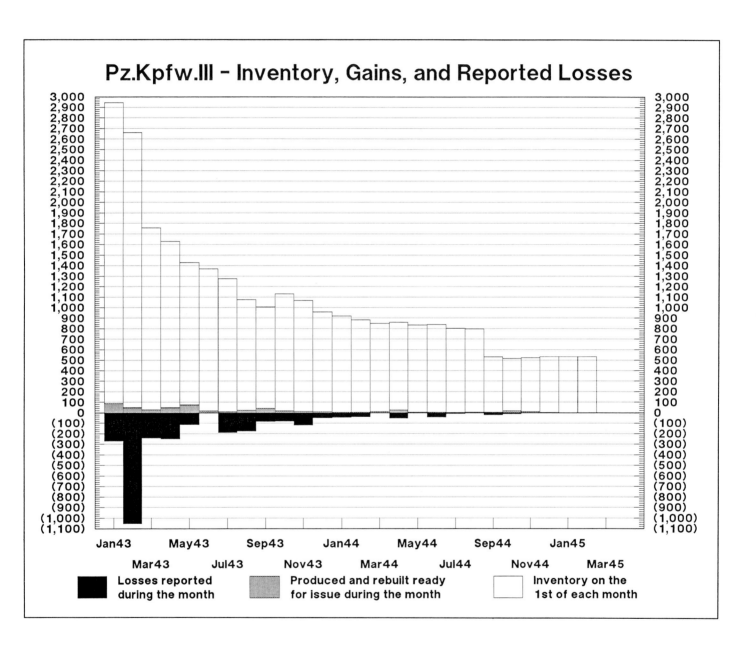

Pz.Kpfw.III – Inventory, Gains, and Reported Losses

Losses reported during the month

Produced and rebuilt ready for issue during the month

Inventory on the 1st of each month

APPENDIX B4 - PANZERKAMPFWAGEN IV (7.5 cm Kw.K.) Sd.Kfz.161

	Produced During Month	Ready for Issue During Month		Losses During Month	Inventory on the 1st of the Month
		New	Rebuilt		
Jan43	163	140	6	93	1077
Feb43	171	182	11	345	1130
Mar43	205	159	9	136	975
Apr43	213	195	6	130	1018
May43	272	299	7	156	1077
Jun43	253	256	25	5	1211
Jul43	244	211	16	290	1472
Aug43	283	272	23	280	1374
Sep43	289	256	17	184	1360
Oct43	328	292	13	199	1574*
Nov43	238	269	14	262	1672
Dec43	354	322	17	316	1689
Jan44	300	323	13	274	1668
Feb44	252	246	20	152	1710
Mar44	310	424	23	121	1821
Apr44	299	256	23	277	2132
May44	302	253	30	83	2119
Jun44	300	284	31	270	2304
Jul44	300	205	28	426	2336
Aug44	300	303	19	368	2128
Sep44	180	236	20	752	2037*
Oct44	187	203	14	141	2039
Nov44	200	188	8	81	1605
Dec44	195	149	5	158	1710
Jan45	170	170	4	287	1684
Feb45	160	165	1	??	1571
Mar45	55	117	3	??	??
Apr45	??	27+	??	??	??

* Inventory adjusted on original report

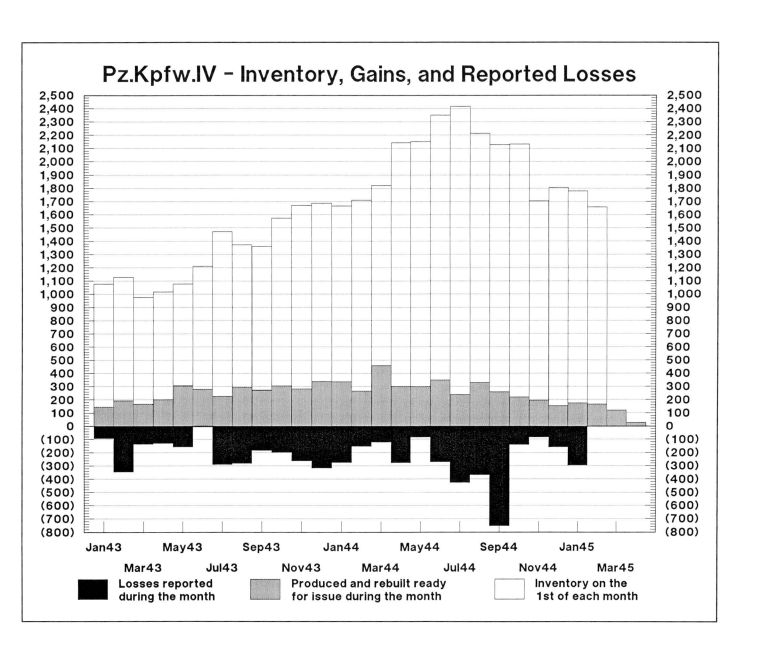

Pz.Kpfw.IV - Inventory, Gains, and Reported Losses

Losses reported during the month | Produced and rebuilt ready for issue during the month | Inventory on the 1st of each month

APPENDIX B5 - PANZERKAMPFWAGEN PANTHER (7.5 cm Kw.K.) Sd.Kfz.171

	Produced During Month	Ready for Issue During Month		Losses During Month	Inventory on the 1st of the Month
		New	Rebuilt		
Jan43	4*	4*			
Feb43	18*	17*			4*
Mar43	59*	40*			21*
Apr43	78*	0*	0		61*
May43	324	235	16		22**
Jun43	160	176	10	0	273
Jul43	202	176	4	84	447
Aug43	120	150	3	43	553
Sep43	197	155	4	80	650
Oct43	257	234	1	112	728**
Nov43	209	222	0	80	851
Dec43	299	309	0	94	989
Jan44	279	283	0	130	1177
Feb44	256	245	12	127	1323
Mar44	270	291	6	19	1451
Apr44	311	276	8	247	1736
May44	345	370	16	117	1773
Jun44	370	338	11	138	2038
Jul44	380	341	5	373	2249
Aug44	350	393	15	290	2211
Sep44	335	377	4	692	2304**
Oct44	278	256	5	294	1963
Nov44	318	357	13	133	1898
Dec44	285	253	7	243	2135
Jan45	211	230	4	252	2151
Feb45	126	172	5	??	2133
Mar45	102	94	5	??	??
Apr45	??	64+	??	??	??

* With the exception of three Panthers that had been provided to Wa Pruef 6 for testing, all the Panthers completed from January through April were returned, rebuilt, and included in the 324 Panthers reported as accepted in May 1943.
** Inventory adjusted on original report

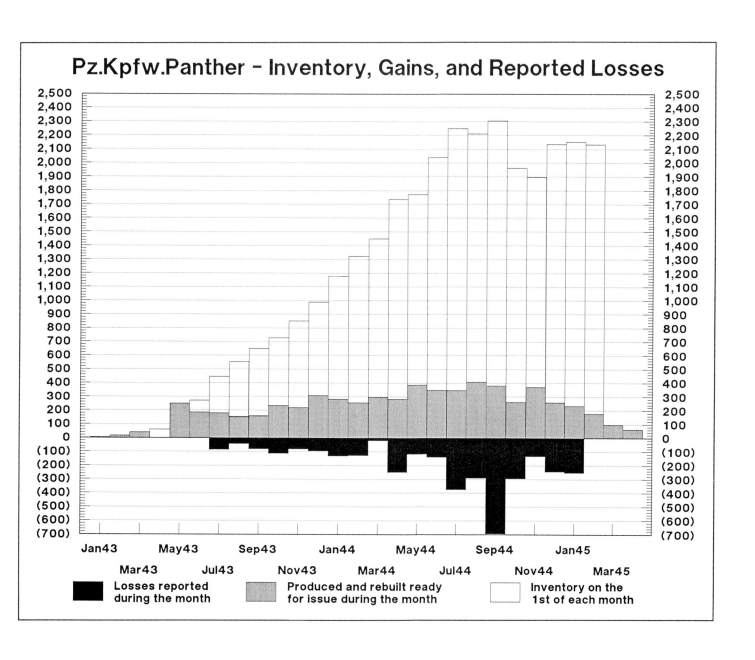

Pz.Kpfw.Panther - Inventory, Gains, and Reported Losses

Losses reported during the month

Produced and rebuilt ready for issue during the month

Inventory on the 1st of each month

APPENDIX B6 - PANZERKAMPFWAGEN TIGER I (8.8 cm Kw.K.) Sd.Kfz.181

	Produced During Month	Ready for Issue During Month		Losses During Month	Inventory on the 1st of the Month
		New	Rebuilt		
Jan43	35	30	1	11	65*
Feb43	32	33	0	3	85*
Mar43	41	39	0	16	108*
Apr43	46	47	0	4	134
May43	50	47	0	17	177
Jun43	60	55	0	0	207
Jul43	65	57	0	34	262
Aug43	60	74	0	41	286
Sep43	85	55	0	34	319
Oct43	50	85	0	37	339*
Nov43	56	36	0	29	387
Dec43	67	80	0	65	394
Jan44	93	87	0	62	409
Feb44	95	102	1	13	434
Mar44	86	88	1	32	526
Apr44	104	94	3	96	583
May44	100	85	5	21	584
Jun44	75	104	5	92	654
Jul44	64	65	8	195	671
Aug44	6	16	11	94	549
Sep44	0	0	6	125	433*
Oct44			1	39	314
Nov44			18	19	276
Dec44			4	2	274
Jan45			2	62	276
Feb45			3	??	216
Mar45			0	??	??
Apr45			??	??	??

* Inventory adjusted on original report

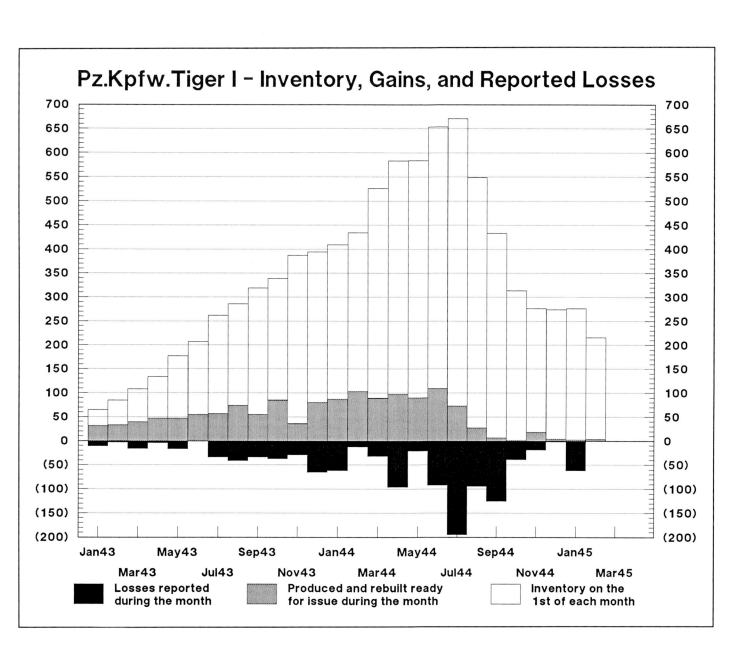

Pz.Kpfw.Tiger I - Inventory, Gains, and Reported Losses

Losses reported during the month

Produced and rebuilt ready for issue during the month

Inventory on the 1st of each month

APPENDIX B7 - PANZERKAMPFWAGEN TIGER II (8.8 cm Kw.K.) Sd.Kfz.182

	Produced During Month	Ready for Issue During Month		Losses During Month	Inventory on the 1st of the Month
		New	Rebuilt		
Oct43	0				
Nov43	1				
Dec43	0				
Jan44	5	0			
Feb44	5	5			0
Mar44	6	1			5
Apr44	6	6			6
May44	15	19			12
Jun44	32	24			31
Jul44	45	49			55
Aug44	94	77			104
Sep44	63	86		23	83*
Oct44	26	13		10	146
Nov44	26	31	4	11	149
Dec44	56	51		30	174
Jan45	40	40	2	11	195
Feb45	42	35	1	??	226
Mar45	30	25		??	??
Apr45	0	0	??	??	??

* Inventory adjusted on original report

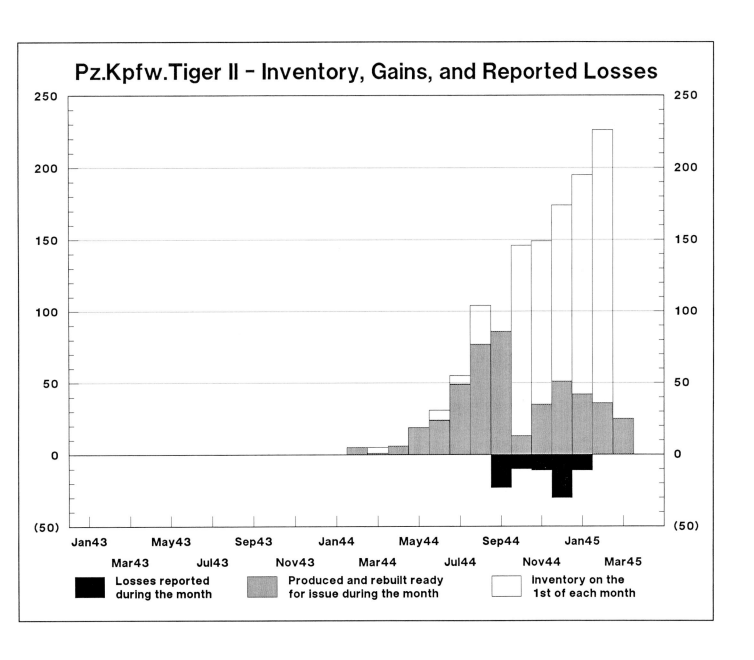

Pz.Kpfw.Tiger II - Inventory, Gains, and Reported Losses

Losses reported during the month

Produced and rebuilt ready for issue during the month

Inventory on the 1st of each month

APPENDIX B8 - PANZERBEFEHLSWAGEN Sd.Kfz.265-268

	Produced During Month	Ready for Issue During Month		Losses During Month	Inventory on the 1st of the Month
		New	Rebuilt		
Jan43	13	18	1	17	278
Feb43	1	9	3	40	280
Mar43		9	1	30	252
Apr43			7	5	310*
May43			23	2	312
Jun43			38	0	333
Jul43			30	15	371
Aug43			26	15	376
Sep43			8	10	377
Oct43			1	16	416*
Nov43			4	20	401
Dec43			2	17	385
Jan44			2	23	370
Feb44			0	17	348
Mar44			0	9	327
Apr44			2	21	318
May44			0	4	299
Jun44			1	11	295
Jul44			5	16	285
Aug44			3	6	274
Sep44			0	0	271
Oct44			0	0	271
Nov44	Not reported after October 1944				
Dec44					
Jan45					
Feb45					
Mar45					
Apr45					

* Inventory adjusted on original report

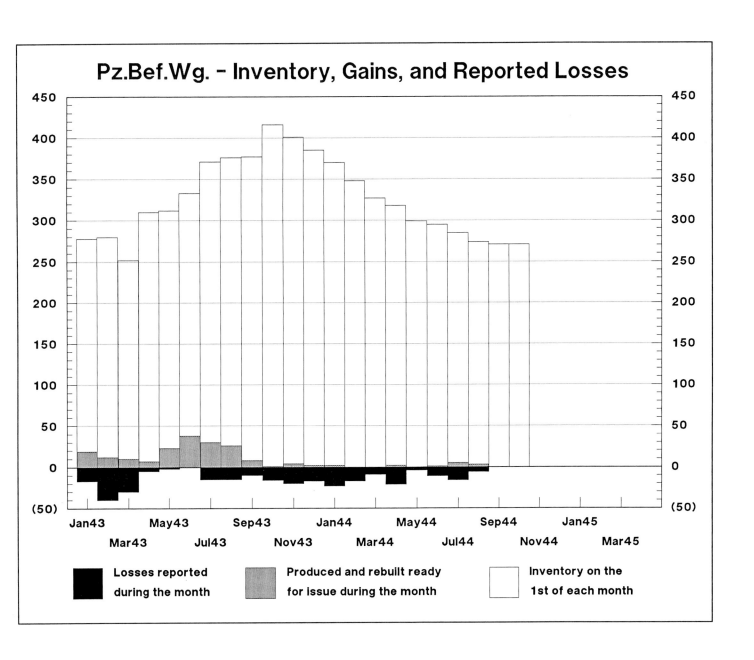

APPENDIX C1 - TECHNICAL SPECIFICATIONS OF AMERICAN TANKS

	Grant I	M3 Medium	M4 Medium	M4A3(76) HVSS	Sherman VC
Combat Weight (tons)	28	27.9	30.4	33.7	32.7
Maximum Speed (km/hr)	40.2	=	=	41.8	40.2
Crew	6	6 or 7	5	=	4
Main Gun (cm/caliber)	37 L/56 75 L/31	= =	75 L/40	76	76.2
Machine Guns	1	3	3	3	2
Main Gun Ammunition	50-75 182-37	= 178-37	97	71	77
M.G. Ammunition	3100	9200	5050	6850	6170
Power/Weight (HP/ton)	14.3	=	13.2	14.8	13.0
Ground Pressure (kg/cm^2)	1.2	=	1.1	0.77	0.96
Ground Clearance (m)	0.43	=	=	=	=
Fording Depth (m)	1.0	=	=	0.91	1.07
Range on Road (km)	177	193	=	161	=
Range Cross Country (km)					
Fuel Capacity (l)	662	=	=	636	606
Armor	Rolled & Cast	= =	= =	= =	= =
Hull Front (mm)	38.1-50.8	=	50.8	50.8-108	50.8
Hull Side (mm	38.1	=	=	=	=
Hull Rear (mm)	38.1	=	=	=	=
Hull Roof (mm)	12.7	=	19	=	=
Hull Belly (mm)	12.7-25.4	=	=	=	=
Turret Front (mm)	50.8-76.2	50.8	76.2	63.5-88.9	76.2-88.9
Turret Side (mm)	50.8	=	=	63.5	50.8
Turret Rear (mm)	50.8	=	=	63.5	50.8
Turret Roof (mm)	31.8	22.2	25.4	=	=
Length (m)	5.90	5.63	5.89	7.54	7.77
Width (m)	2.75	2.72	2.62	3.00	2.67
Height (m)	3.02	3.12	2.74	2.97	2.74
Drive Sprocket	Front	=	=	=	=
Motor	Continental	Wright	=	Ford	Chrysler
Type	Gasoline	=	=	=	=
Cooling	Air	=	=	Water	=
Power (HP)	400	=	=	500	425
Maximum rpm	2400	=	=	2600	2850
Capacity (l)	15.9	=	=	17.9	33.1
Bore/Stroke (mm)	127/140	=	=	137/152	111/114
Cylinders	9	=	=	8	30
Motor Efficiency (HP/l)	25.2	=	=	27.9	12.8
Transmission	5F,1R	=	=	=	=
Speed 1.Gear (km/hr)	3.9	=	=	4.0	3.9
Speed 2.Gear (km/hr)	9.4	=	=	9.8	9.4
Speed 3.Gear (km/hr)	16.5	=	=	17.1	16.5
Speed 4.Gear (km/hr)	26.4	=	=	27.5	26.4
Speed 5.Gear (km/hr)	40.2	=	=	41.8	40.2
Steering	Cletrac	=	=	=	=
Turning Circle (m)	21	19	=	=	21
Roadwheels	6	=	=	=	=
Tires	Rubber	=	=	=	=
Diameter/Width (mm)	508/229	=	=	521/159	508/229
Pressure on Wheel (kg/cm)	106	=	115	184	124
Suspension	Volute Springs	= =	= =	HVSS	Volute Springs
Roadwheels/Spring	2	=	=		
Type of Track	Rubber	=	=	=	=
Width/Pitch (mm)	420/152	=	=	584/152	420/152
Steering Ratio	1.77	=	=	1.91	1.77

APPENDIX C2 - TECHNICAL SPECIFICATIONS OF BRITISH TANKS

	Crusader Mk.II	Cromwell Mk.V	Valentine Mk.I	Churchill Mk.III	Churchill Mk.VII
Combat Weight (tons)	18.8	27.9	16.0	39.1	40.1
Maximum Speed (km/hr)	41.8	27.9	26.1	26.4	21.7
Crew	4	5	3	5	5
Main Gun (cm/caliber)	4.0 L/52	7.5 L/40	4.0 L/52	5.7	7.5 L/40
Machine Guns	1	3	1	3	3
Main Gun Ammunition	130	64	52	74	82
M.G. Ammunition	4950	5550	3150	7575	7125
Power/Weight (HP/ton)	18.0	21.5	8.4	8.3	8.7
Ground Pressure (kg/cm²)	1.09	1.05	0.72	0.92	0.94
Ground Clearance (m)	0.41	0.41	0.42	0.53	=
Fording Depth (m)	1.0	1.37	0.91	=	=
Range on Road (km)	160	266	112	198	228
Range Cross Country (km)					
Fuel Capacity (l)	455	527	255	682	=
Armor	Rolled	Cast & Rolled	Rolled	= & Cast	=
Hull Front (mm)	20-40	63-57	60	102	152-139
Hull Side (mm	14+14	32	60	76	95
Hull Rear (mm)	14-28	32	60	50	=
Hull Roof (mm)	7	20	10-20	19	=
Hull Belly (mm)	6.4-10.4	14-6	7-20	19	25
Turret Front (mm)	49	76	65	89	152
Turret Side (mm)	23.5	63	60	76	95
Turret Rear (mm)	20-30.7	57	65	76	95
Turret Roof (mm)	12	20	10-20	19	20
Length (m)	5.98	6.50	5.46	7.35	7.37
Width (m)	2.77	3.05	2.62	3.25	3.33
Height (m)	2.24	2.46	2.10	2.78	=
Drive Sprocket	Rear	=	=	=	=
Motor	Nuffield	Meteor	AEC	Bedford	=
Type	Gasoline	=	Diesel	Gasoline	=
Cooling	Water	=	=	=	=
Power (HP)	340	600	135	325	350
Maximum rpm	1500	2550	1900	2200	=
Capacity (l)	27.0	26.9	9.64	21.3	=
Bore/Stroke (mm)	127/178	137/152	120/142	127/140	=
Cylinders	12	=	6	Twin 6	=
Motor Efficiency (HP/l)	12.6	22.3	14.0	15.2	16.4
Transmission	4F,1R	5F,1R	5F,1R	4F,1R	=
Speed 1.Gear (km/hr)	5.7		2.5		
Speed 2.Gear (km/hr)	9.8		5.3		
Speed 3.Gear (km/hr)	22.0		9.8		
Speed 4.Gear (km/hr)	41.8		19.0	26.4	21.7
Speed 5.Gear (km/hr)		61.2			
Steering	Single Radius Clutch	Controlled Differential	Clutches	Controlled Differential	=
Turning Circle (m)	9.0		7.9		
Roadwheels	5	5	6		
Tires	Rubber	=	Rubber	Steel	=
Diameter/Width (mm)	812/90x2	803/254	2x610/135 4x495/135		
Pressure on Wheel (kg/cm)	100		99		
Suspension	Christi	=	Coil Springs	= =	
Roadwheels/Spring	1	1	3	1	=
Type of Track	Unlubricated	=	=	=	=
Width/Pitch (mm)	246/103	356/100	365/159	559/211	=
Steering Ratio	1.67	1.50	1.40	1.73	=

APPENDIX C3 - TECHNICAL SPECIFICATIONS OF GERMAN PANZERS

	Pz.Kpfw.IV Ausf.H-J	Pz.Kpfw.Panther Ausf.D-A	Ausf.G	Pz.Kpfw.Tiger Ausf.E	Ausf.B
Combat Weight (tons)	25	44.8	45.5	57	69.8
Maximum Speed (km/hr)	38	55	=	45.4	41.5
Crew	5	=	=	=	=
Main Gun (cm/caliber)	7.5 L/48	7.5 L/70	=	8.8 L/56	8.8 L/71
Machine Guns	2	=	=	=	=
Main Gun Ammunition	87	79	82	92	84
M.G. Ammunition	3150	5100	4800	4800	4800
Power/Weight (HP/ton)	10.6	15.5	15.5	12.3	10
Ground Pressure (kg/cm^2)	0.89	0.73	0.75	0.74	0.78
Ground Clearance (m)	0.40	0.56	=	0.47	0.49
Fording Depth (m)	0.80	1.9	=	1.60	1.60
Range on Road (km)	235 (320J)	200	=	195	170
Range Cross Country (km)	120 (210J)	100	=	110	120
Fuel Capacity (l)	470 (680J)	730	=	540	860
Armor	Rolled	=	=	=	=
Hull Front (mm)	80	80-60	80-50	100	150-100
Hull Side (mm)	30	40	50-40	80-60	80
Hull Rear (mm)	20	40	=	80	80
Hull Roof (mm)	10	16	=	25	40
Hull Belly (mm)	11	16	=	25	40-25
Turret Front (mm)	50	100	100	120-100	180
Turret Side (mm)	30	45	45	80	80
Turret Rear (mm)	30	45	45	80	80
Turret Roof (mm)	16-25	16	16	25	40
Length (m)	7.02	8.86	=	8.45	10.29
Width (m)	2.88	3.44	3.42	3.70	3.76
Height (m)	2.68	3.10(2.99A)	2.98	3.00	3.09
Drive Sprocket	Front	=	=	=	=
Motor	HL120TRM	HL230P30	=	HL230P45	HL230P30
Type	Gasoline	=	=	=	=
Cooling	Water	=	=	=	=
Power (HP)	300	700	=	=	=
Maximum rpm	3000	3000	=	=	=
Capacity (l)	11.9	23	=	=	=
Bore/Stroke (mm)	105/115	130/145	=	=	=
Cylinders	12	=	=	=	=
Motor Efficiency (HP/l)	22.3	30.4	=	=	=
Transmission	6F,1R	7F,1R	=	8F,4R	=
Speed 1.Gear (km/hr)	4.2	4.1	=	2.8	2.6
Speed 2.Gear (km/hr)	8.1	8.4	=	4.3	3.8
Speed 3.Gear (km/hr)	13.8	13.3	=	6.2	5.6
Speed 4.Gear (km/hr)	20.8	20.8	=	9.2	8.3
Speed 5.Gear (km/hr)	29.5	30.8	=	14.1	12.8
Speed 6.Gear (km/hr)	38	42.5	=	20.9	19.0
Speed 7.Gear (km/hr)		55	=	30.5	27.3
Speed 8.Gear (km/hr)				45.4	41.5
Steering	Differential	Single Radius	=	Double Radius	=
Turning Circle (m)		8.7	=	7	
Roadwheels	8x2	8x2	=	8x2	9x2
Tires	Rubber	=	=	Steel	=
Diameter/Width (mm)	470/90	860/100	=	800/75	=
Pressure on Wheel (kg/cm)	87	140	142	238	258
Suspension	Leaf Spring	Torsion Bars	=	=	=
Roadwheels/Spring	4	2	=	2	2
Type of Track	Unlubricated	=	=	=	=
Width/Pitch (mm)	400/120	660/150	=	725/130	800/300
Steering Ratio	1.43	1.50	=	1.28	1.48

APPENDIX C4 - TECHNICAL SPECIFICATIONS OF SOVIET TANKS

	T-70	T-34-76	T-34-85	KV-1Ss	IS-2
Combat Weight (tons)	10	26.3	30	42.5	46
Maximum Speed (km/hr)	45	47.0	47.0	38.0	37
Crew	2	4	5		4
Main Gun (cm/caliber)	4.5 L/46	7.62 L/41	8.5 L/53	7.62 L/41	12.2
Machine Guns	1	2	2	4	4
Main Gun Ammunition	90	77	56	114	28
M.G. Ammunition	945	4420	1955	3087	2631
Power/Weight (HP/ton)	17.0	19	17	14.1	11.3
Ground Pressure (kg/cm^2)	0.7	0.64	0.87		0.82
Ground Clearance (m)	0.3	0.38	0.4	0.45	0.42
Fording Depth (m)	0.9	1.12	0.9	1.6	1.3
Range on Road (km)	360	455	300	200	240
Range Cross Country (km)	180	260	160	160	210
Fuel Capacity (l)	480	480	480		820
Armor	Rolled	=	=	Rolled	
Hull Front (mm)	45	45	45	75+30	120-90
Hull Side (mm	45	45	45	75	95-90
Hull Rear (mm)	35	40	45-40	75	60
Hull Roof (mm)	10	20	30	40	30-20
Hull Belly (mm)	10	15	20	40-30	30-20
Turret Front (mm)	60	45	55-45	90-95	160
Turret Side (mm)	35	45	55-50	100	160-100
Turret Rear (mm)	35	40	50	95	90
Turret Roof (mm)	10	16	20	30	30
Length (m)	4.42	5.93	7.53	6.95	9.9
Width (m)	2.47	3.02	3.00	3.25	3.09
Height (m)	2.08	2.46	2.50	2.64	2.73
Drive Sprocket	Front	Rear	=	=	=
Motor	GAZ-203	W2	=	=	V-2-IS
Type	Gasoline	Diesel	=	=	=
Cooling	Water	=	=	=	=
Power (HP)	170	500	=	600	520
Maximum rpm	3750	1700	1700	2000	2200
Capacity (l)	3.48	38.9	=	=	=
Bore/Stroke (mm)	82/	150/180	=	=	=
Cylinders	2x6	12	=	=	=
Motor Efficiency (HP/l)		12.9	=	15.4	13.4
Transmission	4F,1R	4F,1R	=	2x4F,1R	8F,2R
Speed 1.Gear (km/hr)	7	7.2	=	3.8	
Speed 2.Gear (km/hr)	15	15.1	=	5.5	
Speed 3.Gear (km/hr)	25	29.5	=	7.8	
Speed 4.Gear (km/hr)	45	47.0	=	10.8	
Speed 5.Gear (km/hr)				13.4	
Speed 6.Gear (km/hr)				19.3	
Speed 7.Gear (km/hr)				27.6	
Speed 8.Gear (km/hr)				38.0	37
Steering	Clutches	=	=	=	=
Turning Circle (m)		7.7	=	9.5	
Roadwheels	5	5	=	6	6
Tires	Rubber	=	Steel	=	=
Diameter/Width (mm)	540/80	825/150x2	=	590/110x2	535/250
Pressure on Wheel (kg/cm)	125	88	100	161	153
Suspension	Torsion Bars	Christi	=	Torsion Bars	= =
Roadwheels/Spring	1	1	=	1	1
Type of Track	Unlubricated	=	=	=	=
Width/Pitch (mm)	300/111	560/170	=	700/163	650/162
Steering Ratio		1.5	=	1.7	

APPENDIX D - PENETRATION CAPABILITIES OF TANK GUNS

Name	Type of Ammunition	Weight Kg	Vo m/s	Thickness of Armor (mm) Perforated at 30° Angle				
				100	500	1000	1500	2000
M.G.34	S.m.K.	0.0115	785	8	3			
	S.m.K.H.			13	8			
2 cm Kw.K.30 & 38	2 cm Pzgr.	0.148	780	20	14			
	Pzgr.40	0.100	1050	40	20			
3.7 cm Kw.K. L/45	Pzgr.	0.685	745	35	29	22	20	
	Pzgr.40	0.368	1020	64	31			
3.7 cm Kw.K.34(t)	Pzgr.(t)	0.850	675	35	30	23	21	
	Pzgr.(t)umg.	0.815	675	34	29	25	22	
	Pzgr.40	0.368	980	60	39			
3.7 cm Kw.K.38(t)	Pzgr.(t)	0.850	741	36	31	24	22	
	Pzgr.(t)umg.	0.815	750	41	33	27	24	
	Pzgr.40	0.368	1040	64	33			
5 cm Kw.K. L/42	Pzgr.	2.06	685	53	43	32	24	
	Pzgr.39	2.06	685	55	47	37	28	
	Pzgr.40	0.925	1050	94	55			
5 cm Kw.K. L/60	Pzgr.	2.06	835	67	57	44	34	
	Pzgr.39	2.06	835	69	59	47	37	
	Pzgr.40	0.925	1180	130	72			
	Pzgr.40/1	1.07	1130	116	76			
7.5 cm Kw.K. L/24	K.Gr.rot Pz.	6.80	385	41	38	35	32	30
	Gr.38 HI/A	4.40	450	70	=	=	=	
	Gr.38 HI/B	4.57	450	75	=	=	=	
	Gr.38 HI/C	4.80	450	100	=	=	=	
7.5 cm Kw.K.40 L/43 and L/48	Pzgr.39	6.80	740	99	91	81	72	63
	Pzgr.40	4.10	920	126	108	87		
	Gr.38 HI/B	4.57	450	75	=	=	=	
	Gr.38 HI/C	4.80	450	100	=	=	=	
7.5 cm Kw.K.42 L/70	Pzgr.39/42	6.80	925	138	124	111	99	88
	Pzgr.40/42	4.75	1120	194	174	150	127	106
8.8 cm Kw.K.36 L/56	Pzgr.39	10.2	773	120	110	100	91	84
	Pzgr.40	7.30	930	170	155	138	122	110
	Gr.39 HI	7.65	600	90	=	=	=	=
8.8 cm Kw.K.43 L/71	Pzgr.39-1	10.2	1000	202	185	165	148	132
	Pzgr.40/43	7.30	1130	237	217	193	170	152

FRENCH AND RUSSIAN GUNS TESTED BY WA PRUEF

Name	Type of Ammunition	Weight Kg	Vo m/s	100	500	1000	1500	2000
2.5 cm Kw.K.121(f)	Pzgr.122(f)	0.32	920	35	29	20		
3.7 cm Kw.K.144(f)	Pzgr.144(f)	0.39	600	25	19			
3.7 cm Kw.K.143(f)	Pzgr.146(f)	0.70	705	29	23	16	12	
4.7 cm Kw.K.173(f)	Pzgr.176(f)	1.62	660	39	33	26	20	
4.5 cm Pak 184(r)	Pzgr.(r)	1.43	760	42	35	28	23	
7.62 cm Kw.K.L/30.5	Pzgr.39 rot	7.6	575	72	66	58	51	
7.62 cm Kw.K.L/41.5	Pzgr.39 rot	7.6	625	82	75	67	60	54

APPENDIX E - RECOMMENDED BOOKS

The Eastern Front by Steve Zaloga and James Grandsen, Published by Squadron/Signal Publications, Carrolton, Texas.

Die Geschichte der deutschen Panzerwaffe 1916-1945 by General Walther K. Nehring, Published by Motorbuch Verlag, Stuttgart Germany.

German World War II Organizational Series by Leo W.G. Niehorster, Published by Dr.Niehorster, Hannover, Germany.
> Volume 5/I - Mechanized Army Divisions (4.07.1943)
> Volume 5/II - Mechanized GHQ Units and Waffen-SS Formations (4.07.1943)
> Volume 7/I - Mechanized Army Divisions (6.06.1944)
> Volume 7/II - Mechanized GHQ Units and Waffen-SS Formations (6.06.1944)
> Volume 8/I - Mechanized Army Divisions (16.12.1944)
> Volume 8/II - Mechanized GHQ Units and Waffen-SS Formations (16.12.1944)

Tobruk and El Alamein by Barton Maughan, Published by Australian War Memorial, Canberra.

Panzer Battles by Major General F.W. von Mellenthin, Published by Ballantine Books, New York.

Panzer Leader by General Heinz Guderian, Published by Ballantine Books, New York.

Stalingrad to Berlin, The German Defeat in the East by Earl F. Ziemke, Published by U.S.Army Center of Military History, Washington, D.C.

Northwest Africa: Seizing the Initiative in the West by George F. Howe, Published by U.S.Army Center of Military History, Washington, D.C.

Cross Channel Attack by Gordon A. Harrison, Published by U.S.Army Center of Military History, Washington, D.C.

Breakout and Pursuit by Martin Blumenson, Published by U.S.Army Center of Military History, Washington, D.C.

Abteilung Abt. - battalion with less than five companies
Abwehr defense
Allgemeines Heeresamt army department over general staffs including In 6
Armeewagen 20 first code name for Grosstraktor
Armee army
Armee Oberkommando A.O.K. - army command
Art type
Artillerie artillery
Aufklaerung reconnaissance
Ausbildung training
Ausfuehrung Ausf. - model designation

Bataillon battalion of five companies
Batterie artillery battery
Befehlspanzer command tank
Begleitwagen B.W. - code name for the Pz.Kpfw.IV
Beobachtungs observation
Berge recovery
Bergepanther recovery vehicle with Panther chassis
Bergezug recovery platoon
Beute-Panzer captured tanks
Breitkeil reverse "V" formation

Chef der Heeresleitung early title for army chief of staff
Chef des Stabes chief of staff

Einsatz employ
Ersatzheer reserve army
Ersatzstaffel replacement section

Fahrgestell chassis
Fallschirmjaeger parachute troops
Fall Gelb code name for plans to attack west
Fall Weiss code name for plans to attack Poland
Faustpatrone shaped charge anti-tank weapon fired by infantry
Feldgrau field grey
Feldheer activated field army
Feldwebel army rank equivalent to American army sergeant
Ferdinand 8.8 cm tank destroyer
Fla anti-aircraft
Flak anti-aircraft gun
Flakpanzer anti-aircraft tank
Flakvierling quad anti-aircraft guns
Flammenwerfer flamethrower
Flammpanzer tank with a flamethrower
Fliegerabwehr Fla - anti-aircraft
Fuehrer leader

Fuehrer-Panzerwagen fully tracked armored command vehicle
Funk Fu - radio
Funkgeraet FuG - radio set
Funklenk F.L. or Fkl - radio controlled
Gebirgs-Jaeger mountain troops
Gefechtstross combat trains
Gefreiter army rank equivalent to American army corporal
Gemischte mixed
Generalstab des Heeres GenStdH - army chief of staff
Gepanzerte armored
Geschuetz gun
Gliederung organization
Gr.38 HL shaped charge shell
gr.Pz.Bef.Wg. large armored command vehicle
Grosstraktor large tank
Gruppe section

Hafthohlladung hand-held shaped charge
Halbzug section
Haubitze howitzer
Hauptmann army rank equivalent to American army captain
Heeres German army
Heeresgruppe command over several armies
Heeresmotorisierung army motorization
Heerestruppen independant army units
Heereswaffenamt army ordnance department
Heeres Zeugamt H.Za - army ordnance depot
Hohlgranate HL - shaped charge shells
Hohlraumgranate shaped charge shells
Hohlraummunition shaped charge shells

Inspektorat 6 In 6 - inspector for motorized units
Infanterie infantry
Inspektion inspection
Inspekteur inspector
Instandsetzung repair

Jagdpanther tank destroyer with Panther chassis
Jagdpanzer tank destroyer
Jagdtiger tank destroyer with Tiger chassis

Kampfgruppe battle group
Kampfstaffel small mixed combat unit
Kampfwagen early generic name for tank
Kampfwagen-Abwehr anti-tank
Kavallerie cavalry
kl.Pz.Bef.Wg. small armored command vehicle
Kleintraktor small tank

Kommando Kdo. - command
Kommando der Panzertruppen command over all panzer units
Kompanie Kp. - company
Kompanie-Trupp Kp.Tr. - company headquarters
Korps corps
Korps-Truppen units assigned to a corps
Kradschuetzen motorcycle borne infantry
Kraftfahr-Kampftruppen motorized combat troops
Kraftfahrlehrkommando Kf.Lehr-Kdo. - motorized training command
Kraftfahrtruppen motorized troops
Kraftfahrversuchsstab experimental automotive staff
Kranken-Panzer-Wagen armored ambulance
Kreuz cross
Kriegsausrustungsnachweisungen K.A.N. - wartime equipment table
Kriegsmarine navy
Kriegsstaerkenachweisungen K.St.N. - wartime organization table
Krupp-Traktor code name for early Pz.Kpfw.I chassis
Kuebelwagen small car such as the VW
Kurz kz - short
Kw.K. tank gun

Landespolizei state police
La.S.100 code name for the Pz.Kpfw.II
Landwirtschaftlicher Schlepper La.S. - agricultural tractor - code name for the Pz.Kpfw.I
Lang lg - long
Lastkraftwagen trucks
Lehrgaenge training course
Lehrtrupp training company
leichte light
Leichttraktor light tank
Leutnant army rank equivalent to American army second lieutenant
Luftwaffe air force

Mannschaftstransportwagen M.T.W. - crew transport vehicle - code name for the Sd.Kfz.251
M.G.-Kampfwagen early name for the Pz.Kpfw.I
M.G.-Panzerwagen early name for the Pz.Kpfw.I
Minenraeum mine clearing
mittlere medium
mot abbreviation for motorized
Munition ammunition

Nachrichten signals
Nachrichtenblatt news bulletin
Nahkampfwaffen close defense weapon
Nebelgranate smoke shells
Nebelkerzen smoke candles
Neu new
Neubau Fahrzeug Nb.Fz. - code name for a medium tank

Oberarzt head doctor
Oberbefehlshaber des Heeres commander of the army
Obergefreiter army rank with no American equivalent, between a corporal and a sergeant
Oberfeldwebel army rank equivalent to staff American army sergeant
Oberkommando des Heeres OKH - army high command
Oberkommando des Wehrmacht OKW - armed forces high command
Oberleutnant army rank equivalent to American army first lieutenant
Oberquartiermeister high command quartermaster
Oberst army rank equivalent to American army colonel
Oberstleutnant army rank equivalent to American army lieutenant colonel
Ob.West OKW command over Western Front
Ostheeres army on the Eastern Front

Pak anti-tank gun
Panzer-Abwehr anti-tank
Panzer-Abteilung armored battalion
Panzer-Armee armored army
Panzerbefehlswagen armored command vehicle
Panzerbeobachtungswagen armored artillery observation vehicle
Panzer-Brigade armored brigade
Panzer-Division armored division
Panzergranate Pzgr. - armor-piercing shell
Panzergranate 38 Pzgr.38 - capped armor-piercing shell
Panzergranate 39 Pzgr.39 - capped armor-piercing shell with a ballistic cap
Panzergranate 40 Pzgr.40 - solid high density core armor piercing round
Panzer-Grenadiere armored infantry
Panzer-Gruppe German army command higher than a corps but lower than an army
Panzer-Jaeger anti-tank unit
Panzer-Jagd-Kommandos tank hunter teams
Panzerkampfwagen Pz.Kpfw. - generic name for tank
Panzer-Kompanie armored company
Panzerkopfgranate armor piercing shells
Panzer-Regiments armored regiment
Panzerspaehwagen armored car
Panzertruppen armored troops, after February 1943 used to designate a separate branch of the army
Panzer-Vernichtungstrupps tank hunter teams
Panzer-Waffe armor as a branch of the army
Panzerwagen early generic name for a tank
Panzer-Zug armored platoon
Personalamt personnel department
Pionier combat engineer

Radfahr bicycle mounted unit
Reichsheeres German army
Reichswehr German armed forces

Reihe formation of tanks in a row
Reiter-Regiments cavalry regiment
Ritterkreuztraeger person awarded the knight's cross
Rollbahn main route

Sanitaets medics
Schokakola high energy ration of chocolate with a high caffeine content
Schiesschule gunnery school
schnellen Truppen title for the branch of the army containing the mobile units - later renamed Panzertruppen
S.m.K. steel core ammunition
S.m.K.H. special hard core ammunition
Schuerzen side skirts on tanks
Schuetzen motorized infantry
Schuetzenpanzerwagen SPW - armored infantry carrier - name for the Sd.Kfz.251
Schule school
Schulfahrgestell tank chassis for driver's training
Schulfahrzeuge training vehicles
Schwadron squadron
schwere heavy
Schwerpunkt primary area selected for concentrating an attack or a concentrated point for defense
schwerster Art heaviest type
Sd.Kfz. special vehicle
Sehstab observation periscope
Selbsfahrlafette Sfl. or Sf. - self-propelled
Sicherungs security
Sonder special
Sondergeraet special equipment
Spezial Sp - special, designation used in North Africa for Panzers with the longer guns
Splittergranate high-explosive fragmentation shell
Sprenggranaten Sprgr. - high-explosive fragmentation shells
Sprengstofftraeger explosives carrier
Stab headquarters
Stabsfeldwebel army rank equivalent to American army staff sergeant

Stabskompanie headquarters company
Staffel section with reserve tanks
Stuetzpunkt defensive position prepared for all-round defense
Sturmgeschuetz assault gun
Sturmhaubitze 10.5 cm assault gun
Sturm-Moerser 38 cm assault gun on Tiger chassis
Sturmpanzer 15 cm assault gun
Sturmtiger 38 cm assault gun on Tiger chassis

Tauchpanzers submersible tanks
Teil-Einheit sub unit
Tiefladeanhaenger low-bed trailers
Tropen tropical

Verband unit
verlastet transported
Versorgung supply
Versuchs experimental
Versuchsstelle experimenting station

Waffe weapon or branch of service
Waffenamt ordnance department
Waffenzug weapons platoon
Wa Prw 6 automotive design office under the Heeres Waffenamt
Wehrkreise army districts
Wehrmacht armed forces encompassing the Heeres, Luftwaffe, and Kriegsmarine
Weisung directive
Werkstatt-Kompanie maintenance company

z.b.V. for special employment
Zuege platoons
Zug platoon
Zugfuehrerwagen Z.W. - code name for the Pz.Kpfw.III
Zugkraftwagen three-quarter tracked towing vehicle
Zugmaschine towing vehicle

Also from the publisher

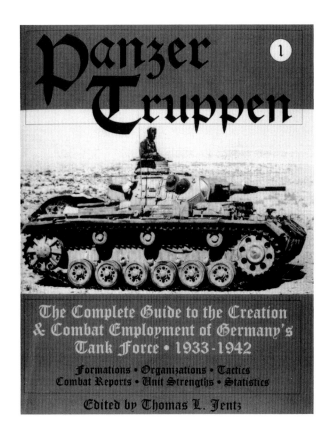

PANZERTRUPPEN
The Complete Guide to the Creation & Combat Employment
of Germany's Tank Force • 1933-1942

Edited by Thomas L. Jentz.

This first volume presents the offensive phase up to October 1942. The second volume covers the defensive phase to the end of the war.
Size: 8 1/2" x 11" over 200 b/w photos
288 pages, hard cover
ISBN: 0-88740-915-6 $49.95

GERMANY'S PANTHER TANK
The Quest for Combat Supremacy

Thomas L. Jentz

Over 20 years of research went into the creation of this history of the development, characteristics, and capabilities of the Panther.
Size: 8 1/2" x 11" over 170 b/w photos, line drawings
160 pages, hard cover
ISBN: 0-88740-812-5 $45.00

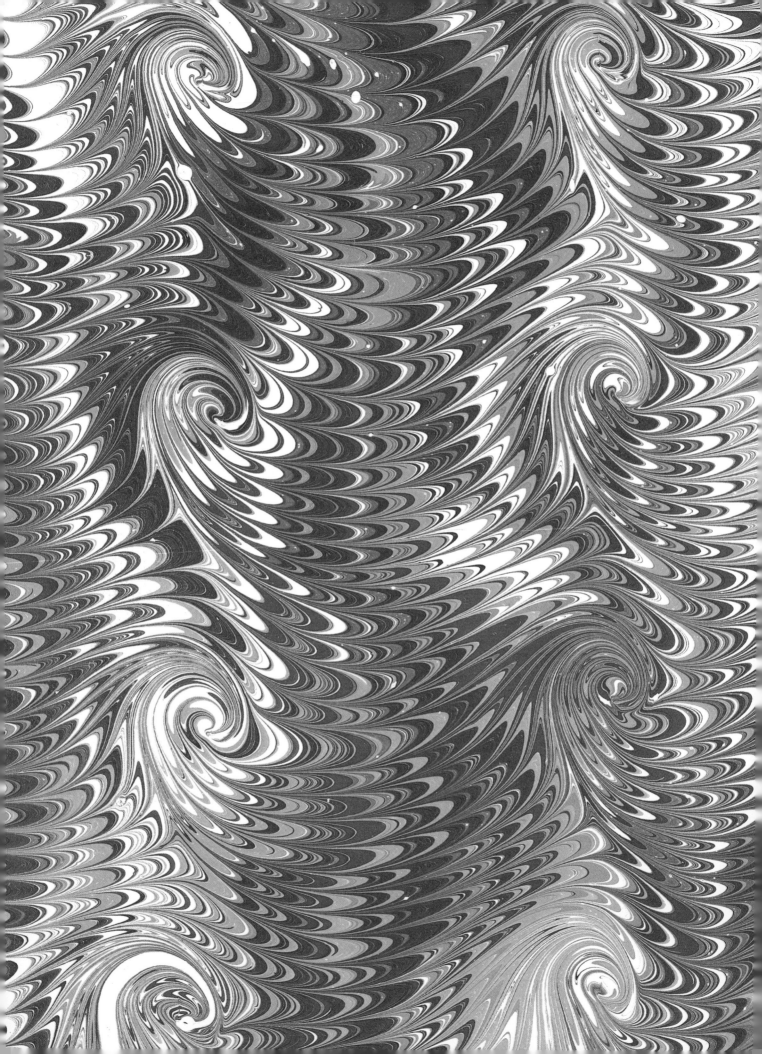